T0142354

Communications
in Computer and Information Science　　　1796

Rationale

The CCIS series is devoted to the publication of proceedings of computer science conferences. Its aim is to efficiently disseminate original research results in informatics in printed and electronic form. While the focus is on publication of peer-reviewed full papers presenting mature work, inclusion of reviewed short papers reporting on work in progress is welcome, too. Besides globally relevant meetings with internationally representative program committees guaranteeing a strict peer-reviewing and paper selection process, conferences run by societies or of high regional or national relevance are also considered for publication.

Topics

The topical scope of CCIS spans the entire spectrum of informatics ranging from foundational topics in the theory of computing to information and communications science and technology and a broad variety of interdisciplinary application fields.

Information for Volume Editors and Authors

Publication in CCIS is free of charge. No royalties are paid, however, we offer registered conference participants temporary free access to the online version of the conference proceedings on SpringerLink (http://link.springer.com) by means of an http referrer from the conference website and/or a number of complimentary printed copies, as specified in the official acceptance email of the event.

CCIS proceedings can be published in time for distribution at conferences or as post-proceedings, and delivered in the form of printed books and/or electronically as USBs and/or e-content licenses for accessing proceedings at SpringerLink. Furthermore, CCIS proceedings are included in the CCIS electronic book series hosted in the SpringerLink digital library at http://link.springer.com/bookseries/7899. Conferences publishing in CCIS are allowed to use Online Conference Service (OCS) for managing the whole proceedings lifecycle (from submission and reviewing to preparing for publication) free of charge.

Publication process

The language of publication is exclusively English. Authors publishing in CCIS have to sign the Springer CCIS copyright transfer form, however, they are free to use their material published in CCIS for substantially changed, more elaborate subsequent publications elsewhere. For the preparation of the camera-ready papers/files, authors have to strictly adhere to the Springer CCIS Authors' Instructions and are strongly encouraged to use the CCIS LaTeX style files or templates.

Abstracting/Indexing

CCIS is abstracted/indexed in DBLP, Google Scholar, EI-Compendex, Mathematical Reviews, SCImago, Scopus. CCIS volumes are also submitted for the inclusion in ISI Proceedings.

How to start

To start the evaluation of your proposal for inclusion in the CCIS series, please send an e-mail to ccis@springer.com.

Yuan Tian · Tinghuai Ma · Qingshan Jiang ·
Qi Liu · Muhammad Khurram Khan
Editors

Big Data and Security

4th International Conference, ICBDS 2022
Xiamen, China, December 8–12, 2022
Proceedings

 Springer

Editors
Yuan Tian [iD]
Nanjing Institute of Technology
Nanjing, China

Qingshan Jiang [iD]
Chinese Academy of Sciences
Shenzhen, China

Muhammad Khurram Khan [iD]
King Saud University
Riyadh, Saudi Arabia

Tinghuai Ma [iD]
Nanjing University of Information Science
and Technology
Nanjing, Jiangsu, China

Qi Liu [iD]
Nanjing University of Information Science
and Technology
Nanjing, China

ISSN 1865-0929   ISSN 1865-0937 (electronic)
Communications in Computer and Information Science
ISBN 978-981-99-3299-3   ISBN 978-981-99-3300-6 (eBook)
https://doi.org/10.1007/978-981-99-3300-6

Preface

This volume contains the papers from the 4th International Conference on Big Data and Security (ICBDS 2022). The event was held in Xiamen and Quanzhou, and was organized by Nanjing Institute of Technology, Xiamen University, JiangSu Computer Society, and IEEE Broadcast Technology Society.

The International Conference on Big Data and Security (ICBDS 2022) brings experts and researchers together from all over the world to discuss the current status and potential ways to address security and privacy regarding the use of Big Data systems. Big Data systems are complex and heterogeneous; due to their extraordinary scale and the integration of different technologies, new security and privacy issues are introduced and must be properly addressed. The ongoing digitalization of the business world is putting companies and users at risk of cyber-attacks more than ever before. Big data analysis has the potential to offer protection against these attacks. Participation in workshops on specific topics of the conference was expected to achieve progress, and global networking in transferring and exchanging ideas.

The papers come from researchers who work in universities and research institutions, and give us the opportunity to achieve a good level of understanding of the mutual needs, requirements, and technical means available in this field of research. The topics included in the second edition of this event include the following fields connected to Big Data: Security in Blockchain, IoT Security, Security in Cloud and Fog Computing, Artificial Intelligence/Machine Learning Security, and Cybersecurity and Privacy. We received 211 submissions and accepted 54 papers. All the accepted papers were peer reviewed by three qualified reviewers chosen from our technical program committee based on their qualifications and experience.

The proceedings editors wish to thank the dedicated Scientific Committee members and all the other reviewers for their efforts and contributions. We also thank Springer for their trust and for publishing the proceedings of ICBDS 2022.

January 2022

Yuan Tian
Tinghuai Ma
Qingshan Jiang
Qi Liu
Muhammad Khurram Khan

Organization

General Chairs

Ting Huai Ma   Nanjing University of Information Science and Technology, China
Yi Pan   Georgia State University, USA
Muhammad Khurram Khan   King Saud University, Saudi Arabia
Yuan Tian   Nanjing Institute of Technology, China

Organization Chair

Zhong Tan   Xiamen University, China

Technical Program Chairs

Victor S. Sheng   University of Central Arkansas, USA
Qi Liu   Nanjing University of Information Science and Technology, China

Technical Program Committee Members

Eui-Nam Huh   Kyung Hee University, South Korea
Heba Abdullataif Kurdi   Massachusetts Institute of Technology, USA
Omar Alfandi   Zayed University, UAE
Dongxue Liang   Tsinghua University, China
Mohammed Al-Dhelaan   King Saud University, Saudi Arabia
Päivi Raulamo-Jurvanen   University of Oulu, Finland
Zeeshan Pervez   University of the West of Scotland, UK
Adil Mehmood Khan   Innopolis University, Russia
Wajahat Ali Khan   Kyung Hee University, South Korea
Qiao Lin Ye   Nanjing Forestry University, China
Pertti Karhapää   University of Oulu, Finland
Farkhund Iqbal   Zayed University, UAE
Muhammad Ovais Ahmad   Karlstad University, Sweden
Lejun Zhang   Yangzhou University, China

Linshan Shen	Harbin Engineering University, China
Ghada Al-Hudhud	King Saud University, Saudi Arabia
Lei Han	Nanjing Institute of Technology, China
Tang Xin	University of International Relations, China
Mznah Al-Rodhaan	King Saud University, Saudi Arabia
Yao Zhenjian	Huazhong University of Science and Technology, China
Thant Zin Oo	Kyung Hee University, South Korea
Mohammad Rawashdeh	University of Central Missouri, USA
Alia Alabdulkarim	King Saud University, Saudi Arabia
Elina Annanperä	University of Oulu, Finland
Soha Zaghloul Mekki	King Saud University, Saudi Arabia
Basmah Alotibi	King Saud University, Saudi Arabia
Mariya Muneeb	King Saud University, Saudi Arabia
Maryam Hajakbari	Islamic Azad University, Iran
Miada Murad	King Saud University, Saudi Arabia
Pilar Rodríguez	Technical University of Madrid, Spain
Zhiwei Wang	Hebei Normal University, China
Rand. J	Shaqra University, Saudi Arabia
Jiagao Wu	Nanjing University of Posts and Telecommunications, China
Weipeng Jing	Northeast Forestry University, China
Yu Zhang	Harbin Institute of Technology, China
Nguyen H. Tran	University of Sydney, Australia
Hang Chen	Nanjing Institute of Technology, China
Sarah Alkharji	King Saud University, Saudi Arabia
Chunguo Li	Southeast University, China
Babar Shah	Zayed University, UAE
Tianyang Zhou	State Key Laboratory of Mathematical Engineering and Advanced Computing, China
Manal Hazazi	King Saud University, Saudi Arabia
Amiya Kumar Tripathy	Edith Cowan University, Australia
Shaoyong Guo	Beijing University of Posts and Telecommunications, China
Shadan AlHamed	King Saud University, Saudi Arabia
Cunjie Cao	Hainan University, China
Linfeng Liu	Nanjing University of Posts and Telecommunications, China
Chunliang Yang	China Mobile IoT Company Limited, China
Patrick Hung	University of Ontario Institute of Technology, Canada
Xinjian Zhao	State Grid Nanjing Power Supply Company, China

Workshop Chairs

Mohammad Mehedi Hassan   King Saud University, Saudi Arabia
Asad Masood Khattak   Zayed University, UAE

Publication Chair

Vidyasagar Potdar   Curtin University, Australia

Organization Committee Members

Fan Lin   Xiamen University, China
Yuyao Zhang   Xiamen University, China
Jalal Al-Muhtadi   King Saud University, Saudi Arabia
Geng Yang   Nanjing University of Posts and
                            Telecommunications, China
Qiao Lin Ye   Nanjing Forestry University, China
Pertti Karhapää   University of Oulu, Finland
Lei Han   Nanjing Institute of Technology, China
Yong Zhu   Jingling Institute of Technology, China
Bin Xie   Hebei Normal University, China
Dawei Li   Nanjing Institute of Technology, China
Jing Rong Chen   Nanjing Institute of Technology, China
Thant Zin Oo   Kyung Hee University, South Korea
Alia Alabdulkarim   King Saud University, Saudi Arabia
Rand. J   Shaqra University, Saudi Arabia
Hang Chen   Nanjing Institute of Technology, China
Jiagao Wu   Nanjing University of Posts and
                            Telecommunications, China

Contents

Big Data and New Method

Artificial Intelligence and Machine Learning Security

Data Technology and Network Security

Cybersecurity and Privacy

IoT Security

Big Data and New Method

Data-Driven Energy Efficiency Evaluation and Energy Anomaly Detection of Multi-type Enterprises Based on Energy Consumption Big Data Mining

Xiangguo Liu[(⊠)], Jian Geng, Zhonglong Wang, Lingyao Cai, and Fanjiao Yin

State Grid Shandong Electric Power Company, Tai'an Power Supply Company, Tai'an 271000, China
wbystu@163.com

Abstract. In view of the continuous improvement of the current energy consumption data of many types of enterprises, the effective monitoring of enterprise energy consumption and the early warning of different reward energy use will be the top priority. This paper proposes a data-driven energy efficiency evaluation and energy anomaly detection method for multi-type enterprises based on energy consumption big data mining. This method uses K-means Clustering algorithm identifies the energy consumption patterns of different enterprises, which is convenient for the evaluation of enterprise energy efficiency. Then, on the basis of pattern division, the outlier detection of enterprise energy consumption data is completed by CEEMDAN-LOF algorithm, and the abnormal energy consumption detection and research of enterprises are realized. The example uses the real energy consumption data of power grid enterprises, and the simulation results show the effectiveness of the proposed method.

Keywords: Early warning of abnormal energy use · big data mining · K-means clustering · outlier detection

1 Introduction

Energy conservation and emissions reduction has become the consensus of the whole society, is the only way to sustainable development [1, 2], so in the continuous improvement of the enterprise energy consumption data, the effective use of enterprise energy consumption data for energy consumption can effectively monitor and abnormal use of early warning is the most important [3], identification of abnormal energy consumption to reduce energy consumption of enterprises improves the management level of the power grid provides the positive support.

Project Supported by Science and Technologyleft-248285 Project of State Grid Shandong Electric Power Company "Research on the key technologies for intelligent research and judgment of energy efficiency anomalies of multi type enterprises based on massive data mining" (5206002000QW).

Reference [4] proposed the concept of multi-energy system to obtain the optimal energy ratio through energy efficiency and energy consumption ratio. Reference [5] proposed the establishment of a comprehensive energy system evaluation index body through the related architecture of energy Internet. Reference [6] proposed a Stacking ensemble model for anomaly monitoring based on five ML models. Reference [7] designed different screening methods for measurement anomalies based on the differences in massive data features.

2   Determination of the Optimal Number of Clusters

Evaluation index, SC is a common clustering algorithm for arbitrary bunch of class C_j and a single sample of SC calculation formula is:

$$s = \frac{b - a}{max(a, b)} \tag{1}$$

where:

$$a = \frac{1}{n_1} \sum_{x_i \in C_j} (x_i - c_j)^2 \tag{2}$$

$$b = \frac{1}{m} \sum_{x_i \in C_j} \sum_{x_k \in C_l} (x_i - x_k)^2 \tag{3}$$

where: S is the contour coefficient of a single sample; A is the average distance between samples and all other points in class C_j; B is the average distance between the samples in class C_l and all points in the samples in the nearest class C_j; C_j is the center of mass of class C_j; M and N represent the number of samples in class C_j and C_l, respectively.

However, SC will be overrepresented on convex clusters. Therefore, GSA algorithm is considered to be introduced on the basis of SC. GSA can estimate the optimal number of clusters in the dataset, and the effect is obvious in the scenario where the number of clusters is set at a low value.

The clustering dispersion of K clusters is defined as:

$$W(K) = \sum_{i=1}^{K} \sum_{x_i \in C_j} (x_i - c_j)^2 \tag{4}$$

The main idea of GSA algorithm is to calculate the natural logarithm of the corresponding cluster dispersion for each set cluster number K, and compare it with the threshold, so as to determine the optimal cluster number. After natural logarithm processing, the data situation tends to be more linearized, which makes it easier to determine the Gap value Gap(K) between clustering dispersion and threshold. The Gap value is defined as follows:

$$Gap(K) = E \ln[W_r(K)] - \ln[W(K)] \tag{5}$$

where: R is the selected reference dataset, and E is the mathematical expectation of the reference dataset. The Gap (K) value contains the information of clustering dispersion between the data set to be tested and the reference distribution. With the change of K, the Gap (K) value will also change, and the analysis of Gap (K) can determine the optimal number of clusters.

The above describes the algorithm principles of GSA and SC respectively. However, the determination of the optimal clustering number by simply using GSA or SC methods may lead to misjudgment, resulting in insignificant clustering effect. Therefore, in order to improve the accuracy of clustering results, GSA-SC fusion algorithm was introduced to determine the optimal number of clusters, and the average value of Gap(K) and S was calculated to construct a new clustering evaluation index G, as shown in the following equation.

$$G = \frac{Gap(K) + s}{2} \tag{6}$$

3 Energy Consumption Pattern Recognition Based on K-Means Clustering

K-means is based on partition clustering algorithm. Its main idea is that, for a data set given multiple data objects, it can be divided into several dissimilar clustering clusters by partition method, and the data objects of each cluster cannot belong to another cluster. The partition process is shown as follows (Fig. 1):

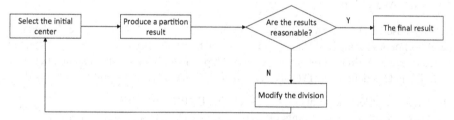

Fig. 1. Flowchart of partitioning based clustering algorithm

K-means clustering algorithm was proposed by MacQueen in L976, and its main idea is to divide the data set with N objects into K clusters. K-means algorithm generally uses Euclidean distance to measure similarity, and the evaluation function S of clustering effect can be defined as follows.

$$S = \sum_{i=1}^{k} \sum_{j=1}^{n} D_{ij} \|x_i - h\|^2 \tag{7}$$

The end of the partition is marked by the minimum sum of squared distances of data objects in each cluster. However, in the actual experiment, it is impossible to minimize the sum of squared distances of each cluster, and the partitioning algorithm will fall into the local optimal solution. The execution steps of K-means clustering algorithm are divided into the following four steps:

Step 1: Randomly select the initial K cluster center points, c_i;

Step 2: Traverse the points in the data space to obtain the nearest initial clustering center to the point, and finally merge this point into the class.

Step 3: Calculate the mean of the sum of squared distances of points within each cluster, and take the mean as the next cluster center.

Step 4: If the sum of squared distances of points in the cluster does not change, end the clustering; otherwise, iterate step 2 and step 3 continuously.

The time complexity of k-means algorithm is $O(nkd)$, where n represents the number of data points, K represents the number of clustering centers, and D represents the dimension of data points. For k-means algorithm, the time taken for each iteration is $O(nkd)$). If the number of iterations is T, then the time complexity of K-mean clustering algorithm is $O(nkd)$. In fact, most of the time spent by k-means algorithm is to calculate the distance between data points. Future improvement direction can be aimed at reducing the time consumption and the nearest neighbor problem.

4   Abnormal Analysis of Energy Consumption Data

In this module, the abnormal analysis of energy consumption data is completed by combining CEEMDAN algorithm and LOF algorithm, and the data analysis helps enterprises to better improve energy monitoring and abnormal detection of energy consumption data.

4.1 LOF Algorithm

Density-based LOF algorithm is based on the definition of KTH distance, k-distance neighborhood, reachable distance and local reachable density of data objects. Related concepts are as follows: For a given dataset D, $p \in D$ and $O \in D$, the distance between point P and O is denoted as D (p, O), and the KTH distance $k(p)$ of point P is defined as:

(1) There are at least k points $O' \in D$, such that $D (P, O') \leq D (P,O)$:
(2) There are at most $k-1$ points $O'' \in D$ such that $D (P, O'') < D (P, O)$ holds.

The set of points whose distance is not greater than the KTH distance of P is the k-distance neighborhood of point P, which is defined as follows.

$$N_k(p) = \{q \in D - \{p\}|d(p, o) \leq k(p)\} \tag{8}$$

For a given dataset D, $p \in D$, $O \in D$, the KTH distance of point O and the maximum distance between point P and O are the reachable distance, and the calculation formula is as follows:

$$r_r(p, o) = max\{k(o), d(p, o)\} \tag{9}$$

It can be understood that when point p is far away from point O, the reachable distance is the actual distance between the two points; When point P is close to point O, the reachable distance is the K distance of point p. That is, for a point o in $N_k(p)$, when the reachable distance $r_k(p, o)$ is taken as the distance (p, o) between two points, it indicates that K of point P from point O is more likely to be far away from a point in the

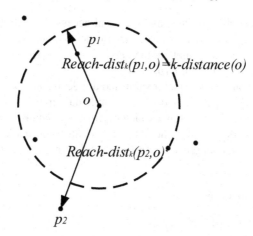

Fig. 2. When $k = 4$, reach distance (P_1, O) and reach distance (P_2, O)

neighborhood. On the contrary, if $r_k(p, o)$ takes $k(O)$, then for the point O in $N_k(p)$, the probability that point p is in the neighborhood of K distance of point O is large (Fig. 2)

The reciprocal of the average reachable distance of all points in the K-neighborhood $N_k(p)$ based on point P is the local reachable density of point P, and the calculation formula is:

$$l_k(P) = \frac{|N_k(p)|}{\sum_{o \in N_k(p)} r_k(p, o)} \tag{10}$$

According to the local reachable density, the greater the distance between a data point and its neighbors, the smaller the density between them, and vice versa. That is, the locally accessible density reflects the density of the local area around the data point. The local anomaly factor is expressed as the average of the ratio between the local accessible density of other points in $N(P)$ and the local accessible density of point P. The calculation formula is as follows:

$$L_k(p) = \frac{\sum_{o \in N_k(p)} l_k(o)}{|N_k(p)| l_k(p)} \tag{11}$$

The local anomaly factor reflects the degree of outliers between point P and its neighbors. If the value of $L_k(p)$ approaches 1, it means that the local density of point P is close to that of its neighbors. If the value of $L_k(p)$ is greater than 1 and larger, it means that point P is more distant from neighboring points and can be regarded as a possible outlier. Therefore, the outlier degree of any point P in the data set can be judged by calculating $L_k(p)$.

The calculation flow of LOF algorithm is as follows:

(1) Determine the parameter, k, and calculate the k-th distance. For a given dataset D, there is one sample data $P_i \in D$, $i = 1, 2, n$, k is a positive integer. Determine the value of parameter k and calculate each point P in dataset D and its k distance $k(p_i)$ in its neighborhood $N_k(p_i)$.

(2) Calculate the accessible distance and the local accessible density. $k(p_i)$ obtained from the upper dragon was used to calculate the accessible distance between p: and the k distance from all the points in the neighborhood $N_k(p_i)$, thus calculating the local accessible density of p of $l_k(p_i)$

(3) Calculate the local anomalous factor value and divide the anomalous data set. Local anomaly factor $l_k(p_i)$ is calculated for all sample data in data set D and compared with the threshold 1. If local anomaly factor $l_k(p_i) \leq 1$, data P is considered normal and otherwise outliers. The local anomaly factor of all points in the dataset compared to 1. For comparison, data greater than 1 are divided into anomalous data sets, and the algorithm ends.

4.2 CEEMDAN Algorithm

The specific steps of CEEMDAN are as follows:

(1) Add white Gaussian noise εωi (n) to the signal X(n) to be decomposed: x(n) = x(n) + εωi (n), where ω I (n) represents the white Gaussian noise added in the ith experiment, ε represents the amplitude of the noise, and the first IMF component can be obtained by using EMD algorithm to decompose the above expression for I times and calculate the mean value:

$$\overline{IMF_1(n)} = \frac{1}{I} \sum_{i=1}^{I} IMF_1(n) \tag{12}$$

$\overline{IMF_1(n)}$ denotes the first IMF component obtained using CEEMDAN.

(2) By subtracting the first F-component from the original signal to be decomposed, the margin after the first step of decomposition can be obtained: $r_1(n)$: $r_1(n) = x(n) - IMF_1(n)$;

(3) The second IMF can be obtained by 1 decomposition experiment of R_1 (n) = x(n) − IMF$_1$(n) using EMD [8] algorithm and taking the average value;

(4) For k = 2, 3 … K, calculate the KTH allowance r_k(n), The k + 1 IMF component can be obtained by decomposing $r_k(n) + E_k[\varepsilon\omega^i(n)]$ I times and taking the average value:

$$\overline{IMF_{k+1}(n)} = \frac{1}{I} \sum_{i=1}^{I} E_i \left\{ \pi_k(n) + \varepsilon E_k \left[\omega^i(n) \right] \right\} \tag{13}$$

where $\overline{IMF_{k+1}(n)}$ represents the k + 1 IMF component obtained using CEEMDAN algorithm.

(5) Repeat until you can't break it down.

5   Example Simulation and Analysis

The example data adopts the historical energy consumption data of a cement enterprise as the research sample to study the abnormal data detection proposed in this section. Daily level data of the enterprise from January 1, 2020 to December 31, 2020 are selected as the detection data, a total of 365 data.

5.1 Enterprise Energy Consumption Mode Division

The historical energy consumption data of enterprises were normalized. The figure shows the distribution of the actual and normalized values of the enterprise's historical energy consumption. It can be seen from the figure that the energy consumption is mainly distributed within the interval [0, 2.5], but there is an isolated point (the actual value is 20.45). If the traditional clustering algorithm is used for analysis, because the number of clusters is a hyperparameter, it needs to be artificially input, which leads to the optimal number of clusters of samples is not easy to determine and has strong randomness. Therefore, the GSA-SC fusion algorithm is considered to determine the optimal clustering number of energy consumption set (Fig. 3).

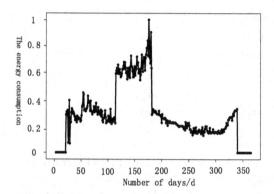

Fig. 3. Schematic diagram of historical energy consumption distribution of enterprises

Due to the shut-down and refurbishment during the data statistics period, the total energy consumption, coal consumption and power consumption of the enterprise are all 0 data, so this type of 0 data is ignored, and the preprocessed data is shown in Fig. 4.

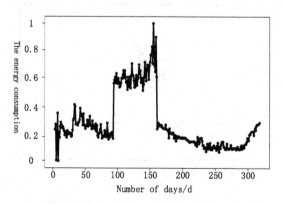

Fig. 4. Data display after preprocessing

In order to verify the superiority of the GSA-SC algorithm presented in this paper, GSA and SC are respectively used for comparative analysis, and the results are shown in the table. As can be seen from the table, if only GSA method is used to judge, when K ≥ 3, the change trend of Gap(K) is not obvious, and all values are very similar, leading to the difficulty in determining the optimal cluster number. If only SC algorithm is used for analysis, when K is 2 and 3, its corresponding S value is close, and the optimal cluster number is not easy to determine. When the GSA-SC algorithm proposed in this paper is used, it is easy to determine that when K is 3, G value is the largest, and no neighboring point value is similar to it. Therefore, the optimal number of clusters was selected as 3 (Table 1).

Table 1. Effect comparison of GSA-SC algorithm

K	GSA	SC	GSA-SC
2	0.241	0.42	0.3305
3	0.302	0.43	0.366
4	0.305	0.35	0.3275
5	0.304	0.312	0.308
6	0.311	0.29	0.3

The binary K-means++ algorithm was used for cluster analysis to obtain different energy consumption patterns. The clustering results are shown in the figure, and the details of cluster classes are shown in the table. According to the information in the table, the energy consumption data are divided into three clusters: A, B and C. Before normalization, the standard interval of cluster A is [5.01 TCE, 10.54 TCE], the standard interval of cluster B is [11.9 TCE, 16.6 TCE], and the standard interval of cluster C is [4.56 TCE, 9.04 TCE].

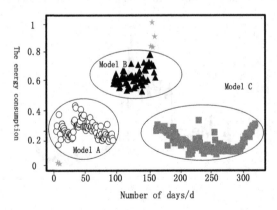

Fig. 5. Clustering results of enterprise energy consumption data

Table 2 shows the data clustering results achieved by combining IBM SPSS Statistics software. As can be seen from the table, when the number of cluster classes is set to the optimal number of cluster classes 3, the final cluster center and the number of cases in each cluster are completely consistent with the situation in the figure. It can be seen from Table 2 combined with Fig. 5.

Table 2. Number of cases in each cluster class

Clusters of class	A	B	C
Numbers	93	67	158

5.2 Abnormal Energy Consumption Detection for Enterprises

As shown in Fig. 6, the solid red line is the running trend of the energy consumption time series curve of enterprises. Figure 7 shows that the low-frequency recombination sequence obtained by CEEMDAN is relatively flat and has the ability to resist outliers, which can well represent the running trend of the energy consumption time series curve of enterprises.

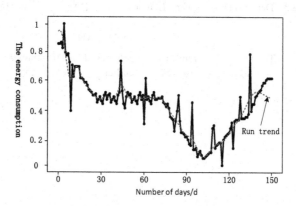

Fig. 6. Comparison of energy consumption data and operation trend of enterprises

Figure 7 for the primitive LOF detection under the temporal sequence $k = 30$ result diagram, as shown in Fig. 7, you can see the serial number 0–20 and other time data is identified as the discrete points, this is because the test results by this period enterprise regular changes in the energy use, lead to the results of the discriminant deviation, thus unable to accurately identify outlier data points.

As shown in Fig. 8, compared with the original outlier detection, CEEMDAN-LOF outlier data detection method adopted in this paper takes into account the running trend of time series, and LOF values of outlier data and normal data are significantly different, which is convenient to distinguish group data from normal data.

The detailed diagnostic results of the two algorithms are shown in Table 3. When k = 10, 20, 30, and 40, there are many false and missed values when the original sequence

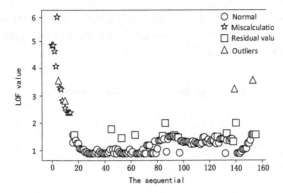

Fig. 7. Adopts LOF outlier data detection method

is used to detect the outlier data. However, there is no false or missed values when CEEMDAN is used to detect the outlier data after eliminating the sequence running trend. It further validates the effectiveness of the method used in this paper to detect abnormal data.

Table 3. Detection results using LOF and CEEMDAN-LOF algorithms

K	LOF			CEEMDAN-LOF		
	Number of outliers	The number of residual	Number of mistakes	Number of outliers	The number of residual	Number of mistakes
10	10	7	0	17	0	0
20	15	8	6	17	0	0
30	17	13	13	17	0	0
40	18	11	12	17	0	0

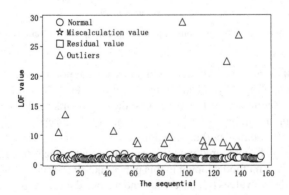

Fig. 8. CEEMDAN-LOF outlier data detection method

6 Conclusion

Driven by the presented data based on the energy consumption of big energy efficiency evaluation and the type of data mining enterprises can use anomaly detection method to solve the energy consumption of the anomaly detection problem under the huge amounts of data, and for different types of enterprise energy consumption data monitoring and puts forward the corresponding method of energy efficiency for the enterprise, the power grid to improve the management level.

References

1. Guo, Y., Zhang, X., Jiang, F., Zhang, J.: Research and management of water supply energy saving technology based on carbon peaking and carbon neutralization target. Water Supply Drainage 1–5 (2022). Accessed 28 Aug 2022
2. Zhang, B., Lan, C.: Research on the present situation and countermeasures of energy-conservation and emission-reduction in China's iron and steel industry. In: 2010 Asia-Pacific Power and Energy Engineering Conference, pp. 1–4 (2010)
3. Zhang, J., Lei, Y.: Research on the multi-objective optimized model of power generation dispatching based on low-carbon economy and energy-conservation. In: The 27th Chinese Control and Decision Conference (2015 CCDC), pp. 1651–1655 (2015)
4. Tian, Y., Yu, Z., Zhao, N., Zhu, Y., Xia, R.: Optimized operation of multiple energy inter-connection network based on energy utilization rate and global energy consumption ratio. In: 2018 2nd IEEE Conference on Energy Internet and Energy System Integration (EI2), pp. 1–6 (2018)
5. Liu, H., Li, Z., Cheng, Q., Yao, T., Yang, X., Hu, Y.: Construction of the evaluation index system of the regional integrated energy system compatible with the hierarchical structure of the energy Internet. In: 2020 IEEE 4th Conference on Energy Internet and Energy System Integration (EI2), pp. 342–348 (2020)
6. Jian, S., Li, W., Peng, X., Yan, Z., Cheng, C., Yuan, H.: Abnormal detection of power consumption based on a stacking ensemble model. In: 2021 4th International Conference on Energy, Electrical and Power Engineering (CEEPE), pp. 1021–1026 (2021)
7. Li, Z.: Abnormal energy consumption analysis based on big data mining technology. In: 2020 Asia Energy and Electrical Engineering Symposium (AEEES), pp. 64–68 (2020)
8. Han, Z., Zhang, C., Gao, M.: Hybrid energy storage planning for island-type integrated energy system based on EMD decomposition. Therm. Power Gener. **2022**(09), 72–78 (2022). Accessed 28 Aug 2022
9. Arkhangelski, J., Abdou-Tankari, M., Lefebvre, G.: Efficient abnormal building consumption detection by deep learning LSTM IOT data classification. In: 2022 11th International Conference on Renewable Energy Research and Application (ICRERA), pp. 125–129 (2022)
10. Zhang, W., Dong, X., Li, H., Xu, J., Wang, D.: Unsupervised detection of abnormal electricity consumption behavior based on feature engineering. IEEE Access **8**, 55483–55500 (2020)

Research on Data-Driven AGC Instruction Execution Effect Recognition Method

Haiyang Jiang[1], Hongtong Liu[2(✉)], and Yangfei Zhang[2]

[1] State Grid Heilongjiang Electric Power Company, Harbin 150090, Heilongjiang, China
[2] School of Electric Power Engineering, Nanjing Institute of Technology, Nanjing 211167, Jiangsu, China
liuht@njit.edu.cn

Abstract. With the high penetration of random energy such as wind power and photovoltaic in the power grid, the influence of the accuracy of regulation of traditional thermal power units on the operation of the power grid is gradually increasing. Aiming at the problem of the deviation between the actual output of thermal power units and the AGC command of the power grid, this paper proposes a data-driven AGC command execution effect identification method. Firstly, based on Kernel Principal Component Analysis (KPCA), a data preprocessing method is proposed, which maps feature datasets into low-dimensional vectors to achieve dimensionality reduction. Secondly, the Independent Recurrent Neural Network (IndRNN) is used to process and predict the dimensionality reduction data, so as to realize the accurate perception of the adjustment effect of the unit execution command. Finally, the real power grid data is used to simulate and verify the proposed method. The results show that the model can effectively reduce the deviation of instruction execution.

Keywords: recurrent neural network · kernel principal component analysis · Long short-term memory network · gated recurrent unit

1 Introduction

Automatic generation control (AGC) has become increasingly mature and widely used after years of research [1, 2], in recent years, the installed capacity of renewable energy, mainly wind energy and photovoltaic energy, has increased year by year, due to the uncertainty of renewable energy output, it is necessary for the generator to undertake heavy output regulation task for a long time, however, the regulating capacity of thermal power units is far from meeting the demand of frequency modulation [3]. Therefore, it is urgent to improve the regulation capacity of thermal power units to deal with the problems caused by new energy grid connection. In the field of active power scheduling under the background of new energy generation, it is difficult to improve the regulation ability of thermal power units by traditional frequency modulation strategy optimization. However, with the rise of intelligent algorithms in recent years, more and more scholars use intelligent algorithms to improve the regulation ability of thermal power units. Literature [4] proposed a multi-model predictive function control strategy and applied it to the design of power regulation control system to achieve better primary frequency modulation performance of thermal power units. Literature [5] proposed a deep fusion learning model based on convolutional neural network and fully connected neural network for short-term wind power generation prediction.

In addition, in recent years, the regulation technology based on artificial intelligence technology has been gradually paid attention to by researchers. Literature [6] proposed an online decision method for unit recovery based on deep learning and Monte Carlo search and obtained an online recovery scheme with high robustness. Literature [7] proposed a self-learning decision-making method for unit combination based on long-term deep learning network. Compared with traditional methods, the decision accuracy and efficiency are improved, and the decision results are more robust.

The strategies proposed in the above literatures are still based on the premise that thermal power units can accurately respond to AGC instructions, and they cannot overcome the problems caused by low response accuracy of thermal power units.

To solve the above problems, this paper firstly uses deep recurrent neural network (DRNN) to predict and perceive the accuracy of AGC control command execution. Secondly, a preprocessing strategy for the input parameters of the deep network model is proposed to improve the overall training speed and output accuracy of the model. Finally, the real unit operation data in a provincial power grid is used for simulation analysis, and the advantages of the proposed preprocessing strategy in model training and convergence are verified. It is proved that the prediction model proposed in this paper can accurately predict the unit AGC command.

2   Independent Recurrent Neural Network

2.1   Recurrent Neural Network

Recurrent neural network [8] (RNN) is a commonly used model for predicting time series. Its most important feature is that the state of cyclic neurons at a certain time not only depends on the current input, but also can be affected by the input before the current time. Such characteristics make it very suitable for solving time series prediction problems. The RNN is not only fully connected from layer to layer, but also the output and input of the hidden layer are connected through a specific arithmetic unit, forming a feedback loop and forming a flip-flop like structure, which endows the RNN unit with the ability to remember the state of the previous cycle.

Figure 1 shows a standard single-layer RNN network.

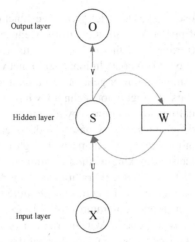

Fig. 1. Structure diagram of recurrent neural network

Where X represents the value of the Input layer, S represents the value of the Hidden layer, O represents the value of the Output layer, U represents the Input weight matrix represents the Output weight matrix, and W represents the cyclic weight matrix.

To solve more complex problems, the RNN network can be superimposed to build a deep recurrent neural network (DRNN) model. The DRNN model has more nonlinear features and weight parameters and can fit more complex functions. Figure 2 shows the structure diagram of a DRNN with three hidden layers.

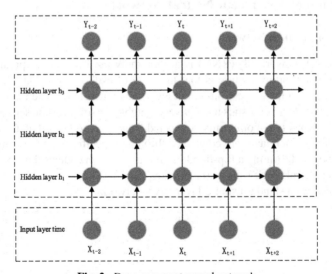

Fig. 2. Deep recurrent neural network

2.2 Improvement of Deep Recurrent Neural Network

To solve the problem of gradient disappearance or gradient explosion in DRNN network, an improvement is made on the basis of RNN, long short-term memory network [9] (LSTM) and gated recurrent unit [10] (GRU) are proposed. These two network structures improve the problem of gradient disappearance or gradient explosion to a certain extent. However, because tanh or sigmoid is used as the activation function, the gradient attenuation between network layers is caused, and it is difficult to construct and train RNN-based deep LSTM or GRU.

The above problems can be solved effectively by using Independent Recurrent Neural Network (IndRNN). The status update formula of IndRNN is:

$$h_t = \sigma(Wx_t + Uh_{t-1} + b_h) \tag{1}$$

Stands for Hadamard product, This is the biggest difference with traditional RNN networks. A neuron in the cell of IndRNN at each time is only related to the corresponding neuron in the cell of other time, and has nothing to do with other neurons. Therefore, the connections between neurons can be achieved by stacking multiple layers of IndRNN units, making the IndRNN expand to deeper layers.

For the n neuron, the hidden state at time t can be calculated as follows:

$$h_{n,t} = \sigma\left(W_n x_t + u_n \odot h_{n,t-1} + b_n\right) \tag{2}$$

IndRNN presents a new perspective of aggregating spatial patterns (via W) independently over time steps (via U). By stacking multiple layers of neurons, each neuron in the next layer independently processes the output of all neurons in the previous layer, which reduces the difficulty of building deep network structures and enhances the processing ability of long sequence problems.

3 KPCA Preprocessing Process

The input preprocessing process based on KPCA is as follows:

1) The parameters of KPCA preprocessing model are adjusted. The Grid Search (GS) algorithm with k-fold cross-validation was used to Search for the optimal KPCA preprocessing model hyperparameters.
2) Data normalization stage. The feature variables were input into the model in the form of vectors, and the corresponding data sets of the feature variables were standardized to map the data within the range of 0–1.
3) Calculate eigenvalues and eigenvectors. Firstly, the preprocessed data is mapped to a high-dimensional space by constructing a kernel function. Secondly, the covariance moments are obtained by calculating the eigenvectors and eigenvalues of the covariance matrix in the high-dimensional space. Finally, the calculated eigenvalues are sorted.

4) Principal components are determined by calculating the contribution rate of eigenvalues. First, calculating the contribution rate of each characteristic value, the characteristics of the contribution rate is greater than the fixed threshold value in a collection of C, and calculate the collection C characteristic value in the cumulative contribution rate, and if the cumulative contribution rate is greater than the threshold, then determine the characteristic value from the set of feature vector of the principal component number, and will get the number of principal component dimension reduction after save to set U; If the cumulative contribution rate is less than the threshold, adjust the parameters and repeat step (4).

5) Judge whether GS algorithm completes the traversal of parameters. If so, select the KPCA model with the optimal parameters according to the maximization of the principal component contribution rate, and output the set U of the optimal KPCA model. If not, return to step 3.

Figure 3 is the flow chart of input preprocessing based on KPCA.

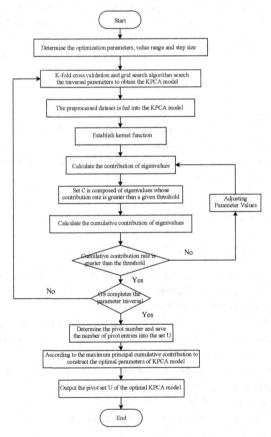

Fig. 3. Flow chart of input variable preprocessing based on KPCA

4 Identification Process of AGC Instruction Execution Effect

The identification process of AGC instruction execution effect based on KPCA preprocessing strategy and DIndRNN model is as follows:

1) Data preprocessing. The original data of unit operation were normalized.
2) Construct DIndRNN model. The preprocessed data set was used as input to construct DIndRNN model.
3) Train DIndRNN model. The preprocessed training data is input into the model, and the predicted value obtained is compared with the training label. The weight of DIndRNN model is updated through back propagation, and step (3) is repeated until the training of DIndRNN model is completed.
4) DIndRNN model deployment. The preprocessed test data set is input into the trained DIndRNN model, and the predicted response value of the unit to AGC instruction is output, so as to realize the identification of the effect of the unit executing AGC instruction (Fig. 4).

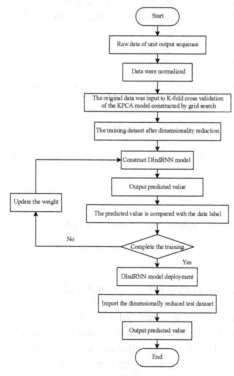

Fig. 4. Flowchart of AGC instruction execution effect identification algorithm

5 Example Analysis

5.1 Basic Information of the Example

To verify the validity and rationality of the model and control method proposed in this paper, real data of power grid are introduced as the analysis object. The data time span is half a year, the sampling frequency is 1 min, and the original data is 262,080 pieces. The models used in the examples are built by Tensorflow2.0, a deep learning framework owned by Google. The language is python3.7.6; The computer used is configured with Intel(R)Core(TM)i7-9750HCPU@2.60 GHz and 16G memory.

5.2 Comparative Analysis of Training Set and Validation Set

Randomly selected 80 predicted points, the prediction accuracy of DIndRNN model on training set and validation set is compared, and the single-step prediction result is shown in Fig. 5. It can be clearly seen from the figure that, in both the training set and the validation set, DIndRNN model can better give the output prediction results of the unit under AGC command, which reflects the good generalization ability of DIndRNN model, that is, it can also have a good effect on the data not in the training set.

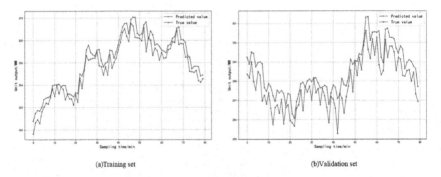

(a)Training set   (b)Validation set

Fig. 5. Comparative analysis of prediction results of training set and validation set

5.3 Comparative Analysis of DIndRNN Model and MLP Model

Figure 6(a) shows the prediction results of DIndRNN model and MLP model. The red broken line represents the DIndRNN model prediction result, the blue broken line represents the MLP model prediction result, and the green broken line represents the real unit output value. MLP model presents a large error in predicting unit output sequence, while DIndRNN model has a higher prediction accuracy. This is because the MLP model cannot store sequence information and is difficult to process sequence data. DIndRNN has the ability of memory and has a good effect on sequence prediction.

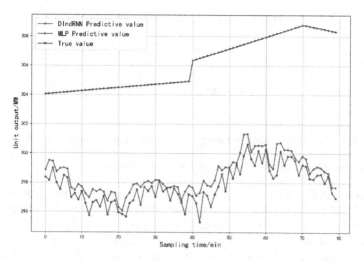

(a)Comparison between DIndRNN model and MLP model

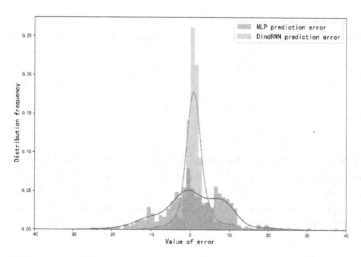

(b) Compared with the MLP model prediction error distribution DIndRNN model

Fig. 6. DIndRNN model and MLP model analysis

Figure 6(b) shows the prediction error distribution of DIndRNN model and MLP model in the form of histogram. The horizontal coordinate of the histogram is each interval of the error distribution, and the vertical coordinate is the proportion of the model prediction error within the interval. The curve in the figure is the kernel density fitting curve. The orange histogram represents the error distribution of the DIndRNN model, while the blue histogram represents the error distribution of the MLP model. As can be seen from Fig. 6(b), the error distribution of DIndRNN model is far more concentrated than that of MLP model. This also shows from another aspect that DIndRNN model has a smaller error value (Table 1).

Table 1. DIndRNN model and MLP model evaluation index

Evaluation index	DIndRNN	MLP
MAE	3.4211	8.5662
MSE	46.3561	132.1398

5.4   Influence of Preprocessing Strategy on Model Prediction Accuracy

1) Comparison of different dimensionality reduction models.

In order to verify the effectiveness of the KPCA dimensionality reduction model, the KPCA dimensionality reduction model, local linear embedding (LLE) and principal component analysis (PCA) models are compared and analyzed in this section. Different dimensionality reduction models are used to process the original data, and DIndRNN model is used to output the data after processing. The evaluation indexes of the prediction results are shown in Table 2.

Table 2. Different pretreatment strategy prediction precision quantitative contrast

The evaluation index	KPCA	LLE	PCA
MAE	7.3239	16.3661	138.9642
MSE	110.2366	588.6422	36142.6866

As can be seen from the table, the linear dimensionality reduction method PCA has been unable to effectively process the data set in this paper, and too much effective information has been lost in the dimensionality reduction process, leading to the failure of the model to give prediction results. The nonlinear dimensionality reduction methods KPCA and LLE perform much better. Among them, KPCA model is better than LLE model.

2) Analysis of model prediction accuracy based on dimensionality reduction.

Table 3 shows the prediction accuracy of DIndRNN model under different dimensionality reduction dimensions.

Table 3. Comparison of model training errors in different dimensions

The evaluation index	3d	4d	5d
MAE	11.8624	7.3239	7.6322
MSE	368.2402	110.2366	14.6988

It can be seen from Table 3 that the prediction accuracy is better in 4d than in 3d. However, when the dimension changes from 4d to 5d, the prediction accuracy drops slightly. Dimension 4 is the optimal parameter.

3) The influence of preprocessing on the model training process.

Figure 7 shows the error reduction of DIndRNN model in the training process whether KPCA dimensionality reduction preprocessing process is adopted.

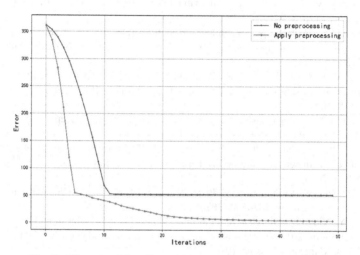

Fig. 7. Diagram of the effect of preprocessing on model training

It can be seen from the orange broken line that the error decreases rapidly in the first five iterations, and the rate of decline is faster than that of the blue broken line. In addition, after 30 iterations, both kinds of broken lines tend to be flat. Compared with the blue curve, the error value of the yellow curve is smaller, which indicates that the KPCA dimension reduction strategy effectively simplifies the model.

6 Conclusion

In this paper, an AGC instruction identification method based on independent recurrent neural network is proposed. The main conclusions are as follows:

1) The KPCA dimension reduction model constructed in this paper can effectively eliminate the factors that have little correlation with unit output.
2) Compared with the traditional recurrent neural network model, the DIndRNN prediction model constructed in this paper has better prediction accuracy.
3) Using KPCA preprocessing strategy and DIndRNN model, the dimensionality of data can be reduced under the premise of retaining as much effective information as possible, shorten the training time of the model, and improve the prediction accuracy.

References

1. He, C., Wang, H., Wei, Z., et al.: Distributed collaborative real-time control of wind farm and AGC unit. Acta Electr. Eng. Sin. **35**(02), 302–309 (2015)
2. Liao, X., Liu, K., Le, J., et al.: Coordinated control strategy for cross regional AGC units based on bi level model predictive structure. Acta Electr. Eng. Sin. **39**(16), 4674–4685+4970 (2019)
3. Lin, L., Zou, L., Zhou, P., Tian, X.: Multi-angle economic analysis on deep peak regulation of thermal power units with large-scale wind power integration. Autom. Electr. Power Syst. **41**(07), 21–27 (2017)
4. Shu, J., et al.: Primary frequency modulation control strategy in deep peak load cycling state for thermal power units based on multi-model predictive control. Boiler Technol. **51**(06), 12–17 (2020)
5. Hossain, M.A., Chakrabortty, R.K., Elsawah, S., Gray, E.M., Ryan, M.J.: Predicting wind power generation using hybrid deep learning with optimization. IEEE Trans. Appl. Supercond. **31**(8), 1–5 (2021)
6. Sun, R., Liu, Y.: Online decision making of unit recovery based on deep learning and Monte Carlo tree search. Power Syst. Autom. **42**(14), 40–47 (2018)
7. Yang, N., Ye, D., Lin, J., et al.: Research on intelligent decision-making method of unit commitment with self-learning ability based on data-driven. Chin. J. Electr. Eng. **39**(10), 2934–2945 (2019)
8. Zhao, H., Xue, W., Li, X., et al.: Multi-mode neural network for human action recognition. IET Comput. Vis. **14**(8), 587–596 (2020)
9. Xuejun, Y., Yiqun, Z., Shuxian, S., et al.: LSTM network for carrier module detection data classification. In: 2019 International Conference on Smart Grid and Electrical Automation (ICSGEA), Xiangtan, China (2019)
10. Dong, M., Grumbach, L.: A hybrid distribution feeder long-term load forecasting method based on sequence prediction. IEEE Trans. Smart Grid **11**(1), 470–482

Research on Day-Ahead Scheduling Strategy of the Power System Includes Wind Power Plants and Photovoltaic Power Stations Based on Big Data Clustering and Filling

Feng Qi[1], Qiang Wang[2], Xiaoqiang Wei[1], Yiping Zhang[1], Wenbin Wu[1], Donyang He[1], Taicheng Wang[3(✉)], and Suyang Shen[3]

[1] State Grid Heilongjiang Electric Power Co., Ltd., Harbin 150090, Heilongjiang, China
[2] Jixi Power Supply Company of State Grid Heilongjiang Electric Power Co., Ltd., Jixi 158100, China
[3] School of Electric Power Engineering, Nanjing Institute of Technology, Nanjing 211167, Jiangsu, China
wang-tc@hotmail.com

Abstract. Traditional power system scheduling optimization methods cannot fully deal with the massive data brought by the increase of new energy penetration. Aiming at the above problems, this paper proposes a day-ahead scheduling optimization method based on big data clustering and filling for power system includes wind power plants and photovoltaic power stations. Firstly, according to the collected historical data of power grid, the K-means clustering method of big data is used to generate representative load, wind power and solar illumination scene sets. Secondly, a missing value filling method based on historical data assisted scene analysis was proposed. Finally, the day-ahead scheduling model of power system with wind power plants and photovoltaic power stations is established and solved by improved particle swarm optimization algorithm. The simulation results show that this method can improve the filling accuracy of the missing value of the day-ahead dispatching historical data of the power system, and meet the development demand of the power system with new energy.

Keywords: Data filling · Power system includes new energy · Scene analysis · Wave cross correlation analysis · Reactive power optimization

1 The Introduction

With the continuous improvement of power grid automation and the wide application of power grid data intelligent acquisition system, the power grid data collection system is becoming mature. However, the lack of frequency and accuracy in the collection process of power grid data inevitably leads to some missing values in the data, so as to interfere with the process of data analysis and affect the final identification effect of the model. Therefore, how to effectively fill the missing value of power grid data has gradually become a difficult problem to be solved.

Y. Tian et al. (Eds.): ICBDS 2022, CCIS 1796, pp. 25–36, 2023.
https://doi.org/10.1007/978-981-99-3300-6_3

In recent years, the research on big data [1] has been upsurge around the world. Big data technology has injected fresh blood into the development of smart grid and achieved good results [2].

Literature [3] proposes a medium and long-term load forecasting method for power system based on big data clustering. The calculation results show that the big data clustering algorithm can effectively cluster and partition a large number of load data, realize the discrimination and prediction of loads with different growth characteristics, and has high prediction accuracy. Literature [4] proposes complete compatibility classes based on the incomplete data fill algorithm, the energy consumption of large data management model, to help green data center, effective management of solar energy and other resources to match the utility to provide stable and adequate power supply, thus providing efficient service system for the whole data center energy services. Literature [5] proposes a missing data filling algorithm for the unified data model of panoramic regulation, which uses the improved Markov Monte Carlo method to estimate the missing data according to the known data, and obtains the best parameters of incomplete regulatory data through fewer iterations, thus improving the accuracy of missing data estimation.

This paper proposes a day-ahead scheduling optimization strategy of power system based on big data clustering and filling. Firstly, the K-means clustering method of big data is used to generate representative load, wind power and solar illumination scene sets. Then, a missing value filling method of power grid data based on multi-parameter IOT fusion technology is proposed. The fluctuation cross-correlation analysis is carried out according to the historical data of power grid. By combining the weights and the dynamic time warping distance to measure a certain date missing attribute data is similar to the date of the known data integrated similarity to find out the attribute the date of the highest similarity, and the date at the same time to missing data combined with the linear fitting curve data attribute data fill further improved the precision of data missing value fill. Finally, the day-ahead scheduling model of the power system includes wind power plant and photovoltaic power station is established, and the improved particle swarm optimization algorithm is used to solve the problem. The simulation results show that the data after clustering can meet the requirements of data integrity and accuracy including day-ahead scheduling optimization of system with wind power plants and photovoltaic power stations.

2   K-Means Clustering Method for Massive Power Grid Data

The process of grouping a collection of physical or abstract objects into multiple classes consisting of similar objects is called clustering. A cluster generated by clustering is a collection of data objects that are similar to objects in the same cluster but different from objects in other clusters. Dissimilarity is calculated according to the membership value of the description object, and distance is often used as a measure.

With the increasing perfection of the power grid information collection system, a large amount of network data can be collected. Therefore, the selected clustering method is required not only to be able to cluster quickly and accurately when the amount of information is not large, but also to adapt to the demand of increasing data volume and to output the clustering results timely and quickly. Because k-means algorithm can deal with large data sets, has good scalability and high efficiency, is simple and fast, can adapt to the demand of real-time processing of data volume growth, and is widely used in large-scale data clustering, so K-means algorithm is selected to cluster samples in this paper.

The steps of classical k-means algorithm are as follows:

1) Determine the number of clusters N and the maximum number of iterations M.
2) Choose any N objects in the sample as the initial clustering center.
3) Calculate the Euclidean distance between the samples and N objects, and classify the samples according to the size of the Euclidean distance. The Euclidean distance is defined as:

$$d_{ij} = \sqrt{\sum_{k=1}^{p} (x_{ik} - x_{jk})^2} \tag{1}$$

In the formula: x_{ik} represents the observed value of the ith variable of the kth sample; p represents the number of samples; d_{ij} Represents the Euclidean distance between sample j and sample i.

4) Calculate the average value of various objects and update the clustering center.
5) Calculate the square error criterion function to determine whether convergence conditions are met. If convergence occurs, the algorithm ends. If it does not converge, judge whether the number of iterations is greater than M. if it is less than M, go to the third step, otherwise, the algorithm ends. The squared error criterion function is:

$$E = \sum_{i=1}^{k} \sum_{x_q \in C_i} (x_q - m_i)^2, \quad m_i = \sum_{x_q \in C_i} \frac{x_q}{n_{C_i}} \tag{2}$$

6) Output clustering results

The validity of clustering can be from two aspects of the distance between the class and class distance measure, class distance means that the condensation degree of similar samples, the distance between the class means that between different classes of separating degree, thus a good clustering results, should meet the distance between the class, class distance is small, so the greater the similarity of the same class, the greater the difference of the sample in different classes. Contour coefficient is an index that comprehensively reflects the similarity and difference between classes, so it can be used to evaluate the quality of clustering and determine the reasonable number of clusters. The contour coefficient S is defined as:

$$S = \sum_{i=1}^{n} \frac{s_i}{n} \tag{3}$$

In the formula, n represents the total number of samples; s_i represents the contour coefficient of sample i, its definition is:

$$s_i = \frac{y_i - x_i}{\max\{x_i, y_i\}} \tag{4}$$

In the formula, x_i represents the average distance between the ith sample in class x and other samples in class x, and represents the degree of cohesion in the class; Calculate the average of distances between x_i and samples in all classes except x, and denote y_i as the minimum value of this average. Obviously, the larger the value, the higher the clustering quality.

3   Missing Data Processing Strategy Based on Historical Data Assisted Scene Analysis

In the field of day-ahead reactive power optimization of new energy grids, the accuracy and completeness of data have a great impact on the line loss analysis results. However, with the exponential growth of collected data, the problem of missing voltage data caused by manual input and acquisition device failure occurs frequently, so the missing data need to be identified or completed. The traditional maximum expected value algorithm [6], K-proximity algorithm [7] and other methods provide solutions, but the filling effect is not ideal because historical data are rarely used as the analysis basis. In recent years, the world raised a hot wave of big data research, big data technology for smart grid development injected fresh blood, and good results were obtained, therefore this section presents a missing value based on historical data aided scenario analysis to fill method, further improve the missing value in the line loss analysis fill precision at the same time, meet the demand of power grid development, The overall process is shown in Fig. 1:

The specific steps are as follows:

Step 1: Obtain the historical data of the power grid and go to Step 2.
Step 2: The fluctuation cross-correlation between the known attribute data and the missing attribute data at the same time was calculated by the fluctuation cross-correlation analysis algorithm, and then Step 3 was performed.

The calculation steps are as follows:

1) Certain two time series of equal length x_i and y_i, $i = 1, 2, \cdots, N$
2) Calculate the sum of differences between x_i, y_i and the average value:

$$\begin{cases} \Delta x(l) = \sum_{i=1}^{l} (xi - \bar{x}), l = 1, 2, \cdots, N \\ \Delta y(l) = \sum_{i=1}^{l} (yi - \bar{y}), l = 1, 2, \cdots, N \end{cases} \tag{5}$$

In the formula, l represents the sampling length, $\Delta x(l)$ and $\Delta y(l)$ respectively represent the sum of differences between x_i, y_i and the average value at sampling length l, $\bar{x}$ and $\bar{y}$ respectively represent the average value of x_i and y_i.
3) Calculate the forward difference representing x_i and y_i autocorrelation respectively:

$$\begin{cases} \Delta x(l, l_0) = x(l_0 + l) - x(l_0), l_0 = 1, 2, \cdots, N - l \\ \Delta y(l, l_0) = y(l_0 + l) - y(l_0), l_0 = 1, 2, \cdots, N - l \end{cases} \tag{6}$$

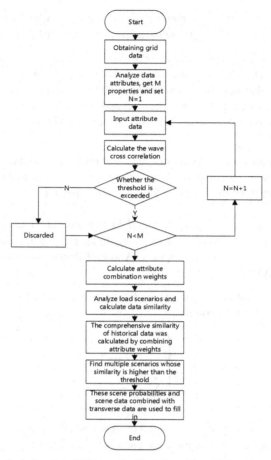

Fig. 1. Flowchart of missing data filling method based on historical data assisted scene analysis

4) Calculate the covariance of x_i and y_i:

$$Covxy(l) = \sqrt{\left[\Delta x(l, l_0) - \overline{\Delta x(l, l_0)}\right] \times \left[\Delta y(l, l_0) - \overline{\Delta y(l, l_0)}\right]} \qquad (7)$$

$$\begin{cases} \overline{\Delta x(l, l_0)} = \frac{1}{N-l} \sum_{l_0}^{N-l} \Delta x(l, l_0) \\ \overline{\Delta y(l, l_0)} = \frac{1}{N-l} \sum_{l_0}^{N-l} \Delta y(l, l_0) \end{cases} \qquad (8)$$

In the formula: $Cov_{xy}(l)$ represents the covariance of x_i and y_i, $\overline{\bullet}$ represents the average of $\bullet$.

5) Calculate the cross-correlation number of fluctuations of x_i and y_i: if x_i and y_i have certain correlation, then $Cov_{xy}(l)$ satisfies the power-law distribution $Cov(l) \sim m^{h_{xy}}$.

In the formula, h_{xy} represents the correlation degree of x_i and y_i, namely the fluctuation correlation coefficient. The fluctuation correlation coefficient h_{xy} can be obtained by fitting the power-law distribution. When $h_{xy} = 0$ means x_i and y_i are unrelated; When $h_{xy} > 0$, it means x_i and y_i are positively correlated; When $h_{xy} < 0$, it means that x_i and y_i are negatively correlated; A higher value of h_{xy} indicates a higher degree of correlation between x_i and y_i.

Step 3: If the fluctuation correlation between a known attribute data and the missing attribute data exceeds the comparison threshold, the known attribute data is retained and the missing attribute data goes to Step 4. Otherwise, the known attribute data is discarded.

Step 4: The attributes corresponding to the M known attribute data retained are called *Know* attributes, and the attributes corresponding to the missing attribute data are called *Unknow* attributes. The combined weights of *Know* attributes and *Unknow* attributes are calculated respectively.

In this step, the combined weight w_j of *Know* attribute j and *Unknow* attributes are calculated by the following formula:

$$\begin{cases} w_j = \dfrac{c_j}{\sum\limits_{j=1}^{M} c_j} \\ \sum\limits_{j=1}^{M} w_j = 1 \end{cases} \tag{9}$$

In the formula: M represents the number of *Know* attributes $j = 1, 2, \ldots, M$, cj represents the fluctuation correlation coefficient between *Know* attribute j and *Unknow* attributes.

Step 5: The scene analysis was carried out on the date containing *Unknow* attributes, and the H most similar scenes were found after clustering historical data of the power grid. The date with attribute *Unknow* is called the missing date, and The H most similar scenes found are called H similar scenes.

Step 6: Firstly, the time period of the missing attribute data in the missing date is determined. Then, for the same time period of each similar scene, the similarity between each *Know* attribute data of the missing date and each *Know* attribute data of each similar scene is measured by the dynamic time-bending distance.

The specific steps are as follows:

1) Set the occurrence time of missing attribute data as time t_n, select n time points backward at time t_n, select n time points forward at time t_n, and finally form the time period (t_n, t_{2n}) of missing attribute data in the missing date, including $2n + 1$ time points $t_0, t_1, \ldots, t_{2n}$; Let M *Know* attributes retained after comparison threshold judgment and screening be denoted as $A_1, A_2, \ldots, A_M$, *Unknow* attribute be denoted as A_0;

2) The *Know* attribute data $A_1, A_2, \ldots, A_M$ at time $t_0, t_1, \ldots, t_{2n}$ of the hth similar scene are denoted as $D_{(1,h)}, D_{(2,h)}, \ldots, D_{(M,h)}$ respectively. $D_{(j,h)} = \sum\limits_{g=0}^{2n} d_{(j,h,g)}$, $d_{(j,h,g)}$ denotes the attribute data of *Know* attribute j at time t_g in the hth similar scene, $j = 1, 2, \ldots, M, h = 1, 2, \ldots, H, g = 1, 2, \ldots, 2n$;

3) The dynamic time-bending distance is used to measure the similarity $S_{(j,h)}$ between the *Know* attribute data A_j at time $t_0, t_1, \ldots, t_{2n}$ in the hth similar scene and the attribute data $D_{(j,h)}$ at time $t_0, t_1, \ldots, t_{2n}$ in the missing date. p represents the missing date.

Step 7: Combined with the combined weights of each *Know* attribute and *Unknow* attribute, the comprehensive similarity of *Unknow* attribute of each similar scene is calculated using the following formula:

$$C_h = \sum_{j=1}^{M} \sum_{h=1}^{H} w_j \times S_{(j,h)} \tag{10}$$

In the formula, C_h represents the comprehensive similarity of *Unknow* attribute in the hth similar scene.

Step 8: After finding N scenes whose comprehensive similarity of *Unknow* attribute is within the threshold, the data T_1 of the *Unknow* attribute at the time t_n of the scene is extracted from the ith scene as the longitudinal filling data. At the same time, the linear fitting of the curve for the *Unknow* attribute was used to find out the data T_2 at time t_n of this scene as the transverse filling data, and the filling value of the missing attribute data in this scene was solved:

$$\begin{cases} T_i = \alpha \times T_1 + \beta \times T_2 \\ \quad\quad \alpha + \beta = 1 \end{cases} \tag{11}$$

In the formula, time t_n is the occurrence time of missing attribute data, α is the weight of T_1, and β is the weight of T_2.

Call the probability of each scenario p_i, the final imputation value of missing attribute data is obtained by multiplying the imputation value of each scene by its scene probability:

$$T = \sum p_i T_i$$

4 Construction of Power System Optimization Model Including Wind Power Plant and Optical Power Station

4.1 Doubly-Fed Asynchronous Fan

The relationship between DFIG active power P_{DFIG} output and wind speed v [8] is as follows:

$$P_{DFIG} = \begin{cases} 0, & v \le v_i, v \ge v_o \\ k_1 v + k_2, & v_i < v \le v_e \\ P_e, & v_o > v > v_e \end{cases} \tag{12}$$

In the formula, P_e is DFIG rated power; v_i is the cut in wind speed; v_e is the rated wind speed; v_o is the cut out wind speed; k_1 and k_2 are the parameter of the fan power generation system.

The relation expression of active and reactive power output in DFIG is as follows:

$$\begin{cases} \left(\frac{P_{DFIG}}{1-s}\right)^2 + Q_{DFIG}^2 = (3U_s I_s)^2 \\ \left(\frac{P_{DFIG}}{1-s}\right)^2 + \left(Q_{DFIG} + 3\frac{U_s^2}{X_s}\right)^2 = \left(3\frac{X_m}{X_s}U_s I_r\right)^2 \end{cases} \tag{13}$$

In the formula: s is the slip rate; U_s is the stator side voltage; I_s is the stator winding current; X_s is the stator leakage reactance; X_m is excitation reactance; I_r is the rotor side converter current.

4.2 Photovoltaic Power Array

The active power output of PV array shall meet the following equation:

$$p_{PV} = E\eta A \tag{14}$$

In the formula, η - photoelectric conversion efficiency; A - Effective light area.
Reactive power output characteristics of PV array shall meet the following equation:

$$|Q_{PV}|_{max} = \sqrt{S_{PV}^2 - P_{PV}^2} \tag{15}$$

In the formula: $|Q_{PV}|_{max}$ - maximum reactive power regulation capacity of PV; S_{PV} - grid-connected inverter capacity of PV system; P_{PV} - Active power output of PV system.

4.3 The Objective Function

The objective is to minimize the active power loss, and its objective function is as follows:

$$\min y = P_{loss} = \sum_{k=1}^{N_l} G_k(U_i^2 + U_j^2 - 2U_i U_j \cos\theta_{ij}) \tag{16}$$

In the formula, P_{loss} is the active power loss of the system; U_i and U_j are node i and node j voltage amplitudes respectively; N_l is the number of system branches; G_k is the conductance of the branch; θ_{ij} is the voltage phase Angle difference between node i and node j.

4.4 The Constraint

1) System power flow constraint

$$\begin{cases} P_{Li} - P_{DGi} = U_i \sum_{k \in i} U_k (G_{ik} \cos \delta_{ik} + B_{ik} \sin \delta_{ik}) \\ Q_{Li} - Q_{DGi} = U_i \sum_{k \in i} U_k (G_{ik} \sin \delta_{ik} - B_{ik} \cos \delta_{ik}) \end{cases} \tag{17}$$

In the formula, node k is all the nodes connected with the node; P_{Li}, Q_{Li} are the active and reactive power injected into node i; P_{DGi}, Q_{DGi} are the active and reactive power of DG or battery injected into node i; δ_{ik} is the phase Angle difference of nodes at both ends of branch ik; G_{ik}, B_{ik} are the real and imaginary parts of admittance on branch ik; U_i, U_k are the voltage amplitudes of node I and node k respectively.

2) Node voltage constraint

$$U_{i\,min} \leq U_i \leq U_{i\,max} \quad i = 1, 2, \ldots, n \tag{18}$$

In the formula, n is the number of system nodes; U_i, $U_{i\,max}$, $U_{i\,min}$ are respectively the node voltage of the node and its allowed maximum and minimum values.

3) Constraints on DG operation conditions

$$Q_{DGi\,min} \leq Q_{DGi} \leq Q_{DGi\,max} \tag{19}$$

In the formula, Q_{DGi}, $Q_{DGi\,max}$, $Q_{DGi\,min}$ are the reactive power output of DG of station I (group) and its allowable maximum and minimum value respectively.

5 Example Analysis

5.1 The Example Described

In this paper, an improved IEEE14 node power system simulation analysis is adopted, as shown in Fig. 2. Node 9 is connected to a large-scale wind power plant, node 5 is connected to a centralized photovoltaic power station, and node 2 and node 10 are connected to 10 sets of switchable capacitor banks with a reactive power capacity of 200 kVar each. It is assumed that the transformer between branch 5–6 and branch 4–9 is a 17-level transformer with load adjusting sub, and the improved particle swarm optimization algorithm is used to optimize the solution [9]. The voltage reference value of the power system is 220 kV, and the capacity reference value is 100 MVA.

The fan inlet wind speed, rated wind speed and cut out wind speed are 4 m/s, 12 m/s and 25 m/s, respectively, with a rated capacity of 8 MW. The effective illumination area of the photovoltaic power station is 30000 m^2, the conversion efficiency is 0.9, and the rated capacity is 8 MW. The allowable range of the node voltage is ±6% of the rated voltage; The population of the improved PSO algorithm is 50, the number of iterations is 150, the GAMA parameter is 0.95, and the learning factor is C1 = C2 = 0.5.

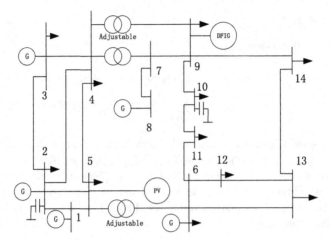

Fig. 2. Improved IEEE14 node system

5.2 Analysis of Optimization Results

An electrical network of typical years of historical data as fill the database, and assumes that one of the typical day has the problem of the missing data, will fill it as object, the method proposed in this paper after data packing on that day, part of the extract containing fill data into the improved IEEE14 node in the system, and a scheduling optimization.

The optimization results of control variables are shown in Fig. 3:

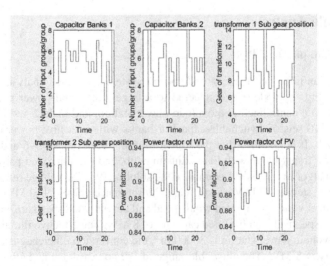

Fig. 3. Optimization results of control variables

The result of active power loss of the whole system for a whole day under various conditions is shown in the Table 1.

Table 1. The simulation results contrast

The layer number	Situation name	Value of loss (kW)	The error rate from the true value
1	The loss of the original system	345.77	5.01%
2	The loss of the system before reactive power optimization with real data	341.62	3.75%
3	The loss of the system after reactive power optimization with real data	329.28	0%
4	The loss after clustering and filling in out possible scenarios with big data	327.53	0.532%

Standard system is the first case IEEE14 node in the table of a scheduling cycle loss, the second is in the system after modification is not a scheduling a scheduling cycle loss, and the third is the transformation system has a scheduling cycle loss after scheduling optimization, the fourth case is to use the clustered scene data to fill in the missing data, and carry out day-ahead scheduling optimization to optimize the loss of a scheduling cycle.

According to the data in the table, the method proposed in this paper is used to fill the grid data, and then the grid with the data filled is optimized for day-ahead scheduling. The results obtained are close to accurate data, which can meet the requirements of data integrity and accuracy for day-ahead scheduling optimization of new energy grid.

This paper proposes a day-ahead scheduling optimization method for power systems including wind power plants and photovoltaic power stations based on big data clustering and filling. The main conclusions are as follows:

1) The proposed missing value filling method based on historical data assisted scenario analysis can improve the filling accuracy of the missing value of the historical data of the day-ahead scheduling of the power system.
2) The load, wind power and photoelectric scene sets obtained by K-means clustering method of big data can be accurately represented.
3) Establish day-ahead scheduling model of power system including wind power plants and photovoltaic power stations, and use improved particle swarm optimization algorithm to solve it. The simulation results show that this method can improve the filling accuracy of the missing value of the day-ahead dispatching historical data of the power system, and meet the development demand of the power grid with new energy.

References

1. Li, G., Cheng, X.: Big Data Research: a major strategic field of future technology and economic and social development – research status and scientific thinking of big data. Proc. Chin. Acad. Sci. **27**(06), 647–657 (2012)
2. Song, Y., Zhou, G., Zhu, Y.: Current status and challenges of smart grid big data processing technology. Power Grid Technol. **37**(04), 927–935 (2013)
3. Xu, Y., Cheng, X., Li, Y., Zhang, H., Yu, W., He, B.: Medium and long-term load forecasting of power system based on big data clustering. J. Electr. Power Syst. Autom. **29**(08), 43–48 (2017)
4. Yuan, J., Zhong, L., Yang, G., Chen, M., Gu, J., Li, T.: Research on filling and classification algorithm of incomplete energy consuming big data in green data center. Chin. J. Comput. **38**(12), 2499–2516 (2015)
5. Tang, L., Wang, R., Wu, R., Fan, B.: Missing data filling algorithm for panoramic regulation unified data model. Autom. Electr. Power Syst. **41**(01), 25–30+87 (2017)
6. Mallick, P., Chen, Z., Zamani, M.: Reinforcement learning using expectation maximization based guided policy search for stochastic dynamics. Neurocomputing **484**, 79–88 (2017)
7. Kim, Y.K., Kim, H.J., Lee, H., Chang, J.W.: Privacy-preserving parallel kNN classification algorithm using index-based filtering in cloud computing. PLoS ONE **17**(5), e0267908 (2017)
8. Lang, Y., Zhang, X., Xu, D., Ma, H., Hadianmrei, S.R.: Reactive power analysis and control strategy for doubly-fed wind farm. Proc. CSEE **2007**(09), 77–82 (2007)
9. Hematpour, N., Ahadpour, S.: Execution examination of chaotic S-box dependent on improved PSO algorithm. Neural Comput. Appl. **33**(10), 5111–5133 (2020)

Day-Ahead Scenario Generation Method for Renewable Energy Based on Historical Data Analysis

Hong Wang[1], Yang Liu[1], Chao Yin[1], Xuesong Bai[1], Bo Sun[1], Menglei Li[2(✉)], and Xiyong Yang[2]

[1] State Grid Heilongjiang Electric Power Company, Harbin 150090, Heilongjiang, China
[2] Nanjing Institute of Technology, Nanjing 211167, Jiangsu, China
lml20000617@xina.com

Abstract. With the massive application of new energy, the contradiction of power grid regulation has become increasingly prominent. How to effectively predict the range of the power grid is a huge challenge faced by the day-ahead dispatch of power system. Aiming at this problem, this paper proposes a method for generating day-ahead scenarios for renewable energy based on historical data analysis. First, the deep embedding clustering (DEC) algorithm is used to analyze historical data, and periods with similar characteristics are divided into one group. Then the conditional deep convolutions generative adversarial network (C-DCGAN) model generates a day-ahead scenario set for renewable energy. At last, the Belgian Elia renewable energy data is used for simulation analysis, and the results show that the proposed method can accurately describe the uncertainty of renewable energy.

Keywords: Renewable energy · Cluster analysis · Conditional deep convolutional generative adversarial networks · Day-ahead scenario set

1 The Introduction

Global energy is undergoing a deep transformation with renewable energy becoming the focus of energy development [3]. However, due to the uncertainty of renewable energy, it brings huge challenges to the power system [4]. How to accurately describe the uncertainty is one of the key issues to overcome these challenges.

The stochastic optimization method uses the scenario analysis method to deal with the uncertainty of renewable energy [1]. Scholars has used statistical methods to generate renewable energy scenarios: Class method, time series simulation method, Markov chain, scene tree generation method, autoregressive moving average model, etc. [2, 3]. The output of renewable energy is easily affected by various factors such as geographical environment, climate and weather.

In recent years, with the rapid development of artificial intelligence, deep learning algorithms have become popular. Compared with statistical methods, renewable power output scenarios generated by deep learning models can accurately describe the uncertainty of renewable energy due to excavating multi-feature and high-dimensional raw

© The Author(s), under exclusive license to Springer Nature Singapore Pte Ltd. 2023
Y. Tian et al. (Eds.): ICBDS 2022, CCIS 1796, pp. 37–46, 2023.
https://doi.org/10.1007/978-981-99-3300-6_4

data. Main deep learning models include: variational auto-encoder (VAE) [4], deep belief network (DBN) [5], generative adversarial networks (GAN) [6]. In recent years, a large number of scholars have studied the method of new energy output scenarios based on unsupervised learning models. Reference [7] proposed a method for new energy output scenarios based on variational autoencoders. Using variational autoencoders to extract non-Euclidean correlation features and temporal correlation features and effectively describe the correlation between multi-source scenarios. Reference [8] uses GAN to find the time-space correlation features of new energy output and introduce Wasserstein distance to improve the training quality of the model. Reference [9] proposes a renewable energy day-ahead scenario generation method based on a conditional generative adversarial network (CGAN), learning the relation between the noise distribution and the day-ahead scenarios through the training of the adversarial network. Compared with the Markov chain scenario generation method, it can describe the uncertainty of wind power more accurately.

Although a series of research has achieved a lot, there are few studies on the generation methods of day-ahead scenarios with new energy access. Aiming at such problems, this paper proposes a method for generating day-ahead scenarios for renewable energy based on historical data analysis. First, the deep embedding clustering (DEC) algorithm is used to cluster and analyze historical data, and time periods with similar characteristics are collected together; second, the conditional deep convolutional generative adversarial network (C-DCGAN) model generates a set of renewable energy day-ahead scenarios; finally, the simulation analysis is carried out with the Belgian Elia renewable energy data to verify the effect of the method in this paper. The example results show that the method proposed in this paper can more accurately describe the uncertainty of renewable energy.

2 General Framework of Day-Ahead Scenario Generation Method for Renewable Energy

Figure 1 shows the framework of the day-ahead prediction method under the high proportion of renewable energy, which is mainly divided into three steps:

Step 1: Collect historical data and use autoencoder to get low-dimensional features; use K-means clustering to get initial clustering results; calculate rework loss and clustering loss function and use the K-means algorithm to iterate repeatedly until the clustering result is within the set deviation range.

Step 2: Establish a C-DCGAN model for each cluster; collect historical prediction data and actual data, input into C-DCGAN for training. After training, the model can learn the relationship between the noise and the actual output.

Step 3: Obtain the prediction value of the new energy output, judge its feature and select the C-DCGAN model, input the prediction value, and day-ahead scenario is generated multiple times to form a scenario set; calculate the prediction interval.

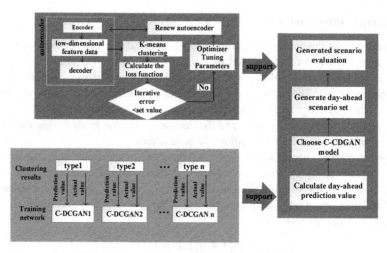

Fig. 1. Daye-ahead prediction method framework

3 Cluster Analysis Based on Deep Embedding Clustering

3.1 Overall Framework of Deep Embedding Clustering Algorithm

The overall network framework is shown in Fig. 2. The first part is to train the stacked autoencoder and use the encoder to convert the data after the normalization into low-dimensional data. In the second part, the low-dimensional data is clustered and analyzed, and the clustering results are obtained by the joint optimization of feature extraction and clustering process.

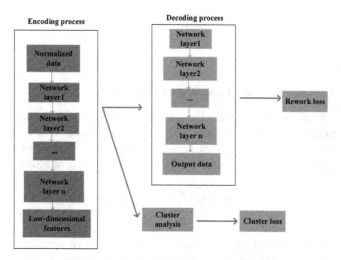

Fig. 2. Cluster algorithm network framework

3.2 Stacked Autoencoder

As a typical deep unsupervised training model, autoencoder can learn effective low-dimensional features from unlabeled high-dimensional data; it is similar to common unsupervised learning algorithms such as principal component analysis and independent component analysis. The autoencoder can extract low-dimensional and representative features, which can improve the clustering accuracy and efficiency; the training of the autoencoder consists of the encoder and the decoder, using the gradient descent method and back-propagating the error to adjust the parameters.

In order to extract useful low-dimensional data, this paper adopts stack autoencoder, which is combined by stacking several autoencoders, and the results are more representative. Assume the training data is $x = [x_1, x_2, \ldots, x_i, \ldots, x_n]$, x_i represents the normalized data, and n represents the time series; the encoding and decoding process of autoencoder data is as follows:

$$h^k = \begin{cases} f\left(w_1^k x + b_1^k\right), k = 1 \\ f\left(w_1^k h^{k-1} + b_1^k\right), 1 < k \leq K \end{cases} \tag{1}$$

$$r^k = \begin{cases} g\left(w_2^k h^k + b_2^k\right), k = 1 \\ g\left(w_2^k r^{k-1} + b_2^k\right), 1 < k \leq K \end{cases} \tag{2}$$

In the formula, h^k and r^k are the output of the layer k in the encoding and decoding processes, K is the maximum number of layers in the process, w_1^k and w_2^k are the network weights of the layer k in the process, b_1^k and b_2^k are the offset of the layer k in the process; h^K is the low-dimensional output of the encoder, and its dimension is much smaller than x; r^k is the final output of the decoder, and its dimension is equal to x.

In this paper, the mean square error (MSE) is used as the loss function, and the formula is as follows:

$$L_r = \frac{\sum_{i=1}^{n} (r_i^K - x_i)^2}{n} \tag{3}$$

3.3 Initial Clustering of Low-Dimensional Features

In this paper, the K-Means algorithm is used for iterative clustering solution. Selecting the optimal number of clusters is the key to cluster analysis. Because we do not know the optimal number of scenario categories, according to the idea of elbow rule [8], we use the sum of squared errors (SSE) as an indicator [9]. The formula of SSE is as follows:

$$E = \sum_{j=1}^{m} \sum_{z \in C_j} |z - \mu_j|^2 \tag{4}$$

E represents the sum of squared errors of the clustering results, which represents the tightness of the sample data in each cluster; m represents the number of clusters, z represents the sample data, and μ_j represents the center of cluster j, C_j represents the sample set of cluster j.

3.4 Joint Optimization

If the low-dimensional data is extracted from the autoencoder and analyzed, the disadvantage of the method is that feature extraction and clustering are independent of each other, and it is hard to obtain optimal clustering results [10]; so the joint optimization of low-dimensional feature extraction and clustering is necessary.

In the reference [11], a clustering loss function is constructed with KL divergence to train the autoencoding network. The loss function formula is as follows:

$$L_c = KL(P\|Q) = \sum_j \sum_i P_{ij} \log \frac{p_{ij}}{q_{ij}} \tag{5}$$

q_{ij} represents the probability that the low-dimensional feature z_i obtained by the autoencoder belongs to the cluster center μ_j, and p_{ij} is the auxiliary target distribution function.

Reference [11] uses a more robust heavy-tailed distribution to represent q_{ij}, and its expression is as follows:

$$q_{ij} = \frac{(1 + \|z_i - \mu_j\|^2/\alpha)^{\alpha+1/2}}{\sum_{j=1}^{m} (1 + \|z_i - \mu_j\|^2/\alpha)^{\alpha+1/2}} \tag{6}$$

α represents the degree of freedom of the distribution t.

In order to improve the clustering performance, we adopt p_{ij} as auxiliary objective distribution function, and improve the clustering accuracy through the square term of q_{ij}; the expression of p_{ij} is as follows:

$$p_{ij} = \frac{q_{ij}^2/\sum_i q_{ij}}{\sum_j (q_{ij}^2/\sum_i q_{ij})} \tag{7}$$

Reference [11] only considers the clustering loss, which influences the feature space, resulting in meaningless and unrepresentative features.

The loss function of the network is modified as:

$$L = L_r + \gamma L_c \tag{8}$$

In the formula, L_r is the reconstruction loss, L_c is the clustering loss; γ is the coefficient that controls the distortion degree of the embedding space.

4 Day-Ahead Scenario Generation Based on C-DCGAN

A C-DCGAN model is established for each cluster of data with similar characteristics to generate day-ahead scenario [12]. In this way, the interference of different clusters of data on the training can be avoided, and the problems of training can be solved.

4.1 Conditional Deep Convolution GAN

GAN is an unsupervised generative model proposed by Goodfellow et al. in 2014. The system consists of a generator and a discriminator. The generator is used to generate the potential distribution of actual data, and the discriminator used to judge whether the input data is real data or fake data; the system improves the accuracy of the samples generated by the generator through the mutual game between the generator and discriminator.

C-DCGAN adds a convolutional network on the basis of CGAN, and uses the powerful feature extraction capability of the convolutional layer to improve the effect of CGAN. The basic structure of C-DCGAN is shown in Fig. 3.

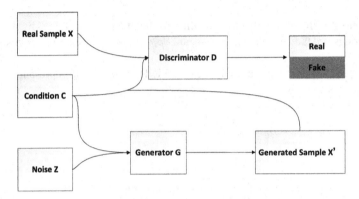

Fig. 3. Basic structure of C-DCGAN

4.2 Building Models Based on C-DCGAN

According to the national technical specifications for the wind and solar power plants, the power field needs to report the power generation prediction curve of the field from 0 to 24 h of the next day, and the time gap is 15 min. If the energy output is stable, the prediction value of wind and solar power output is added to the maximum output of the stable energy source to obtain the prediction curve of the local maximum power output.

Taking the prediction value of the new energy output day as the condition and the actual output as the sample, the two are respectively sent to the C-DCGAN model for training.

4.3 Training of the C-DCGAN Model

The input of the C-DCGAN generator is the combined matrix of noise z and condition c, the output generated sample is $x' = G(z|c)$, the probability distribution of the generated sample is p(x'), the real sample is x, and the probability distribution of the real sample is p(x). The loss functions of the generator and discriminator in C-DCGAN are as follows:

$$L_G = -E_{x'-p(x')}[D(c|x')] \tag{9}$$

$$L_D = -E_{x-p(x)}[D(c|x)] + E_{x'-p(x')}[D(c|x')] \tag{10}$$

E is the expected value of the distribution and D(~) is the discriminator function. The generator is to minimize L_G, the discriminator is to maximize L_D. Combining the above two formulas, the objective function of the C-DCGAN training process can be described:

$$\min_G \max_D V(D, G) = E_{x-p(x)}[D(c|x)] - E_{x'-p(x')}[D(c|x')] \tag{11}$$

5 Determination and Evaluation of the Day-Ahead Value

5.1 Determination of the Day-Ahead Prediction Value

First, obtain the day-ahead prediction value of new energy output, send it into the trained autoencoder to extract low-dimensional data and calculate the Euclidean distance between the extracted low-dimensional value and the center of each cluster. The calculation formula is as follows:

$$D_j = \sqrt{\sum_{i=1}^{n} (h_i - u_i^j)^2} \tag{12}$$

D_j is the distance from the low-dimensional data to the center of the cluster j, h_i is the low-dimensional data of the prediction value, and u_i^j is the data of the center of the cluster j. Second, compare each D_j, and select the cluster with the smallest D_j as the cluster category to which should belong, and then the C-DCGAN model corresponding to the cluster is selected to generate the day-ahead scenario set. Finally, calculate the maximum and minimum values at each moment in the day-ahead scenario set.

5.2 Evaluation of the Day-Ahead Prediction Value

The day-ahead scenario set can be used to describe the uncertainty and the Coverage Rate (CR) and Interval Average Width (IAW) can be used to evaluate the credibility of the gap confidence interval. The calculation formulas of CR and IAW are as follows:

$$CR = \left(\frac{N_r}{N_{all}}\right) \times 100\% \tag{13}$$

N_r is the total number of actual values falling into the prediction interval, and N_{all} is the total number of samples.

$$IAW = \frac{1}{N_{all}} \sum_{n=1}^{N_{all}} (g_n^{max} - g_n^{min}) \tag{14}$$

g_n^{max} is the maximum value of the gap interval of the sampling point n, g_n^{min} is the minimum value, $g_n^{max} - g_n^{min}$ is the width of the gap interval of the sampling point n.

6 Example Analysis

The method in this paper is a combination of DEC and C-DCGAN, so DEC-C-DCGAN is used to represent the method proposed in this article.

6.1 Day-Ahead Scenario Generation

The calculation example uses the renewable energy power data of Belgium on one day as a sample. The data interval is 1 h, and the example takes 24 groups of data in one day. Extract the prediction value of renewable energy and 100 sets of noise and splice them, day-ahead scenarios and actual value are shown in Fig. 4:

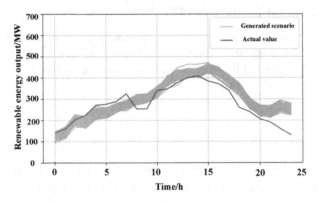

Fig. 4. DEC-C-DCGAN renewable energy day-ahead scenario Set

The yellow line in Fig. 4 represents 100 day-ahead scenarios generated by the generator. It can be seen that the output trend of the day-ahead scenarios generated by DEC-C-DCGAN is consistent with the actual value, and is not much different from the actual value.

6.2 Method Comparison

In order to verify the accuracy of the scenario generation method proposed in this paper, the calculation example compares the DEC-C-DCGAN method with the C-DCGAN method. The confidence interval of the day-ahead scenario set generated by the two methods is shown in Fig. 5.

As can be seen in Fig. 7, the day-ahead scenario set generated by the C-DCGAN method has a wider confidence interval, while the day-ahead scenario set generated by the DEC-C-DCGAN can better describe the prediction error range and uncertainty of new energy under the corresponding prediction value.

In order to avoid the lack of rigor in the sample, the example simulates the sample, calculates the coverage rate and the interval average width, and compares the two methods, the calculation results are shown in Table 1.

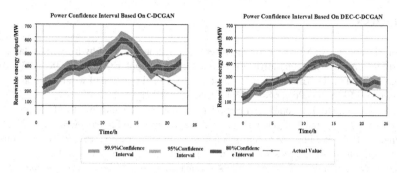

Fig. 5. Power confidence interval of the day-ahead scenario set

Table 1. Scenario generation index results

Confidence	DEC-C-DCGAN		C-DCGAN	
	Coverage rate %	Interval average width/MW	Coverage rate %	Interval average width/MW
99.9%	83.56	74.21	60.60	119.31
95%	65.65	56.12	30.32	95.21
80%	50.56	37.36	15.52	79.64

It can be seen from the table that the DEC-C-DCGAN method has higher coverage rate than the C-DCGAN method, but the interval average width of the DEC-C-DCGAN method is smaller than that of the C-DCGAN method.

In conclusion, the DEC-C-DCGAN method can describe the day-ahead output uncertainty of renewable energy more accurately than the C-DCGAN method.

7   Conclusion

This paper proposes an improved renewable energy day-ahead scenario generation method, and analyzes the output characteristics of renewable energy. In the calculation example. This paper concludes:

1) DEC-C-DCGAN can better adapt to the problem of new energy day-ahead scenario generation.
2) This paper compares the proposed DEC-C-DCGAN method with the C-DCGAN method. The results show that the DEC-C-DCGAN method can accurately describe the uncertainty of the day-ahead output of new energy.
3) The method proposed in this paper does not involve explicit feature analysis and has broaden applicability.

References

1. Wei, H., Zhang, H., Yu, D., et al.: Short-term optimal operation of hydro-wind-solar hybrid system with improved generative adversarial networks. Appl. Energy **250**, 389–403 (2019)
2. Sturt, A., Strbac, G.: Efficient stochastic scheduling for simulation of wind-integrated power systems. IEEE Trans. Power Syst. **27**(1), 323–334 (2012)
3. Li, Y., Xie, K., Hu, B.: Copula-Arma model for multivariate wind speed and its applications in reliability assessment of generating systems. J. Electr. Eng. Technol. **8**(3), 421–427 (2013)
4. Kingma, D.P., Welling, M.: Auto-encoding variational Bayes. IEICE Transactions on Fundamentals of Electronics, Communications and Computer Sciences (2013)
5. Hinton, G.E., Osindero, S., The, Y.-W.: A fast learning algorithm for deep belief nets. Neural Comput. **18**(7), 1527–1554 (2006)
6. Goodfellow, I.J., Pouget-Abadie, J., Mirza, M., et al.: Generative adversarial nets. In: Proceedings of the 27th International Conference on Neural Information Processing Systems, pp. 2672–2680. MIT Press, Montreal (2014)
7. Wang, X., Li, Y., Dong, X., et al.: Multi source-load scenario generation method of active distribution network based on variational autoencoder. Power Syst. Technol. **45**(8), 2962–2969 (2021)
8. Chen, Y., Wang, Y., et al.: Model-free renewable scenario generation using generative adversarial networks. IEEE Trans. Power Syst. **33**(3), 3265–3275 (2018)
9. Dong, X., Sun, Y., Pu, T.: Day-ahead scenario generation of renewable energy based on conditional GAN. Proc. CSEE **40**(17), 5527–5535 (2020)
10. Yu, P.: Variational autoencoder-based representation learning and deep embedding clustering with attributed networks. Zhejiang University (2019)
11. Yang, J., Liu, J., et al.: A method for generating scenes of uncertain sources of water light charge based on deep embedding clustering. Chin. Soc. Electr. Eng. **40**(22), 7296–7306 (2020)
12. Zhnag, C., Shao, Z., et al.: Renewable power generation data transferring based on conditional deep convolutions generative adversarial network. Power Syst. Technol. **46**(06), 2182–2190 (2022)

A High-Frequency Stock Price Prediction Method Based on Mode Decomposition and Deep Learning

Weijie Chen[1,2], Qingshan Jiang[1(✉)], Xibei Jia[2(✉)], Abdur Rasool[1,3], and Weihui Jiang[2]

[1] Shenzhen Institute of Advanced Technology, Chinese Academy of Sciences, Shenzhen 518055, China
qs.jiang@siat.ac.cn
[2] Shenzhen Audaque Data Technology Co., Ltd., Shenzhen 518057, China
xibei.jia@audaque.com
[3] Shenzhen College of Advanced Technology, University of Chinese Academy of Sciences, Shenzhen 518055, China

Abstract. The modeling and prediction of stock prices is the core work in securities investment, and it is of enormous significance to reducing decision-making risks and improving investment returns. Existing research mainly focuses on mid or low-frequency stock price prediction, which is challenging to apply to intraday high-frequency trading scenarios. Meanwhile, the model accuracy face limitation due to the neglect of the influence of random noise and the refinement of the price sequence law. This paper proposes a high-frequency stock price prediction method based on mode decomposition and deep learning to improve intraday stock price prediction accuracy. Firstly, this method stabilizes the stock price series through empirical mode decomposition to tackle the issue of random noise interference. Then the convolutional neural network is introduced to extract the high-dimensional data features hidden in the stock price series by using multiple convolution kernels. Furthermore, the gated recurrent unit is used to process time-sequential data and to predict the stock prices at the minute level. The experimental result indicates that the proposed high-frequency stock price prediction method can achieve a significant forecasting effect, and its accuracy outperforms the existing methods.

Keywords: High-Frequency Price Prediction · Empirical Mode Decomposition · Convolutional Neural Network · Gated Recurrent Unit

1 Introduction

The stock market in China is still in a weakly efficient state due to multiple factors, such as market supply and demand, information transparency, and investor sentiment. It is difficult to predict the exact price value due to its strong nonlinearity and non-stationarity. On the other hand, modeling and accurate forecasting of stock prices through real transaction data help to understand the influencing factors of stocks, and it is a benefit to discover the potential relationship between current prices and historical information. Moreover, accurate predictions can effectively reduce decision-making risks and improve investment returns. Therefore, stock price prediction has been a problematic and essential issue in securities investment [1–3].

The price prediction of stocks can be divided into low-frequency, mid-frequency, and high-frequency predictions according to different time scales. Here the high-frequency prediction especially refers to the prediction for the next several minutes, such as 1 min, 5 min, or 10 min, etc. [4, 5]. The data used for high-frequency prediction usually includes market snapshots, transactions, and entrustment records released by the exchange. Unlike the low and mid frequency counterparts, which mainly focus on the daily or weekly scenario, the high-frequency prediction has the following characteristics. Firstly, the transaction behavior is more random in high-frequency trading, resulting in larger non-stationary noise in original price data. Thus the high-frequency price series needs to be stabilized. Secondly, the usable high-frequency trading data of stocks is limited, which only contains micro information such as transaction price and trading volume. To achieve a more accurate prediction, it is necessary to further mine high-dimensional features from the original price-volume data. Thirdly, the high-frequency price data has a stronger trend. The rise and fall process of price has a strong continuity in a short period, so it is noteworthy to consider the causality of sample data in modeling.

According to the above characteristics, this paper proposes a high-frequency stock price prediction method based on mode decomposition and deep learning. This method first stabilizes the price series through Empirical Mode Decomposition (EMD) [6] to reduce random noise interference. Then uses Convolutional Neural Network (CNN) [7] to abstract hidden properties of the stock price sequence, which is a benefit for modeling by introducing more usable inputs. In addition, the Gated Recurrent Unit (GRU) [8] is used to integrate the feature data, learn the sequential law of price series and calculate the price prediction result at the next moment. The primary purpose of this method is to enhance the prediction ability for stock prices in high-frequency scenarios. To inspect the effectiveness of the proposed method, the accuracy of prediction results is analyzed through four indicators, and the comparison with different parameters and different prediction methods is also demonstrated.

2 Related Work

The high-frequency stock price prediction methods can be classified into three categories: technical prediction, time series, and deep learning. The technical prediction method uses historical price and volume data to form multiple technical indicators and then predict the future price according to the indicator values. Liu [9] constructed 15 technical indicators, including price trend, oscillation, and momentum, and used them to predict the stock price for the next 5 min. Gu [10] constructed 97 derivative indicators based on price change rate, volatility, and Bollinger bands and used a regression model to predict the price direction after 5 min. Kong [11] constructed 18 technical indicators such as price change rate, volume change rate, and their moving average values to predict price fluctuations. Chandar [12] constructed 16 technical indicators from historical data and used three different models to predict the next minute closing price of selected stocks. The core of the technical prediction method lies in the design of high-frequency technical indicators. Good indicators can bring benefits to forecasting effects. However, with the popularization of programmed trading, various possible indicators have been repeatedly applied and gradually become invalid. It is challenging to solve the problem of high-frequency price prediction simply by constructing new indicators.

The time series prediction method fits the historical price data with a specific model, such as the difference autoregressive moving average model, autoregressive conditional heteroskedasticity model, or spline function model, and then predicts the future price by data extrapolation. Song [13] used the differential autoregressive moving average model to predict the 5-min prices of the CSI 300 index and introduced adaptive filtering to optimize the parameters. On the basis of the differential autoregressive moving average model, Li [14] used the information criterion to determine the model parameters and used the support vector machine as an auxiliary to fit the residual quantity of the model, which could improve the prediction accuracy of 5-min high-frequency prices. Based on the limit order book data, Huang [15] used the spline basis function to fit the real-time buying and selling supply and demand curve and predicted the high-frequency price in 15 s. The principle of the time series prediction method is simple and easy to implement. However, due to the strong randomness and high volatility of prices in high-frequency trading, it is difficult to meet the assumption of data stationarity. In addition, the accurate calibration of model parameters is difficult for this method, resulting in relatively low accuracy in prediction.

Deep learning uses massive amounts of historical data to train a model and complete specified classification or regression tasks according to the model prediction results. The high-frequency trading data of stocks has a fast update frequency and rich data details, which make it especially suitable for deep learning. Taroon [16] built a long short-term memory network and several variants to predict the next minute high frequency stock price movement. Solis [17] used convolutional neural models, recurrent networks and densely-connected neural networks to construct a combined model to predict the 2 min and 5 min short term stock price. Chong [18] used the component analysis techniques and restricted Boltzmann machine to reduce the input dimension and trained a deep neural network to predict the stock price after 5 min. Lachiheb [19] analyzed the correlation between stocks and classified the stocks with similar properties into the same category. Models for each group are trained independently. The empirical result shows that the grouping modeling method can improve the 5-min price prediction accuracy. Lanbouri [20] predicted the high-frequency prices for the next 1 min, 5 min, and 10 min based on recurrent networks and analyzed the impact of different input indicators on the prediction effect. The deep learning model is not limited by the number of input variables and supports more hidden layers and more complex network structures. However, if the original input data is contaminated by random noise, the prediction result will be inevitably biased and thus lead to a large prediction error. Existing research used original stock price data as input directly for model training. The noise interference in high-frequency price prediction was not fully considered, and the hidden features in data were not fully mined; thus, the prediction accuracy is limited.

3   Methodology

In view of the shortcomings and challenges of existing approaches, we propose a novel method based on mode decomposition and deep learning for high-frequency stock price prediction. The architecture of the proposed method is shown in Fig. 1.

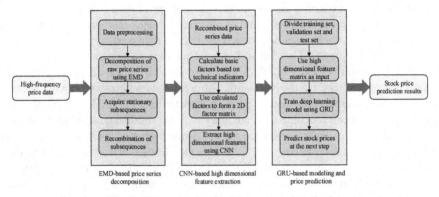

Fig. 1. The architecture of the proposed method

As illustrated in Fig. 1, the input of this method is the high-frequency stock price data, and the output is the prediction result of future prices. Here, the high-frequency stock data refers to the historical transaction data, entrust data, and snapshot data released by the exchange. The prediction target is the price value of the next 5 min. The core part of the method is mainly divided into three modules:

(1) EMD-based price series decomposition. In this method, the empirical mode decomposition technology decomposes nonlinear price signals into several stationary subsequences, thus eliminating noise interference.
(2) CNN-based high dimensional feature extraction. Owing to few usable features in high-frequency data, the convolutional network is used to extract hidden property from the existing data, thus enriching input information for modeling.
(3) GRU-based modeling and price prediction. After feature extracting, the high dimensional feature matrix is input for model training. The gated recurrent unit is then used to learn the input data's time series law and predict the future price.

3.1   EMD-Based Price Series Decomposition

Empirical mode decomposition is an automatic signal analysis technique [21] that disassemble nonlinear and dynamic time series into several stationary subsequences. Compared with traditional signal decomposition techniques, EMD will not enforce pre-set parameters and does not depend on subjective experience of researchers, thus suitable for adaptive signal stabilization and noise elimination. The overall process of EMD-based time series decomposition can be listed as follows.

Step 1: Set the input time series $x(t)$, and assign it to a new time series $x^*(t)$.

Step 2: Find all the maximum and minimum elements in $x^*(t)$ based on a specific frequency, and fit the extremum points through the cubic spline interpolation function to obtain the upper envelope $e_{max}(t)$ and lower envelope $e_{min}(t)$.

Step 3: Compute the average between two envelopes to acquire the mean sequence $m(t)$, and then calculate the difference between $x^*(t)$ and the sequence:

$$m(t) = (e_{max}(t) + e_{min}(t))/2 \tag{1}$$

$$h(t) = x^*(t) - m(t) \tag{2}$$

Step 4: If the number of crossings between the extremum points and the zero points is equal to 1, and the average of upper and lower envelopes are both equal to 0, let $h(t)$ be the intrinsic mode function (IMF) of this round and enter Step5. Otherwise, let $x^*(t) = h(t)$, and return to Step2.

Step 5: Calculate the ith residual component $r_i(t)$ of the original time series:

$$r_i(t) = x^*(t) - c_i(t) \tag{3}$$

Step 6: If $r_i(t)$ is non-monotonic, then let $x^*(t) = r_i(t)$, and return to Step2. Otherwise, if $r_i(t)$ is monotonic, then the time series decomposition is completed.

After the decomposition process mentioned above, the relationship between the original series $x(t)$, the components $c_i(t)$ and the residual $r_n(t)$ are described as:

$$x(t) = \sum_{i=1}^{n} c_i(t) + r_n(t) \tag{4}$$

In this paper, the original high-frequency price data is firstly preprocessed. Since the real trading time is random and uncertain, the time interval between two transactions is inconsistent, which means the EMD cannot be applied directly. Therefore, the 4-h trading time of a whole day is evenly divided into 4800 units, with 3 s per unit. The missing price will be filled, and a complete price sequence with 4800 values is formed. The price series is then regarded as the input $x(t)$ for EMD decomposition. Finally, the first and second-order high-frequency noises will be removed, and the remaining stationary subsequences will be recombined as a new series.

3.2 CNN-Based High-Dimensional Feature Extraction

The convolutional neural network [22] has aptitude for representation learning and is widely used for feature extraction. The CNN structure usually consists of the input, convolution, and pooling layers. Assume that the input layer is a $N \times N$ matrix, and the size of the convolution kernel is $F \times F$, then the output value after convolution is:

$$v_{i,j} = f\left(\sum_{k=0}^{F-1}\sum_{m=0}^{F-1} w_{k,m} V_{i+k,j+m}\right) \tag{5}$$

where $v_{i,j}$ is the convolution result at row i and column j. $w_{k,m}$ is the weight of the row k and column m in the convolution kernel. $V_{i+k,j+m}$ is the origin input at row $i + k$ and column $j + m.f$ is the excitation function. After the convolution operation, an $E \times E$ output matrix of can be obtained, where $E = N - F + 1$.

To improve modeling efficiency, several basic factors will be constructed based on classic technical indicators and human experience before CNN processing. This paper constructs 16 basic factors from the price change rate and amplitude perspective.

Factor 1 is the latest transaction price p_t at the current moment, and factors 2 to 6 are the rate of change between the latest price and the previous 5 to 25 min:

$$F = p_t / p_{t-i*20} \qquad (6)$$

where $i = 5, 10, \ldots, 25$. Since the data samples every 3 s, it contains 20 data points for each minute. Factors 7 to 11 are the difference between the highest price and the lowest price in the previous 5 to 25 min:

$$F = \max(p_{t-i*20}, p_{t-i*20+1}, \ldots, p_t) - \min(p_{t-i*20}, p_{t-i*20+1}, \ldots, p_t) \qquad (7)$$

Factors 12 to 16 are the average prices for each time interval:

$$F = avg(p_{t-i*20}, p_{t-i*20+1}, \ldots, p_t) \qquad (8)$$

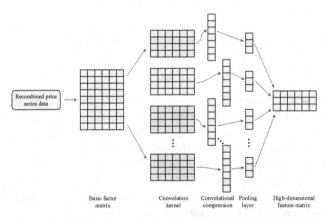

Fig. 2. CNN-based high-dimensional feature extraction

The feature extraction process based on CNN is presented in Fig. 2. Firstly, a $d \times n$ basic factor matrix is constructed according to the step mentioned above, where $d = 4800$, $n = 16$. Then the input matrix will be scanned by several convolution kernels and be compressed into several feature vectors. The pooling layer will further refine the vector information by average pooling. Finally, the pooled feature vectors are spliced horizontally to form a high-dimensional feature matrix.

3.3 GRU-Based Modeling and Price Prediction

A Gated recurrent unit is developed from the classic long short-term memory model [23]. GRU introduces the reset gate and updates gate to tackle the gradient disappearance and gradient explosion problems in backpropagation, and meanwhile effectively reduce the complexity and training time. Assume that the input state variable is x_t, then the reset gate r_t as well as the update gate z_t will be:

$$r_t = \sigma(x_t w^r + h_{t-1} W^r + b^r) \tag{9}$$

$$z_t = \sigma(x_t w^z + h_{t-1} W^z + b^z) \tag{10}$$

where w^r, W^r, w^z, W^z are the weight coefficient matrices of the reset gate and the update gate. b^r and b^z are the gate offsets. h_{t-1} denotes the previous hidden state and σ represents the sigmoid function.

After obtaining the two gate states, the output state of the latest moment h_t can be calculated as follows:

$$h' = \tanh(x_t w^h + (h_{t-1} \bullet r_t) W^h + b^h) \tag{11}$$

$$h_t = (1 - z_t) \bullet h_{t-1} + z_t \bullet h' \tag{12}$$

where h' is temporary state, and b^h is its offset. w^h and W^h are the weight coefficient matrix. The tanh is the excitation function and $\bullet$ denotes dot product operation. The final state will be transmitted to the next layer of the model.

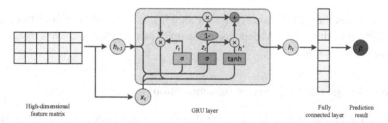

Fig. 3. GRU-based modeling and price prediction

The GRU-based time series modeling and prediction process is presented in Fig. 3. Firstly, the high-dimensional feature matrix extracted by CNN is used as input. At time step t = 0, the first sample of the feature matrix will be transmitted to h_{t-1} and x_t simultaneously. At each time step, new samples will be input, and the hidden state will be updated through the internal operation of GRU [24]. Finally, the last state will be transmitted to the fully connected layer and mapped to a real scalar, which is the final prediction result. After the above three-stage processing flow, a prediction price sequence with the same length as the original price sequence can be obtained.

4   Results Evaluation

4.1   Datasets and Evaluation Metrics

The high-frequency price data utilized in this paper comes from the released data of the Shanghai and Shenzhen stock exchanges, including the trading time, price, and volume of each transaction. The data time range is from 2022/1/4 to 2022/8/31. The data from

January to June is choosen as the training part, the data in July is the validation part, and the data in August is regarded as the test part. The research object is the constituent stocks of the CSI 300 Index. For each moment in the prediction, the historical price data of the previous 25 min will be used to construct the basic factor matrix. Then the stock price is predicted according to the method described in Sect. 3. The prediction target is the future stock price in the next 5 min.

Since the output of the method in this paper is a price prediction value, which belongs to a regression problem, we choose the commonly used accuracy indicators such as RMSE, MAE, MAPE, and R2 [25] as the evaluation metrics:

$$RMSE = \sqrt{(\sum_{i=1}^{N} (y_i - \tilde{y}_i)^2)/N} \tag{13}$$

$$MAE = (\sum_{i=1}^{N} |y_i - \tilde{y}_i|)/N \tag{14}$$

$$MAPE = (\sum_{i=1}^{N} \left| \frac{y_i - \tilde{y}_i}{y_i} \right|)/N \times 100\% \tag{15}$$

$$R^2 = 1 - \frac{\sum_{i=1}^{N} (y_i - \tilde{y}_i)^2/N}{\sum_{i=1}^{N} (\overline{y}_i - \tilde{y}_i)^2/N} \tag{16}$$

where y_i denotes the real stock price at time step i. $\tilde{y}_i$ is the predicted stock price based on the method in this paper. N denotes the sample quantity and $\overline{y}_i$ is the average of all real prices in the sample.

4.2 High-Frequency Price Series Decomposition

Since the trading behavior in the real market is random and uncertain, the time intervals between two transactions are inconsistent. Discontinuous data is unable to be applied to EMD, and thus in this paper, the discontinuous price series is firstly discretized and aligned with fixed intervals. Thereafter, the price series is decomposed by EMD and is split into several subsequences with different frequencies. By taking the price data of 601318.SH PingAn Insurance on 2022/8/1 as an example, the high-frequency price series decomposition result is reported in Fig. 4.

It can be analyzed from Fig. 4 that the original high-frequency price series is decomposed into nine subsequences, including IMF1–IMF8 and a residual sequence. Since high-frequency trading only focuses on a relatively short time, the time window here is from 10:00 am to 11:00 am. As shown in the figure, the oscillation frequency of the curve decreases as the order number increases. The first two subsequences show strong randomness, which reflects the unstable factors in high-frequency stock trading and thus need to be excluded. Those curves with higher order display less oscillation, reflecting the actual trend of the stock. Based on the above analysis, we remove the high-frequency noise terms IMF1 and IMF2 and use the remaining subsequences to build a new stable sequence, thereby reducing the impact of random noise.

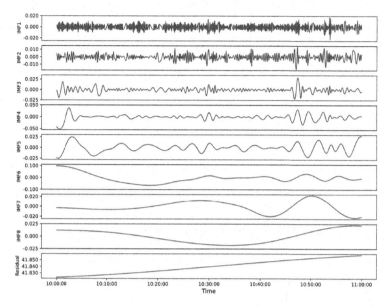

Fig. 4. High-frequency price series decomposition of 601318.SH PingAn Insurance

4.3 High-Frequency Stock Price Prediction Results

The decomposed price data will be input to CNN and GRU for feature extraction and time series modeling. The CNN layer contains 128 convolution kernels, and their size is 100×16. The rectified linear unit is chosen as the activation function. The average pooling operation is adopted in the pooling layer; the average value of every two adjacent features is taken as the representative for data refinement. By applying the convolution calculation above, the correlation information of the basic factors can be fully extracted, and a high-dimensional feature matrix is obtained.

The dimension of the GRU unit, which represents the length of the output sequence in a single step, is set to 128. The number of input features is also 128, which is consistent with the number of convolution kernels output by CNN. Different from traditional non-sequential models, GRU takes three-dimensional samples with step size as input, so the high-dimensional feature matrix needs to be transformed. Here, each sample at each moment is merged with previous data over a short period to form a three-dimensional tensor. The output of the GRU layer is a 128×1 vector. Finally, the vector is mapped into a single scaler by the fully connected layer, which is the predicted result of the high-frequency stock price in the next moment.

The training process of the proposed method is given in Fig. 5. As demonstrated in the figure, the loss function values of the training set and the validation set both decrease rapidly in the first 50 iterations, which reflects the rapid convergence ability of the model. Some basic factors have been built by classic technical indicators before model training, which reduces the complexity of model training. After that, the iteration curve oscillates randomly within a certain range and then gradually converges.

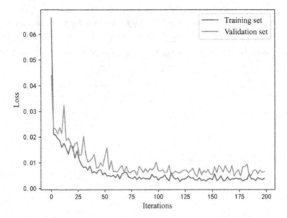

Fig. 5. Loss function iteration process for model training

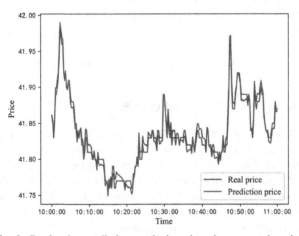

Fig. 6. Stock price prediction results based on the proposed method

The price series prediction result based on the proposed method is shown in Fig. 6, where the blue curve is the real price of the stock, and the red curve denotes the predicted price. Here we carry out the experiment in an iterative fashion; that is, the data of the previous 25 min from the current time step will be used for factor construction and feature extraction and the model will provide a prediction result about the price of the next 5 min. Therefore, each time step has an independent prediction value to show the detailed difference between the real and predicted data. To be consistent with Sect. 4.2, the stock 601318.SH PingAn Insurance on 2022/8/1 is adopted here as an example for demonstration. As illustrated from the figure, the proposed model can accurately predict the high-frequency stock price, and the predicted price curve always keeps the same trend as the curve of the real price, which reflects the good prediction ability of the model.

Table 1. Stock price prediction error of the proposed method

	Min	Max	Mean
RMSE	0.0475	0.0646	0.0528
MAE	0.0382	0.0579	0.0416
MAPE (%)	0.2657	0.3120	0.2909
R^2	0.9519	0.9804	0.9741

To quantify the prediction effectivity of the method, the RMSE, MAE, MAPE, and R2 are counted, as given in Table 1. The table shows the minimum, maximum, and means errors for all constituent stocks in the CSI 300 index, which can reflect the best and worst performances of the model. It can be analyzed from the table that the maximum value of RMSE for all stocks is 0.0646, and the maximum value of MAE is 0.0579, which are all within a reasonable range. Since the research sample already contains stocks of different industries and styles, the results above show that the prediction is less affected by the stock properties, which reflects the method's stability.

5 Discussion and Analysis

In Sect. 4, we verify the prediction accuracy of the proposed method, where the experiment is conducted with fixed parameters. In order to further verify the method's robustness, in this section, we examine the model effectiveness with different parameter settings. Besides, to compare the performance of different methods and show the superiority of the proposed method, we will study and analyze the results of the other four prediction methods on the same data in the experiment.

5.1 Comparative Analysis of Different Model Parameters

A reasonable set of parameters has an important influence on the accuracy of model output. Therefore, we examine the model performance by adjusting different parameter values. This section analyzes the batch sizes of the input sample, and the quantities of convolution kernels in the CNN layer, units in the GRU layer, neurons in the fully connected layer, respectively. For a clear comparison, when one parameter is being examined, the other three parameters will remain the default values. For example, when the batch size is being analyzed, the number of CNN Kernels, GRU units, and fully connected units will remain to be 128, 128, and 64, respectively. The prediction error on different parameter settings is shown in Table 2.

The batch size refers to the sample quantity selected in a single process during model training, which has an important impact on the model's learning rate and optimization effect. The number of CNN kernels and the number of GRU units are the core parameters of the model. The higher value is conducive to the data fitting of the training set, but at the same time, it may reduce the generalization ability. The neurons quantity in the fully connected layer is also important for the stability of the model. As demonstrated

Table 2. Statistics of prediction error on different parameter values

Metrics	Batch Size			Number of CNN Kernels		
	32	64	128	64	128	256
RMSE	0.0597	0.0528	0.0640	0.0596	0.0528	0.0637
MAE	0.0538	0.0416	0.0576	0.0537	0.0416	0.0573
MAPE (%)	0.3761	0.2909	0.4028	0.3765	0.2909	0.4016
R^2	0.9634	0.9741	0.9584	0.9587	0.9741	0.9537
Metrics	Number of GRU Units			Number of Fully Connected Units		
	64	128	256	32	64	128
RMSE	0.0586	0.0528	0.0632	0.0568	0.0528	0.0552
MAE	0.0528	0.0416	0.0568	0.0512	0.0416	0.0497
MAPE (%)	0.3695	0.2909	0.3992	0.3582	0.2909	0.3481
R^2	0.9621	0.9741	0.9552	0.9638	0.9741	0.9649

in Table 2, different model parameters have significant influence to the final prediction accuracy. As the value of the model parameters increases, the prediction accuracy will first increase and then be followed by a decrease, which means that the model parameters have a reasonable value range. From the statistics, it is concluded that the model performs best when it contains 64 samples in a batch, 128 CNN convolution kernels, 128 GRU units and 64 neurons in the fully connected layer.

5.2 Comparative Analysis of Different Prediction Methods

In order to further examine the proposed method, namely EMD-ConvGRU, we make a horizontal comparison with other similar prediction methods in this section to demonstrate the advantages of the method in high-frequency price prediction. Here, the classical technical prediction method Naive [26], the time series prediction method ARIMA [27], the single CNN model [28], and the GRU model [29] are selected for comparison.

Naive: The traditional technical indicator model uses the moving average convergence divergence (MACD) as the prediction indicator. This method calculates the moving average of convergence and differences in the past time and then uses the calculated value as the stock price prediction result.

ARIMA: The autoregressive integrated moving average model, which obtains the optimal model parameters by fitting the historical data of the stock price series, and predicts the future price through data extrapolation.

CNN: The convolutional neural network model, which collects the historical data of the stock in the recent period for model training. The same as that in Sect. 3.2, we use the 16 basic factors as model input. However, different from the proposed method, the EMD and GRU are neglected here but only use the single CNN model.

GRU: The gated recurrent unit model can obtain the data interdependence in time domain and adaptively search the optimal mode of the input series. Similar to the CNN method, the single GRU structure is used here.

In order to ensure the fairness of the comparison, the division of the training set, validation set, and test set of various models is consistent with those described in Sect. 4.1. The difference between the models is as follows. The Naive model only uses the MACD single indicator for modeling, and the calculated indicator value is directly adopted as the predicted value of the future price. The ARIMA model applies extrapolation by using the correlation information of the price series itself and does not contain any factors. The CNN and GRU models can be regarded as part of the proposed EMD-ConvGRU but do not include the EMD noise processing, which is used to compare the effectivity of the single model and the hybrid model proposed in this paper. The stock price prediction results of the above different models are provided in Fig. 7.

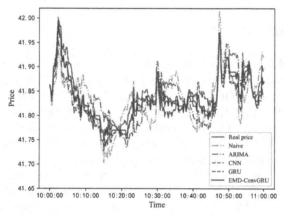

Fig. 7. Comparison of high-frequency stock price prediction results based on different methods

The figure shows the high-frequency price data of 601318.SH PingAn Insurance from 10:00 am to 11:00 am on 2022/8/1. As can be seen from Fig. 7, the prediction accuracy of the traditional Naive method is the lowest. Although it can basically follow the trend of the real price from the macro level, there is still a significant difference between the predicted and real values. The ARIMA model only performs a simple fit to the price series, so the prediction effect is relatively weak. CNN and GRU refine the data features from the perspective of space and time, respectively, and the prediction accuracy is improved. Among them, GRU performs relatively better because it captures the fluctuation law of high-frequency data. However, neither of them considers the influence of random noise. There are several spikes in some areas of the prediction curve, which indicates instability in the model. Overall, the prediction accuracy of the models above is still lower than the proposed method.

Table 3. Error comparison of different stock price prediction methods

	Naive	ARIMA	CNN	GRU	**EMD-ConvGRU**
RMSE	0.1844	0.1646	0.1249	0.1134	**0.0528**
MAE	0.1661	0.1483	0.1014	0.0979	**0.0416**
MAPE(%)	1.1618	1.0368	0.7086	0.6851	**0.2909**
R^2	0.7572	0.7934	0.8345	0.8634	**0.9741**

Statistics on the errors of different stock price prediction methods are compared in Table 3. As listed in Table 3, the proposed EMD-ConvGRU can obtain the best prediction effect. The RMSE obtained by the test set samples is 0.0528, the MAE is 0.0416, the MAPE is 0.2909%, and the R^2 is 0.9741. Compared to other similar methods, the method in this paper comprehensively considers the influence of random noise, the extraction of high-dimensional features, and the time series characteristics hidden in price series. Thus the prediction accuracy is significantly improved.

6 Conclusion

The existing challenges in stock prediction, i.e., lack consideration of random noise interference, insufficient usable features for high-frequency modeling, and ignoring the time sequence regularity of the price data, motivated us to design a new method to solve these problems. This paper proposes a novel method using mode decomposition and deep learning techniques to improve stock price prediction accuracy. This method first uses EMD to stabilize the original price series, then uses CNN to extract local features in stock price data, and finally uses GRU to model and make prediction for the future price of the next 5 min. The experimental results demonstrate that the proposed method performs better than similar existing methods. Since a large amount of high-frequency data is needed for model training, we recommend to equip an exclusive server with large storage and high calculational efficiency to satisfy the capacity and speed requirement in practical use. In the future, we will combine this high-frequency price prediction method with specific stock selection and timing methods to construct an efficient strategy for practical stock intraday trading.

Funding. This work is supported by the National Key Research and Development Program of China under fund number 2021YFF1200104, and the Key Technologies Research and Development Program of Guangdong Province under fund number 2020B010165003.

References

1. Long, J., Chen, Z., He, W., et al.: An integrated framework of deep learning and knowledge graph for prediction of stock price trend: an application in Chinese stock exchange market. Appl. Soft Comput. **91**, 106205 (2020)

2. Yuan, X., Yuan, J., Jiang, T., et al.: Integrated long-term stock selection models based on feature selection and machine learning algorithms for China stock market. IEEE Access **8**, 22672–22685 (2020)
3. Aslam, S., Rasool, A., Jiang, Q., et al.: LSTM based model for real-time stock market prediction on unexpected incidents. In: 2021 IEEE International Conference on Real-time Computing and Robotics (RCAR), pp. 1149–1153. IEEE (2021)
4. Guo, Y., Han, S., Shen, C., et al.: An adaptive SVR for high-frequency stock price forecasting. IEEE Access **6**, 11397–11404 (2018)
5. Akyildirim, E., Bariviera, A.F., Nguyen, D.K., et al.: Forecasting high-frequency stock returns: a comparison of alternative methods. Ann. Oper. Res. **2022**, 1–52 (2022)
6. Liu, T., Luo, Z., Huang, J., et al.: A comparative study of four kinds of adaptive decomposition algorithms and their applications. Sensors **18**(7), 2120 (2018)
7. Dhillon, A., Verma, G.K.: Convolutional neural network: a review of models, methodologies and applications to object detection. Prog. Artif. Intell. **9**(2), 85–112 (2020)
8. Shen, G., Tan, Q., Zhang, H., et al.: Deep learning with gated recurrent unit networks for financial sequence predictions. Proc. Comput. Sci. **131**, 895–903 (2018)
9. Liu, Z.: Strategy optimization of stock technical analysis under high-frequency trading: method based on Adaboost neural network. Shanghai Normal University (2019)
10. Gu, Y., Yan, D.: Price forecast with high-frequency finance data: an autoregressive recurrent neural network model with technical indicators. In: Proceedings of the 29th ACM International Conference on Information & Knowledge Management, pp. 2485–2492 (2020)
11. Kong, A., Zhu, H., Azencott, R.: Predicting intraday jumps in stock prices using liquidity measures and technical indicators. J. Forecast. **40**(3), 416–438 (2021)
12. Kumar Chandar, S.: Stock price prediction based on technical indicators with soft computing models. In: Chen, J.-Z., Tavares, J.M.R.S., Shakya, S., Iliyasu, A.M. (eds.) ICIPCN 2020. AISC, vol. 1200, pp. 685–699. Springer, Cham (2021). https://doi.org/10.1007/978-3-030-51859-2_62
13. Song, Y., Sun, Y.: High frequency financial time series prediction: ARIMA model based on adaptive filtering. J. Jilin Bus. Technol. Coll. **37**(2), 82–86 (2021)
14. Li, Z., Han, J., Song, Y.: On the forecasting of high-frequency financial time series based on ARIMA model improved by deep learning. J. Forecast. **39**(7), 1081–1097 (2020)
15. Huang, S.-F., Guo, M., Chen, M.-R.: Stock market trend prediction using a functional time series approach. Quant. Finan. **20**(1), 69–79 (2020)
16. Taroon, G., Tomar, A., Manjunath, C., et al.: Employing deep learning in intraday stock trading. In: Fifth International Conference on Research in Computational Intelligence and Communication Networks, pp. 209–214 (2020)
17. Solís, E., Noboa, S., Cuenca, E.: Financial time series forecasting applying deep learning algorithms. In: Salgado Guerrero, J.P., Chicaiza Espinosa, J., Cerrada Lozada, M., Berrezueta-Guzman, S. (eds.) TICEC 2021. CCIS, vol. 1456, pp. 46–60. Springer, Cham (2021). https://doi.org/10.1007/978-3-030-89941-7_4
18. Chong, E., Han, C., Park, F.C.: Deep learning networks for stock market analysis and prediction: methodology, data representations, and case studies. Expert Syst. Appl. **83**, 187–205 (2017)
19. Lachiheb, O., Gouider, M.S.: A hierarchical deep neural network design for stock returns prediction. Proc. Comput. Sci. **126**, 264–272 (2018)
20. Lanbouri, Z., Achchab, S.: Stock market prediction on high frequency data using long-short term memory. Proc. Comput. Sci. **175**, 603–608 (2020)
21. Ma, A., Yu, T.: Technical analysis with empirical mode decomposition: a case in the Hong Kong stock market. J. Wealth Manag. **24**(1), 41–48 (2021)
22. Chen, W., Jiang, M.: A novel graph convolutional feature based convolutional neural network for stock trend prediction. Inf. Sci. **556**, 67–94 (2021)

23. Li, C., Xiao, F., Fan, Y.: An approach to state of charge estimation of lithium-ion batteries based on recurrent neural networks with gated recurrent unit. Energies **12**(9), 1592 (2019)
24. Hong, W., Li, S., Hu, Z.: Improving relation extraction by knowledge representation learning. In: 2021 IEEE 33rd International Conference on Tools with Artificial Intelligence, pp. 1211–1215. IEEE (2021)
25. Lu, W., Li, J., Wang, J., et al.: A CNN-BiLSTM-AM method for stock price prediction. Neural Comput. Appl. **33**(10), 4741–4753 (2021)
26. Wang, J., Kim, J.: Predicting stock price trend using MACD optimized by historical volatility. Math. Probl. Eng. **2018**, 1–12 (2018)
27. Khanderwal, S., Mohanty, D.: Stock price prediction using ARIMA model. Int. J. Mark. Hum. Resour. Res. **2**(2), 98–107 (2021)
28. Hoseinzade, E., Haratizadeh, S.: CNNpred: CNN-based stock market prediction using a diverse set of variables. Expert Syst. Appl. **129**, 273–285 (2019)
29. Gupta, U., Bhattacharjee, V., Bishnu, P.S.: StockNet-GRU based stock index prediction. Expert Syst. Appl. **207**, 117986 (2022)

A Cross-Platform Instant Messaging User Association Method Based on Supervised Learning

Pei Zhou[1], Xiangyang Luo[2(✉)], Shaoyong Du[2], Wenqi Shi[2], and Jiashan Guo[1]

[1] School of Cyber Science and Engineering, Zhengzhou University, Zhengzhou 450000, China
[2] State Key Laboratory of Mathematical Engineering and Advanced Computing, Zhengzhou 450000, China
luoxy_ieu@sina.com

Abstract. To solve the multi-platform user association problem of complex trajectory matching process and high time cost in cross-platform association positioning of instant messaging users, and at the same time make full use of the information in user trajectories, this paper proposes a supervised learning-based cross-platform instant messaging user association positioning method. The algorithm firstly places probes in the area where the target may appear to obtain user information; then gets user trajectories through the obtained user distance information and time information; selects user features through the classification algorithm of supervised learning, and designs a cross-platform instant messaging user association localization method based on supervised learning, so as to increase the association efficiency and accuracy of cross-platform instant messaging user association. The method conducts specific experiments for the most commonly used instant messaging tools in China, WeChat and Stranger users, and the results show that the method can achieve efficient and reliable association for these two types of instant messaging users.

Keywords: Instant Messaging · User trajectory · Supervised learning · Cross-platform user association

1 Introduction

With the rapid development of mobile Internet technology and wireless positioning technology, mobile social networks have gradually emerged and profoundly changed and affected people's lives [1–3]. The combination of smart devices and social platforms has become a new development trend, and gradually produced a variety of location-based social networks [4, 5], such as Twitter, WeChat [6], Momo, Foursquare, Weibo, etc. Location-based social networks can use the location information of mobile devices to combine the network world with the real world and provide people with more convenient services [7–9]. Location-based friendships in instant messaging applications enable ordinary users to get in-formation such as nicknames, signatures, and gender of other users in the vicinity based on their current location, and to obtain distance information of nearby users. Typical examples of such services are WeChat "Nearby", Weibo "Nearby", Momo "Nearby", etc. (in this paper we collectively refer to them as "Nearby (in this paper, we collectively refer to them as "nearby people" services). User behavior data is different because of different instant messaging tools' functions. Identifying and matching the corresponding account of the same user in multiple instant messaging tools can fully integrate multiple IM platform data sets and construct complete user information, which is of great significance for instant messaging user positioning.

The existing cross-platform instant messaging user association methods are mainly based on similarity calculation of instant messaging user attribute information, as well as for the sequential features of trajectories to determine whether a user exists in a relationship by location co-occurrence and distance matching between user location nodes for the time period used. The main process for the similarity of user attribute information as a classification feature of the supervised learning classification algorithm is shown in Fig. 1. The matching method based on user attribute information can be used to correlate the information of multi-platform users. However, as users' privacy awareness increases, instant messaging users may choose other user attribute information such as user names that are completely unrelated to their real identities. Therefore, it is difficult to accurately correlate and locate instant messaging users through user attribute information. User trajectory information is an important feature to characterize user identity, and the cross-platform association of instant messaging users can be accurately achieved through location co-occurrence and distance matching of sequential features of trajectories, but the method calculates the similarity of user trajectories and has high time complexity when processing user trajectories, resulting in low efficiency of user matching.

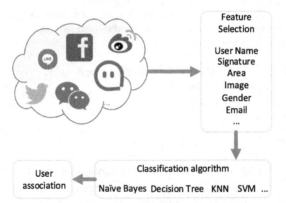

Fig. 1. Cross-platform association method for instant messaging based on user attribute information.

To address the above problems, this paper proposes a cross-social platform instant messaging user trajectory matching method based on supervised learning. The method designs a cross-platform instant messaging user association localization method based on supervised learning by means of a classification algorithm; finally, the trajectory information of users in several different instant messaging tools is matched to accurately and efficiently associate users. In this paper f experiments are conducted on public dataset and real instant messaging application s dataset respectively to verify the efficiency and accuracy of the proposed algorithm.

The main work of this paper is as follows:

(1) Suitable user matching features based on trajectory information are selected, as well as a cross-platform instant messaging user association localization algorithm based on super-vised learning is proposed, which fully solves the problem of large time cost of complex user trajectory matching and significantly improves the efficiency of cross-platform user trajectory matching.

(2) Based on the open data set of Microsoft Research Asia and the well-known instant messaging applications WeChat and Momo, the data set of data collection and processing were carried out and the experimental results show that the proposed method is more effective and efficient than the existing methods.

The rest of this paper is organized as follows: Sect. 2 introduces the existing related work and analyzes its shortcomings; Sect. 3 proposes a cross-platform instant messaging user association method based on supervised learning and explains the key steps in detail; Sect. 4 conducts comparative experiments based on existing public datasets and real instant messaging applications and analyzes the experimental results; Sect. 5 concludes the whole paper.

2 Background and Related Work

The current cross-platform association localization method for instant messaging users based on user attribute information is mainly based on similarity calculation of instant messaging user attribute information as a classification feature for supervised learning classification algorithm. Malhotr in paper [10], obtains user attribute information such as, user ID, user nick-name, user gender, profile image, location, personality signature, etc. For user ID, user nick-name, and location, a score in the range of [0,1] is given by using a complex string matching method, and the similarity of the two strings is discerned by judging the magnitude of the score. For personality signatures, the range of similarity between two personality signature sets can be obtained by using TF-IDF vector space model, preprocessing by removing punctuation and discontinued words, and then calculating the cosine similarity between two personality signature sets, and considering each personality signature set as a document. For profile images, the image similarity is obtained by converting the scalar product of RGB component vectors of the target user image into a vector of gray scale coefficients thus analyzed by mean square error, peak signal to noise ratio, and Levenshtein. Through feature selection of user attribute information, supervised learning based classification algorithm models such as plain Bayesian, decision tree, KNN and SVM algorithms are trained and tested to achieve cross-platform association localization of instant messaging users.

Paula in the paper [11] describes the user's interests and intentions through a scalable auto-mated user analysis technique by extracting his URL from publicly available tweet information, and using semantic ontologies. To improve the performance of the method, the interest and intent categories of the user summary ontology are found by using the website categories provided by OpenDNS and the DBpedia collective knowledge database. In the above case, the user summary ontology is populated by these collective categories, individual assertions, and relationships of interests and intentions. Liu proposed a solution framework HYDRA in paper [12]. This model is able to handle large amount of information loss and avoid dimensionality disasters when dealing with high-dimensional sparse representations. Extensive experiments with 10 million users on seven popular social networking platforms show that HYDRA correctly identifies real user links across platforms from a large number of noisy user behavior data records, and outperforms existing optimal methods by 20% in different settings and by a factor of 4 in most cases. Li presents the UGC-based user identification problem in paper [13], and then proposed a UGC-based user identification model. A solution based on supervised machine learning is proposed. Experimental results show that the method achieves F1 values of 89.79%, 86.78%, and 86.24% on three real datasets, respectively. This work presents the possibility of matching user accounts with accessible online data.

Cross-platform user association based on user behavioral features mainly associates users through their behavioral features such as activity trajectories, friend relationships and other information. The user trajectory information partly reflects the user's movement trajectory in the real world and becomes a strong behavioral information to characterize the user's identity. Hao et al. in [14] divided the whole map into many grids, and then represented each user's trajectory into a sequence composed of several small grids, and used the Term Frequency-Inverse Document Frequency (TF-IDF) model to transform each user's trajectory into a vector. In [15], Chen et al. propose a cross domain trajectory to vector algorithm (CDTrajectory) based on Paragraph2vec to match user trajectories across social networks. Vector algorithm (CDTraj2vec). They used the PV-DM model in the Paragraph2vec algorithm to extract the location access order features in the trajectory sequence to obtain the vector representation of user trajectories, and finally determine whether the trajectories match by the user trajectory vectors. in the paper [17], Zhou et al. determined the cross-platform instant The association of cross-platform instant messaging users is determined by calculating the similarity of user trajectories and the distance distribution of location nodes in user trajectories at the same time.

3 Cross-Platform Instant Messaging User Association Based on Supervised Learning

In this paper, we study how to match users' trajectory information in different instant messengers, match account information belonging to the same user in different instant messengers, so as to achieve cross-platform association localization of instant messenger users and further enrich user trajectory information, and propose a supervised learning-based cross-platform instant messenger user association localization method. Using a dataset of matched accounts known to belong to the same user, this paper uses feature-specific similarity techniques to compare the corresponding features of trajectory information for each instant messenger. By analyzing user trajectories, a similarity vector is generated for each pair of accounts belonging to the same entity in the form of <similarity of user trajectories based on TF-IDF algorithm, similarity of user trajectories based on TF-IWF algorithm, number of co-occurrence grids, maximum distance between corresponding co-occurrence grids, ratio of co-occurrence grid pairs to matching grid pairs, sum of time differences of trajectory matching points>. This vector is used as a training instance for the supervised classifier. Similar vectors are generated for trajectory information known to belong to different users. In this paper, the use of these vectors is tested using four classifiers: plain Bayes, KNN, decision tree and SVM.

This chapter specifies the process of cross-platform instant messaging user association localization method based on supervised learning. The method obtains the attribute information of the instant messaging target user and the notice distance between the querier and the target user through the probe, and uses a suitable instant messaging location algorithm to obtain the geo-graphic location information of the target user according to the strength of the privacy protection policy of the instant messaging tool, and obtains the user time trajectory sequence by combining the target user's time of using the instant messaging location-based service; the user's spatial time trajectories are respectively The spatial-temporal trajectories of users are gridded and vectorized respectively, and the calculation results are weighted; the similarity of user trajectories based on TF-IDF and TF-IWF algorithm models and the gridded information of user trajectories are statistically calculated respectively to build a complete cross-platform association localization feature of instant messaging users. Through the training experiments of four classification models, namely, plain Bayesian, KNN, decision tree and SVM, and the test experiments of association localization, the cross-platform association localization of instant messaging users is realized. The general framework of the method is shown in Fig. 2.

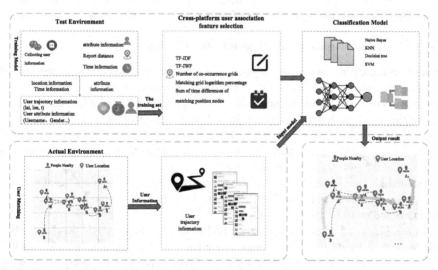

Fig. 2. A general framework for cross-platform instant messaging user association methods based on supervised learning.

The main steps of the method are as follows:

(1) User information acquisition and information pre-processing. The probes are strategically placed in the vicinity of the instant messaging target users to sense "nearby people". The user trajectories are obtained by using the distance and time information of other users' announcements; the trajectories are gridded and vectorized respectively, and the results are weighted and normalized to calculate the instant messaging user trajectories. Inverse document frequency similarity based on word frequency and inverse word frequency similarity based on word frequency.

(2) Cross-platform user association feature selection. The similarity calculation of nicknames and personality signatures of users of different instant messengers is carried out by editing distance and TF-IDF algorithm model. We also obtain the trajectory sequences based on small grid numbers by gridding the trajectory information of instant messaging target users, analyze and calculate the distribution of multi-platform instant messaging target user trajectory sequences, and obtain the number of co-occurring grids, the maximum distance between corresponding co-occurring grids, the ratio of co-occurring grid pairs to matching grid pairs, the sum of time difference of trajectory matching points, and other features for feature selection.

(3) Classification model training and testing. The public dataset and the real instant messaging user dataset are divided into the training and testing sets for the classification model. The dataset is pre-processed and input to the model for classification training, and the test data are input for prediction to determine the cross-platform association relationship of instant messaging users.

(4) Cross-platform user association. Cross-platform association localization of instant messaging users is achieved through supervised learning based on plain Bayesian, KNN, decision tree, and SVM classification algorithms to efficiently determine the association relationship of multi-platform instant messaging users.

3.1 Get User Information and Trajectory Information

In this paper, the probe will be deployed to obtain the notification distance information between the inquirer and the target user through the function of "nearby people" of WeChat and record the online time of the target user, and locate the target user through the positioning algorithm based on the trilateral measurement of the notification distance between the probe and the target user and the spatial division positioning algorithm based on the statistical analysis of the notification distance. The location of the target user is located, and the time trajectory sequence of the target user using the instant messenger is obtained by combining the time of the target user using the location-based service. The dataset is collated and classified for training to build a model and for evaluating the validity of the model during model testing.

In this paper, we strategically arrange probes to sense and collect "people nearby" information of instant messaging users. Since the instant messaging "people nearby" service is a service principle to sense users in a circular area with the query point as the center, based on this, we arrange probes in the target user's area and number them so that each neighboring probe can form a positive hexagon, which not only can sense and collect the instant messaging user's "The number of probes can also be minimized to reduce the cost of collecting cross-platform user-related location information of instant messaging users. In addition, by deploying probes in a hexagonal shape, it is easier to locate users based on trilateral measurements.

The user's temporal trajectory information contains three-dimensional data, which are the latitude and longitude information of the target user's geographic location and the time when the target user used the location-based service of instant messaging. Usually, the target user trajectory nodes are represented by a three-dimensional array lat, lon, t.

The user location in the track is divided into a small grid. Determine a rectangular user activity area according to the latitude and longitude coordinates of the user trajectory. The user activity area corresponds to a latitude range of lat_1, lat_2 and a longitude range of lon_1, lon_2. Then the side length of the grid is set according to the positioning error, which determines the number of rows l and the number of columns r of the grid. Finally, all the geographical position coordinates in the trajectory are converted into grid number g_i by Eqs. (1)–(3). Where lat, lon denotes the coordinate point of any geographic location in the trajectory, g_x denotes the row number where the grid is located, and g_y denotes the column number where the grid is located.

$$g_x = \left\lfloor \frac{(lat - lat_1) * l}{lat_2 - lat_1} \right\rfloor \tag{1}$$

$$g_y = \left\lfloor \frac{(lon - lon_1) * r}{lon_2 - lon_1} \right\rfloor \tag{2}$$

$$g_i = (r^*(g_x - 1) + g_y) \tag{3}$$

The time and space points in the user trajectory are represented by a grid. First, set each hour as a time slot. Then the user's geographic coordinate grid is combined with the time period to form the user's trajectory grid. The user trajectory is represented as $T = \{h_{t_1}^{g_1}, h_{t_2}^{g_2}, h_{t_n}^{g_i}\}$, where g_1, g_2, ..., g_i denotes the number of the geolocation grid in the trajectory, t_1, t_2, ..., t_n denotes the time point when the user appears in the g_i grid, and $h_{t_n}^{g_i}$ denotes the temporal point of the user.

3.2 Cross-Platform User Association Feature Selection

A user's personal information on any instant messenger can be considered as an N-dimensional vector, where each dimension is user attribute information, e.g., username, nickname, age, personality signature, etc., and user behavior information e.g., trajectory information, etc. A subset of these features from an IM tool user e.g., username, user trajectory, etc., can be used to match the same user in another IM tool. We choose to study user trajectory features of WeChat and Momo users for matching. In this paper, we will discuss the user features used to match users in cross-platform association targeting of instant messaging users.

(1) Similarity of user trajectories based on word frequency inverse document frequency

Since instant messaging user activity trajectories are similar to text structures, both being sequences composed of discrete data objects, the paper [14] proposes a user association algorithm based on word frequency inverse text frequency. The algorithm also divides the user's trajectory into grids and replaces the target user location nodes with grid serial numbers. That is, the target user's location area is divided into small grids of moderate size according to the localization error of instant messenger, and the user's trajectory sequence is constructed as a sequence of grid ordinal number estimation. By calculating the target user weight vector based on the word frequency inverse document frequency algorithm, the similarity of the weight vectors is compared to determine the association relationship of different instant messenger users.

The frequency value TF of the i grid in trajectory j can be expressed as:

$$tf(g_i, T_j) = \log(1 + f_{i,j}) \tag{4}$$

The inverse document value IDF of the mesh in both trajectories can be expressed as:

$$idf(g_i, S)\frac{1}{\log(1 + |\{i|f_{i,j} > 0\}|)} \tag{5}$$

$$v(T_j) = (tf - idf(g_1, T_j), tf - idf(g_2, T_j), \ldots, tf - idf(g_i, T_j)) \tag{6}$$

The weight vector $v(T_j)$ is formed and normalized for user trajectory vector similarity calculation

(2) Similarity of user trajectories based on word frequency inverse word frequency

The user association algorithm based on word frequency inverse text frequency can effectively screen out the noisy nodes in user trajectory information that cause mis-judgment of results and can effectively judge the association relationship of multi-platform instant messaging users. However, as the number of instant messaging user trajectory information increases, the simple word-frequency inverse document frequency algorithm cannot make the extracted trajectory key locations effectively reflect the importance and distribution of location nodes. Therefore, this paper chooses the word frequency inverse word frequency based user trajectory similarity as the most important feature of multi-platform instant messaging user association. The IWF approach more accurately expresses the importance of key location nodes in the user trajectory to be matched. At the same time, the calculation result of TF-IWF can just solve the problem of too small TF-IDF weights close to 0.

The trajectory vector calculation method based on the TF-IWF algorithm model, first calculates the frequency value TF of the i grid in the trajectory j, then calculates the co-occurrence frequency value IWF of the grid in the two trajectories T_j, and finally calculates the TF-IWF value of each grid in the trajectory. The trajectory vector is formed $v(T_j)$. By normalizing this vector, the user trajectory vector is calculated for similarity. The algorithm of user trajectory vector generation based on TF-IDF and TF-IWF algorithms is shown in Table 1.

Table 1. TF-IWF based user trajectory vector generation algorithm.

algorithm 1 User trajectory vector generation algorithm based on TF-IDF and TF-IWF algorithms
Input: $T_a = \{h_{t_1}^{c_1}, h_{t_2}^{c_2}, \ldots, h_{t_n}^{c_i}\}$, $T_b = \{h_{t_1}^{c_1}, h_{t_2}^{c_2}, \ldots, h_{t_n}^{c_i}\}$
Output: $sim_{tf-idf}(T_a, T_b)$, $sim_{tf-iwf}(T_a, T_b)$
1    $S_V = \{T_a, T_b\}$;
2   *for each* $h_{t_n}^{c_i}$ *in the set* S_V **do**:
3   *Calculate tf of the grid in the trajectory* T_a *to appear in the trajectory* T_a
4   *Calculate the idf value of the user grid* c_i *in the trajectory* T_a
5   *Calculate the value of iwf for the grid in the trajectory* T_a *in* S_v
6   **end for**
7    $v(T_a)_{idf} = \{tf \cdot idf(c_1), tf \cdot idf(c_2), \ldots, tf \cdot idf(c_i)\}$
8    $v(T_a)_{iwf} = \{tf \cdot iwf(c_1), tf \cdot iwf(c_2), \ldots, tf \cdot iwf(c_i)\}$
9   *for each* $h_{t_n}^{c_i}$ *in the set* S_V **do**:
10   *Calculate tf of the grid in the trajectory* T_b *to appear in the trajectory* T_b
11   *Calculate the idf value of the user grid* c_i *in the trajectory* T_b
12   *Calculate the value of iwf for the grid in the trajectory* T_b *in* S_v
13   **end for**
14   $v(T_b)_{idf} = \{tf \cdot idf(c_1), tf \cdot idf(c_2), \ldots, tf \cdot idf(c_i)\}$
15   $v(T_b)_{iwf} = \{tf \cdot iwf(c_1), tf \cdot iwf(c_2), \ldots, tf \cdot iwf(c_i)\}$

(3) Number of co-occurring grids

After gridding for the target user trajectory, the location nodes in the target user trajectory are divided into individual divided small grids. In this paper, the location nodes of the instant messaging target user trajectory are replaced by the number of each grid. The location nodes of the instant messaging target user trajectory are com-posed into a sequence of grid serial numbers according to the user sequential access feature. Based on the trajectory temporality feature, the more the number of grid co-occurrences of instant messaging user trajectory location nodes in different platforms at the same time, the more similar the user trajectory matching results are, and the higher the degree of cross-platform association of instant messaging users.

(4) Number of co-occurring grid pairs as a percentage of matched grid pairs

In the previous feature, the day is divided into 24 time periods, while the location nodes of instant messenger target user trajectories are replaced by grid serial numbers by gridding the instant messenger target user trajectories. Due to the existence of instant messaging system errors and positioning errors, instant messaging users in the same location may be located in different but similar small grids in different instant messenger trajectory information. Since the more the number of user trajectory matching location nodes in the same grid in multi-platform instant messaging user matching trajectory, the higher the degree of user association, the proportion of the number of target user co-occurrence grid in the overall matching trajectory grid is an important feature of cross-platform instant messaging user association method.

(5) The sum of the time difference of the track matching points

Existing cross-platform instant messaging user association methods often calculate the similarity of instant messaging user trajectories of different platforms by analyzing the activity pattern and location node distribution of the target users, without considering the temporal characteristics of user trajectories, which increases the error of cross-platform instant messaging user association. Considering the temporality of instant messaging user trajectories, this paper divides a day into 24 time periods, i.e., one hour is a time period, and calculates user online time in the process of locating instant messaging targets and takes the sum of absolute values of time differences of trajectory matching points as an important feature of cross-platform instant messaging user association methods based on supervised learning.

3.3 Classification Model Training and Testing

In the previous section, feature selection for the classification training model was introduced to preprocess the dataset to generate the training set for the classifier. By processing the dataset feature values and target values, the dataset is divided into training set and test set, and the feature values of the training set as well as the test set are normalized and fed into the classification algorithm model. After training the classifier, they classify the two dataset pairs as "matching" or "mismatching" by testing them as inputs. A "match" means that the two instant messaging user trajectory information matches belong to the same user, while a "mismatch" means that they do not belong to the same user. To further evaluate the effectiveness of the adopted similarity metrics, the classification model is tested on two datasets with different feature selection, and the data prediction calculation and accuracy are performed (Fig. 3).

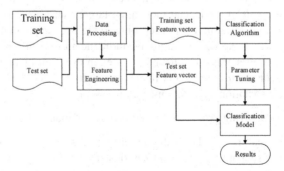

Fig. 3. Supervised learning classification model formation process.

3.4 Cross-Platform User Association

User trajectory information is an important feature to characterize user identity, and user attribute information is an important feature to filter trajectory matching users to improve user association accuracy. Through supervised learning-based plain Bayesian, KNN, decision tree, and SVM classification algorithms can effectively determine the association relationship of multi-platform instant messaging users and achieve cross-platform association location of instant messaging users. Acquiring any instant messenger target user location information can achieve target user localization, and acquiring and fusing multiple instant messenger location information extends the tar-get user trajectory, improves the completeness of target user localization, and refines the location granularity of target users.

4 Experiments

In order to verify the performance of the proposed algorithm in this paper, the pro-posed algorithm is experimentally compared on four different supervised learning classification algorithms, and the experimental results are analyzed by comparing the matching accuracy of different algorithms on the target user trajectories.

4.1 Experimental Dataset and Evaluation Criteria

In this paper, we validate the proposed algorithm on the public dataset GeoLife project [17] from Microsoft Research Asia and on a dataset based on real instant messaging applications. In this paper, a single spatio-temporal data set is divided into two parts, and then the two parts are used for trajectory matching. When splitting each user trajectory, each segment of user trajectory is cross-sectioned into two parts D_{Geo1} and D_{Geo2} in turn, as shown in Fig. 4.

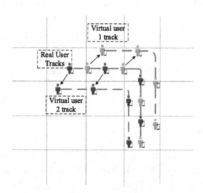

Fig. 4. Spatio-temporal dataset partitioning methods.

In the process of acquiring real experimental data, instant messaging tools WeChat and Momo were respectively run every 10 min NoxPlayer[1] to obtain user information.

---

[1] NoxPlayer: https://www.yeshen.com.

In the area of Zhengzhou (a rectangular area of 220 km²), 312 probes were set up and numbered with a distance of 2 km between probes, and the information of users appearing in the "People Nearby" interface of Momo and WeChat was read respectively. Read the user information of "nearby people" in Momo and WeChat respectively, and save the information in the local computer in turn. The specific data set information is shown in Table 2.

Table 2. Experimental data set information.

Data source	Geolife		Real user experiment	
Divide the data set	D_{Geo1}	D_{Geo2}	D_{LBSD1}	D_{LBSD2}
Number of user trajectory	1325	1325	668	668
Coordinate Points	21212	19650	6312	7048
Range of grids	lat:39–41 lon:115–117	lat:39–41 lon:115–117	lat: 34.652–34.87 lon: 113.53–113.96	lat: 34.652–34.87 lon: 113.53–113.96
Time Range	2007.4–2012.8	2007.4–2012.8	2021.7–2021.8	2021.7–2021.8

This section uses Precision, Recall and F1 Score as criteria to evaluate the performance of the algorithm, defined as follows:

$$precision = \frac{\sum_{(i \in [1,N])} TP_i}{\sum_{(i \in [1,N])} TP_i + \sum_{(i \in [1,N])} FP_i} \tag{7}$$

$$recall = \frac{\sum_{(i \in [1,N])} TP_i}{\sum_{(i \in [1,N])} TP_i + \sum_{(i \in [1,N])} FN_i} \tag{8}$$

$$F1 = \frac{2 * precision * recall}{precision + recall} \tag{9}$$

4.2 Experimental Setup

The user matching features and their descriptions are shown in Table 3. The experimental parameters are set as shown in Table 4. Most of the positioning errors of wechat and Momo users are within the range of [60 m and 80 m], so the side length of the small grid is set to 100 m, making it possible for users to locate in the grid. Small grid of rows and columns is based on user activity area range of latitude and longitude, by small grid side length calculation. The time information partition threshold of the trajectory is 1 h, and the trajectory similarity threshold is 0.9. Since this paper is a cross-platform user association based on instant messaging, experiments on the Geolife dataset are also conducted according to the above parameters.

Table 3. Features and Description.

Feature item serial number	Feature Description	Feature representation
0	TF-IDF similarity	tf-idf
1	TF-IWF similarity	tf-iwf
2	Number of co-existing grids	co-occurrence
3	Number of co-occurring grid pairs as a percentage of matched grid pairs	scale
4	The sum of the time difference of the track matching points	t

Table 4. Parameter meaning and setting.

variable	value	illustrate
g	100 m	Side length of the grid
R_G	2224	The number of rows of the grid in Geolife
C_G	1728	The number of columns of the grid in Geolife
R_Z	418	The number of rows of the real user experiment grid
C_Z	571	The number of columns of the real user experiment grid

4.3 Comparative Analysis of Experimental Results

In order to obtain the best performance of the algorithm in this paper, different features are selected for different data in this paper to analyze the performance of the classification model for cross-platform association of instant messaging users. There-fore, we study different datasets in this paper. In both datasets, <tf-idf, tf-iwf, co-occurrence, scale, t> are chosen as the training features for the classification model in this paper (Fig. 5).

In this paper, four supervised learning classification algorithms are used to match instant messaging target user trajectory information and partial user attribute informa-tion. The classification model features <tf-idf, tf-iwf, co-occurrence, scale, t> are used in GeoLife, a public dataset from Microsoft Asia Research Institute, and real instant messaging user application dataset, and the experimental results are shown in Fig. 6 and Fig. 7. The experimental results show that the results of each classifier have high accuracy except KNN, where the plain Bayesian, decision tree, and SVM algorithms have high accuracy recall for the real instant messaging user information dataset. Using the most effective feature selection and similarity measures, this paper achieves an accuracy of 98.0% for cross-platform instant messaging user association localization. Compared to the literature [17] method with higher accuracy, the algorithm in this paper requires 72% less time overhead when processing the same number of data samples in both datasets with 98% accuracy, which requires significantly less time overhead. As shown in Fig. 8 the user association localization method based on supervised learning proposed in this

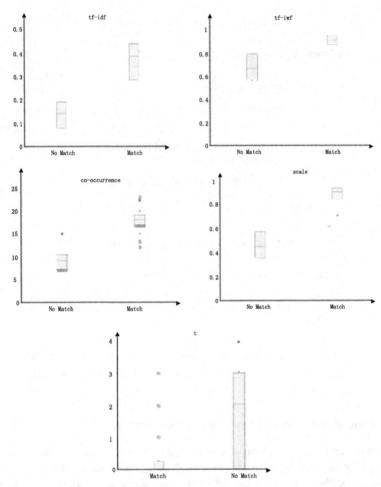

Fig. 5. Box-whisker diagram for each feature of matching and non-matching classes.

paper has a higher accuracy performance compared to other methods on different classification algorithms, and the accuracy is improved by 15.2% compared to the optimal supervised learning classification algorithm based on user attribute information.

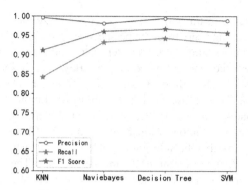

Fig. 6. Geolife dataset results graph.

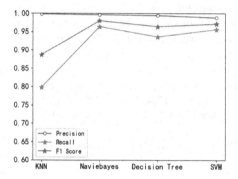

Fig. 7. Real instant messaging user dataset results graph.

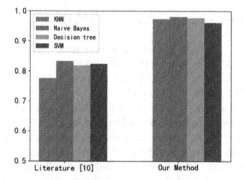

Fig. 8. Comparison of experimental results.

5 Conclusion

In this paper, we work on selecting user matching features based on trajectory information, and targeting these user features by selecting different supervised learning classification algorithms for information association across different instant messaging platforms. In the process of trajectory matching, we analyze the association of cross-platform instant messaging users from the perspective of similarity of "people nearby" information of instant messaging users. We determine whether the target users are related or not by using supervised learning based on plain Bayesian, KNN, decision tree and SVM classification model algorithms. By introducing trajectory features after gridding, training and testing of classification models, the ability of eliminating models to negate user attribute information from each other is evaluated. Experiments on cross-platform instant messaging user association localization based on WeChat and Momo based on supervised learning prove that the algorithm improves the efficiency of user association while accurately associating different instant messaging tools. The method proposed in this paper solves the problem of complex time cost of user trajectory matching, significantly improves the efficiency of cross-platform user trajectory matching, and can quickly analyze user trajectory features and locate cross-platform users by association in a large amount of user trajectory data. In future work, we will focus on the selection of user association features and accurate association based on richer user information. This study hopes to provide time-sensitive technical support for malicious social network instant messaging users.

Funding Statement. This work was supported by the National Natural Science Foundation of China (No. U1804263, 61872448, 62172435, and 62002386) and the Zhongyuan Science and Technology Innovation Leading Talent Project (No. 214200510019).

Conflicts of Interest. The authors declare that they have no conflicts of interest to report regarding the present study.

References

1. China Internet Network Information Center: The 47th China Statistical Report on Internet Development (2021)
2. Li, J., Yan, H., Liu, Z., Chen, X.: Location-sharing systems with enhanced privacy in mobile online social networks. IEEE Syst. J. **11**(2), 439–448 (2017)
3. Wang, H., Li, Y., Chen, Y.: Co-location social networks: linking the physical world and cyberspace. Proc. SPIE **4445**, 119–129 (2001)
4. Yuan, F., Jose, J.M., Guo, G.: Joint Geo-Spatial Preference and Pairwise Ranking for Point-of-Interest Recommendation, pp. 46–53. ICTAI, San Jose, CA, USA (2016)
5. Wang, R., Xue, M., Liu, K.: Data-Driven Privacy Analytics: A WeChat Case Study in Location-Based Social Networks, pp. 561–570. ICTAI, San Jose, CA, USA (2016)
6. Number of monthly active WeChat users from 2nd quarter 2011 to 2nd quarter 2021. https://www.statista.com/statistics/255778/number-of-active-wechat-messenger-accounts
7. Kim, J., Lee, J.G., Lee, B.S.: Geosocial co-clustering: a novel framework for geosocial community detection. ACM Trans. Intell. Syst. Technol. **11**(4), 1–26 (2020)
8. Xie, R., Chen, Y., Lin, S., Zhang, T.: Understanding Skout users' mobility patterns on a global scale: a data-driven study. World Wide Web **22**(11) (2018)
9. Nurgaliev, I., Qiang, Q.U., Bamakan, S.: Matching user identities across social networks with limited profile data. Front. Comput. Sci. **16**(4), 1–14 (2020)
10. Malhotra, A., Totti, L., Meira, W.: Studying user footprints in different online social networks. In: ASONAM, Istanbul, Turkey (2012)

11. Penas, P., Del Hoyo, R., Vea-Murguía, J.: Collective knowledge ontology user profiling for Twitter – automatic user profiling. In: ICWIIAT, Atlanta, GA, USA (2013)
12. Liu, S., Wang, S.: Structured learning from heterogeneous behavior for social identity linkage. IEEE Trans. Knowl. Data Eng. **27**(7), 2005–2019 (2015)
13. Li, Y., Zhang, Z., Peng, Y.: Matching user accounts based on user generated content across social networks. Future Gener. Comput. Syst. **83**, 104–115 (2018)
14. Hao, T., Zhou, J., Cheng, Y., Huang, L., Wu, H.: User identification in cyber-physical space: a case study on mobile query logs and trajectories. In: SIGSPATIAL, California, CA, USA (2016)
15. Chen, X., Xu, Q., Huang, R.: A cross-social network user identity recognition algorithm based on user trajectory. J. Electron. Inf. Technol. **40**(11) (2018)
16. Zhou, P., Luo, X., Du, S., Li, L., Yang, Y., Liu, F.: A cross-platform instant messaging user association method based on spatio-temporal trajectory. In: Sun, X., Zhang, X., Xia, Z., Bertino, E. (eds.) ICAIS 2022. CCIS, vol. 1587, pp. 430–444. Springer, Cham (2022). https://doi.org/10.1007/978-3-031-06761-7_35
17. Zheng, Y., Xing, X., Ma, W.Y., Liu, F.: Bull. Tech. Comm. Data Eng. **33**(2), 32–39 (2010)

Research on Data Watermark Tracing System in Hadoop Environment

Wenyu Qiao[1] and Jiexi Wang[2(✉)]

[1] China Electric Power Research Institute Co., Ltd., Beijing 100192, China
[2] Nanjing Wensi Haihui Beijing Branch, Beijing 100192, China
347039414@qq.com

Abstract. The application of big data requires effective tracing of data transmission and flow processes, so as to achieve effective determination of data authenticity and security. If network data is not effectively supervised, unexpected events such as data loss, leakage or tampering will occur, resulting in network data threats and risks that cannot be traced and responded to. The traditional data tracing methods are found difficult to meet the processing needs of massive data. Hence, data tracing in Hadoop environment is considered to better deal with the risk of data loss, tampering and leakage in the process of multiple data distribution. In this paper, the Hadoop environment system and its application in the field of data watermark tracing is explored. By analyzing the data tracing model and its implementation, a data watermark tracing system in Hadoop environment is established and the tracing process is examined. The experiments are designed and the efficiency of the proposed system is validated.

Keywords: Watermark Tracing · Data Security · Hadoop Environment

1 Introduction

The current information technology represented by big data has greatly improved the level and capability of data processing, computing and services. However, the huge amount of data also brings a serious challenge to how to track the source and destination of data efficiently and in real time [1]. In the network environment, the privacy, authenticity and security of data are essential to establish a healthy and sustainable network environment [2]. The application of big data requires effective tracing of data transmission and flow channels, so as to achieve effective determination of data authenticity and security [3]. Without effective supervision of network data, data may be lost, leaked or tampered, leading to uncontrolled events, which will cause untraceable threats and risks to the network environment [4].

There are still some key problems in the current application of data watermark tracing technology that need further solutions and breakthroughs, and the traditional stand-alone data watermark tracing technology cannot efficiently meet the current processing needs of large-scale data sets [5]. Hadoop based data watermark tracing technology can effectively improve the occupation of data storage and algorithm resource optimization, and play an important role in data security, data transmission and evolution tracking [6]. Meanwhile, it can guarantee the authenticity, accuracy and security of data sources and better meet the application requirements of the actual environment by establishing a high-complexity data tracing model in the face of massive data tracking and processing requirements [7].

At present, the research and application of data watermark tracing technology are mostly focused on small-scale, low-complexity structured data, and as the volume of data continues to rise, the application of these data watermark tracking processing technology becomes more difficult [8]. Data tracing in Hadoop environment can better avoid and cope with the risk of data loss, tampering and leakage in the process of multiple data distribution [9]. In this paper, to over the shortcomings of existing data tracing technologies, a data watermark tracing system based on the Hadoop environment is proposed. By using the data tracing algorithm, it can quickly locate the transmission path of data and effectively record the actions and processes of data events, which is expected to provide application value.

2 Data Tracing Model

2.1 Data Tracing Technology

Data tracing technology includes data annotation algorithm, watermark tracing algorithm and block-chain-based tracing algorithm, etc. [10]. Among them, data security protection mode is introduced in data annotation technology, which can annotate the security of data and guarantee the security of data source and processes. The annotation process of this technology is shown in Fig. 1 where D and R denote documents and records respectively. The flow direction and process of data are demonstrated, so that the corresponding annotation records will be generated in each iteration of data.

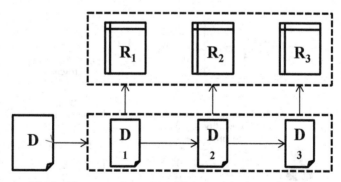

Fig. 1. The annotation process of data annotation technology

Secondly, the data tracing algorithm based on block-chain can better guarantee the privacy of data, and the effective trust relationship between data nodes can be established with the distributed storage and encryption characteristics of block-chain technology. The block-chain-based data tracing algorithm can track the status of data in real time and realize the shared distribution and verification of data nodes, which makes data difficult to be tampered with.

In addition, the data watermark-based tracing algorithm further optimizes the data screening and storage capacity. The watermark is embedded in the data association tuple so as to detect the capacity of the data tuple and the combination of attributes, and the optimal combination of data attributes is obtained based on the detection results [11]. The sorted tuple attribute data can quickly obtain the location information of the watermark identifier, which makes the robustness of the data significantly improved and optimized. Thanks to the embedding property of the tuple data, the watermark features can be recovered and preserved to a larger extent in the malicious deletion database.

2.2 Data Watermark Tracing Model

Data traceability can effectively locate the real data information, and effectively review, standardize and protect the data content [14]. The quality of data mainly depends on two key factors, namely, the source of data and the iterative process of data. With the rising volume of data transactions in the big data environment, the flow of data has numerous links, which makes it more difficult to trace the data watermark. By adding tags to the data flow and processing procedure, the location, time and date of data flow can be recorded in details. Data watermark tracing can effectively screen out information leakage and malicious interception events during the data flow, thus assisting big data security agencies in data security protection and response.

The main goal of data watermark tracing is to record and trace the process of data flow, and to record the origin of data or database by adding traceable marks to the data [12]. For example, the data watermarking process can be recorded and traced with the help of log records, or by extracting the annotation information injected in the data, the secure data flow process can be judged and traced, and the tracing process is shown in Fig. 2.

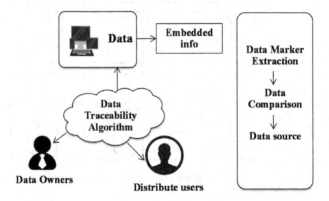

Fig. 2. Process of data watermark tracing

Since the data source needs to carry out specific log audits for different stages in the process of data distribution, a large arithmetic power occupation is generated in this process, thus leading to a high cost of data watermark tracing [13]. Secondly, the information annotation process of data also brings a lot of data occupation. Although these data help to realize the process of data traceability, they will also bring new data tracing problems while occupying memory. In addition, how to protect the privacy and security of user data in the process of data watermark tracing also requires attention in the process of watermark tracing.

Embedding watermarks in data and using intelligent algorithms to process and distribute data in Hadoop environment can timely process risk data in case of suspicious data leakage. Both embedded information marking and direct data marking contain data user distribution information, and the Hadoop environment can be disturbed and affected by many factors, so it also needs to have data security protection capability.

Building a data tracing model in Hadoop environment enables more accurate analysis of data tuples with less correlation between data sources [15]. Data watermark tracing using identification technology can effectively identify the security and the level of data. Since the data in large databases have large uncertainties, the development trend of data is difficult to predict, and the high degree of intersection and correlation between data makes the production and flow of data more and more complicated. In order to reduce the impact of source data distortion, data deficiency and data roughness in the process of data tracing, it is necessary to effectively manage the data in the database, and its management process is shown in Fig. 3. Through the definition and construction of data models, scenarios that effectively match with data tracing applications are generated. The data storage mode in the index is optimized to improve the efficiency of data analysis and processing.

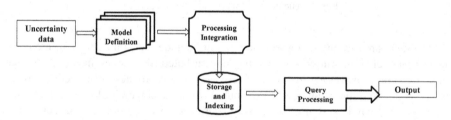

Fig. 3. Management process of database

3 Hadoop Environment Architecture

In the process of analyzing and extracting data watermarks, the metadata model is used to effectively record and react to the static characteristics of the data. In order to further clarify the evolution and correlation between data, and visually display and analyze, it is necessary to manage the database as a whole, so as to record the evolution process of data and directly react to it. Traditional data tracing is mainly carried out based on typical databases, which has the shortcomings of low efficiency and large arithmetic power occupation, making it difficult to meet the realistic needs of efficient data batch tracing in the big data environment. In the big data environment, the existence of a large amount of unstructured data makes it more complicated and challenging to establish the relationship model between data. Therefore, it is necessary to build data watermark tracing applications with the help of Hadoop technology.

As the volume of data processing in various industries continues to rise, the requirements for real-time data tracing, integration and processing are becoming higher. As an open and distributed computing environment, Hadoop platform can establish a clear system framework for users. The ecosystem architecture of Hadoop is shown in Fig. 4 below, which mainly includes data warehouse module, data stream processing module and database mining module. In addition, its ecosystem includes tools for installation, deployment, configuration and management, as well as subsystems and functional modules such as the distributed file subsystem.

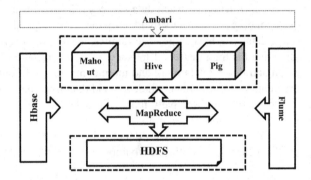

Fig. 4. The ecosystem architecture of Hadoop

The main architecture of the Hadoop system includes several subsystem modules such as parallel computing program module, distributed file system, master node and local file system, as shown in Fig. 5. These subsystem modules are effectively built to guarantee the implementation of distributed storage and parallel functions, and the stability of the whole system is effectively guaranteed by incorporating master nodes in the system. By integrating numerous decentralized servers, the entire system server is called to carry out data integration and processing, and the operational status of the server is effectively monitored. These modules give Hadoop system localized data analysis ability, and make the data calculation of the system platform stable, open and redundant.

The Hadoop system model is capable of encoding and recording data and regrouping the collected data. The data collected by the system model contains data feature values, which need to be trained on the set. The Hadoop environment system model hierarchy consists of three layers: the data representation layer, the data numerical information layer, and the data evolution layer.

The data under Hadoop will further produce a complex lineage branch architecture in the flow process, which can visually record and store the data storage and flow process.

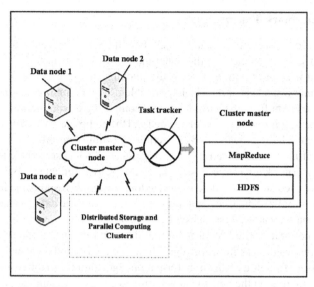

Fig. 5. The main subsystem modules of the Hadoop system

4 Data Watermark Tracing System in Hadoop Environment

To address the shortcomings of traditional data watermark tracing technology, intelligent algorithms need to be set up to target the data according to its type. By integrating the watermark in the data, it can guarantee real-time tracking and recording of the data flow process without affecting the functionality and security of the original data. With the continuous expansion of data capacity, watermarking in the database has important research and application value.

4.1 Data Watermarking Method

The process of adding identification information to the data requires deriving the simulation data and the annotation rules of the data. Generally, numerical and non-numerical data should be injected with the corresponding data attributes using methods such as random number production and database data dictionaries. The annotation calculation algorithm to annotate the generated virtual data to the original data is shown in Eq. (1), where k is the key, v is the virtual data tuple and o_i is the calculated primary key, and the final hash value of the data tuple is obtained.

$$H = h(k, v, o_i) \tag{1}$$

The virtual data tuple is injected into a specific row, thus making the arrangement of data random and realistic. In addition, for different groups of users, the data watermark information needs to be distributed in a targeted manner. For multi-level data sharing and circulation, the tracing process needs to be able to pass the validity test. In the multi-level distribution of watermark data, low-level watermark data cannot affect the effectiveness of high-level watermark data. Effectiveness testing and traceability need to be verified independently.

4.2 Data Watermark Tracing System

In order to ensure the security of data, especially in the security event after the effective tracing, it is necessary to capture the watermark information in the leaked data and obtain the data user information through the tracking of the watermark. By tracking the data watermark, the loss of data leakage problems can be minimized. By extracting the watermark content from the leaked data and comparing it with the stored watermark information, the user information is determined and the complete trace of the data leakage path is achieved. The data watermark detection algorithm can effectively capture the watermark identification of leaked data and determine all data users in the leakage path.

The data watermark tracing process in the Hadoop environment is shown in Fig. 6, in which the distributed storage module in the Hadoop system is responsible for collecting and storing the initialized data and capturing user data during the data collection process. Next, the distributed data analysis subsystem is mainly used to transpose the data, such as time-frequency transformation of the initial data, and inject the watermark into the data by using the watermark injection algorithm. The distributed data analysis and processing subsystem further uses the transformation algorithm to perform time-frequency inverse transformation on the embedded watermarked data to obtain the processed data containing the watermark.

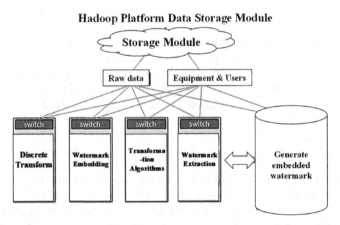

Fig. 6. The data watermark tracing process in the Hadoop environment

The data processing task subsystem in the Hadoop environment is responsible for handling the data scheduling issues, including the allocation, integration, aggregation and analysis of resources. The data resource management process architecture in the Hadoop environment is shown in Fig. 7.

The resource management module in Hadoop environment can allocate the excess resources to make the task processing more balanced. In the process of data watermark tracing, the collected device and user information together construct the watermark plus the dense data. Discrete transformation in the Hadoop environment is calculated as shown in Eqs. (2) and (3), where M is the coefficient matrix and m is the dimension of the data matrix, a, b are the coordinates of pixel points and x, y are the values of $T(x, y)$

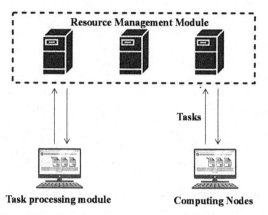

Fig. 7. The data resource management process architecture

after discrete transformation.

$$M = \sqrt{\frac{2}{m}} \left[\begin{array}{cccc} \cos\dfrac{\pi}{2m} & \cos\dfrac{3\pi}{2m} \ldots \ldots \cos\dfrac{(2m-1)\pi}{2m} \\ \cos\dfrac{(m-1)\pi}{2m} & \cos\dfrac{(m-1)3\pi}{2m} \ldots \cos\dfrac{(2m-1)(m-1)\pi}{2m} \end{array} \right] \qquad (2)$$

$$T(x, y) = \frac{2}{m} \sum_{a=0}^{m-1} \sum_{b=0}^{m-1} T(a, b) \cos\frac{(2a+1)x\pi}{2m} \cos\frac{(2b+1)y\pi}{2m} \qquad (3)$$

Through the distributed storage, integrated resource management and distributed processing subsystem modules in Hadoop environment, efficient data reception, arithmetic power allocation, resource optimization and watermark generation and capture are implemented respectively, so as to ensure the feasibility of real-time data tracking ability. In addition, the algorithm module is used to perform time-frequency transformation and inverse transformation on the initial data to achieve lossless embedding of the data watermark and guarantee the stability and robustness of the data. In the process of data watermark injection and extraction, the unordered algorithm is used to embed the watermark into the data, which improves the security of the data, better resists the risk of data leakage, and ensures the traceability of the data.

5 Validation of System Performance

The data watermark tracing verification platform under Hadoop environment consists of multiple hardware and software systems, and the architecture of this verification platform is shown in Fig. 8. The Hadoop environment platform integrates and interconnects the subsystem modules of different nodes, and the node servers are formed in a distributed manner. After the configuration of the node servers is completed, the login key command is set so as to realize the flow of data between different nodes.

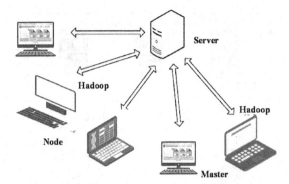

Fig. 8. The architecture of data watermark tracing verification platform

5.1 Verification Parameters

The validation of data watermark tracing in Hadoop environment uses several parameters such as acceleration ratio, number of computation nodes and data volume to measure and evaluate the accuracy and efficiency of data watermark tracing. The tracing accuracy of data watermarking is a measure of the accuracy of the whole system application in the Hadoop environment, which is obtained by calculating the ratio of the correctly traced data to the total data. The data watermark tracing efficiency is an important criterion to measure the stability and adaptability of the whole system, which is obtained by the calculation of the node computation time.

As important evaluation parameters for the effectiveness of data watermark tracing, the acceleration ratio and constant efficiency scalability can be used to visually verify the performance of the data watermark tracing system in the Hadoop environment. Among them, the arithmetic performance P_s of the data watermark tracing system in the Hadoop environment is calculated as shown in Eq. (4) where, t_r is the algorithm running time and t_i is specific node i executing algorithm task time.

$$P_s = \frac{t_r}{t_i} \tag{4}$$

The efficiency of the data watermark tracing system in Hadoop environment is calculated as shown in Eq. (5) where C is the cost of the algorithm in the execution of simultaneous operations at a particular moment.

$$E_t = \frac{P_s}{i} = \frac{1}{1 + \frac{C}{t_r}} \tag{5}$$

5.2 Verification Results

Based on these two key core evaluation parameters metrics, and dynamic adjustment of the calculation parameters can evaluate the operational performance of the whole system. Table 1 shows the data watermark tracing verification settings.

Table 1. Test environment settings

No.	Environment	Servers numbers	Servers code
1	Environment I	3 Servers	Node 2, 4
2	Environment II	4 Servers	Node 3, 5, 7
3	Environment III	7 Servers	Node 1, 4, 6

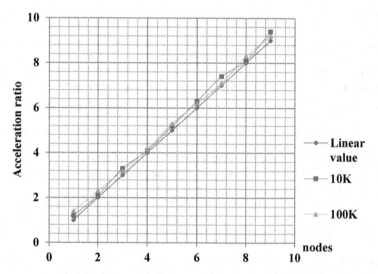

Fig. 9. The performance results of acceleration ratio

The performance results of data watermark tracing acceleration ratio in Hadoop environment are shown in Fig. 9.

From Fig. 9, it can see that the tracing acceleration ratio of the whole system is positively correlated with the distribution of the number of servers where "Linear value" provides the reference line. It can be seen that there is a linear correlation between the operation efficiency of the system and the computing nodes. For the different scales of datasets, the performance between 10 K and 100 K is close, which means that the increase of datasets may not affect the performance of the system.

6   Conclusion

In summary, Hadoop-based data watermark tracing system can achieve effective improvement in data storage occupancy and arithmetic resource optimization, and play an important role in data security, data dissemination and evolutionary tracking. In this paper, a data watermark tracing model in Hadoop environment is built to achieve accurate and efficient tracing of datasets. Meanwhile, the Hadoop environment system and its application in the field of data watermark tracing is studied. Furthermore, based on the analysis of the system architecture of data tracing and corresponding algorithms, this paper establishes a data watermark tracing system where the processing procedure is designed. The experiments for verification is finally established and the results show the effectiveness of the proposed system. However, there are still many limitations in this paper at the level of data availability and flexible storage, and the research on the modular design on Hadoop environment platform needs to be further optimized in the future research.

References

1. Wang, L., Zhou, G., Wang, L., Peng, Z.: Attribute level lineage and probabilistic computation of uncertain data. J. Softw. **25**(04), 863–879 (2014)
2. Prabhune, A., Zweig, A., Stotzka, R., Hesser, J., Gertz, M.: P-PIF: a ProvONE provenance interoperability framework for analyzing heterogeneous workflow specifications and provenance traces. Distrib. Parallel Databases **36**(1), 219–264 (2017). https://doi.org/10.1007/s10 619-017-7216-y
3. Hondo, F., et al.: Data provenance management for bioinformatics workflows using NoSQL database systems in a cloud computing environment. In: 2017 IEEE International Conference on Bioinformatics and Biomedicine (BIBM), pp. 1929–1934 (2017)
4. Gort, M.L.P., Olliaro, M., Cortesi, A.: Reducing multiple occurrences of meta-mark selection in relational data watermarking. IEEE Access **10**, 62210–62231 (2022)
5. Chen, L., Shi, C., Yu, P., Shen, W., Gao, X., Yang, R.: Research and application of digital watermark tracing technology in data security protection of power grid. In: 2020 IEEE 3rd International Conference of Safe Production and Informatization (IICSPI), pp. 530–533 (2020)
6. Li, D., Li, Y., Yuan, C., Chen, H., Zhang, L.: Research on private cloud platform of seed tracing based on Hadoop parallel computing. In: 2015 4th International Conference on Computer Science and Network Technology (ICCSNT), pp. 134–137 (2015)
7. Shen, X., Zhang, Y., Wang, T., Sun, Y.: Relational Database watermarking for data tracing. In: 2020 International Conference on Cyber-Enabled Distributed Computing and Knowledge Discovery (CyberC), pp. 224–231 (2020)
8. Darwish, S.M., Selim, H.A., Elsherbiny, M.M.: Distortion free database watermarking system based on intelligent mechanism for content integrity and ownership control. J. Comput. **13**(9), 1053–1066 (2018)
9. Dwivedi, A.K., Sharma, B.K., Vyas, A.K.: Watermarking techniques for ownership protection of relational databases. Int. J. Emerg. Technol. Adv. Eng. **4**(1), 368–375 (2014)
10. Tosh, D.K., Shetty, S., Liang, X., Kamhoua, C., Njilla, L.: Consensus protocols for blockchain-based data provenance: challenges and opportunities. In: 2017 IEEE 8th Annual Ubiquitous Computing, Electronics and Mobile Communication Conference (UEMCON), pp. 469–474 (2017)
11. Liang, X., Shetty, S., Tosh, D., Kamhoua, C., Kwiat, K., Njilla, L.: ProvChain: a blockchain-based data provenance architecture in cloud environment with enhanced privacy and availability. In: 2017 17th IEEE/ACM International Symposium on Cluster, Cloud and Grid Computing (CCGRID), pp. 468–477 (2017)
12. Siledar, S., Tamane, S.: A distortion-free watermarking approach for verifying integrity of relational databases. In: 2020 International Conference on Smart Innovations in Design, Environment, Management, Planning and Computing (ICSIDEMPC), pp. 192–195 (2020)
13. Kamal, M., Tariq, S.: Light-weight security and data provenance for multi-hop internet of things. IEEE Access **6**, 34439–34448 (2018)

14. Elkhodr, M., Alsinglawi, B., Alshehri, M.: Data provenance in the internet of things. In: 2018 32nd International Conference on Advanced Information Networking and Applications Workshops (WAINA), pp. 727–731 (2018)
15. Goyal, M., Anuranjana: Demonetization-Twitter data analysis using big data & Hadoop. In: 2019 Amity International Conference on Artificial Intelligence (AICAI), pp. 156–158 (2019)

Application of RFID Tag in the Localization of Power Cable Based on Big Data

Zhenyu Zhang[1], Shuming Feng[1]([✉]), Min Xiao[2], Yongcheng Yang[1], and Gangbo Song[1]

[1] Jiangsu Electric Power Information Technology Co., Ltd., Nanjing, China
401945335@qq.com
[2] Nanjing Institute of Technology, Nanjing, China

Abstract. At present, cable labels have problems that labels are easy to knock and fall off during the storage and allocation of equipment. The binding falls off affected by the external environment and time, which cannot effectively support the unified coding and full life management of the equipment. A cable fault positioning algorithm based on big data is designed, which combines the positioning algorithm of uhf UHF RFID electronic label with the positioning algorithm of active label to realize the work safety monitoring management of inspection personnel and the automatic positioning reporting management of circuit barrier problems. The read-write conflict and interference problem in the passive UHF RFID electronic tags and the active UHF electronic tags are introduced in the original algorithm. The simulation of the algorithm is analyzed, and the simulation results prove that the present algorithm can solve the problem better than the original one. The algorithm can effectively locate the cable fault, and has certain engineering and theoretical value.

Keywords: Cable positioning · Radio frequency identification · Interference problem · Cable distribution · Big data · Cable channel model

1 Introduction

Power cable is an important basic product of the power grid, which can be used for the transmission and distribution of electric energy. At present, under the influence of the big data of the power grid, the cable management system has developed many advantages. In the city power grid, limited by the limitation of space, the electric cable becomes the main line of the city power supply [1–3]. Therefore, power cable plays an important role of vascular and nerve in urban power transmission and distribution, and is an indispensable basic product of urban informatization and electrification in the future [4–6].

With the continuous development of urban economy, the scale of the city has been continuously expanded [7, 8], and the lifeline of the city has been continuously laid. Due to the acceleration of urban construction speed, urban road transformation and the crossing of various pipelines, leading to the multiple cable multiple displacement transformation, so that the reference above the original underground cable channel changes,

Y. Tian et al. (Eds.): ICBDS 2022, CCIS 1796, pp. 92–104, 2023.
https://doi.org/10.1007/978-981-99-3300-6_8

resulting in some cable lines are not clear [9]. In addition, the power cable is laid underground, the operating environment is hidden, and the cable identification in the parallel cable trench is difficult, which is not conducive to the arrangement and positioning of faults, resulting in the difficulty of fault processing and low economic benefits. Therefore, the effective management of urban underground power cable needs to be solved urgently [10–12].

At present, the RFID labels used in the cable field are mainly UHF back adhesive electronic label, UHF tape electronic label and electronic identification device of underground pipeline [1]. RFID electronic label is mainly dominated by UHF communication technology, which has the advantages of long non-contact communication distance and wide scanning range, but it also has poor practicability in accurate differentiation of cluster cables and portable read identification [5–7]. Especially in recent years, with the surge of various kinds of mobile operation terminals [8], a variety of front-line operation terminals, causing the problem of "one person operation, multiple machines carrying", which greatly affects the actual application effect of RFID electronic label, and urgently needs simple, practical, convenient and economic electronic label reading means.

2   UHF RFID Technology

The traditional underground cable identification method adopts ordinary signs and color band, after a period of time, ordinary signs are easy to lose from the cable, color strip color off, can not achieve the purpose of the cable identification. Compared with the traditional cable identification method that can not be used for a long time, the cable intelligent inspection and identification device can completely solve the long-term and accuracy of the cable identification problems [13]. The cable intelligent inspection and identification device implants the cable and cable channel data into the passive electronic identification plate, and the electronic identification plate adopts ring buckle and embedded type to greatly reduce the possibility of logo loss. The handheld terminal is used to read at a long distance and in multiple ways, which reduces the difficulty of checking the information of cable. The computer software is used to write different collection units in each subsystem, facilitate reading and background management, and provide the environmental information of power cables and channels to relevant managers in real time and accurately, so as to reduce the workload of maintaining cable data. The main advantages of this method are reflected in further improving the level of informatization and intelligence of the cable, and its remarkable characteristics are reflected in the adaptability, accuracy and real-time of the new technology applied to the cable interior, and meet the technical indicators of cable operation and information management [14].

The wireless identification technology is used to develop intelligent electronic signs suitable for city cables and channels. The cable information is implanted into the electronic sign plate, and the power cable information is read by using close range wireless identification technology on the site. The installation of the sign adopts the watch cover mode, anti-fouling and waterproof, convenient and firm installation, to adapt to the outdoor well environment. Develop intelligent electronic identification for cable well cover plate. The cable well information is implanted into the electronic sign, integrated and embedded into the cover plate, and the cable channel information is read through the UHF technology. Develop electronic identification reading terminal [15]. Read the electronic identification information and interact with the background system. It usually takes three to five minutes to identify traditional cable labels. Putting cable data into the electronic label and being read by reading equipment will greatly reduce the time for cable identification and positioning.

Ultra-high Frequency Radio Frequency Identification (UHF RFID) belongs to one of the core technologies of the Internet of Things, is a kind of contactless automatic identification technology working in the 860–960 MHz frequency band [16], the technology integrates semiconductor, electronic information, cryptography and other fields, because UHF RFID has the advantages of long distance, low cost and low power consumption, has been widely used in many industries (Fig. 1).

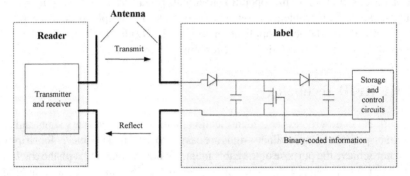

Fig. 1. System block diagram for the RFID

The basic working principle of RFID system is that the reader and writer sends a specific radio frequency signal through the transmitting antenna. When the electronic label enters the effective working area, the AC transformer field generates induction voltage at both ends of the antenna, so that the energy is activated, so that the electronic label transmits its own coded information through the built-in antenna. The receiving antenna of the reader and writer receives the modulation signal sent from the label, transmits it to the reader signal processing module through the modulator of the antenna, and sends the effective information to the background host system for related processing. The host system identifies the identity of the label according to the logical operation, makes corresponding processing and control for different Settings, and finally sends out a signal to control the reader and writer to complete different read and write operations. In terms of the communication and energy induction mode between electronic tags and readers, the RFID system can generally be divided into inductance coupling system and electromagnetic backscattering coupling system [17]. The RFID chip of 900 MHz UHF belongs to the scattering coupling of electromagnetic reverse. According to the free propagation theorem of electromagnetic waves, the radiation range of electromagnetic waves emitted by the reader antenna in free space is approximately a sphere. Assuming that excluding the interference of other electromagnetic signals such as WiFi signals, when the reader continuously transmits electromagnetic waves to the RFID label, the power density from the reader to the antenna is shown in the following equation

$$S_{TA} = \frac{EIRP}{4\pi d^2} = \frac{P_{RA}G_{RA}}{4\pi d^2} \tag{1}$$

EIRP is the effective omnidirectional radiation power of the UHF RFID reader antenna, P_{RA} is its emission power, G_{RA} is its antenna gain, and d is the distance between the reader and the label. Ignoring the polarization loss of the tag antenna, ideally, the maximum, total received power $P_{TA\,max}$ obtained from the tag at the reader antenna d is shown in the following equation

$$P_{TA\,max} = S_{TA} \cdot A_{Tag} = \frac{P_{RA}G_{RA}}{4\pi d^2} \cdot \frac{\lambda^2 G_{TA}}{4\pi} = (\frac{\lambda}{4\pi d})^2 \tag{2}$$

Judging from the equation, when P_{RA}, G_{RA} and operating frequencies remain certain, $P_{TA\,max}$ is inversely proportional to d^2, that is, the electromagnetic wave energy received by the label is inversely proportional to the square of the distance between the UHF RFID readers. It can also be said that when the energy required for the label is not large, the recognition distance is long if the system communication recognition sensitivity is ignored. It is further known that the path loss P_{loss} of the transmitted electromagnetic waves propagating in free space is shown in the following equation [18]

$$P_{Loss} = 10\log\frac{P_{RA}}{P_{TA\,max}} = -10\log\frac{\lambda^2 G_{RA}G_{TA}}{(4\pi d)^2} \tag{3}$$

Similarly, when P_{RA}, G_{TA} and working frequency remain certain, P_{loss} is proportional to d^2. The path loss of the forward link of the UHF RFID system changes in the same direction with the square of the distance between the tag and the writer, and the path loss increases with the distance between the two. However, when the path loss is small, it also means that the farther the identifiable distance of the system is. UHF RFID works in the 900 MHz band and electronic tags do not require external battery power. The label chip is mainly composed of three parts, control logic, memory and RF analog front end. Its structure block diagram is shown in the figure below (Fig. 2).

The rectifier circuit is responsible for converting the RF signal to the DC, and the voltage regulator circuit is responsible for stabilizing the DC signal above the operating voltage required for the secondary circuit. The voltage regulator circuit is able to output a stable voltage when the operating distance between the reader and the label varies substantially. When the demodulation circuit obtains the signal envelope, the envelope is shaped to produce a baseband signal from the digital circuit. Modulation circuit (modulator) uses the reverse scattering principle to modulate the RF signal. The label itself does not produce the carrier, but reflects the received continuous carrier, and modulates its amplitude according to the baseband signal. In order to make the baseband circuit work normally, the oscillator and o-electric reset circuit on the chip are required to generate clock signal and reset signal respectively. In the above circuit modules, all circuits outside the baseband circuit are collectively referred to as the RF analog front end circuit, so that the label can be divided into three components: the antenna, the RF analog front end and the baseband circuit.

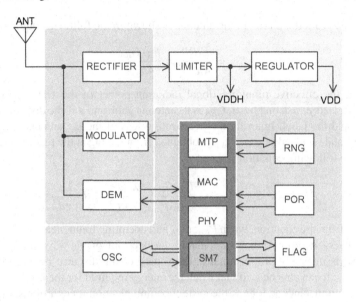

Fig. 2. Block diagram of the chip structure for the UHF RFID tags

3   Positioning Algorithm of Faulty Cables Based on RFID

3.1   Deployment Plan for Positioning

Passive uhf UHF RFID electronic tags are mainly buried near the pipeline to be located, and the ring marker on each cable is managed by a unique cable channel master marker. Assuming that the length, width and height of the cable trench are L, W, and H, respectively, the deployment scheme is shown in Table 1. In them, the number of labels or collection points is calculated down.

Table 1. Occupancy of cables

Level of density	The spacing of labels	Number of labels
1	0.8	0.64
2	1.0	1
3	1.2	1.44
4	2.0	4

Based on the deployment situation of the localization environment, the calibration of PDA signal intensity is required, so that the intensity of PDA emission signal increases linearly.

At the same time, different signal intensity levels need to be divided according to the signal intensity of different electronic labels read by PDA. The signal intensity level requires PDA to support received signal intensity detection (RSSI). The grading method of signal intensity allows to estimate the estimated distance from the reader to the target label, assumed to have N moving measurement points of PDA, then the estimated distance set M from PDA to the target tag is as follows

$$M = \{L_1, L_2, ...L_N\} \tag{4}$$

N is the number of PDA moving measurement points. Three distances taken from the estimated distance set M were selected for the calculation of the three-sphere intersection, thus yielding a set of estimated coordinates for the target tag. The calculation formula for the intersection of three-balls can be expressed as follows.

$$\begin{cases} (x_1 - x_0)^2 + (y_1 - y_0)^2 + (z_1 - z_0)^2 = L_1^2 \\ (x_2 - x_0)^2 + (y_2 - x_0)^2 + (2z - z_0)^2 = L_3^2 \\ (x_3 - x_0)^2 + (y_3 - y_0)^2 + (z_3 - z_0)^2 = L_3^2 \end{cases} \tag{5}$$

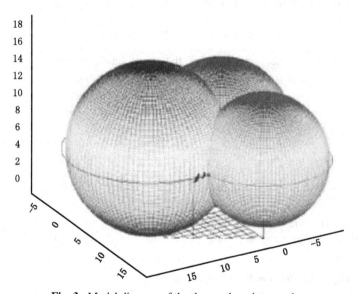

Fig. 3. Model diagram of the three-sphere intersection

Where a is the coordinate of PDA, (x_0, y_0, z_0) is the coordinate of the unknown target labels, and the three-sphere intersection model is shown in Fig. 3.

It uses the least squares plane to reduce the error in the estimated coordinates of the target label. This paper uses a least squares plane fit to reduce the error in the estimated coordinates of the target label. The unrelated model variable $t_1, t_2, t_3...t_q$ can form a linear function of least squares $y(t_1, t_2, t_3..t_q, b_1, b_2, b_3...b_q) = b_0 + b_1 t_1 + ...b_q t_q$. The matrix form is as follows

$$
\begin{pmatrix}
1 & t_{11} & \cdots & t_{1j} & \cdots & t_{1q} \\
1 & t_{21} & \cdots & t_{2j} & \cdots & t_{2q} \\
\cdots & & & & & \\
1 & t_{i1} & \cdots & t_{ij} & \cdots & t_{iq} \\
\cdots & & & & & \\
1 & t_{n1} & \cdots & t_{nj} & \cdots & t_{nq}
\end{pmatrix}
\cdot
\begin{pmatrix}
b_0 \\
b_1 \\
\cdots \\
b_j \\
\cdots \\
b_q
\end{pmatrix}
=
\begin{pmatrix}
y_0 \\
y_1 \\
\cdots \\
y_i \\
\cdots \\
y_n
\end{pmatrix}
\tag{6}
$$

With t_{ij} as the data matrix A, the parameter b_j as the parameter vector b, and the observation y_j as Y, the matrix of the above equation is $Ab = Y$, and the corresponding square difference form is $Ab = Y$. The corresponding squared difference form is $mi \ n_b = \|Ab - Y\|_2$.

The feasible coordinate set r of the target label is obtained by the previous calculation. The discrete point in note R is (x_i, y_i, z_i) and the linear plane equation fitted using least squares is $\min(\sum_{i=1}^{n} b_0 + b_1 x_i + b_2 y_i - z_i)^2$. Solving the fitting equation coefficient (b_0, b_1, b_2), the calculation formula of the target label coordinates is

$$
z(x_1, y_1; b_0, b_1, b_2) = b_0 + b_1 x_1 + b_2 y_1 \tag{7}
$$

When calculating the coordinates of the target label, we obtain the estimated coordinates of the target label according to the following formula

$$
\begin{cases}
x = \dfrac{\sum_{i=1}^{i=n} x_i}{n} \\[2mm]
y = \dfrac{\sum_{i=1}^{i=n} y_i}{n} \\[2mm]
z = \dfrac{\sum_{i=1}^{i=n} (b_0 + b_1 x_i + b_2 y_i)}{n}
\end{cases}
\tag{8}
$$

where (x_i, y_i, z_i) is the feasible solution of the middle 1/3 part of the discrete points in the feasible estimation target coordinate set R, sorted by the x coordinate.

3.2 The Algorithm for Fault Localization

In the actual application environment, the identification of passive UHF RFID electronic tags will be affected by various interference, which increases the code error rate, slow the identification speed and reduce the identification distance. Therefore, for the conflict interference problem of RFID reading and writing, the read and write anti-interference strategy is added to the algorithm.

The steps of the positioning algorithm for the passive UHF RFID electronic tags are as follows (Fig. 4):

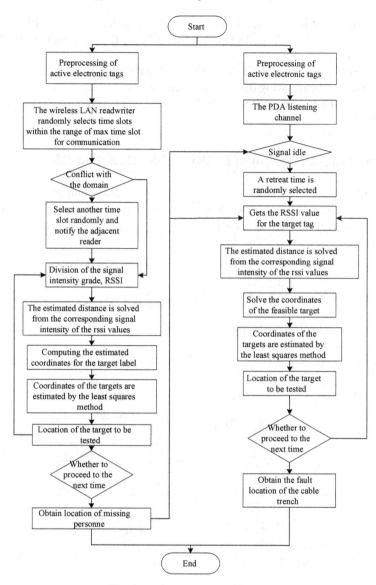

Fig. 4. Flow chart of the algorithm

In the first step, deploy the passive uhf UHF RFID electronic tag in the cable trench to record the signal strength of the electronic tag, the coordinates of the electronic tag, and the configuration information.

The second step, before transmitting the signal, PDA must listen to whether there are other readers in the channel, and read the label if the channel is idle. If the channel is busy, you will randomly choose a retreat time, and then continue to read. Based on the signal intensity of the PDA reads, the signal intensity is divided into the maximum and minimum signal intensity levels, and the estimated distance between PDA and the target tag is estimated from the electronic tag set between the maximum and minimum signal intensity levels.

In the third step, the estimated coordinates of the target label are calculated using a formula based on the receiving distance between the label and the PDA.

Finally, the least squares plane fit was used to obtain the estimated coordinates of the target labels.

4 Positioning Algorithm of Faulty Cables Based on RFID

Based on RFID positioning label, the cable channel safety inspection and fault positioning algorithm designed is composed of safety inspection system and fault positioning system. The system structure diagram is shown in Fig. 5.

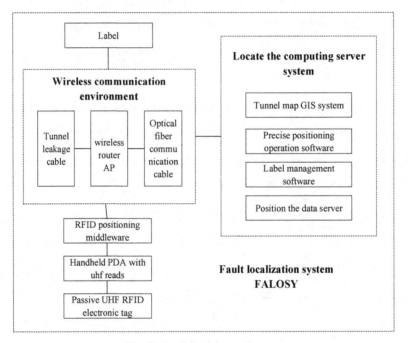

Fig. 5. System structure diagram

4.1 Single-End Traveling Wave Ranging Principle

Considering that the medium of the same power cable is consistent, the propagation speed, amplitude size and waveform of the traveling wave do not change. When the transmission is uneven, the energy of the traveling wave signal is redistributed. Therefore, we can consider the single-end injection traveling wave to observe the reflected wave change for fault ranging. Because the test traveling wave is usually high-frequency pulses, it cannot be analyzed with the power cable model of universal sets.

The distribution parameter model of power cable divides the whole line into unit length, and the unit resistance and inductance are consistent. Therefore, the power cable can be considered as a uniform transmission line, and the traveling wave advances at a uniform speed. Reflection occurs when an impedance mismatch is encountered during the transmission of the traveling wave, and the reflection factor is defined as

$$r = \frac{Z_2 - Z_1}{Z_2 + Z_1} \tag{9}$$

Z_1 and Z_2 in the formula respectively indicate the different impedances passed by the traveling wave during transmission. When there is a fault, the resistance of the power cable changes, that is, the reflection factor changes, then the reflection waveform changes. By fault-ranging the time difference between the emission wave and the first reflected wave, the measured distance is

$$L = (\Delta t \times v)/2 \tag{10}$$

In the formula, v, is the traveling wave speed corresponding to the cable insulation material.

4.2 Single-End Traveling Wave Ranging Principle

In the process of single-end traveling wave ranging, when a fault is encountered, the waveform state will jump, with non-stationary and non-linear characteristics, and the empirical mode decomposition algorithm (EMD) has the advantages of non-linear and non-stationary signal processing and adaptive processing ability, so the EMD algorithm is used to handle traveling wave noise reduction.

The EMD algorithm can decompose the input signal into narrow-band components of multiple frequencies, as shown in Eq.

$$x(t) = \sum_{i=1}^{n} f_i(t) + r_n(t) \tag{11}$$

In the formula, $f_i(t)$ is the multiple intrinsic mode function components, $r_n(t)$ is the residual signal.

From the formula, the core of the empirical mode decomposition algorithm is the choice of the IMF component, which must satisfy the following conditions. In the whole range, the number of poles is the same or at most one different from the number of over zeros, at any time the envelope defined by the local maximum and the envelope defined by the local minimum, the mean is zero.

5 Simulation Results

It can be found from the figure that the denoising method shown in the article can effectively filter out white noise. For large burr, such as when the sampling point is 170, the signal trend can be judged by the EMD algorithm, so as to remove large burr, which has a good denoising effect (Figs. 6 and 7).

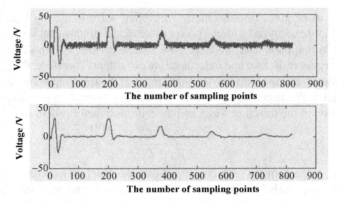

Fig. 6. Open-circuit waveform before and after noise reduction

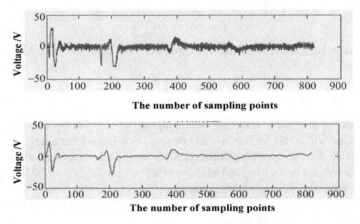

Fig. 7. Short-circuit waveform before and after noise reduction

This paper presents a performance simulation of the algorithm for cable channel safety patrol and fault localization based on the RFID tag. The comparison results of the error simulation of the signal intensity grades are shown in the figure. The figure shows the broken line with the block is the fault positioning algorithm designed by the present invention, the dot broken line is the performance of the algorithm without the anti-interference strategy, and the broken line with the triangle is the performance of the original algorithm without any improvement. It can be seen from the figure that when the signal intensity level is divided into more signal intensity levels, the positioning error of all the algorithms will gradually decrease, and the algorithm designed by the present invention has the optimal error performance.

6 Conclusion

Cable labels have problems that labels are easy to knock and fall off during the storage and allocation of equipment. The binding falls off affected by the external environment and time, which cannot effectively support the unified coding and full life management of the equipment. A cable fault positioning algorithm is designed, which combines the positioning algorithm of uhf UHF RFID electronic label with the positioning algorithm of active label to realize the work safety monitoring management of inspection personnel and the automatic positioning reporting management of circuit barrier problems. The read-write conflict and interference problem in the passive UHF RFID electronic tags and the active UHF electronic tags are introduced in the original algorithm. The simulation of the algorithm is analyzed, and the simulation results prove that the present algorithm can solve the problem better than the original one. The algorithm can effectively locate the cable fault, and has certain engineering and theoretical value.

References

1. Ding, K., Chan, F.T.S., Zhang, X., et al.: Defining a Digital Twin-based Cyber-Physical Production System for autonomous manufacturing in smart shop floors. Int. J. Prod. Res. **57**(20), 6315–6334 (2019)
2. Zhuang, C., Liu, J., Xiong, H.: Digital twin-based smart production management and control framework for the complex product assembly shop-floor. Int. J. Adv. Manuf. Technol. **96**(1–4), 1149–1163 (2018). https://doi.org/10.1007/s00170-018-1617-6
3. Tao, F., Cheng, J., Qi, Q., Zhang, M., Zhang, H., Sui, F.: Digital twin-driven product design, manufacturing and service with big data. Int. J. Adv. Manuf. Technol. **94**(9–12), 3563–3576 (2017). https://doi.org/10.1007/s00170-017-0233-1
4. Liu, Q., Zhang, H., Leng, J., et al.: Digital twin-driven rapid individualised designing of automated flow-shop manufacturing system. Int. J. Prod. Res. **57**(12), 3903–3919 (2019)
5. Mittal, S., Khan, M.A., Romero, D., et al.: Smart manufacturing: characteristics, technologies and enabling factors. Inst. Mech. Eng. **233**(5), 1342–1361 (2017)
6. Sihan, H., Guoxin, W., Yan, Y., et al.: Blockchain-based data management for digital twin of product. J. Manuf. Syst. **54**, 361–371 (2019)
7. Rosen, R., Wichert, G., Lo, G., et al.: About the importance of autonomy and digital twins for the future of manufacturing. IFAC-Papers OnLine **48**(3), 567–572 (2015)
8. Simons, S., Abé, P., Neser, S.: Learning in the AutFab-the fully automated industrie 4.0 learning factory of the University of Applied Sciences Darmstadt. Proc. Manuf. **9**, 81–88 (2017)
9. Tao, F., Liu, W., Zhang, M., et al.: Five-dimension digital twin model and its ten applications **25**(01), 1–18 (2019)
10. Tao, F., Zhang, H., Liu, A., et al.: Digital twin in industry: state-of-the-art. IEEE Trans. Industr. Inf. **15**(4), 2405–2415 (2019)
11. Shen, C., Jia, M., Chen, Y., et al.: Digital twin of the energy internet and its application. J. Glob. Energy Interconnect. **3**(01), 1–13 (2020)
12. Song, X., Jiang, T., Schlegel, S., Westermann, D.: Parameter tuning for dynamic digital twins in inverter-dominated distribution grid. IET Renew. Power Gener. **14**(5), 811–821 (2020)
13. Jain, P., Poon, J., Singh, J.P., et al.: A digital twin approach for fault diagnosis in distributed photovoltaic systems. IEEE Trans. Power Electron. **35**(1), 940–956 (2020)

14. Tang, W., Chen, X., Qian, T., et al.: Technologies and applications of digital twin for developing smart energy systems. Strateg. Study CAE **04**, 1–12 (2020)
15. Zhou, M., Yan, J., Feng, D.: Digital twin framework and its application to power grid online analysis. CSEE J. Power Energy Syst. **5**(3), 391–398 (2019)
16. Fei, T., He, Z., Qinglin, Q., et al.: Ten questions towards digital twin: analysis and thinking. Comput. Integr. Manuf. Syst. **26**(01), 1–17 (2020)
17. Negri, E., Berardi, S., Fumagalli, L., et al.: MES-integrated digital twin frameworks. J. Manuf. Syst. **56**, 58–71 (2020)
18. Schroeder, G.N., Steinmetz, C., Pereira, C.E., et al.: Digital twin data modeling with AutomationML and a communication methodology for data exchange. IFAC-PapersOnLine **49**(30), 12–17 (2016)

Research Hotspots and Evolution Trend of Virtual Power Plant in China: An Empirical Analysis Based on Big Data

Yan Zhang[1], Pengcheng Liu[2], Hao Xu[1(✉)], and Mulan Wang[1]

[1] School of Economics and Management, Nanjing Institute of Technology, Nanjing 211167, China

{zhangyan,xhnjit,wangml}@njit.edu.cn

[2] School of Electrical Engineering, Nanjing Institute of Technology, Nanjing 211167, China

Abstract. **[Objective]** Due to the 14th Five-Year Plan and the "30·60" double carbon targets advocates energy reform, the number of articles on virtual power plant (Abbreviation is VPP) has surged, the annual number of articles published has maintained a positive growth trend. In the context of big data, the research track of VPP is sorted out by literature measurement method and visual knowledge graph. It will provide a reference direction for the following scholars' research and accelerate the combination of emerging technologies and VPP. **[Methods]** Through the data collection of CNKI related literature on VPP in China in the past 20 years, Using CiteSpace to process and analyze big data, rapidly form a visual map to reveal the development and evolution trajectory of VPPs, and make it easier to track research hotspots and core frontier technologies. **[Result/Conclusion]** The knowledge map generated by big data reveals the research hotspots of VPP and the evolution trajectory of research hotspots, and the conclusion obtained is more reasonable and realistic significance. Through the map, the main technological research directions of VPP were controllable load, distributed energy resource, communication and energy storage. It aims to achieve the stability of massive distributed energy resource grid-connection, fast and safe communication, expansion of energy storage capacity and overall economic benefits, etc. Combined with the current research on VPP in China, the research on VPP in the future will closely follow the trend of national policies, and the emergence of new energy will gradually disperse and diversify the research on VPP.

Keywords: Virtual Power Plant · CiteSpace · Big Data · Knowledge Graph · Research Hotspot

1 Introduction

National policies are now advocating energy reform and promoting the transformation of the traditional power industry. The increasing demand for electricity from the customer side and the diversification of new forms of power generation have contributed to the interest of researchers in the field of "virtual power plant" (VPP), resulting in a rapid

Y. Tian et al. (Eds.): ICBDS 2022, CCIS 1796, pp. 105–121, 2023.
https://doi.org/10.1007/978-981-99-3300-6_9

increase in the number of publications on VPP. Most of the research has been carried out in the area of technology. Many advances have been made in theoretical methods and advanced technologies, but there are few literatures that take existing big data as the research object and integrate bibliometrics and visual analysis methods to carry out related research on this field systematically. While scientific knowledge mapping can extract and filter structured knowledge sequences from big data, show the evolution of research hotspots based on keywords and other titling information, map the interactions between knowledge groups. The scientific knowledge map can extract and filter structured knowledge sequences from a large amount of literature data to show the evolution of research hotspots and map the cross-interaction between knowledge communities based on keywords and other titling information, thus enabling the mining of hotspots and emerging trends [1] provides a reference for promoting research on VPP.

In the context of the "era of big data", CNKI was used to collect literature data on VPP in the past twenty years (2002–2021), visualize and analyze the imported literature data based on CiteSpace, draw a knowledge map of co-occurrence, identify the research hotspots, evolutionary processes and other key information in the field of VPP research based on the results of the information visualization analysis, and count the number of articles about VPP published by journals, judge and divide the core area of journals in this field, and finally This study aims to provide a systematic overview of the current status of research in the field of VPP in China, in order to provide effective assistance to other scholars in the field and promote the development of the field.

2   Related Work

The essence of this research is to process and analyze the big data about VPP, and reveal the research hotspots of VPP, the correlation between research hotspots, the evolution of research trends, research cutting-edge technologies, core published journals and other characteristics.

2.1   Status Quo of Literature Big Data Mining

Literature is an important research achievement of researchers, including research purpose, research object, research method, research content and research conclusion, etc. The quantity of literature output in a field is the most direct reflection of its research progress. Data mining in literature big data mainly takes structured metadata such as keywords, authors, topics, author institutions, published journals and publication time as objects, which can analyze a certain field from multiple perspectives [2]. At present, data mining researchers in China mainly focus on universities and research projects supported by the government. Compared with foreign countries, there are fewer researchers in enterprises. At present, the main research directions of data mining include: data analysis, data model construction and evaluation, data risk assessment and quality optimization, Chinese text mining, data mining algorithm, etc. [3]. Under the background of the era of big data, from the past in view of the structured data mining to dig out the hidden information from unstructured data, and the hidden information in unstructured data mining will be the future research focus and development trend of the era of big data

[3], through the scientific method from the data resources in the mining of deep value to serve social development and progress, Only when the value of big data resources is fully utilized by researchers can the era of big data truly come.

2.2 Research Status of VPP

"Aggregated distributed energy resources (DER)" and "communication speed and security" are the two core technologies of virtual power plant, and the current related research mainly focuses on the technical aspects. Yang et al. [4] introduce the scheduling mechanism of the internal resources of a VPP, and sort out the domestic and international power market bidding problems from three aspects: time scale, optimization model and uncertainty factors. Li Bin et al. [5] take the problems of distributed power trading presenting centralized network verification and low market competitiveness as the starting point, analyze the advantages and disadvantages of blockchain technology applied to VPP, and provide research ideas for future blockchain application to VPP from three aspects: security, sharing, and consensus. Wei Zhinong et al. [6] analyses the core ideas, key technologies, operational framework and development prospects of VPP based on the vast amount of literature distilled. Yang Zijun et al. [7] Through an example analysis of VPP applied to the Jiangsu power grid, some specifications and implementation processes are proposed for VPP to participate in the market mechanism in order to improve the speed of dispatch. However, few researchers mine the value information of VPP from literature big data to reveal the relevant characteristics of VPP from all aspects and multiple dimensions.

3 Data Sources and Research Design

3.1 Data Collection

In order to collect high-quality and representative literature on VPP, based on the advanced search function in CNKI, this study collected literature on VPP in March 2022, with the search scope set to "Chinese retrieval" and the search topic set to "VPP". The first research on VPP in China was published in 2002 [8]. Since only 17 articles were collected for three months in 2022, the results of 2022 were not included in the article for the convenience of research. A total of 837 documents were retrieved from CNKI, and 815 Chinese documents were finally obtained through manual sorting and screening, which constitute the basic data of this study.

3.2 Building Knowledge Graphs Based on CiteSpace

This study used CiteSpace version 5.8.R3 (software available at https://citespace.podia. com/download) to map and analyze the literature knowledge map of the VPP using CiteSpace software. CiteSpace is based on the textual data format of the WOS database as the standard, and also provides data format conversion for CNKI, CSSCI, SDSS and NSF databases, among others, also provide data format conversion functions [9], so the collected knowledge network data were imported into CiteSpace and converted to WOS data format using Data's data conversion function. CiteSpace generates keyword co-occurrence map, keyword clustering map, keyword emergence map and source journals from the converted literature data to reveal related characteristics in the field of VPP.

Algorithm 1 Feature reveal algorithm

Input: Literature data collected in CNKI in refworks format

Procedure.

1. Using CiteSpace to generate keyword co-occurrence maps based on keywords in literature data to mine research hotspots

2. Clustering of keyword co-occurrence maps using LLR clustering algorithms to uncover correlations between research hotspots

3. Using the Burstiness function of the CiteSpace to judge the research hotspots of sudden change in a short time and explore the potential research topics

4. a few journals are the main focus of publications in a research area, and the Bradford coefficient algorithm (**Algorithm 2**) is used to determine the "core area" of publications in that area

Output: Research hotspots of VPP in China, correlation between hotspots, potential research themes, cutting-edge technologies and "core areas" of publications, etc.

The design framework of this study is as follows:

1. Analysis and design of the trend of annual publication volume of VPP: Import the collected data into CiteSpace software, export the data table of annual publication volume, analyze the trend of publication volume of VPP, analyze the trend change of research popularity and the factors affecting the change of research popularity;

2. Analysis and design of research hotspots in the VPP field: A research field is bound to have research hotspots, so the author imported collected data into CiteSpace to generate keyword co-occurrence maps and analyzed the main research directions in this field.

3. Analysis and design of the relationship between VPP research hotspots: Since the keyword co-occurrence map cannot directly reflect the complex cross-relationship between research hotspots, on this basis, LLR clustering algorithm is used to cluster keywords to generate the keyword cluster map and analyze the relationship between core research directions.

4. the VPP emphases research hot spots formation time analysis and design: research hotspots will change over time, this study will be sent to you by CiteSpace Burstiness function derived the distribution of the main research direction of time, analysis of the reasons that result in the change of research direction;

5. Design of the "core area" analysis of VPP articles: The publications related to VPP are mainly distributed in a few journals. According to the Bradford coefficient algorithm,

the "core area" of the publications of VPP is judged. The articles of these journals have high recognition and reference value in the research field of VPP, and provide valuable information for scholars in this research field.

Algorithm 2 Bradford coefficient algorithm [11]

Input: Euler coefficient (E=0.5772), total number of posts in the statistics (Y).
Output: core journal load (M), to determine the core area is judged to be the journal with more articles published than the core journal.
Procedure:
1. Obtain the article data from **CNKI** from 2002-2021 and count the total number of articles published Y
2. Count the number of articles in each journal from the database (N_i) and sort them in descending order
3. Calculate $M = (e^E \cdot Y)^{1/3}$, (e^E =1.781)
4. Compare the sizes of N_i and M in descending order in step 2 until N_i is smaller than M and go to step 5
5. Output M, names of journals with more than M articles and their number of articles
6. End

Single keywords can reflect the limited meaning of words, while word co-occurrence can reveal deeper content of literature, and words can be automatically extracted through co-citation coupling analysis to generate clustering mapping. CiteSpace has three algorithms for keyword clustering: the LSI algorithm (Latent Semantic Indexing algorithm) removes common words from the data and retains important words, the LLR algorithm (Log Likelihood Ratio algorithm) measures the most likely words based on a probability density function, and the MI algorithm (Mutual Information algorithm) weighs the most appropriate words by a pairwise comparison [10]. The LLR algorithm (log-likelihood algorithm) measures the maximum possible words based on a probability density function, and the MI algorithm (mutual information algorithm) weighs the more appropriate words by comparing them with each other [9]. Since LLR is more realistic, the LLR clustering algorithm was used for the generation of the map in this study.

The clustering effect and reliability of this cluster map can be judged according to two indicators, namely, the clustering module value Modularity (Q value) and Mean Silhouette (S value) [10]. Knowledge graph is based on knowledge domain, is an image that highlights the relationship between the development of scientific knowledge and structure [12, 13]. The construction of a qualified knowledge map usually requires complete data, clear mapping and reasonable interpretation to derive information on the research hotspots, development trajectories and trends of a professional field.

4   Research Findings

4.1   VPP Area Research Heat Analysis

Figure 1 gives the results related to the volume of publications in the field of VPP research, where the change in the annual volume of publications can indirectly reflect the hotness of research in a certain knowledge area, whether it is a current research hotspot, and to a certain extent reflects the current level of scholarly attention to the field. The figure can divide the overall volume of literature published on VPP into two phases, with a clear trend of increasing publication around 2012.

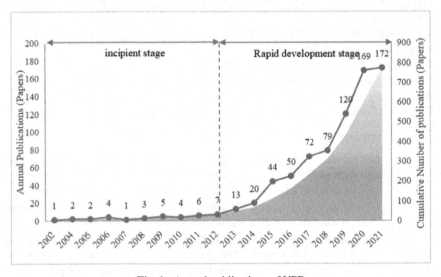

Fig. 1. Annual publications of VPP

The VPP in 2002 has just entered the view of the domestic scholars, the author from the domestic first research paper [8] concluded that parts of domestic residents faced peak at that time, the capacity can't meet the demand of electricity in time, the electricity is low, and will produce excessive energy waste generation problem, through the construction of VPP at a low investment, the contradiction between power generation side and power consumption side is solved and obvious economic benefits are produced. As can be seen from Fig. 1, the research of VPP can be divided into "incipient stage" and "rapid development stage":

1. incipient stage

The number of articles published between 2002 and 2012 was low and fluctuating, accounting for only 4.52% of the total number of articles published, probably due to the fact that the concept of VPP has just been introduced and has not yet attracted much attention from domestic scholars.

2. rapid development stage

Since 2013, there has been an obvious growth trend in the number of articles published every year, and so far it has always maintained an increasing trend. Between 2018 and 2021, the number of annual publications shows an explosive growth trend, accounting for 69.78% of the total number of publications in four years.

4.2 Hot Topics of VPP

Keywords are the main content of a piece of literature. In order to extract the research hotspots of VPP, this research hotspot analysis starts from the frequency and centrality of keywords, and the top 15 high-frequency keywords and high-centrality keywords of VPP are counted as shown in Table 1. From the table, we can see that the research hotspots of VPP mainly revolve around the type of DER, transaction security, communication speed and stability after integration into the grid, the frequency and centrality of keywords such as "electric vehicles", "optimal dispatch", "energy storage" and "uncertainty" are all ranked highly, implying that VPP are now mainly involved in these areas and have formed a more complete knowledge system. Further research reveals that, firstly, there is a rich volume of publications on electric vehicles. Zhang Weiguo [14] et al. consider the electricity demand of electric vehicles and DER generation revenue, and propose a hierarchical approach to power system scheduling to achieve load balancing management of VPP, so as to ensure the safety and economy of the power system. Secondly, the modeling of DER output is an important basis for pricing and grid connection of VPP. Shihong Miao [15] et al. propose an accurate modeling of various types of DERs to optimize the scheduling strategy of VPP, help VPP to reasonably arrange unit output and adjust market quotations in a timely manner, and improve the economy and reliability of VPP by forecasting wind power and load which are highly volatile. In addition, energy storage technology can largely improve the stability and economic efficiency of the system after the DER is connected to the grid. Wang Kaike [16] et al. propose a two-layer optimal operation model for VPP participating in energy storage systems on the basis of ensuring the stable operation of the power system and the profitability of the overall operation, to achieve collaborative optimization and realize the flexibility of the storage side of the large-scale DER to participate in the grid and promote the sustainable development of the power system.

In order to further reveal the research hotspots in the field of VPP, this paper further portrays the research hotspots in the field of VPP research based on keyword co-occurrence analysis. In this paper, the keyword co-occurrence map of the VPP is drawn with the help of CiteSpace software, and the association between the keywords is further profiled to accurately portray the research hotspots in the field. The result is shown in Fig. 2.

Figure 2 reveals a total of 382 nodes, 635 connecting lines and a network density of 0.0087, reflecting the more frequent co-citation between keywords. Using one year as the length of the time slice, Pathfinder's cropping algorithm was used to extract the main association relationships in the network structure, and the less important edges

Table 1. High frequency and betweenness centrality keywords of VPP papers

NO.	High frequency keywords	Frequency	High betweeness centrality keywords	Centrality
1	Virtual Power Plant	817	Virtual Power Plant	0.81
2	Uncertainty	87	Electric Vehicles	0.18
3	Optimized scheduling	67	Demand response	0.14
4	Electric Vehicles	63	Optimized scheduling	0.08
5	Demand response	61	Energy storage	0.08
6	Electricity market	60	Uncertainty	0.07
7	Electric to gas	47	Internet of Things	0.07
8	Blockchain	40	Simulation	0.07
9	Cooperation game	31	Information interaction	0.06
10	Economic Dispatch	29	Blockchain	0.05
11	Energy storage systems	29	Economic Dispatch	0.05
12	Master-slave game	27	Wind Power Consumption	0.05
13	Cogeneration	23	New Energy	0.05
14	Optimized operation	23	Smart Grid	0.05
15	Consensus mechanisms	23	Electricity market	0.04

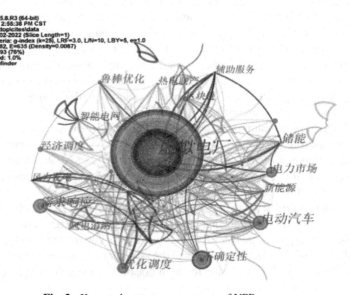

Fig. 2. Keywords co-occurrence map of VPP

were compressed and cropped to draw a more accurate knowledge map. Compared to the keyword statistics, the keyword co-occurrence graph for VPP is a clearer reflection of the more researched areas and the degree of association between the various areas. The node threshold was set at 10 to identify the key areas of focus for the VPP research. "Electric Vehicles", "Uncertainty", "Demand Response", "Optimal Scheduling", "Electricity Markets", "ancillary services", "blockchain", "energy storage", and these research directions are also the directions with a good research base for VPP, with a certain research foundation and a high level of research enthusiasm.

4.3 Clustering Mapping Analysis of Keywords in the Field of VPP Research

It is generally accepted that a Q value > 0.3 means that the clustering structure is obvious [9], an S value > 0.5 means that the clustering results are reasonable and an S value > 0.7 means that the results are convincing [12]. The clustering results of this study Q = 0.6773 and S = 0.917 indicate that the clustering structure is obvious and has a certain degree of reliability, the relevant results are shown in Fig. 3, and based on the node size it is inferred that the VPP is currently popular research topics mainly include: "Energy storage systems", "Ancillary services", "The master-slave game", "New energy", "Electro-to-gas", "Distributed electricity trading", "Uncertainty" and "Smart grids" etc.

It can be seen from the Fig. 3 that clustering results have a high degree of overlap, and there are many common concerns between fields, but at the same time, there are also many differences. For example, the number of nodes for the keywords of energy storage system is second only to that of VPP and there is more overlap with other clustering modules, indicating that the research area of VPP focuses on the breakthrough of energy storage technology and combines with other research directions. Similarly, auxiliary services, master-slave game, new energy and distributed power transactions overlap each other deeply and have a large number of nodes, indicating that these research directions are the main research directions of VPP in China and focus on cross research between them, while smart grid, modelling and collision detection are more independent research fields, indicating that these research directions are specific to certain areas of VPP and the connection with other directions needs to be further studied.

In order to further analyses the data of each cluster of the clustering module, the data of the most 8 clustering modules were exported (as shown in Table 2), from which it can be concluded that the value of S is greater than 0.7, indicating that the results of clustering are reasonable and credible, and the number of nodes involved in these clusters are greater than 10, meaning that the research heat of these clusters is high, and the author will carry out mapping interpretation on some of the labels with high popularity in research.

In the divided cluster, the main feature quantities include: scale, contour value, representative year and cluster label. When the cluster scale is large, it can be explained that the clustering results are representative. Table 2 shows that the scale of the 8 clusters in the cluster is more than 20, which means they are representative. The contour value of the cluster is close to 1, indicating a high degree of similarity among cluster members.

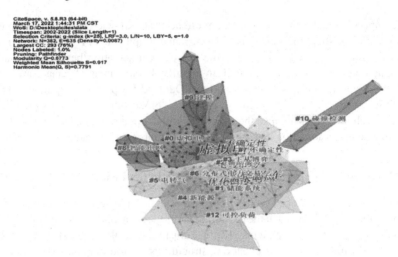

Fig. 3. Keywords Cluster mapping

The contour value of the 8 clusters in the result is all greater than 0.7, indicating a high degree of similarity among cluster members.

1. **Cluster #0**: which contains the largest number of literature, echoing the previous keyword frequency results, responding to the literature collected in this study mainly around VPP, the current form of new energy generation is developing towards diversification, DER participation in the power industry power generation has the advantages of environmental protection, reliability and flexibility, etc., but also has the disadvantages of large quantities, uneven distribution, randomness and intermittency of power generation. The large number of DERs connected to the grid puts enormous pressure on the stability of the power system, frequency regulation and voltage regulation. The new concept of the VPP offers a solution to these problems by bringing together various DERs such as controllable loads, energy storage systems, electric vehicles and DGs and then using communication technology to match the demand side with the supply side in a more rapid and stable manner. The VPP does not change the connection between the grid and the load, but acts as an "intelligent housekeeper" in the power system, using communication technology and smart metering technology to allow the DERs and the customer side to self-regulate. These aggregated DERs complete their own dispatch with the customer, unlike the unified dispatch of traditional power systems.

2. **Cluster #1**: The diagram clearly shows that the energy storage system has a large overlap with auxiliary services, new energy and distributed power trading, implying that the energy storage system is associated with these fields, and that energy storage is a research hotspot that the power industry has been focusing on. At present, energy storage in Jiangsu and Guangdong is developing well, mainly in the form of electrochemical energy storage. In a visit to Nanjing Power Supply Company, also found that the national grid is currently exploring a "new" model of energy storage to achieve

Table 2. Cluster module data sheet

Cluster NO.	Nodes amount	Profile values	Average year of cluster membership	The main research keywords involved in clustering (LLR) [TOP5]
#0	56	0.974	2014	Virtual power plants; Fuzzy c-mean algorithm; Aggregate regulation; Transaction settlement; Aggregate clustering method
#1	40	0.887	2015	Auxiliary services; Bidding strategy; Time domain response performance; Classification methods; Energy storage
#2	40	0.796	2015	Energy storage systems; Optimal scheduling; q-value migration; Multi-campus integrated energy systems; Deep reinforcement learning
#3	31	0.886	2015	Master-slave game; Nash equilibrium; Operational optimization; Multi-microgrid markets; Economic dispatch
#4	24	0.914	2017	New Energy; Energy Storage Batteries; National Grid Corporation; Generation Costs; Interconnection
#5	21	0.934	2013	Power to gas; Energy saving; Carbon recycling; Carbon capture from gas-fired units; Wind power consumption
#6	20	0.918	2015	Distributed power trading; Privacy and security; Data synchronization; Consensus mechanism; Blockchain

(*continued*)

Table 2. (*continued*)

Cluster NO.	Nodes amount	Profile values	Average year of cluster membership	The main research keywords involved in clustering (LLR) [TOP5]
#7	20	0.952	2016	Uncertainty; Wind power; Photovoltaic power; Smart energy; Distributional robust optimization

a "breakthrough" in energy storage development and safe operation, applying super-star micro-storage to solve the problem of stability brought about by new energy and diverse load access. It is worth noting that these resources are often blended together at present, and are not single-functional. Such hybrid resources facilitate the maximization of resource utilization and better maintain the stable operation of the power system. Wang Ruidong [17] et al. based on the fact that electric vehicles have the role of energy storage, applying electric vehicles to VPP can reduce the impact on grid stability by allowing them to be charged and discharged in an orderly manner when they are integrated into the grid, while also increasing the benefits to the VPP.

3. **Cluster #2**: Ancillary services play an important role in the electricity market, used to maintain stable operation of the power system. Compared to the past participation of thermal power plants generation in ancillary services, VPP aggregate a variety of DERs to optimize the electricity market structure, which can more quickly meet market demand response, reduce thermal power plants regulate pressure and improve overall economics. Guan Shufeng [18] et al. propose a set of indicators reflecting the frequency regulation performance of controllable loads, classify controllable loads, and consider the performance indicators of these controllable loads to participate in the auxiliary service bidding of VPP.

4.4 Research Hotspots Evolutionary Trends

Compared with the keyword clustering mapping, the size of the central node can reflect the research heat of this node, a research hotspot emergence map can more intuitively reflect the research hotspots and evolutionary trends at a certain stage [9]. The evolution of research hotspots was plotted using the Burstiness function of the CiteSpace software (shown in Fig. 4), where the frequency of keywords spiked within a short period of time to form hotspots. A total of 17 mutant words were found with a minimum duration of 1 year. In Fig. 4, Begin, End and Strength represent the start of year, end year and strength of keyword emergence, respectively. Through the analysis of keywords, it is found that there is an obvious time trend in related research fields of VPP in China:

1. Between 2002 and 2014, "delay control", "framework design", "data synchronization", "cost optimization ", "data mining", "power scheduling", "generalized energy storage", "multilayer networks ", "bidding strategies" and "digital twins" were early research hits in the field of VPP knowledge, and it can be found that the research on

the first stage of the VPP is mainly about how to optimize the transaction between the VPP and the power market when a large number of converged DER is put into the power plant. VPP should simultaneously consider key information such as operation parameters of DER, marginal cost and load prediction, as well as the stability of power system operation and overall economic benefits after grid connection, which means timely synchronization of data, design and bidding, power generation scheme and cost information after successful bidding.

From 2010 to 2015, the research heat of "smart grid" surged, and its strength was the highest, because of the promotion of "12th Five-Year Plan" and the state Grid Corporation of China determined the basic principles and overall goal of building a strong smart grid in 2010, until 2015, the stage of comprehensive construction. The emergence of key words is often time-continuous, which can be used to predict the hot spots of subsequent research. It can be seen from the figure that "wind power", "wind power consumption", "flexible load" and "distribution network" have been hot in 2017 until now. It can be concluded that the emergence of new energy leads to the current research direction is mainly to optimize the distribution network technology to improve the stability of the power system.

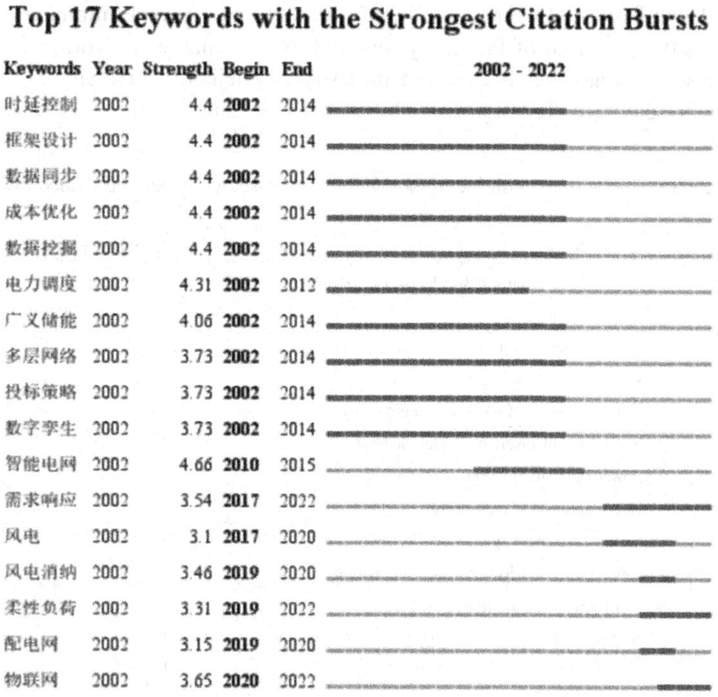

Top 17 Keywords with the Strongest Citation Bursts

Keywords	Year	Strength	Begin	End	2002 - 2022
时延控制	2002	4.4	2002	2014	
框架设计	2002	4.4	2002	2014	
数据同步	2002	4.4	2002	2014	
成本优化	2002	4.4	2002	2014	
数据挖掘	2002	4.4	2002	2014	
电力调度	2002	4.31	2002	2012	
广义储能	2002	4.06	2002	2014	
多层网络	2002	3.73	2002	2014	
投标策略	2002	3.73	2002	2014	
数字孪生	2002	3.73	2002	2014	
智能电网	2002	4.66	2010	2015	
需求响应	2002	3.54	2017	2022	
风电	2002	3.1	2017	2020	
风电消纳	2002	3.46	2019	2020	
柔性负荷	2002	3.31	2019	2022	
配电网	2002	3.15	2019	2020	
物联网	2002	3.65	2020	2022	

Fig. 4. Key words emergent mapping

4.5 Journal Distribution

In 1934 the British mathematician and library scientist (S.C. Bradford) found that research papers in a field were distributed in a regular pattern across different journals, with most papers being published in a few journals. He divided all journals in a field into three zones: core, relevant and non-relevant, each containing an almost equal number of papers. Bradford also points out that counting the distribution of source journals for research papers can clarify the spatial distribution of research papers in the field, and counting the core journals in the field provides more effective resource information for relevant researchers.

In 1986, Leo Egghe, a Belgian intelligence scientist, proposed the Bradford coefficient calculation based on Bradford's law [11]. And carried out statistical calculation of the number of articles of 815 published journals on virtual power plants through this law. It is concluded that the number of core journals of virtual power plant research should be: $M = (e^E \cdot Y)^{1/3} \approx 11.32$, that is, the journals with more than 11 articles are in the core area of journal distribution. The journals with more than 11 articles are selected and plotted in Table 3. Which are "North China Electric Power University (Beijing)", "Power Grid Technology", "Electric Power Construction", "Power System Automation", "Chinese Journal of Electrical Engineering", "North China Electric Power University", "Electric Power Demand Side Management", "Power Automation Equipment", "Southeast University", "Journal of Power System and its Automation", "North China Electricity Industry", "Shanghai Jiao Tong University", "Zhejiang University", "Changsha University of Science & Technology", "Electric Measurement and Instrumentation".

Table 3. Top 15 journals with the highest number of research papers published on VPP

Rank	Journal Name	Amount of articles
1	North China Electric Power University (Beijing)	57
2	Grid technology	44
3	Power Construction	39
4	Power system automation	35
5	Chinese Journal of Electrical Engineering	27
6	North China University of Electric Power	26
7	Power Demand Side Management	22
8	Power automation equipment	17
9	Southeast University	16
10	Journal of Power Systems and Automation	16
11	North China Electricity	15
12	Shanghai Jiao Tong University	14
13	Zhejiang University	13
14	Changsha University of Science & Technology	13
15	Electrical measurement and instrumentation	12

Among them, master's and doctoral theses from universities are a major force, with six journals run, accounting for 40% of the total. These universities are mainly engaged in research in the electrical field, which is relatively well recognized and academic in the academic community, and is therefore the first choice for scholars considering publishing their research results. The remaining nine journals are also core journals with high impact factors, which are more professional and relevant to the study of VPP and can provide important research and reference values for scholars in this field.

5   Conclusion and Outlook

5.1   Conclusion

In order to mine the research hotspots and evolution trends of VPP in China in 20 years from 2002 to 2021, this study needs big data to support and ensure that the research results are in line with the actual situation and which were conducted by big data technology. Therefore, the database of (CNKI) was selected, and the literature on VPP was selected as the research object. The relevant literature big data were collected, and the visual atlas was generated by CiteSpace software for analysis. It is interpreted that there are cross studies among research hotspots, but at the same time focusing on research on energy storage, electric vehicles, ancillary services, distributed power trading, etc.; changes in national policies directly influence the direction of research trends; and research content focuses on integration with emerging technologies. This study can provide scientific reference for other scholars to research hot spots, core technologies, cutting-edge technologies and core journals of VPP in the future. Under the background of national policies, we should focus on the research of core technologies while integrating emerging technologies to achieve innovation. The main reasons for the constant turnover of research hotspots, analyzed through the data of this study, are as follows.

1. The trajectory of research hotspots is highly relevant to policy developments

Through the contents of the diagram, it is found that the research hotspots of VPP show the characteristics of stages, from the beginning of the initial stage in 2002, when China's power supply was in short supply and the "three electricity offices" were implemented, which means that the demand-side electricity consumption was controlled by administrative means. The main research directions at this time were the efficiency and security of data transmission, the timeliness of the supply and demand side, and cost optimization. The 12th Five-Year Plan and the "Opinions on Accelerating the Construction of Strong Smart Grid" formulated by the State Grid Corporation in 2010 directly contributed to the growth of research on smart grids from 2010 to 2015. The "14th Five-Year Plan" and the "30·60" double carbon target proposed to promote the structural reform of the energy supply side, as can be seen from the mapping of the number of articles published, the research on VPP from 2015 to the present is at a " The number of articles published annually has been increasing, and the hot spots have been related to "carbon neutrality", "carbon trading", "new energy" and "electric vehicles". "It is clear that VPP are a hot area of research at the moment, and that new policies are emerging to promote new research hotspots in this area.

2. Changes in research directions reveal technological developments in the field

The main research directions of VPP are how to store energy in large capacity, improve the stability of grid connection, efficient and safe communication, guarantee economic benefits, etc. In recent years, the number of electric vehicles has proliferated, and scholars have considered applying electric vehicles to VPP. Through the existence of differences in electricity prices at different times, research has allowed electric vehicles to be charged in an orderly manner when the price is low (i.e., at the trough of electricity consumption) to reduce the impact of grid connection of electric vehicles on system stability, so the overall economy and energy use will be improved. At the same time, further research and application of new energy technologies in the country has led to an increasing number of DERs being connected to the grid, but unlike conventional centralized coal power plants, according to these DER power generation uncertainties, domestic scholars to improve the situation of the research heat is rising.

5.2 Outlook

This study only collects and analyzes domestic literature big data related to VPP, and does not analyze foreign research in this field, so it is not comprehensive to summarize the cutting-edge technologies of VPP. At the same time, this paper has not conducted research on the authors and institutions with a large number of publications in the field of VPP, and has not deeply revealed the relationship between research hotspots and academic communities. Therefore, in the follow-up work, data sources will be expanded, such as WOS database, to fully reveal the hot spots and research trends in the field, and carry out relevant comparative studies.

Acknowledgments. The research was supported by 2022 POSTGRADUATE EDUCA TION AND TEACHING REFORM PROJECT IN JIANGSU PROVINCE: Grant number JGKT22_B029, 2022YJYJG01; JIANGSU PROVINCIAL SOCIAL SCIENCE FOUNDA-TION YOUTH PROJECT: Grant number 21TQC003; MAJOR PROJECT OF PHILOSOPHY AND SOCIAL SCIENCE RESEARCH IN UNIVERSI TIES OF JIANGSU PROVINCE: Grant number 2021SJZDA178; THE INNOVATION FUND GENERAL PRO-JECT I OF NANJING INSTI-TUTE OF TECHNOLOGY, Grant number CKJB202003; The TEACHING REFORM AND CONSTRUCTION PROJECT OF NANJING INSTITUTE OF TECH-NOLOGY, Grant number JXGG2021031; and Graduate Student Education and Teaching Reform Project of Nanjing Institute of Technology in 2023(NO. 2023YJYJG12); National Alliance for the Development of Graduate Education in Applied Universities of 2022(NO. AGED2022YB08); and JIANGSU PROVINCE EDUCATION SCIENCE "14TH FIVE-YEAR PLAN" 2021 ANNUAL PROJECT, Grant number C-c/2021/01/62.

References

1. Wu, Y.N., Wang, H.J., Wang, Z.X., et al.: Knowledge mapping analysis of rural landscape using Citespace. Sustainability **12**(01), 66 (2020)
2. Tian, J., Li, G., Zhang, A.: Spatio-temporal big data mining based on Citespace5.5R2: a case study of geographic information system discipline literature of CNKI. Surv. Mapp. Eng. **31**(03), 46–53(2022). (in Chinese)
3. Yang, X.: A survey of domestic research on data Mining. Comput. Program. Skills Maint. **2020**(08), 115–117 (2020). (in Chinese)

4. Yang, X., Luo, Z., Ye, G.: A review of virtual power plant scheduling and market bidding under energy interconnection. Zhejiang Electr. Power **40**(12), 46–53 (2021). (in Chinese)
5. Li, B., Yang, F., Zhao, Y.: A review of blockchain algorithm application research for distributed power trading. Power Grid Technol. 1–16, 1236 (2022). (in Chinese)
6. Wei, Z., Yu, S., Sun, G.: The concept and development of virtual power plants. Power Syst. Autom. **37**(13), 1–9 (2013). (in Chinese)
7. Yang, Z., Jing, J., Deng, X.: Discussion on the participation of virtual power plants in th-e auxiliary service market of Jiangsu power grid. Power Demand Side Manag. **23**(04), 90–95 (2021). (in Chinese)
8. Hebei Province to build a "virtual peaking power plant". Power Demand Side Manag. (04), 13 (2002). (in Chinese)
9. Zhao, J.: A study on CiteSpace visualization process and analysis paradigm. Knowl. Econ. **2014**(16), 105–107 (2014). (in Chinese)
10. Bian, X., Zhang, L., Zhou, B.: A review of domestic and international research on electricity market based on knowledge graph. J. Electr. Eng. Technol. 1–13 (2022). (in Chinese)
11. Leo, E.: The dual of Bradford's law. JASIS **37**(4), 246–255 (1986)
12. Chen, Y., Chen, C., Liu, Z.: Methodological functions of CiteSpace knowledge graphs. Scientol. Res. **33**(02), 242–253 (2015). (in Chinese)
13. Newman, M., Girvan, M.: Finding and evaluating community structure in networks. Phys. Rev. E **69**(2), 423–433 (2004)
14. Zhang, W., Song, J., Yang, L.: A load balancing management strategy for virtual power plant's considering electric vehicle charging demand. Power Syst. Autom. 1–12 (2022). (in Chinese)
15. Lin, Y., Miao, S., Yang, W.: Optimal scheduling strategy of virtual power plant day be-fore for multiple uncertainty environment. Power Autom. Equip. **41**(12), 143–150 (2021). (in Chinese)
16. Wang, K., Nan, D., Li, Y.: Virtual power plant participation in two-layer optimal operation strategy of energy storage side of large-scale new energy system. J. Electr. Eng. **15**(02), 24–33 (2020). (in Chinese)
17. Kong, Y., Gao, H., Zhang, T.: Exploring the application of 5G communication technology for virtual power plants. Power Inf. Commun. Technol. **18**(08), 80–85 (2020). (in Chinese)
18. Guan, S., Wang, X., Jiang, C.: Research on the classification and aggregation method of virtual power plants based on the difference of controllable load response performance and the bidding strategy of auxiliary service market. Power Grid Technol. **46**(03), 933–944 (2022). (in Chinese)

Influencing Factors Analysis and Prediction Model of Pavement Transverse Crack Based on Big Data

Yuqin Zhu[✉], Wengang Ma, Ling Cong, Chengtao Li, and Shixiang Hu

School of Economics and Management, Nanjing Institute of Technology, Nanjing 211167, China
zhuyuqin@njit.edu.cn

Abstract. Transverse cracks dominated by reflective cracks are one of the most common diseases of expressways in our country. In order to improve the structural integrity and driving comfort, this study relied on big data stored in the PMS of Jiangsu Province to analyze the development law and influencing factors of transverse cracks in semi-rigid base asphalt pavement. Two index types, node index and development index, were proposed, and the evaluation results and significant influencing factors of these two evaluations indexes were analyzed respectively. The fitting model function in JMP software was used to statistically analyze the traffic and structural influence factors of the transverse crack in the total mileage of 854 km of 291 original road sections. Then the SCB test was carried out to obtain the fracture energy of each sublayer of the sections. At last, a TCS prediction model was constructed by the significant influencing factors and the composite fracture energy representing the overall crack resistance level of the asphalt layer. The results of this study show that 85% of the road sections cracked for the first time within 3–9 years of opening to traffic. The first 5 years after opening to traffic was the slow development stage of transverse cracks, and the 5–10 years was the stage of rapid development of transverse cracks. 10–15 years later, the development speed of transverse cracks tended to slow down. The main factors affecting the generation and development of transverse cracks are traffic volume, the gradation type of each layer, the thickness of modified asphalt layer and the type of base material.

Keywords: pavement maintenance · transverse cracks · influencing factors · semi-rigid base asphalt pavement · big data · prediction model

1 Introduction

Transverse crack dominated by reflective crack is one of the most common diseases of highways in our country. The existence of transverse cracks not only poses hidden dangers to the integrity and strength of the pavement structure, but also seriously affects the driving comfort of the pavement. Transverse cracks can be caused by temperature shrinkage or by reflection of cracking from the semi-rigid base layer to the road surface.

Alaswadko [1] found that road age has a greater impact on crack formation and development than other variables. During the crack development, the impact of pavement

© The Author(s), under exclusive license to Springer Nature Singapore Pte Ltd. 2023
Y. Tian et al. (Eds.): ICBDS 2022, CCIS 1796, pp. 122–138, 2023.
https://doi.org/10.1007/978-981-99-3300-6_10

strength is greater than that of traffic load at any time; low temperature has a significant impact on the generation and propagation of transverse cracks [2]; parameters such as the thickness, modulus, and temperature shrinkage coefficient of the surface layer and base layer have a certain influence on inhibiting the expansion of reflective cracks [3]; and Xia Ruifang's research shows that when traffic loads and temperature loads act together, the low-temperature shrinkage stress can effectively reduce the shear stress intensity factor caused by the traffic eccentric load [8].

In terms of materials, fallah found that the stiffness of the cracking layer and the cover layer is the main factor to directly improve the service life of the anti-reflection crack of the cover layer [4]; the asphalt mixture has a high ultimate fracture energy release rate, which can improve the reflection fatigue life of surface layer [1]; a change in fracture energy of 25 J/m² will result in a significant difference in pavement thermal cracking performance [5]; Surface layer paved with HMA type of SMA-13 has less crack density, compared with AK-13 or PAC-13 [2].

Throughout the research on reflection crack prediction at home and abroad, it mainly focuses on the modeling and simulation of finite element software or indoor test simulation. For a long time, transverse cracks in semi-rigid base asphalt pavement, as a typical disease of domestic expressways, lacked the analysis and mining of actual performance testing data. The development process of expressways in Jiangsu Province is very consistent with the development process of expressways in our country and thus has a strong representation. Based on the data related to expressways in Jiangsu Province in the Pavement Maintenance Management System (PMS) developed by Professor Ni Fujian of Southeast University, this paper screened 291 unrepaired road sections with a total mileage of 854.18 km. According to the pavement structure, traffic volume, climate and environmental information of each road section, the development law and main influencing factors of transverse cracks in semi-rigid base asphalt pavement based on big data are studied. The fracture energy of each layer of the current typical pavement structure is obtained through laboratory experiments. And a prediction model for transverse cracks in pavement was constructed based on the significantly influencing factors and tested fracture energy.

2 Evaluation of Transverse Cracks in Asphalt Pavement with Semi-rigid Base

2.1 Evaluation Indicators

This study defines two types of evaluation indexes: node index and development index. The node index is used to evaluate the spatial distribution of transverse cracks in a road section at a certain time node. In this study, the transverse crack spacing (TCS) is chosen as the node index [7–10], which is further subdivided into 5-year transverse crack spacing (TCS-5y), 10-year transverse crack spacing (TCS-10y), and 15-year transverse crack spacing (TCS-15y). The development index is used to evaluate the development speed of transverse cracks in the road section with time. In this study, two development indicators were newly defined, namely, Age for firstly Cracking (AFC, year) and increment in the number of transverse cracks per kilometer (INTC, amount/year). The definitions and specific evaluation objectives of these two indicators are shown in Table 1.

Table 1. Development-type evaluation index of transverse cracks

Evaluation indicators, unit	Definition	Evaluation target
AFC, year	The road age when the transverse joint spacing is less than 300 m for the first time	The time taken for transverse cracks to propagate to the road surface after opening to traffic
INTC, amount/year	Average of the increments of the number of transverse joints per kilometer per year	The growth rate of the number of transverse joints in each road section

2.2 Evaluation Results

Evaluation Results of the Node Index. The frequency distribution diagram of the current TCS is shown in Fig. 1. According to the TCS grading standard determined by reference [8], the current TCS grade distribution for the studied sections is shown in Fig. 2.

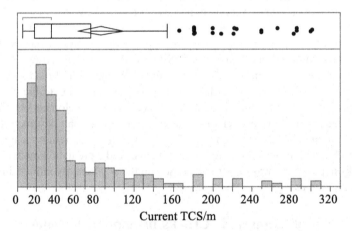

Fig. 1. Current Frequency of TCS on unmaintained sections

From the above statistical diagram, the maximum TCS of the current sections without any treatment is 2000 m, while the minimum value is 5.12 m; the median value is 36.63 m; the average value is 91.6 m; the standard deviation is 207.32 m; and the variable coefficient is 226.34%. It reveals that due to multiple influencing factors, the distribution of TCS is relatively scattered. According to the classification standards in the reference [8], 19% of the TCS is on the "excellent" level, 40% is on the "medium" level, and 41% is on the "poor" level. The proportion of road sections on the "medium" and

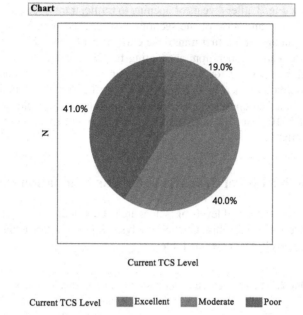

Fig. 2. Current Degree Distribution of TCS on unmaintained sections

"poor" level is relatively high, which is also consistent with the unmaintained situation of these sections.

Evaluation Results of the Development Index. Along with the operation, transverse cracks begin to appear on each section gradually. Figure 3 shows the proportion of cracked mileage to total section mileage as a function of road age.

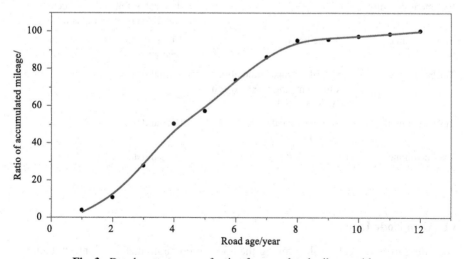

Fig. 3. Development curve of ratio of accumulated mileage with age

As shown in the Fig. 3, after 4 years of opening to traffic, transverse cracks appeared in half of the sections, and 85% of the sections first cracked within 3 to 9 years of operation. The mean age of the first transverse crack is 5.14 years. Most sections first cracking after 4–5 years of operation, accounting for 21% of the total length, which followed by sections operated for 6–7 years, accounting for 18%. According to the data statistics, the first 5 years after opening to traffic is the slow development stage of transverse cracks, and the transverse cracks on most sections have a rapid progress stage within the age of 5–10 years. 10 years later, the development speed in most sections slow down gradually.

3   Influencing Factors of Transverse Cracks Evaluation Index

In this study, different types and levels of factors are subdivided according to pavement structure and traffic volume for this statistical analysis. Specific influencing factors (IF) and corresponding levels are shown in Table 2.

Table 2. Influencing factors of transverse crack evaluation index

Type of IF	Name of IF	Level of IF
Pavement structure	Thickness of pavement/cm	71, 73, 74, 75, 76, 77, 78, 80
Pavement structure	Thickness of modified asphalt layer/cm	4, 10, 18
Pavement structure	Gradation type of Upper layer	AK-16, AK-13, SMA-13, OGFC-13, SUP-13
Pavement structure	Gradation type of Middle layer	AC-20, AC-25, SUP-20
Pavement structure	Gradation type of Lower layer	AC-25, SUP-25
Pavement structure	Base type	Two ash stabilized base, cement stabilized base, composite base
Traffic volume	Traffic level	Light, medium, heavy, extremely heavy
Traffic volume	Annual average cumulative equivalent single axle loading (AESAL/10e4)	Actual data
Traffic volume	Average annual daily traffic (AADT)	Actual data
Traffic volume	Truck ratio/%	Actual data

3.1   IF of Node Index

According to statistical results, among the 854 km unmaintained sections studied, the total mileage with TCS-5y is 566 km, the average TCS of which is 880 m, and the length of whose TCS exceeding 100 m accounts for 83%. The total length of the road sections with TCS-10y is 696 km, the average TCS of which is 111 m, and the length of whose TCS exceeding 100 m accounts for 26%. The total length of the road segment with TCS-15y is 442 km, the average TCS of which is 43 m, and the length of whose TCS exceeds 100 m accounts for 18%.

IF of TCS-5y. Whether the target factor X in the analysis has significant influence on the evaluation index Y is shown in Table 3. Figure 4 shows the average comparison results of all significant factors using Turkey Kramer HSD TEST average comparison method (this method is used in the following) by JMP software. The circles on the right side of the statistical graph represent different levels of a factor, and the circle radius represents the dispersion degree of y value corresponding to the factor X at a certain level. The farther away the center of the circle is, the more significant the influence of factor X on target y.

Table 3. The significance analysis results of the influencing factors of TCS-5y

IF(X)	Degrees of freedom	Sum of square	F ratio	Probability of > F
Gradation type of Upper layer	4	1.43E+06	0.79	0.5330
Gradation type of Middle layer	2	1.55E+06	1.71	0.1830
Gradation type of Lower layer	1	2.76E+02	0.00	0.9803
Base type	2	7.18E+05	0.79	0.4542
Thickness of modified as-phalt layer/cm	1	1.36E+06	2.99	0.0853
Thickness of pavement/cm	1	6.02E+06	13.27	0.0003*
Traffic level	3	4.07E+06	2.99	0.0319*
Annual average cumulative equivalent single axle loading (AESAL/10e4)	1	9.39E+04	0.21	0.6496
Truck ratio (TR/%)	1	6.55E+04	0.14	0.7042
Average annual daily traffic (AADT)	1	1.10E+06	2.43	0.1208

According to the analysis results of the TCS-5y after the opening to traffic, the factors that have a significant effect on the it in the early stage of the opening to traffic are the pavement thickness and traffic level. In addition, the probability value of modified asphalt layer thickness>F is 0.0853, which is slightly larger than the judgment level of 0.05, and far smaller than the probability value of other insignificant factors. The TCS in the early days increases with the thickness of the pavement, indicating that the path length of the reflection cracks has a more significant effect on the early cracks than the gradation type of each layer. The early TCS of the road sections with 2–3 layers of modified asphalt is significantly better than that of the sections with 0–1 layers of modified asphalt. There is a significant difference between the TCS-5y of extremely-heavy/heavy traffic sections and that of medium traffic/light traffic. The average TCS-5y values of the sections under

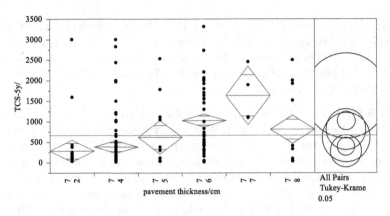

(a) Pavement thickness

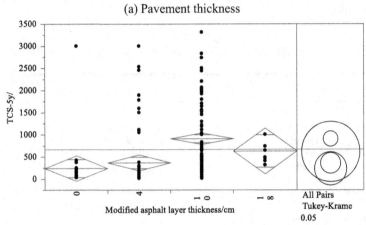

(b) Modified asphalt layer thickness

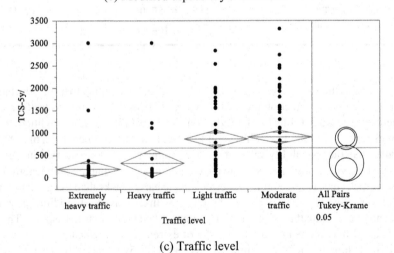

(c) Traffic level

Fig. 4. Significant influence factor mean comparison results of TCS-5y

extremely-heavy traffic, heavy traffic, medium traffic and please traffic are 194.81 m, 328.83 m, 869.70 m and 909.77 m respectively.

IF of TCS-10y. Whether the target factor X in the analysis has a significant impact on the evaluation index Y is shown in Table 4. Figure 5 shows the partly results of the mean comparison of the significant factors of TCS-10y.

Table 4. The significance analysis results of the influencing factors of TCS-10y

IF(X)	Degrees of freedom	Sum of square	F ratio	Probability of > F
Gradation type of Upper layer	3	4.29E+05	6.56	0.0003*
Gradation type of Middle layer	2	2.59E+05	6.99	0.0011*
Gradation type of Lower layer	1	1.01E+03	0.05	0.8155
Base type	1	1.40E+05	6.43	0.0122*
Thickness of modified as-phalt layer/cm	1	1.07E+05	4.92	0.0280*
Thickness of pavement/cm	1	1.11E+04	0.51	0.4774
Traffic level	3	2.36E+05	4.26	0.0058*
AESAL	1	5.86E+03	0.27	0.6047
AADT	1	1.48E+03	0.07	0.7950
TR	1	2.19E+03	0.10	0.7516

5–10 years opening to traffic for 5–10 years is the stage of rapid development of transverse cracks in most road sections. TCS-10y is significantly affected by many factors such as pavement structure and traffic level, including the gradation type of upper level, middle level, base, modified Asphalt layer thickness and traffic level. The difference between the composite base and the semi-rigid base is mainly accounts for the significant influence of TCS-10y by the type of base. The average TCS-10y values of the road sections of the composite base, the cement stabilized base and the lime-and fly-ash stabilized base are 252.04 m, 82.57 m and 81.96 m respectively. In addition to base type, TCS-10y is also significantly affected by the thickness of the modified asphalt layer and increases with the thickness of the asphalt layer. The average TCS-10y values of the road sections with 0 layer, 1 layer and 2 layers of modified asphalt are 57.67 m, 81.75 m and 102.62 m, respectively. TCS-10y is still significantly affected by traffic level.

IF of TCS-15y. Whether the target factor X in the analysis has a significant impact on the evaluation index Y is shown in Table 5. Figure 6 shows the results of the mean comparison of the significant influencing factors of TCS-15y.

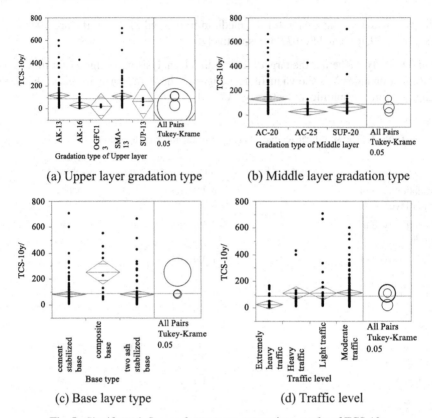

Fig. 5. Significant influence factor mean comparison results of TCS-10y

Table 5. The significance analysis results of the influencing factors of TCS-15y

IF(X)	Degrees of freedom	Sum of square	F ratio	Probability of > F
Gradation type of Upper layer	3	1.91E+04	2.91	0.0392*
Gradation type of Middle layer	1	8.72E+01	0.04	0.8422
Gradation type of Lower layer	0	0.00E+00	.	.
Base type	1	2.65E+02	0.12	0.7286
Thickness of modified asphalt layer/cm	1	8.43E-01	0.00	0.9844
Thickness of pavement/cm	1	1.15E+02	0.05	0.8189
Traffic level	3	1.53E+03	0.23	0.8735
AESAL	1	1.07E+03	0.49	0.4853
AADT	1	5.71E+03	2.61	0.1098
TR	1	5.57E+03	2.55	0.1141

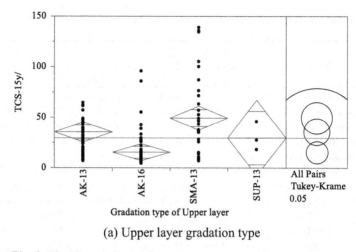

Gradation type of Upper layer

(a) Upper layer gradation type

Fig. 6. Significant influence factor mean comparison results of TCS-15y

After 10 to 15 years of opening to traffic, the development speed of transverse cracks in most road sections slow down, and the cracks in the base layer have gradually reflected to the road surface. The significant influencing factor of TCS-15y is only the gradation type of upper layer. For the sections of AK-16 gradation type, SUP-13 gradation type, AK-13 gradation type and SMA-13 gradation type, the average TCS-15y values are 20.31 m, 29.70 m, 37.51 m and 51.10 m, respectively. In terms of traffic level, the TCS-15y is relatively close after 15 years of operation. According to the statistical analysis between the three node evaluation indicators and the traffic level above, the influence of the traffic level on the TCS is gradually weakened.

3.2   IF of Development Index

IF of AFC.   Whether the target factor X has a significant impact on the evaluation index Y is shown in Table 6. Figure 7 shows the mean comparison results for all significant factors.

According to the analysis results, except the pavement thickness, other factors have a significant impact on AFC. The probability value of modified asphalt layer thickness>F is 0.0875, which is slightly larger than the judgment level of 0.05, and much smaller than the probability value of the factor of pavement thickness. It can be considered that it also has a significant impact on the road age with transverse cracking. Compared with the typical semi-rigid base pavement structure, the thickness of the asphalt layer increases and the thickness of the semi-rigid base decreases, which prolongs the development path of shrinkage cracks in the semi-rigid base, and the transverse cracks appear about 2 years later. From the perspective of traffic volume factors, the traffic level factors significantly affect AFC. According to the order of traffic levels from light to heavy, the average AFC

Table 6. Significance analysis results of influencing factors of AFC

IF(X)	Degrees of free-dom	Sum of square	Mean square	F ratio	Proba-bility of > F
Gradation type of Upper layer	4	66.1474	16.5369	3.2422	0.0124*
Gradation type of Middle layer	2	69.6315	34.8157	6.8761	0.0012*
Gradation type of Lower layer	1	58.8046	58.8046	11.5782	0.0007*
Base type	2	96.5997	48.2999	9.549	<.0001*
Thickness of modified asphalt layer/cm	3	8.9929	2.99763	0.5645	0.0875
Thickness of pavement/cm	5	52.0037	10.4007	1.9918	0.6321
Traffic level	3	141.1943	47.0648	8.0548	<.0001*
AESAL	121	1233.5575	10.1947	3.5041	<.0001*
AADT	122	1180.7789	9.67852	3.0883	<.0001*
TR	109	1146.815	10.5212	3.3853	<.0001*

values correspond to 8.6/6.2/6.3/4.6 years, respectively. The AFC of light traffic sections is 4 years later than it of extremely heavy traffic sections.

IF of INTC. The calculation of INTC is to average the annual increase in the number of transverse cracks per kilometer of each road section. Whether the target factor X in the analysis has a significant impact on the evaluation index Y is shown in Table 7.

Table 7. Significance analysis results of influencing factors of INTC

IF(X)	Degrees of free-dom	Sum of square	Mean square	F ratio	Probability of > F
Gradation type of Upper layer	4	66.1474	16.5369	3.2422	0.0124*
Gradation type of Middle layer	2	69.6315	34.8157	6.8761	0.0012*
Gradation type of Lower layer	1	58.8046	58.8046	11.5782	0.0007*
Base type	2	96.5997	48.2999	9.549	<.0001*
Thickness of modified asphalt layer/cm	3	8.9929	2.99763	0.5645	0.0875
Thickness of pavement/cm	5	52.0037	10.4007	1.9918	0.6321
Traffic level	3	141.1943	47.0648	8.0548	<.0001*
AESAL	121	1233.5575	10.1947	3.5041	<.0001*
AADT	122	1180.7789	9.67852	3.0883	<.0001*
TR	109	1146.815	10.5212	3.3853	<.0001*

According to the analysis results, the factors that have a significant impact on INTC are the gradation type of upper layer, the type of base layer, the proportion of trucks, and the traffic level. The mean values of INTC for the sections under extremely heavy traffic, heavy traffic, medium traffic and light traffic are 7.75/year, 4.81/year, 4.19/year and 4.06/year respectively.

Therefore, based on the above analysis, the main factors affecting the generation and development of transverse joints are the traffic level, the gradation type of each layer, the thickness of the modified asphalt layers, the total thickness of the pavement and the type of base. The composite base is not a typical semi-rigid base, therefore only TCS prediction model for sections with cement stabilized was established. However, the influence of the thickness of the modified asphalt layer of the surface material and the different gradation types would cause different crack resistance capability, which could be quantified by the fracture energy test.

4 Fracture Energy Test and Correlation Analysis with TCS

Semi-Circular Bending Test, referred to as SCB test, has been gradually used to analyze and evaluate the crack resistance of asphalt mixtures. According to the research experience at home and abroad, fracture energy is a common index for evaluating the crack resistance of pavement materials. In this study, core samples of representative sections of semi-rigid base asphalt pavement in Jiangsu Province were drilled to carry out − 10 °C non-slit SCB test. The correlation analysis between the test results and the TCS is used. The effectiveness of crack resistance provides theoretical and data support for the establishment of TCS prediction models [11–19].

The cylindrical specimen was cut into semicircular specimens with the dimensions shown in Table 7, and then the SCB test was carried out in layers. The SCB test device is shown in Fig. 8, in which the distance between the fulcrums of the two round bars is 12 cm, which is equivalent to 0.8 times of the semicircle specimen (Table 8).

Table 8. Specimen size in SCB test

Layers	Thickness/mm	Diameter/mm
Upper layer	40	150
Middle layer	50	150
Lower layer	50	150

Through the SCB test, the force-displacement curve during the failure process of the specimen is shown in Fig. 8, and the fracture energy is calculated by formula (1). The experimental results are shown in Table 9.

$$G_f = \frac{w_f}{Area_{ing}} * 10^6 \tag{1}$$

where G_f——fracture energy (J/m^2);
  w_f——work of fracture (J);

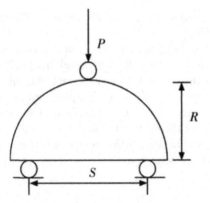

Fig. 7. SCB test device

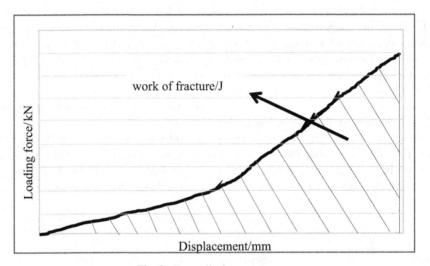

Fig. 8. Force-displacement curve

$Area_{ing}$——fracture surface area (mm^2).

The correlation between the fracture energy of a single certain layer and the measured value of TCS is not very high. Therefore, the fracture energy of the upper, middle and lower layers is taken as a weighted average with respect to the thickness of each layer to establish a composite fracture energy G_{f_c}. The composite fracture energy is fitted with the measured value of TCS, and the fitting result is shown in Fig. 9. As showed in the figure, the correlation between G_{f_c} and TCS is relatively enhanced.

Table 9. SCB test results of each road section and corresponding TCS

Section ID	Pavement thickness/cm	Upper layer fracture energy /J/m²	Middle layer fracture energy /J/m²	Lower layer fracture energy /J/m²	TCS/m
1	75	2484.95	2439.14	1279.05	36.41
2	75	2505.00	2466.66	1409.04	39.94
3	76	2835.62	2464.16	1362.44	44.03
4	76	2829.00	2531.54	1552.84	46.87
5	75	3878.95	3641.62	2837.80	68.11
6	74	3005.62	2783.32	1257.65	48.49
7	74	1994.62	2188.60	1389.59	31.82
8	74	2149.61	2756.28	1269.11	48.96
9	74.25	2161.16	2757.20	1416.82	49.03
10	77	2229.70	2816.40	2165.55	52.03
11	77	2744.92	3134.62	2646.23	58.47
12	76	3184.12	2690.67	2575.88	54.23
13	75	3292.60	2342.61	2475.04	55.48
14	73	3624.00	3192.26	2917.51	58.53
15	80	2937.00	3404.92	2951.22	59.49
16	74	3102.00	3592.44	2920.03	61.48

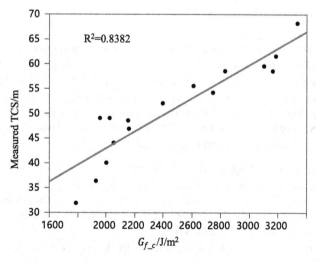

Fig. 9. Statistical results of correlation between G_{f_c} and TCS measured values

5   TCS Prediction Model Construction

According to the factors that have significant impacts on TCS obtained from the above analysis, the TCS prediction model is constructed, as shown in Eq. (2).

$$TC = Ah^{Bk_1} G_{f\_c}^{Ck_2} \left(\frac{1}{N}\right)^{Dk_3} \tag{2}$$

where

TCS——TCS/m;
G_{f_c}——composite fracture energy of asphalt pavement under-10 °C/J/m^2;
h——asphalt layer thickness/cm;
N——the cumulative number of equivalent axle loads/10 e4 times;
k_1, k_2, k_3——Calibration coefficient, the default value is 1.0;
A, B, C, D——model coefficients.

The coefficients in formula (2) are fitted using the data of the unmaintained road section above. Due to the different degree of influence of traffic volume, each road section is fitted according to the 0 ~ 5 years, 5 ~ 10 years and 10 ~ 15 years of opening to traffic, and the fitting results are shown in formula (3), Where t represents the years after opening to traffic. R^2 of each stage is 0.8075, 0.8862 and 0.7863, respectively.

$$TCS = \begin{cases} 0.1695h^{0.2257k_1} G_{f_c}^{2.1888k_2} \left(\frac{1}{N}\right)^{1.5785k_3}, 0 < t \le 5; \\ 0.1195h^{0.0179k_1} G_{f_c}^{2.2381k_2} \left(\frac{1}{N}\right)^{1.4794k_3}, 5 < t \le 10; \\ 0.0004h^{0.0247k_1} G_{f\_c}^{2.0488k_2} \left(\frac{1}{N}\right)^{0.6785k_3}, 10 < t \le 15. \end{cases} \tag{3}$$

6   Conclusions

Based on the big data stored in the PMS system, an evaluation system for transverse cracks in asphalt pavement was constructed, and the corresponding evaluation results and influencing factors of the node index and development index were analyzed respectively. The significant influencing factors of TCS node index and development index were obtained using JMP software for statistical analysis. According to the influence of various factors on TCS, a prediction model was established for semi-rigid base asphalt pavement. The main research conclusions and results are as follows:

(1) The gradation type of upper layer significantly affects AFC, INTC, TCS-10y and TCS-15y; the gradation type of middle layer significantly affects TCS-10y; the gradation type of lower layer significantly affects AFC. The thickness of modified asphalt layer significantly affects AFC, TCS-5y and TCS-10y, and the total pavement thickness significantly affects TCS-5y.
(2) The type of base significantly affects AFC, INTC and TCS-10y. Compared with the traditional semi-rigid base, the road section with a composite base of asphalt-stabilized gravel and cement-stabilized gravel has a larger AFC and a lower development rate of transverse cracks. The TCS condition of sections using cement stabilized base is better than that using lime-and-ash stabilized base.

(3) The traffic volume significantly affects the speed and process of the reflection of the shrinkage cracks from the base to the surface to form transverse cracks, but the degree of influence gradually weakens as the energy within the pavement structure is gradually released in this process.

(4) Finally, the three parameters of the pavement thickness, the cumulative number of axle loads, and the G_{f_c} at -10 °C were used to construct a prediction model for the TCS, and the models were fitted for 0 ~ 5 years, 5 ~ 10 years and 10 ~ 15 years respectively.

References

1. Alaswadko, N., Hassan, R., Meyer, D., et al.: Probabilistic prediction models for crack initiation and progression of spray sealed pavements. Int. Pavement Eng. 1–11 (2016)
2. Wang, J., Wang, H., Wang, X., et al.: Study on the development law of transverse cracks in asphalt pavement with semi-rigid base. In: CICTP 2019, pp. 1058–1067 (2019)
3. Song, J., Bai, P., Guan, X.: Modeling analysis of reflective crack of semi-rigid base asphalt pavement. Highw. Eng. **42**(03), 40–44+51 (2017)
4. Fallah, S., Khodaii, A.: Evaluation of parameters affecting reflection cracking in geogrid-reinforced overlay. J. Cent. South Univ. (Engl. Vers.)**22**(3), 10 (2015)
5. Wang, X., Huang, X., Bian, G.: Analysis on mechanism of using LSPM for preventing reflective cracks in asphalt pavement with semi-rigid base. J. Highw. Transp. Res. Dev. **33**(07), 12–18 (2016)
6. Yarrapureddi, H.K.R., Souliman, M.: Model for Predicting Reflection Cracking in Asphalt Overlay Pavements (2020)
7. Zhou, L.: Research on Performance Evaluation and Prediction of Asphalt Pavement of Expressway. SoutheastUniversity (2015)
8. Zhu, Y.: Research on Design Control Index of Semi-rigid Base Asphalt Pavement. SoutheastUniversity (2019)
9. Xu, H.: Research on Reflection Crack Propagation and Fatigue Life of Semi-rigid Base Asphalt Concrete Pavement. Guangxi University (2012)
10. Zhou, L., Ni, F., Zhao, Y.: Evaluation method for transverse cracking in asphalt pavements on freeways. Transp. Res. Rec. **2153**, 97–105 (2010)
11. Pérez-Jiménez, F., et al.: Effect of load application rate and temperature on the fracture energy of asphalt mixtures. Fénix and semi-circular bending tests. Constr. Build. Mater. **48**(Complete), 1067–1071 (2013)
12. Archilla, A.R., Diaz, L.G.: Effects of asphalt mixture properties on permanent deformation response. Transp. Res. Rec.: J. Transp. Res. Board (2011)
13. Gu, F., Luo, X., West, R.C., et al.: Energy-based crack initiation model for load-related top-down cracking in asphalt pavement. Constr. Build. Mater. **159**, 587–597 (2018)
14. Onifade, I., Birgisson, B., Balieu, R.: Energy-based damage and fracture framework for viscoelastic asphalt concrete. Eng. Fract. Mech. **145**, 67–85 (2015)
15. Carpenter, S.H., Lytton, R.L., Epps, J.: Environmental factors relevant to pavement cracking in West Texas. Environ. Impacts (1974)
16. Zhang, Y.Q., Jia, S.Y.: Evaluation method for asphalt pavement performance of freeway. J. Changan Univ. (2005)
17. Lancaster, I.M., Khalid, H.A., Kougioumtzoglou, I.A.: Extended FEM modelling of crack propagation using the semi-circular bending test. Constr. Build. Mater. **48**(Complete), 270–277 (2013)

18. Mahmoud, E., Saadeh, S., Hakimelahi, H., et al.: Extended finite-element modelling of asphalt mixtures fracture properties using the semi-circular bending test. Road Mater. Pavement Des. **15**(1), 14 (2014)

19. Liu, H.J.: Fatigue life evaluation of asphalt rubber mixtures using semi-circular bending test. Adv. Mater. Res. **255–260**, 3444–3449 (2011)

Research on the Evolution of New Energy Industry Financing Ecosystem Under the Background of Big Data

Hairong Wang[1,2,3](✉) and Qiuchi Wu[3]

[1] International Joint Laboratory of Green and Low Carbon Development, Nanjing 211167, Jiangsu, China
wanghr@nuaa.edu.cn
[2] The Key Laboratory of Carbon Neutrality and Territory Optimization, Ministry of Natural Resources, NJIT Research Center, Nanjing 211167, Jiangsu, China
[3] Nanjing Institute of Technology, Nanjing 211167, Jiangsu, China

Abstract. As a disruptive technological change in IT industry, big data has changed the traditional information asymmetry and physical area barrier, which has brought profound changes to the strategic management, organizational structure, business decision-making and operating model of modern enterprises. Data and information have become important emerging factors of production, changing the management and financing methods of new energy industry. At the same time, ecological theory is extended to the field of new energy industry financing, and it becomes a new trend to study the new energy industry financing ecosystem. Based on the in-depth analysis of big data and new energy industry financing ecosystem, we combine the life cycle theory and construct logistic model to analyze the evolution process of new energy industry financing ecosystem in the context of big data, and find that China's new energy industry financing ecosystem has entered the growth stage, but it has not yet achieved efficient collaborative evolutionary development. By reshaping the new energy industry financing ecosystem with big data as the core resource, constructing a big channel of data exchange for the new energy industry financing ecosystem in all aspects, innovating the key business and processes in the system with big data as the core, and obtaining the competitive advantage of the new energy industry financing ecosystem, building a big data information sharing platform to promote open collaborative innovation in the new energy industry financing ecosystem. We can provide strong support for the continuous optimization and collaborative evolution of the new energy industry financing ecosystem in the context of big data.

Keywords: Big Data · New Energy Industry · Financing Ecosystem · Synergistic Evolution

1 Introduction

" Big data" is formed by the huge and complex volume of information, and the diversity, complexity and real-time nature of big data are of high value. According to McKinsey & Company, "Data, which has penetrated every industry and business function today, has

Y. Tian et al. (Eds.): ICBDS 2022, CCIS 1796, pp. 139–154, 2023.
https://doi.org/10.1007/978-981-99-3300-6_11

become an important production factor. "Big Data" will play an irreplaceable role in driving business development [1, 2]. The importance of big data in modern society can be summarized as "the new age oil" because of the importance of big data information in the context of an information-driven era [3]. In the context of "big data", the operation and ecology of the industry are becoming increasingly networked and dynamic. By reshaping the interaction between the industry and social media, netizens, customers, employees, upstream and downstream cooperative enterprises and competitors, the industrial ecological chain resources are integrated to build a new industrial ecosystem with multi-group cooperation and symbiosis. New models and new business models for the development of the new energy industry are emerging [4], and new energy data is reshaping the business model and financing model of the new energy industry, promoting the opening of new energy markets and industrial upgrading, and forming new economic growth points. Similar to the biological world, the financing activities of the new energy industry involve the circulation of funds between different transaction subjects, just like the flow of energy between different organisms, and the financing activities are influenced by the transaction subjects and their external environment. In the process of financing, new energy enterprises gradually form an interdependent and mutually influential financing ecosystem with their stakeholders and the surrounding environment, and continuously exchange material, energy and information, which is characterized by openness, diversity, self-adaptation and self-organized evolution. This ecosystem is open, diverse, adaptive and self-organizing. It has become a new trend to extend ecological theory to the field of new energy industry financing and to study the ecosystem of new energy industry financing. Especially in the big data environment, the proliferation of massive data and the iteration of value network have endowed the intricate complexity and collaborative balance of the financing ecosystem of the new energy industry more worthy of further investigation.

Taking a comprehensive view of the relevant theoretical research and practical application at home and abroad, the research of big data is still in the initial stage. The theoretical research focuses on macro analysis, while the practice focuses on the auxiliary decision of data mining results. Most of the existing research results of big data focus on the information science aspects such as the acquisition, storage, processing, mining and information security of big data. From the perspective of industry management, it is relatively short of discussing the changes and impacts brought by big data on industrial strategy, decision making and co-evolution. With the rising of big data and its all-round application, relevant theories and practical researches will continue to expand and promote the creation and application scope of information and data in industrial development. Based on the in-depth analysis of big data and new energy industry financing ecosystem, this paper analyzes the evolutionary process of new energy industry financing ecosystem by combining life cycle theory and logistic model, empirically tests its evolutionary development stage by substituting data, and condenses the collaborative evolutionary strategy of new energy industry financing ecosystem in the context of big data, so as to provide theoretical guidance and reference for the continuous optimization and collaborative evolution of new energy industry financing ecosystem in the context of big data.

2   Theoretical Basis

2.1   Big Data

Big data, also known as massive data, is a data phenomenon resulting from the rapid development of computer technology and Internet technology, and IBM proposes that big data has the characteristics of quantity, speed, variety, value and authenticity. As of 2020, according to relevant statistical results, more than 50 billion different devices have been Internet-connected and connected to net-works around the world [5]. According to McKinsey, "Big Data" refers to a vast amount of data that surpasses the capabilities of conventional database software tools in terms of gathering, storing, handling, and scruti-nizing [6]. These massive data usually originate from the conduct of digital transactions, the receipt and delivery of emails, the playback of videos and audios on the Web, the clicks on Web blogs, the interaction of replies to online social software, and the retrieval of search engines [7, 8]. At the same time, a large amount of information can be used to optimize cur-rent communication methods, such as: making information delivery more visible and popular [9]. The research institute Gartner defines "big data" as follows. "Big data" is de-fined as a large scale, extremely fast growing and diverse information asset, and this new definition requires newer processing responses to increase its ability to optimize information processing processes. In order to handle such a large amount of data, it is important to identify the more valuable and meaningful data, and to process it in a large amount and efficiently. The process of analyzing and utilizing "big data" has gradually formed a new type of industry, which aims at distinguishing a large amount of data, extracting the useful parts and processing them twice, and adding value to the local data by processing them from the huge data as a whole. This industry is gradually maturing in the big data environment, and this kind of data and information processing and processing has become an important new production factor in the context of the times [10]. Therefore, based on the development of the big data processing industry, new management methods and more innovative financing methods are bound to emerge in the new energy sector [8].

2.2   New Energy Industry Financing Ecosystem in the Context of Big Data

Similar to the composition of the natural ecosystem [11], in the process of financing the new energy industry, the new energy enterprises, as the ultimate demander and user of funds, together with the providers of funds, financing institutions and financing methods, constitute the main body of financing, which constantly exchanges materials and information with the financing ecosystem, and through the conversion of data values, thus constituting the new energy industry financing ecosystem, as shown in Fig. 1. In the new energy industry financing ecosystem, the value exchange relationship between the capital providers, financing institutions and new energy enterprises through financing methods is called the new energy enterprise financing value chain. In the real new energy enterprise financing, due to the huge number of capital providers, financing institutions and new energy enterprises, they constitute a long and short financing chain, complex and simple, these value chains are intertwined in the new energy industry financing ecosystem and woven into a net-like institution that connects the components together, called the new energy enterprise financing value network. These value networks evolve under the synergy of biotic and abiotic ecological factors of new energy industry financing, and help funds flow along the financing value chain from fund providers to new energy enterprises.

According to the analysis of the characteristics of natural ecosystem, the financing ecosystem of new energy industry also has the characteristics of diversity, interdependence, evolution, openness and stability. Given the diversity of financing providers, financing institutions and new energy enterprises, their financing methods and financing value chains are also diverse, so their financing ecosystems also have diverse characteristics.

As different new energy enterprises have their own ecological niches based on their use of various financing ecological resources, the intense intra-species competition in the new energy industry has led to the need to expand the scope of ecological resources, resulting in the proximity of the ecological niches of two new energy industries and intensifying inter-species competition in the new energy industry. According to the principle of competition and mutual exclusion, a new energy enterprise or new energy industry may die out or survive through the differentiation of ecological niches, and through the effective differentiation of ecological niches, a new energy industry cluster with a variety of new energy enterprises will often be formed. In new energy industry clusters, new energy enterprises tend to complement each other rather than compete directly, and these competitive and complementary relationships create an interdependent financing ecosystem. For the new energy industry financing ecosystem, the financing value chain of the new energy enterprises needs to adapt to the changes in the financing ecosystem in order to obtain limited capital flow. Once they are unable to adapt to the changes in the financing ecosystem, the financing value chain of new energy companies will break and be quickly replaced by other dominant new energy companies.

In the ecological environment of "survival of the fittest", the financing ecosystem of the new energy industry must make full use of the support of big data to maintain the evolutionary momentum, so as to maintain sufficient competitiveness and achieve sustainable development. The new energy industry financing ecosystem will gradually establish a mutually coordinated system structure relationship through evolutionary adaptation, and through the intervention of appropriate negative feedback, it can strengthen its resistance and resilience by using the stable play of self-regulation ability, thus forming a stable equilibrium state of the new energy industry financing ecosystem.

According to the analysis of the characteristics of natural ecosystem, the financing ecosystem of new energy industry also has the characteristics of diversity, interdependence, evolution, openness and stability. Given the diversity of financing providers, financing institutions and new energy enterprises, their financing methods and financing value chains are also diverse, so their financing ecosystems also have diverse characteristics.

In the ecological environment of "survival of the fittest", the new energy industry financing ecosystem must fully leverage the advantages of big data and evolve to maintain sufficient competitive ability to achieve sustainable development. The new energy industry financing ecosystem will gradually establish a mutually coordinated system structure relationship after evolutionary adaptation, and through the intervention

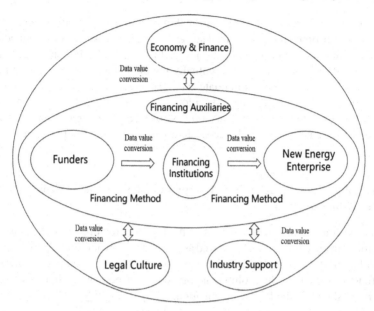

Fig. 1. New energy industry financing ecosystem structure map in the Context of Big Data

of appropriate negative feedback, it can strengthen its resistance and resilience by using the stable play of self-regulation ability, thus forming a stable equilibrium state of the new energy industry financing ecosystem.

3 Analysis of the Evolutionary Process of New Energy Industry Financing Ecosystem Based on Logistic Equation in the Context of Big Data

In view of the bionic nature of the new energy industry financing ecosystem, life cycle theory can be introduced into the new energy industry financing ecosystem in the context of big data for analysis to study its systematic evolutionary process. Life cycle in biology refers to the whole process of an organism with life characteristics from birth, growth, maturity, aging to death. The introduction of this concept into economics and management theory has produced product [12], enterprise [13] and industrial life cycle theory [14]. Gort and Klepper [12] divided the product life cycle based on the number of vendors in the industry and derived five stages (G-K model), including introduction, mass entry, stabilization, mass exit, and maturity. On the basis of the G-K model research, subsequent scholars have studied the differences in strategies, restructuring and mergers, and organizational structures of firms in different industrial life cycle stages, and their research perspective has gradually shifted from a single product life cycle to the overall industrial life cycle.

In summary, the main conclusion of the research on the evolutionary process of industries is that industries basically need to go through four processes: Gestation period, Growth period, Maturity and Decline period. In 1845, mathematician Pierre-François

Vélule proposed and named the logistic growth model to describe the process of population growth over time, in a generalized sense The logistic curve is an S-shaped distribution, indicating that the initial population growth is exponential; then the growth rate slows down and tends to saturation; eventually the population reaches the top limit of what the real ecosystem can accommodate and the population stops growing. In view of its own development characteristics and ecological constraints, the logistic function can also be used to explain the evolutionary process of many ecosystems, that is, with the continuous development of time, the ecosystem will tend to the limit state until it stops growing.

3.1   An Evolutionary Model of New Energy Industry Financing Ecosystem Based on Logistic Equation

In view of the connotation characteristics of the logistic growth model, the new energy industry financing ecosystem can be viewed as a continuous evolutionary process, similar to the evolution of biological population systems in nature, so this paper chooses the logistic function to analyze the evolutionary process of the new energy industry financing ecosystem, as shown in the following equation.

$$\frac{dE(t)}{dt} = rE(t)\left(1 - \frac{E(t)}{M}\right) \tag{1}$$

$E(t)$ is the operating efficiency of the new energy industry financing ecosystem at moment t (new energy industry financing efficiency), M is the limit of new energy industry financing efficiency (constrained by the new energy industry financing ecosystem) and $M > 0$, and r is the natural growth rate of new energy industry financing efficiency. When $t = 0$, the initial value of new energy industry financing efficiency is $E(t_0) = E_0$ and $0 < E_0 < M$, $(1 - \frac{E(t)}{M})$ is the obstruction coefficient of new energy industry financing efficiency development, which is also called logistic coefficient. It means that the evolution of the financing efficiency of the new energy industry will be influenced by its current efficiency value, but given that its evolutionary process has already consumed the available resources, resulting in its evolutionary speed will be limited.

By deforming and solving Eq. (1), the new energy industry financing efficiency $E(t)$ can be calculated as:

$$E(t) = \frac{M}{1 + \left(\frac{M}{E_0} - 1\right)e^{-rt}} \tag{2}$$

Equation (2) is the evolution equation of the operational efficiency of the financing ecosystem of the new energy industry, which can be derived from the dynamic changes of the financing efficiency of the new energy industry during the evolution process. From the above equation, we can derive $\lim_{t \to +\infty} \frac{M}{1 + (\frac{M}{E_0} - 1)e^{-rt}} = M$, when time progresses backward, the financing efficiency of new energy industry will tend to the maximum M that the financing ecology can accommodate, which also represents that the financing ecosystem of new energy industry has reached the limit that the ecology can carry.

Since the logistic function image is an S-shaped curve, in order to deeply analyze the evolutionary process of the financing efficiency of the new energy industry and the change of its development rate, the second order derivative of Eq. (2) can be obtained as follows:

$$\frac{d^2E(t)}{d_{t2}} = r^2E(t)\left(1 - \frac{E(t)}{M}\right)\left(1 - \frac{2E(t)}{M}\right) \tag{3}$$

Equation (3) represents the efficiency growth equation of the new energy industry financing ecosystem, and also the efficiency acceleration equation. When $\frac{d^2E(t)}{d_{t2}} = 0$, $\frac{dE(t)}{dt} = \frac{rM}{4}$, at this time $\frac{dE(t)}{dt} = \frac{rM}{4}$, $t^* = \frac{\ln(\frac{M}{E_0}-1)}{r}$, the inflection point of the original logistic function, the concavity of the function will change at this moment; when $E(t) < \frac{M}{2}$, $\frac{d^2E(t)}{d_{t2}} > 0$, at which time the development speed of the financing efficiency of the new energy industry will increase; when $E(t) > \frac{M}{2}$, $\frac{d^2E(t)}{d_{t2}} < 0$, at which time the development speed of the financing efficiency of the new energy industry will gradually decrease.

Continuing the derivative of Eq. (3) yields the third order derivative of $E(t)$.

$$\frac{d^3E(t)}{d_{t3}} = r^3E(t)\left(1 - \frac{E(t)}{M}\right)\left[M - \left(3 - \sqrt{3}\right)E(t)\right] * \left[M - \left(3 + \sqrt{3}\right)E(t)\right] \tag{4}$$

When $\frac{d^3E(t)}{d_{t3}} = 0$, two solutions are obtained as $E_1(t) = \frac{M}{3+\sqrt{3}}$ and $E_2(t) = \frac{M}{3-\sqrt{3}}$, respectively.

Substitute into Eq. (4) to get $t_1^* = \frac{\ln[(2-\sqrt{3})(\frac{M}{E_0}-1)]}{r}$, $t_2^* = \frac{\ln[(2+\sqrt{3})(\frac{M}{E_0}-1)]}{r}$.

The positions corresponding to these two points are the two extreme points of the development acceleration of the financing efficiency of the new energy industry. The development speed of financing efficiency of new energy industry corresponding to t_1^* and t_2^* is $\frac{dE(t)}{dt}|_{t=t_1^*} = \frac{dE(t)}{dt}|_{t=t_2^*} = \frac{rM}{6}$.

3.2 The Evolutionary Process of New Energy Industry Financing Ecosystem Based on Logistic Equation

According to the above model derivation process, the evolutionary process and growth rate curve of the operational efficiency of the new energy industry financing ecosystem over time can be derived, as shown in Fig. 2.

From the analysis of Fig. 2, it can be seen that the operational efficiency of the new energy industry financing ecosystem changes over time, showing an S-curve growth trend within a restricted growth interval, and the overall evolutionary process can be divided into four stages:

1. Gestation period $(0 < t < t_1^*)$.

    At this stage, the operational efficiency of the new energy industry financing ecosystem $\frac{dE(t)}{dt} > 0, \frac{d^2E(t)}{d_{t2}} > 0, \frac{d^3E(t)}{d_{t3}} > 0$, the acceleration and growth rate of the system operational efficiency are greater than 0, and the financing efficiency is growing positively and exponentially. When the efficiency develops to t_1^* moment, the efficiency speed is $\frac{rM}{6}$ and the efficiency reaches $E_1(t) = \frac{M}{3+\sqrt{3}}$, at which time the

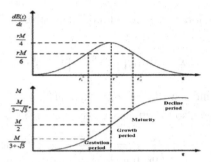

Fig. 2. The evolutionary process of the operational efficiency of the new energy industry financing ecosystem and its evolutionary speed equation curve

acceleration of the financing efficiency of the new energy industry reaches the maximum, the gestation period is completed and the financing efficiency enters the rapid growth stage. During the gestation period of the financing ecosystem of new energy industry, the overall system scale is small and the synergistic operation mechanism is uncoordinated, so the system operation efficiency is slow, which is a process of accumulating strength. As the internal structure of the system becomes stable, the financing ecosystem system will gradually take shape, and the overall system operation efficiency will enter the growth period stage when the functions of the system are stably played.

2. Growth period $\left(t_1^* < t < t^*\right)$

At this stage, the operational efficiency of the new energy industry financing ecosystem $\frac{dE(t)}{dt} > 0$, $\frac{d^2E(t)}{d_t2} > 0$, $\frac{d^3E(t)}{d_t3} < 0$, the growth rate of the system operational efficiency is still large, but the acceleration will indeed gradually shrink. At the moment when the efficiency develops to t^*, the efficiency speed is $\frac{rM}{4}$, and the efficiency reaches $E(t) = \frac{M}{2}$, when the operational efficiency speed of the new energy industry financing ecosystem reaches the maximum in the evolutionary range, and the overall system ushers in the best period. This stage is the rapid growth stage of the operational efficiency of the financing ecosystem of new energy industry, and the momentum accumulated in the previous gestation stage is gradually released, the state of the system and its stability will be greatly improved, and the self-organized operation mechanism will appear within the system, and the evolutionary role of the financing ecosystem is increasingly prominent, and the financing ecosystem of new energy industry enters a benign development track.

3. Maturity $(t^* < t < t_2^*)$

The operational efficiency of the new energy industry financing ecosystem $\frac{dE(t)}{dt} > 0$, $\frac{d^2E(t)}{d_t2} < 0$, $\frac{d^3E(t)}{d_t3} < 0$, the acceleration and growth rate of the operational efficiency of the system are gradually weakening, and the efficiency evolution is underpowered. At the moment of efficiency development to t_2^*, the efficiency speed is $\frac{rM}{6}$ and the efficiency reaches $E_2(t) = \frac{M}{3-\sqrt{3}}$, when the acceleration of the operating efficiency of the new energy industry financing ecosystem reaches the negative maximum, and the system operating efficiency tends to stabilize before this node, and the new energy industry financing ecosystem ushers in the maturity stage. Based on the accumulated efficiency evolutionary momentum in the early stage is given full play, the system operation efficiency enters a steady growth period, but due to the constraints of the financing ecology, the evolution of the new energy industry financing ecosystem gradually appears a bottleneck, and this stage is the key trend point for the operation of the new energy industry financing ecosystem. If the system can have the function of financing and allocation of funds to meet the new market demand, the system operation efficiency will enter the next virtuous development cycle of breeding-growth-maturity, while if the system cannot form a new round of growth breakthrough, the system operation efficiency will only stay at the original development level until it gradually tends to decline.

4. Decline period $(t_2^* < t < +\infty)$

The operational efficiency of the new energy industry financing ecosystem $\frac{dE(t)}{dt} > 0$, $\frac{d^2E(t)}{d_{t2}} < 0$, $\frac{d^3E(t)}{d_{t3}} > 0$, the system operational efficiency growth rate decreases while the acceleration is increasing negatively, the financing efficiency shows negative exponential growth and will gradually reach the growth limit until it stops growing completely. At this stage, the financing ecosystem of the new energy industry is seriously underpowered, and the operating efficiency gradually reaches the limit of the financing ecosystem's capacity. This decline may cause the system's demise, or it may promote the expansion of the financing ecosystem to generate new power and enter the next round of evolution.

In a comprehensive manner, the evolutionary process of the financing ecosystem of the new energy industry in the context of big data is the result of the positive and negative feedback mechanism between the financing ecosystem and the financing subject. In the early and late evolutionary process, the growth rate of operational efficiency of the financing ecosystem of new energy industry is low, but the growth rate of operational efficiency in the middle stage of evolution is high, and the operational efficiency of the whole cycle has gone through the gestation period, growth period, maturity period and decline (or regeneration) period, showing a curve evolution.

4   An Empirical Test of the Evolution of New Energy Industry Financing Ecosystem Based on Logistic Equation in the Context of Big Data

The evolutionary process of the new energy industry financing ecosystem is described above by constructing logistic equations. In the empirical study, it is necessary to derive estimates of the parameters to determine the evolutionary development stage of the new energy industry financing ecosystem. According to the equation $E(t) = \frac{M}{1+(\frac{M}{E_0}-1)e^{-rt}}$, assuming $A = \frac{M}{E_0} - 1$, then it can be derived that:

$$E(t) = \frac{M}{1 + Ae^{-rt}} \tag{5}$$

Therefore, the accuracy of the estimation of the parameters M, A and r determines the effectiveness of the Logistic curve fitting. Transforming both sides of Eq. (5) logarithmically yields.

$$\ln \frac{M-E(t)}{E(t)} = \ln A - rt \tag{6}$$

Assuming that M is a known number, let $Y = \ln \frac{M-E(t)}{E(t)}$, $X = \ln A$, and linear transformation of Eq. (6) yields.

$$Y = -rt + X \tag{7}$$

The estimated values of X and r can be derived by using SPSS linear regression, and the parameter A is calculated by substituting $X = \ln A$, and then the estimated values of parameters M, A and r are used as the initial values of nonlinear regression iterations for logistic growth curve fitting. With the help of Logistic growth model to fit the evolutionary process of the financing ecosystem of new energy industry, this paper uses the financing efficiency values of new energy industry from 2011 to 2020 as the fitting index to explore the evolutionary trend of the system of financing ecology and financing efficiency of new energy industry over time, divide the growth stages and identify the characteristics of each stage.

Efficient financing pertains to the capacity to promptly consolidate capital with minimum expense and vulnerability, and to leverage the consolidated capital for optimal gains, which is a reflection of the operational efficiency of the financing ecosystem of the new energy industry [15]. The key elements to measure financing efficiency include financing cost, financing risk, and financing speed; allocation efficiency refers to the ability of enterprises to use the integrated funds to bring maximum returns, and the indicators to quantify it can be measured from the profitability, operational capacity, and development capacity of enterprises. The quantitative indicators can be selected from three aspects: profitability, operating capacity and development capacity. The specific financing efficiency evaluation index system is shown in Table 1 [15].

Table 1. New energy industry financing efficiency evaluation index system

Inputs/ Outputs	Indicator Name	Indicator Variables	Calculation formula
Input Indicators	Financing Costs	Debt financing cost	Interest expense / (short-term borrowings + long-term borrowings + bonds payable)
		Equity Financing Costs	Capital Asset Pricing Model
	Financing Risks	Equity ratio	Total liabilities / Total shareholders' equity

(*continued*)

Table 1. (*continued*)

Inputs/ Outputs	Indicator Name	Indicator Variables	Calculation formula
	Financing time	Funding Speed	Sales proceeds/net cash inflow from financing activities
Output Indicators	Profitability	Net Asset Margin	Net Profit / Average Total Assets
	Operating Capacity	Total assets turnover ratio	Sales revenue / Average total assets
	Development capacity	Net profit growth rate	Increase in total net income for the year/ total net income for the previous year

To thoroughly assess the comprehensive progress of financial efficiency in China's new energy sector, it is essential to implement an effective evaluation method, and selects listed companies in the new energy industry from them according to the 2017 annual industry classification report of listed companies by the China Securities Regulatory Commission and combined with Wind database and RESSET concept stock classification, and excludes The annual financial data of 130 listed companies were selected for analysis based on the annual industry classification report of the China Securities Regulatory Commission for 2017, combined with Wind database and RESSET concept stock classification, and excluding companies with abnormal financial status and listed after 2011. The index data of the sample companies from 2011 to 2020 to measure the financing efficiency of the new energy industry were substituted into the Super Efficiency DEA model (as shown in Eq. 8), and the time series data of the average value of the operating efficiency of the new energy industry financing ecosystem were obtained as shown in Fig. 3.

$$
\text{Min} \, \theta = \theta_0 - \varepsilon \left(\sum_{r=1}^{s} S_r^+ + \sum_{i=1}^{m} S_i^- \right)
$$

$$
s.t \begin{cases} \sum_{\substack{j=1 \\ j \neq h}}^{N} \lambda_j x_{ij} + S_i^- = \theta x_{r0} \\ \sum_{\substack{j=1 \\ j \neq h}}^{N} \lambda_j y_{rj} - S_r^+ = y_{r0} \\ \lambda_j \geq 0, S_r^+ \geq 0 \\ S_i^- \geq 0, r = 1, 2, 3, \ldots, s \\ j = 1, 2, 3, \ldots, N, i = 1, 2, 3, \ldots m \end{cases} \tag{8}
$$

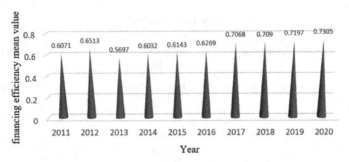

Fig. 3. New energy industry financing efficiency time series data 2011–2020

The operational development of the financing ecosystem of the new energy industry is influenced by the interaction of factors such as financing subjects and financing ecology, and its efficiency cannot grow indefinitely. The limit value of the operational efficiency of the financing ecosystem of new energy industry under the joint action of its ecological factors is M. Since the maximum value of financing efficiency of new energy industry in 2011–2020 is 2.425, since the maximum value of financing efficiency of new energy industry from 2011 to 2020 is 2.425, the maximum value of financing efficiency mean E can be assumed to be 2.425. Using Python for linear regression, the linear equation fitted to the sample points of the mean of the financing efficiency of the new energy industry $Y = -0.022t + 1.147, R^2 = 0.848$, according to which it was decided that $A = e^{1.147} = 3.148$ and $r = 0.022$. Using Python with E(t) as the dependent variable and $M = 2.245, A = 3.148, r = 0.022$ as the initial values of the parameters, a nonlinear regression iteration was performed, and the nonlinear iteration yielded an extremely large number of M results, which may be caused by too few observations. Therefore, extrapolation of the current regression equation was used to obtain the predicted values of financing efficiency for the subsequent 10 periods as shown in Fig. 4.

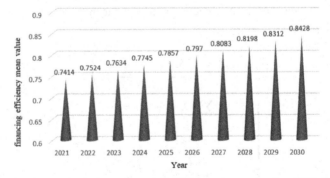

Fig. 4. New energy industry financing efficiency time series data 2021–2030

The new energy industry financing efficiency data for the above 20 periods were re-run as a non-linear regression, and the regression model parameter estimates are shown in Table 2, which shows that $R^2 = 0.872$, indicating a good fit of the logistic growth model to the observed values of the new energy industry financing efficiency.

Table 2. Nonlinear regression model parameter estimates

Parameters	Estimated value	Standard Deviation (SD)	95% Confidence interval	
			Lower limit	High limit
M	2.425	6.744	−10.352	18.548
A	3.1487	0.426	−15.761	20.784
r	0.022	0.004	−0.057	0.026

The final fitted logistic growth model is $E(t) = \frac{2.425}{1+3.148e^{-0.022t}}$, where t = year-2010, which leads to the conclusion that the evolutionary trajectory of the financing ecosystem of the new energy industry in China from 2011 to the present is consistent with the logistic model. From the fitted M = 2.425, it can be seen that the efficiency value E(t) $\in$ $(\frac{M}{3+\sqrt{3}}, \frac{M}{2})$ of the current operation of the new energy industry financing ecosystem in China, the evolution of the new energy industry financing ecosystem has entered the growth phase stage, but has not yet achieved an efficient synergistic evolutionary development.

5   Co-Evolutionary Strategy of New Energy Industry Financing Ecosystem in the Context of Big Data

In the era of "big data", information exchange and sharing among new energy enterprises is more convenient and faster [17]. The interaction between the new energy industry financing ecosystem and the external environment has become more and more frequent under the industrial integration promoted by "big data" [18, 19], and the value association between industries has a new form of expression. The use of "big data" technology not only provides the possibility of mutual benefit and symbiosis between individuals, populations and the external environment in the new energy industry financing ecosystem, but also becomes a new way to finance the new energy industry.

In view of the fact that the new energy industry financing ecosystem has not yet achieved efficient collaborative evolutionary development, in order to promote the new energy industry financing ecosystem to accelerate the maturity stage, it is urgent to condense the evolutionary strategy of the new energy industry financing ecosystem in the context of big data [20, 21], so as to grasp the changes of the financing subject and the external environment in real time as a whole, realize dynamic self-adaptation to the environment, and enhance the evolutionary Dynamics of the new energy industry financing efficiency ecosystem operation.

(1) Establish a new energy industry financing ecosystem with big data as the core resource, and build a large channel for data exchange in the new energy industry financing ecosystem in all aspects. The pursuit of economies of scale for big data resources can trigger the outward expansion of the new energy industry financing value chain with big data as its core, which in turn can lead to changes in the value proposition, business distribution, financing methods and collaborative development network of the new energy industry financing ecosystem and promote the

formation of a new financing value chain in the financing ecosystem. At the same time, because big data resources have the characteristics of large quantity, wide coverage, rich variety and fast operation, they cannot be sensed, collected and processed by traditional information technology within the observable time in general. Therefore, it is necessary to build a big channel of data exchange in the financing ecosystem of new energy industry in all aspects by improving the infrastructure for carrying big data and obstructing various effective data transmission channels, so as to Therefore, it is necessary to realize seamless data connection and sharing within the financing ecosystem, and form a comprehensive data processing system and knowledge sharing system, so as to achieve synergistic development among the transaction subjects, between populations and with the external environment within the financing ecosystem.

(2) Innovation of key business and processes in the system with big data as the core to obtain the competitive advantage of the new energy industry financing ecosystem. In the context of big data, the transaction subjects, shared resources, value network, ecological structure and other elements within the new energy industry financing ecosystem are in a dynamic evolutionary process and continuous reconfiguration. By driving the financing value chain of the new energy industry ecosystem through big data assets, it can enhance the same-side and cross-side network effects among groups, promote the reconstruction of the financing value chain, realize the characteristics of the financing model embodied in the benefit-sharing mechanism among transaction subjects of the new energy industry financing ecosystem, and integrate with the characteristics of the application embodied in the technical architecture of shared data, and promote the In this way, we can effectively guide and coordinate the interaction and synergy among multiple groups in the new energy industry financing ecosystem, and share the value appreciation and sustainable profits brought by the synergy effect of the system as a whole, thus reshaping the entire new energy industry financing ecosystem. In this process, we will obtain the competitive advantage of the new energy industry financing ecosystem and accelerate the evolution and upgrading of the new energy industry financing ecosystem.

New management concepts and decision-making models emerge in the context of big data with the deepening of enterprise management practices. Analyzing the evolution of the financing ecosystem of new energy industry in the era of big data from the perspective of life cycle, combining the big data generated by the financing process of multilateral groups, conducting theoretical research and practical tests on the evolution of the financing ecosystem of new energy industry in the environment of big data, and reshaping the new energy It is important for the future financing strategy management and decision-making of modern enterprises, and also provides reference for government agencies to formulate relevant policies and laws and regulations, and provide decision-making for sustainable economic development, industrial structure optimization, and economic growth model transformation. It will also provide realistic guidance for the development of a coordinated development strategy of "collaborative evolution of enterprise ecology" in the digital economy.

(3) Building a big data information sharing platform to promote open collaborative innovation in the new energy industry financing ecosystem. The collaboration among factions in the financing ecosystem of the novel energy industry is grounded on

reciprocal reliance, and establishing a trust system in the milieu of voluminous data can be accomplished by developing a platform for sharing big data information, facilitating effortless data linkage and regulation of boundaries. Based on the sharing and acquisition of big data, it makes the competing relationship between groups within the ecosystem closer, builds a structural big data information support platform on which the financing ecosystem of new energy industry depends, and using the accumulated billions of massive data, it can change the execution side of value creation activities and the interaction with participants in the financing model, continuously enhances the interaction between new energy enterprises and groups inside and outside the financing ecosystem, constructs and builds symbiotic synergistic relationships with acceleration, and realizes open collaborative innovation in the financing ecosystem of new energy industry.

Acknowledgment. The project was supported by National social science foundation project (19BTJ016), National Social Science Foundation, Jiangsu Universities Philosophy and Social Sciences Research Project (2021SJA0452), The Open Research Fund of NJIT Research Center, The Key Laboratory of Carbon Neutrality and Territory Optimization, Ministry of Natural Resources (No. CNT202203), The Open Research Fund of NJIT Institute of Industrial Economy and Innovation Management (JGKB202002).

References

1. Wang, J.Y., Zhao, Q.C.: Collaborative evolution of business ecosystem in big data environment. J. Shandong Univ. (Philos. Soc. Sci. Ed.) **05**, 132–138 (2014)
2. Pantelis, K., Aija, L.: Understanding the value of (big) data. In: IEEE International Conference on Big Data, pp. 38–42. IEEE (2013)
3. Hirsch, D.D.: The glass house effect: Big Data, the new oil, and the power of analogy. Me. L. Rev. **66**, 373 (2013)
4. Munford, M.: Rule changes and big data revolutionise Caterham F1 chances. The Telegraph (2014)
5. Gerhardt, B., Griffin, K., Klemann, R.: Unlocking Value in the Fragmented World of Big Data Analytics, vol. 7. Cisco Internet Business Solutions Group (2012)
6. Manyika, J., Chu, M.: Big data: the next frontier for innovation, competition and productivity. Mc Kinsey Q. (5), 27–30 (2011)
7. Eaton, C., Deroos, D., Deutsch, T., Lapis, G., Zikopoulos, P.C.: Understanding Big Data: Analytics for Enterprise Class Hadoop and Streaming Data. Mc Graw-Hill Companies 978-0-07-179053-6 (2012)
8. Schneider, R.D.: Hadoop for Dummies, Special John Wiley & Sons, Canada (2012). 978-1-118-25051-8
9. Madden, S.: From databases to big data. IEEE Internet Comput. **16**(3), 4–6 (2012)
10. Zi, W.C.: The evolution and construction of enterprise ecosystem in the era of "Big Data." Soc. Sci. **12**, 55–62 (2013). (in Chinese)
11. Lin, B., Xu, B.: How to promote the growth of new energy industry at different stages? Energy Policy **118**, 390–403 (2018)
12. Gort, M., Klepper, S.: Time paths in the diffusion of product innovations. Econ. J. **92**(367), 630–653 (1982)

13. Haire, M.: Psychological problems relevant to business and industry. Psychol. Bull. **56**(3), 169–194 (1959). https://doi.org/10.1037/h0041259
14. Zhang, H.H.: On industrial life cycle theory. Finance Trade Res. (06), 7–11 (2004). (in Chinese)
15. Wang, H.R., E Y Z: Research on financing efficiency of jiangsu new energy industry under the threshold of ecological synergy. East China Econ. Manag. **32**(05), 14–19 (2018). (in Chinese)
16. Xue, X.F., Liang, J.W., Li, X.Z.: Research on collaborative logistics ecosystem in the context of "big data." Mon. Price Mag. **04**, 63–67 (2016). (in Chinese)
17. Moore, J.F.: Business ecosystems and the view from the firm. The Antitrust Bull. **51**(1), 31–75 (2006)
18. Zhang, H.: Research on the synergistic development of commerce ecosystem based on big data. Reform Strategy **31**(08), 31–33 (2015). (in Chinese)
19. Sagiroglu, S., Sinanc, D.: Big Data. In: A review.2013 international conference on collaboration technologies and systems (CTS), pp. 42–47. IEEE (2013)
20. Agrawal, D., Bernstein, P, Bertino, E., et al.: Challenges and opportunities with Big Data 2011-1 (2011)
21. George, G., Haas, M.R., Pentland, A.: Big data and management. Acad. Manag. J. **57**(2), 321–326 (2014)

A Survey of the State-of-the-Art and Some Extensions of Recommender System Based on Big Data

Lixin Jia[1], Lixiu Jia[2], and Lihang Feng[1]([✉])

[1] Nanjing Tech University Nanjing, Nanjing, China
lfeng8@njtech.edu.cn
[2] Nanjing Institute of Technology, Nanjing, China

Abstract. Recommender systems (RSs) based on big data have been shown to be very powerful tools for solving the information overload to assist the choice-making when dealing with the massive amount information in the age of big data and artificial intelligence. This paper presents an overview of the state-of-art RS that can be classified into four categories: content-based algorithms (CR), collaborative filtering-based algorithms (CF), and knowledge-based algorithms (KR), as well as hybrid recommendation-based algorithms (HR). The popular CF-based recommender algorithms are especially focused by classifying them into the memory-based algorithms, and model-based algorithms as they show the advantages of great rating prediction without contextual features compared to the rest of RS approaches. By reviewing the current RS and understanding their limitations, the emerging solutions or possible extensions that would improve recommendation capabilities involving deep learning, knowledge graphs, and parallel computing techniques are significantly discussed for future RS research direction. At the same time, by identifying current problems, some possible solutions will be shown in the last part.

Keywords: Recommender System · Deep Learning · Knowledge Graph · Big Data · Parallel Computing

1 Introduction

Nowadays, all kinds of information flood our daily life. Despite the benefits of such information, the vast flow of information can also make the decision-making process more complex, which leads to a problem: Information overload [1–6]. Information overload costs a lot of energy to make decisions in the face of massive amounts of information, so it is vital for assisting people to make a correct decision. There are two main types of tools: one is the search engine [7], and the other is the recommender system based on big data. Compared with search engines, personalized recommender systems based on big data tend to have more advantages in information precise positioning. Recommender systems (RSs) based on big data are widely used in various domains, such as music (QQMusic), movies (Douban Film), travel (Ctrip), shopping (Taobao shopping, Dangdang shopping), etc.

The research on recommender systems based on big data originated in the late 20th century and is an interdisciplinary subject integrating multiple fields. The development of recommender systems base on big data can be roughly divided into two stages:

- Basic stage: Malone et al. adopted a content-based semi-structured module to implement the Information Lens [8] which was an email filtering system. Marko et al. proposed an intelligent agent feedback update mechanism LIRA [9] for web page recommendation, which improved the personalized search accuracy of search engines, Armstrong et al. created a web browsing path recommendation agent WebWatcher [10] by referring to the historical recommendation data of the recommender system and the historical browsing behavior of users, which can recommend hyperlinks matching the user model to target users; Palo Alto developed a collaborative filtering-based email recommender system-Tapestry [11] which established the prototype and framework of collaborative filtering. A team called Grouplens developed the MovieLens recommender system based on the active collaborative filtering system [12] and released the MovieLens dataset [13].
- Grow stage: With the establishment of the Netflix Prize competition by Netflix, various excellent recommendation algorithms such as SVD++ [14] have emerged one after another. Later, Kaggle, Tianchi, and other competitions also produced excellent models such as XGBoost [15] and LightGBM [16].

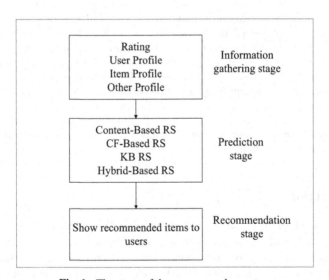

Fig. 1. The stage of the recommender system

The stage of the recommender system based on big data is shown in Fig. 1, and there are three stages as follows:

- Information collection and integration stage: the information is formatted and integrated by collecting rating information, user feature information, item feature information, user comment information, social network information, etc.

- Prediction stage: through a series of algorithms calculate the above-integrated information, and finally obtain the target users' predicted score and recommended items.
- Recommendation stage: the above recommendation results are displayed to the user through the front end, and the user feedbacks on the preferences of the recommended items to the user after receiving the recommendation to further optimize the recommendation accuracy of the recommendation system.

All kinds of extended recommender systems based on big data are detailed in this paper. Nevertheless, before doing this, the background to the development of recommender systems based on big data is firstly introduced. The classification of recommender systems based on big data is presented in Sect. 2. As collaborative filtering-based recommender systems based on big data are most widely used today, more details are described in this section. Section 3 summarizes the most current technologies and their integration into recommender systems based on big data. In the last section, the existing problems in recommender systems based on big data today are identified and some possible solutions and future works are shown.

2 Recommender System Approaches

The recommender system based on big data is defined as [3]: Suppose C is the set of all target users, suppose S is the set of all recommended items, suppose u is a utility function which is usually the rating situation of a user for the item, suppose $c \in C$, we want to select a group $s^i \in S$ to maximize the utility of users, to be precise in Eq. (1):

$$\forall c \in C, s_c^i = argmax\, u(c, s), s \in S \tag{1}$$

The core problem of recommender systems based on big data is to extend the scope of the utility function from a partial subset to the whole space. In short, from the items that users have rated to the entire items that users have not rated.

The recommender system based on big data has four branches according to the type of recommendation, which are content-based approach, collaborative filtering-based approach, knowledge-based and hybrid approach.

2.1 Content-Based Approach

According to the user historical preferences, the user-preferred tags are extracted, and the similarity between the user-preferred tags and the item feature tags is matched, and finally, a similar item set is recommended to the target user. The main process of the algorithm is as follows: Firstly, according to the user's history selection (explicit feedback, such as rating; Implicit feedback, such as views, reviews, etc.) to extract the user (Such as user type, age, hobbies, etc.), and meanwhile extraction project portrait (Such as the type of film, director, release date and so on.), then user and calculated through user portrait portraits and project to predict similarity of the project, according to the similarity of the project recommended to the user (Fig. 2).

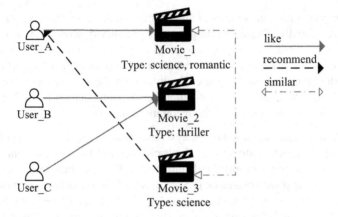

Fig. 2. Content-based recommendation system

As the content-based recommender algorithm is predictive based on tags and content-based recommender algorithm doesn't require a rating matrix, the algorithm can fully exploit items of user preferences handily, but in real life, there are many difficulties in extracting user-profiles and there can be cold start problems for new users.

2.2 Collaborative Filtering Approach

The collaborative filtering-based recommender algorithm is one of the most popular recommender algorithms because the advantage of the collaborative filtering recommendation algorithm is that it can complete rating prediction without contextual features. However, in real life, users' ratings for items are often sparse, so the recommendation effect is often unsatisfactory, and there will be the problem of user cold start. In order to improve user satisfaction, some improved CF algorithms as shown in Table 1 and these algorithms will be detailed in the next part. These improved algorithms are detailed in the next part.

Memory-Based CF Approach

Memory-based collaborative filtering recommendation algorithms include item-based collaborative filtering recommendation algorithms and user-based collaborative filtering recommendation algorithms. For the item-based collaborative filtering recommendation algorithm, the core idea of the algorithm is: "Like attracts like". First, the similarity between items is calculated, and then the book recommendation ranking is calculated according to the user's historical ratings combined with the similarity between items. Finally, the top N books are selected to recommend to the target user. For the user-based collaborative filtering recommendation algorithm, the core idea of the algorithm is: "People by groups", by calculating the similarity between the user and the user. Finally, through the similarity between users and the rating of items for scoring prediction.

Memory-based collaborative filtering algorithm (Fig. 3) is to read all the rating data into the memory and then operates, which is suitable for the case of a small amount of data. When the amount of data is particularly large, the operation efficiency of this

Table 1. Improved CF algorithms.

Topic	Research	Main Contribution
Memory-Based Approach	Lemire et al. [17]	Improves scoring initialization problem and realizes dynamic update rating
	Huang [18]	Improves Slope one algorithm and adds dynamic factor
Model-Based Approach	Wang [21]	Proposes the Mat Mat Framework which improves scoring matrix space consumption issues
	Wang [22]	Introducing situational awareness based on the MatMat Framework
	Xu et al. [26]	Improves the HIN and the LMFE, and comprehensively improves the prediction accuracy
	Barathy et al. [27]	Proposes a new scoring matrix initialization method that reduces the sparsity of the scoring matrix
	Han et al. [30]	Proposes a method in order to reduce the influence of social noise

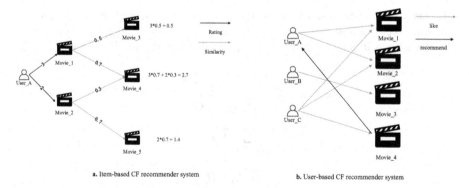

a. Item-based CF recommender system   b. User-based CF recommender system

Fig. 3. Memory-based CF recommendation system

method is greatly reduced. Figure 3.a shows the instances of collaborative filtering recommendation systems based on content. Suppose that the rating of a user to a movie is from 1 to 5 points, the rating of *user A* to *movie 1* and *movie 2* is 3 points and 2 points respectively. We can recommend movies to users according to rating and similarity. A sample user-based collaborative filtering recommendation algorithm is shown in Fig. 3.b, user A likes movie 1 and movie 2, user C likes movie 1, movie 2, and movie 4, and the similarity between user C and user A is the closest, so movie 4 in user C is recommended to user A.

An improved item-based collaborative filtering algorithm called the slope one algorithm is proposed [17] which includes the static slope one algorithm which is suitable for infrequently updating item ratings and the dynamic slope one algorithm which is suitable for frequently updating item ratings. Two types are as follows:

- Static slope one algorithm calculates the mean of the rating difference between known items, combines the mean with the historical rating of the target user, and predicts the unknown rating. The specific method first calculates the average score difference between items through the following equation, then calculates the predicted score according to Eq. (2), and finally selects the top N high-scoring items to recommend to the target user.

$$D_{i,j} = \frac{\sum_{u \in N(i) \cap N(j)} (r_{ui} - r_{uj})}{|N(i) - N(j)|} \tag{2}$$

r_{uj} represents the rating situation of user u on item j, $N(i)$ represents the set of users who have rated item i, $D_{i,j}$ represents the average rating difference between item i and item j.

$$R_{i,j} = \frac{\sum_{i \in N(u)} |N(i) \cap N(j)| (r_{ui} - D_{i,j})}{\sum_{i \in N(u)} |N(i) \cap N(j)|} \tag{3}$$

$N(u)$ is the set of items that have been rated by user u, and r_{ui} is the rating of item i by user u.

- Dynamic slope one algorithm realizes dynamic update based on algorithm [18] which m introduces dynamic factors $c_{j,i}$ and $b_{j,i}$, and changes the average score difference between items in Slope one by $c_{j,i}$ and $b_{j,i}$. as shown in Eq. (4), Eq. (5) and Eq. (6).

$$\hat{R}_{u,j} = \frac{\sum_{i \in I_u - \{j\}} (b_{j,i}/c_{j,i} + R_{u,i}) c_{j,i}}{\sum_{i \in I_u - \{j\}} c_{j,i}} \tag{4}$$

$$b_{j,i} = \sum_{u \in U_i \cap U_j} R_{u,j} - R_{u,i} \tag{5}$$

$$c_{j,i} = |U_i \cap U_j| \tag{6}$$

Model-Based CF Approach

The model-based collaborative filtering algorithm models the historical ratings of users on items and uses the data to fit the model and then uses the trained model to predict the items that have not been rated by the target user. The model-based collaborative filtering algorithm has a significant effect on sparse matrix rating prediction, but there are problems of poor interpretation and low user satisfaction.

A collaborative filtering algorithm based on matrix factorization [19, 20] is one of the most popular model-based collaborative filtering algorithms. The main process of the algorithm like Fig.4 is to first decompose the user rating matrix $R_{m \times n}$ into two low-dimensional user vectors U and item vector I. $R_{m \times n}$ is decomposed into $U_{m \times k}$ and $I_{k \times n}$,

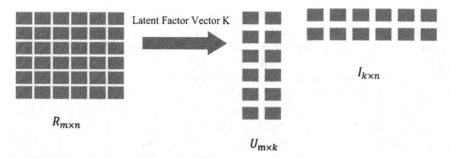

Fig. 4. Matrix decomposition process

and then the loss function is minimized by the optimization algorithm. With the update of the gradient, the user vector and the item vector are obtained.

The loss function is shown in Eq. (7). $r_{i,j}$ denotes the rating of item j by user i, β is a regularization parameter to prevent overfitting, $U_i I_j^T$ denotes predicted scores, $||U_i||^2$ denotes user vector norm, and $||I_j||$ denotes item vector norm.

$$J = \sum_{i,j \in R} (r_{i,j} - U_i I_j^T)^2 + \frac{\beta}{2}(||U_i||^2 + ||I_j||^2) \tag{7}$$

The updated equation of the user vector and item vector is shown in Eq. (8) and Eq. (9) (Taking the stochastic gradient descent algorithm as an example):

$$U_i^{(t)} = U_i^{(t-1)} + \alpha \left(2\left(r_{i,j} - U_i I_j^T\right)I_j - \beta U_i\right) \tag{8}$$

$$I_j^{(t)} = I_j^{(t-1)} + \alpha \left(2\left(r_{i,j} - U_i I_j^T\right)U_i - \beta I_j\right) \tag{9}$$

Here α is the learning rate. Firstly, the user vector and the item vector are randomly initialized, and the inner product of the two is closer and closer to the true value by stochastic gradient descent. Until the predetermined loss threshold is reached or the specified training rounds are reached.

MatMat framework [21] which is a matrix factorization model is proposed for the space consumption of matrix factorization, which replaces the traditional matrix factorization method by the product of user characteristic matrix and item characteristic matrix. It fits the model by the product of the user characteristic matrix and item characteristic matrix. Literature [22] improves on literature [21] and integrates the MatMat framework with context-aware information based on the LDOS-CoMoDa movie dataset as shown in the specific Eq. (10). Experiments show that the recommendation system has improved the prediction accuracy and running speed.

$$R_{i,j} = \begin{bmatrix} \frac{r_{i,j}}{\max(r)} & \frac{daytype}{\max(daytype)} & \frac{season}{\max(season)} \\ \frac{weather}{\max(weather)} & \frac{r_{i,j}}{\max(r)} & \frac{location}{\max(location)} \\ \frac{emotion}{\max(emotion)} & \frac{mood}{\max(mood)} & \frac{r_{i,j}}{\max(r)} \end{bmatrix} \tag{10}$$

In Eq. (10), function max () denotes getting the maximum value, $r_{i,j}$ denotes the rating of item i by user j. Day type, Season, Weather, Location, Emotion, and Mood respectively represent the day of the week, season, weather conditions, geographical location, the internal mood of the audience, and the external performance of the audience. The above scenario information is numerically represented in the LDOS-CoMoDa dataset, so the above factors can be further analyzed and predicted.

Based on the Heterogeneous Information Network (HIN) (An effective auxiliary data modeling method) in literature [23–25] and the Local Low-rank Matrix Approximation embodied in literature [21] (LLORMA) method, a method called Local Matrix Factorization with Social Network Embedding (LMFE [26]) is proposed, which uses social network and user rating data to build HIN. By extracting the feature representation of users and items to create a submatrix, and then by weighting the submatrix prediction score, finally, the prediction score of the comprehensive prediction matrix is obtained. The performance of the recommendation system is further optimized by this method.

A solution for the problem of data sparseness degree grading initialization user rating-based method is proposed [27]. Firstly, the common ratings of the target user and similar users are summed, and then the number of similar users whose similarity to the target user is greater than the threshold is calculated. Finally, the quotient of the above values is calculated and the value is updated to the unrated ratings. Compared with the experiment without data processing, the recommendation accuracy of this method is improved.

Given the lack of dealing with social noise in the existing research, based on the SoRec model [28] and TrustMF model [29], a noise-aware asymmetric social collective matrix factorization model called AsySocialCoMF [30] is proposed. This model proposes a new method to calculate trust value by using an asymmetric trust network, which can effectively reduce the influence of social noise. At the same time, this model proposes a matrix factorization method to capture the overall information distribution based on spectral regularization. The model not only improves the prediction accuracy but also has a good improvement for the cold start problem.

2.3 Knowledge-Based Approach

Since a large amount of scoring data cannot be obtained in a certain item and the data scored by a certain item is very small, content-based recommendation algorithms and collaborative filtering-based recommendation algorithms often fail to achieve satisfactory results. A knowledge-based recommender algorithm (KB) [31] is proposed for solving the above problem. The main process of the algorithm is to first customize the user's needs, then recommend items that users may like according to the needs, and then feedback on the user's needs for the recommended items, using the user's feedback as a parameter into a knowledge-based recommender system based on big data.

Knowledge-based recommendation algorithms can effectively solve the problem of user cold start and KB doesn't depend on user rating of items, but there are difficulties in knowledge acquisition and knowledge sorting [32].

2.4 Hybrid Approach

Compared to a single recommendation algorithm, the performance of the hybrid recommendation algorithm will be improved. Hybrid-based recommendation algorithms are mainly classified into weighted, hierarchical, feature-combined, and threshold algorithms. For weighted hybrid recommendation algorithms, the scores obtained by multiple recommendation algorithms are weighted and combined to finally obtain the ratings of the candidate items by the target user. For hierarchical recommendation algorithms, the results obtained by one recommendation algorithm are used as input to another recommendation algorithm, which predicts the ratings. The feature-combined recommendation algorithm fuses multiple recommendation algorithms and sends information extracted from various types of data to the model for final prediction scores. For the threshold hybrid recommendation algorithm, the threshold is set according to different problem contexts and situations, and different recommendation algorithm strategies are employed around the threshold.

Because the hybrid recommendation algorithm is the integration of other algorithms, the effect will be greatly improved compared with a single recommendation algorithm, but the hybrid recommendation algorithm still has the problems of sparse user-rating matrix and cold start of users.

3 Emerging Approach

Following the traditional recommendation algorithm, more recommender algorithms integrated with other fields emerge in an endless stream. The emerging recommendation algorithms from the following three sections will be shown in Table 2. These algorithms are optimized from the perspectives of dealing with data noise, reducing data sparsity through auxiliary information, and improving model training speed and some details will be described in the next part.

3.1 Deep Learning-Based Approach

Although traditional machine learning methods in the treatment of low-dimensional data have an effective prediction, for high-dimensional data, the generalization of traditional machine learning methods tend to have many deviations, for data calibration and feature extraction, frequently have a lot of artificial, deep learning as a branch of machine learning, can be obtained from the data automatic features. The fitting and prediction of the model are driven by big data.

Common neural network models are Convolutional Neural Networks, Recurrent Neural Networks, and Autoencoder Neural Networks.

Convolutional Neural Network [33] mainly includes three basic layers, which are the convolutional layer, the pooling layer, and the fully connected layer. The three basic layers cooperate to reduce the scale of data on the basis of retaining the original data characteristics. Convolutional Neural Network reduces the complexity of the model and prevents the overfitting problem [34].

Autoencoder Neural Network has natural advantages in the prediction of recommender systems based on big data [35]. The autoencoder is divided into two parts: The encoder reconstructs the rating data in the input layer, and the decoder reconstructs the predicted rating in the output layer. At the same time, it can learn and predict the user vector and item vector. Finally, the rating was predicted by the product of the user vector

Table 2. Emerging algorithms.

Topic	Research	Main Contribution
Deep Learning-Based Approach	Liu et al. [35]	Improves prediction accuracy by fusing the autoencoder with the graph structure
	Chen et al. [36]	Improves graph neural networks by fusing heterogeneous graph neural networks with recurrent neural networks
	Yao et al. [37]	Deals with the noise of data and the problem of poor interpretability of recommendation results
Knowledge Graphs-Based Approach	Cao [38]	Proposes a method of fusing recurrent neural networks and weight-based knowledge graphs
	Xu [39]	Alleviates the prediction bias
	Deng [42]	Proposes a method that solves the data sparsity problem of accidental groups
	Lu [43]	Proposes a strategy to avoid calibrating exercises
Parallel Computing-Based Approach	Gurbuz et al. [44]	Proposes a series of indicators that are instructive for parallel computing deployment recommender schemes
	Li et al. [45]	Proposes a parallelization method for improving the speed of MF
	Zhao [46]	Uses offline computing and online computing to complete real-time recommendation and offline recommendations

and the rating vector. A graph-based autoencoder rating prediction method is proposed [36], which is combined with the graph structure on the basis of the original autoencoder and converted the rating prediction into a link prediction problem. On this basis, it is combined with the social influence model, and experimental results show that it can significantly improve prediction accuracy.

A collaborative filtering recommendation algorithm based on heterogeneous graph attention neural network and recurrent neural network (HGANTRec) is proposed [36], which uses a heterogeneous graph neural network to mine the hidden features between users and items in the data, and then uses the attention mechanism to learn the weights

of different types of edges. Finally, according to the user behavior time attribute information. Compared with the traditional graph neural network algorithm, this method can
better depict user preferences and further improve prediction accuracy.

Aiming at the problem of data noise and poor interpretability of recommendation
results when users purchase items in MOBA Games. A hierarchical attention-based
recurrent neural network recommendation framework (eaLSTM) is proposed [37]. The
LSTM framework and attention mechanism are integrated; at the same time, the event
attention and matching attention methods are used. The event attention assigns different
events different weights, and the matching attention assigns different weights to different
competitions. Compared with LSTM, experiments show that eaLSTM improves the
accuracy of recommendations.

3.2   Knowledge Graphs-Based Approach

The knowledge graph is a kind of heterogeneous figure which specific implementation
process is as follows. At first, the construction of a knowledge graph aims to optimize the
search engine. It uses entities as nodes and edges between entities as relations between
entities. Each edge is represented by a triplet (Head entities, Relationships, Tail entities),
and applying a knowledge graph to the recommender system based on big data can further
improve the prediction accuracy of the recommender system based on big data.

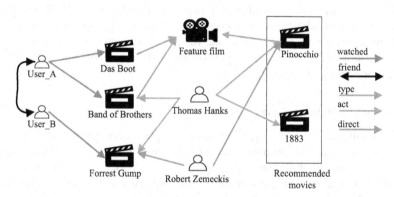

Fig.5. Recommender system based on the knowledge map

In Fig. 5, users, actors, directors, and feature file as entities at the same time, viewing
record, friend relationship, movie genre, starring role as edges in the knowledge graph.
Pinocchio and *1883* are recommended to *user A* and *user B* through various relationships
between entities and edges. The specific reasons for recommendation are as follows: The
relationship between the two users is friends, and the movie recommendation is carried
out by analyzing the types, starring roles, and actors of the movies they have watched.

A method of fusing recurrent neural networks and weight-based knowledge graphs
(RNWKG) is proposed [38]. This method controls the propagation direction of the target
user in the knowledge graph by setting the weight, and it further improves the efficiency
of model training and prediction by removing the noise of data. The entity is embedded

into the user vector and the item vector through the representation learning method of the knowledge graph, and then the user preference information is further mined by the recurrent neural network, and finally, recommendation sets are generated.

In order to alleviate the prediction bias, a fair representation learning model of a recommender system based on a knowledge graph on the basis of graph embedding debiasing algorithm is proposed [39], which further constrains the fairness of multiple sensitive attribute groups by mining the potential association between sensitive attributes. The adversarial learning framework is introduced to remove the sensitive attribute information in the user representation generated by using the sensitivity graph and the original knowledge graph.

Based on the group-based SIGR model [40] and GroupSA model [41], an end-to-end knowledge graph which is based on the attention group recommendation method (KGAG) is proposed [42], which solves the data sparsity problem of accidental groups. The specific process is as follows: First by figure convolution neural network to build a knowledge graph and calculating interest similarity between users, then the attention mechanism is used to construct a user within the group's influence, to learn more by the ideas of the marginal loss distinct groups and the vector representation of the item. Target users are modeled through social networks in literature [40], and structured information based on the item side is used in the literature [42]. Compared with the modeling method based on social networks, the data sparsity of the modeling method based on the item side is greatly reduced.

A kind of elementary mathematics exercises recommended strategy [43] is proposed. Traditional recommendation methods need calibration. Starting from the semantic content of the topic, the triple is used as the feature of the topic, and the personalized recommendation of the target user's topic is completed through the same-level diffusion and multi-hop propagation strategy.

3.3 Parallel Computing-Based Approach

Compared with serial computing, which uses a single processing resource to execute tasks in sequence, parallel computing divides tasks into multiple subtasks and completes these subtasks through different processing resources. Distributed computing is a kind of parallel computing, but these subtasks in distributed computing are independent of each other. Cloud computing is the development of parallel computing and distributed computing, which is a computing model. Computing resources are linked through the cloud, and large-scale computing tasks are completed by distributing computing tasks to the cloud.

The problem of existing parallel computing metrics is summarized [44]. A series of green computing indicators that are meaningful for the analysis of energy-saving deployment alternatives are summarized, such as CPU utilization, throughput, CPU energy consumption, computing cost, and other indicators. These indicators are summarized by this research and this research has guiding significance for parallel computing deployment schemes.

A CUDA-based SGD parallelization method (CUMSGD) is proposed to improve the speed of MF [45]. By eliminating the dependence on user-item pairs and decomposing the MF task into multiple independent subtasks, GPU was used to complete each subtask in parallel. On the basis of CUMSGD, a multi-GPU strategy (MCUSGD) is adopted to further improve the parallel speed by extending tasks to distributed platforms (Spark, Hadoop, and other platforms).

A recommender system based on the Hadoop framework is proposed [46]. The recommender system can be divided into two modules which are the online recommended module and offline recommended modules. Online module is shown in Fig.6.a. The user's request validity checking through the gateway, when after the inspection, on the one hand, the request to the recommendation engine, on the other hand, records the user's behavior to the Flume. Flume collects data through the web server, stores the collected data in HBase, and transmits the collected data to the offline module and Spark through Kafka respectively. The data flowing into Spark is processed and passed to the recommendation engine, and the data passed into the offline module is used for offline processing. The offline module (Fig.6.b) is divided into three parts: the data layer, the recall layer, and the ranking layer. The data layer standardizes the original data and stores these data in different storage systems. The recall layer is responsible for generating the recommendation set through user behavior. The ranking layer is responsible for ranking the recommendation set by using various models.

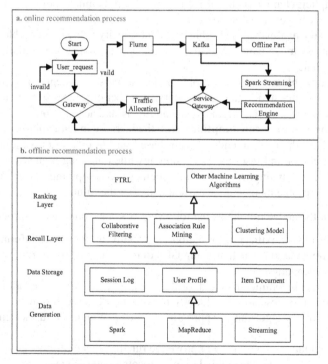

Fig. 6. Comprehensive recommendation system

A kind of parallel computing method based on user characteristics is proposed [47]. The rating matrix is divided into blocks according to the row vector, and each block is given to a process for processing so that multiple processes are executed concurrently.

The score for not making a prediction is obtained by averaging the sum of the computed results for each parallel process. Through the verification of the Yahoo Music dataset, compared with the sequential execution method, the running time of the proposed method is shorter under the same prediction effect.

For individual abnormal data and model to predict the problem of slow, a method of cross-entropy which is used to calculate similarity is proposed [48]. In the high noise data set, the similarity calculation method based on cross-entropy is more accurate than the traditional similarity calculation method.

4   Conclusions and Discussion

The recommender system based on big data plays an indispensable role in the present era of information overload. There are still many problems with RSs including:

- **Data mining problem:** In order to improve the prediction accuracy, the traditional prediction based on score often can't predict efficiently, so the implied characteristics of digging [36] are very important. In recent years, a variety of hidden features of mining is emerging endlessly, but these are done based on humans, often inadequate for the implicit characteristics of the mining. There is much room for improvement in the processing of social noise [30].
- **Data sparsity problem:** The problem of data sparsity is the main problem faced by the current recommendation system based on big data, which is essentially a problem of missing data.
- **Cold start problem:** Cold start problem of data sparseness degree is a special case. It mainly is manifested in the newly established user or project so as to be unable to establish contact with the original data and timely and accurate prediction.
- **Computing resource consumption:** With the increase in data volume and computing resources, the recommender system based on big data often generates a large amount of computing resource consumption while obtaining higher accuracy. How to comprehensively improve prediction accuracy and computing power consumption is one of the problems facing the current and even the future.

In view of the above problems, the following possible solutions are proposed:

- Integrating more auxiliary information (Especially implicit side information) into user recommendations, such as using GPS to integrate past travel routes into scenic spot recommendations.
- Using a fusion recommendation algorithm for a specific recommendation scenario.
- As mentioned in these articles [49, 50], in order to prevent recommendation simplification, a novelty algorithm is appropriately added. Which can further improve user satisfaction
- Parallel computing is a trend to improve the running speed of models. In the future, parallel computing will be applied to more recommendation systems.

To sum up, the recommender system based on big data is a discipline that integrates multiple fields. The research on the recommender system based on big data will integrate more advanced technologies, apply them to more industrial fields, and promote the development of the industry.

Acknowledgement. This work is supported by the grant of National Natural Science Foundation of China (62103184), in part by China Postdoctoral Science Foundation (2021M690630), in part by Basic Science (Natural science) Research project of Jiangsu Province(No.22KJB510022), in part by Jiangsu Provincial Double-Innovation Doctor Program (No. (2020)30696), in part by Scientific Research Foundation of Nanjing Institute of Technology of China (No.YKJ201978).

References

1. Hdioud, F., Frikh, B., Ouhbi, B.: A comparison study of some algorithms in Recommender Systems. In: 2012 Colloquium in Information Science and Technology, pp. 130–135 (2012)
2. Lekakos, G., Giaglis, G.M.: Improving the prediction accuracy of recommendation algorithms: approaches anchored on human factors. Interact. Comput. **18**(3), 410–431 (2006)
3. Adomavicius, G., Tuzhilin, A.: Toward the next generation of recommender systems: a survey of the state-of-the-art and possible extensions. IEEE Trans. Knowl. Data Eng. **17**(6), 734–749 (2005)
4. Ghazanfar, M.A., et al.: A scalable, accurate hybrid recommender system. In: 2010 Third International Conference on Knowledge Discovery and Data Mining, pp. 94–98 (2010)
5. Hornick, M., Tamayo, P.: Extending recommender systems for disjoint user/item sets: the conference recommendation problem. IEEE Trans. Knowl. Data Eng. **24**(8), 1478–1490 (2012)
6. Munoz-Organero, M., et al.: A collaborative recommender system based on space-time similarities. IEEE Pervasive Comput. **9**(3), 81–87 (2010)
7. Liang, F., et al.: Search engine for the internet of things: lessons from web search, vision, and opportunities. IEEE Access **7**, 104673–104691 (2019)
8. Malone, T.W., et al.: The information lens: an intelligent system for information sharing in organizations. Acm Sigchi Bull. **17**(4), 1–8 (1986)
9. Balabanović, M.: An adaptive Web page recommendation service. In: Proceedings of the first International Conference on Autonomous Agents, pp. 378–385 (1997)
10. Armstrong, R., et al.: Webwatcher: a learning apprentice for the world wide web. In: AAAI Spring Symposium on Information Gathering from Heterogeneous, Distributed Environments, vol. 93, p. 107. Stanford (1995)
11. Goldberg, D., et al.: Using collaborative filtering to weave an information tapestry. Commun. ACM **35**(12), 61–70 (1992)
12. Maltz, D., Ehrlich, K.: Pointing the way: active collaborative filtering. In: Proceedings of the SIGCHI Conference on Human Factors in Computing Systems (1995)
13. Harper, F.M., Konstan, J.A.: The movielens datasets: history and context. ACM Trans. Interact. Intell. Syst. **5**(4), 1–19 (2015)
14. Jiao, J., et al.: A novel learning rate function and its application on the SVD++ recommendation algorithm. IEEE Access **8**, 14112–14122 (2020)
15. Chen, T., et al.: Xgboost: extreme gradient boosting. R package version 0.4–2, pp. 1–4 (2015)
16. Ke, G., et al.: Lightgbm: a highly efficient gradient boosting decision tree. Advances in Neural Information Processing Systems 30 (2017)
17. Lemire, D., Maclachlan, A.: Slope one predictors for online ratingbased collaborative filtering. In Proceedings of the 2005 SIAM International Conference on Data Mining, pp. 471–480 (2005)
18. Huang, M.: Design and Implementation of Incremental Music Recommendation System Based on Slope One Algorithm. Chongqing University (2016)
19. Do, M.P.T., et al.: Model-based approach for collaborative filtering. In: 6th International Conference on Information Technology for Education, pp. 217–228 (2010)

20. Luo, X., et al.: An efficient non-negative matrix-factorization-based approach to collaborative filtering for recommender systems. IEEE Trans. Industr. Inf. **10**(2), 1273–1284 (2014)
21. Wang, H.: MatMat: matrix factorization by matrix fitting. In: 2021 IEEE 4th International Conference on Information Systems and Computer Aided Education (ICISCAE), pp.99–101 (2021)
22. Wang, H.: MovieMat: context-aware movie recommendation with matrix factorization by matrix fitting. In: 2021 7th International Conference on Computer and Communications (ICCC), pp. 1642–1645 (2021)
23. Jamali, M., Lakshmanan, L.: Heteromf: recommendation in heterogeneous information networks using context dependent factor models. In: Proceedings of the 22nd international conference on World Wide Web, pp. 643–654 (2013)
24. Shi, C., et al.: Semantic path based personalized recommendation on weighted heterogeneous information networks. In: Acm International on Conference on Information and Knowledge Management, pp. 453–462 (2015)
25. Sun, Y., Han, J.: Mining heterogeneous information networks: a structural analysis approach. ACM SIGKDD Explor. Newsl. **14**(2), 20–28 (2013)
26. Xu, J., et al.: Local matrix factorization with social network embedding. In: 2021 IEEE International Conference on Artificial Intelligence and Industrial Design (AIID), pp. 492–495 (2021)
27. Barathy, R., et al.: Applying matrix factorization in collaborative filtering recommender systems. In: 2020 6th international conference on advanced computing and communication systems (ICACCS), pp. 635–639 (2022)
28. Ma, H., et al.: Sorec: social recommendation using probabilistic matrix factorization. In: Proceedings of the 17th ACM Conference on Information and Knowledge Management, pp. 931–940 (2008)
29. Yang, B., et al.: Social collaborative filtering by trust. IEEE Trans. Pattern Anal. Mach. Intell. **39**(8), 1663–1747 (2013)
30. Han, J., Pan, Y.: A noise-aware asymmetric spectral regularization collective matrix factorization algorithm for recommender system in cloud services. In: 2020 IEEE 13th International Conference on Cloud Computing (CLOUD), pp.502–506 (2020)
31. Laseno, F.U.D., et al.: Knowledge-based filtering recommender system to propose design elements of serious game. In: 2019 International Conference on Electrical Engineering and Informatics (ICEEI), pp.158–163 (2019)
32. Tran, T.: Combining collaborative filtering and knowledge-based approaches for better recommendation systems. J. Bus. Technol. **2**(2), 17–24 (2007)
33. Zhou, F.Y., Jin, L.P., Dong, J.: Review of convolutional neural network. Chin. J. Comput. **40**(6), 23 (2017)
34. Yan, C., Shi, Y.: A personalized location recommendation based on convolutional neural network. In: 2020 IEEE 5th Information Technology and Mechatronics Engineering Conference (ITOEC), pp. 1516–1519 (2020)
35. Liu, J.: Research on Application of Autoencoder in Recommendation System. Tianjin University of Technology (2022)
36. Chen, R.: Recommendation Algorithm Based on Heterogeneous Graph Attention Network and Recurrent Neural Network. Chongqing University (2021)
37. Yao, Q., Liao, X., Jin, H.: Hierarchical attention based recurrent neural network framework for mobile MOBA game recommender systems. In: 2018 IEEE Intl Conf on Parallel & Distributed Processing with Applications, Ubiquitous Computing & Communications, Big Data & Cloud Computing, Social Computing & Networking, Sustainable Computing & Communications (ISPA/IUCC/BDCloud/SocialCom/SustainCom), pp. 338–345. (2018)

38. Ruimeng, C.: Research and Application of Recommendation Algorithm Based on Recurrent Neural Network and Weighted Knowledge Graph. Chongqing University of Technology (2021)
39. Xu, B.: Research on Fairness of Recommendation System Based on Knowledge Graph. School of Computer Science and Engineering (2022)
40. Yin, H., et al.: Social influence-based group representation learning for group recommendation. In: 2019 IEEE 35th International Conference on Data Engineering (ICDE), pp. 566–577 (2019)
41. Guo, L., et al.: Group recommendation with latent voting mechanism. In: 2020 IEEE 36th International Conference on Data Engineering (ICDE), pp. 121–132 (2020)
42. Zhiyi, D.: Research on the Solution of Data Sparsity Problem of Recommendation System Based on Knowledge Graph. School of Computer Science and Engineering (2022)
43. Yinren, L.: Enhanced Personalized Learning Recommender System Based on Knowledge Graph. School of Computer Science and Engineering (2022)
44. Gürbüz, H.G., Tekinerdogan, B.: Software metrics for green parallel computing of big data systems. In: 2016 IEEE International Congress on Big Data (BigData Congress), pp. 345–348 (2016)
45. Li, H., et al.: MSGD: a novel matrix factorization approach for large-scale collaborative filtering recommender systems on GPUs. IEEE Trans. Parallel Distrib. Syst. **29**(7), 1530–1544 (2017)
46. Zhao, X.: A study on e-commerce recommender system based on big data. In: 2019 IEEE 4th International Conference on Cloud Computing and Big Data Analysis (ICCCBDA), pp. 222–226 (2019)
47. Koohi, A., Homayoun, H.: Parallel multi-view graph matrix completion for large input matrix. In: 2019 IEEE 9th Annual Computing and Communication Workshop and Conference (CCWC), pp. 0337–0341 (2019)
48. Sun, J., et al.: A parallel recommender system using a collaborative filtering algorithm with correntropy for social networks. IEEE Trans. Netw. Sci. Eng. **7**(1), 91–103 (2020)
49. Al-Doulat, A.: Surprise and curiosity in a recommender system. In: 2018 IEEE/ACS 15th International Conference on Computer Systems and Applications (AICCSA), pp. 1–2 (2018)
50. Abbas, F.: Serendipity in recommender system: a holistic overview. In: 2018 IEEE/ACS 15th International Conference on Computer Systems and Applications (AICCSA), pp. 1–2 (2018)

An Innovative AdaBoost Process Using Flexible Soft Labels on Imbalanced Big Data

Jinke Wang[1], Biao Song[1(✉)], Xinchang Zhang[1], Yuan Tian[2], and Ran Guo[3]

[1] Nanjing University of Information Science and Technology (NUIST), Nanjing, China
bsong@nuist.edu.cn
[2] Nanjing Institute of Technology (NJIT), Nanjing, China
[3] Cyberspace Institute Advanced Technology, Guangzhou University, Guangzhou, China

Abstract. DNNs (Deep Neural Networks) have been proved to be a successful technique in many areas. Understanding the reasons behind DNN is, however, quite important in assessing trust, which is fundamental if one plans to take action based on leaning results, or when choosing whether to deploy a new model. Lack of insights into the model can be an obstacle that hinders the development and application of the DNN. AdaBoost is a well-known boosting learning technique with better interpretability, combining many relatively weak and inaccurate rules to increase the performance. And as it modified sample weights in the training process, it shows excellent adaptability even in complex cases as it can alleviate overfitting. In the paper, we propose a method training the nets by the AdaBoost based on the soft label, which we call flexibly soft-labeling AdaBoost (FSL AdaBoost). Our soft labels are made in a novel and sequential way, adding further interpretability and adaptability to the learning process. Experimental results on several well-known datasets have validated the effectiveness and novelty of FSL AdaBoost.

Keywords: deep learning · AdaBoost · soft label · noise reduction

1 Introduction

With the rapid development of deep learning, the performance of deep neural networks are getting better and better. It has been proved that deep networks could approximate continuous functions, though the complexity of computation often demands large capacity [1]. In such context, if a network has sufficient capacity, such as parameters, it can even "memorize" every example [2] instead of summarizing the rules, which is not the result we want. In fact, most of the networks have enough capacity to fit, even memorize the training samples [3]. As the net is a "black box" to us, we are unable to know whether it memorize the samples or conclude the laws. Although networks use simple hypotheses to learn the pattern and generalize laws first, it is proved that deep networks have the ability to fit the noise even the noise is complete random noise [4, 5]. Deep networks have

The authors extend their appreciation to National Key Research and Development Program of China (International Technology Cooperation Project No. 2021YFE014400) and National Science Foundation of China (No. 42175194) for funding this work.

been applied to more and more complicated tasks in real life, such as facial expression recognition, network intrusion detection [35], software defect pre-diction [36, 37], and cell detection[38]. In these scenarios, our datasets are often full of noise or have various features, and the datasets are imbalanced in usual [32], making networks difficult to work and often just fit over the training set instead of getting ex-tensive experience. This is the reason why many successful networks have excellent performance in training datasets but can't be applied in real life. All the problems above diminish the adaptability of CNNs.

AdaBoost has show great adaptability to deal with these problems [33]. As a kind of ensemble learning, its core is combing several weak classifiers into a strong classifier by modifying the samples constantly. The advantage of AdaBoost is that by adjusting weights in every round, we could make our model pay more attention to samples matter lot. This could not only raise the efficiency of our model but also enhance the ability to deal with over-fit. Additionally, the datasets in real life are usually imbalanced, which means different classes have different numbers of samples in datasets. By modifying the sample weights, AdaBoost can settle this problem to a certain extent [6, 7].

However, since AdaBoost's tactic of modification is decreasing weights of the sam-ples predicted right and give wrong ones a bigger weight, it is sensitive to the ab-normal samples and noise [18], may cause unknown risks. Especially under the complex envi-ronment, 0 or 1 label is not perfect and accurate. If a sample is inaccurate itself or outlier compared to the other ones, AdaBoost may pay too much attention to the ab-normal sam-ples. If nothing is done, the wrong feature will be concluded, causing a chain reaction and making more wrong predictions.

To deal with the label noise, we combine AdaBoost with soft-label and propose a method named FSL AdaBoost that can provide more information while avoiding over-fitting. As soft labels use several probabilities to represent the features of the samples, it can encompass more dimensions of information. Just like the facial expression is often consisted of several types of feelings [9], a hard label can't reflect it precisely. In our method, we make several classifiers with different subjects to evaluate the samples. In this way, we can strengthen the monitorship of training and increase the interpretability of the process. According to the different performance of the samples under classifiers, we take different measure to construct their soft labels. The high-quality samples will be given the "sharp" soft label to stress the main feature of sample, this can help net conclude the laws. The low-quality samples, in other word, the samples contain complicated feature, will get a "gentle" soft label to augment the label information and eliminate the label loss of the hard label in the beginning, Even the samples difficult to be predicted right can provide useful information and experience when it is predicted wrong in the AdaBoost part, preventing the estimator to conclude the wrong laws from the low-quality samples in the AdaBoost part when the wrong samples have the higher weights. As we make soft labels in different ways under different condition, the labels are more flexible and contain less label noise than the used one, increasing the adaptability and applicability of method.

In this paper, we unite the advantages of AdaBoost and soft label to enhance the ability of the network. In Sect. 2, we will introduce the two methods particularly and the other researches on them. Section 3 shows the main process and principle of FSL

AdaBoost. Our experiments can be seen in Sect. 4. Lastly, a conclusion and our future work are presented in Sect. 5.

2   Related Work

In this section, we will introduce some characteristics of AdaBoost and soft-label and related work about the two methods.

2.1   AdaBoost

Ensemble learning has shown outstanding effects in the past years, which com-bines some weak learners to create a strong learner. It has been proved that if a concept could be weakly learned, it is strongly learnable absolutely [14]. AdaBoost is one of the most important and effective ensemble methods without a doubt. Since AdaBoost was proposed, variants of it have been created continuously. Such as Discrete AdaBoost, Real AdaBoost, and Gentle AdaBoost [15, 16]. No doubt that AdaBoost has a great effect, but the reason behind the high efficiency is not so clear. Michiel Collins and Robert E. Schapire give a unified explanation of boosting and logistic regression learning problems, using optimization of Bregman distances [17]. Carlos Domingo and Osamu Watanabe came up with an optimized method named MadaBoost that can mend some problems of AdaBoost, which are that AdaBoost is unable to be used in the boosting by filtering framework and AdaBoost seems to not good at resisting noise [18]. Wenyang Wanga and Dongchu Sun presented two improved AdaBoost algorithms: the Enhanced AdaBoost and Reinforced AdaBoost by adjusting the weights of weaker classifiers, including global error rate and the positive class accuracy rate, and to enhance the effect, the new algorithms consider the degree of imbalance. It has been shown that Enhanced AdaBoost aims to the datasets whose degree of imbalance is big and the Reinforced AdaBoost is more adept at dealing with the slightly imbalanced ones [19]. Jingjing Cao et al. propose a noise-detection AdaBoost by labeling the noisy instances at each iteration and adding a regeneration condition to control the ensemble training error bound. And their experiments show that there will be different effects when the function is different: The method based on K-NN is better than EM-based method [20]. Boosting algorithms emphasizing on choosing subset of features to construct ensembles of classifiers is a different direction compared to selecting subset of instances to generate new weight distribution [20]. Random subspace method (RSM) is a standard method to randomly choose a subspace from the original feature space, which could be composed from any base classifier [28]. In [29], Satoshi et al. empirically showed that combining RSM and AdaBoost algorithm could decrease generalization error compared to using RSM and AdaBoost, respectively. Additionally, Nicolas et al. improved the performance of the RSM-based AdaBoost by paying attention to the discriminate information among subspaces [30].

2.2   Soft Label

Soft-label has proved better performance in many cases as it can connect each sample with complicated classes. Yanling Gan et al. proposed a soft-label constructor based on CNN, through which each class can get a new label and use a soft label perturbation strategy to enhance discrimination ability[8]. X. Geng used a bivariate Gaussian function to construct soft labels to describe the smooth transition characteristic of head poses [24]. Labels are an important part of training, however, it's time-consuming and human-annotated labels are not right forever [34]. By contraries, unlabeled samples are available easily. The soft label can address this problem to a certain extent. As the semi-supervised method has been shown more effective than using unlabeled samples only [10]. Mingbo Zhao et al. presented a new method propagating the label information from labeled to enhance conventional LDA performance [10]. Tianyu Liu et al. have proposed a noise-tolerant method for extracting distantly-supervised relation depending on the soft label which could correct wrong labels during training dynamically [11]. Quang Nguyen et al. researched on active learning and wanted to get better models by getting more information from the labeled samples. Their works depend on the classical algorithm but allow to learn with both binary class and soft label information [12]. Görkem Algan and Ilkay Ulusoy proposed a new framework based on meta soft label that can resist labels noise [13]. Luhui Xu et al. used a smooth Gaussian function as input to construct soft labels and optimized soft labels by two types of objective functions: KL divergence loss and Jeffreys divergence loss. And then applied the labels into a regularized convolutional neural network architecture that has proved more robust and stable[25]. To address the cross-database recognition problem, Xiaoqing Wang et al. used GAN to generate samples. In the process of training CNN based on the unlabelled GAN generated samples, they introduced a distributed pseudo label method (DPL). In their method, domain adaptation can be achieved with limited target data without ground truth labels [26]. Barsoum et al. relabeled the FER-2013 database with soft labels according to the manual annotation results of 10 taggers, showing that the multiple labels per image boost the classification accuracy compared with the traditional approach of single label from majority voting [27].

3 Methodology

In this Section, we will introduce the main process of FSL-AdaBoost.

3.1 The General Framework

The main structure of the FSL AdaBoost includes two parts, making soft labels and training based on the AdaBoost. In the labels-making stage, we propose to flexibly generate individual soft labels for every sample through a novel and meaningful process rather than using existing class-unified soft labels. We will train different kinds of classifiers to evaluate the samples. Different samples have different ways to get their label depending on the performance of the different estimators, so the label can adapt itself to the feature, having a more flexible choice to broaden the method's applicability. The second part is the AdaBoost. In this part, we will train the estimators with the soft labels we construct before. Though continuously adjusting sample weights and training new estimator in dependence on the updated weights, the final estimator constructed by the combination of the previous estimators can have a better performance. From the Fig. 1, we can see the general structure of FSL.

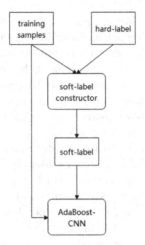

Fig. 1. The General Structure of FSL.

3.2 Creating Soft Labels

Firstly, the individual soft label is constructed in a sequential way. In the beginning, we create weakened classifiers by training C different estimators $\{W_0, W_1, \ldots W_{C-1}\}$, where C is the total number of the classes. The W_i classifier will be trained by the train data where the sample weights of class i. are deliberately reduced to be smaller than that of other classes. We will set a parameter β. (greater than one at least) to control the degree of weight modification. The sample weights of class i. are set to $1/\beta$. And the others are set to 1. In such condition, if the W_i classifier could predict the i_{th} class samples right, the right ones will be given the hard label which they are used to be. The second classifier is the normal one where we give every sample the same weight and train a estimator N. The samples can be predicted right in the second classifier but wrong in the weakened one will be given the soft label, which is estimator's output, a C-dimensional vector in the form of one-hot code. In the third stage, we will train C classifier $\{S_0, S_1, \ldots S_{C-1}\}$ again just like the first stage. The difference, however, is that the S_i classifier will be trained by the train data that the sample weights of class i are bigger than other classes, in the other words, in this condition, the i_{th} class sample weights atrengthened. We will give samples of class i the weight of β and the others the weight of 1. If the i_{th} class samples could be predicted by the S_i classifier but wrong in the first two kinds of classifiers, we will give them the soft label, too. But the different point ithat, unlike the second stage, we will do such modification by (1) instead give the output only.

$$L_x = softmax(\sqrt{S_j^0(x)}, \sqrt{S_j^1(x)}, \sqrt{S_j^2(x)} \ldots \ldots \sqrt{S_j^{C-1}(x)}) \tag{1}$$

where L_x is the new label of the sample x, $(S_j^0(x), S_j^1(x), S_j^2(x), \ldots \ldots S_j^{C-1}(x))$ is the output vector of the estimator S_j when the input is sample x, and j is the real class of the sample x. The *softmax* activation is a type of normilization, which is defined in (2). Through this activation, we can not only ensure each sample has the same weight in the beginning, preventing the trainning stage is unfair, but also can reflect the possibility of each class intuitively by mapping the number to the number between 0 and 1 and accelerate the convergence [31].

$$L_x^i = \frac{e^{\sqrt{S_j^i(x)}}}{\sum_{k=0}^{C-1} e^{\sqrt{S_j^k(x)}}} \tag{2}$$

In the last stage, there are still some samples not labeled the first three stages, we will remove them from the training set.

The general process and some samples could be show in Fig. 2 below. And the Table 1 is the pseudo code of this part. Firstly, the dataset will be predicted by the weakened classifiers. Every sample will be predicted by the classifier corresponding to the sample's real class. If the sample is predicted right, just like the first sample above, it will be given the hard label just as the label it used to be. And then, other samples will be transmitted to the normal classifier. The samples predicted right by the normal one will get the soft label that is the same as the output of the classifier, just like the second sample in Fig. 2. The samples, however, predicted wrong again will be transmitted to the strengthened classifiers corresponding to the sample's class. Under this circumstance, if the sample could be classified correctly, the output of the classifier will be calculated by (1) (2) and then the computation will be given to the sample, just like the third sample in Fig. 2. The output is the [0.05 0.02 0.81 0.02 0.1 0] and the new label is [0.149128 0.13736197 0.29330066 0.13736197 0.16360025 0.11924715]. Lastly, there are still remaining samples without labels, this part will be deleted and the others with their new labels will become a new dataset as a whole.

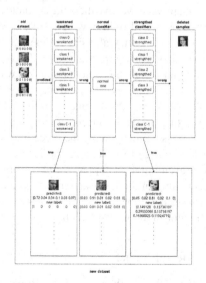

Fig. 2. Soft Label Generation Process.

Table 1. Pseudo code of making soft labels

In the beginning, we have the training set $\{X, Y\}$, and set a parameter β.
1) for i = 0 to $C - 1$, where C is the number of classes:
 $weights[Y == i] = 1/\beta$.
 $weights[Y! = i] = 1$.
use $\{X, Y\}$ and $weights$ to train an estimator W_i.
 the i_{th} class samples that can be predicted right will be given the hard
label.
2) use $\{X, Y\}$ to train a estimator N.
all the unlabeled samples that can be predicted right will be given the soft label
$N(x)$.
3) for i=0 to $C - 1$:
 $weights[Y == i] = \beta$.
 $weights[Y! = i] = 1$.
use $\{X, Y\}$ and $weights$ to train an estimator S_i
 the unlabeled samples of the i_{th} class that can be predicted right will be
given the soft label calculated by (1).
4) delete the unlabeled samples from X and get a new input set X', using X'
and the new label set Y' form a new set $\{X', Y'\}$.
save $\{X', Y'\}$.

The process above is not difficult to understand. Samples can be classified into the right class even when the right class has a smaller weight comparatively. This means these samples have evident features so we give them the absolute hard label. The samples at the second stage could be predicted right have relatively evident features, too. But, worse than the first ones. This means they also have some features of other classes, so we make them have the soft label. The samples at the third stage are the ones predicted right only when they have bigger weights. It is not hard to know that this kind of sample has the feature of the right class, but not evident, and they have complicated features so the soft labels are no doubt the choice. As the output of the estimator is created under the circumstance that the right class is enhanced, we use square root to maintain the leading position of the right class while reducing the preceding degree of the right class. Then, we use softmax activation (2) to normalize the labels to make the sum of the label's elements equals 1, preventing the samples' weights from becoming unbalanced. The feature of samples remaining in the last stage may be too complicated to classify, even their label may be wrong in the beginning. If we reserve them, they could cause deviation and take the estimator in the wrong direction.

3.3   AdaBoost Based on the Soft Label

After the soft-label stage, we will enter the stage of AdaBoost. The traditional method is commonly applied to the two-class classification problem, and CNN has too deep structures and too many learning parameters which will reduce the effect if we decrease the weights of the right predicted samples, so we adopt the multi-class AdaBoost method proposed by Zhu et al. [21] and AdaBoost-CNN proposed by Aboozar Taherkhania et al. [22] which combines AdaBoost with the multi-class classification.

In AdaBoost-CNN, samples weights will be initialized by $1/n$, where n. . is the number of samples, and updated by (3)(4) after every round.

$$w_i^{m+1} = w_i^m \exp\left(-\alpha \frac{C-1}{C} L_i \cdot \log\left(G^m(x_i)\right)\right), i = 0, 1, 2 \ldots \ldots n - 1 \qquad (3)$$

$$w_i^{m+1} = \frac{w_i^{m+1}}{\sum_{t=1}^{n} w_t^{m+1}} \qquad (4)$$

where w_i^m is thre weight of the ith sample which will be used by the mth round's estimator, α is the learning rate, and L_i is the updated soft label of the ith sample. $G^m(x_i)$ is the output vector of the mth rnd's estimator when the input is the ith sample. After updating the weights, they are normalized by dividing them by the sum of the weights to limit the sum to 1 (4).

For the large number of learning parameters, the number of weakly trained samples seems smaller. Then the subsequent estimators will concentrate on the weakly trained part only, making estimators become over fitted on the untrained part [22]. So AdaBoost-CNN take advantage of transfer learning, changing the way of training the CNN, from starting with a random initial condition to training in dependence of the previous estimator. After i^{th} round, we will get estimator G_i and update the sample weights. And then, the $i + 1^{th}$ round will start, the updated weights will be transmitted to the estimator G_{i+1} and train it.

At last, we will get a list of estimators $\{G_1, G_2, \ldots G_M\}$, they will be assembled and the result of the total estimators will be obtained by (5).

$$class(x) = argmax \sum_{m=1}^{M} h_c^m(x) \qquad (5)$$

where $h_c^m(x)$ is C-dimensional vector calculated by (6) and M is the number of the rounds, and the number of estimators, too.

$$h_c^m(x) = (C - 1)\left(\log(G^m(x)) - \frac{1}{C}\sum_{\tilde{c}=1}^{C} \log(G_{\tilde{c}}^m(x))\right) \qquad (6)$$

where $G^m(x)$ the output vector of the estimator G_m when the input is x, and $G_{\tilde{c}}^m(x)$ is the $\tilde{c}^{th}$ element of $G^m(x)$. The main process is shown below in Fig. 3.

4 Experiments

We will introduce the experiments in the folllowing section, including the datasets and experiment results and analyze the methhod according results. In the experiments, we borrow and modify the code of Aboozar Taherkhani in [22] (https://github.com/a-taherk hani/AdaBoost_CNN) to realize the AdaBoost part.

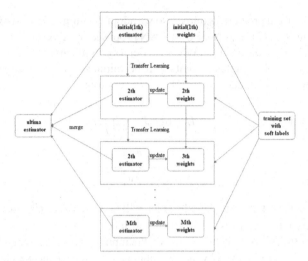

Fig. 3. Schematic plot of the AdaBoost based on the updated labels

4.1 Datasets

To evaluate FSL AdaBoost completely, we utilise FER-2013 [23] as our experiments' datasets.

FER-2013 is the dataset used for FER competition in ICML 2013 challenges in representation learning. It contains a train set with 28,709 pictures, a validation set with 3,589 pictures, and a test set with 3,589 pictures. All the 35,887 pictures are divided into seven classes: anger, disgust, fear, happiness, sadness, surprise, and neutral. Each picture is a gray level image which has the size of 48 × 48 pixels. There are some samples in Fig. 4. Different from usual datasets, FER-2013 is closer to reality. First, the dataset is unbalanced. There is a big gap between numbers of different classes, the general condition could be seen in Fig. 5. In addition, there may be some pictures consist of different emotions which are difficult to be classified. It means that even the labels could be imprecise or wrong, making noise in the dataset.

Fig. 4. Samples in FER-2013

4.2 Experiments Results

This section will show the results of the experiments. To rule out the influence of chance, every experiment below will be conducted ten times at least. And the data be-low are the average number of the results of the several experiments.

We compare the method with the single CNN and AdaBoost-CNN. The results of the experiments can be seen in Fig. 5. The results show that AdaBoost needs enough epochs to train for every estimator. When the number of epochs is small, the estimator can't be trained enough and this results in wrong predictions. If a estimator is not trained enough, the updating of sample weights after training will cause errors, decreasing accuracy rate. Additionally, AdaBoost-CNN based on hard label loses efficacy in this experiment. Through analysis, we know the reason. By observing the training process, we find that the estimators except the first one in the AdaBoost have terrible performance. As the dataset has a mass of label noise, the estimator is difficult to generalize the laws and predict right. And the core of AdaBoost is paying more attention to the wrong predicted samples, this causes a vicious circle: more noise a sample has, more easily it will be predicted wrong, then it gets higher weight and more wrong laws the estimator will generalize. So the updating of the samples will lose its balance and the estimator trained based on this sample weights will learn nothing in the end. FSL AdaBoost has another advantage is that it can resist the overfit to a certain extent. The figure shows that with the increasing of epochs, the accuracy of a single CNN will decrease instead when the number of epochs is big enough, the main reason is the phenomenon of overfitting. If the number of training epochs is too big, the estimator will learn too much, even the noise of the dataset. Although AdaBoost-CNN trains a new estimator based on the old one, it will modify the weight of samples after each round, meaning that the new

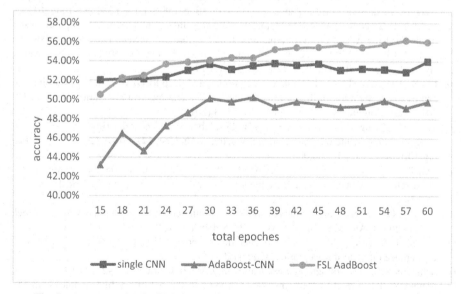

Fig. 5. Accuracy of a single CNN, AdaBoost-CNN and FSL AdaBoost on FER-2013

estimator convergence forward a new direction different from the old one, resisting the phenomenon of overfitting.

5 Conclusion

In this paper, we propose a new method called FSL AdaBoost that combines AdaBoost with soft weights. Compared to the traditional method, FSL AdaBoost performs better in a complicated environment full of noise especially the label noise. The hard label can't encompass all the information if the sample is complicated. To deal with this problem, the soft label is a good choice. As the data in real life is not always normative, the quality of data varies widely. This is a huge obstacle for training. We use a novel method to obtain the soft weight by evaluating the quality of samples and use different ways to treat them to resist the discrepancy among samples.

References

1. Cybenko, G.: Approximation by superpositions of a sigmoidal function. Math. Control Signals Syst. **2**(4), 303–314 (1989). https://doi.org/10.1007/BF02551274
2. Goodfellow, I., Bengio, Y., Courville, A.: Deep Learning. MIT Press (2016). http://www.dee plearningbook.org
3. Zhang, C., Bengio, S., Hardt, M., Recht, B., Vinyals, O.: Understanding deep learning requires rethinking generalization. arXiv preprint arXiv:1611.03530 (2016)
4. Krueger, D., et al.: Deep nets don't learn via memorization (2017)
5. Arpit, D., et al.: A closer look at memorization in deep networks. In: Proceedings of the 34th International Conference on Machine Learning-vol. 70, pp. 233–242 (2017)
6. Lee, W., Jun, C.H., Lee, J.S.: Instance categorization by support vector machines to adjust weights in AdaBoost for imbalanced data classification. Inf. Sci. (Ny) **381**, 92–103 (2017)
7. Lima, N.H.C., Neto, A.D.D., De Melo, J.D.: Creating an ensemble of diverse support vector machines using Adaboost. In: International Joint Conference on Neural Networks (2009)
8. Gan, Y., Chen, J., Xu, L.: Facial expression recognition boostedby soft label with a diverse ensemble. Pattern Recogn. Lett. **125**, 105–112 (2019)
9. Li , S., Deng, W., Du, J.: Reliable crowdsourcing and deep locality-preserving learning for expression recognition in the wild. Computer Vision and Pattern Recognition (CVPR). In: 2017 IEEE Conference on IEEE, pp. 2584–2593 (2017)
10. Zhao, M., Zhang, Z., Chow, T.W.S., Li, B.: Soft label based linear discriminant analysis for image recognition and retrieval. Comput. Vis. Image Underst. **121**, 86–99 (2014). https://doi. org/10.1016/j.cviu.2014.01.008
11. Liu, T., Wang, K., Chang, B., Sui, Z.: A soft-label method for noise-tolerant distantly super-vised relation extraction. In: Proceedings of the 2017 Conference on Empirical Methods (2017)
12. Nguyen, Q., Valizadega, H., Hauskrecht, M.: Learning classification models with soft-label information. J. Am. Med. Inform. Assoc. **21**, 501–508 (2014)
13. Algan, G., Ulusoy, I.: Meta soft label generation for noisy labels. In: 2020 25th International Conference on Pattern Recognition (ICPR) (2021)
14. Schapire, R.E.: The strength of weak learnability. Mach. Learn. **5**, 197–227 (1990)
15. Freund, Y., Schapire, R.E.: Experiments with a new boosting algorithm. In: Machine Learning: Proceedings of the Thirteenth International Conference, Morgan Kauman, SanFrancisco, pp. 148–156 (1996)

16. Lienhart, R., Kuranov, A., Pisarevsky, V.: Empirical analysis of detection cascades of boosted classifiers for rapid object detection. In: Michaelis, B., Krell, G. (eds.) DAGM 2003. LNCS, vol. 2781, pp. 297–304. Springer, Heidelberg (2003). https://doi.org/10.1007/978-3-540-45243-0_39

17. Collins, M., Schapire, R.E., Singer, Y.: Logistic regression, adaboost and bregman distances. In: Thirteenth Conference on Computational (2000)

18. Domingo, C.: MadaBoost: A modification of AdaBoost. In: Proceedings of the 13th Conference on Computational Learning Theory (2013)

19. Wang, W., Sun, D.: The improved AdaBoost algorithms for imbalanced data classification. Inform. Sci. **563**, 358–374 (2021)

20. Cao, J., Kwong, S., Wang, R.: A noise-detection based AdaBoost algorithm for mislabeled data. Pattern Recog. **45**(12), 4451–4465 (2012)

21. Ji, Z., Hui, Z., Rosset, S., Hastie, T.: Multi-class AdaBoost. Stat. Its Interface **2**, 349–360 (2009)

22. Taherkhani, A., Cosma, G., McGinnity, T.M.: AdaBoost-CNN: an adaptive boosting algorithm for convolutional neural networks to classify multi-class imbalanced datasets using transfer learning. Neurocomputing **404**, 351–366 (2020)

23. Goodfellow, I.J., et al.: Challenges in representation learning: a report on three machine learning contests. In: Lee, M., Hirose, A., Hou, Z.-G., Kil, R.M. (eds.) ICONIP 2013. LNCS, vol. 8228, pp. 117–124. Springer, Heidelberg (2013). https://doi.org/10.1007/978-3-642-42051-1_16

24. Geng, X., Xia, Y.: Head pose estimation based on multivariate label distribution. In: Proceedings of the IEEE Conference on Computer Vision and Pattern Recognition, pp. 1837–1842 (2014)

25. Xu, L., Chen, J., Gan, Y.: Head pose estimation with soft labels using regularized convolutional neural network. Neurocomputing **337**, 339–353 (2019)

26. Wang, X., Wang, X., Ni, Y.: Unsupervised domain adaptation for facial expression recognition using generative adversarial networks. Comput. Intell. Neurosci. **2018**, 1–10 (2018). https://doi.org/10.1155/2018/7208794

27. Barsoum, E., Zhang, C., Ferrer, C.C., Zhang, Z.: Training deep networks for facial expression recognition with crowd-sourced label distribution. In: Proceedings of the 18th ACM International Conference on Multimodal Interaction, ACM, pp. 279–283 (2016)

28. Ho, T.: The random subspace method for constructing decision forests. IEEE Trans. Pattern Anal. Mach. Intell. **20**(8), 832–844 (1998)

29. Shirai, S., Kudo, M., Nakamura, A.: Comparison of bagging and boosting algorithms on sample and feature weighting. In: Benediktsson, J.A., Kittler, J., Roli, F. (eds.) MCS 2009. LNCS, vol. 5519, pp. 22–31. Springer, Heidelberg (2009). https://doi.org/10.1007/978-3-642-02326-2_3

30. García-Pedrajas, N., Ortiz-Boyer, D.: Boosting random subspace method. Neural Netw. **21**(9), 1344–1362 (2008)

31. Rao, Q., Yu, B., He, K., Feng, B.: Regularization and Iterative Initialization of Softmax for Fast Training of Convolutional Neural Networks. In: 2019 International Joint Conference on Neural Networks (IJCNN), 30 Sep 2019

32. Masko, D., Hensman. P.: The Impact of Imbalanced Training Data for Convolutional Neural Networks. Bachelor thesis, KTH, Sch. Comput. Sci. Commun. (2015)

33. Hu, W., Maybank, S.: AdaBoost-based algorithm for network intrusion detection. In: IEEE Transactions on Systems, Man, and Cybernetics, Part B: Cybernetics, 1 Apr 2008

34. Ahfock, D., McLachlan, G.J.: Harmless label noise and informative soft-labels in supervised classification. Comput. Stat. Data Anal. **161**, 107253 (2021)

35. Ochiuddin Miah, M., Shahriar Khan, S., Shatabda, S., Farid, D.M.: Improving detection accuracy for imbal-anced network intrusion classification using cluster-based under-sampling with random forests. In: 2019 1st International Conference on Advances in Science, Engineering and Robotics Technology (ICASERT), pp. 1–5. IEEE (2019)
36. Bennin, K.E., Keung, J., Phannachitta, P., Monden, A., Mensah, S.: Mahakil: diversity based oversampling approach to alleviate the class imbalance issue in software defect prediction. IEEE Trans. Software Eng. **44**(6), 534–550 (2017)
37. Song, Q., Guo, Y., Shepperd, M.: A comprehensive investigation of the role of imbalanced learning for software defect prediction. IEEE Trans. Software Eng. **45**(12), 1253–1269 (2018)
38. Cruz-Roa, A.A., Ovalle, J.E.A., Madabhushi, A., Osorio, F.A.G.: A deep learning architecture for image representation, visual interpretability and automated basal-cell carcinoma cancer detection. In: Salinesi, C., Norrie, M.C., Pastor, Ó. (eds.) Advanced Information Systems Engineering: 25th International Conference, CAiSE 2013, Valencia, Spain, June 17-21, 2013. Proceedings, pp. 403–410. Springer Berlin Heidelberg, Berlin, Heidelberg (2013). https://doi.org/10.1007/978-3-642-40763-5_50

Artificial Intelligence and Machine Learning Security

Feature Fusion Based IPSO-LSSVM Fault Diagnosis of On-Load Tap Changers

Honghua Xu[⊠], Laibi Yin, Ziqiang Xu, Qian Xin, and Mengjie Lv

State Grid Nanjing Power Supply Company, Nanjing 320105, China
`honghuawl@126.com`

Abstract. Aiming at the problem of single characteristic quantity and low accuracy of traditional on-load tap changers, this paper presents a fault diagnosis algorithm of on-load tap changers based on IPSO-LSSVM. Firstly, the time-frequency signal extracted from the vibration signal and the improved scale permutation entropy form a multi-feature fusion matrix; Then, considering the redundancy and high computational complexity of the multi-dimensional feature matrix, the principal component analysis is used to screen the feature subset and obtain the sensitive feature subset; Finally, IPSO-LSSVM is used to select and classify the initial feature subset. Experimental results show that the classification accuracy of IPSO-LSSVM is improved by at least 5% compared with other methods.

Keywords: On load tap changers · IPSO-LSSVM · principal component analysis · classification accuracy

1 Introduction

On-load tap changer (OLTC) is one of the core equipment of the power system, and its operation is of great significance to the operation reliability of the whole power system. According to relevant statistics in recent years, OLTC mechanical faults account for 27.8% of the total transformer faults [1, 2]. Therefore, based on developing the mechanical state of OLTC, the research of the common fault diagnosis and recognition algorithm of tap changers has become one of the hot spots in the electrical field [3, 4].

The vibration signal of contact opening and closing during OLTC switching contains a large amount of mechanical state information of equipment [5–10]. This idea was first proposed by Bengtsson et al. of ABB in 1990, and then it has been paid more and more attention at home and abroad, and some effective. OLTC diagnosis methods have been put forward [11]. In view of the nonstationary and strong time-varying characteristics of OLTC vibration signal, various OLTC vibration signal analysis methods have been proposed from different angles at home and abroad. P Kang et al. used continuous wavelet transform (CWT) to analyze the vibration signal of OLTC. The state database of OLTC is established by the "Ridge back distribution map" of two-dimensional wavelet coefficients, and the "Ridge back map" of different types of faults is compared with the database. On this basis, the paper proposes an OLTC mechanical diagnosis method based on Kohonen's self-organizing map, which has been applied in the field [12–14]. In [15,

Y. Tian et al. (Eds.): ICBDS 2022, CCIS 1796, pp. 187–199, 2023.
https://doi.org/10.1007/978-981-99-3300-6_14

16] the empirical mode decomposition method and the variational mode decomposition method decompose the vibration signal to obtain the natural mode component. Then the optimized autocorrelation vector machine and the support effect finite support vector machine are used to analyze and diagnose the mechanism jam, main contact looseness, spring looseness and other faults of OLTC. However, the above methods fail to analyze the signal essence of OLTC, thus affecting the fault diagnosis accuracy of OLTC. According to this, the phase space reconstruction method is used in [17] to reconstruct the vibration from low dimension to high dimension signal. The phase point spatial distribution coefficient is used to realize the fault diagnosis of OLTC. Similarly, based on phase space reconstruction in [18], the K-means algorithm and the OLTC fault diagnosis method of cluster displacement vector center are proposed, and the different working conditions of OLTC are judged. However, the characteristics obtained by this method do not have regularity. In [19], aiming at the defects of the K-means clustering algorithm, the locust algorithm is adopted to improve it. Its fault diagnosis method based on the chaos principle and GOA-K-means is proposed. The proposed eigenvector has certain regularity and can identify typical OLTC faults.

In fault diagnosis and identification, the support vector machine method [20], Markov chain method [7], and Convolutional Neural Network (CNN) [21] method are commonly used. A support vector machine is suitable for small sample fault diagnosis, but it is sensitive to initial parameters. In [7] proposes an OLTC fault diagnosis method based on the Hidden Markov model (HMM). But this method has the problem that the characteristic signal is ignored as a noise signal due to the data synchronization. In [7], the CNN model is used to diagnose different faults of OLTC. However, deep learning requires big data training to reach the ideal state, while OLTC has few fault samples, which is difficult to meet the actual needs. Based on the above analysis, this paper proposes a fault diagnosis method for on-load tap changers based on feature fusion and IPSO-LSSVM.

2 Construction of Characteristic Matrix Based on OLTC Vibration Signal

2.1 Time Domain Feature Extraction

When the OLTC fails, the mechanical state will change. Therefore, the amplitude and frequency components of the vibration signal of OLTC will change. Therefore, this paper uses the time-domain statistical method to extract the vibration characteristics of OLTC.

(1) Root mean square value

$$C_1 = \sqrt{\frac{1}{N} \sum_{i=1}^{N} (x_i)^2} \tag{1}$$

(2) Kurtosis value

$$C_2 = \left(1 / N \sum_{i=1}^{N} x_i \middle/ \sqrt{\sum_{i=1}^{N} (x_i - t_m)^2 / N} \right)^4 \tag{2}$$

(3) Skewness index

$$C_w = \frac{\sqrt{n(n-1)}}{n-2} \frac{\frac{1}{n}\sum\limits_{i=1}^{n}(x_i - \bar{x})^2}{(\frac{1}{n}\sum\limits_{i=1}^{n}(x_i - \bar{x})^2)^{\frac{3}{2}}} \tag{3}$$

(4) Waveform index

$$S_t = \frac{(\frac{1}{n}\sum\limits_{i=1}^{n}x_i^2)^{1/2}}{\frac{1}{n}\sum\limits_{i=1}^{n}|x_i|} \tag{4}$$

(5) Peak index and pulse index

$$I_p = \frac{X_p}{(\frac{1}{n}\sum\limits_{i=1}^{n}x_i^2)^{1/2}} \tag{5}$$

$$C_f = \frac{X_p}{\frac{1}{n}\sum\limits_{i=1}^{n}|x_i|} \tag{6}$$

where, I_P and C_F represent peak quality assurance and pulse index respectively. Through the above feature analysis, the time-domain statistical feature vector of the vibration signal is obtained as follows:

$$X_t = [C_1, C_2, C_w, S_f, I_P, C_f] \tag{7}$$

2.2 IMPE Feature Extraction

Multi-scale permutation entropy (MPE) is an index to measure the complexity of a signal. The more complex the signal sequence is, the larger the entropy value is. By changing the time scale, more minute features of the signal sequence can be characterized. The calculation steps of multi-scale arrangement entropy are as follows [24]:

(1) Assuming that the signal sequence is $x(T)$, the signal sequence is coarsened as shown in Eq. (8), and a reconstructed sequence $y(T)$ is formed, wherein the number of parameters is N/τ.

$$y_j^\tau = \frac{1}{\tau} \sum_{i=(j-1)\tau+!}^{j\tau} x_i, 1 \leq j \leq \left[\frac{N}{\tau}\right] \tag{8}$$

where $\left[\frac{N}{\tau}\right]$ represents the rounding function.

(2) When the embedding dimension is equal to m, the signal reconstruction sequence is mapped to the phase space, and the multi-scale arrangement entropy is calculated according to the order of the row vectors in the phase space, it is shown as Eq. (9):

$$MPE(x, \tau, m, \tau) = PE(y_j^\tau, m, \delta) \tag{9}$$

For the above arrangement entropy calculation method, the main problems are as follows: ① when the signal is coarse grained, the mean value is taken as the reconstruction parameter, so it is sensitive to signal mutation. ② MPE requires a high number of signal sequences. When the time scale increases, the accuracy of MPE also decreases. The specific improvement steps are as follows:

1) First, the coarse granulation process of IMPE(improved multiscale permutation entropy) is to divide the signal sequence x (T) into $x(t)(x_1, x_2, ..., x_{1+\tau})$, $(x_2, x_3, ..., x_{2+\tau})$, $(x_3, x_4, ..., x_{3+\tau})$ ...The mean value is obtained in an incremental manner, and a new signal sequence $z_i^{(\tau)}(i = 1, 2, \cdots, \tau)$ is formed.

$$\begin{cases} z_i^{(\tau)} = \{y_{i,1}^{(\tau)}, y_{i,2}^{(\tau)}, \cdots, y_{i,n}^{(\tau)}\} \\ y_{i,j}^{(\tau)} = \dfrac{\sum\limits_{f=0}^{\tau-1} x_{f+i+(j-1)\tau}}{\tau} \end{cases} \tag{10}$$

2) Then the reconstructed signal sequence is reconstructed. When the embedding dimension is equal to m, the time scale is equal to τ. The MPE values of each group were calculated [25]:

$$MPE(x, \tau, m, \delta) = PE(z_i^\tau, m, \delta) \tag{11}$$

3) Finally, the different MPE values of τ group were averaged to obtain the IMPE value.

By improving the multi-scale permutation entropy to measure the complexity of the signal, the detailed components are more refined in the process of signal coarsening, and the signal characteristics can be accurately characterized when the number of signal sampling points is small, further improving the accuracy of traditional multi-scale permutation entropy calculation.

2.3 Construction of Feature Fusion Matrix

Combined with the above features, the time domain features and IMPE features are fused in this paper. Firstly, the CEEMD [25] algorithm is used to decompose OLTC vibration signals to obtain K IMFs, and the IMPE value is calculated for each IMF component. The matrix representation of IMPE is as follows:

$$IMPE = \begin{bmatrix} IMPE_{1,1} & IMPE_{1,2} & \cdots & IMPE_{1,s} \\ IMPE_{2,1} & IMPE_{2,2} & \cdots & IMPE_{2,s} \\ \vdots & \vdots & \ddots & \vdots \\ IMPE_{k,1} & IMPE_{k,2} & \cdots & IMPE_{k,s} \end{bmatrix} \tag{12}$$

where, $IMPE_{k,s}$ represents the IMPE value obtained from the Kth IMF element under the scale factor S, and the average value of IMF from 1 to k is calculated as follows:

$$\overline{IMPE} = [\overline{IMPE}_1, \overline{IMPE}_2, \cdots, \overline{IMPE}_s] \tag{13}$$

Combined with time-frequency features, the specific representation of all features after fusion is shown as follows:

$$Q = [X_f, \overline{IMPE}] \tag{14}$$

3 OLTC Fault Diagnosis Model Based on IPSO-LSSVM

3.1 IPSO Algorithm

Aiming at the problem that the traditional PSO algorithm is prone to fall into local optimization and early convergence, the reverse learning strategy and the inertia weight nonlinear decreasing strategy are introduced into the basic PSO algorithm. The specific improvements are as follows:

(1) The particle population was initialized by the reverse learning mechanism [26]:

$$\bar{x} = a + b - x \tag{15}$$

where, $x \in [a,b]$, x is a real number, $\bar{x}$ and is the reverse point.

(2) Aiming at the defects of PSO algorithm, such as premature and falling into local optimization in the later stage ω. The weight reduction strategy is adopted as follows:

$$\omega = (\omega_{max} - \omega_{min})(\frac{k}{T_{max}})^2 \tag{16}$$

where in ω_{max} is the maximum value of inertia weight, ω_{min} is the minimum value of inertia weight, K is the current iteration number, and T_{max} is the maximum iteration number. $\omega_{max} = 0.9$, $\omega_{min} = 0.4$。

(3) Particle velocity and position update

$$V_i^{t+1} = \omega \cdot v_i^t + c_1 \cdot rand_1 \cdot (pbest_i - X_i^t) + c_2 \cdot rand_2 \cdot (gbest_i - X_i^t) \tag{17}$$

$$X_i^{t+1} = X_i^t + V_i^{t+1} \tag{18}$$

where w represents the inertia weight, which measures the influence weight of the previous generation particles on the current generation particles in the particle learning process, c_1 and c_2 represent the learning factor, $rand_1$ and $rand_2$ represent the selection between 0 and 1, $pbest_i$ represents the individual extreme value of the i-th particle, $pbest_i$ represents the extreme global value of the i-th particle, V_i^{t+1} represents the speed of the i-th particle at the $t + 1$ iteration, represents the position of the ith particle at the $t + 1$ iteration, and X_i^{t+1} represents the position of the i-th particle at the $T + 1$ iteration.

3.2 LSSVM Algorithm

LSSVM is an extension of the support vector machine, considering data samples (x_i, y_i) $(i = 1,2,...,l)$, where $x_i \in R^n$, $y_i \in R^n$, are sample input and sample output, respectively, and l is the number of samples. Through nonlinear transformation, input samples x can be mapped to high-dimensional space [28]:

$$f(x) = w^{\mathrm{T}}\phi(x) + c \tag{19}$$

where, w is the weight of the hyperplane, c is a constant, and $\phi(\cdot)$ is a spatial transformation function.

The objective function of least squares support vector machine is defined as:

$$\begin{cases} \min J = \frac{1}{2}w^{\mathrm{T}}w + \gamma \sum_{i=1}^{l} e_i^2 \\ s.t. y_i = w^{\mathrm{T}}\phi(x) + c + e_i \end{cases} \tag{20}$$

The Lagrange function is constructed as follows:

$$L(w, b, e, a_i) = \frac{1}{2}w^{\mathrm{T}}w + \gamma \sum_{i=1}^{l} e_i^2 - \sum_{i=1}^{l} a_i[w^{\mathrm{T}}\phi(x) + c - y_i + e_i] \tag{21}$$

where, a_i is Lagrange multiplier, and according to KKT condition, it can be obtained as follows:

$$\begin{cases} \frac{\partial L}{\partial w} = 0 \rightarrow \sum_{i=1}^{l} a_i\phi(x_i) = 0 \\ \frac{\partial L}{\partial c} = 0 \rightarrow \sum_{i=1}^{l} a_i = 0 \\ \frac{\partial L}{\partial e_i} = 0 \rightarrow a_i + \gamma e_i = 0 \\ \frac{\partial L}{\partial a_i} = 0 \rightarrow w^{\mathrm{T}}\phi(x_i) + c - y_i + e_i = 0 \end{cases} \tag{22}$$

By solving Eq. (22), the mathematical model of LSSVM can be obtained as follows:

$$f(x) = \sum_{i=1}^{l} a_i K(x, x_i) + c \tag{23}$$

where, $K(\cdot)$ is the kernel function of the model, and the RBF kernel function is usually used, as shown below:

$$K_{\mathrm{RBF}} = \exp(-\frac{\|x - x_i\|^2}{2\delta^2}) \tag{24}$$

where, δ is a kernel function parameter. Therefore, LSSVM model performance depends on γ and δ.

3.3 OLTC Fault Diagnosis Model Based on IPSO-LSSVM

The main steps of IPSO algorithm to optimize LSSVM parameters are as follows:

(1) Initialize particle swarm. Set the population size of the particle swarm $N = 30$ and the maximum number of iterations $T_{max} = 100$; The range of parameter optimization is $\lambda \in [0.01, 1000]$, $\delta \in [0.01, 100]$; to use random functions to generate the initial position and initial velocity of particles.
(2) Determine the fitness value. According to Eq. (25), the fitness value of each formula is calculated, the particles at each position are evaluated, and the initial local fitness value and global optimal fitness value of each particle are determined. Equation (25) is calculated as follows:

$$f = \frac{1}{N} \sum_{i=1}^{N} \left| \frac{F_c}{F_c + T_c} \right| \times 100\% \qquad (25)$$

(3) Update particles. The particle updates its velocity and position through Eqs. (17) and (18).
(4) Update the global best search position of the whole population.
(5) Update the local optimal search position of each particle.
(6) Determine whether the maximum number of iterations is reached. If not, return to step (3) to continue the search. If it is, at the end of the algorithm, the global optimal position $pbest_i$ is output, and its corresponding (λ, σ) is the optimal solution for LSSVM model parameters.

4 Experimental Verification and Analysis

4.1 Experimental Data Acquisition

In this paper, the CMIII-500-63B-10193W tap changer is used for experimental simulation. As shown in Fig. 1 three vibration sensors are respectively attached to the top and side of OLTC, and the vibration signals during operation are collected by the sensors with a sampling frequency of 50 kHz. The signal is transmitted by cable to a computer for signal storage and analysis. Among them, the sensor uses a CTCAC102 type acceleration sensor [29].

The OLTC was set to four operating conditions, including the normal operation of contact, contact shedding, contact burning, and contact loosening, with 60 groups respectively, of which 40 groups were used for training and 20 groups were used for testing. Vibration signals under normal operating conditions are shown as follows in the Fig. 2 (Fig. 3).

Fig. 1. Sensor installation position diagram

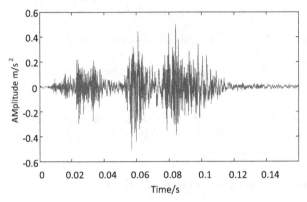

Fig. 2. Vibration diagram under normal working conditions (a) Time domain diagram of CEEMD (b) Frequency domain diagram of CEEMD.

According to the [30], the relevant parameters of IMPE are selected for comparison when the scale factors $S = 20$, $\tau = 1$, $m = 3$, and $m = 7$. The vibration signals under four different working conditions were decomposed, and each working condition included 10 groups of sample values, and the number of samples in each group was $N = 6880$. The IMPE value of IMF obtained from each CEEMD decomposition was calculated, and the average value was calculated 10 times so as to obtain the variation trend of scale factor S with IMPE, as shown in Fig. 5: As can be seen from the figure, when m = 7, the effect of change stability obtained by the four different working conditions is significantly better than that obtained by $m = 3$, and when $m = 7$, the four different working conditions can be well distinguished, especially the three different fault states, and the discrimination degree is obvious. In summary, $\tau = 1$, $m = 7$, and $S = 20$ are selected as the feature selection parameters of IMPE in this paper. As shown in the Fig. 4.

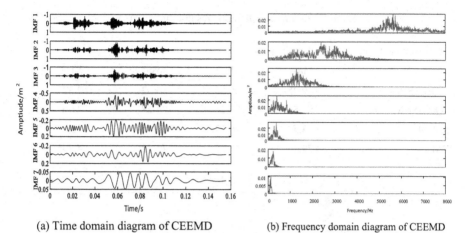

(a) Time domain diagram of CEEMD   (b) Frequency domain diagram of CEEMD

Fig. 3. Time-frequency domain decomposition diagram of normal operation state

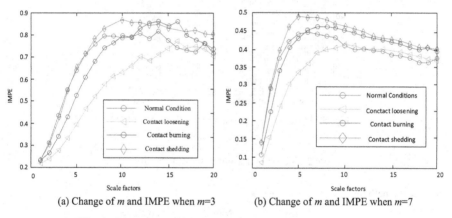

(a) Change of m and IMPE when $m=3$ (b) Change of m and IMPE when $m=7$

Fig. 4. The relationship of m and IMPE in different conditions

4.2 Comparison of Calculation Results

To verify the effectiveness of the proposed method, the proposed method is compared with the other three methods. As can be seen from Table 1 and Fig. 5, IPSO-LSSVM is 1.97% higher than PSO-LSSVM [32], LSSVM, and SVM [32] without PCA [33], indicating that IPSO-LSSVM has the highest diagnostic accuracy among all methods (Table 2, Fig. 6).

Table 1. Accuracy recognition results without PCA

comparison methods	Accuracy %			
	Max	Min	Average	STD
IPSO-LSSVM	89.25	85.55	86.52	2.325
PSO-LSSVM	86.56	83.25	84.28	2.562
LSSVM	83.52	80.52	81.56	3.532
SVM	79.25	75.55	76.52	4.895

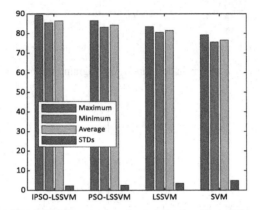

Fig. 5. Different comparison methods without PCA

Table 2. Accuracy recognition results with PCA

comparison methods	Accuracy %			
	Max	Min	Average	STD
IPSO-LSSVM	95.83	87.5	93.53	1.325
PSO-LSSVM	90.25	85.5	87.58	1.952
LSSVM	85.50	82.55	83.85	2.456
SVM	83.35	81.25	82.55	3.625

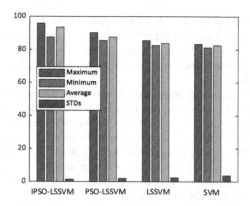

Fig. 6. Different comparison methods with PCA

5 Conclusion

In this paper, feature fusion and IPSO-LSSVM for mechanical fault feature selection of on-load tap changers are proposed. Firstly, PCA was used to screen the high-dimensional features and obtain the sensitive feature subset so as to overcome the problems of high redundancy and complexity of fusion features. Then, the improved particle swarm optimization algorithm was used to optimize LSSVM, and the sensitive subset was selected and classified. Finally, the data of OLTC 4 different fault states are selected and compared with other algorithms. Through the analysis and comparison of experimental data, the effectiveness of the proposed method is verified, and the necessity of PCA feature selection is emphasized.

Acknowledgments. This research was funded by the key technology projects of State Grid Jiangsu Electric Power Co., Ltd. (grant number J2022047).

References

1. Yan, Y., Ma, H., Wen, M., Dang, S., et al.: Multi-feature fusion-based mechanical fault diagnosis for on-load tap changers in smart grid with electric vehicles. IEEE Sens. J. **21**(14), 15696–15708 (2021)
2. Xu, Y., Zhou, C., Geng, J., Gao, S., Wang, P.: A method for diagnosing mechanical faults of on-load tap changer based on ensemble empirical mode decomposition, Volterra model and decision acyclic graph support vector machine. IEEE Access **7**, 84803–84816 (2019)
3. Wang, C., Lu, L., Ma, H., et al.: Diagnosis for loose switching contact fault of on-load tap-changer in transformer. In: CICED 2010 Proceedings, pp. 1–6. Nan Jing (2010)
4. Simas, E.F., de Almeida, L.A.L., de Lima, A.C.: Vibration monitoring of on-load tap changers using a genetic algorithm. In: Proceedings of IEEE Instrument Measurement Technology Conference, vol. 3, pp. 2288–2293. IEEE, Canada (2005)
5. Lin, C., Zhang, D., Huang, Q., Yang, R., et al.: Influence of load current on vibration signal of on-load tap changers. In: 2018 International Conference on Power System Technology, pp. 3262–3268. IEEE PES, Guangzhou (2018)

6. Duan, R., Wang, F.: Fault diagnosis of on-load tap-changer in converter transformer based on time–frequency vibration analysis. IEEE Trans. Ind. Electron. **63**(6), 3815–3823 (2016)

7. Li, Q., Zhao, T., Zhang, L., Lou, J.: Mechanical fault diagnostics of onload tap changer within power transformers based on hidden Markov model. IEEE Trans. Power Delivery **27**(2), 596–601 (2012)

8. Cao, H., Wu, X., Zhou, J., et al.: Research progress on mechanical fault diagnosis of on-load tap changer based on vibration analysis. In: 2021 IEEE International Conference on Power Electronics, Computer Applications (ICPECA), pp. 948–951. IEEE (2021)

9. Secic, A., Krpan, M., Kuzle, I.: Using deep neural networks for on-load tap changer audio-based diagnostics. IEEE Trans. Power Delivery **37**(4), 3038–3050 (2022)

10. Kim, W., Kim, S., Jeong, J., et al.: Digital twin approach for on-load tap changers using data-driven dynamic model updating and optimization-based operating condition estimation. Mech. Syst. Signal Process. **181**, 1–17 (2022)

11. Bengtsson, C.: Status and trends in transformer monitoring. IEEE Trans. Power Delivery **11**(3), 1379–1384 (1996)

12. Kang, P., Birtwhistle, D.: Condition monitoring of power transformer on-load tap-changers. Part 1: automatic condition diagnostics. IEE Proc. – Gener., Transm. Distrib. **148**(4), 301–306 (2001)

13. Kang, P., Birtwhistle, D.: Condition monitoring of power transformer on-load tap-changers. Part II: detection of ageing from vibration signatures. IEE Proc. – Gener., Transm. Distrib. **148**(4), 307–311 (2001)

14. Kang, P., Birtwhistle, D.: Condition assessment of power transformer on-load tap changers using wavelet analysis and self-organizing map: field evaluation. IEEE Trans. Power Delivery **18**(1), 78–84 (2003)

15. Jinxin, L., Guan, W., Tong, Z., et al.: Fault diagnosis of on-load tap-changer based on variational mode decomposition and relevance vector machine. Energies **10**(7), 946–959 (2017)

16. Duan, X., Zhao, T., Li, T., Liu, J., Zou, L., Zhang, L.: Method for diagnosis of on-load tap changer based on wavelet theory and support vector machine. The J. Eng. **2017**(13), 2193–2197 (2017)

17. Zhao, T., Li, Q., Chen, P.: Dynamic analysis method for feature extraction of mechanical vibration signals of on-load tap changers. Trans. China Electrotech. Soc. **22**(1), 41–46 (2007). (in Chinese)

18. Zhou, X., Wang, F., Fu, J., et al.: Mechanical condition monitoring of on-load tap changers based on chaos theory and K-means clustering method. Proc. CSEE **35**(6), 1541–1548 (2015). (in Chinese)

19. Ma, H., Yan, Y.: Analysis and calculation method of on-load tap changers state characteristics based on chaos theory and grasshopper optimization algorithm-K-means algorithm. Trans. China Electrotech. Soc. **36**(07), 1399–1406 (2021)

20. Wang, F., Xu, S.: Tap-changer fault diagnosis of transformer based on improved PSO-SVM. Electr. Meas. Technol. **39**(11), 190–194 (2016)

21. Zeng, Q., Wang, F., Zhang, Y., et al.: Fault recognition of on-load tap-changer in power transformer based on convolutional neural network. Autom. Electr. Power Syst. **44**(11), 144–151 (2020)

22. Saucedo-Dorantes, J.J., Delgado-Prieto, M., et al.: Multi-fault diagnosis method applied to an electric machine based on high-dimensional feature reduction. IEEE Trans. Ind. Appl. **53**(3), 3086–3097 (2017)

23. Van, M., Kang, H.-J.: Bearing-fault diagnosis using non-local means algorithm and empirical mode decomposition-based feature extraction and two-stage feature selection. IET Sci. Meas. Technol. **9**(6), 671–680 (2015)

24. Guo, Z., Liu, M., Wang, Y., Qin, H.: A new fault diagnosis classifier for rolling bearing united multi-scale permutation entropy optimize VMD and cuckoo search SVM. IEEE Access **8**, 153610–153629 (2020)
25. Feng, Y., Tang, B., Zhao, N.: JTC state detection based on improved multi-scale permutation entropy and fuzzy algorithm. J. Railway Sci. Eng. **18**(12), 3337–3346 (2022)
26. Ye, D., Xie, F., Hao, Z.: A novel identification scheme of lightning disturbance in HVDC transmission lines based on CEEMD-HHT. CPSS Trans. Power Electr. Appl. **6**(2), 145–154 (2021)
27. Yan, Y., Ma, H., Li, Z.: An improved grasshopper optimization algorithm for global optimization. Chin. J. Electr. **30**(3), 451–459 (2021)
28. Zhou, S.: Sparse LSSVM in primal using Cholesky factorization for large-scale problems. IEEE Trans. Neural Netw. Learning Syst. **27**(4), 783–795 (2016)
29. Chen, B., Yan, Y., Wang, L., Chen, M., et al.: One dimension NLM denoising method based on hasudorff distance and its application in OTLC. In: 2019 IEEE Asia Power and Energy Engineering Conference (APEEC), pp. 75–79. Chengdu (2019)
30. Li, R., Wang, J.: Interacting price model and fluctuation behavior analysis from Lempel-Ziv complexity and multi-scale weighted-permutation entropy. Phys. Lett. A **380**, 117–129 (2016)
31. Song, X., Zhao, J., Song, J., et al.: Local demagnetization fault recognition of permanent magnet synchronous linear motor based on S-transform and PSO–LSSVM. IEEE Trans. Power Electron. **35**(8), 7816–7825 (2020)
32. Yang, Y., Wang, J., Yang, Y.: Exploiting rotation invariance with SVM classifier for micro-calcification detection. In: 2012 9th IEEE International Symposium on Biomedical Imaging (ISBI), pp. 590–593. Spain (2012)
33. He, R., Hu, B.-G., Zheng, W.-S., et al.: Robust principal component analysis based on maximum correntropy criterion. IEEE Trans. Image Process. **20**(6), 1485–1494 (2011)

Graphlet-Based Measure to Assess Institutional Research Teams

Shengqing Li[(✉)] and Jiulei Jiang

Changshu Institute of Technology, Suzhou 215500, Jiangsu, China
chq_lee@qq.com

Abstract. This paper identifies the microstructural characteristics of the research teams of academic institutions using graphlet-based measures. The results provide references for the evaluation and development of research teams. Scientific collaboration networks in the Top 20 institutions were evaluated using papers published in the past 6 years on computer image recognition in the field of artificial intelligence. The structural features of 3–5 node graphlets were extracted and analyzed. Significant graphlet structures were distinguished, and graphlet-based measures were used to determine the similarities and differences in the scientific collaboration networks. It was found that the graphlet structures contained significant information, and the graphlet correlation measures could be used to distinguish the similarities and differences of scientific research teams. The data can be used to investigate collaboration efficiency and develop and expand research teams.

Keywords: Institutional Research Team · Graphlet · Structural Measure

1 Introduction

Scientific cooperation is relatively common in scientific research [1]. Due to the strengthening of academic exchange activities, there are increasing interdisciplinary innovation opportunities [2], more complex scientific research problems, and more scientific cooperation. Moreover, scientific research and development are accelerating, and the output of scientific research has increased. The structure, scale, influence, and efficiency of scientific research cooperation have become crucial [3–7]. Research cooperation is divided into inter-institutional virtual research cooperation [1] and intra-institutional research cooperation. Inter-institutional research cooperation is relatively common and promotes the speed and efficiency of research innovation. In contrast, intra-institutional research cooperation has unique advantages in academic exchanges and unique development characteristics due to the geographical proximity of the researchers. Cooperation and competition coexist. The development of cooperative research relationships in an institution is related to the evaluation and performance of research institutions [4]. The importance and influence of research institutions in the industry have been the focus of scientific evaluation. Research achievements obtained through cooperation (inter-institutional or intra-institutional) determine the status of research institutions, the ability to obtain funding for research projects, and the development of scientific and technological talents, which are related to the future growth and development of research institutions [7]. Many achievements have been made in inter-institutional research cooperation [7], but few studies investigated intra-institutional research cooperation.

This study focuses on hotspot research areas in the emerging artificial intelligence industry in the recent 6 years, especially computer image recognition. We analyze research cooperation networks in the Top 20 institutions and extract the 3–5 node graphlet characteristics to distinguish the salient features in the graphlets. We compare the microstructure of the scientific research teams of Chinese and foreign institutions to determine the similarities and differences in scientific research teams.

2 Related Work

Research cooperation has three dimensions: macro, meso, and micro, including inter-regional research cooperation [8], international research cooperation [9, 10], inter-industry research cooperation [11], inter-institutional research cooperation [12, 13], and intra-institutional research cooperation [6]. Scholars have investigated research cooperation at the micro level from multiple dimensions, such as nodes [14], edges [15], triplets [16], models [17, 18], and graphlets [19]. The research topics cover the establishment of research teams [1], composition [3], cooperation model [20], role analysis [4], performance [5], evaluation [6], dynamic evolution [21], knowledge transmission [21], cooperation recommendations [22, 23].

Studies on scientific research cooperation have focused on the analysis of nodes [14], edges [15], and communities [24] in the network of scientific research cooperation. The importance evaluation of nodes and edges and the division of communities have always been a research focus. However, nodes and edges do not reflect the local characteristics of scientific research cooperation. The microstructure of scientific research must to analyzed in-depth. In recent years, many achievements have been made in the measurement of the microstructure of scientific research. Network motifs [18] and multi-node graphlets [25] have become hot spots; However, only a few studies focused on analyzing the microstructure using graphlets [18]. Graphlets with 3–5 nodes have been used [26]. More nodes have not been analyzed due to limitations in computing power.

The comparative analysis of similarities and differences in the network structure is an essential issue in network science [27–30] and has been widely used in sociology [30], medicine [31, 32], physics [24], biology [26], and other fields. A comparison of the similarities and differences in network structures provides information on the frequency and distribution of substructures with similar structures and functions, enabling the evaluation of the stability and robustness of network structures and their evolution [33, 34]. The similarities and differences in the network structure can be measured by the graphlet structure [18], relative graphlet frequency distance, graphlet degree distribution, and graphlet correlation distance [25]. A comparison of the network structure can identify differences in the microstructure of two networks, and the comparison of the structural similarities and differences of research cooperation networks in different institutions in the same field [35–37] can clarify the relationship between similar competitors.

3 Data and Methods

3.1 Data Source and Preprocessing

Basic Data. Artificial intelligence has become an important sector in China's strategic development of emerging industries and new infrastructure planning. Fierce competition exists in this field domestically and internationally. The output of scientific research is high, the output of corporate products is high, and the establishment and development of scientific research teams are crucial. We selected scientific and technological publications in computer image recognition in the field of artificial intelligence. The selected period was nearly 6 years (2015–2020) (data download time is January 2021), and the search string was "subject: (deep learning) aND Subject: (image* or computer vision*)". We used the Science Citation Index (SCI) included in the Web of Science database (www.webofknowledge.com) and obtained 20,268 full records on scientific and technological papers. As shown in Table 1, the number of publications in this field has approximately doubled annually. There were 65079 authors and 11216 scientific research institutions in the field of computer image recognition in the past 6 years, and the average team size was 6 people.

Table 1. Papers on image recognition in the field of artificial intelligence published in the past 6 years

Year	Number of papers	Increase over the previous year
2015	164	203.70%
2016	390	137.80%
2017	1046	168.21%
2018	2668	155.07%
2019	5839	118.85%
2020	10161	74.02%

Establishment of Institutional Collaboration Networks. This article focuses on the similarities and differences between scientific research teams in institutions with important influence in this field. The research teams in the Top 20 institutions were selected for analysis. We extracted the institution information and research collaboration networks in the C1 field of each record using a custom Python program. As shown in Fig. 1, an undirected weighted network was created based on the co-occurrence relationship of the institutions in the C1 field in the records of each paper. The nodes in the network are the institutions, and the edges are the co-occurrence frequencies of the institutions.

Acquisition of Information on Institutions and Authors. We obtained the relevant information on the institutions and authors using data from the basic data. We extracted the institution information and author information from the C1 field of each record using a custom Python program, as shown in Fig. 2.

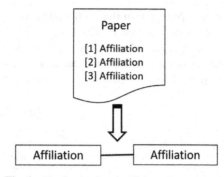

Fig. 1. The institutional collaboration networks

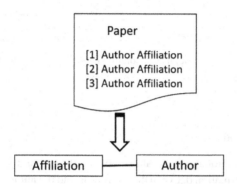

Fig. 2. The author-institution affiliation

The Author's Collaboration Network. The Author's collaboration network is a scientific research team. The author information in the AF field in each record and the collaboration relationship with other authors were extracted using a custom Python program. An undirected weighted network was established based on the co-occurrence relationship of the authors in the AF field in each paper record (Fig. 3). The nodes in the network are the authors, and the edges are the co-occurrence frequencies of the authors.

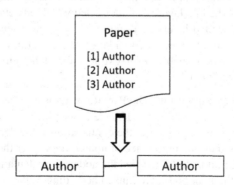

Fig. 3. The author's collaboration network

The Research Collaboration Network in the Institution. The members of the institution have internal and external research collaborations. The internal collaboration network of the institution was extracted using the relationship information between the institution, the authors, and the collaborative network. As shown in Fig. 4, two collaboration networks were established: affiliation1 and affiliation2.

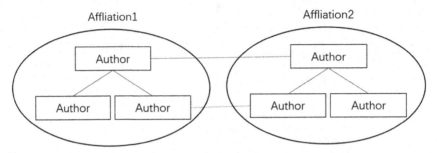

Fig. 4. The research collaboration network in the institution

3.2 Research Method

We combined the institutional collaboration network, the author's collaboration network, and the affiliation information between the institution and the author into a two-layer network. We used the PageRank algorithm to find the Top 20 institutions in the institutional cooperation and the affiliations between the institution, author, and the author's collaboration network to obtain information on the collaboration between scientific research teams of each institution. The network characteristics were obtained by graphlet extraction and an analysis of the institutional scientific research cooperation network using graphlet-related indicators.

Multi-layer Network Modeling. Multi-layer network modeling [38] is used to determine the different types of nodes and edges in a network. This method enables the integration of multi-dimensional node and edge information for the subsequent analysis. As shown in Fig. 5, the first layer is an undirected weighted network of institutional collaboration, and the second layer is an undirected weighted network of author collaboration. The relationship between the two layers is the institution-author affiliation. The organization information can be used to extract the collaboration information of the authors using cross-layer connections.

PageRank Importance Evaluation. The PageRank algorithm [39] was used to determine the relationship between the nodes. If node i has a link to node j, j contributes a value of i to this node. The magnitude of the contribution value depends on the importance of node i. The greater the importance of node i, the higher the contribution value by node j is. Due to the mutual links between the nodes, the calculation of the score is an iterative process, and the final nodes are ranked according to the score. The PageRank

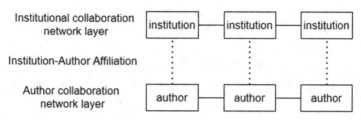

Fig. 5. The multi-layer network of the institution-author affiliation and the collaboration network

value of a node (represented by *PR*) is calculated by Eq. (1):

$$PR(p) = (1 - d)/N + d \sum\nolimits_{i=1}^{n} \frac{PR(T_i)}{C(T_i)} \tag{1}$$

where PR(p) represents the PageRank value of node p; $T_i (i = 1, 2, ..., n)$ represents the other nodes pointing to node p; d is the probability that the user arrives at a node randomly; its range is 0 and 1 (usually 0.85); $C(T_i)$ is the number of links pointing to node T_i; $PR(T_i)/C(T_i)$ represents the value of PR given to p by the in-node of node p, and N represents the total number of nodes. Generally, the initial *PR* value of each node is set to 1, and the *PR* value of each node is recursively calculated by Eq. (1) until the value becomes stable.

Graphlet-Based Measurements. Graphlets are subnets extracted from the overall network [25]. The subnets are interconnected and heterogeneous microstructures. They are generally divided into 2-node, 3-node (2 types), 4-node (6 types), and 5-node graphlets (21 types), etc. a 3–5 node graphlet is typically used to analyze various network structures. Due to differences in the symmetry within the graphlet, the role of the nodes is different in different graphlets. The graphlets of each node are shown in Fig. 6. Due to a large number of graphlets with more than 6 nodes, the computational complexity is high. Novel methods are required to address this problem.

The graphlet concentration is used [18] to extract the significant graphlet types in the 3–5 node graphlets. The graphlet concentration is the ratio of a certain type of graphlet to the total number of graphlets; it describes the salient characteristics of a particular graphlet type. If the number of n-node graphlets of type i is N_i, the graphlet concentration of the n-node graphlet of type i can be calculated by Eq. (2):

$$C(i) = N_i / \sum\nolimits_i N_i \tag{2}$$

We used the relative graphlet frequency distance [25] to compare the number of graphlet microstructures at the 3–5 nodes and determine the similarities and differences between the scientific research teams of different institutions. The relative graphlet frequency distance is the sum of the differences in the graphlet concentration of each type of n-node graphlet in the two networks. This index indicates the similarities and differences between different networks at the graphlet structure level. The relative graphlet frequency distance is calculated by Eq. (3):

$$D(G, H) = \sum\nolimits_i |F_i(G) - F_i(H)| \tag{3}$$

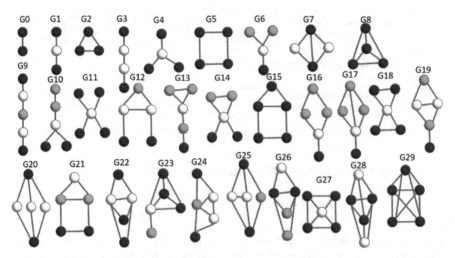

Fig. 6. Graphlet structure and features [40]

where G and H are different networks, and $F_i(G) = C(i)$. This parameter minimizes the influence of the number of high-frequency n-node graphlets on the calculation results.

Comparison of the Network Structure Similarity. The graph edit distance [41] is a commonly used similarity measure for networks and is similar to the Levenshtein distance for strings. We calculated the graph edit distance of two graphs, i.e., we replaced, added, deleted, and edited the points and edges in the two graphs to achieve the fewest editing steps to achieve the isomorphism of the two graphs.

4   Case Study

We processed the 20,268 records from 2015 to 2020 in computer image recognition and established a multi-layer collaboration network, author collaboration network, and information on the institutions and authors. The PageRank algorithm was used to obtain the top 20 influential institutions in the institutional cooperation network, and the relationship between the institutions, authors, and the authors' collaboration networks were obtained. We extracted 2–5 node graphlets from the information and visualized it to identify the significant graphlet structure using the concentration measure. We determined the similarities and differences in the graphlet structure of different scientific research teams using the relative graphlet frequency distance. Finally, the similarities and differences in the subnets of typical graphlets were obtained [27].

4.1   Choice of Top 20 Institutions

The PageRank value of each organization and the Top 20 organizations are shown in Table 2. The domestic research institutions and their ranking are Chinese Academy of Sciences (1), Zhejiang University (2), Sun Yat-sen University (3), University of Chinese Academy of Sciences (6), Shanghai Jiaotong University (7), Chinese University of Hong Kong (10), Peking University (11) Wuhan University (12), Beijing University of Aeronautics and Astronautics (16), and Shenzhen University (19). The foreign scientific research institutions and their rankings are Stanford University (4), Harvard Medical School (5), Oxford University (8), Technical University of Munich (9), Johns Hopkins University (13), University of California, Berkeley (14), University of Tokyo (15), University of Illinois (17), National University of Singapore (18), and University of Washington (20). China's scientific research institutions show high rankings, accounting for 50% of all organizations. Other domestic institutions are also high-ranked, such as Tsinghua University (31), Xiamen University (33), University of Electronic Science and Technology (39), and Tongji University (41). These data show that China has a high academic status and influence in computer image recognition in the field of artificial intelligence, with the Chinese Academy of Sciences ranking in first place for betweenness centrality, proximity centrality, degree centrality, eigenvector centrality, and PageRank. This institution also shows high performance for the other indicators; thus, its scientific research team can be used as a model for other institutions.

Table 2. Top 20 institutions for image recognition research in the field of artificial intelligence

Sort	Institution	PageRank value
1	Chinese Acad Sci	0.008139411
2	Zhejiang Univ	0.003659141
3	Sun Yat Sen Univ	0.003481924
4	Stanford Univ	0.003301128
5	Harvard Med Sch	0.003268185
6	Univ Chinese Acad Sci	0.003138859
7	Shanghai Jiao Tong Univ	0.002927247
8	Univ Oxford	0.002544074
9	Tech Univ Munich	0.002490833
10	Chinese Univ Hong Kong	0.002409168
11	Peking Univ	0.002376065
12	Wuhan Univ	0.002281621
13	Johns Hopkins Univ	0.002262477
14	Univ Calif Berkeley	0.00225594
15	Univ Tokyo	0.002178998
16	Beihang Univ	0.002125124
17	Univ Illinois	0.002113429
18	Natl Univ Singapore	0.0020504
19	Shenzhen Univ	0.002025922
20	Univ Washington	0.002023505

4.2 Distribution of Connected Subgraphs of Research Teams in the Top 20 Institutions

The members of scientific research teams in the institutions collaborate with teams internally and externally. This article mainly considers the collaboration of scientific research teams within the institution. The scientific research collaboration networks of the Top 20 institutions, such as the Chinese Academy of Sciences, are extracted one by one using the institution-author collaboration multi-layer network in Fig. 5. Some of the authors at these institutions are independent (collaborative relationships with authors outside the institution, and no collaborative relationships with authors within the institution), and some authors have collaborative relationships with authors at the same institution. Some individual authors may not be considered; therefore, it is necessary to analyze the scale of each connected subgraph. Table 3 shows the distribution of the internal communication subgraphs of the top 20 institutions in image recognition in the field of artificial intelligence. The scientific research teams at each institution show aggregation and differentiation, and some institutional members are part of research teams in large and closely connected institutions. In these teams, many institutional members have little contact within the institution and collaborate more with members outside of the institution. Among the 10 domestic scientific research institutions, the largest connected subgraph exceeds the scale of the other connected subgraphs, indicating clusters of scientific research teams in some institutions in China.

In the past 6 years, most institutions have seen a clustering of research teams. The scientific research teams in the largest connected subgraph have a significant advantage, such as the Chinese Academy of Sciences. The number of nodes and the sum of the edge weights of the largest connected subgraph in the scientific research collaboration network accounted for 79.3% and 89.8%, respectively, of the entire institutional network. For a convenient comparison, we focus on the largest connected subgraph of the scientific research collaboration network within the institution.

Table 3. Distribution of subgraphs within the top 20 institutions in image recognition in the field of artificial intelligence

Sort	Institution	Number of Unicom subgraphs	The size of the top 10 Unicom subgraphs
1	Chinese Acad Sci	122	[1297, 13, 11, 8, 7, 7, 7, 7, 7, 7]
2	Zhejiang Univ	83	[475, 14, 10, 9, 8, 8, 8, 7, 7, 6]
3	Sun Yat Sen Univ	60	[460, 11, 10, 7, 7, 7, 7, 7, 6, 6]

(*continued*)

Table 3. (*continued*)

Sort	Institution	Number of Unicom subgraphs	The size of the top 10 Unicom subgraphs
4	Stanford Univ	78	[225, 22, 20, 16, 15, 14, 13, 9, 9, 9]
5	Harvard Med Sch	74	[69, 43, 15, 14, 13, 12, 9, 8, 8, 7]
6	Univ Chinese Acad Sci	110	[510, 10, 8, 8, 7, 7, 6, 6, 6, 5]
7	Shanghai Jiao Tong Univ	74	[256, 18, 10, 10, 10, 9, 9, 8, 8, 7]
8	Univ Oxford	54	[27, 13, 12, 12, 12, 11, 6, 5, 5, 5]
9	Tech Univ Munich	47	[36, 36, 18, 14, 12, 10, 7, 7, 7, 5]
10	Chinese Univ Hong Kong	31	[111, 12, 8, 5, 4, 4, 3, 2, 2, 2]
11	Peking Univ	65	[164, 12, 9, 8, 8, 7, 5, 4, 4, 4]
12	Wuhan Univ	48	[505, 9, 7, 7, 6, 5, 5, 5, 4, 4]
13	Johns Hopkins Univ	43	[98, 25, 22, 13, 10, 7, 7, 5, 4, 4]
14	Univ Calif Berkeley	55	[19, 18, 16, 12, 11, 7, 4, 4, 4, 4]]
15	Univ Tokyo	59	[52, 26, 19, 17, 14, 12, 8, 8, 7, 7]
16	Beihang Univ	58	[275, 10, 8, 7, 6, 4, 4, 4, 4, 4]
17	Univ Illinois	60	[13, 12, 12, 8, 8, 7, 6, 6, 5, 5]
18	Natl Univ Singapore	40	[51, 48, 9, 8, 8, 8, 7, 7, 5, 5]
19	Shenzhen Univ	37	[247, 7, 7, 6, 6, 6, 5, 5, 4, 3]
20	Univ Washington	42	[41, 6, 6, 5, 4, 4, 4, 3, 3, 3]

4.3 The Graphlet Structure of the Largest Connected Subgraph of the Scientific Research Team of the Top 20 Institutions

The largest connected subgraph was extracted from the scientific research collaboration network in the Top 20 institutions, and 29 graphlets were extracted from the largest connected subgraph corresponding to each institution using the 3–5 node graphlet structure extraction method. The frequency information of the 3–5 node graphlet is shown in Fig. 7. The frequency distance of some graphlets is larger than that of the other graphlets. The frequency of the graphlets G4, G6, G10, G12, G17, G19, G23, G27, and G29 in Fig. 6 is significantly higher than that of the other graphlets. However, due to the influence of high frequencies in Fig. 7, the structural features of some graphlets cannot be determined.

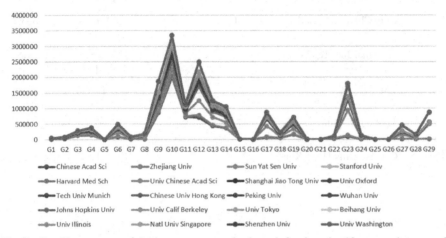

Fig. 7. Graphlet structure of the largest connected subgraph for the scientific research teams of the Top 20 institutions

The graphlet concentration was calculated to prevent the problem shown in Fig. 7 and obtain a quantitative measure of the frequency. The graphlet concentration of each type of 3–5 node graphlet in the largest connected subgraph in the Top 20 organization is

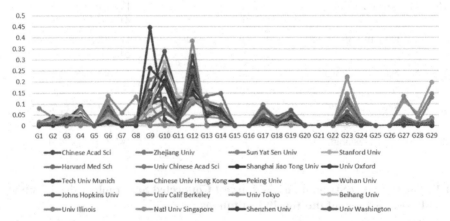

Fig. 8. Graphlet concentration of the largest connected subgraph for the scientific research teams of the Top 20 institutions

shown in Fig. 8. The results show that the graphlet concentration of G4, G6, G10, G12, G17, G19, G23, G27, and G29 is significantly higher than that of the other graphlets.

4.4 Similarity Analysis of the Largest Connected Subgraph of Top 20 Institutional Research Teams

The frequency statistics of the graphlet and the graphlet concentration only describe the structural characteristics of the scientific research teams within a single institution but do not reflect the similarities and differences of the scientific research teams between institutions. The relative graphlet frequency distance and the correlation measure based on the relative graphlet frequency provide information on the similarities and differences between the two graphs.

(1) The relative graphlet frequency distance of the largest connected subgraph for the scientific research teams of the Top 20 institutions

The distance matrix of the relative graphlet frequency distance of the largest connected subgraph for the scientific research teams of the Top 20 institutions is shown in Fig. 9. The relative graphlet frequency distance is small, and the graphlet concentration of the largest interconnected subgraph in the corresponding organization is similar. If the relative graphlet frequency distance is large, the graphlet concentration of

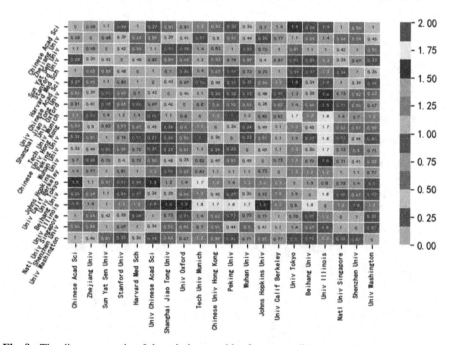

Fig. 9. The distance matrix of relative graphlet frequency distance to the largest connected subgraph for the scientific research teams of the Top 20 institutions

212   S. Li and J. Jiang

the largest interconnected subgraph in the corresponding organization has a large difference. The index reflects the similarities and differences of the graphlet concentration of the largest connected subgraph in the organization. For example, the following distances between two institutions were obtained: Chinese Academy of Sciences-University of Chinese Academy of Sciences (0.27), Chinese Academy of Sciences-Peking University (0.32), Chinese Academy of Sciences-Wuhan University (0.36), Chinese Academy of Sciences-Beijing University of Aeronautics and Astronautics (0.26), Stanford University-Zhejiang University (0.39), Stanford University-Sun Yat-sen University (0.42), Stanford University-Harvard Medical School (0.48), Stanford University-Johns Hopkins University (0.4), Stanford University-National University of Singapore (0.35), Stanford University-University of Washington (0.33). Capturing the shared characteristics helps to find a shared teamwork structure in these institutions with similar graphlet concentration.

(2) The largest connected subgraph for the scientific research teams of the top 20 institutions is based on the graphlet concentration measure

The relative graphlet frequency distance between the two graphs can be used to evaluate the distribution of the graphlet concentration in the two graphs. The similarities and differences of the overall graphlet concentration are difficult to capture. The correlation matrix of the graphlet concentration of the largest connected subgraph for the research teams of the institution is shown in Fig. 10. The higher the correlation of

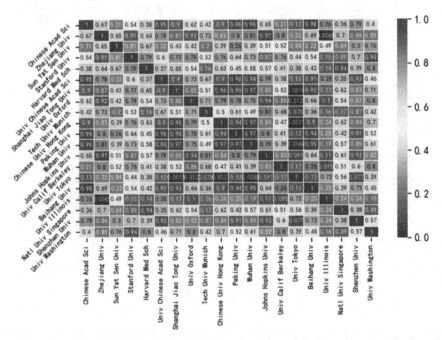

Fig. 10. The correlation matrix of the graphlet concentration of the largest connected subgraph for the scientific research teams of the Top 20 institutions

the graphlet concentration, the more similar the graphlet concentration of the largest interconnected subgraph in the organization is and vice versa. This measure reflects the similarities and differences in the graphlet concentration of the largest interconnected subgraph in the organization. For example: Chinese Academy of Sciences-University of Chinese Academy of Sciences (0.95), Chinese Academy of Sciences-Shanghai Jiaotong University (0.9), Chinese Academy of Sciences-Chinese University of Hong Kong (0.9), Chinese Academy of Sciences-Peking University (0.96), Chinese Academy of Sciences-Wuhan University (0.96), Chinese Academy of Sciences-Beijing University of Aeronautics and Astronautics (0.98), Stanford University-Zhejiang University (0.91), and Stanford University-Washington University (0.94). Capturing the shared characteristics facilitates finding institutions with similar graphlet concentration and identifying collaboration and competition among institutions.

(3) Similarity measure based on a typical graphlet structure

The Chinese Academy of Sciences and Beijing University of Aeronautics and Astronautics have relatively small distances to the graphlet frequencies and high similarity in the graphlet concentration. These two institutions are selected to analyze the similarity of their structures. The largest connected subgraph is used, the graphlets of each type of 3–5 nodes are extracted, and the graphlet concentration is calculated. The graphlet concentration in Fig. 8 shows that G10 (See G10 in Fig. 6) and G12 (See G12 in Fig. 6) are significant. We extract the G10 and G12 subnets from the largest connected subgraph for the scientific research collaboration networks of the Chinese Academy of Sciences

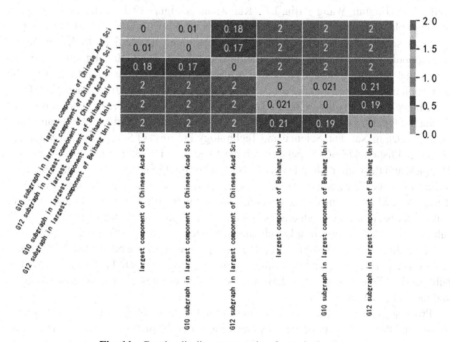

Fig. 11. Graph edit distance matrix of a typical subnet

and Beihang University and calculate the graph edit distance. The graph edit distance matrix is shown in Fig. 11. There is a significant difference in the graph edit distance between and within the institutions, indicating differences in the collaboration modes between the different institutions. Within the two institutions, there is a negligible difference between the connected subgraph and the subnet, indicating close collaboration within the institution and a distinctive collaboration model.

(4) Analysis of typical graphlet structures in Top 20 institutional research cooperation networks

Figure 7 indicates that the two graphlet structures G10 (see G10 in Fig. 6) and G12 (see G12 in Fig. 6) are significant. The subnets of G10 and G12 in the maximum link subgraph of the scientific research cooperation network of Wuhan University and Sun Yat-sen University were extracted. We selected the subnet with the maximum subnet side weight. One G10 subnet ['Bo_Du', 'Liangpei_Zhang', 'Jing_Li', 'Huanfeng_Shen', 'Yanfei_Zhong'] was extracted from Wuhan University. Four subnets of G12 at Wuhan University were obtained ['Wei_Yu', 'Kai_Zhang', 'Jing_Li', 'Jiayi_Ma', 'Shu_Zhang'], ['Wei_Yu', 'Kai_Zhang', 'Pengwei_Liang', 'Jing_Li', 'Shu_Zhang']. [' Wei_Yu ', 'Kai_Zhang', 'Jing_Li', 'Zhiqi_Zhang', 'Jiayi_Ma']. ['Wei_Yu', 'Kai_Zhang', 'Pengwei_Liang', 'Jing_Li', 'Zhiqi_Zhang']. Two G10 subnets at Sun Yat-sen University were extracted ['Wenjia_Cai', 'Yi_Zhu', 'Xiaonan_Yang', 'Jing_Li', 'Haotian_Lin'], ['Wenjia_Cai', 'Chuan_Chen', 'Xiaonan_Yang', 'Jing_Li', 'Haotian_Lin'], Sun Yat-sen University G12 type 2 subnets ['Haotian_Lin', 'Jun_Chen', 'Xiaohang_Wu', 'Jinghui_Wang', 'Kai_Zhang'], ['Haotian_Lin', 'Xiaohang_Wu', 'Jinghui_Wang', 'Bin_Li', 'Kai_Zhang']. Figure 12 shows the different types of subgraphs. They have similar structure and morphology as G10 and G12 in Fig. 6.

Since some scholars do not have published resumes, it is difficult to determine the corresponding authors. Only a few examples are listed. The G10 subgraph in Fig. 12 shows that the core member is located at the intersection of the three branches. The corresponding Chinese authors are Du Bo, Zhang Liangpei, Li Jing, Shen Huanfeng, and Zhong Yanfei. Professor Zhang Liangpei is at the center of the network. Professor Zhang Liangpei has won the first prize in Natural Science at the Ministry of Education and the first prize in National Science and Technology Progress of Surveying and Mapping. He has published 478 SCI papers, which have been cited 24,350 times. Each was cited 51 times, and the author's h index is 80. This author is a highly cited scientist in the field of Earth science. The main research area of this subnet is remote sensing image analysis using artificial intelligence. The academic homepages of the scholars indicate that all collaborators are highly productive scholars in this field. The Wuhan University G12 4 subnets include Professor Jing Ulrich and associate Professor Yu Wei in core positions. Professor Jing Ulrich has published 188 SCI papers, which have been cited 3,687 times. Each was cited 20 times, and the author's h index is 26. Associate Professor Yu Wei has published 59 SCI papers, which have been cited 1,078 times. Each was cited 18 times, and the author's h index is 14.

Professor Lin Hao-tian is at the center of the two G10 subnets of Sun Yat-sen University and the core figure of the cooperative network. Professor Lin Hao-tian has won

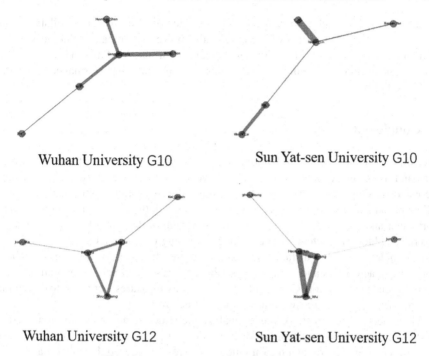

Wuhan University G10   Sun Yat-sen University G10

Wuhan University G12   Sun Yat-sen University G12

Fig. 12. Examples of typical graphlet structures

the first prize of the Outstanding Youth Foundation and the Zhong Nanshan Young Science and Technology Innovation Award. He has published 184 SCI papers, which have been cited 1,914 times. Each was cited 11 times. He is a young scientist born after 1980 and has an h index of 22. The main research area of this subnet is the use of artificial intelligence to identify multiple diseases in eye images. The academic homepages of the scholars show that all collaborators have published extensively in the field of medical image recognition. Professor Lin Hao-tian and Professor Zhang Kai hold the core positions in the G12 Sun Yat-sen University subnets. Professor Zhang Kai has published 111 SCI papers, which have been cited 6282 times. Each was cited 57 times, and the author's h index is 21.

The results indicate that researchers with important academic contributions can be identified using graphlet analysis.

5   Discussion

We analyzed the collaboration of authors at research institutions using a multi-layer network, extracted the core research institutions, and investigated the research collaboration network. Graphlets were created and decomposed. It was found that the frequency and distribution of the graphlets differed for different collaboration networks.

The similarities and differences in the research collaboration between different research institutions were obtained by determining various graphlet parameters. The advantages of the graphlet parameters for characterizing the research collaborations were investigated. The results of the case study showed significant differences in the academic performance of different research teams. Our proposed methods can be used to select and evaluate academic research teams with outstanding performance in specific academic fields.

6 Conclusion

This study investigated the collaboration characteristics of research teams in institutions and the similarities and differences between institutions using graphlet analysis. We established a multilayer network describing the institution-author affiliation and collaboration and used the PageRank algorithm to select the core institution in the network layer and extract the largest connected subgraph of the scientific research teams. Several graphlet parameters were extracted, including the graphlet concentration, relative graphlet frequency distance, and graph editing distance, to evaluate the salient graphlet characteristics and structure describing the research team collaborations with and between the institution. Commonly used centrality measures were used to determine the similarities and differences in the graphlet structure.

The objective of this study was to analyze the structure and collaboration characteristics of scientific research teams of institutions and determine their commonalities and differences using graphlet measurements. The results showed the collaboration and competition between research teams in different institutions.

This study has certain limitations. The proposed network cannot distinguish the roles of authors and their importance in the establishment of research teams. A functional analysis of the different graphlet structures in the research team was not conducted. Follow-up research on these topics will be conducted in the future.

Acknowledgments. This work was supported by the Young Scholars Project of the Humanities and Social Sciences of the Ministry of Education in China (GrantNo.18YJC870011), the School Research Start-up Fund (Grant No. KYZ2018008Q), and the school's key funding for team projects (Grant No. TD22016). We thank the editor and reviewers for their comments that improved our paper.

References

1. Zhu, J.: Network epistemology in scientific collaboration: how do scientists' social interactions influence cognitive interactions. Social Sciences **5**, 122–130 (2021)
2. Zhang, X., Liu, H., Zhang, Z.: Research on the relationship between interdisciplinarity and academic influence of literature under different collaboration modes. J. Intelligence **40**(8), 164–172 (2021)
3. Sang, G., Han, X.: The equilibrium property in scientific collaborations. J. Univ. Elec. Sci. Technol. China **48**(5), 786–793 (2019)
4. He, C., Wu, J., Wei, Z., et al.: Research dominance between institutions and its proximity mechanism in research collaboration: a case study of China's biomedical field. J. China Soc. Sci. Tech. Info. **39**(2), 148–157 (2020)

5. Chen, X., Zhang, Z.: Article title. A Review of the Impact of International Collaboration on Research Performance **63**(15), 127–139 (2019)
6. Cui, B., Dong, K., Xu, H.: Research on the influence and action path of patent cooperation on technology transfer: a case study of a scientific research institution of China. Info. Stud. Theory & Application **43**(12), 103–110 (2020)
7. Zhang, Y., Long, M., Zhu, G.: The influence of Chinese research university's participation in industry-university-research cooperation on academic performance from the perspective of research team. Sci. Technol. Progr. Poli. **36**(1), 132–141 (2019)
8. Gui, Q., Liu, C., Du, D.: The structure and dynamic of scientific collaboration network among countries along the belt and road. Sustainability **11**(19), 5187 (2019)
9. Liu, F., Mao, J., Li, G.: The characteristics of scientific research collaboration and spatial agglomeration pattern in the field of scientometrics. Information Science **40**(1), 166–175 (2022)
10. Wang, L., Wang, X., Philipsen, N.J.: Network structure of scientific collaborations between China and the EU member states. Scientometrics **113**(2), 765–781 (2017). https://doi.org/10.1007/s11192-017-2488-6
11. Feng, S., Kirkley, A.: Mixing patterns in interdisciplinary co-authorship networks at multiple scales. Scientific Reports (10), 7731 (2020)
12. Li, Y., Li, H., Liu, N., Liu, X.: Important institutions of interinstitutional scientific collaboration networks in materials science. Scientometrics **117**(1), 85–103 (2018). https://doi.org/10.1007/s11192-018-2837-0
13. Wen, P., Zheng, X., Lai, T., et al.: Research on the science research relationship and development trend of NSF institutions in US. Journal of Modern Information **41**(4), 154–161 and 177 (2021)
14. Zhou, J., Zeng, A., Fan, Y., Di, Z.: Identifying important scholars via directed scientific collaboration networks. Scientometrics **114**(3), 1327–1343 (2017). https://doi.org/10.1007/s11192-017-2619-0
15. Yu, C., Lin, A., Zhong, Y., et al.: Scientific collaboration recommendation based on network embedding. J. China Soc. Sci. Techni. Info. **38**(5), 500–511 (2019)
16. Sarajlić, A., Malod-Dognin, N., Yaveroğlu, Ö.N., et al.: Graphlet-based characterization of directed networks. Sci. Rep. **6**(1), 35098 (2016)
17. Milo, R., Shen-Orr, S., Itzkovitz, S., et al.: Network motifs: simple building blocks of complex networks. Science **298**(5594), 824–827 (2002)
18. Dey, A.K., Gel, Y.R., Poor, H.V.: What network motifs tell us about resilience and reliability of complex networks. Proc. Natl. Acad. Sci. **116**(39), 19368–19373 (2019)
19. Tamara, D., Kristijan, P., Ljupcho, K.: Graphlets in Multiplex Networks. Scientific Reports **10**(1), 1–13 (2020)
20. Yan, W., Wen, X.: Following and cooperation: an analysis of online academic relationship networks and behavior patterns of research users. Info. Stud. Theory & Application **45**(4), 75–82 (2022)
21. Han, T., Wang, L., Xu, X.: Evolution of scientific research cooperation network in the yangtze river delta city group: empirical analysis based on SCIE and SSCI papers. Info. Stud. Theory & Application **43**(10), 151–156 (2020)
22. Huang, L., Ni, X., Cheng, K., et al.: Identification of potential research partners based on two-mode network analysis. J. China Soc. Sci. Techni. Info. **39**(9), 906–913 (2020)
23. Lin, Y., Wang, K., Liu, H., et al.: Application of network representation learning in the prediction of scholar academic cooperation. J. China Soc. Sci. Techni. Info. **39**(04), 367–373 (2020)
24. Pelacho, M., Ruiz, G., Sanz, F., Tarancón, A., Clemente-Gallardo, J.: Analysis of the evolution and collaboration networks of citizen science scientific publications. Scientometrics **126**(1), 225–257 (2020). https://doi.org/10.1007/s11192-020-03724-x

25. Tantardini, M., Ieva, F., Tajoli, L., et al.: Comparing methods for comparing networks. Sci. Rep. **9**(1), 17557 (2019)
26. Pržulj, N.: Biological network comparison using graphlet degree distribution. Bioinformatics **23**(2), 177–183 (2007)
27. Schieber, T.A., Carpi, L., Díaz-Guilera, A., et al.: Quantification of network structural dissimilarities. Nature Communications **8**, 13928 (2017)
28. Du, Z., Yu, S., Luo, H., et al.: Consensus convergence in large-group social network environment: Coordination between trust relationship and opinion similarity. Knowl.-Based Syst. **217**, 106828 (2021)
29. Perez, C., Ting, I.H.: Can you hold an advantageous network position? The role of neighborhood similarity in the sustainability of structural holes in social networks. Decision Support Systems 113783 (2022)
30. Benson, A.R., Gleich, D.F., Leskovec, J.: Higher-order organization of complex networks. Science **353**(6295), 163–166 (2016)
31. Fang, J., Zhang, P., Zhou, Y., et al.: Endophenotype-based in silico network medicine discovery combined with insurance record data mining identifies sildenafil as a candidate drug for Alzheimer's disease. Nature Aging **1**(12), 1175–1188 (2021)
32. Calderone, A., Formenti, M., Aprea, F., et al.: Comparing Alzheimer's and Parkinson's diseases networks using graph communities structure. BMC Syst. Biol. **10**(1), 25 (2016)
33. Zhao, W., Luo, J., Fan, T., et al.: Analyzing and visualizing scientific research collaboration network with core node evaluation and community detection based on network embedding. Pattern Recogn. Lett. **144**, 54–60 (2021)
34. Duan, D., Xia, Q.: Evolution of scientific collaboration on COVID-19: A bibliometric analysis. Learned Publishing **34**(3), 429–441 (2021)
35. Wang, Y., Yang, X., Yu, H., et al.: The collaboration pattern and comparative analysis of research teams in the artificial intelligence field. Journal **64**(20), 14–22 (2020)
36. Zhang, M., Ge, S., Jia, Y., et al.: Analysis of cohesion characteristics of research cooperation network based on K-core. Systems Engineering –Theory & Practice **40**(7), 1821–1831 (2020)
37. Zhang, L., Tian, D., Qu, J.: Article title. Journal of the China Society for Scientific and Technical Information **39**(7), 719–730 (2020)
38. Kivelä, M., Arenas, A., Barthelemy, M., et al.: Multilayer networks. Journal of complex networks **2**(3), 203–271 (2014)
39. Shi, J., Yang, R., Jin, T., et al.: Realtime top-k personalized pagerank over large graphs on GPUs. Proceedings of the VLDB Endowment **13**(1), 15–28 (2019)
40. Pržulj, N., Corneil, D.G., Jurisica, I.: Modeling interactome: scale-free or geometric? Bioinformatics **20**(18), 3508–3515 (2004)
41. Serratosa, F.: Graph edit distance: restrictions to be a metric. Pattern Recogn. **90**, 250–256 (2019)

Logical Relationship Extraction of Multimodal South China Sea Big Data Using BERT and Knowledge Graph

Peng Yufang[1(✉)], Xu Hao[1], Jin Weijian[1], and Yang Haiping[2]

[1] Nanjing Institute of Technology, Nanjing 211167, China
laisitianshi@163.com
[2] Nanjing University, Nanjing 210023, China

Abstract. In recent years, massive multi-source heterogeneous South China Sea data have been widely used in the construction of South China Sea digital resources, such as the South China Sea Sovereign Evidence Chain Project. Due to the data sparsity, a large number of isolated data are generated, which seriously affects the analysis effect of the South China Sea Big Data. In this paper, we proposed a novel data association method. We collected data from the South China Sea Library Digital Resources as South China Sea evidence data, which is a sentence or paragraph containing time, place, people, institutions and events can prove the sovereignty of the South China Sea. According to the definition of the evidence weight by the International Court of Justice, the logical relationship of South China Sea evidence data was constructed. Firstly, we randomly selected 3068 data from 21174 evidence data to label the logical relationship. Secondly, we used the BERT pre-training model to extract the logical relationship of evidence data. Finally, the Knowledge Graph technology is used to retrieve and visualize the logical relationship of evidence data. In this paper, we applied the BERT to extract the logical relationships of evidence data with an accuracy of 0.78, which indicates that the model has some feasibility. This paper could help to improve the correlation of the South China Sea Big Data and to enhance the ability of data processing.

Keyword: Logical Relationship · The South China Sea Big Data · Deep learning · Knowledge Graph

The authors extend their appreciation to the Young Foundation of Ministry of Education Project of Humanities and Social Sciences in China (Grand Nos: 22YJC870012), the General Project of Philosophy and Social Science Research in Colleges and Universities in Jiangsu Province in China (Grand Nos: 2022SJYB0444) and the School Research Foundation Project of Nanjing Institute of technology in China(Grand Nos: YKJ202231).

Y. Tian et al. (Eds.): ICBDS 2022, CCIS 1796, pp. 219–233, 2023.
https://doi.org/10.1007/978-981-99-3300-6_16

1 Introduction

In the era of Big Data, the importance of data was more and more obvious, who owns the data will take the initiative. Big data security also involves national security. Especially the South China Sea issue has always been a hot topic in territorial sovereignty disputes. Therefore, we research the association of South China Sea big data.

Since the Western Han Dynasty, the Chinese had already found the Spratly Islands. A large number of records of the South China Sea were reserved by China. Especially with the rapid development of information technology, more and more the South China Sea data are being mined. For example, books, thesis, archives, map, audio and video, newspapers, porcelain, temples, stone tablets and various marine antiques. The massive multimodal and scattered of the South Sea big data, which made it more difficult to do association analysis.

In this paper, we applied DNN to extract the fine-grained data from multimodal South China Sea big data from the South China Sea Library Digital Resources, which is a sentence or paragraph can prove the territorial sovereignty of the South China Sea, taking them as the South China Sea evidence data. To further improve the correlation of the South China Sea big data, according to the definition of evidence weight by the International Court of Justice, BERT is applied to extract the logical relationship of the South China Sea evidence data. And knowledge graph technology is applied to achieve evidence data retrieval and visualization.

2 Related Work

2.1 Research on the South China Sea Big Data

In recent years, a large number of the South China Sea digital resources have been discovered, many scholars have flocked to study the South China Sea issue. It is the key way to solve the South China Sea issue by collecting, organizing, analyzing and using the South China Sea big data. From the theoretical level to organize the South China Sea evidence data. For example, from a historical perspective to organize the historical rights and evidence catalogues in the South China Sea [1]. Based on the information organization theory to construct the knowledge system framework of the South China Sea data [2]. Based on the definition of the evidence weight by the International Court to construct the South China Sea evidence chain [3], etc. From the application level of computer technology to organize the South China Sea data. For example, the fine-grained South China Sea data were extracted by machine learning and deep learning [4], the multimodal South China Sea data were classified by using deep learning [5], based on the knowledge graph to visualize the South China Sea documentary data catalogue [6], based on the GIS technology to organize the South China Sea map data [7], etc.

2.2 Research on the Logical Relationship Extraction

In this paper, logical relationship extraction of the South China Sea data belongs to the information extraction in natural language processing [8]. Information extraction is becoming more and more mature both in terms of application areas and technical aspects [9].

Logic, in a narrow sense, refers to the laws of thinking, in a broad sense, it refers to laws, including thinking laws and objective laws. Semantics and logic have different emphases. The former focuses on the expression of the content, structure and meaning of things, while the latter focuses on the speculation on the objective laws of things. Logic includes formal logic and mathematical logic. Formal logic includes inductive logic and deductive logic [10, 11]. The cognitive basis of logic, and described in detail informal logic, legal logic, inductive logic and artificial intelligence logic. In particular, legal logic believes that scientific legal reasoning mode is a necessary condition for realizing judicial justice, and advocates the organic combination of formal logic and informal logic [12]. It can be seen that legal logic is particularly important for judicial decisions.

Research on logical relationship, from the application field level, including (1) knowledge extraction of entity relationship logical reasoning in open text [13]; (2) logical relationship in computer hardware detection [14]; (3) knowledge evaluation logical relationship extraction [15]; (4) multi-level logical relationship of electronic medical records [16]; (6) causal event extraction from financial texts [17], etc. From the technical level: (1) the quantification of logical relationship of financial risk using BERT [18]; (2) the application of event graph and knowledge graph to target recommendation [19, 20]; (3) causality extraction based on Deep Learning [21], etc.

In summary, it is difficult to analyze the sovereignty of the South China Sea from the vast and scattered South China Sea big data, therefore, it is very necessary to deeply explore the relationship of the South China Sea big data. However, there is little research literature on the extraction of logical relationship from South China Sea data, especially on the extraction of logical relationship from the fine-grained South China Sea data. It is particularly important to realize the intelligent extraction of logical relationship of evidence data from a large number of modal evidence materials for building a proof system that can prove the facts of a case. Therefore, this paper constructed the logical association rules of evidence data through the definition of evidence weight by the International Court of Justice, and applied the BERT to extract the logical relationship of the South China Sea big data.

3　Data and Methods

3.1　Data Collection and Preprocessing

We collected data from the South China Sea Library Digital Resources. This paper conducts further research on the basis of fine-grained evidence data extraction results [4]. That is, we collected 21174 the fine-grained South China Sea data (a sentence or paragraph) from 409 multimodal South China Sea Digital Resources (for example: Books, papers, newspapers, maps, archives, audio and video, etc.) by using DNN. We took the 21174 data as the South China Sea evidence data which could prove the territorial sovereignty of the South China Sea. Then This paper randomly selects 3068 samples from 21174 evidence data. Due to the limited number of samples, it is impossible to purposefully find all logical correlations, so only randomly selected samples are labeled and counted. According to statistics, 3068 data have a total of 13 labels. The labels corresponding to the largest number of samples is 564 and the smallest is 76. The samples are relatively uniform on the whole, but there is a problem of small sample size. The sample size distribution of manual labeling is shown in Table 1 and Fig. 1.

Table 1. Sample Size Distribution for Logical Relationship Labeling

Label	Number of samples
111 Chinese official records	564
112 Chinese private records	271
113 History recorded by the claimant	207
114 Historical data recorded by third parties	255
12 International treaties related to China's sovereignty	386
221 Administration in Modern China (1840–1949)	373
222 Administration in Contemporary China (1949-present)	179
311 Maps officially published before the establishment of the government of the Republic of China (before 1912)	76
312 Officially published maps during the Republic of China (1912–1949)	212
313 Official maps published after the founding of New China (1949-present)	126
32 Official maps published by the countries surrounding the South China Sea	88
33 Maps drawn by third parties	224
34 privately drawn maps	107

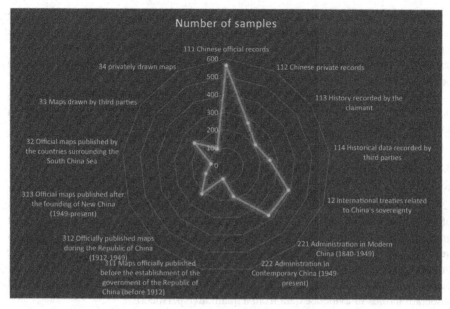

Fig. 1. Sample Size Distribution for Logical Relationship Labeling

3.2 Methods

3.2.1 BERT

BERT [22] is a deep learning-based language representation model proposed by Google AI in October 2018. The main model structure of BERT is the Transformer encoder. BERT is a language model composed of bidirectional multi-head self-attention encoders. [23] As a practical and effective general framework model for natural language processing, BERT is favored by more and more researchers. For example, Lu Xueqiang et al. [24] combined BERT and semantics to handle multi-label classification, Jiang Yanting et al. [25] BERT-based book multi-label classification, etc. The Structure of BERT in Text Classification, as shown in Fig. 2.

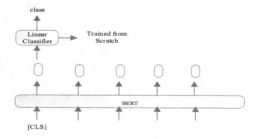

Fig. 2. BERT in Text Classification

The BERT model consists of a multi-layer Transformer model (the Transformer model is represented by Trm in the figure). The basic mechanism of the Transformer Encoder layer expanded on the right includes a multi-attention mechanism layer, a residual normalization layer, and a feedforward linear conversion layer. Finally, do one more normalization.

Logical relationship extraction of the South China Sea data, which can help to improve data correlation and reduce data fragmentation. BERT has a good effect on small sample data classification and extraction.

3.2.2 Building the Logical Association Rules

Whether Wigmore proposed the relevance of evidence in law [26] or logical relevance [27], all reflect the logical character of the evidence. This paper is based on the definition of the evidence weight of the International Court of Justice, that is, the evidence weight gradually decreases from top to bottom, as shown in Table 2. Because it is difficult to quantify the evidence weight, because the same evidence has different probative power in different contexts, and the same type of evidence is produced in different ages, the evidence weight is not easy to quantify. Therefore, this paper constructed the logical association rules of evidence data from a qualitative perspective.

Table 2. Definition of the evidence weight by the International Court of Justice

Name of the evidence weight	Content of the evidence weight
Effective international treaties and agreements	Various border treaties such as Cairo Declaration, Potsdam Proclamation, etc
Documents and reports from international agencies, such as UN documents, NGO reports, etc	United Nations reports, official United Nations working documents, United Nations resolutions, statements, etc., documents, certifications and resolutions of other international institutions, etc
Legislation and other legal documents in colonial period, keeping possession of legal documents more than effective control of laws	The weight of domestic legislation is greater than that of official records, diplomatic declarations, official documents and official declarations; the weight of colonial legislation is in a higher priority, followed by the weight of documentary evidence and graphic evidence reflecting the legal rights of the territory; official documents and official declarations are greater than maps and other graphic materials, audiovisual materials, affidavits, satellite imagery, evidence from third parties

(*continued*)

Table 2. (*continued*)

Name of the evidence weight	Content of the evidence weight
Evidence of effective control during colonial times	Domestic judicial acts, administrative management acts, and acts of effectively exercising territorial jurisdiction, the weight of official acts is generally greater than that of private acts, and the weight of colonial legislation is in a higher priority, followed by written evidence, maps and related graphic materials that reflect territorial legal rights, audiovisual materials, affidavits, satellite images, evidence from third parties
Evidence of effective control in the postcolonial period, the weight of the evidence of effective domination is generally greater than that of the initial evidence	Domestic judicial acts, administrative management acts, and acts of effectively exercising territorial jurisdiction, the weight of official acts is generally greater than that of private acts
initial evidence of entitlement	e.g. "discover"
Other evidence such as ineffective treaties, defective legal acts, etc	
other	

Based on the definition of the evidence weight by the International Court of Justice, and on the basis of Professor Zhang W.B's research on the chain of evidence, this paper puts forward a conception of the logical relationship of evidence data, as shown in Table 3.

Table 3. Logical Relationship of the South China Sea evidence data

(1) first logical name for evidence data	(2) Secondary logical name for evidence data	(3) Tertiary logical name for evidence data	(4) Four-level logical name for evidence data
1 Historical evidence/treaty	11 historical data	111 Chinese official records	
		112 Chinese private records	
		113 History recorded by the claimant	
		114 Historical data recorded by third parties	
	12 International treaties related to China's sovereignty		

(*continued*)

Table 3. (*continued*)

(1) first logical name for evidence data	(2) Secondary logical name for evidence data	(3) Tertiary logical name for evidence data	(4) Four-level logical name for evidence data
	13 Peace Treaty and Island Jurisdiction Plan between China and Claimant		
2 Maintain possession/effective jurisdiction	21 Keep Possession	211 China's Remaining Possession	2111 Official Records
			2112 Private Records
			2113 Claimant Records
			2114 Third Party Records
		212 Acquiescence or acknowledgment of claimant	2121 Recognition or acquiescence of the colonial suzerain before the claimant's independence
			2122 Recognition or acquiescence of claimant after independence
	22 Effective Jurisdiction	221 Administration in Modern China (1840–1949)	
		222 Administration in Contemporary China (1949-present)	
3 Maps	31 Officially published maps of China	311 Maps officially published before the establishment of the government of the Republic of China (before 1912)	
		312 Officially published maps during the Republic of China (1912–1949)	
		313 Official maps published after the founding of New China (1949-present)	
	32 Official maps published by the countries surrounding the South China Sea	321 The official map before independence	
		322 The official map after independence	
	33 Maps drawn by third parties		
	34 privately drawn maps		
4 Audiovisual materials/press reports/satellite graphics	41China-related audiovisual materials/news reports/satellite graphics		
	42 Audiovisual materials/press reports/satellite graphics related to the claimant		

(*continued*)

Table 3. (*continued*)

(1) first logical name for evidence data	(2) Secondary logical name for evidence data	(3) Tertiary logical name for evidence data	(4) Four-level logical name for evidence data
	43 Third-party related audiovisual materials/press reports/satellite graphics		
5 Private conduct without the authorization or consent of a government authority	51 China-related unauthorized private conduct		
	52 Unauthorized private conduct in relation to the claimant		
	53 Unauthorized private conduct related to third parties		

According to the above logical association rules, the South China Sea evidence data set is organized into an organic whole, as shown in Fig. 3.

Historical evidence/treaty in the logical relationship, in which the historical data is divided into official and private, Ma Aihong wrote "Research on the History of South China Sea Documents" [28]. If court archives, official histories or documents of official institutions are considered "official" evidence, they may also be classified as private evidence. Private historical materials, such as the archives collected by Zheng Ziyue and Mai Yunyu. There are differences between official and privately published maps in China, referring to the modern map management written by Wang Jun et al. [29]. The maps officially published by China refer to the attached drawings of the Department of General Affairs, the Ministry of the Navy, the Ordnance Survey, government documents or treaties. In addition, maps approved by the state and attached with the license of the Land and Water Map Review Committee are equivalent in effect to the standard map. Official map. Maps drawn by third parties: No other probative force should be given to those altruistic maps drawn with no connection to the facts or with a subjective purpose. Privately drawn maps: The existence may involve or imply that the country's "first occupation" by a country forms a country's preliminary rights to a certain territory, such as: ancient Chinese maps. In view of the fact that the research in this paper is mainly about the construction of the evidence chain association model, and the research on the value of evidence is the next stage of the task, the logical relationship of the map in this study is my country's official map, the surrounding claimant country map, the third-party map, and the private map. Administration in contemporary China (1949-present): domestic legislation, domestic laws, judicial acts, government declarations, patrols, effective control, effective ruling acts, judicial acts before key dates, domestic official declarations, public statements, official records, administration management, etc.

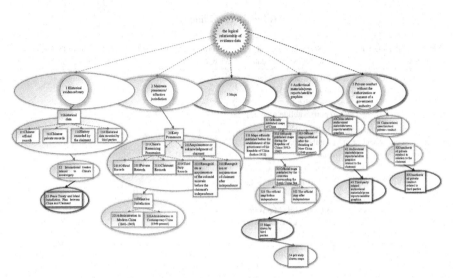

Fig. 3. Logical relationship of the South China Sea evidence data

4 Logical Relationship Extraction of the South China Sea Evidence Data Based on BERT

4.1 Experimental Dataset

3068 pieces of data were selected at any time from 21,174 pieces of evidence for logical relationship labeling. Randomly shuffle the data, and then divide the training set, validation set, and test set according to 8:1:1, and get 2454 training sets; 307 validation sets; and 307 test sets.

4.2 Experimental Environment

This paper uses the PyTorch deep learning framework to build a BERT-based multi-label data classification model. Install cuda10.2 on the Ubuntu20.04.1 LTS system to configure the GPU to train and debug the model. The specific experimental environment configuration is shown in Table 4.

Table 4. Experimental environment configuration

Item	Environment
Development language	Python3.8
Deep Learning Framework	PyTorch1.7.0
Graphics card	Nvidia GeForce GTX 1080ti
RAM	64G memory 32 cores

4.3 Experimental Design and Evaluation Metrics

4.3.1 Hyperparameter Settings for the Model

In this paper, the model parameters are set during the experiment. Data length: unified padding length of 256, fill 0 if less than 256, and cut if it exceeds 256; BatchSize: According to the current graphics card capacity, select 16 samples per batch for training; select the optimizer AdamW; the learning rate of the BERT part is 2e-5; The learning rate of the fully connected layer is 1e-3; the learning rate is optimized by the warmup method; the Epoch is 20; the earlystop is 10; the dropout is set to 0.1, the detailed hyperparameter settings, as shown in Table 5.

Table 5. Hyperparameter setting

Hyperparameter	Value
Number of Transformer	12
Dropout	0.1
Batch_size	16
Max_length	256
Feature dimension	768
Number of epochs	20
lr-BERT	2e-5
lr-FFN	1e-3
Optimiser	AdamW

4.3.2 Backbone Network

The pre-trained Chinese BERT of Harbin Institute of Technology is selected as the basic architecture, and the model uses the super-large-scale Chinese Wikipedia corpus to perform mask self-supervised learning, so as to obtain basic prior knowledge. When training a new task, just finetune it again. The network is constructed by splicing the coding layers of 12-layer transformers.

4.3.3 Loss Function

The loss function in this paper uses the cross entropy loss function, and the specific formula is as follows:

Loss function:

$$L = (1 - \alpha)L_{BCE} + \alpha \sum_{i=1}^{M} L_{LCA}$$

4.3.4 Evaluation Indicators

The evaluation indicators select the evaluation indicators commonly used in multi-label classification problems, such as accuracy, recall, precision, and F1.

$$Accuracy = (TP + TN)/(TP + TN + FP + FN) \tag{1}$$

$$Precision = TP/(TP + FP) \tag{2}$$

$$Recall = TP/(TP + FN) \tag{3}$$

$$F1 = 2PR/(P + R) \tag{4}$$

4.4 Experimental Results and Analysis

Since the number of samples in this paper is only 3068, for the BERT pre-training model, the larger the number of samples, the better the training effect of the model. The experimental results of this model: Acc: 0.78, precision: 0.75, recall: 0.72, F1: 0.68, the overall effect is OK, and the model is feasible. If a large number of samples are increased in the later stage, the effect of the model will be significantly improved.

5   Visualization of Logical Relationship of the South China Sea Evidence Data Based on Knowledge Graph

In order to show the logical relationship of the South China Sea evidence data clearly, the Knowledge Graph technology was used to visualize and retrieve these data. Retrieve a topic in the search box, and get all the evidence data sets. These evidence data sets have a label that is the logical relationship between the evidence data, and a tree-like visualization result is constructed through the logical relationship. The logical relationship of the evidence data in this paper, the same layer is the "brother relationship", the higher the importance is at the top. Each layer is subdivided below, and there is a "parent-child relationship" between them and the previous layer. The higher the ranking, the higher the importance, as shown in Fig. 3.

In view of the complexity and certain difficulties of visualization in Fig. 4, this paper simply presents the visualization of logical relationship of the South China Sea evidence data. By importing the logical relationship data of the evidence data into the Neo4j graph database, the visualization of the logical relationship is preliminarily realized, as shown in Figs. 4 and 5.

From Fig. 5, it can be clearly shown that "evidence: In December 1936, Kaiyang Industrial Company of Hirata Sueji sent personnel to Taiping Island to explore phosphate mines", which belongs to the logical relationship of "53 unauthorized private acts related to third parties". Through the visualization of the evidence chain based on logical correlation, historical evidence and legal basis are fully integrated, providing more voice for rights protection in the South China Sea.

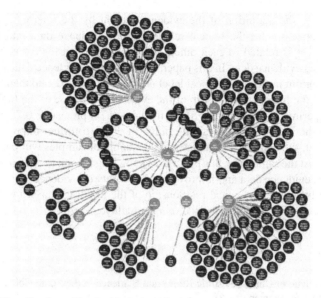

Fig. 4. Visualization of Logical Relationship for the South China Sea Evidence Data

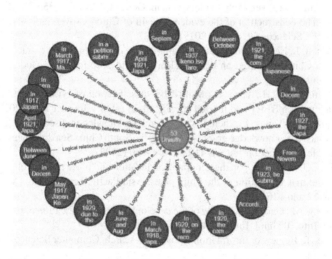

Fig. 5. Visualization of Logical relationship for the South China Sea evidence data

6 Conclusion and Future Work

In the age of big data, hundreds of millions of digital resources are generated, a large amount of isolated data is also generated, which seriously affects the effect of data analysis. The South China Sea big data also faces such problems. Therefore, this study based on the definition of evidence weight by the International Court of Justice, the logical relationship of evidence data is constructed to enhance the relevance of the South China Sea big data.

According to the definition of the evidence weight by the International Court of Justice, this paper divides the logical relationship of evidence data into five logical layers, each layer is related to each other, and finally forms a logical network of the South China Sea evidence data. In this paper, 3068 pieces of evidence data are randomly selected, the bottom layer of the logical label is manually labeled, and then the BERT is used to extract the logical relationship of the evidence data. Due to the limited sample size of the experiment, the accuracy of the model is 0.78, precision: 0.75, recall: 0.72, F1: 0.68, and the model has a certain usability. In order to further improve the model extraction effect, the number of samples and the quality of samples will be increased in the later stage. At the same time, this paper uses knowledge graph to visualize the logical relationship of evidence data and improve the readability of evidence data. Meanwhile, in order to fully reflect the logical relationship of the South China Sea evidence data, the later research will further ensure the sample quality.

References

1. Li, J.: Catalogue of China's Historic Rights and Evidence in the South China Sea. Xiamen University Press, Xiamen (2018)
2. Chen, S., Wu, S., Xie, Q.: Research on the construction of AI knowledge management system for South China Sea sovereignty evidence chain. Ocean Information **35**(01), 52–56 (2020)
3. Zhang, W.: The construction of the evidence chain of China's sovereignty over the Nansha Islands. Social Sciences **09**, 85–96 (2019)
4. Peng, Y., Chen, J., He, Z.: Comparison and application of evi dence data extraction algorithms in the South China sea based on machine learning and deep learning. Modern Intelligence **42**(02), 55–69 (2022)
5. Peng, Y., Shi, J., Xu, H., Yang, H.: Multi-label classification of evidence data in the South China Sea based on BERT and faceted classification. Library Journal 1–15 [2022-05-13]
6. Wang, Y., Situ, L., Yang, H., Cheng, W.: Research on knowledge discovery of documentary catalogues based on knowledge graph——taking the South China Sea documentary catalogue as an example. Information Journal **41**(03), 173–180 (2022)
7. Xu, P., Shen, G.: A research on the geographical location and place name evolution of "North Island" in the map exhibition of the Philippines. Asia-Pacific Security and Ocean Research (04), 102–112 and 126 (2016)
8. Zhao, J., Song, M., Gao, X.: A review of the development and ap plication of natural language processing. Info. Technol. Info. **07**, 142–145 (2019)
9. Guo, X., He, T.: Review of information extraction research. Computer Science **42**(02), 14–17 and 38 (2015)
10. Qin, C., Zhu, T., Zhao, P., Zhang, Y.: Research progress of natural language semantic analysis. Library and Information Work **58**(22), 130–137 (2014)
11. Copi, I.M., Copi, C, Copi, I.M., et al.: Introduction to Logic. Renmin University of China Press, Beijing (2014)
12. Xiong, M.: Logic and Cognition. Acta Social Sciences, 2002-11-14 (003)
13. Liu, H., Xue, Y., Li, R., Ren, H., Chen, H., Zhang, P.: Knowledge extraction of open text-oriented logical reasoning and exploration of event influence reasoning. Journal of Chinese Information **35**(10), 56–63 (2021)
14. You, J.: Logic design and implementation of arbitrary waveform synthesis module based on sampling rate conversion technology. University of Electronic Science and Technology of China (2021)

15. Ma, N.: Research on Knowledge Extraction Technology of Trap Evaluation Based on Ontology. Northeast Petroleum University (2021)
16. Wu, C., Xu, L., Qian, Y., He, Q., Wang, Z.: Exploration of multi-level information extraction methods from Chinese electronic medical records. China Digital Medicine **15**(06), 29–31 (2020)
17. Luo, Z.: Research on Causal Event Extraction from Chinese Financial Texts. Jiangxi University of Finance and Economics (2020)
18. Jia, M., Wang, X.: Quantification method of financial risk logical relation ship based on BERT and mutual information. Data Analysis and Knowledge Discovery: 1-16 [2022-05-15]
19. Wu, X.: Research on tourism route recommendation method integrating affair graph and knowledge graph. Harbin Institute of Technology (2021)
20. Han, Y.: Research on Logical Relationship Extraction Technology in Knowledge Graph. Chongqing University of Posts and Telecommunications (2020)
21. Zheng, Y.: Research on BLTGM Causal Relationship Extraction Model Based on Time Relationship and Deep Learning. Jilin University (2021)
22. Devlin, J., Chang, M.W., Lee, K., et al.: BERT: Pre-Training of Deep Bidirectional Transformers for Language Understanding. arXiv Preprint, arXiv: 1810.04805
23. Duan, R., Chao, W., Zhang, Y.: Application of pre-trained language model BERT in downstream tasks. J. Beijing Univ. Info. Sci. Technol. (Natural Science Edition) **35**(06), 77–83 (2020)
24. Lv, X., Peng, C., Zhang, L., Dong, Z., You, X.: Multi-label text classification method integrating BERT and label semantic attention. Computer Applications: 1–8 [2021-10-21]
25. Jiang, Y., Hu, R.: Research on book representation learning and multi-label classification based on BERT model. New Century Library (09), 38-44 (2020)
26. Lempert, R.O., Salzburg, S.A.: A Modern Approach to Evidence:Text, Problem, Tran scripts and Cases. West Group, 153 (1982)
27. Montrose, J.: Basic Concepts of the Law of Evidence. Law Quarterly Re view **70**, 127 (1954)
28. Ma, A.: A Textual Research on South China Sea Documents and Historical Ma terials. Science and Technology Document Information Management **29**(3), 28–31 and 35 (2015)
29. Wang, J., Zhang, X.: Topographic mapping and map management in mod ern China. In: International Symposium on Review and Prospect of Modern Science and Technology in China, pp. 358–362. Chinese Academy of Engineering, Beijing (2002)

Research on Application of Knowledge Graph in War Archive Based on Big Data

Huang Yongqin[⊠], Chen Xushan, Yang Anlian, and Ping Shuo

Department of Military Information and Public Opinion, Political College of National Defense University PLA, Shanghai 200433, China
yqhuang163@163.com

Abstract. War archive is a quintessential big data issue about national history and military data security in urgent need of exploitation. Knowledge graph is one of the core technologies of knowledge engineering in the era of big data. With the ability of deep knowledge reasoning and progressively expanding cognition, knowledge graph has become a key technology for the construction and application in the field of military big data. Most of the existing knowledge graph is general knowledge graph for general fields, but there is no mature method of knowledge graph construction and application for the military archival big data. Taking the archival data of the War to Resist U.S. Aggression and Aid Korea as an example, this paper, based on the special needs for military archive fields, explores the construction path of knowledge graph from the aspects of knowledge modeling, knowledge extraction, knowledge fusion and knowledge management. At the same time, the application of knowledge retrieval, archive resource linking, knowledge Q & A, knowledge recommendation and other scenarios are explored.

Keywords: Knowledge Graph · Archival Data · War Archive · Military Big Data · Military Data Security · the War to Resist U.S. Aggression and Aid Korea

1 Introduction

In the era of big data, the contradiction between the explosive growth of information and the limited processing cognitive ability of users has become increasingly prominent, as well as the phenomenon of information overload and knowledge disorientation. With its powerful semantic processing and deep knowledge reasoning capability, knowledge graph (KG) has become one of the key technologies for the development and application of big data and artificial intelligence, which is widely used in big data analysis, intelligent question and answer, personalized recommendation and other fields. War archive is an important component of military big data, which is related to national history and military data security, and its development and utilization possess specific practical value, while knowledge graph is one of the important big data solutions to achieve this goal. The 14th

The authors extend their appreciation to the Young Foundation of National Social Science in China (Grand Nos: 2019-SKJJ-C-064, 19CTQ033).

Five-Year National Archives Development Plan, revealed in 2021, has also proposed the exploration of knowledge graph, artificial intelligence and digital humanities on the deep processing and utilization of archival big data.

Current research hotspots mainly consist of two aspects. On one hand of archive, some scholars focus on the construction of domain-specific knowledge graph, such as anti-epidemic COVID-19 archival big data [1], electronic archive management [2], electronic medical record archive [3], knowledge service [4], etc. On the other hand, in military field, the wide application scenarios of knowledge graph include weapons and equipment big data [5], military terminology [6], operational elements [7], Command big data information System [8], etc. Nowadays, few studies pay close attention to the development of war archival data, except that Chen Haiyu [9] constructs a knowledge aggregation framework of anti-Japanese war archive resource, and selects "Nanchang Uprising" as an example to display the knowledge aggregation and visualization of anti-war archive resource based on the theoretical approach of digital humanities. Also, Jesús Robledano-Arillo [10] presents a linked open data (LOD) comprehensive distributed systems of knowledge representation, which can be queried through SPARQL language. Eetu Mäkelä [11] collected more than ten different authoritative big data sources about the First World War based on the CIDOC conceptual reference models (CIDOC-CRM), the dataset includes events, places, agents, times, keywords, and themes related to the war. The content is harmonized into Resource Description Framework (RDF), and published as a WW1LOD Linked Open Data service. Mikko Koho [12] presents the WarSampo knowledge graph, a shared semantic infrastructure, and a linked open data service for World War II big data, used both WarSampo knowledge graph and CIDOC-CRM to enable linked and semantic integration of open big data on military history of World War II distributed in different countries and heterogeneous nationalities. In summary, it shows that knowledge graph is feasible to be applied in the field of military archival big data, and the open standards such as CIDOC-CRM, WW1LOD, and WarSampo mentioned in the existing research results can simultaneously provide references for the knowledge graph applications in this study. However, it must also be considered that these standards are not mainly focused on the archive domain, research must be conducted in conjunction with professional and widely used archival standards, as well as the data characteristics of war archive.

Taking the military archival big data of the War to Resist U.S. Aggression and Aid Korea as an example, this paper explores the construction and application of knowledge graph based on the following reasons: (a) from the perspective of archive resources, there is a vast amount of military archive with different types of data structure for this war, which is a typical big data problem that need to be developed and utilized at a deep level. (b) From the perspective of operational work, the practice of the compilation and research of military archive is mainly qualitative and text-based battle case studies, lacking macroscopic and visualized display results from the viewpoint of big data. (c) From the perspective of user needs, the interview and investigation found that there was a strong demand for the use of archive of the war to resist US aggression and aid Korea in the construction of their history museum and honor room, military history research, military big data security strategy and the battle case teaching. Knowledge graph is one of the best ways to solve the above needs, and at the same time, this paper hopes that the research can provide reference for the construction path of knowledge graph for military archival big data.

2 Construction of Knowledge Graph

Based on the knowledge graph life cycle theory [13], in the process of constructing the knowledge graph in archival big data for the War to Resist U.S. Aggression and Aid Korea, there are mainly the following life cycles: knowledge modeling, knowledge extraction, knowledge fusion, and knowledge management. Each link iterates in the construction process.

2.1 Knowledge Modeling

Knowledge graph is essentially a large-scale semantic network, and knowledge modeling is the process of organizing and expressing different types of knowledge through ontology-based knowledge representation, and obtaining semantic information about knowledge by using formal knowledge representation. The purpose of knowledge modeling is to acquire the basic concepts in a specific knowledge domain, the relationships among those concepts and the attribute composition of such concepts, etc., then outputting the knowledge framework and forming a domain semantic network with the acquired knowledge instances. In summary, ontology is the core realization path of knowledge modeling, and the path to realize standardization, normalization, and structured processing of knowledge. The specific processes of the ontology design are as follows.

(1) **Concept extraction**. The main approach is a combination of top-down and bottom-up methods.

Application of top-down method. The domain terms required for knowledge framework construction, i.e., entity type names, attribute names, relationship names and other key elements, are extracted from knowledge resources. First, the texts in the above standards and resources are analyzed by using natural language processing tools to extract candidate terms; then the statistical features of the terms are used to filter the terms of lower quality among them; finally, the screened terms are merged and the terms of same concepts are aggregated and converted into concepts. Among the knowledge sources used for top-down concept extraction include (a) archival industry standards, such as national military standards for the archival industry, electronic archival metadata schemes, archival description and retrieval models, Open Archival Information System (OAIS)- Reference model and records retention models (ISO 14721); (b) military knowledge resources, such as military terminology, military encyclopedias, military archive thesaurus, archives compilation and research achievements; (c) data standards of Libraries Archives & Museums (LAMs), including FRBR family series standards, CIDOC-CRM, Cataloging Cultural Objects: A Guide to Describing Cultural Works and Their Images (CCO), Visual Resources Association Core Categories (VRA Core) etc.; (d) multimedia content description standards, such as MPEG-7, MPEG-21, etc.

Application of bottom-up method. Combining the wisdom of experts, we analyzed the specific composition of archival content, and then summarized and refined the relevant concepts in the archival data. Finally, comparing the concepts extracted top-down from the knowledge sources, we formed a preliminary conceptual framework system.

(2) **Relationship extraction**. After completing concept extraction, the relationship between concepts needs to be further defined. The main steps include: (a) Classification system construction. Using auxiliary tools such as narrative tables to obtain the contextual relationships between different concepts. (b) Attribute definition and relationship extraction. The attributes and relations of the above concepts are extracted in a way like the domain concept extraction, and firstly, the set of candidate attributes and relations is obtained; then the low-quality attributes and relations are evaluated and filtered out, with finally the attributes and relations expressing the same meaning aggregated and converted into attributes and relations of the war domain concepts. When necessary, it also needs to define some rules or constraints on the attributes and relations, which can be used for knowledge disambiguation to improve the quality of the graph.

CIDOC-CRM [14] is a set of conceptual reference models for information integration applied to cultural heritage developed by the International Documentation Committee (CIDOC) of the International Council of Museums (ICOM). As the preceding review shows, CIDOC-CRM has been used to describe relevant elements of warfare with remarkable effectiveness, but there is also an insufficient match with data from the archival domain. The Records in Contexts Conceptual Model (RiC-CM) released in 2016 and the Records in Contexts-Ontology (RiC-O) released in 2019 by the International Council on Archives (ICA) [15] are new international standards for the semantic description and contextual organization of archival resources, which can effectively promote the application of data-based semantic transformation of archival resources. In the research practice, RiC-CM is selected as the basis of ontology concept model for the archives of the War to Resist U.S. Aggression and Aid Korea, CIDOC-CRM is used as the semantic framework reference, and a combination of top-down and bottom-up design ideas is adopted. RDF data standard [16] and Ontology Wed Language (OWL)[17] are used to knowledge representation, and Protégé [18] is chosen as the construction tool. We used the seven-step method of parsimonious knowledge engineering proposed by Noy and McGuinness [19] to construct the ontology.

As shown in Table 1.

(a) Six core concepts such as E01 Time, E06 Location, E10 Combatants, E20 Troops, E26 Battles, and E33 Message are extracted as the top-level concepts of the domain archive ontology.

(b) The mapping relationship between the six concept classes and CIDOC-CRM and RiC-CM is shown in the Table 1, where E01 Time and E06 Place are designed in a reorganized way, and E10 Combatant, E20 Combat Troop and E33 Message are designed in an upgraded way, while E26 Campaign follows the existing standard.

(c) Data attributes indicate the intrinsic properties and specific characteristics of the class. 32 data attributes are defined for the six concept classes as shown in the table.

(d) Object attributes indicate the relationships between classes. Object attributes are defined according to the war process, and eight object attributes are defined with reference to the relationships described in the CIDOC-CRM framework and the RiC-CM model: relevance, participation, took place, start, finish, consists of, affiliation, and transmit.

Table 1. Ontology knowledge framework

Class	Method	Mapping with CIDOC-CRM	Mapping with RiC-CM	Data Property	Object Property
E01 Time	Reorganization	—	RiC-E18 Date	E02 Start Time E03 Persistent Time E04 Finish Time E05 Other Time	**Start**: E02 Start Time ↔ E27 Campaign Name **Finish**: E04 Finish Time ↔ E27 Campaign Name
E06 Place	Reorganization	E53 Place	RiC-E22 Place	E07 Historical Place E08 Current Place E09 Latitude-Longitude	**Relevance**: E07 Historical Place ↔ E08 Current Place
E10 Combatant	Upgrade	E21 Person	RiC-E08 Person	E11 Name E12 Alias E13 Native E14 Birth Date E15 Death Date E16 Nationality E17 Position E18 Achievements E19 Political Stand	**Participation**: E11 Combatant ↔ E27 Campaign Name **Affiliation**: E11 Combatant ↔ E16 Nationality **Relevance**: E11 Name ↔ E11 Name (e.g., Calling)
E20 Combat Troop	Upgrade	E74 Group E39 Actor	RiC-E09 Group	E21 Troop Name E22 Troop Abbreviation E23 Superior Troop E24 Subordinate Troop E25 History of the Combat Troop	**Consists of**: E21 Troop Name ↔ E11 Combatant
E26 Campaign	Follow	E5 Event	RiC-E14 Event	E27 Campaign Name E28 Campaign Alias E29 Campaign Causes E30 Campaign Process E31 Campaign Results E32 Historical Status and Significance	**Took place**: E07 Historical Place ↔ E27 Campaign Name

(continued)

Table 1. (*continued*)

Class	Method	Mapping with CIDOC-CRM	Mapping with RiC-CM	Data Property	Object Property
E33 Message	Upgrade	E31 Document	RiC-E02 Record Resource	E34 Operational Command E35 Instruction E36 Announcement E37 Request for report E38 General messages	**Transmit**: E34 Operational command ↔ E10 Combatant

2.2 Knowledge Extraction

Knowledge extraction is the process of extracting knowledge instances from archival metadata and archival contents, which mainly includes entity recognition and relationship extraction. Specifically, knowledge acquisition techniques such as entity recognition, relationship recognition, attribute recognition, and event recognition are used to semantically extract text data in data resources, and techniques such as image recognition, speech recognition, and video summarization are used to extract features from other media data in big data resources, and finally output entities, attributes, and interrelationships among entities, form a normalized semantic network structure. Based on data types, there are three methods: (1) for structured data, we analyzed the data characteristics, then specified mapping rules in combination with expert knowledge, and prepared a mapping matching procedure according to the mapping rules, while finally extracted archival event knowledge by executing the mapping procedure; (2) for semi-structured data, the data is parsed according to its composition, and semi-structured knowledge extraction methods such as manual generation method, wrapper generation method and automatic extraction method are used for knowledge acquisition; (3) for unstructured data, a part of the data resources is taken out as training data, this part is manually labeled, and then Hidden Markov Model and Conditional Markov Model are selected for model training, and under the condition that the model meets the requirements of accuracy and recall, the model is used for the knowledge acquisition task of the remaining data resources.

We compiled experimental sample in the format of archival chronology by collecting public data, pictures, audio, and video materials of the War to Resist U.S. Aggression and Aid Korea [20]. As shown in Fig. 1, the main work of knowledge extraction includes.

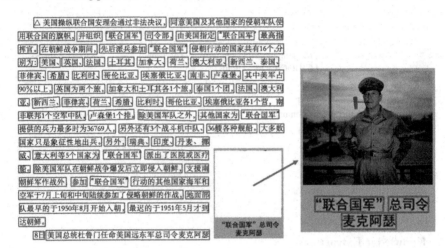

Fig. 1. Schematic Diagram of Text Extraction

(1) **Layout analysis**. The separation of the text region and the image region is achieved through analysis, which facilitates the next step of recognition operation for the different characteristics of the two regions respectively. The Mask R-CNN network [21] is used to detect and segment the images in the page, and each image is positioned as a separate object through the bounding box, with finally the pixel-level coordinates of the image and the document layout after removing the image are obtained.

(2) **Text detection**. Since the number of images and the typographic position of each page are different, if the text detection algorithm based on preset shape candidate boxes is used, there may be certain defects, so that a text detection algorithm based on U-Net [22] image segmentation is used to classify at the pixel level, to determine whether each pixel point belongs to a text target and its connection with surrounding pixels, and then the results of adjacent pixels are integrated into a text box. So, we formulate the skip pathway like: let $x^{i,j}$ denotes the output of node $X^{i,j}$ where i indexes the down-sampling layer along the pixel point and j indexes the convolution layer of the dense block along the detect pathway. The stack of feature images represented by $x^{i,j}$ is computed as shown in Eq. (1).

$$x^{i,j} = \begin{cases} H\left(x^{i-1,j}\right), j = 0 \\ H\left(\left[\left[x^{i,\kappa}\right]_{\kappa=0}^{j-1}, \mu\left(x^{i+1,j-1}\right)\right]\right), j > 0 \end{cases} \tag{1}$$

Using this algorithm, the text of the legend below the image and the document layout after removing the image are processed for text detection respectively, and the coordinates of the text box of the legend and the coordinates of the text box of the document are obtained.

(3) **Text recognition**. This includes the text recognition in the text box of the legend and the text box of the document. Firstly, Recurrent Neural Network (RNN) model [23] is used to describe text sequences, and for further integration of contextual semantic

information, Bi-directional Long Short-Term Memory (Bi-LSTM) [24] is used to integrate contextual information at the same time to improve model accuracy and solve the problem of semantic long-range drift. Secondly, a sequence-to-sequence architecture based on encoding-decoding is adopted, consisting of an encoder that reads the text input sequence and a decoder that generates the output one, which is used to train the above network to map a variable-length text sequence to another variable-length output sequence. Finally, in order to reduce the complexity of the model, shorten the training time and improve the training efficiency, an attention mechanism [25] is introduced in the model training by first reading the whole sentence or paragraph to obtain the focus of the current text expression and then focusing on different parts of the input sentence to collect the semantic details needed to generate the next output word.

After the above three steps, the pixel-level coordinates of the image, the document text recognition content and the legend text recognition content are unified and integrated into a JSON file for saving and outputting to provide data support for generating the knowledge graph.

It is worth pointing out that in the specific construction process, knowledge modeling and knowledge extraction are carried out simultaneously and influence each other. The knowledge framework generated in knowledge modeling can form a top-down and well-structured concept hierarchy, which facilitates the entities, relations, and attributes of knowledge extraction to correspond directly to the concepts; the entities, relations and attributes of knowledge acquisition can improve the knowledge framework from the bottom-up, which facilitates the formation of new concepts and the correction of outdated and wrong concepts.

2.3 Knowledge Fusion

It refers to the fusion and validation of the knowledge contained in the initially constructed graphs, which specifically includes.

(1) **Knowledge fusion**. The initially constructed graphs are fused and unified at multiple levels and perspectives. It mainly includes the fusion of the framework layer and the data layer. (a) The framework layer fusion adopts the ontology evolution management toolset to achieve framework alignment and bridge the lexical heterogeneity and semantic ambiguity among different frameworks. (b) The data layer fusion follows the steps of entity alignment, attribute alignment, and attribute value fusion to complete the disambiguation, de-duplication, and error correction of tuples (entities, relations, and attributes) between different schemas. The knowledge fusion model specifically includes the elements of entity acquisition, entity linking, entity fusion matching, and knowledge evaluation. In the research, the internal entity disambiguation of the knowledge graph was carried out. For example, the chief of staff of the volunteer army "Xie Fang", formerly known as "Xie Ruchuan", was also known as "Xie Peiran", so we use attributes such as Alias to assist in the identification and disambiguation of entities. In order to facilitate machine understanding, we use the RDF data model to represent knowledge as < entity, attribute, attribute value > or < subject, predicate, object >, for example, (a) the association of "entity-entity" can be represented as < MacArthur, order, Walker > < 38th Army, affiliated to, 13th corps >; (b) the association of "entity-attribute" can

be represented as < MacArthur, position, commander-in-chief of the United Nations Command >.

(2) **Graph quality control**. The quality control is realized by designing the knowledge inference model, which mainly includes missing knowledge completion, error knowledge correction and outdated knowledge update in the graph. Among them, (a) missing knowledge completion includes entity type completion, inter-entity relationship completion and entity missing attribute value completion. Error knowledge correction includes error entity type detection; (b) error entity relationship detection, and error attribute value detection. The update of outdated knowledge mainly targets the information related to timestamps and hot events in the graph. The knowledge inference model specifically includes elements of training model design, training data set preparation, graph inference algorithm selection, model training, model evaluation, and model generation.

As shown in Fig. 2, the main work includes:

(1) The JSON format files (see Fig. 2- a) output from the knowledge extraction session are extracted, and the text data are imported into the annotation tool. Combining the ontology knowledge framework described in the previous section, the text is annotated by relying on a combination of model extraction and manual correction (see Fig. 2- b).

(2) After data inspection, export the annotated text data into a unified structured format (see Fig. 2- c), then based on the LOD model, the text is subjected to entity relationship extraction, fusion, validation and other processing operations (see Fig. 2- d) based on the RDF data standard in order to form a high-quality triple dataset (see Fig. 2- e).

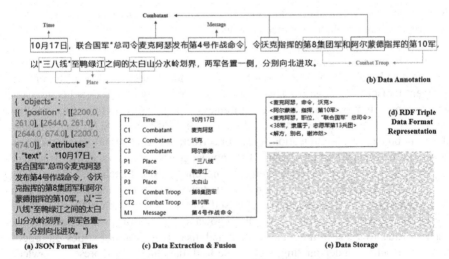

Fig. 2. Schematic diagram of data processing

2.4   Knowledge Management

Knowledge management refers to the management of high-quality graphs, providing efficient storage, indexing and access to graphs, and supporting the realization of graph-based knowledge services, specifically including:

(1) **Graph storage**. Neo4j [26] is a Java-based graph database management system, which has received more attention and use because of its open source, high performance and lightweight advantages. The knowledge graph of the Archival Data for the War to Resist U.S. Aggression and Aid Korea adopts Neo4j as the storage and management platform, and represents the nodes, edges and attributes in the attribute map in the form of fixed-length records as the data format stored on the disk, and the node records maintain the pointers to their adjacent edges and attributes, while the edge records maintain the pointers to their adjacent nodes and attributes, and the attribute records are maintained to point to their corresponding specific attribute values.

(2) **Graph indexing**. The disambiguation, de-duplication, and error correction of words in the knowledge fusion process, as well as the merging of synonyms and near-synonyms, the construction of targeted indexed word lists, and then the establishment of indexing strategies, can more quickly locate the graph knowledge. We established various subgraph indexes of the graph, including sub-structure index, path index, keyword index, etc. According to the indexes, we can quickly get the candidate subgraphs that satisfy the conditions when querying, and avoid searching on the whole graph.

(3) **Graph query**. SPARQL [27] is a query language developed by W3C for RDF data, and is a widely supported query language for graph databases. The SPARQL is used to realize various types of queries such as subgraph query, path query and keyword query of the graph. At the same time, when the user inputs requirements, the retrieval system should reason and associate as much as possible to retrieve query results that meet the user's needs.

3   Application of Knowledge Graph

After completing the construction of the knowledge graph in archival big data for the War to Resist U.S. Aggression and Aid Korea, a prototype service application system was developed based on the graph database Neo4j, which initially realized applications such as knowledge retrieval, archive resource linking, knowledge Q&A and knowledge recommendation.

(1) **Knowledge retrieval**. Entity search and relationship search can be realized simultaneously. As shown in Fig. 3, the entity search with "MacArthur" can get the relationship between MacArthur and related entities, and display the knowledge graph in a visual way. Each node in the retrieval result can be used as a new retrieval point to realize knowledge navigation. In addition, the graph-based reasoning can also get the direct or indirect relationship between two entities based on the input of the two entities using the path-based reasoning algorithm.

Fig. 3. Search results for the "MacArthur" entity

(2) **Archive resource linking**. The retrieval results can not only display the relevant entities, but also click on the links to further correlate with the relevant documents, pictures, audio and video materials corresponding to the entity, so that users can directly browse the original archives. Figure 3 shows the original photo archives corresponding to the "MacArthur" entity.

(3) **Knowledge Q&A**. Unlike the traditional archive retrieval based on the "keyword", the knowledge graph service system can realize reasoning based on ontology and complete question and answer interaction in the form of natural language. As shown in Fig. 4, which presents the user asking, "Who were the commanders of the U.S. 8th Army Group in this war?" and the system intelligent answer, "Walton Walker, Matthew Ridgway, James Van Fleet, Maxwell Taylor". If the user further pursues, "What were the dates of Matthew Ridgway's command of the 8th Army Group?", the system will invoke and present the archival data in the knowledge base, by extracting the concept of "time" and answering: December 26, 1950 - April 11, 1951.

(4) **Knowledge recommendation**. Based on the user's question and retrieval behavior, the system can recommend relevant personalized knowledge services based on the user model and user big data portrait, as shown in the Fig. 4, after the user asks the question about the date of Matthew Ridgway's command of the 8th Army Group, the system automatically recommends "Do you want to know the start and end dates of James Van Fleet 's command of the 8th Army Group " to the user, and the user can click on the question link if he/she wants to know, the system can automatically answer it.

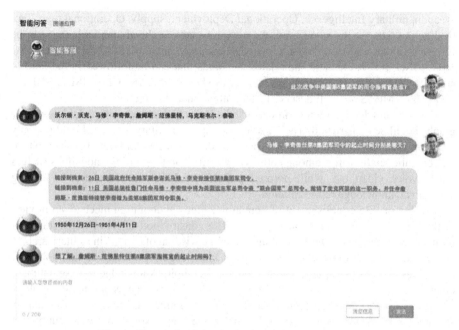

Fig. 4. Knowledge Q&A in the form of natural language

4   Discussion and Future Work

The paper explores the construction and application of knowledge graph in archival big data for the War to Resist U.S. Aggression and Aid Korea. (a) For construction of knowledge graph, the construction path mainly includes knowledge modeling, knowledge extraction, knowledge fusion and knowledge management. Based on the analysis of archival data, the paper draws on CIDOC-CRM and RiC-CM to build an ontology of the archive for the War to Resist U.S. Aggression and Aid Korea, as well as propose the knowledge Framework. In addition, the study also carries out layout analysis, text detection, text recognition, data annotation, data extraction, data representation in RDF triple format, data fusion, etc.

(b) For application of knowledge graph, this study mainly explores the application scenarios of knowledge retrieval, archival resource linking, knowledge Q&A and knowledge recommendation from the perspective of big data.

At present, the application of knowledge graph is still based on the pilot of typical projects and typical scenarios, and is rapidly developing and gradually taking shape. The construction of knowledge graph in archival data for the War to Resist U.S. Aggression and Aid Korea can provide useful reference for the application of the knowledge graph in military big data. Combining with the actual situation, the following work and trends should be paid attention to in the future:

(1) Further expansion of the ontology and enrich the knowledge framework is needed. Only six concept classes have been constructed in the research, which can still be further added and expanded, such as Strategic security, Operational Determination, Weather,

Weapon, military Intelligence, Operational Deployment, supply, Operational map, Tactical action, etc. At the same time, the comprehensive archival standards that can be followed in the field of archival knowledge ontology, such as ISO 30300 series, ISO 16175, ISO 21127, etc., and the related standards that can be followed in the field of archival cataloguing (sub)ontology, such as ISAD (G), ISAAR (CPF), ISDF, SDIAH, ISO 23081, METS, etc., all deserve further attention and reference.

(2) The knowledge graph form needs to be innovated and a multimodal knowledge graph should be constructed. The knowledge graph of military archive should not only focus on the archival content with Structured data as the main body, but also extend the semantic relationships among entities and entities under multiple modalities such as image, voice, video, etc., while portraying multimodal big data association and fusing multimodal knowledge representation.

(3) Reasonable establishment of human-machine collaboration mechanism in view of the difficulties of application scenarios. The construction of knowledge graph for military archive must be good at making use of the wisdom of experts in military archive domain, in order to refine the granularity of knowledge representation and solve the difficulties of sparse samples, diverse scenes and complex knowledge representation in practical applications; good at making use of technologies such as automatic ontology construction and graph representation reasoning to reduce the reliance on human in the process of construction and application of the graph, so as to realize automatic, large-scale and high-quality construction of knowledge graph.

(4) Strengthen cross-disciplinary research and explore the integration and application of artificial intelligence and other big data technologies. In the process of building the knowledge graph of military archival big data, it is necessary to deeply integrate technologies such as natural language processing (NLP) and deep learning (DL), and enhance the role of machine intelligence in the process of construction and application for the knowledge graph, to support the broader practice of the knowledge graph in related fields.

References

1. Shu, Z., Zhang, P., Li, X., et al.: Construction of Archival Knowledge Graph of Serious Social Incidents under the Context of Digital Memories. Zhejiang Archives (2021)
2. Xu, C., Xu, J.: Provenance method of electronic archives based on knowledge graph in big data environment. Journal of Information Hiding and Privacy Protection (2021)
3. Wang, H., Miao, X., Pan, Y.: Design and implementation of personal health record systems based on knowledge graph. In: 2018 9th International Conference on Information Technology in Medicine and Education (ITME) IEEE Computer Society (2018)
4. Yang, J., Qi, T.: From Electronic Records to Knowledge Graph: A New Approach of Knowledge Service Based on Electronic Records. Archives Science Bulletin (2020)
5. Liao, F., Ma, L., Yang, D.: Research on construction method of knowledge graph of US military equipment based on BiLSTM model. In: 2019 International Conference on High Performance Big Data and Intelligent Systems (2019)
6. Zhao, Q., Huang, H., Ding, H.: Study on Military Regulations Knowledge Construction based on Knowledge Graph. In: 2021 7th International Conference on Big Data and Information Analytics (2021)

7. Leskinen, P., Koho, M., Heino, E., Tamper, M., et al.: Modeling and Using an Actor Ontology of Second World War Military Units and Personnel. International Semantic Web Conference Springer (2017)

8. Yoo, D., No, S., Ra, M.: A Practical Military Ontology Construction for the Intelligent Army Tactical Command Information System. INT J COMPUT COMMUN (2014)

9. Chen, H., Xiang, Q., He, J.: Research on the aggregation and visualization of anti-japanese war archives resources oriented to knowledge service. Archives Science Study (2021)

10. Robledano-Arillo, J., Navarro-Bonilla, D., Cerdá-Díaz, J.: Application of linked open data to the coding and dissemination of spanish civil war photographic archives. Journal of Documentation ahead-of-print (2019)

11. Mäkelä, E., Törnroos, J., Lindquist, T., Hyvönen, E.: WW1LOD: an application of CIDOC-CRM to World War 1 linked data. Int. J. Digit. Libr. **18**(4), 333–343 (2016). https://doi.org/10.1007/s00799-016-0186-2

12. Koho, M., Ikkala, E., Leskinen, P., et al.: WarSampo knowledge graph: Finland in the Second World War as Linked Open Data. Semantic Web (2020)

13. Xing, M., et al.: Research on the Construction and Application of Knowledge Graph in Military Domain. International Conference on AI and Big Data Application (2019)

14. CIDOC-CRM. https://cidoc-crm.org/,2022-08-16

15. ICA: Records In Context: A Conceptual Model for Archival Description (2016)

16. Klyne, G., Carroll, J.J., et al.: Resource Description Framework (RDF): Concepts and Abstract Syntax. w3c recommendation (2004)

17. Kunal, S., Pascal, H.: Web Ontology Language (OWL). Encyclopedia of Social Network Analysis and Mining (2014)

18. Protégé: https://protege.stanford.edu/,2021-11-16

19. Noy, N.F., Mcguinness, D.L.: Ontology Development 101: A Guide to Creating Your First Ontology. Stanford Medical Informatics (2001)

20. Chronicle of the War to Resist U.S. Aggression and Aid Korea. https://news.12371.cn/2014/10/23/ARTI1414065228514997.shtml,2014-10-23

21. He, K., Gkioxari, G., Dollár, P., et al.: Mask R-CNN. IEEE Transactions on Pattern Analysis & Machine Intelligence (2020)

22. Zhou, Z., Siddiquee, M.R., Tajbakhsh, N., et al.: UNet++: A Nested U-Net Architecture for Medical Image Segmentation. 4th Deep Learning in Medical Image Analysis Workshop (2018)

23. Gregor, K., Danihelka, I., Graves, A., et al.: DRAW: A Recurrent Neural Network for Image Generation. Computer Science (2015)

24. Jin, C., Weihua, L.I., Chen, J.I., et al.: Bi-directional long short-term memory neural networks for chinese word segmentation. Journal of Chinese Information Processing (2018)

25. Bahdanau, D., Cho, K., Bengio, Y.: Neural machine translation by jointly learning to align and translate. Computer Science (2014)

26. Protégé: https://protege.stanford.edu/products.php,2022-07-26

27. Sqarql 1.1 query language. https://www.w3.org/TR/sparql11-query/, 2021-03-21

Semi-supervised Learning Enabled Fault Analysis Method for Power Distribution Network Based on LSTM Autoencoder and Attention Mechanism

Haining Xie[1(✉)], Liming Zhuang[1], and Xiang Wang[2]

[1] State Grid Shanghai Municipal Electric Power Company Electric Power Research Institute, Shanghai, China
xiehn@sh.sgcc.com.cn
[2] Nanjing Liandi Information System Co., Ltd, Nanjing, China

Abstract. By upgrading the existing distribution network fault statistical analysis system of Shanghai Institute of Electrical Science and Technology, comprehensive research is needed to investigate the hardware configuration and system functions of the system, optimize the system structure, meet the needs of the company's distribution network business department, and provide strong support for the daily operation and management of the distribution network. In this paper, we present a semi-supervised learning enabled fault analysis method for power distribution network based on LSTM autoencoder and attention mechanism. We make the LSTM autoencoder's loss function more robust so that it may be affected by both labeled and unlabeled input. Next, by minimizing the loss function, we can learn how the distribution of both types of data is distributed. We also added an attention mechanism to make the model performance more stable as the weight of the marked data changes. We apply the improved experience of LSTM autoencoder to the LSTM prediction model and realize the LSTM prediction model under semi-supervised learning. The proposed algorithm can effectively solve the problems of strong dependence of time series data and high cost of marking, so as to obtain better fault detection results of power distribution network.

Keywords: Semi-supervised learning · fault analysis method · power distribution network · LSTM autoencoder · attention mechanism

1 Introduction

At present, State Grid Shanghai Institute of Electrical Science and Technology has deployed a set of distribution network fault statistical analysis system, which is responsible for the monitoring, statistics and analysis of the whole Shanghai distribution network trip fault information, as well as the fault filling process of each power supply company, fault impact scope analysis and other work. The system was put into use in 2015 and has been running for many years. The operation data of distribution network equipment obtained through the system provides accurate and comprehensive data and technical support for the company's distribution network operation and maintenance management.

Figure 1 shows the distribution network fault statistics analysis system hardware topology status diagram. At present, the following problems are found in the operation and use of the distribution network fault statistical analysis system of Shanghai Institute of Electrical Science and Technology:

- The performance of the existing acquisition server is unable to meet the requirements of the full data acquisition and capture of the eleven stations; The architecture of a single-host application system has potential reliability risks and needs to be upgraded to a dual-host system.
- The existing disk array has a capacity of 5TB, which is mainly used for the storage of the existing system data and the management of historical data generated over the years; Due to the requirement of the implementation of the data storage in 11 locations, a new disk array of no less than 10TB is needed for the storage and management of all the data collected by various companies. The amount of all the data is very large, especially the historical data.
- Lack of distribution network reliability analysis and other related functions, which cannot meet the needs of business departments in this aspect.
- The external interface function needs to be improved to meet the current industry trend of micro services.

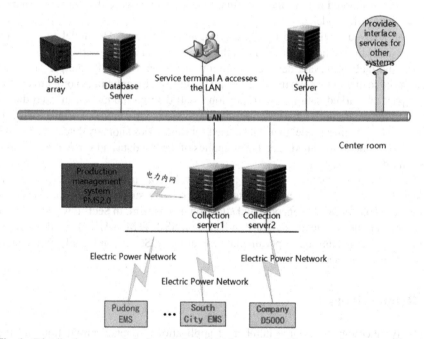

Fig. 1. Distribution network fault statistics analysis system hardware topology status diagram

Learning enabled fault analysis method for power distribution network has recently received increasingly attentions. In the time series of unsupervised anomaly detection algorithm research and supervision of anomaly detection algorithm on the basis of the research has got certain development, how to make the experience of the supervision of anomaly detection algorithm and time sequence of unsupervised anomaly detection algorithm, the combination of form can be used, high performance supervision and time sequence anomaly detection algorithm become one of the focus in the study of this article. To detect time series anomalies, this work suggests a semi-supervised anomaly detection model based on LSTM and an attention mechanism. The proposed method mainly includes two parts: model construction and anomaly detection.

In the construction of the model structure, we combine the unsupervised LSTM autoencoder algorithm and the semi-supervised SVDD algorithm to establish a semi-supervised anomaly detection model based on LSTM and attention mechanism. The model is composed of an autoencoder module and an attention-mechanism module. The unsupervised LSTM autoencoder is improved into a semi-supervised LSTM autoencoder model. A small amount of labeled data is used to strengthen the learning ability of the data distribution of the model, so as to improve the overall performance of the model. In order to solve the problem of information loss in the LSTM autoencoder, an attention mechanism is introduced between the encoder and the decoder to focus on the information related to the current state and improve the performance of the model when reconstructing data. To the extent that marked data plays a role in the whole loss function, this paper adds a hyperparameter to the loss term of marked data to determine the weight of marked data in the loss function, so as to explore the impact of marked data on the whole model.

In anomaly detection, we used the constructed LSTM-AAE model to carry out anomaly detection of time series. Firstly, the time series data set is preprocessed, including data normalization and data segmentation operation. Secondly, the pre-processed data is used to distinguish the training set and the test set. Meanwhile, in order to explore the impact of marked data in the proportion of all data on the model, marked data in the training set should be divided. Thirdly, the LSTM-AAE model is trained with the training set to obtain a model that can be used for time series anomaly detection. Finally, the trained model is used to detect the anomalies of the test data and verify the reliability of the model.

The rest of this article is organized as follows. Literature review is briefly reviewed in Sect. 2. In Sect. 3, we present the system model of semi-supervised anomaly detection model based on LSTM autoencoder and attention mechanism. In Sect. 4, we describe the time series anomaly detection algorithm based on SS-LSTM-AAE. The validity of the method is presented through experimental evaluations in Sect. 5, and finally we conclude the entire paper in Sect. 6.

2 Related Work

Anomaly detection has a large number of applications in actual production and life. For example: find out potential fraud or cash out records from credit card transaction records, find out illegal traffic participants in traffic surveillance videos, find out pathological tissues in medical images, find out intruders in the network, Find out abnormal transmission etc. from the signal transmitted by IoT.

Most of the current anomaly detection scenarios are highly dependent on manual work, and there is a large demand for manpower. In the future, as the aging population increases and the working population decreases, it will be a general trend to use algorithms to replace manual abnormalities.

The current mainstream anomaly detection algorithms are usually based on deep learning technology, and can be divided into supervised methods, unsupervised methods, and semi-supervised methods according to the supervision information used. In addition, there are also some anomaly detection algorithms that combine deep learning techniques with traditional non-deep learning techniques. These methods are introduced separately below.

Time series anomaly detection has been the subject of extensive research [1, 2]. Anomaly identification based on statistical assessments of prediction errors was completed by Fox in his 1972 work, which is the earliest known related work [6]. The majority of research on statistics before machine learning approaches were developed [7, 8]. Anomaly detection in time series has been widely employed since the development of machine learning and deep learning techniques [3]. This paper discusses two distinct theories based on several approaches of time series anomaly identification.

Prediction errors serve as the foundation for regression procedures. This technique makes use of some sort of time series forecasting model, compares observed data to model predictions, and classifies observations based on the forecast error between observed and predicted values. This method's prediction component can be implemented in a number of ways. The Autoregressive Moving Average (ARMA), which is popular across many domains, has been used for time series anomaly identification [9]. The issue that ARMA faces with managing seasonal datasets has been addressed by SARMA (seasonal ARMA) [10] and MLP (multi-layer perceptron) techniques [11]. Chou proposed a novel method for sequence prediction that combines his ARMA model and his MLP [12]. To identify anomalies in incorrect predictions, a simple fixed threshold is used.

The properties of univariate time series data can now be more accurately simulated by LSTM and GRU thanks to the invention of recurrent neural networks (RNN) [4, 5]. We outline a technique to show how neural networks excel at simulating the variability found in univariate systems [13]. RNNs are employed in regression in an article by Shipmon et al. [14] to compare data with a threshold to detect anomalies before going to the accumulator. Data is designated as anomalous and the accumulator is incremented when it exceeds the threshold. Solav et al. [15] propose an Anomaly Detection in Online Time Series Using Deep RNN. Incrementally retraining the neural network enables the neural network to adapt to dataset drift, demonstrating the applicability of neural networks. In this approach, we put up a number of distinct time steps and score techniques based on the prediction errors at various time steps to assess anomalies. Despite some advances in time series forecasting, RNNs still have difficulties classifying anomalies based on forecast inaccuracy. I'm sorry for making you wait. To examine the prediction error, process the RNN model's output, and then output the aberrant decision outcome, we employ a Gaussian Naive Bayesian model [16]. Bontesmps et al. establish the minimum time interval during which collective anomalies take place. Do centralized population anomaly monitoring and calculate error measurements throughout time [17]. Hendman and other people. Unsupervised thresholding with non-fixed values and dynamic changes has been proposed [18]. Using this method, there is no need to make Gaussian assumptions about the past smooth forecast error distributions, and in some ways, difficulties that could occur if parametric assumptions are broken are also avoided. The threshold under the effect of the present forecast error sequence is established for anomaly identification by locating the extremum of the smoothed prediction error.

The non-regressive category includes methods that depend on reconstruction mistakes. This type of technique often uses an autoencoder model, sending the actual observations to a hidden layer with few neurons where the original data is compressed and expanded to the output layer in accordance with the format of the actual observations and reconstructed values. To categorize reconstruction errors between the actual and reconstructed values, the reconstructed values are compared to the actual observed values. For autoencoder reconstruction, Luo et al. collected cellular sequence data over time from resource-constrained sensor devices, and they identified abnormalities based on shallow autoencoder network reconstruction errors [19].

The two types of feature extraction are temporal feature extraction and spatial feature extraction. For anomaly detection, the majority of current research only takes one of these features into account. Convolutional neural networks (CNNs) and RNNs have been coupled in several research to investigate the extraction of temporal and spatial features. Researchers have been able to use CNN on time series due to its good effect on spatial feature extraction in prior studies. Yastmastmastmastmastmastmastmastmastmastmas, and. We must change the format of the time series because they are often univariate or multivariate series, which are incompatible with a 2D convolution kernel. Kings. CNNs are appropriate for extracting spatial features from time series because of a method that has been presented to project a univariate time series onto a 2D picture [20]. Liu and co. It has been suggested that multivariate CNNs be used to categorize multivariate time data. These techniques offer a productive strategy to extract spatial characteristics from time series and enhance the functionality of various classifiers [21]. Nevertheless, removing merely the spatial features from the time series results in the loss of the data's temporal feature information [22].

The above briefly introduce the implementation steps of two typical deep unsupervised anomaly detection algorithms. As can be seen from the above steps, unsupervised anomaly detection algorithms usually judge whether there is a fault by calculating the difference between the reconstructed or generated image and the actual image. Although this method does not require abnormal samples and is more suitable for actual scenarios, it has obvious disadvantages—the ability to resist noise interference is relatively poor. Since pixel-level differences are not necessarily caused by actual faults, they may also be caused by innocuous disturbances such as stains, and deep unsupervised anomaly detection algorithms cannot distinguish these different differences. Therefore, in practical applications, deep unsupervised anomaly detection Algorithms usually have more false positives.

3 System Model

The proposed semi-supervised anomaly detection model (SS-LSTM-AAE) based on LSTM autoencoder and attention mechanism is described in this section. The SS-LSTM-AAE model consists of a semi-supervised LSTM autoencoder module and an attentional mechanism module. In order to solve the problem of tag all data of high labor costs and unmarked data can help to determine the searching space of unsupervised learning algorithm and the search direction, based on the discrete data sets on a semi-supervised learning algorithm experience, LSTM automatic encoder of unsupervised algorithm was improved, forming a semi-supervised LSTM automatic encoder model, At the same time, the attention mechanism is introduced to solve the information loss problem of the automatic encoder.

3.1 Unsupervised LSTM Autoencoder

Encoder and decoder are the two components that make up an autoencoder (AE). The decoder reconstructs the hidden representation h_t and outputs the reconstruction result after the encoder transforms the input x_t into a hidden representation h_t using a function map. As shown in Fig. 2 below, the encoder performs feature mapping to output transformation after extracting time features from the input time series data using LSTM:

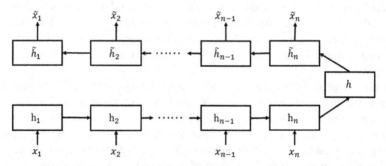

Fig. 2. The working principle of unsupervised LSTM autoencoder

An encoder based on LSTM will update the time series $x = (x_1, x_2, \ldots, x_t) \in R^{n \times t}$ input encoder after the hidden state:

$$h_t = f(h_{t-1}, x_t)$$

where $h_t \in R^m$ is the time step t corresponding to the hidden state of the encoder, The hidden unit's size is m, and the activation function is f. The cell state, which is the foundation of LSTM, is updated or deleted by the LSTM network through the gate. Here is how it works:

$$f_t = \sigma(W_f \cdot [h_{t-1}, x_t] + b_f)$$

$$i_t = \sigma(W_i \cdot [h_{t-1}, x_t] + b_i)$$

$$\tilde{C}_t = \tanh(W_C \cdot [h_{t-1}, x_t] + b_C)$$

$$C_t = f_t * C_{t-1} + i_t * \tilde{C}_t$$

$$o_t = \sigma(W_o \cdot [h_{t-1}, x_t] + b_o)$$

$$h_t = o_t \tanh(C_t)$$

where the connection between the current input x_t and the previous hidden state $[h_{t-1}, x_t] \in R^{m+n}$ exists. The activation function is σ, and * denotes multiplication of elements. The weights for the forget gate, input gate, and output gate are W_f, W_i, W_o, respectively. Offsets are b_f, b_i, and b_o. The hidden state h_t may be regarded as encoded data or as intermediate data with temporal properties that will be used for decoding. The decoder must learn the mapping from h_t to x_t and reduce the error between x_t and x_t according to the output h_t in order to achieve the goal of finally reconstructing the data distribution.

3.2 Attention Mechanism

Classical learning decoder - encoder structure has certain defects, namely the encoder may hide the last step of state vector as the output, decoder by using the hidden state vector refactoring, refactoring process relies too heavily on the entire data compressed into fixed output vector, inevitably lead to the loss of information, the result of reconstruction is not accurate.

To solve the problem of information loss, the model needs to focus on the information relevant to the current state and ignore other irrelevant information. Based on the above requirements, the attention mechanism calculates the degree of matching between the current input sequence and the output vector, and the information with a high degree of matching is defined as the focus of attention. In order to further explore the feasibility of semi-supervised algorithms in the field of autoencoders, this paper uses the attention mechanism of LuongAttention structure to improve the classic autoencoder and test the semi-supervised learning algorithm.

Although the LuongAttention structure is similar to the Bahdanau structure, Luong et al. have formed several key differences by simplifying and summarizing the original structure.

LuongAttention has several improvements compared to BahdanauAttention, which is why this paper chose LuongAttention:

- LuongAttention simply uses hidden states in the top LSTM layer of the encoder and decoder, while BahdanauAttention mechanism uses hidden state connections of bidirectional RNN in the bidirectional encoder.
- The calculation path of LuongAttention is simpler than that of BahdanauAttention;
- Compared with BahdanauAttention, which only uses concat alignment function, LuongAttention uses multiple alignment functions and proves the other alignment functions have better effect through experiments.

3.3 Semi-supervised LSTM Autoencoder

By including a new loss term for labeled data, the model learns how labeled data are distributed. With labeled normal data ($y_s = 0$), we choose the same loss term as the unsupervised LSTM autoencoder to teach the model the appropriate data distribution. The reconstruction of anomalous data must deviate from the original data distribution because this study opts to penalize the inverse of the reconstruction error for tagged anomalies ($y_s = 1$). When adding a new loss item, adjust the weighted hyperparameter for the loss item to control the significance of learning from labeled data and unlabeled data. Model training will concentrate more on the labeled data when $\gamma > 0$; when $\gamma > 1$. The model will place more emphasis on the unlabeled data distribution when there is a discrepancy between $\gamma < 1$ and the data distribution.

4   Time Series Anomaly Detection Algorithm Based on SS-LSTM-AAE

In this section, a time series anomaly detection algorithm is proposed using the proposed SS-LSTM-AAE model. The method consists of two stages: data preprocessing, model training, and anomaly detection. Data preprocessing mainly includes data normalization and data segmentation operations.

This study responds to the following research queries by performing experiments on three widely used time series datasets:

- In terms of anomaly detection using semi-supervised algorithms, do autoencoder models perform better than unsupervised techniques? Can the semi-supervised method enhance the model's performance after adding the attention mechanism?
- Can the semi-supervised algorithm maintain or increase the enhancement effect of the autoencoder model under different marker data proportions?
- Tag weight Does the weight of the tag data in the loss function significantly affect the performance of the semi-supervised autoencoder model?

Detailed descriptions in this paper are shown in Table 1:

Table 1. Time series data sets detail description

Dataset	Data	Size
Yahoo! Webscope A1Benchmark	Untagged data sets	17114
	Tagged data set	16970
	The test set	10782
Yahoo! Webscope A2Benchmark	Untagged data sets	17052
	Tagged data set	17178
	The test set	22736
NAB	Untagged data sets	16128
	Tagged data set	16128
	The test set	8066

The Webscope S5 dataset from Yahoo! is a labeled dataset for anomaly identification that includes both genuine and fake time series data. The full dataset is made up of four benchmark subsets: A1 benchmarks for certain samples of real production traffic data from Yahoo!, and the other three benchmarks based on artificial time series. The benchmarks A1 and A2 are used to assess anomaly detection models. Only 1,669 out of the 94,866 total data points in the A1 benchmark are anomalous. Using the publicly available Yahoo! Webscope data set, a study was conducted to ensure the validity of the experiment. We selected a data set with no or few abnormal points at the end and removed a small number of abnormal points to create an unlabeled data set that contained both abnormal points and data sets with a large number of both normal and abnormal points. A test set is created from a labeled data set that is randomly chosen from a number of files. Following screening, we obtained 17114 unlabeled data, 16670 labeled data, 10782 test set data, and 17052 unlabeled data, 17178 labeled data, and 22736 test set data based on A1 and A2 benchmarks, respectively.

Dataset NAB More than 50 unlabeled real-time and human-time data files make up the NAB dataset, an unlabeled anomaly detection dataset. In this study, the model is judged using generated datasets with and without anomalies. Artificial No Anomaly uses the majority of its data as an unlabeled dataset and the remaining portion as a training set. In this manner, a test set with 8066 data, a labeled data set with 16128 data, and an unlabeled data set with 16128 data are all produced.

5   Performance Evaluation and Analysis

This section's main focus is on how semi-supervised techniques affect unsupervised models more favorably. The semi-supervised models are compared to the unsupervised LSTM autoencoder (LSTM-AE) and the LSTM autoencoder with additional attention mechanism as a consequence (LSTM-AAE).

- Use only the experiment data set and test set that are not indicated as encoder or decoder for the automatic encoder (LSTM-AE to LSTM).
- LSTM - AAE in LSTM - AE, on the basis of increased LuongAttention mechanism to further enhance the model performance, use only the unmarked experiment data set and test set.
- SS - LSTM - AE to LSTM - AE's loss function was improved, using no data sets and marking data set for training.
- SS - LSTM - AAE in SS - LSTM - AE, on the basis of increased LuongAttention mechanism, without using data sets and marking data set for training.

This section uses Python3.7 as the programming language and the CUDA version of TensorFlow3.0 as the neural network framework. In terms of model parameter setting, due to the purpose of comparing the performance difference between unsupervised and semi-supervised models, the corresponding models all use the same parameters except the loss function. In addition, the anomaly depends on whether the reconstruction error is greater than the set threshold, and the threshold is determined on different data and according to experience.

5.1   Evaluation Index

The experiments in this section address the topic of anomaly detection as a classification problem and assess the precision, recall rate, and F1-score of several models. If the typical case in a binary problem is marked as an exception, the error is displayed as a false positive (FP). An incorrect marking of the aberrant occurrence as normal is known as a false negative (FN). Again, normal conditions are accurately detected, and true positive (TP) and true neg-ative (TN) signify abnormalities. The following criteria can be applied to many indicators:

$$\text{precision} = \frac{TP}{TP + FP}$$

$$\text{recall} = \frac{TP}{TP + FN}$$

$$\text{F1} - \text{score} = 2 \times \frac{precision \times recall}{precision + recall}$$

5.2 Experimental Results

1) Abnormal detection

Table 2 shows how well the same kind of autoencoders perform on tasks involving anomaly detection in unsupervised and semi-supervised environments. Better performance in these environments is highlighted below, and the best performance is highlighted in bold.

Table 2 shows that: 1) For all three data sets, most of the semi-supervised algorithm's indicators outperform those of the unsupervised method; 2) Combining Figs. 3 and 4, it can be found that after adding the attention mechanism, the unsupervised model and the semi-supervised model The performance indicators of the supervision model have been improved, and the improvement of the attention mechanism has an impact on the performance of the automatic encoder model. Secondly, the performance of the attention mechanism after half supervision model has also improved compared to the unsupervised model, indicating that the semi-supervised algorithm is adding attention. The performance of the autoencoder model can still be improved after the mechanism. In summary, the performance of the supervised autoencoder algorithm is better than that of the unsupervised autoencoder algorithm, and the model effect can be further improved steadily through the attention mechanism.

2) Mark the weight

In the semi-supervised algorithm, this paper improves the loss function of the unsupervised autoencoder by adding a loss term and defining a hyperparameter γ to determine the weight of the new loss term in the whole loss function. This section analyzes the $\gamma \in \{0.5, 1.0, 1.5, 2.0\}$ in the data set Yahoo! Experiments are carried out on A1Benchmark, and the experimental results are shown in Table 3.

Then the two models were tested under different γ on Yahoo! A1Benchmark and Yahoo! Experiments were carried out on two data sets of A2Benchmark. F1-score of the model was taken out for line graph drawing Results in Fig. 5.

It can be observed from Table 3 that adjusting the value of γ for the same data set does not make much difference. Combined with Fig. 3.16, it can be found that when γ is increased

Table 2. Abnormal detection result

Model	Yahoo! A1Benchmark			Yahoo! A2Benchmark			NAB		
	pre	recall	F1-score	pre	recall	F1-score	pre	recall	F1-score
LSTM-AE	**0.9950**	0.5708	0.7254	0.5467	1.0	0.7069	0.4440	0.5963	0.5090
SS-LSTM-AE	0.8244	0.6980	0.7560	0.7014	0.9996	0.8244	0.8063	**0.6133**	0.6967
LSTM-AAE	0.6880	0.9102	0.7837	0.5486	**1.0**	0.7085	0.7357	0.4575	0.5641
SS-LSTM-AAE	0.6983	**0.9282**	**0.7970**	0.7055	0.9992	**0.8270**	**0.9317**	0.5991	**0.7293**

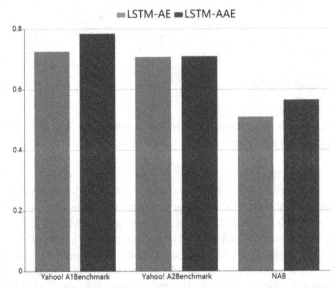

Fig. 3. Comparison of F1-score changes in unsupervised autoencoders before and after the addition of attention mechanism

from 1.0 to 1.5, the performance of the model declines in most cases. When γ is increased from 1.5 to 2.0, although the performance of the model is improved, it is almost the same as that when the value of 1.0 is increased. Meanwhile, in Fig. 5, comparing the change of model performance with the increase of Fig. 5 before and after adding the attention mechanism, it is found that the change of SS-LSTM-AAE performance after adding the attention mechanism is more stable than that of SS-LSTM-AAE, indicating that the increase of the attention mechanism improves the learning degree of the autoencoder model to the data distribution. The model can better learn the distribution of source data.

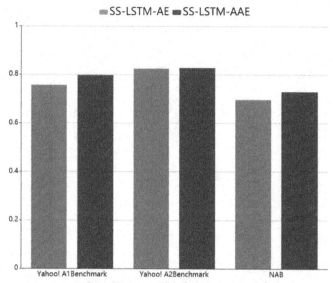

Fig. 4. Comparison of F1-score changes in semi-supervised autoencoders before and after the addition of attention mechanism

Table 3. The influence of γ on Yahoo! A1Benchmark test results

γ	SS-LSTM-AE			SS-LSTM-AAE		
	pre	recall	F1-score	pre	recall	F1-score
0.5	0.8092	0.6992	0.7502	0.6964	0.9252	0.7947
1.0	0.8244	0.6980	0.7560	0.6983	0.9282	0.7970
1.5	0.8841	0.6975	0.7798	0.7052	0.9282	0.8015
2.0	0.7935	0.7004	0.7440	0.7032	0.9256	0.7992

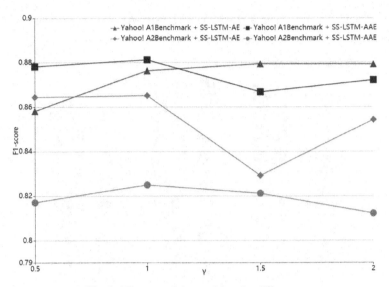

Fig. 5. F1-score of the model under different γ

6 Conclusion

The main output of this study is a distribution network time series anomaly detection system based on an attention mechanism and an LSTM autoencoder. An improved attention mechanism based on an unsupervised LSTM autoencoder and a semi-supervised LSTM autoencoder are both included in the framework of the LSTM autoencoder-based semi-supervised anomaly detection model. This model improves the loss function of the semi-supervised LSTM autoencoder. The learning data distribution contains a small amount of labeled data, which improves the model's ability to learn the full data distribution. Also, by include the attention mechanism, the problem of information loss in autonomous learning is addressed. a steady drop. The time series anomaly detection technique based on SS-LSTM-AAE is detailed in the second portion of this study and consists of two steps: data preparation and anomaly identification. Data normalization and time division are both parts of data preprocessing. Experiments were carried out on three publicly accessible time series data sets to show that a semi-supervised learning framework is more effective at detecting abnormalities in time series. The performance work of the unsupervised framework and the half-supervised framework was compared using the identical network configuration. Unsupervised LSTM encoders are less effective at spotting faults than semi-automatic supervised encoders.

References

1. Chandola, V., Banerjee, A., Kumar, V.: Anomaly detection: a survey. ACM Comput. Surv. **41**(3), 1–58 (2009)
2. Cook, A., Misirli, G., Fan, Z.: Anomaly detection for IoT time-series data: a survey. IEEE Internet Things J. **7**(7), 6481–6494 (2019)

3. Ian, G., Yoshua, B., Aaron, C.: Deep Learning. The MIT Press (2016)
4. Kim, J., Kim, J., Thu, H.L.T., et al.: Long short term memory recurrent neural network classifier for intrusion detection. In: 2016 International Conference on Platform Technology and Service (PlatCon), pp. 1–5. IEEE (2016)
5. Malhotra, P., Vig, L., Shroff, G., et al.: Long short term memory networks for anomaly detection in time series. In: Proceedings, vol. 89, pp. 89-94. Presses universitaires de Louvain (2015)
6. Fox, A.J.: Outliers in time series. J. Roy. Stat. Soc.: Ser. B (Methodol.) **34**(3), 350–363 (1972)
7. Burman, J P., Otto, M.C.: Census bureau research project: Outliers in time series. Bureau of the Census, SRD Res. Rep. CENSUS/SRD/RR-88114 (1988)
8. Vallis, O., Hochenbaum, J., Kejariwal, A.: A novel technique for long-term anomaly detection in the cloud. 6th {USENIX} workshop on hot topics in cloud computing (HotCloud 14) (2014)
9. Wold, H.: A Study in the Analysis of Stationary Time Series. Almqvist & Wiksell (1938)
10. Kadri, F., Harrou, F., Chaabane, S., et al.: Seasonal ARMA-based SPC charts for anomaly detection: application to emergency department systems. Neurocomputing **173**, 2102–2114 (2016)
11. Zhang, G.P., Qi, M.: Neural network forecasting for seasonal and trend time series. Eur. J. Oper. Res. **160**(2), 501–514 (2005)
12. Chou, J.S., Telaga, A.S.: Real-time detection of anomalous power consumption. Renew. Sustain. Energy Rev. **33**, 400–411 (2014)
13. Fu, R., Zhang, Z., Li, L.: Using LSTM and GRU neural network methods for traffic flow prediction. In: 2016 31st Youth Academic Annual Conference of Chinese Association of Automation (YAC), pp. 324–328. IEEE (2016)
14. Shipmon, D.T., Gurevitch, J.M., Piselli, P.M., et al.: Time series anomaly detection; detection of anomalous drops with limited features and sparse examples in noisy highly periodic data. arXiv preprint arXiv:1708.03665 (2017)
15. Saurav, S., et al.: Online anomaly detection with concept drift adaptation using recurrent neural networks. In: Proceedings of the ACM India Joint International Conference on Data Science and Management of Data, pp. 78–87 (2018)
16. Xie, X., Wu, D., Liu, S., et al.: IoT data analytics using deep learning. arXiv preprint arXiv: 1708.03854 (2017)
17. Bontemps, L., McDermott, J., Le-Khac, N.A.: Collective anomaly detection based on long short-term memory recurrent neural networks. In: International Conference on Future Data and Security Engineering, pp. 141-152. Springer, Cham (2016)
18. Hundman, K., Constantinou, V., Laporte, C., et al.: Detecting spacecraft anomalies using lstms and nonparametric dynamic thresholding. In: Proceedings of the 24th ACM SIGKDD International Conference on Knowledge Discovery & Data Mining, pp. 387–395 (2018)
19. Luo, T., Nagarajan, S.G.: Distributed anomaly detection using autoencoder neural networks in wsn for iot. In: 2018 IEEE International Conference on Communications (ICC), pp. 1–6. IEEE (2018)
20. Wang, W., Zhu, M., Wang, J., et al.: End-to-end encrypted traffic classification with one-dimensional convolution neural networks. In: 2017 IEEE International Conference on Intelligence and Security Informatics (ISI), pp. 43–48. IEEE (2017)
21. Liu, C.L., Hsiao, W.H., Tu, Y.C.: Time series classification with multivariate convolutional neural network. IEEE Trans. Industr. Electron. **66**(6), 4788–4797 (2018)
22. Kim, T.Y., Cho, S.B.: Web traffic anomaly detection using C-LSTM neural networks. Expert Syst. Appl. **106**, 66–76 (2018)

Fault Detection Method for Power Distribution Network Based on Ensemble Learning

Haining Xie[1(✉)] and Lijuan Chao[2]

[1] State Grid Shanghai Municipal Electric Power Company Electric Power Research Institute, Shanghai, China
xiehn@sh.sgcc.com.cn
[2] Nanjing Liandi Information System Co., Ltd., Nanjing, Jiangsu, China

Abstract. The State Grid Shanghai Institute of Electrical Science and Technology fault statistics system requires implementation of data analysis and index control capability improvement. This requires the purchase of corresponding hardware and ongoing algorithm and rule optimization in accordance with the application's actual needs. By enhancing the loss function of the unsupervised LSTM prediction model based on the enhanced experience of the semi-supervised time series anomaly detection algorithm based on LSTM autoencoder and attention mechanism, a semi-supervised LSTM prediction model is proposed in this paper to address the issue that the prediction model is affected by the abnormal data in the training set. This paper further proposes a semi-supervised anomaly detection algorithm based on ensemble learning after verifying the enhanced semi-supervised LSTM prediction model. The algorithm consists of two parts: an anomaly detection model based on LSTM autoencoder and attention mechanism, and a semi-supervised LSTM prediction model. In order to create a semi-supervised model with superior performance, we combined the semi-supervised LSTM prediction model with the semi-supervised LSTM autoencoder model after applying the improved experience of the LSTM autoencoder to the LSTM prediction model. Both algorithms can successfully address the issues of high marking costs and significant time series data reliance in order to produce improved time series anomaly detection results.

Keywords: Fault detection · power distribution network · ensemble learning · LSTM autoencoder

1 Introduction

The Performance Improvement and Transformation of the State Grid Shanghai Institute of Electrical Science and Technology Distribution Network Fault Statistical Analysis System was carried out in 2018 by the Institute of Electrical Science and Technology. The intelligent operation and maintenance management and control platform of the distribution network was constructed using the PMS2.0 system as its primary support mechanism. The fault monitoring function of the DAS main station system of the Shanghai distribution network was added. This feature was included on the basis of the EMS dispatch fault monitoring and the statistical analysis of the main network. It is now possible to install functions such as the service audit process function, the data access and statistics function of the main station of the distribution network, the fault data application analysis module, and so on. It does not, however, enable distribution network reliability analysis, fault GIS display, or micro-service support at this time.

LSTM is responsible for the creation of an unsupervised prediction model, which serves as the fundamental basis for traditional time series anomaly detection and prediction technologies. The LSTM-based unsupervised time series prediction model has the capability to swiftly react to abrupt changes in the development trend of time series. Nevertheless, owing to the drawbacks of unsupervised learning, the training set that only contains normal data is often utilized for model training in order to improve the performance of LSTM prediction models. This is done in order to maximize the effectiveness of the models. As the amount of data grows, it will be harder to filter out abnormal data from a large quantity of data while only retaining regular data. This will make it more difficult to only maintain normal data. So, one of the primary focuses of the second research presented in this work is on the best way to make use of a limited amount of marked data in order to ameliorate the impact that aberrant data has on the overall performance of the prediction model.

A semi-supervised LSTM prediction model is proposed in this chapter to address the issue that the prediction model is affected by the abnormal data in the training set. This issue is addressed by combining the enhanced expertise of the semi-supervised time series anoma-ly detection algorithm based on LSTM autoencoder and attention mechanism with a semi-supervised LSTM prediction model. This paper goes on to propose a semi-supervised anomaly detection algorithm based on ensemble learning. The algorithm is divided into two parts: the anomaly detection model based on LSTM autoencoder and attention mechanism, and the semi-supervised LSTM prediction model, which is verified after the improved semi-supervised LSTM pre-diction model is verified. Both of these parts are comprised of the semi-supervised LSTM prediction model. The majority of the information in this chapter is devoted to the development of a semi-supervised anomaly detection model that is based on ensemble learning and to the creation of a time series anomaly detection model that is based on SS-LSTM-PAAE.

The semi-supervised LSTM prediction model is established in the building of the semi-supervised anomaly detection model based on en-semble learning. The unsupervised LSTM prediction model is improved based on the experience of SS-LSTM-AAE, and the unsupervised LSTM prediction model is enhanced based on the experience of SS-LSTM-AAE. The unsupervised LSTM prediction model is augmented using the SS-LSTM-AAE enhanced loss function technique in this model. As a result, the new model is able to handle the problem of anomalous data in the unlabeled data by learning from the labeled data. Finally, we develop a semi-supervised anomaly detection model based on en-semble learning by combining the semi-supervised LSTM prediction model with the SS-LSTM-AAE. This model uses semi-supervised en-semble learning (SS-LSTM-PAAE). The model first reconstructs the data using SS-LSTM-AAE, then predicts the reconstruction results with a semi-supervised LSTM prediction model, and then utilizes the final prediction results to detect anomalous data. All of these steps are performed by the model.

In the first step of the procedure for identifying anomalies in time series using SS-LSTM-PAAE, the gathered public data set is subjected to preprocessing. This step involves the operations of data normalization and data segmentation. After that, the trained model was generated by putting the data that had been preprocessed through the SS-LSTM-PAAE model's training procedure. The trained model is applied to the test data set in order to identify any time series abnormalities. This is done in order to validate the dependability of the model.

The remaining parts of this article will be organized in the following way. In Part 2, the literature review is summarized once again for your convenience. In Sect. 3, we provide our proposal for the system model of the ensemble learning-based semi-supervised anomaly detection technique. In Sect. 4, we will discuss the SS-LSTM-PAAE-based time series anomaly detection method that we developed. In the next section, we provide experimental assessments of the validity of the technique, and in the last section, we bring the whole work to a conclusion.

2   Related Work

Reconstruction error-based modeling is included in the realm of non-regression modeling. With this sort of method, an automated encoder model is used rather often. It extends the original data according to the format of the actual observed value to the output layer, compresses it, transfers the actual observed value to a hidden layer that has less neurons, and then outputs the rebuilt value. The comparison and classification process begins with a comparison of the reconstruction error, which is the difference between the value that was reconstructed and the value that was actually served. Luo et al. used the reconstruction error of the shallow auto-encoder network to discover discrepancies in the sequence data from mobile phones acquired over time from resource-constrained sensor devices [1]. This was accomplished by using the shallow auto-encoder network.

There are two different kinds of feature extraction: temporal feature extraction and spatial feature extraction. The vast bulk of the research that has been done up to this point simply looks at one of the characteristics to determine whether or not there is an abnormality. In research that combines recurrent neural networks (RNN) with convolutional neural networks (CNN), researchers take into consideration the extraction of temporal and spatial data (RNN). Researchers are able to utilize CNN to investigate time series since it did so well in earlier experiments when extracting information about spatial relationships. Convolutional Neural Networks (CNNs) are so popular for image processing that the convolution kernel only has two dimensions. Due to the fact that time series almost always belong to either the univariate or the multivariate category, neither of which corresponds to the two-dimensional convolution kernel, these series need to be modified. CNN is a valuable tool for extracting spatial information from time series, as indicated by Wang et al. [2], who proposed a technique for projecting univariate time series into two-dimensional pictures. According to Liu et al., a multivariate CNN might be used to classify multi-variate temporal data. These approaches effectively remove geographical information from time series while simultaneously improving the performance of numerous classifiers [3]. The simple process of extracting spatial information from time series will result in a loss of the data's temporal understanding [4].

RNN is a kind of neural network that is well-suited for the processing of time series because of its ability to capture relationships between data that span both space and time. The RNN will set aside some of the input data as historical data at each time step by making use of hidden units in the process. The past data will be wiped clean due to the limited storage space available and the inability of disguised devices. When the time series is longer than the maximum time period for which the RNN is able to accurately record the data relationship, the gradient will, as a consequence, become indistinguishable. The LSTM and GRU systems both incorporate gate units that replicate memory and forgetting functions. This allows the systems to tackle the problem of gradient disappearance that is caused by long-term storage. The advantages that RNN offers in the process of extracting temporal characteristics have led to its widespread use in the field of time series data analysis. CNN and LSTM with attention processes were proposed by Karim et al. [5] as a method for extracting features from time series data. The findings of the experiment indicate that LSTM works to enhance the overall functioning of the convolutional network. In the automatic en-coder model that was suggested by Sutskever et al., the RNN-based encoder collects and stores the temporal properties of the input sequence that is received at each time step, and the RNN-based decoder receives the decoded data and reconstructs it [6]. Both of these processes are carried out by the RNN. When Malhotra et al. deployed the LSTM-based autoencoder for the first time to identify time series anomalies [7], the experimental findings revealed that the autoencoder performed better than the prediction-based technique when it came to unexpected data. The Mal-hotra et al method only uses normal data to train the automated encoder. This is done in order to grasp the properties of the normal data distribution and to make use of the discrepancy between the decoded and original data in order to identify anomalies.

In the setting of massive data sets, the cost of time series data labeling is mostly resolved by the two ways that were just described, each of which takes an entirely different approach. Nevertheless, there are certain restrictions on the application and efficiency of unsupervised learning algorithms. These restrictions may be found in the algorithms themselves. The development of semi-supervised learning occurs when the data are often only partly annotated. As compared to the use of either labeled or unlabeled data alone, the semi-supervised technique is able to more effectively use both types of data to boost model performance [8]. Cheng et al. proposed a semi-supervised layered stacking TCN model via the use of temporal convolutional networks (TCN) [9]. The findings of the experiment demonstrated that the semi-supervised learning technique resulted in an improvement in the performance of the model. The semi-supervised DEEP SVDD methodology was presented for the very first time in Ruff et al. [10]. In order to enhance the overall functionality of the model, the processes of data mapping and information entropy extraction were modified to make use of marked data.

3 Construction of Semi-supervised Anomaly Detection Model for Electric Power Networks Based on Ensemble Learning

This section gives an overview of the semi-supervised anomaly detection model (SS-LSTM-PAAE) that is based on ensemble learning that is suggested in this research. The semi-supervised LSTM prediction model and the SS-LSTM-AAE model combine to form the SS-LSTM-PAAE model. This research enhanced the unsupervised LSTM prediction model to produce a semi-supervised LSTM prediction model and integrated it with SS-LSTM-AAE to form an SS-LSTM-PAAE model based on the experience of SS-LSTM-AAE in the improvement of loss function. Figure 1 displays the suggested model's general architecture.

3.1 Unsupervised LSTM Prediction Model

The unsupervised LSTM prediction model is composed of LSTM neural network and fully connected layer. The LSTM neural network learns the input data, outputs the results, and then maps the output results of the LSTM neural network to the result space of the sample data through the fully connected layer to output the final prediction results. Assume that the obtained time series is $T = \{x_1, x_2, \cdots x_n\}$, where x_t is the data of the current time series at time t. Set a sliding window of length K, sliding step length is 1, T divided into data set $S = \{(s_1, y_1), (s_2, y_2), \cdots, (s_{n-K}, y_{n-K})\}$ and $(s_t, y_t) = (\{x_t, x_{t+1}, \cdots x_{t+K-1}\}, x_{t+K})$. The unsupervised LSTM prediction model takes the data set composed of s_t as the input and the data composed of y_t as the output for training to learn the data development trend in the time series data.

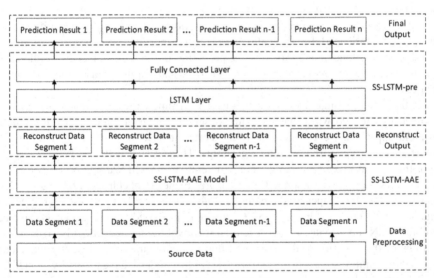

Fig. 1. Structure diagram of SS-LSTM-PAAE model for false detection of electric power distribution network

Unsupervised LSTM prediction model through the LSTM neural network to learn s_t, and through the connection layer will study results output to $\tilde{y}_t$. $\tilde{y}_t$ and y_t is LSTM numerical gap between prediction error of prediction model, in order to guarantee the LSTM correct prediction model on the data distribution of study, you will need to minimizing the prediction error. Therefore, we took the prediction error as the loss function of the unsupervised LSTM prediction model, and completed the learning task of the prediction model through the following functions:

$$\min \sum_{i=1}^{n-K} \|y_i - \tilde{y}_i\|_2$$

After the training of the prediction model, the prediction error is also taken as abnormal fraction to judge whether the current data is abnormal data in the test experiment of the prediction model. In this step, a threshold σ is set to compare the prediction error with the threshold σ. If the prediction error is higher than the threshold, the data is marked as abnormal. If the prediction error is lower than the threshold, the data is marked as normal:

$$\text{is\_anomaly} = \begin{cases} 1 \ error > \sigma \\ 0 \ error < \sigma \end{cases}$$

3.2 Semi-supervised LSTM Prediction Model

The unsupervised LSTM pre-diction model, like the unsupervised LSTM autoencoder, makes sure that training data in the majority of studies only comprises normal data in order to accurately understand the distribution of data and prevent the impact of abnormal data on model learning. The expense of eliminating anomalous data from unlabeled data is rising steadily in the context of large data, nevertheless. As a result, it is essential to investigate how to remove anomalous data from training data. In the study without tag data distribution, can also learn the marked data distribution, to achieve the goal of learning data distribution correctly. Considering the actual scene, in addition to the unmarked data, generally there will exist a small number of labeled data. This article obtains from this part marked data, will be a tag data into the training data, for unsupervised LSTM prediction model was improved.

3.3 Semi-supervised Anomaly Detection Model Based on Ensemble Learning

In order to guarantee the effectiveness of each method, ensemble learning gathers a variety of learning strategies and generates multiple distinct models. By combining the rules of various models, ensemble learning is created, increasing the generalization power and learning precision of the underlying model. This study examines the use of semi-supervised learning in the field of time series anomaly identification from two perspectives and divides unsupervised time series anomaly detection into prediction error-based and reconstruction error-based categories. After confirming that the two models, SS-LSTM-AAE and SS-LSTM-pre, were available, this article combined the two models using ensemble learning's sequential integration method to create a semi-supervised anomaly detection model (SS-LSTM-PAAE).

In order to integrate the two models, it is necessary to ensure that the output of one model can be used as the input of the other model for further analysis. Therefore, considering that the dimensions of the reconstructed model input and output data are the same, we decide to take SS-LSTM-AAE as the first part of SS-LSTM-PAAE. Input the source data into SS-LSTM-AAE, output the result of the reconstruction of SS-LSTM-AAE, and then use the reconstruction result as the input of SS-LSTM-pre for prediction operation, and finally output the prediction result of SS-LSTM-pre, which is the output result of the model SS-LSTM-PAAE.

SS-LSTM-AAE and SS-LSTM-pre are trained individually during the training procedure to guarantee the performance of each model. The input and output dimensions of SS-LSTM-AAE and SS-LSTM-pre must match up while building the model since the output results of SS-LSTM-AAE must be directly entered into SS-LSTM-pre. In the SS-LSTM-PAAE model proposed in this paper, unmarked time series x_u and marked time series x_{label} are divided into data segments by using a sliding window of length 1 to obtain unmarked time series data segment set $S_u = \{(s_1, r_1, y_{s1}), (s_2, r_2, y_{s2}), \ldots, (s_m, r_m, y_{sm})\}$ and marked time series data set $S_{label} = \{ (\overline{s}_1, \overline{r}_1, \overline{y}_{s1}), (\overline{s}_2, \overline{r}_2, \overline{y}_{s2}), \ldots, (\overline{s}_n, \overline{r}_n, \overline{y}_{sn})\}$, including s_i and $\overline{s}_i$ said the case of a data segment, r_i and $\overline{r}_i$ said the i-th a data after the data segment, the predicted results and y_{si} and $\overline{y}_{si}$ said the ith a data segment of the tag. In the process of training SS-LSTM-AAE, using only the s_i, $\overline{s}_i$, y_{si} and $\overline{y}_{si}$ four attribute values, and in the process of training SS - LSTM - pre is used by all attribute values.

SS-LSTM-PAAE model to determine the anomaly score based on the SS-LSTM -pre final output results with the source data r_i and $\overline{r}_i$ between prediction error, namely:

$$\text{score}_{\text{error}} = E[r_i : \tilde{r}_i] = \frac{1}{l} \|r_i - \tilde{r}_i\|_2$$

4 Time Series Anomaly Detection Algorithm Based on SS-LSTM-PAAE

In this section, a time series anomaly detection algorithm is established by using the proposed SS-LSTM-PAAE model. The algorithm includes three stages: data preprocessing, model training and anomaly detection. Data preprocessing steps mainly include data normalization and data segmentation operation. The model training stage includes the training of two independent models and the partitioning of data sets.

4.1 Data Preprocessing

Suppose that the obtained data set to be trained is $T = \{x_1, x_2, \cdots x_n\}$, where the maximum value of the data is x_{max} and the minimum value is x_{min}. Due to the different value ranges of time series data in different time periods, in order to avoid the decline of data distribution learning ability caused by inconsistent data units, this paper uses min-max standardization to normalize the value ranges of all data. The conversion function is as follows

$$\tilde{T} = \{x | \tilde{x}_i = \frac{x_i - x_{min}}{x_{max} - x_{min}}, i = 1, 2, \cdots, n\}$$

The $\tilde{T}$ for normalization after the training data set, x_i is the original value of the i-th a data, $\tilde{x}_i$ by x_i corresponding numerical after normalization.

4.2 Training Process of the Proposed SS-LSTM-PAAE Model

In this section, the process of SS-LSTM-PAAE model training using the data after data preprocessing will be described. The implementation process is as follows:

- Step1: Initialize the model parameters, and unify the input and output dimensions of SS-LSTM-AAE and the input dimensions of SS-LSTM-pre. Set the maximum number of iterations, number of hidden layers, number of neurons, and batch size.
- Step2: Use the training data respectively to train SS-LSTM-AAE in SS-LSTM-pre, and save the model parameters after training.
- Step3: Adjust the hyperparameter γ in the loss function of the two models, train the two models again, and save the trained model parameters.
- Step4: Distinguish the proportion of marked data for the training data, form three training data sets with the proportion of 20% marked data, 30% marked data and 50% marked data. Then train the two models and save the model parameters after training.

In the training process, Step1 and Step2 are a basic process of the training model. Step3 aims to answer the research question of the weight of the marker, and Step4 aims to answer the research question of the scale of the marker. Several model parameter files were saved in the training process, which also reduced the work burden for the subsequent anomaly detection.

4.3 Abnormal Detection

This part solves the following research issues by doing experiments on three typical time series data sets, similar to SS-LSTM-AAE:

- LSTM prediction model in the case of a semi-supervised anomaly detection algorithm of anomaly detection performance is better than unsupervised algorithm under the LSTM prediction model? After the integration of SS-LSTM-AAE and SS-LSTM-pre, is the performance of time series anomaly detection better than the two models or close to the higher performance of the two models?
- Tag size under the different mark data share, a semi-supervised algorithms effect to the promotion of LSTM prediction model can maintain or get higher? Will the enhancement effects of the model be maintained or improved after integration?
- Weight marking data share in the loss function can greatly affect a semi-supervised LSTM prediction model and the performance of the integrated model?

Web-scope S5 data set contains 17,114 unmarked data, 16,670 marked data, and 10,782 test sets based on A1 benchmark, as well as 17,052 unmarked data, 17,178 marked data, and 22,736 test sets based on A2 benchmark. The experimental data set that is used in this section is identical to the experimental data set that is used in SS-LSTM-AAE, which is derived from Yahoo! This object is comprised of 16,128 unmarked data sets, 16,128 marked data sets, and 8066 tested data sets taken from the artificialNoAnomaly and arti-ficialWithAnomaly categories of NAB.

5   Experimental Results and Analysis

5.1   Experiment Settings

The improvement effect of the semi-supervised algorithm on the unsupervised prediction model and the performance improvement effect of the integrated model on the single model are the main topics of discussion in this section. In order to compare the two models, the semi-supervised LSTM prediction model and the unsupervised LSTM prediction model (LSTM-PRE), respectively (SS-LSTM-pre). Also employed is the integration model (SS-LSTM-PAAE), which is built on SS-LSTM-AAE and SS-LSTM-pre.

- **LSTM-pre**: LSTM as prediction model of unsupervised network structure, use only the unmarked experiment data set and test set.
- **SS-LSTM-pre**: LSTM-pre's loss function was improved, using no data sets and marking data set for training.
- **SS-LSTM-PAAE**: SS -LSTM-AAE and SS-LSTM- pre method according to the sequence of integration of the thinking of integrated model, using no data sets and marking data set for training.

This section uses Python3.7 as the programming language and the CUDA version of TensorFlow3.0 as the neural network framework. In terms of model parameter setting, due to the purpose of comparing the performance difference between unsupervised and semi-supervised models, the corresponding models all use the same parameters except the loss function. In addition, the anomaly depends on whether the reconstruction error is greater than the set threshold, and the threshold is determined on different data and according to experience.

5.2   Experimental Results of Semi-supervised LSTM Prediction Model

In this part, the validity of the proposed semi-supervised LSTM prediction model and the integrated model SS-LSTM-PAAE model is verified, including the experimental results of the SS-LSTM-pre model on three research problems and the performance improvement results of the SS-LSTM-PAAE model on three research problems on a single model.

The same LSTM prediction model's performance in anomaly detection tasks under unsupervised and semi-supervised settings is shown in Table 1 below. Unsupervised and semi-supervised models perform better, as bolded in the table below.

Table 1.   Abnormal detection results

Model	Yahoo! A1Benchmark			Yahoo! A2Benchmark			NAB		
	pre	recall	F1-score	pre	recall	F1-score	pre	recall	F1-score
LSTM-pre	0.5910	**0.8096**	0.6832	0.7163	**1.0**	0.8347	0.3405	0.9530	0.5018
SS-LSTM-pre	**0.8487**	0.7288	**0.7842**	**0.7757**	0.9676	**0.8611**	**0.3620**	**0.9736**	**0.5278**

It can be observed from Table 1 that under the three data sets, while some of the second half of the supervision model of recall index compared with a drop in the unsupervised model, but in the rest of the indicators, a semi-supervised model has a certain even great advantages, so you can get half under the supervision of LSTM prediction model performance than unsupervised performance good conclusion.

We chose the corresponding percentage of marked data for each data set and ran numerous tests with various marked data proportions in order to further investigate the effect of marked data on the model. Table 2 compares the effectiveness of supervised and unsupervised algorithms at various proportions.

Table 2 shows that: 1) The performance of the semi-supervised algorithm is better than that of the unsupervised method, regardless of the proportion of marked data in the entire training set; 2) When combined with Figs. 2, 3, and 4, and compared to the unsupervised model, the semi-supervised model will stabilize one index in pre and recall while significantly improving the other index, resulting in the final improvement of F1-score, with the exception of the improvement of all indexes in the NAB data set. The performance of the semi-supervised method steadily improves as the amount of marked data increases, but as the proportion rises, so does the algorithm's performance improvement window. More specifically, performance of each model was greatly enhanced when the markup data was increased from 20% to 30% as opposed to 30% to 50%.

In the semi-supervised algorithm, this paper improves the loss function of the unsupervised LSTM prediction model by adding a loss term and defining a hyperparameter γ to determine the weight of the new loss term in the whole loss function. This section analyzes the $\gamma \in \{0.5, 1.0, 1.5, 2.0\}$ in the data set Yahoo! Experiments are conducted on A1Benchmark, and the experimental results are shown in Table 3.

Table 2. Model performance tables with different markup data ratios

	20%标记数据占比								
Model	Yahoo! A1Benchmark			Yahoo! A2Benchmark			NAB		
	pre	recall	F1-score	pre	recall	F1-score	pre	recall	F1-score
LSTM-pre	0.5910	**0.8096**	0.6832	0.7163	**1.0**	0.8347	0.3405	0.9530	0.5018
SS-LSTM-pre	**0.7432**	0.8100	**0.7752**	**0.7716**	0.9268	**0.8421**	**0.3512**	**0.9709**	**0.5158**

	30%标记数据占比								
Model	Yahoo! A1Benchmark			Yahoo! A2Benchmark			NAB		
	pre	recall	F1-score	pre	recall	F1-score	pre	recall	F1-score
LSTM-pre	0.5910	**0.8096**	0.6832	0.7163	**1.0**	0.8347	0.3405	0.9530	0.5018
SS-LSTM-pre	**0.8663**	0.6977	**0.7808**	**0.7738**	0.9692	**0.8605**	**0.3571**	**0.9722**	**0.5223**

	50%标记数据占比								
Model	Yahoo! A1Benchmark			Yahoo! A2Benchmark			NAB		
	pre	recall	F1-score	pre	recall	F1-score	pre	recall	F1-score
LSTM-pre	0.5910	**0.8096**	0.6832	0.7163	**1.0**	0.8347	0.3405	0.9530	0.5018
SS-LSTM-pre	**0.8487**	0.7288	**0.7842**	**0.7757**	0.9676	**0.8611**	**0.3620**	**0.9736**	**0.5278**

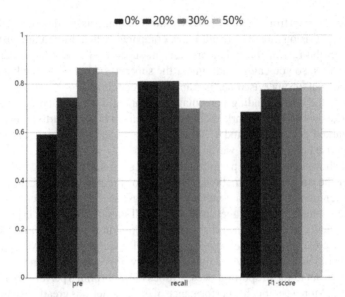

Fig. 2. Comparison diagram of indexes of SS-LSTM-pre under different marked data proportions under Yahoo! A1Benchmark

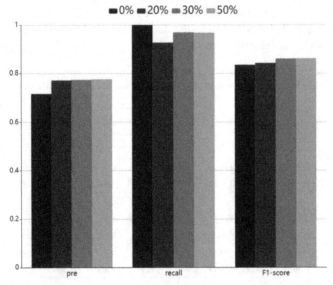

Fig. 3. Comparison diagram of indexes of SS-LSTM-pre under different marked data proportions under Yahoo! A2Benchmark

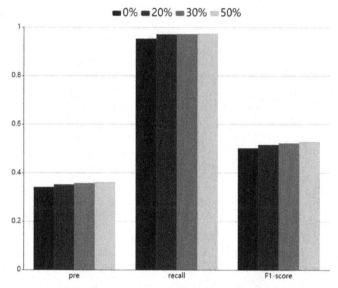

Fig. 4. Comparison of indexes of SS-LSTM-pre under different marked data proportions under NAB

The SS-LSTM-pre model is also tested under different γ in Yahoo! A1Benchmark and Yahoo! Experiments were conducted on two data sets of A2Benchmark. F1-score of the model was taken out for line graph drawing, and the results were shown in Fig. 5.

Table 3. Yahoo! A1Benchmark test results under different γ

γ	SS-LSTM-pre		
	pre	recall	F1-score
0.0	0.5910	0.8096	0.6832
0.5	0.8487	0.7288	0.7842
1.0	0.7466	0.5820	0.6541
1.5	0.7868	0.8028	0.7947
2.0	0.4845	0.8524	0.6178

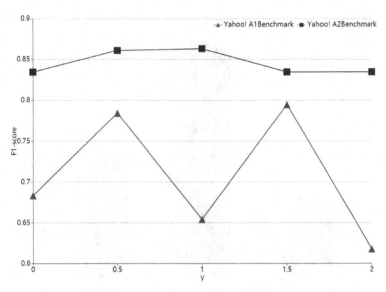

Fig. 5. F1-score of the model under different γ

6 Conclusion

In order to identify defect data in electrical power distribution networks, this research primarily introduces the semi-supervised LSTM prediction model and the semi-supervised anomaly detection approach based on ensemble learning. The semi-supervised anomaly detection approach based on ensemble learning and the semi-supervised LSTM prediction model are introduced first. The two primary models introduced are the semi-supervised anomaly detection model merged with the SS-LSTM-AAE and SS-LSTM-pre model, which is an improvement over the unsupervised LSTM prediction model. The semi-supervised LSTM prediction model enhances the loss function of the unsupervised LSTM prediction model, bringing a small quantity of marked data within the range of learning data distribution, boosting the model's ability to learn the distribution of all the data. By the concept of sequence integration, the semi-supervised anomaly detection model based on ensemble learning combines the SS-LSTM-AAE and SS-LSTM-pre models to create a more effective SS-LSTM-PAAE model. Second, the suggested time series anomaly detection algorithm in this research, which consists of three steps data pre-processing, SS-LSTM-PAAE model training, and anomaly detection is explained. This approach is based on SS-LSTM-pre and SS-LSTM-PAAE. Data normalization and temporal segmentation operations are included in data preprocessing. The training phase of the integrated model is described by the SS-LSTM-PAAE model. Lastly, experiments were carried out on three public time series data sets to confirm that semi-supervised learning and ensemble learning frameworks can better detect abnormalities in time series. First, it is determined that the semi-supervised LSTM prediction model can carry out anomaly detection more effectively than the unsupervised prediction model by comparing the performance of the unsupervised prediction model with the semi-supervised prediction model with the same network topology. Second, it is determined that the integrated model has improved in some circumstances while preserving the superior performance of the two separate models by comparing the performance of the integrated model and two separate models. The effectiveness of the sequence integration method is confirmed in the area of time series anomaly identification.

References

1. Luo, T., Nagarajan, S.G.: Distributed anomaly detection using autoencoder neural networks in WSN for IoT. In: 2018 IEEE International Conference on Communications (ICC), pp. 1–6. IEEE (2018)
2. Wang, W., Zhu, M., Wang, J., et al.: End-to-end encrypted traffic classification with one-dimensional convolution neural networks. In: 2017 IEEE International Conference on Intelligence and Security Informatics (ISI), pp. 43–48. IEEE (2017)
3. Liu, C.L., Hsaio, W.H., Tu, Y.C.: Time series classification with multivariate convolutional neural network. IEEE Trans. Industr. Electron. **66**(6), 4788–4797 (2018)
4. Kim, T.Y., Cho, S.B.: Web traffic anomaly detection using C-LSTM neural networks. Expert Syst. Appl. **106**, 66–76 (2018)
5. Karim, F., Majumdar, S., Darabi, H., et al.: LSTM fully convolutional networks for time series classification. IEEE access **6**, 1662–1669 (2017)
6. Sutskever, I., Vinyals, O., Le, Q.V.: Sequence to sequence learning with neural networks. Adv. Neural Inf. Proc. Syst. 3104–3112 (2014)
7. Malhotra, P., Ramakrishnan, A., Anand, G., et al.: LSTM-based encoder-decoder for multi-sensor anomaly detection. arXiv preprint arXiv:1607.00148 (2016)
8. Shah, M.P., Merchant, S.N., Awate, S.P.: Abnormality detection using deep neural networks with robust quasi-norm autoencoding and semi-supervised learning. In: 2018 IEEE 15th International Symposium on Biomedical Imaging (ISBI 2018), pp. 568-572. IEEE (2018)
9. Cheng, Y., Xu, Y., Zhong, H., et al.: HS-TCN: a semi-supervised hierarchical stacking temporal convolutional network for anomaly detection in IoT. In: 2019 IEEE 38th International Performance Computing and Communications Conference (IPCCC), pp. 1–7. IEEE (2019)
10. Ruff, L., Vandermeulen, R.A., Görnitz, N., et al.: Deep semi-supervised anomaly detection. arXiv preprint arXiv:1906.02694 (2019)

Factors Influencing Chinese Users' Willingness to Pay for O2O Knowledge Products Based on Information Adoption Model

Zhu Zhentao[1]([✉]), Yue Wen[1], Zhang Yan[1], and Wu Qiuchi[2]

[1] School of Economics and Management, Nanjing Institute of Technology, Nanjing 211167, China
{zztnit,zhangyan}@njit.edu.cn
[2] School of Electrical Engineering, Nanjing Institute of Technology, Nanjing 211167, China

Abstract. The China's knowledge payment industry has entered the "pan-knowledge payment" period, and the overall situation of industry is gratifying. O2O paid knowledge platforms, which are not under the public media spotlight, are also developing slowly. The non-standardized knowledge services provided by this type of platform have a unique charm that standardized online knowledge payment products do not have because they can be personalized and socially interacted on site, and their business value is worthy of attention. The research issue of this paper is what factors influencing users' willingness to pay can be identified and verified using statistical models from the user behavior and content information available on a typical China's O2O paid knowledge platform. From the perspective of Information Adoption theory, we construct a model of the factors influencing the willingness to pay for O2O paid knowledge products, which includes two aspects: information quality and source credibility. We collected a total of 9,907 actual behavioral data and topic data from users of the China's O2O paid knowledge platform, "Zaih.com", and used log-linear regression model to verify the hypotheses. The results show that: in terms of information quality, content integrity, information relevance, information applicability and interactive empathy have significant positive effects on users' willingness to pay; in terms of credibility of information sources, the expertise and attractiveness of knowledge providers indicated by integrity of their profile and their high level residence have significant positive effects on users' willingness to pay. The above findings have important guiding implications for the three parties of O2O knowledge payment, especially for the service improvement and personal development of knowledge providers of this type of platform.

Keywords: knowledge payment · information adoption model · user behavior data mining · log-linear regression · O2O knowledge products · willingness to pay

Y. Tian et al. (Eds.): ICBDS 2022, CCIS 1796, pp. 276–295, 2023.
https://doi.org/10.1007/978-981-99-3300-6_20

1 Introduction

In recent years, the rise of self-media and the boom of sharing economy have matured the channels for professionals in various fields to realize content cash, providing a continuous supply of quality resources; at the same time, the information overload brought by the rapid development of society in the transition period and the accelerated speed of knowledge iteration have brought pressure and caused anxiety to people, which also greatly stimulated the demand for knowledge payment; smart hardware and mobile payment have provided strong technical support for both supply and demand [1]. Figure 1 illustrates the transaction model and industry ecology of China's knowledge payment system.

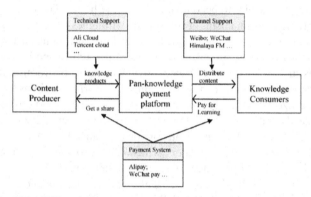

Fig. 1. China's Knowledge payment transaction models and industry ecology

iiMedia Consulting report released in February 2020 said the market size of knowledge payment reached 27.8 billion CNY in 2019, and is expected to exceed 39.2 billion CNY in 2020 [2]. Although the development of various industries was hampered by the epidemic caused by COVID-19 in early 2020, the knowledge payment industry has ushered in a window period, and the number of participants in the "Listen to a book every day" campaign reached 400,000 from January 29 to February 5, taking DeDao App as an example. Currently, knowledge payment has entered the era of pan-knowledge payment, in which knowledge providers package knowledge, experience and information into products or services for knowledge consumers with the help of pan-knowledge payment platforms, forming a value transformation. In this process, knowledge suppliers, pan-knowledge payment platforms and knowledge consumers influence each other, thus obtaining the resources and values required by each [3].

The O2O knowledge payment products studied in this paper are a kind of paid products launched by platforms adopting the O2O (Online to Offline) + C2C (Customer to Customer) model, in which knowledge consumers book knowledge providers online and conduct one-to-one consulting services offline. Compared to online paid knowledge platforms, O2O paid knowledge platforms (such as Zaih.com) adopt the model of online booking and offline consulting, and their development is relatively slow. At present, the head platforms in China's knowledge payment industry are all online platforms, such as Himalaya FM, Dragonfly FM, and Lazy Listening [3], but O2O knowledge payment model has a certain complementary relationship with the online knowledge payment model, and this complementarity is reflected in the fact that O2O consulting provides a non-standardized knowledge payment product that can effectively meet the more personalized needs of knowledge consumers [4].

This model of O2O consulting also has some problems. First, due to information asymmetry, it is difficult for consumers to determine the effective value of products when acquiring knowledge services; second, the number of appointments (which can be interpreted as product sales) for topics and courses offered by providers of knowledge services is clearly bifurcated, with only a few knowledge service products winning the favor of users and paying a high number of fees. How to increase the number of appointments for topics or courses is the key issue for the providers of knowledge services who are not yet mentors or aspire to become mentors in the future. Therefore, exploring the influencing factors and mechanisms of consumers' willingness to purchase such products is not only important for studying the healthy development of this customized knowledge service business model, but also has important theoretical and business values for relevant parties such as knowledge service providers, service platforms and consumers.

A typical representative of the O2O consulting platform website is "Zaih.com". "It is a non-standardized product that allows you to meet with experts in different fields to solve your needs with various personalized restrictions. Figure 2 shows a few of the "topics" under the "startup financing" category on the Zaih.com website. A professional in a certain field is referred to as a "mentor"; a mentor can provide multiple service topics, each of which is called a "topic". The topics of different mentors of similar subjects are marked as different topics by the system. Mentor services are charged by topic, and the price range is mainly from 300 to 600 CNY. Compared with knowledge websites such as DeDao and Zhihu, the public visibility of the mentor is limited, but the unit price of the product is obviously higher because it provides offline meeting scenarios; at the same time, the one-to-one consultation service also enables the mentor to provide more customized and professional services.

Fig. 2. Selected topics in Startup Finance category tab of Zaih.com

In this paper, we use the information adoption model to collect the actual behavioral data of the users of O2O consulting knowledge payment platform (take "Zaih.com" as an example) and combine it with a statistical model to study the factors influencing the users' willingness to pay.

2 Literature Review

In the existing studies, the factors influencing consumers to purchase knowledge service products can be summarized into three dimensions: individual characteristics dimension, product service dimension and external influence dimension.

Individual Characteristics Dimension
Through qualitative research, Shuai Zhang et al. found that the most critical factors influencing users' online knowledge payment behavior are individual needs and information quality, and individual perception is an important influencing factor [5]. Using the MOA theory (Motivation-Opportunity-Ability) to construct an analytical framework for user behavior, Xinya Yang et al. found that interest motivation, perceived usefulness, perceived ease of use, learning ability, and consumption ability were the main influencing factors of Himalaya FM users' payment behavior [6]. Dou and Wang came to a similar conclusion when they studied content subscription service websites: perceived value-added and perceived risk, and users' purpose of use significantly influenced users' willingness to subscribe to content or services [7, 8]. However, Wang did not consider demographic variables in his study, and Punj G addressed this issue by suggesting that the amount users pay for digital content subscription services is related to income and education, but the effects of age and gender are more significant [9].

Product Service Dimension
Cai Shun et al. used Zhihu Live, a paid knowledge platform, as the research object, and constructed a model based on its actual operation data and proposed hypotheses to explore the effect of price on the sales of knowledge products (e.g., Live), and although the factors affecting user payment were not directly studied, the study for sales found that price had a negative effect on the sales of knowledge products [10], but as the number of product reviews increased, the moderating role of price was also suggested by Zhao Y et al. The team used a negative binomial regression model to analyze data collected from Zhihu and found that the reputation and trustworthiness of knowledge contributors positively influenced users' payment decisions [10]. This finding indirectly suggests that consumers are still influenced by price factors when making knowledge payments, which contradicts many scholars who conclude that price does not have a significant effect on willingness to pay.

External Impact Dimension
Based on the theory of information economics, Goyanes used logit regression analysis to conclude that other digital media usage and media usage (mainly Twitter) would affect users' willingness to purchase online news services [12]. Zhang et al. used the theory of planned behavior to find that collective norms significantly affect willingness to pay

for knowledge [13], which is similar to Zhang Shuai's proposal that subjective norms are an important factor influencing users' online knowledge payment [5], where both subjective norms and collective norms emphasize the external pressure on individuals to adopt a certain behavior. Some scholars have also noticed the influence brought by trial experiences. Du et al. argue that the expertise, interestingness, and convenience perceived by the user experience are the main influencing factors in determining users' willingness to pay for knowledge [5]. Based on this view, related scholars have also carried out research on customers' satisfaction with trial and experience services, such as Chen et al. used expectation confirmation theory to study the trial services of paid knowledge platforms as a cognitive evaluation process of "expectation-confirmation-satisfaction", and found that utility value and enjoyment value significantly influenced consumers' satisfaction with. They found that utility value and enjoyment value significantly affected consumers' satisfaction with the trial of knowledge services, while the effect of trial cost was not significant [14].

From the perspective of the theories and models used in the study, the existing studies are mainly divided into two schools of thought, one of which is to study willingness to pay or behavior using technology acceptance models and their derivative models; the other is to study using psychology or consumer behavior; only a few scholars use data analysis to conduct relevant studies [10, 10].

3 Theoretical Model Construction

3.1 Theoretical Model

As an experience-based product, knowledge consumers usually have to make payment decisions without fully understanding the value and quality of the product. In the case of "Zaih.com", for example, users can only decide whether to pay to initiate topic invitations by browsing topic interface information (topic description, topic price, etc.), mentor interface information (mentor introduction, appointment rate, etc.) and relevant comment information. This information can be broadly classified into two categories: topic quality information and mentor trustworthiness information. The IAM (Information Adoption Model) suggests that the process of changing users' attitudes towards information until they adopt it can be achieved through two distinct routes: one is the central route dominated by information quality; the other is the peripheral route dominated by the credibility of the information source. It can be seen that the purchase decision process of O2O consulting knowledge products, the subject of this study, has some adaptability with this model.

The IAM model proposed by Sussman and Siegel (2003) was first applied to the study of online information dissemination and communication [15], and in recent years it has also been applied to the usefulness of reviews on online shopping platforms [14], personalized recommendations for e-commerce [17], and other related studies. The model is constructed based on the Elaboration Likelihood Model (ELM) proposed by Petty et al. (1984) [18] and the Technology Acceptance Model (TAM) proposed by Davis

(1989) [19]. The ELM model assumes that whether information receiver's attitude and behavior change depends on the receiver's ability and motivation. When the receiver receives the information, the receiver's attitudes are transformed will via two distinct routes: the central route and the peripheral route. The processing of information will result in the receiver thinking about the information based on his or her own ability and motivation. Under the central route, the change in the attitude or behavior of the information receiver comes from careful reflection on the quality of the information; under the peripheral route, information-related cues such as the expertise, attractiveness, or trustworthiness of the information sender will be the key to changing the user's attitude, rather than the information itself [20]. The user's likelihood of fine-grained processing of information will determine the user's choice of a specific route, and information from the central route is more likely to be accepted when the likelihood of fine-grained processing is high, and conversely the peripheral route is more effective. Further research by Petty et al. (1986) showed that information quality becomes the main factor influencing information acceptance when information receivers are diligently engaged in the process of receiving information [21]. Sussman et al. built on this research and found that argument quality, and source credibility are the main factors influencing information when the likelihood of fine processing is high and low, respectively. At this point, in the IAM model, the central route shifts to argument quality and the peripheral route shifts to the credibility of the information source. Consumer perceived information usefulness will be directly influenced, and information usefulness further influences information adoption.

This study focuses on O2O paid knowledge platforms and explores the factors that affect knowledge consumers' willingness to pay for topics offered by mentors on O2O paid knowledge platforms. Willingness to pay refers to consumers' subjective evaluation of a good or service in a specific context and their willingness to pay a certain amount to receive the good or service, but the willingness is susceptible to interference in the process of turning into a paying behavior or decision. Since knowledge consumers have the problem of information asymmetry when transacting on online platforms and are unable to judge the true value and utility of a topic, platform users can help reduce the risk in the payment decision process by assessing the quality of information conveyed by the topic and the credibility of the mentor. Therefore, based on the IAM model, this study proposes the following theoretical model and hypotheses applicable to the willingness to pay for O2O consulting knowledge products. The diagram of the theoretical model of this topic is shown in Fig. 3. The plotting style of the conceptual model does not adopt the style of the structural equation method, and the rectangular modules do not represent the observed variables, but the latent variables. The style is consistent with the literature by Liu [4].

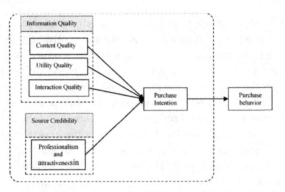

Fig. 3. Model of willingness to pay for O2O consulting knowledge products

Table 1 shows the variables used in the model and their measures, the correspondence of the fields in the data crawled.

Table 1. Description of model variables and their measures

Dimensionality	Variable	Measured variable	Variable Description	Corresponding field
Argument quality	Content quality	Information integrity [22]	Level of detail of the information obtained	Topic description (length of text)
		Quality signals [23]	The price reflects the quality of the product to some extent	Price
	Utility quality	Information relevance [24]	The extent to which the content of the information obtained matches the needs of the user	Number of topic views
		Information Applicability	The extent to which the content of the information received helped the user to solve the problem	Topic Rating

(*continued*)

Table 1. (*continued*)

Dimensionality	Variable	Measured variable	Variable Description	Corresponding field
	Interaction quality	Feedback timeliness [25]	Timeliness and rapidity of mentors' responses to user invitations and feedback	Response time to invitations
		Interaction real-time	Real-time level of follow-up communication between mentors and users	The mentor responds to user review
		Interactive empathy	The extent to which the services provided by mentors are adapted to the habits and characteristics of users	The mentor is also a user
		Service mode	Mentors offer knowledge sharing methods that are not limited to individual appointments, such as phone communication, group appointments	Type
Source credibility	Expertise and attractiveness	Communicator expertise and reputation	Education level, curriculum vitae, city level of residence, etc as reflected in the mentor profile	Mentor profiles (text length), Mentor's region, Appoint acceptance rate

Some of the measured variables in Table 1 are further elaborated below. The basis for using price as the counterpart of quality signals in this paper is the signal of product quality in Signaling Theory (STS). Connelly et al. argue that price is a common signal of product quality [23]. Some mentors in the "Zaih.com" platform are also consumers of "Zaih.com", and they may know more about consumers than mentors who have not experienced the consumer role. This corresponds to interaction empathy.

3.2 Research Hypothesis

Effects of Content Quality on Purchase Intention
Li Jing et al. point out that the content quality of information in the online shopping environment refers to the extent to which the content of information is consistent with objective reality [17]. For each topic opened by the mentors of "Zaih.com", the mentors will explain the content of the topic and inform the knowledge consumers of the main issues and details of the topic, so that consumers can make a preliminary judgment of the content quality of the topic before paying. In general, when two products in the same category have different levels of detailed product descriptions, the more likely consumers are to be willing to purchase the product with detailed descriptions. According to the signal theory, Cai Shun et al. pointed out that the common quality signals of knowledge payment products include price, product description, and advertising expenditure, etc., and concluded through the study that price has a negative impact on the sales of Zhihu Live [10]. Based on the above literature, this paper uses topic description word count and topic price as indicators of content quality and proposes the following hypotheses.

H1a: Topic description word count has a significant positive effect on users' willingness to pay for knowledge.

H1b: Price has a significant negative effect on users' willingness to pay for knowledge.

Effects of Utility Quality on Purchase Intention
Jiahui Xu et al. defined information utility quality as the extent to which it can help subjects to accomplish their work tasks and divided it into two perspectives of applicability and timeliness [26]. According to this formulation, this paper measures the utility quality in terms of information relevance and applicability, and uses the number of topic views and topic ratings as the corresponding fields of the two, respectively. Information relevance refers to the extent to which the information content obtained matches the user's needs. Knowledge consumers with purposeful needs will only enter the topic details page to browse if they think the topic provided by mentors can bring them help, while the number of topic views will have a certain impact on other users' willingness to pay. The applicability of information can be reflected by the topic rating, if the user's desired information content is satisfied and can generate additional perceived value, the user will give a high rating to this topic. The level of rating will affect the willingness of users to pay. Therefore, the following assumptions are made.

H2a: The number of topic views has a significant positive effect on users' willingness to pay for knowledge.

H2b: Topic ratings have a significant positive effect on users' willingness to pay for knowledge.

Effects of Interaction Quality on Purchase Intention
Bing Liu et al. proposed that process service experience and perception is an indicator of the impact of users' perception of service quality and level during information interaction [21]. In this paper, feedback timeliness, interaction real-time, interaction empathy, and topic service type are used to measure interaction quality. Feedback timeliness refers to

the speed of the mentor's timely feedback to the user's invitation; interaction real-time refers to the degree of real-time follow-up communication between the mentor and the user; interaction empathy refers to the degree of adaptation of the service provided by the mentor to the user's habits and characteristics. Some of the mentors in the "Zaih.com" platform are also users, and these double-identity mentors when participating in other mentors' paid topics, they are likely to learn from their experience and have a better grasp of users' habits, thus improving their own services. The type of topic service of "Zaih.com" is gradually enriched with the development of the platform, but still mainly in the form of individual offline appointments, supplemented by group appointments, calls and photography and hair art offline services, etc. From the perspective of effective information transfer and customer perceived value, the form of individual one-to-one appointments is more targeted and interactive than other forms. Based on this, users are more likely to pay for such topics.

H3a: The speed at which mentors respond to invitations has a significant positive effect on willingness to pay for knowledge.

H3b: Mentor responses to user ratings have a significant positive effect on willingness to pay for knowledge.

H3c: Mentors are customers have a significant positive effect on willingness to pay for knowledge.

H3d: One-to-One appointment topic service has a significant positive effect on willingness to pay for knowledge compared to other formats.

Effects of Expertise and Attractiveness on Purchase Intention
Many studies point to trust as an important factor influencing consumer behavior. For the users of the "Zaih.com" platform, the expertise and reputation of mentors are the sources of trust. Zhao, Yuxiang et al. in their study on the factors influencing willingness to pay in knowledge Q&A platforms pointed out that trust positively moderates the relationship between perceived value and willingness to pay [27]. A study by Qiping Liu and others pointed out that users in the field of knowledge payment trust more that the knowledge, experience, and skills possessed by knowledge providers who exhibit strong expertise will meet their needs and are therefore willing to pay for knowledge [4]. Based on the above literature, this paper uses the word count of mentor profiles, the region of the mentor, and appointment acceptance rate as indicators of the reputation of the deliverer, and proposes the following hypotheses.

H4a: Mentor profile word count has a significant positive effect on users' willingness to pay for knowledge.

H4b: The region of the mentor has a significant positive effect on users' willingness to pay for knowledge.

H4c: Appointment acceptance rate pickup has a significant positive effect on users' willingness to pay for knowledge.

4 Research Design

4.1 Data Sources and Variable Descriptions

We use crawling techniques to crawl 14,000 topics provided by nearly eight thousand mentors on the Zaih.com website in October and nearly 110,000 topic reviews left by over 50,000 users. After data pre-processing, nearly 2,000 observations with multiple missing key fields were removed (14.5%). A total of 9907 topic data from 5548 mentors were retained. The fields in this dataset were extracted from the raw data: mentor data, topic data, and user rating data to integrate the required fields. The dependent variable of this study is the number of "want to meet" of the topic created by a certain mentor on "Zaih.com" platform, which is used as a measure of willingness to pay. This is recorded by the number of times the users click the "Want to meet" button on the topic's page. Detailed descriptions of the variables are given in Table 2.

Table 2. Variable description table.

Variable role	Dimensionality	Measured variable	Range of value	notes
Dependent variable	Willingness to pay	The "want to meet" number	1–2339 (0–7.757)	The values in parentheses are taken from the natural logarithm
Independent variable	Content quality	Topic description	63–3269	Unit: word
		price	1–200,000	Unit: CNY
	Utility quality	Number of topic views	1–378	Unit: times
		Topic rating	Bellow 9.2;9.2–9.3;9.3–9.5;9.5or more; Insufficient number of ratings	9.5and more count for 10.15%
	Interaction quality	Response time to invitation	Within 1 day; within 2 day; within half a day; else	Within half a day count for 50.5%
		Reply to user's comments	0: False; 1: True	False count for 73%
		Mentor with user identity	0: False; 1: True	True count for 10.5%

(*continued*)

Table 2. (*continued*)

Variable role	Dimensionality	Measured variable	Range of value	notes
		Topic service type	Individuals; photographic; phone communication; grouping	Individuals count for 70.9%
	Expertise and attractiveness	Word count of mentor profile	1–3251	Unit: word
		Mentor's region	Tier 1; New Tier 1	Tier 1 count for 80%
		Appoint acceptance rate	Medium acceptance rate; high acceptance rate	High acceptance rate count for 89%

The highest price among all the topics is the "Entrepreneur Consulting Service" topic opened by Yao Di, COO (Chief Operating Officer) of GuoKr.com, which aims to provide management guidance for startup teams. Despite this, the topic has received 1,435 "want to meet" and 1 actual appointment, which is highly rated by users. The rating of the topic is divided into 4 levels according to the rating quartile, and the system will not show the rating for topics that the number of topic appointments does not meet the minimum requirement to be rated. The rating of this type of topic is treated as "insufficient rating". The variable "mentor's region" has 9 cities in the original dataset, including Beijing. We divide the nine cities into two levels: "Tier 1" and "New Tier 1" according to the "New City Classification List" released by the First Financial New Tier Cities Institute on May 24, 2019. Tier 1 cities include Beijing, Shanghai, Guangzhou and Shenzhen. Tier 2 and below cities do not appear in the records, probably because the platform's mentors are mostly concentrated in Tier 1 and New Tier 1 cities, and because these cities are where the main market for O2O advice is located.

4.2 Statistical Model

The dependent variable of the topic's "want to meet" number, and from the type, linear regression and Poisson regression can be tried. After preliminary attempts, it is found that the Poission model does not meet the requirement of approximately equal mean and variance, and the results obtained from Poisson regression have the problem of over dispersion. The linear regression model is simple and easy to operate, and the results of the model have good interpretation, which is conducive to exploratory analysis and decision analysis. Because the dependent variable is severely right-skewed and takes a range of values greater than or equal to 1, the dependent variable is conceivably logarithmic in order to make it conform to the assumption of normality and homogeneity of variances of linear regression. Equation (1) is the specific model expression.

$$
\begin{aligned}
\ln & (\text{The}''\text{want to meet}''\text{ number}) \\
= & \beta_0 + \beta_1 \times \textit{topic description word count} \\
& + \beta_2 \times \textit{price} + \beta_3 \times \textit{topic views number} \\
& + \beta_4 \times \textit{topic rating} \\
& + \beta_5 \times \textit{respond time to invitations} \\
& + \beta_6 \times \textit{mentor with user identity} \\
& + \beta_7 \textit{Reply to user's comments} \\
& + \beta_8 \times \textit{topic service type} \\
& + \beta_9 \times \textit{mentor profile word count} \\
& + \beta_{10} \times \textit{mentor's region} \\
& + \beta_{11} \times \textit{appointment acceptance rate} + \in
\end{aligned}
\tag{1}
$$

5 Results

5.1 Descriptive Statistics of the Sample

Table 3 provides descriptive statistics for the continuous type variables in the sample, and a brief description of all qualitative variables can be found in the remarks section of Table 2. Of interest are the three categorical variables of "topic rating", "whether the mentor is a consumer", and "the mentor's region". The "high score" of 9.5 or above in topic rating accounts for only 10.15% of the total, and is mostly distributed in topics with "Internet+" as the theme; the number of mentors who are both mentors and users only accounts for 10.5% of the nearly 5000 mentors; In terms of region distribution, 82.19% of the mentors are located in Beijing and Shanghai, and 89% of the mentors are located in tier-1 cities in terms of city level.

Table 3. Descriptive statistics of the sample

Variable	Min	Max	Mean	Standard deviation	Skewness	Kurtosis
Ln(The "want to meet" number)	0	7.757	4.419	1.12	-0.069	-0.31
Topic description word count	63	3269	465.4	256.07	1.99	7.42
Topic views number	1	378	10.81	16.11	7.404	88.37
Mentor profile word count	1	3251	522.3	359.12	1.912	5.575

Figure 4 shows the distribution of topic's "wants to meet" number. This variable is right skewed, with the majority of topics having "wants to meet" number below 500, and very few topics having "wants to meet" number above 500, with the highest being 2339. Since this paper will be studied using regression analysis, it is necessary to log-transform the dependent variable that is skewed to conform to the normality assumption of the linear regression model.

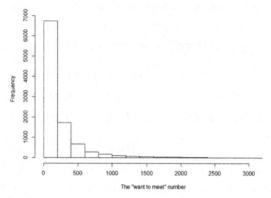

Fig. 4. Histogram of the distribution of the "want to meet" number

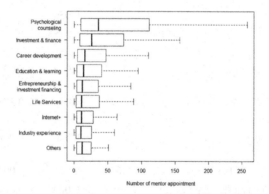

Fig. 5. Box plot of the number of appointments with professional mentors by field

Figure 5 shows that the focus of the users of "Zaih.com" platform is on two areas: psychology counseling and investment finance, which are also the areas with the highest number of courses offered by mentors, and the number of appointments with mentors in these two areas is at the top of the segment.

5.2 Statistical Model Analysis

Table 4 shows the detailed results of the log-linear models under the AIC criterion (Akaike information criterion). The AIC principle and the BIC principle are two common approaches to model selection, and they aim to find the optimal balance between model simplicity and model accuracy. The difference is that the penalty term of BIC is larger than AIC in the case of large samples, and the resulting models are simpler than the AIC criterion, but the accuracy is also relatively lower, while the models filtered under the AIC criterion are models are relatively complex, but with higher precision. Since this paper favors exploratory analysis, we hope that the model is relatively rich in variables, enhances the explanation, and can provide constructive opinions for all parties of knowledge payment, so the AIC criterion is used.

Table 4. Regression results under the AIC criterion

Term	Coefficient	S.E	P-value	Notes
Intercept	3.7548	0.0502	<0.001	
Topic description word count (hundred word)	0.0280	0.0036	<0.001	
price(100CNY)	0.0036	0.0004	<0.001	
Topic views number	0.0173	0.0005	<0.001	
Topic rating- 9.2 below	0.1109	0.0299	<0.001	Baseline:
Topic rating- 9.3–9.5	-0.0096	0.0312	0.758	9.2–9.3
Topic rating- 9.5 and more	0.2030	0.0380	<0.001	
Topic rating- insufficient rating	-0.3319	0.0309	<0.001	
Time length to respond to invitation—within 1 day	-0.0238	0.0355	0.502	Baseline: Within 2 days
Time length to respond to invitation—within half a day	-0.1324	0.0342	<0.001	
Time length to respond to invitation—other else	0.0441	0.0426	0.301	
Reply to user's comments-True	-0.2972	0.0207	<0.001	Baseline: False
Mentor with user identity-True	0.1801	0.0308	<0.001	Baseline: False
Mentor profile word count (hundred word)	0.0001	0.0000	< 0.001	
Mentor's region—Tier1 city	0.4525	0.0301	<0.001	Baseline: New Tier 1
topic service type—phone communication	1.038	0.0232	<0.001	Baseline: Individuals
topic service type—grouping	1.201	0.0437	<0.001	
topic service type—Photography, Hair Service	0.0651	0.1104	0.555	
F-test	F (17,9889) = 444.6		<0.001	$R^2_{adj} = 0.4322$

The overall fit of the model can be obtained from $R^2 = 0.4332$ indicating that 43.32% of the variance in the topic's "want to meet" number could be explained by the independent variables in the model.

The significance test for the model as a whole can be derived from the F statistic, which corresponds to a p-value of less than 0.001 for the F Statistic $F(17,9889) = 444.6$, indicating that the model as a whole is significant at the 0.001 significance level, i.e., at least one of the independent variables has a significant effect on the dependent variable. The F test proves that the model as a whole is significant, and the significance of the individual regression coefficients is next tested (T test). From the results of the model estimation in Table 4, the following interpretation of the significant factors can be made against the coefficient estimates at the 0.001 level of significance.

In the content quality dimension, with other factors unchanged, for every 100-word increase in the number of words in the topic description, the topic's "want to meet" number increases by 2.80% on average, which has a significant effect, and H1a holds, proving that information integrity positively affects knowledge consumers' willingness to pay; for every 100 CNY increase in price, the topic's "want to meet" number increases by 0.36% on average, which shows that price positively affects users' preference for mentors and increases the number of topics they want to see, which does not support hypothesis H1b, This is inconsistent with Shun Cai et al.'s proposal that price has a negative effect on the sales of Zhihu Live. The possible reason is that users see the price of offline appointment-based knowledge payment products as a positive signal of the product's quality, and believe that the price is a reflection of the value of the topics offered by mentors, and the higher the price is, the greater the utility it brings to them, so users' willingness to pay for such topics is higher.

In the quality of usefulness dimension, all other factors being equal, for every increase in the number of topic views, topic's "want to meet" number increases by 1.73% on average, which verifies hypothesis H2a; among the topic ratings, the "want to meet" number of topics with insufficient ratings is the lowest, and the "want to meet" number of topics with ratings above 9.5 is the highest, which is 20.3% higher than the average number of topics with ratings between 9.2 and 9.3, which verifies hypothesis H2b. This is consistent with the significant positive influence of "course rating" on users' selection behavior as concluded by Qiping Liu. This indicates that users' perceived relevance and applicability of information positively influences their willingness to pay for topics offered by mentors.

In the interaction quality dimension, all other factors being equal, the average "want to meet" number of topics opened by mentors who responded to users within half a day was 13.24% lower than that of mentors who responded to users within two days, which does not support H3a. The average "want to meet" number of topics opened by mentors who responded to users' reviews was 29.7% lower than that of mentors who did not respond to users' reviews, which does not support H3b. Although answering users' requests and responding to their evaluations is not as fast and efficient as buying products online, it also reflects the expertise of the mentors. The "want to meet" number of topics opened by those mentors who are both mentors and consumers is on average 18.01% higher than that of mentors who are not users, which verifies H3c, the "want to meet" number of topics whose service type is call and group is on average 104% and 120% higher than that of one-to-one appointments, respectively, which does not support H3d. Although most of the mentors of the platform are concentrated in first-tier cities, but from nearly 100,000 comments data in the "user's city" field shows that nearly half of the consumers are distributed in second-tier cities and below, such users may be more inclined to pay for the call form of topics. The median value of client appointments for such topics is 11, much higher than the level of 4 appointments for all topics.

In the expertise and attractiveness dimensions, under the condition that other factors remain unchanged, for every 100 words increase in the number of words in a mentor's profile, the "want to meet" number of topics opened by the mentor increases by 1.27% on average, which has a significant impact, and H4a holds, indicating that the education level, professional background and personal history contained in a mentor's profile help to convey their expertise and attractiveness to knowledge consumers and win users' trust; the "want to meet" number of topics opened by the mentors live in first-tier cities is 45.25% higher than those in new first-tier cities, which validates H4b. The cities where mentors settle are often a reflection of their ability and status, and this social capital will have a positive impact on users' willingness to pay; In the case of appointments acceptance rate, the sample of "medium acceptance rate and below" is too small to reflect its significant influence, and is excluded from the model under the AIC criterion. In summary, mentor expertise and attractiveness have a significant positive impact on users' willingness to pay, which is consistent with the findings of Zhao Y et al. [10]. To summarize the hypotheses of this paper are shown in Table 5.

Table 5. Summary of hypothesis testing result

Dimensionality	Assumption	Finding
Content quality	H1a: Topic description word count has a significant positive effect on users' willingness to pay for knowledge	Supported
	H1b: Price has a significant negative effect on users' willingness to pay for knowledge	No supported
Utility quality	H2a: The number of topic views has a significant positive effect on users' willingness to pay for knowledge	Supported
	H2b: Topic ratings have a significant positive effect on users' willingness to pay for knowledge	Supported
Interaction quality	H3a: The speed at which mentors respond to invitations has a significant positive effect on willingness to pay for knowledge	No supported
	H3b: Mentor responses to user ratings have a significant positive effect on willingness to pay for knowledge	No supported
	H3c: Mentors with user identity have a significant positive impact on willingness to pay for knowledge	Supported

(*continued*)

Table 5. (*continued*)

Dimensionality	Assumption	Finding
	H3d: The type of topic service being personal has a significant positive effect on willingness to pay for knowledge compared to other forms	No supported
Expertise and attractiveness	H4a: The number of words in a mentor profile has a significant positive effect on users' willingness to pay for knowledge	Supported
	H4b: The location of mentors has a significant positive effect on users' willingness to pay for knowledge	Supported
	H4c: The rate of mentor appointments acceptance has a significant positive effect on users' willingness to pay for knowledge	No supported

6 Conclusions

6.1 Conclusion and Practical Implications

This paper constructs a theoretical model and proposes hypotheses based on the information adoption model from the perspective of knowledge consumers, and conducts a study on the willingness to pay of users of O2O appointment-based paid knowledge platforms. This paper is innovative in the following three aspects: first, it expands the application of information adoption model in the field of knowledge payment; second, in terms of research objects, this paper selects O2O paid knowledge platforms, which are less studied by scholars at present, enriching the research in the field of knowledge payment; third, in terms of research methods, it does not use questionnaires, structured interviews and other methods, but uses actual behavioral data combined with theoretical models for analysis. The study finds that:

1. Under the central route (i.e., in terms of argument quality), the quality of in-formation content, represented by information completeness (word count of topic description) and quality signals (price), has a significant positive effect on users' willingness to pay
2. The quality of information utility, represented by information relevance (number of topic views) and information applicability (topic ratings), has a significant positive effect on users' willingness to pay.
3. Among the four hypotheses of information interaction quality, only "mentor is a consumer has a positive impact on users' willingness to pay" is supported, while the remaining three hypotheses are not supported, indicating that inter-action quality is less important in influencing users' willingness to pay.
4. Under the peripheral route (i.e., in terms of source credibility), the expertise and attractiveness of the deliverer (region of the mentor, word count of the mentor's profile) also have a significant positive effect on users' willingness to pay.
5. The findings of this paper have implications for knowledge providers, consumers and platforms in O2O paid knowledge payment platforms.

6.2 Limitations and Future Research Directions

There are some limitations in this study. Firstly, a considerable part of the observations in the sample data of the study has many missing fields, which are directly deleted in this paper, which may lose some valuable information and affect the representativeness of the sample; Secondly, the model does not consider two original moderating variables in the information adoption model: the expertise and involvement of information recipients, which can be studied in the future on the moderating effect of these two variables on knowledge consumers' willingness to pay. Finally, since the data used in this paper contains a large amount of text data, the research method can consider combining the methods of text analysis, such as using text mining techniques to identify whether the mentor's introduction has a prestigious school background, a famous enterprise background and other features that reflect expertise, and also conducting sentiment word analysis from the user's comments, so as to explore the key words and sentiment preference of user comments which may have impact on consumers' purchase intention.

Acknowledgements. This paper is supported by the National Natural Science Foundation of China (No. 72171102), Major Projects of Jiangsu Universities Philosophy and Social Science (No.2021SJZDA178), the Open Research Fund of Jiangsu Collaborative Innovation Center for Smart Distribution Network, Nanjing Institute of Technology (No. XTCX202212), the Open Research Fund of NJIT Institute of Industrial Economy and Innovation Management (No. JGKA202202).

References

1. iResearch China. 2019 China Knowledge Services Industry Survival Strategy Guidelines [EB/OL] http://report.iresearch.cn/report_pdf.aspx?id=3467, 2019-11-7/2021-9-1 (2019)
2. iiMedia Consulting. Trafficking in anxiety? The current dilemma and trend analysis of the development of China's knowledge payment industry in 2020[EB/OL]. https://www.iimedia.cn/c1020/69216.html, 2020-2-21/2020-3-17 (2020)
3. Analysys Consulting. China Pan Knowledge Payments Market Thematic Analysis 2019 [EB/OL]. https://www.analysys.cn/article/detail/20019604, 2019-12-13/2021-9-1 (2019)
4. Liu, Q., Wang, W., He, G.: Research on user choice behavior of offline knowledge payment platform based on social capital theory. Res. Libr. Sci. (22), 34–41 (2019) (in Chinese)
5. Zhang, S., Wang, W., Li, J.: Research on the influencing factors of users online knowledge payment behavior. Libr. Inf. Serv. **61**(10), 94–100 (2017). (in Chinese)
6. Yang, X., Hu, X.: Factors influencing knowledge payment behaviors on chinese mobile internet from a MOA perspective: taking Ximalaya FM for example. New Century Libr. **10**, 29–36 (2019). (in Chinese)
7. Dou, W.: Will internet users pay for online content? J. Advert. Res. **44**(4), 349–359 (2004)
8. Wang, C.L., Zhang, Y., Ye, L.R., et al.: Subscription to fee-based online services: what makes consumer pay for online content? J. Electron. Commer. Res. **6**(4), 304–311 (2005)
9. Punj, G.: The relationship between consumer characteristics and willingness to pay for general online content: implications for content providers considering subscription-based business models. Mark. Lett. **26**(2), 175–186 (2013)
10. Cai, S., Shi, H.R., Fu, X., et al.: Paying for knowledge in online community: an ex-ploratory study for Zhihu live. J. Ind. Eng./Eng. Manage. (03), 71–83 (2019) (in Chinese)

11. Zhao, Y., Zhao, Y., Yuan, X., et al.: How knowledge contributor characteristics and reputation affect user payment decision in paid Q&A? An empirical analysis from the perspec-tive of trust theory. Electron. Commer. Res. Appl. **31**, 1–11 (2018)
12. Goyanes, M.: An empirical study of factors that influence the willingness to pay for online news. Journal. Pract. **8**(6), 742–757 (2014)
13. Zhang, Z., Deng, Y.: The factors affecting the willingness to pay for knowledge payment behavior. Mod. Educ. Technol. (11), 86–92 (2018) (in Chinese)
14. Chen, H., Jiao, W., Li, W.: Empirical study on consumer's intention to purchase knowledge services-a trial perspective. J. Mod. Inform. (2), 136–143 (2019) (in Chinese)
15. Sussman, S.W., Siegal, W.S.: Informational influence in organizations: an integrated approach to knowledge adoption. Inf. Syst. Res. **14**(1), 47–65 (2003)
16. Zhang, Y., Li, Z., Zhao, Y.: How the Information quality affects the online review usefulness—An empirical analysis based on Taobao review data. Chin. J. Manage. **14**(01), 77–85 (2017). (in Chinese)
17. Li, J., Qi, X., Chen, M.: Understanding the Impact of perceived information quality on information acquisition and information adoption. Inf. Sci. (3), 123–129 (2015) (in Chinese)
18. Petty, R.E., Cacioppo, J.T.: The elaboration likelihood model of persuasion. In: Communication and persuasion, pp. 1-24. Springer, New York, NY (1986)
19. King, W.R., He, J.: A meta-analysis of the technology acceptance model. Inf. Manage. **43**(6), 740–755 (2006)
20. Petty, R.E., Cacioppo, J.T.: The effects of involvement on responses to argument quantity and quality: central and peripheral routes to persuasion. J. Pers. Soc. Psychol. **46**(9), 135–146 (1984)
21. Petty, R.E., Cacioppo, J.T.: Communication and persuasion: central and peripheral routes to attitude change. Springer Science & Business Media (2012)
22. Boritz, J.E.: IS practitioners' views on core concepts of information integrity. Int. J. Account. Inf. Syst. **6**(4), 260–279 (2005)
23. Connelly, B.L., Certo, S.T., Ireland, R.D., et al.: Signaling theory: a review and assessment. J. Manag. **37**(1), 39–67 (2011)
24. Dunk, A.S.: Product life cycle cost analysis: the impact of customer profiling, competitive advantage, and quality of IS information. Manag. Account. Res. **15**(4), 401–414 (2004)
25. Wixom, B.H., Todd, P.A.: A theoretical integration of user satisfaction and technology acceptance. Inf. Syst. Res. **16**(1), 85–102 (2005)
26. Xu, J., Li, Q., Zhang, J.: The impact of information quality on customer information adoption behavior and information quality improvement in shared services platform. Inf. Sci. **37**(05), 148–154 (2019). (in Chinese)
27. Zhao, Y., Liu, Z., Song, S.: Exploring the influencing factors of askers' intention to pay in knowledge Q&A platforms. Data Anal. Knowl. Disc. (8), 16–30 (2018) (in Chinese)

A Survey of Integrating Federated Learning with Smart Grids: Application Prospect, Privacy Preserving and Challenges Analysis

Zhichao Tang, Yan Yan, Dong Wu, Tianhao Yang, Ruixuan Dong, Shuyang Hao, Wei Wang, Yizhi Chen, and Yuan Tian$^{(\boxtimes)}$

School of Electric Power Engineering, Nanjing Institute of Technology, Nanjing 211167, Jiangsu, China
ytian@njit.edu.cn

Abstract. With the widespread promotion of smart grid, the power time series data collected by smart meters also increases rapidly. How to collect these data safely and effectively, analyze and utilize them, and provide better power supply service has become a hot topic of current research. The federated learning technology has attracted much attention from researchers in recent years and various federated learning-based applications have been utilized due to its characteristics of distributed, security, encryption, and reliability. In the development of smart grids, federated learning has been applied for data analytics, privacy preserving, energy management, and so on. This paper is aimed at exploring the feasibility of applying the federated learning framework to the area of smart grids. We conclude the analysis of power time series data, discussing the tribulations and solutions in the process of privacy preserving in the smart grid, and highlighting different challenges of federated learning with the smart grid. We present a summarization among federated learning-based methods with the smart grid for a variety of purposes, with the aim to draw a comparison among federated learning-based methods in the smart grid from different aspects.

Keywords: Federated Learning · Smart Grid · Privacy · Data Analysis · Data Forecasting · Energy Management

1 Introduction

As one of the most important applications on the Internet, smart grids improve the efficiency and reliability of power supply, transmission, distribution, and use. The new generation of technology, technical information, blind cloud computing, and the fifth generation of intelligent energy managers are gray. As a smart meter, you can collect a large amount of information in real time. This intelligent information measurement opens up new perspectives for energy, cleaning agents, and consumers to explore the potential value of information as much as possible. Thus, data analysis and predicting methods in the smart grid are being widely explored. Through analyzing the massive data collected by the smart grid data collection equipment, some hidden characteristics are identified, which is conductive to promote system efficiency and energy savings [1]. In particular, from the perspective of an energy manager, there is a lot of information about energy consumption that can be studied to meet customer needs. Smart meters believe that users will automatically report power consumption after a period of time, so they can analyze the smart grid management system by analyzing the collected data and sending appropriate electronic devices. Due to the benefits brought by the AMI, the extensive research effort goes into smart meter data analytics.

Various methods such as clustering [2], classification [3], and regression [4] have been utilized to extract consumer consumption patterns due to the availability and advantages of the unprecedented amount of smart meter data. In [2], a shape cluster technique via the segmented slope of load profiles is proposed to conduct data mining for the smart meter data. Multi-label classification algorithms are investigated in [3] to infer the operating condition of household appliances from household power consumption. In [4], the decentralized coding used to model and predict individual household energy consumption is compared to traditional methods such as autoregressive and winter hall homogenization embedded in moving averages. Applying these technologies in a centralized manner may lead to a risk of privacy disclosure.

Although the combination of conventional power grid and advanced technology offers convenience to consumers in energy management and control, data privacy and security in smart grid remain momentous issues that need to be tackled urgently. In addition, different retailers hold smart meters and smart meter data in different locations. Given the security and sensitivity of the information carried by smart meters, data owners may not want to share data. In the circumstances, federated learning, as a distributed technique, has been proposed to tackle these challenges. In various learning processes, participants can only send parameters from local educational models to global models built on the server. Therefore, confidential personal information and security can be protected.

However, there are still the risk of privacy disclosure in the federated learning framework even the training data is independently distributed. For example, the participants may upload incorrect collected gradient or updated parameters to the central server. In [5], shared parameters only begin to attack human genomic data that has changed due to improper behavior. Most importantly, people can ask about their symptoms, such as important information and important information. What's more, personal private data can be obtained by attackers such as brute-force ciphertext recovery [6], which will expose patients' symptoms. First, you need to review some local updates to correct the original information [7]. Differences between generic models can also be used to create information [8]. In order to solve the uncertainty issues in various studies, the different strengths of encryption algorithms and local parameters [9].

Despite the shortcomings of federal education, it is still used in many fields, including urban traffic management [10], mobile devices [11], medical diagnosis [12], and so on. To our knowledge, the applications of federated learning have not been widely investigated in the fields of smart grid. So, it is meaningful and significant to do a survey on the applications of the federated learning framework in the smart grid area.

This article concludes the analysis of power time series data, discussing the tribulations and solutions in the process of privacy preserving in the smart grid, and highlighting different applications and challenges of federated learning with the smart grid. This study includes three federal learning frameworks, as well as a meta analysis of materials in the field. We summarize the contributions of this article as follows:

- This article follows the operational steps of federated learning, including local data collection and analysis, data privacy protection, and model framework training.
- We analyze the limiting factors of federated learning in different application fields and user groups, and propose the corresponding federated learning model and application algorithm.
- We summarize the current application challenges based on federated learning in the smart grid to provide an intellectual intuition for readers on developing future algorithms in modern smart grid.

The structure of this article is as follows: In Sect. 2, we summarize research and learning alliances based on intelligent networks. The third part first analyzes the characteristics of intelligent instrument data and solves various challenges brought by large amounts of data. In Sect. 4, we discussed the main weaknesses in smart meter data processing in smart grids, as well as various solutions and algorithms to address these weaknesses when combined with learning. Section 5 gives detailed eyesight to federated learning application challenges in the smart grid environment. Section 6 draws conclusions on this article.

2   Related Work

Many research works have been published regarding exploring AI technology, deep learning and machine learning to cope with challenges in the area of modern smart grid. These techniques are proved powerful and effective to enhance the stability of the power system. To summarize and generalize the current progress of federated learning-based algorithms for energy management, data analytics, data forecasting and other applications in advanced smart grid, different research have been investigated. In this part, we offer an overview of these articles.

In [13], a demand response algorithm is presented to reduce consumers' power demand during spiking periods. In this algorithm, federated learning is applied to determine the parameters with the private data training on the local model. [14] proposes the concept of the FederatedGrids platform and utilizes federated learning and block chain to forecast future energy production and consumption. The platform allows autonomous energy sharing and trading to reduce energy cost and load. Faced with the integration of photovoltaic in the smart grid, [15] proposes a decentralized ML paradigm incorporating federated learning which can provide false data injection attack detection on solar PV dc/dc and dc/ac converters. Federated learning approaches are leveraged in [16] to forecast charging stations' energy demand in the economic-efficiency framework of electric vehicle network. It is proved that this method can improve the accuracy of prediction algorithms in comparison with the other machine learning algorithms. Faced with the training problem of large distribution networks, traditional centralized training algorithms cannot tackle the issue. [17] applies the federated learning framework to enhance the training effect of the model and realize distributed voltage control. Due to the restrictions of privacy and the difficulty of allowing access to all the smart meter data, a Bayesian neural network [18] is projected to disaggregate the distributed solar photo-voltaic generation founded on federated learning. [19] applies federated learning to design a distributed learning algorithm to study the electricity consumption features of power consumers.

Of course, they have done a good job of applying federated learning algorithms to smart grids. Although the survey articles published have paid much attention to the federated learning, there is almost no survey article having a comprehensive learning of the unique superiority of federated learning with smart grid. Thus, it is necessary to launch a compositive survey on the combination of federated learning and the smart grid. As shown in Table 1, we sum up the main points of the article for ready reference.

Table 1. Comparison with related articles

Ref.	Subject	Core issues	Prediction	Security	Management	Technology	Result
[13]	Distribution networks	Demand response	✗	✗	✓	Deep reinforcement learning	Reducing load and cost
[14]	Microgrids	Energy sharing	✓	✗	✓	Blockchain	Reducing load and cost
[15]	Smart grids	False data injection (FDI) attack detection	✗	✓	✗	Machine learning	Providing efficient FDI attack detection for photovoltaic systems
[16]	Electric vehicle networks	Charging stations' profit maximization	✓	✓	✗	Contract theory	Enhancing prediction accuracy and increasing profits
[17]	Distribution networks	Decentralized voltage control	✗	✓	✓	Multi-agent reinforcement learning	Enhancing scalability and privacy
[18]	Distributed photovoltaics	solar photovoltaic generation estimation	✓	✓	✗	Bayesian neural network	Proving effective
[19]	Smart grids	Household characteristic identification	✗	✓	✗	Deep learning network	Proving effective

3   Local Data Collection and Analysis

Constructing a secure and dynamically efficient smart grid (monitoring and evaluation system) inevitably require detecting the faults of the power network and making correct responds timely and accurately. In order to achieve these characteristics of smart grid, the gird requires not only real-time and effective data collection, but also efficient data processing and analysis. Traditional machine learning is required to aggregate data to the center before model training can be performed. During the process of data aggregation, the original data will become uncontrollable and are vulnerable to expose privacy information, which may lead to data privacy disclosure and data security risks. At the same time, with the rapid growth of data volume, the cost of data transmission will multiply. The benefit of federated learning is not to transmit the large amount of raw data collected, but rather to collect data locally and process it only through local models. During joint learning and training, training parameters will be uploaded to the control center unless local encryption algorithms are used. After receiving the training, the teacher's training returned to the station. Combining learning processes can improve the effectiveness and security of data processing and analysis, and reduce operational costs.

Federated learning has been proved feasibly in many research articles in the smart grid. In [20], the author mainly collects electricity data from small-scale housing and service departments and uses federated learning to train and predict user electricity data. This paper validates that the predictions made in the Federal Learning Framework are flexible and personalized. Federal Learning provides strong support for high-precision model building for large data applications by systematically expanding sample size and increasing data dimensions, thus providing richer and better large data services. Federal learning can be used not only for data analysis and prediction, but also for smart grids. On its page, users suggest that energy theft can be transferred to federal government learning about security and privacy. Due to many powerful robbery schemes in software, there is a risk of personal security breaches in the energy sector. In [21], the author proposes that energy theft can be detected while protecting the safety and privacy of users by applying FL. At the same time, the distribution and operation of central information is expensive. But the answer is not immediately available. Therefore, the author's federated learning discovery of theft not only assumes that users are unable to protect themselves from danger, but also reduces information processing costs and corrects the findings given.

As a new machine learning method, federated learning has attracted more and more attention in the rapidly developing field of smart grids. With the development of intelligent networks and the rapid growth of the number of users, the data collected by the network becomes unbalanced, independent, and evenly distributed (non IID). Some [22], [23] and [24] suggest that we solve this problem by assembling federated learning, which is the best federated learning algorithm in engineering. It has been proven that Fedavg can meet under non IID conditions.

4   Data Privacy Protection

4.1   Current Privacy Issues in Modern Smart Grids

In electric power systems, smart meters allow precise measurement and recording of energy use. In this age of big data, data related to the operation of individuals and systems are of great importance to operators and some organizations [25]. Electric utilities control the energy of their customers by deploying "non-intrusive load monitoring (NILM)". The market also needs to predict specific time periods to understand consumer habits, thereby contributing to the safety and efficiency of energy systems. In addition, many technologies can use electricity consumption data to analyze electricity consumption habits in certain regions, thereby inferring consumer behavior and lifestyle in that region. In order to protect the interests of users, we need to protect the privacy of smart meter data without affecting normal use and data collection.

4.2 Effective Solutions to Privacy Issues

To address the above challenges, federated learning is considered effective and widespread approaches in practice. In the actual scenario, federated learning will not be applied in an independent way. It tends to be utilized integrating techniques such as differential privacy [26], homomorphic encryption and others. However, each individual approach has its own advantages and disadvantages [25], so most research constructs new model frameworks for combining algorithms.

Integrating with Homomorphic Encryption. To protect intelligent data tables, federated learning strategies first collect data to train local data models, and then transfer the results to the global security model assembly to process it. The client has a public and private key, and the server has a strict standard algorithm. Ensure that third parties cannot easily access data. Afterward, it is combined with other methods to achieve an optimized mechanism for subsequent privacy protection. We can use homomorphic encryption algorithms to encrypt the data before it is uploaded, and the calculation of the relevant parameters is done locally. Afterward, the information returned from the server is encrypted and the model is trained using the aggregated parameters.

Combined with Differential Privacy. When combining shared learning and algorithm privacy teams, shared learning algorithms are models that combine multiple user data into predictive analysis models, thereby increasing the diversity of training data models. It allows data localization ([27]) and ensures that the data is used later. Shared learning provides a machine learning allocation framework. This framework ensures the utility and privacy of the data and improves efficiency over traditional methods. Differential privacy destroys the query results of adjacent datasets and ensures privacy protection of the entire database. Differential privacy uses a Laplacian mechanism to add noise + to the data transfer and training model, while local differential privacy controls the noise size. Both result sets can be analyzed simultaneously to finally achieve local differential privacy, and it does not affect the final query results.

Hybrid Algorithms in the Federated Learning Framework. Differential privacy can also be combined with homomorphic encryption to form the distributed K-means clustering model. The k-means algorithm is used to achieve high-speed clustering in the iteration of datasets related to differential privacy. At the same time, Homomorphic Encryption is added in [28] to enhance the data protection capability. Not only that, but Homomorphic Encryption can also improve data privacy in the federated learning framework by encrypting the relevant data without changing the original nature, [29] and [30] thus resist attacks.

Adding Rechargeable Batteries. At the same time, the system is equipped with rechargeable batteries for strategic charging and discharging, achieving confidentiality for the fuzzy real power consumption data requirements. The model protects the user's real data in several ways and ensures the protection of privacy.

The data trained by each method differs in privacy, security, accuracy, and efficiency. In the future, there will be increased research on the combination of multiple methods, clustering sampling methods, and predictive models. Some studies suggest that multiple aspects will be evaluated. Thus, the accuracy of the training models and the effective protection of user privacy will be ensured [25–27].

5   Model Training Framework

It is prohibited to use it directly for the exchange of personal and electrical information. Partnership research allows people to study energy together and share artificial intelligence models without compromising local energy information. The energy system is a large geographic system that covers the entire supply. Geography, climate, and design have all changed. This is due to the low quality of local models, independent and unpredictable data distribution, and unpredictability during connectivity. After all, educated alliances are compatible with cloud computing performance. In fact, due to the high cost of communication between the service and many customers, it is difficult to establish a federated learning environment.

To address these issues, volumes [31–33], and [34] include a cloud that intelligently combines learning and protection capabilities between users. Since then, although the Institute has had a negative impact, as part of federal research, a data evaluation mechanism has been established at the local level, and two improvement issues for users and clean energy services have been raised. In particular, the author validated the results of a group model collected to teach network and communication technologies. The experimental results show that the fusion speed of our analysis and sd-ffel results exceeds the requirements of alliance learning architecture. The Norwegian network is used in 35, 36, 37, 38, 39, and 40 countries. Long term memory (LSTM) is between [36] and [11], and is the release of local models learned from long-term digital memory (LSTM), which is one of the characteristics of carbon emissions. Energy projects are more suitable for carbon neutral design. Carbon emissions are considered one of the characteristics of carbon dioxide, and energy design has resulted in more convenient carbon neutral design. In Lithuania (36), it is recommended that the highest dimensions of reducing learning speed, reducing adaptation difficulties, and reducing the difficulty of multiple neural networks are very strong. The previous paragraph is different. [35] and [38] provide as much encryption as possible for neural networks. For the first time, the network has reduced the pressure of updating data links for each gradient client. In [37] Fedbrand, I prepared a method for collecting architects to assemble different particle sizes. Therefore, we have designed a model to improve the efficiency of Fedbatch fusion and model. In fact, we are studying the education and practicality between different sub models. Energy data quality [42] aims to provide security through research and analysis of special education models. This approach, combined with learning and technology exchange, helps establish barriers between the government and powerful companies, and proposes federated learning algorithms between powerful companies. [38–40], and [41]. Learning together is a method of analyzing the weight of each layer of a car learning model and learning with a group of customers.

6 Conclusion

This paper summarizes the latest advances in smart grid efficiency and reliability, as well as popular algorithms in the field of the Internet of Things, including data analysis, privacy protection and energy management. The system studied in this paper shows the artistic state of modern smart grid. The monitoring and evaluation system of smart grid can timely and accurately detect and respond to faults in the grid. In addition, federal learning allows faster, more accurate data processing and analysis, lower operating costs, and excellent privacy protection than traditional machine learning. Federal learning can be used not only for data analysis and prediction, but also for smart grid applications. We hope this article can provide a realistic and comprehensive overview of the development status of smart grid.

Acknowledgement. This work was also supported by the national natural science foundation of China (Project No.42171245), Jiangsu Province Engineering Research Center of IntelliSense Technology and System, the Scientific Research Foundation of Nanjing Institute of Technology (YKJ201922) and NARI Technology Co., Ltd.

References

1. Dhinu Lal, M., Varadarajan, R.: A review of machine learning approaches in synchrophasor technology. IEEE Access **11**, 33520–33541 (2023). https://doi.org/10.1109/ACCESS.2023. 3263547
2. Eddin, M.E., Massaoudi, M., Abu-Rub, H., Shadmand, M., Abdallah, M.: Novel functional community detection in networked smart grid systems-based improved louvain algorithm. In: 2023 IEEE Texas Power and Energy Conference (TPEC), College Station, TX, USA, pp. 1-6 (2023) https://doi.org/10.1109/TPEC56611.2023.10078573.
3. Wang, Y., Bennani, I.L., Liu, X., Sun, M., Zhou, Y.: Electricity consumer characteristics identification: a federated learning approach. IEEE Trans. Smart Grid **12**(4), 3637–3647 (2021)
4. Xiang, Y., et al.: Slope-based shape cluster method for smart metering load profiles. IEEE Trans. Smart Grid **11**(2), 1809–1811 (2020)
5. Tabatabaei, S.M., Dick, S., Xu, W.: Toward non-intrusive load monitoring via multi-label classification. IEEE Trans. on Smart Grid **8**(1), 26–40 (2016)
6. Zhang, Y., Xu, C., Li, H., Yang, K., Zhou, J., Lin, X.: HealthDep: an efficient and secure deduplication scheme for cloud-assisted eHealth systems. IEEE Trans. Industr. Inf. **14**(9), 4101–4112 (2018)
7. Yin, H., Mallya, A., Vahdat, A., Alvarez, J.M., Kautz, J., Molchanov, P.: See through gradients: image batch recovery via gradinversion. In: Proceedings of the IEEE/CVF Conference on Computer Vision and Pattern Recognition, pp. 16337–16346 (2021)
8. Melis, L., Song, C., De Cristofaro, E., Shmatikov, V.: Exploiting unintended feature leakage in collaborative learning. In: 2019 IEEE symposium on security and privacy (SP), pp. 691–706. IEEE (2019) May)
9. Yin, L., Feng, J., Xun, H., Sun, Z., Cheng, X.: A privacy-preserving federated learning for multiparty data sharing in social IoTs. IEEE Trans. Netw. Sci. Eng. **8**(3), 2706–2718 (2021)
10. Liu, Y., James, J.Q., Kang, J., Niyato, D., Zhang, S.: Privacy-preserving traffic flow prediction: a federated learning approach. IEEE Internet Things J. **7**(8), 7751–7763 (2020)

11. Mills, J., Hu, J., Min, G.: Multi-task federated learning for personalised deep neural networks in edge computing. IEEE Trans. Parallel Distrib. Syst. **33**(3), 630–641 (2021)
12. Ngo, T., et al.: Federated deep learning for the diagnosis of cerebellar ataxia: privacy preservation and auto-crafted feature extractor. IEEE Trans. Neural Syst. Rehabil. Eng. **30**, 803–811 (2022)
13. Bahrami, S., Chen, Y.C., Wong, V.W.: Deep reinforcement learning for demand response in distribution networks. IEEE Trans. Smart Grid **12**(2), 1496–1506 (2020)
14. Bouachir, O., Aloqaily, M., Özkasap, Ö., Ali, F.: FederatedGrids: federated learning and blockchain-assisted P2P energy sharing. IEEE Trans. Green Commun. Netw. **6**(1), 424–436 (2022)
15. Zhao, L., Li, J., Li, Q., Li, F.: A federated learning framework for detecting false data injection attacks in solar farms. IEEE Trans. Power Electron. **37**(3), 2496–2501 (2021)
16. Saputra, Y.M., Nguyen, D., Dinh, H.T., Vu, T.X., Dutkiewicz, E., Chatzinotas, S.: Federated learning meets contract theory: economic-efficiency framework for electric vehicle networks. IEEE Trans. Mob. Comput. **21**(8), 2803–2817 (2020)
17. Federated Reinforcement Learning for Decentralized Voltage Control in Distribution Networks Haotian Liu, Graduate Student Member, IEEE, and Wenchuan Wu, Fellow, IEEE
18. Level Behind-the-Meter Solar Generation Disaggregation Jun Lin, Jin Ma, Member, IEEE, and Jianguo Zhu, Senior Member, IEE
19. Lin, J., Ma, J., Zhu, J.: Privacy-preserving household characteristic identification with federated learning method. IEEE Trans. Smart Grid **13**(2), 1088–1099 (2021)
20. Čaušević, S., et al.: Flexibility prediction in smart grids: making a case for federated learning (2021)
21. Wen, M., Xie, R., Lu, K., Wang, L., Zhang, K.: Feddetect: a novel privacy-preserving federated learning framework for energy theft detection in smart grid. IEEE Internet Things J. **9**(8), 6069–6080 (2021)
22. Su, Z., et al.: Secure and efficient federated learning for smart grid with edge-cloud collaboration. IEEE Trans. Industr. Inf. **18**(2), 1333–1344 (2021)
23. Akkaya, K., Rabieh, K., Mahmoud, M., Tonyali, S.: Customized certificate revocation lists for IEEE 802.11s-based smart grid AMI networks. IEEE Trans. Smart Grid **6**(5), 2366–2374 (2015)
24. Popoola, S.I., Ande, R., Adebisi, B., Gui, G., Hammoudeh, M., Jogunola, O.: Federated deep learning for zero-day botnet attack detection in IoT-edge devices. IEEE Internet Things J. **9**(5), 3930–3944 (2021)
25. Gough, M.B., Santos, S.F., Alskaif, T., Javadi, M.S., Castro, R., Catalão, J.P.: Preserving privacy of smart meter data in a smart grid environment. IEEE Trans. Industr. Inf. **18**(1), 707–718 (2021)
26. Wang, H., Zhang, J., Lu, C., Wu, C.: Privacy preserving in non-intrusive load monitoring: a differential privacy perspective. IEEE Trans. on Smart Grid **12**(3), 2529–2543 (2021) https://doi.org/10.1109/Tsmartgrid.2020.3038757
27. Duan, M., Liu, D., Chen, X., Liu, R., Tan, Y., Liang, L.: Self-balancing federated learning with global imbalanced data in mobile systems. IEEE Trans. Parallel Distrib. Syst. 32(1), 59–71 (2021)
28. Jia, B., Zhang, X., Liu, J., Zhang, Y., Huang, K., Liang, Y.: Blockchain-enabled federated learning data protection aggregation scheme with differential privacy and homomorphic encryption in IIoT. IEEE Trans. Industr. Inf. **18**(6), 4049–4058 (2021)
29. Bai, Y., Fan, M.: A method to improve the privacy and security for federated learning. In: 2021 IEEE 6th International Conference on Computer and Communication Systems (ICCCS), pp. 704–708. IEEE (2021) April)

30. Sun, Y., Shao, J., Mao, Y., Wang, J.H., Zhang, J.: Semi-decentralized federated edge learning for fast convergence on non-IID data. In: 2022 IEEE Wireless Communications and Networking Conference (WCNC), pp. 1898–1903. IEEE (2022) April
31. Ammad-ud-din, M., Ivannikova, E., Khan, S.A., Oyomno, W., Fu, Q., Tan, K.E., et al.: Federated collaborative filtering for privacy-preserving personalized recommendation system (2019)
32. Luo, M.Y., Lin, S.W.: From monolithic systems to a federated e-learning cloud system. In: 2013 IEEE international conference on cloud engineering (IC2E), pp. 156–165. IEEE (2013) March
33. Shen, Z., Wu, Q., Qian, J., Gu, C., Sun, F., Tan, J.: Federated learning for long-term forecasting of electricity consumption towards a carbon-neutral future. In: 2022 7th International Conference on Intelligent Computing and Signal Processing (ICSP), pp. 789–793 (2022) https://doi.org/10.1109/ICSP54964.2022.9778813
34. Wang, X., Liang, X., Zheng, X., An, N.: Electricity federated strategies based on restricted solution space. In: 2021 6th International Conference on Communication, Image and Signal Processing (CCISP), pp. 329–333. IEEE (2021) November
35. Li, F.Q., Wang, S.L., Liew, A.W.C.: Watermarking protocol for deep neural network ownership regulation in federated learning. In: 2022 IEEE International Conference on Multimedia and Expo Workshops (ICMEW), pp. 1–4. IEEE (2022) July
36. Freitag, F., Vilchez, P., Wei, L., Liu, C.H., Selimi, M., Koutsopoulos, I.: An experimental environment based on mini-pcs for federated learning research. In: 2022 IEEE 19th Annual Consumer Communications & Networking Conference (CCNC), pp. 927–928. IEEE (2022) January
37. Cui, J., Wu, Q., Zhou, Z., Chen, X.: FedBranch: heterogeneous federated learning via multi-branch neural network. In: 2022 IEEE/CIC International Conference on Communications in China (ICCC), pp. 1101–1106. IEEE (2022) August
38. Kim, H., Kim, Y., Park, H.: Reducing model cost based on the weights of each layer for federated learning clustering. In: 2021 Twelfth International Conference on Ubiquitous and Future Networks (ICUFN), pp. 405–408. IEEE (2021) August
39. Yang, B., Cao, X., Bassey, J., Li, X., Qian, L.: Computation offloading in multi-access edge computing: a multi-task learning approach. In: Proceedings of the IEEE International Conference on Communications, pp. 1–6 (2019)
40. Khan, L.U., Alsenwi, M., Han, Z., Hong, C.S.: Self organizing federated learning over wireless networks: a socially aware clustering approach. In: 2020 international conference on information networking (ICOIN), pp. 453–458. IEEE (2020) January
41. Xiao, Y., Shu, J., Jia, X., Huang, H.: Clustered federated multi-task learning with NON-IID data. In: 2021 IEEE 27th International Conference on Parallel and Distributed Systems (ICPADS), pp. 50–57. IEEE (2021) December
42. Wang, L., Wang, W., Li, B.: CMFL: mitigating communication overhead for federated learning. In: Proceedings of the 39th IEEE International Conference on Distributed Computing Systems, pp. 954–964 (2019)

Application of the Fusion Access Technology of Carrier and 5G in Power Communication

Yang Hu[1], Ming Zhang[1], Yingli He[1], Guangxiang Jin[2], Qi Wei[2], and Jia Yu[1(✉)]

[1] NARI Group Corporation/State Grid Electric Power Research Institute, Nanjing, China
401945335@qq.com

[2] State Grid Economic and Technological Research Institute Co., Ltd., Beijing, China

Abstract. The distribution network storage is sensitive to the channel reliability and delay, especially with the requirements of the new power system construction, the real-time control requirements of the secondary system of the distribution network are further improved. Due to the diversity of technology applications, distribution network communication naturally has multiple heterogeneous networks. The noncorrelation of medium voltage power line carrier and 5G is used. Using the multi-frequency adaptive medium ballast carrier and its fusion access technology with 5G can effectively avoid the impact of the single network channel, such as the wireless random channel index degradation on the service carrying performance. The overall service delay performance, reliability and anti-attack capability of the network are improved through the multi-channel self-operation and dynamic switching mode, so as to meet the new service communication needs of the distribution network in the construction of the new power system.

Keywords: Big data, · Internet of things · 5G communication · Fusion access technology · Low delay technology

1 Introduction

As an important infrastructure in urban and rural areas, the distribution network is a platform to support the grid connection of distributed power supply and carry the flexible adjustment of resources on the user side [1–3]. The distribution network has become an important position to serve the double-carbon goal and build a new power system [4–6]. The future development of the distribution network will face a new situation, new changes and new demand. From the perspective of power grid technology, the development trend of active of power distribution network is obvious, the power transmission changes from one-way to multi-directional, and the power trend distribution changes from certainty to probability [7]. The structure of the distribution network is increasingly diversified and diversified, and the derived new and old scenes of planning, construction, production, operation and maintenance are intertwined [8]. How to build a suitable differentiated technology system, improve the dispatching and operation level, and promote the collaborative interaction between the source network, load, and storage has become a key problem that needs to be solved [9–11]. The main problems in the traditional medium voltage carrier communication technology include low reception sensitivity, single frequency band, vulnerable to the interference of the power grid noise, poor matching with the power grid impedance, and low communication bandwidth that cannot meet the high real-time distribution and adjustment services [12–15]. This paper focuses on how to break professional barriers and data island, based on computing force to minimize the acquisition range, enhance 4G or 5G carrying control business security protection capability, clear terminal fusion terminal access to different business system security isolation boundary, develop massive data integration management, economic and efficient transmission, real-time sharing and interactive application technology solutions, evaluate the data value and scope of application, to provide the distribution network business collaboration and management cohesion strong data support.

2 Research on Communication Technology

2.1 Low Delay Technology for 5G

According to the efficient networking demand of the power 5G network, it is necessary to virtualize the network resources first to realize the efficient utilization of the network resources [16–18]. A network device in a physical network is a device that completes one or more functions such as data collection, generation, storage, forwarding, receiving, and computing, etc. It has static attributes such as type and its own device information, and also has dynamic attributes such as network status and topology structure. Therefore, this topic proposes to use the device node identification NID (node ID) and the behavior description NBD to describe its static and dynamic properties, respectively, definition is as follows [12]:

$$NID \triangleq \omega(N_{type}, N_{device})$$

In the above formula, N_{type} represents the type of network device (transmission components, storage components, etc.), $N device$ represents the network component itself device information, and $\omega(\cdot)$ represents the component identity generation function.

Based on the information perception of the network device, collect the characteristic information of the network device, and propose the concept of the device behavior description NBD, and further describe the function, topology or performance characteristics of the network device, to represent the device behavior. The behavioral description of the network device NBD is defined as follows [20]

$$NBD \triangleq \begin{bmatrix} \{b_L^{NT}, \ b_P^{NT}, \ b_R^{NT}, \ b_C^{NT}, ...\}_T \\ \{b_B^{NT}, \ b_D^{NT}, \ b_L^{NT}, \ b_S^{NT}, ...\}_P \\ \{b_T^{NF}, \ b_F^{NF}, \ b_C^{NF}, \ b_S^{NF}, ...\}_F \end{bmatrix}$$

In the above equation, T P and F correspond to topological, performance and functional behavior, respectively. For NBD, the topological information includes component location bLNT, component affiliation bLNT, component adjacency bLNP, and connectedness, etc. Functional information includes component type bTNF, component function bF, carrier, and security levels.

In the resource adaptation layer, a virtual network identity is used to mark a functional module of a virtual network. The division of the virtual network is based on specific behaviors, and different classes of behaviors can have different division ways. Therefore, the classification mode is one of the most important attributes of the virtual network. After the virtual network is formed, each virtual network will have a certain behavioral similarity, thus forming the unique behavioral characteristics of the virtual network resource module. According to the above virtual network classification mode and behavioral characteristics, a virtual network can be uniquely identified and generated by the virtual network identity FID, as defined as follows [21]

$$FID \triangleq \varphi(F_T, F_P, F_F)$$

In the above formula, FT represents the topological behavior of ethnic group, FP represents the performance behavior of ethnic group, FF represents the functional behavior of ethnic group, and $\varphi()$ represents the ethnic group identity generation function.

To characterize the virtual network behavior, this project introduces the concept of virtual network behavior describing FBD. Behavioral description is a further description of the behavior of a virtual network, mainly including network status, topology, performance, function, etc. Based on the above classification methods and behavioral characteristics, a virtual network can be uniquely identified. The behavior description, FBD, is defined as follows

$$FBD \triangleq \begin{bmatrix} \{b_L^{NT}, \ b_P^{NT}, \ b_R^{NT}, \ b_C^{NT}, ...\}_T \\ \{b_B^{NT}, \ b_D^{NT}, \ b_L^{NT}, \ b_S^{NT}, ...\}_P \\ \{b_T^{NF}, \ b_F^{NF}, \ b_C^{NF}, \ b_S^{NF}, ...\}_F \end{bmatrix}$$

In the above equation, T, P and F correspond to topological, performance and functional behavior, respectively. For FBD, the topological behavior information includes the group location bFLT, the number of components within a group, the distribution of components and the adjacent group relationship.

2.2 The Necessity for Carrier Communication

The following table analyzes and compares the comparison of power distribution services and different communications from the perspectives of business architecture flow, bandwidth, transmission distance, real-time, reliability, security, cost, and technology maturity (Table 1).

Power line carrier as power proprietary communication channel can meet the demand of electricity information collection service. In terms of cost, the power line carrier serves as a special communication network for the power company. Channel construction relies on the existing distribution lines without additional channel investment, and the distribution lines can use the existing line maintenance personnel without operation and maintenance input. In terms of the application effect, the power line carrier can provide a stable and reliable communication channel for the power distribution service, which is better than the wireless communication in the security, stability and reliability. From the demand of power distribution service for communication mode, as well as the

Table 1. A Comparison of the different communications

Classification of business indicators	Valuefactors	Requi remen ts	Medium voltage carrier	fibre communication	Wireless private network	Wireless public network	Beidou communication
Comprehensive matching value	1		0.925	0.868	0.65	0.425	0.365
Business architecture and data flow to	0.1		1	0.75	0.5	0.25	0.95
Bandwidth	0.1	2.4 kbps	5–100 kbps	>30 Mbps	5–10 Mbps	500 kbps–1 Mbps	100 bytes
Transmission distance	0.1	6s	2.59 s	2.46 s	3.2 s	6.48 s	30 s
Reliability	0.2	>99%	>99%	>97%	>97%	>95%	
Security	0.2		1	1	0.75	0.2	0.2
Cost	0.1	0.9	0.5	0.67	0.83	1	0.8
Technical maturity	0.1	0.6	0.83	0.33	0.17	1	0.4

carrier technology security, efficiency and cost comparison and policy support, power line carrier communication technology can fully meet the needs of power service and provide communication support for power distribution automation business.

3 Fusion Access Technology of Carrier and 5G

Using the non-correlation of the carrier and 5G two heterogeneous networks, the impact of single-channel deterioration on the service is avoided by multi-channel automatic switching mode [24], and the reliability of network services is improved. The main working process is shown in the figure below. First the sender in the original business code inserted insert word, and then the code stream copy two copies, sent through two channels, the receiver in the two cache area receive alignment, according to the state delay of the dual channel timely determine switching policy, finally the receiver according to the channel selection results extracted and send to the service terminal or system, in the channel delay does not exceed the length of the data cache, can ensure channel switching (Figs. 1 and 2).

Taking the intelligent distributed feeder automation service as an example, the network of carrier and 5G fusion access application is shown in the figure below. Dual-channel switching device is set at the distribution station side, including from the carrier module and 5G module, respectively through the inductive coupler and 5G empty port access carrier and 5G network, dual-channel switching device between the two distribution stations for dual-channel data transmission and switching according to the above working principle, to achieve reliable interaction of electrical information between sites.

The application scenario of dual-channel switching device is mainly sensitive to channel reliability and delay in the distribution network. Especially with the proposal of new power system construction requirements. Distribution network secondary system real-time control requirements, intelligent distributed feeder automation [25], distribution network protection business application can realize reliable isolation and the fault

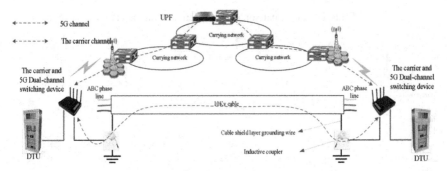

Fig. 1. Application of Carrier and 5G Fusion Access in Intelligent Distributed Feed Automation Service

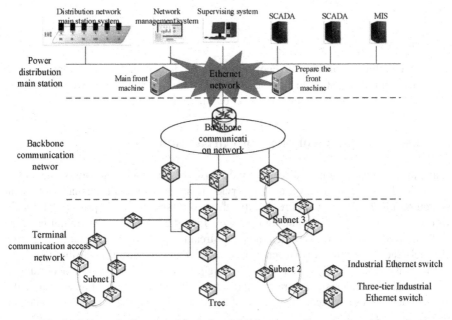

Fig. 2. Schematic diagram of the industrial Ethernet mode network architecture

area rapid safe recovery, the delay requirements from the traditional centralized distribution automation three remote seconds to milliseconds, delay jitter and reliability requirements are further improved. Taking advantage of the advantages of the heterogeneous network with various technologies naturally existing in the distribution network communication, the multi-channel switching mode is of the most important significance to ensure the operation of the distribution network control services requiring higher communication indicators.

The distribution network storage is sensitive to the channel reliability and delay, especially with the requirements of the new power system construction, the real-time control requirements of the secondary system of the distribution network are further improved.

Due to the diversity of technology applications, distribution network communication naturally has multiple heterogeneous networks (Fig. 3).

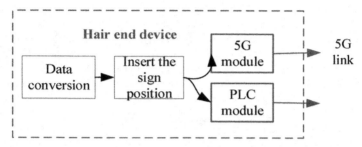

Fig. 3. Architectural diagram of the hair-terminal device

By using the non-correlation of the medium voltage power line carrier and 5G two heterogeneous networks, and using the multi-frequency adaptive medium voltage carrier and its fusion technology with 5G access technology, the impact of a single network channel, such as wireless random channel index deterioration on the service carrying performance, can be effectively avoided. The overall service delay performance, reliability and anti-attack capability of the network are improved through the multi-channel self-operation and dynamic switching mode, so as to meet the new service communication needs of the distribution network in the construction of the new power system (Figs. 4 and 5).

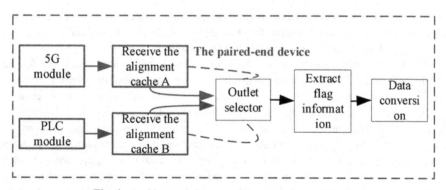

Fig. 4. Architecture diagram of the opposite-end device

A dual-channel switching device is provided in the terminal measurement, including the slave carrier module and 5G module, accessing the carrier data through the inductor coupling device, 5 g empty port and 5G network transmission data, respectively, and realizing the fusion access technology of carrier data and 5G data.

The switching strategy is determined according to the state delay of the double channel. The switching mode includes hard switch and soft switch. The soft switch adopts double distribution and receiving mechanism, which makes the business data without damage during the switching process.

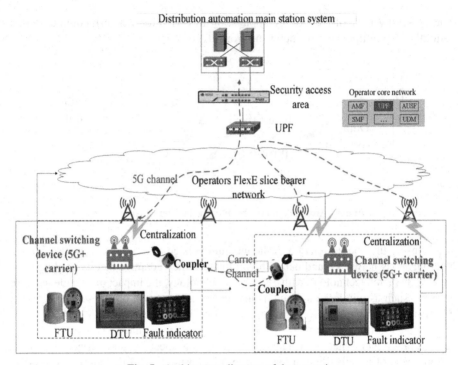

Fig. 5. Architecture diagram of the scenario

The hard switch adopts the mechanism of single single receipt and double-end reverse change. The system switches according to the channel conditions, and the sending and receiving path is consistent before and after the switch.

The 5G and carrier integrated access communication technology is suitable for the distribution network three remote, distributed feeder automation, distribution network direction protection, distribution network area protection and other services sensitive to channel reliability and delay. Intelligent distributed feeder automation, distribution network protection and other business time delay requirements are increased from the three-remote second level of the traditional centralized power distribution automation to the millisecond level, and the time delay jitter and reliability requirements are also further improved. Taking advantage of the advantages of the heterogeneous network with various technologies naturally existing in the distribution network communication, the multi-channel switching mode is of the most important significance to ensure the operation of the distribution network control services requiring higher communication indicators.

4　Testing of the Switching Device

The design purpose of the experiment mainly includes the following aspects, test the cooperation of the main protection manufacturers and communication equipment. Detect the cooperation of the relay protection and communication equipment after accessing the intelligent switching device and the normal operation. Simate the operation of the relay protection device and various channel faults after being connected to the intelligent switching device.

4.1 Design of the Scheme

During the initial operation of the equipment, channels A and B are normal, and to simulate the failure of the single channel, the equipment will automatically switch to another channel. The switch process will last for about 3 s, and the protection should be no action and correct code. One minute apart, the simulated A and B channels failed three times, respectively. During the initial operation of the equipment, channels A and B are normal. When the manual switch (alternating panel keys and network management monitoring center can be used), the equipment will switch to another channel for about 30 s, protected without action and correct code. Repeat one was three, by one three intervals. (Fig. 6)

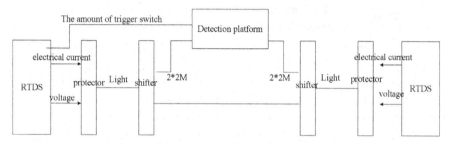

Fig. 6. Schematic diagram of the device connection

Break the A channel, the device should initially run in channel B, the device will not act when the manual switching command is issued. Working in the A channel, B channel respectively loop back, instrument connection, PRBS and other maintenance operations. The equipment shall operate normally in passage B.

4.2 The Results of the Experiment

For the switching device itself test results meet the requirements, the equipment itself support double power supply, network management interface friendly, can accurately record all kinds of events with seconds accuracy, support the query of historical events, can observe events mainly include: single circuit power loss, channel alarm, channel cross alarm, line abnormal alarm, protect abnormal alarm, the current working channel, etc., and can observe the double channel delay difference.

The added additional delay when the unit is operating normally is 400 us. The delay difference between the two channels is less than 12 ms. When the channel switches, the protection device works normally, with no channel abnormality, error code, step and other conditions. When the delay difference of the channel is more than 12 ms, the switch is switched to damage switching each time, which will bring the short time alarm and protection exit of the protection device channel. The channel switching can ensure the consistency of the sending and receiving channel.

When the channel is running on channel A, the operation on b channel will not have any impact on the protection device. When channel B fails, the device believes that the switch should be lossy. After B channel is restored, the switch device will resynchronize the positioning and determine the delay difference of A and B channel.

Equipment alarm is divided into emergency alarm and general alarm, emergency alarm includes, dual power loss, protection letter or dual channel signal interruption, device self-ring test, communication equipment ring back. Ordinary alarm includes single power loss, single channel signal interruption, channel crossing, channel delay difference. The alarm signal can be reflected in the network management program, and can be output through the empty node.

The specific experimental recording data are presented as follows (Figs. 7, 8 and 9).

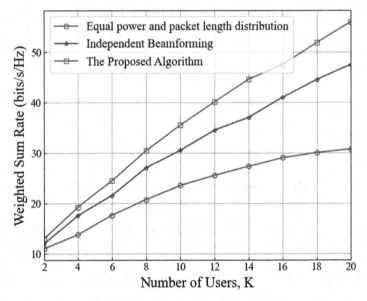

Fig. 7. Test of the symmetric time delay

As can be seen from the figure, compared with the dual transmission scheme and the traditional single transmission scheme. For any signal-dry NR threshold, the average delay of dual transmission scheme is lower than that of dual transmission scheme and traditional single transmission scheme.

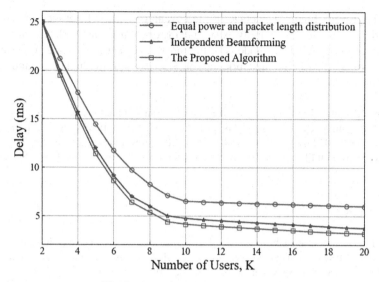

Fig. 8. Test of asymmetric time delay

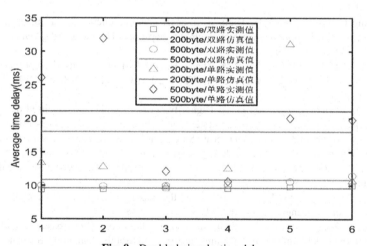

Fig. 9. Double hair selection delay

5   Conclusion

The 5G carrier integrated access communication technology is suitable for the distribution network three remote, distribution network automation, distributed feeder automation, distribution network direction protection, distribution network area protection and other services sensitive to channel reliability and delay. Intelligent distributed feeder automation, distribution network protection and other business time delay requirements from the traditional centralized power distribution automation "three remote" time second level to millisecond level, time delay jitter and reliability requirements are also further improved. Taking advantage of the advantages of the heterogeneous network with various technologies naturally existing in the distribution network communication, the multi-channel switching mode is of the most important significance to ensure the operation of the distribution network control services requiring higher communication indicators.

Acknowledgments. The authors would like to thank the anonymous reviewers and editor for their comments that improved the quality of this paper. This work is supported by scientific project under Grant NO. 5400-202256273A-2-0-XG, the name of the project is Research on Key Technology of Secondary System Planning and Design of Distribution Network for New Power System.

References

1. Yu, J., Zong, P.: The analysis and simulation of communication network in Iridium system based on OPNET. In: The 2nd IEEE International Conference on Information Management and Engineering, Chengdu, China, 16–18 Apr 2010
2. Ding, K., Chan, F.T.S., Zhang, X., et al.: Defining a digital twin-based cyber-physical production system for autonomous manufacturing in smart shop floors. Int. J. Prod. Res. 57(20), 6315–6334 (2019)
3. Zhuang, C., Liu, J., Xiong, H.: Digital twin-based smart production management and control framework for the complex product assembly shop-floor. The Int. J. Adv. Manuf. Technol. 96(1–4), 1149–1163 (2018)
4. Tao, F., Cheng, J., Qi, Q., Zhang, M., Zhang, H., Sui, F.: Digital twin-driven product design, manufacturing and service with big data. The Int. J. Adv. Manuf. Technol. 94(9–12), 3563–3576 (2017)
5. Liu, Q., Zhang, H., Leng, J., et al.: Digital twin-driven rapid individualised designing of automated flow-shop manufacturing system. Int. J. Prod. Res. 57(12), 3903–3919 (2019)
6. Mittal, S., Khan, M.A., Romero, D., et al.: Smart manufacturing: characteristics, technologies and enabling factors. Institut. Mech. Eng. 233(5), 1342–1361 (2017)
7. Sihan, H., Guoxin, W., Yan, Y., et al.: Blockchain-based data management for digital twin of product. J. Manuf. Syst. 54, 361–371 (2019)
8. Rosen, R., Wichert, G., Lo, G., et al.: About the importance of autonomy and digital twins for the future of manufacturing. IFAC-Papers OnLine 48(3), 567–572 (2015)
9. Wang, X, Zong, P., Yu, J.: Link analyzing and simulation of TDRSS based on OPNET. In: The International Conference on Communications and Mobile Computing, Shenzhen, China, 12–14 Apr 2010
10. He, X., Ai, Q., Qiu, R.C., et al.: A big data architecture design for smart grids based on random matrix theory. IEEE Trans. Smart Grid 8(2), 674–686 (2015)
11. Gray, J.: Jim gray on escience: a transformed scientific method. The fourth paradigm: Data-intensive scientific discovery, pp. xvii–xxxi (2009)
12. Hong, T., Chen, C., Huang, J., et al.: Guest editorial big data analytics for grid modernization. IEEE Trans. Smart Grid 7(5), 2395–2396 (2016)
13. Burges, C., Shaked, T., Renshaw, E., et al.: Learning to rank using gradient descent. In: Proceedings of the 22nd International Conference on Machine learning (ICML-05), pp. 89–96 (2005)
14. Yuan, Y., Ardakanian, O., Low, S., et al.: On the inverse power flow problem. arXiv preprint arXiv: 1610.06631 (2016)

15. Chen, Y.C., Wang, J., Domínguez-García, A.D., et al.: Measurement-based estimation of the power flow Jacobian matrix. IEEE Trans. Smart Grid **7**(5), 2507–2515 (2015)

16. Kelly, J., Knottenbelt, W.: Neural nilm: Deep neural networks applied to energy disaggregation. In: Proceedings of the 2nd ACM International Conference on Embedded Systems for Energy-Efficient Built Environments, pp. 55–64. ACM (2015)

17. Xu, S., Qiu, C., Zhang, D., et al.: A deep learning approach for fault type identification of transmission line. Proc. CSEE **39**(1), 65–74 (2019)

18. Boschert, S., Rosen, R.: Digital twin—the simulation aspect. In: Hehenberger, P., Bradley, D. (eds.) Mechatronic Futures, pp. 59–74. Springer, Cham (2016). https://doi.org/10.1007/978-3-319-32156-1_5

Muscle Fatigue Classification Based on GA Optimization of BP Neural Network

Mengjie Zang, Lidong Xing$^{(\boxtimes)}$, Zhiyu Qian, and Liuye Yao

College of Automation Engineering, Nanjing University of Aeronautics and Astronautics, Nanjing 210016, Jiangsu, China
xldnuaa@nuaa.edu.cn

Abstract. The application of medical big data and artificial intelligence algorithms are majorly popular in biomedical field. In this paper, BP neural network optimized by genetic algorithm was used to study the classification of muscle fatigue. Although BP neural network has a strong nonlinear mapping ability by using the gradient descent search method, it is easy to fall into the local minimum during the search process because of the randomness of the initial weights and thresholds generated, which would affect the training rate and the accuracy of muscle fatigue classification. the genetic algorithm was used to complete the configuration of the initial population parameters and the design of fitness function, and the optimal weights and thresholds that met the conditions were output to BP neural network. Finally, the classification results of muscle fatigue were output. The experimental results showed that the GA-BP neural network had a stronger ability to jump out of the local optimization compared with the classification effect of BP neural network. The maximum recognition rate of fatigue state reached 90.4%, and the model running time was 17.1 s, which was relatively reduced by 4.5 s.

Keywords: Medical big data · Artificial intelligence · BP neural network · Genetic Algorithm · Muscle fatigue

1 Introduction

In recent years, the use of artificial intelligence algorithms for classification and recognition in the biomedical field has been widely used. Artificial intelligence algorithms are mainly divided into two categories [1]. The first category is machine learning, such as SVM, Naive Bayesian Bayes classifier, Decision Tree, Random Forest. The second category is deep learning, representative of which are convolutional neural network and BP neural network.

2 Theory and Method

2.1 Characteristics analysis of sEMG signal

Before using the Surface Electromyography (sEMG) signal to complete muscle fatigue classification, characteristic parameters should be extracted as the input sample set of the neural network. Researchers have mainly extracted and analyzed the features of sEMG

Y. Tian et al. (Eds.): ICBDS 2022, CCIS 1796, pp. 318–330, 2023.
https://doi.org/10.1007/978-981-99-3300-6_23

signal from multiple perspectives such as time domain, frequency domain and nonlinear domain, and they have achieved fruitful results. This method also would be used in this paper to complete the extraction of sEMG signal features.

sEMG signal analysis in the time domain

(1) Calculation formula of RMS:

$$RMS = \sqrt{\frac{1}{T} \int_{t}^{t+T} EMG^2(t)dt} \tag{1}$$

Where T is the selected signal length; EMG (t) is the amplitude of sEMG sampled at time t.

(2) Calculation formula of iEMG:

$$iEMG = \int_{t}^{t+T} |EMG(t)|dt \tag{2}$$

sEMG Signal Analysis in the Frequency Domain

(3) Calculation formula of MPF:

$$MPF = \frac{\int_0^{\frac{f_s}{2}} f * P(f)df}{\int_0^{\frac{f_s}{2}} P(f)df} \tag{3}$$

Where f is the frequency of the sEMG signal, f_s is the sampling rate of the signal, $P(f)$ is the power spectral density function.

(4) Calculation formula of MF:

$$MF = \int_0^{\frac{f_s}{2}} P(f)df \tag{4}$$

sEMG Signal Analysis in the Nonlinear Domain

Approximate entropy (ApEn) reflects the complexity of the signal sequence, and the entropy value is positively correlated with the signal complexity [2, 3]. The sequence y (n) are selected as an appropriate pattern dimension m to determine the length of the time window. It is necessary to consider that if the tolerance threshold r value is too small, there will be problems in the estimation of the statistical characteristics of the system; If the parameter is too large, more information will be lost. Generally speaking, the value of r is SD (x) of $(0.1–0.25)$ times, where SD (x) represents the standard deviation of the target data sequence. Then the space is reconstructed, and it forms a set of m-dimensional vectors according to the number of the subscript:

$$Y_m(n) = [y(n), y(n+1), ..., y(n+m-1)]$$
$$n = 1, 2, 3, ..., N - m + 1 \tag{5}$$

$L(Y_m(p), Y_m(q))$ is the maximum absolute value of the element difference corresponding to vector $Y_m(p)$ and $Y_m(q)$, which is simplified as:

$$L(Y_m(p), Y_m(q)) = \max(|y(p+i) - y(q+i)|)$$
$$i = 1, 2, 3, ..., m - 1 \tag{6}$$

Taking any $p = N-m + 1$ and definition:

$$A_p^m(r) = \frac{sum\{L(Y_m(p), Y_m(q)) \leq r, p \neq q\}}{N - m + 1} \tag{7}$$

Adding the dimension of the pattern by one and repeating the above steps:

$$B_p^m(r) = \frac{sum\{L(Y_{m+1}(p), Y_{m+1}(q)) \leq r, p \neq q\}}{N - m + 1} \tag{8}$$

Calculating the natural logarithm of WW and EE respectively, and then the corresponding average value is calculated, which is recorded as:

$$A^m(r) = \frac{\sum_{p=1}^{N-m+1} \ln A_p^m(r)}{N - m + 1} \tag{9}$$

$$B^m(r) = \frac{\sum_{p=1}^{N-m+1} \ln B^m(r)}{N - m + 1} \tag{10}$$

Then the ApEn represents as follows:

$$ApEn = \lim_{N \to \infty} [A^m(r) - B^m(r)] \tag{11}$$

The formula is simplified as:

$$ApEn = A^m(r) - B^m(r) \tag{12}$$

2.2 BP Neural Network

The BP neural network is a multi-layer feed-forward network, it is composed of two processes: forward propagation and back propagation [4, 5]. The input samples are used as the forward input, and the actual calculation result is obtained through the mathematical operation of each hidden layer neuron. The error between the output results and the expected values are calculated. The error values are compared with the predetermined values. If the comparison result is inconsistent and greater than the predetermined value, the algorithm transmits the difference to the neurons of each layer in the opposite direction, and the difference of each layer of neurons in the network model is based on the feedback; the weights and thresholds are dynamically adjusted. The model has been trained many times, and the parameters of the neurons are constantly updated. When the output error decreases below the preset threshold, the best fatigue classification model will be obtained, and if the output error exceeds the pre-set maximum number of training times and the output error has not converged below the set value, the network parameters need to be readjusted to train. Finally, after inputting the test set into the model, it is able to output the classification results of the fatigue levels [6, 7].

Taking a three-layer network as an example, the algorithm is described as follows:

$$y_j = f(net_j) = f(\sum_{i=1}^{M} \omega_{ij} x_i) \tag{13}$$

x_i is the input of the i-th neural network input layer node, and y_j is the output of the j-th neural network hidden layer node. The mathematical definition of o_k for output layer nodes is as follows:

$$o_k = f(net_k) = f(\sum_{j=1}^{H} \omega_{jk} y_j) = f(\sum_{j=1}^{H} \omega_{jk} f(\sum_{i=1}^{M} \omega_{ij} x_i)) \tag{14}$$

$$\frac{\partial E}{\partial \omega_{ij}} = \frac{\partial E}{\partial net_j} \cdot \frac{\partial net_j}{\partial \omega_{ij}} \tag{15}$$

The mathematical definition of the descending gradient δ_j is as follows:

$$\delta_j = -\frac{\partial E}{\partial net_j} = \frac{\partial E}{\partial \delta_j} \frac{\delta_j}{\partial net_j} = -\frac{\sum_k (t_k - o_k)^2}{2 \partial \delta_j} \cdot f'(net_j) \tag{16}$$

$$\delta_j = (t_j - o_j) \cdot f'(net_j)$$

$$\omega_{ji}(t+1) - \omega_{ji}(t) = \eta \delta_i o_j \tag{17}$$

η is the learning rate, which directly determines the amount of weight update.

2.3   BP Neural Network Optimized by GA

Figure 1 shows the process of optimizing the BP neural network by the genetic algorithm. According to the algorithm flow, after features extraction and normalization of the sEMG signals and blood oxygen parameters, the multi-dimensional features set composed of multi-modal data are input into the GA, the GA completes the floating-point number encoding of the population and the design of the fitness function [8, 9].

After three genetic steps of selection, crossover and mutation, the fitness of each individual in the population is counted, and then the individual with the best fitness value is obtained. the worst individuals in the new population will be eliminated. The number of iterations are judged to be less than the iteration, and if the condition is not met, adding 1 to the number of iterations. Otherwise, when the condition is satisfied, the optimal weight and threshold contained in the individual are output to the network, and the results of muscle fatigue classification will be output by the BP neural network after training [10].

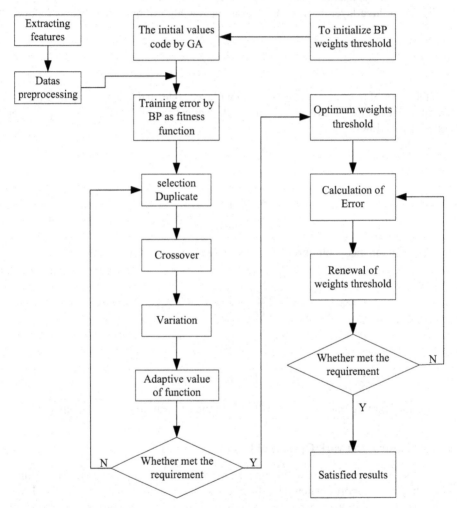

Fig. 1. The process of BP Network optimized with genetic algorithm

3 Experiments

3.1 Classification of Muscle Fatigue

Now there is no "gold standard" for the classification of muscle fatigue in the academic community. Existing studies on muscle fatigue classification generally use the Borg Subjective Fatigue Level Scale. Summarizing existing studies, this paper also used it for the classification of muscle fatigue levels. As shows in Table 1, fatigue of muscle under static isometric contraction is divided into four levels. By dividing the muscle condition into different levels and correlating it with sEMG signals and changes in hemoglobin concentration parameters, the muscle fatigue condition can be classified more scientifically and accurately.

Table 1. Borg Rating of Perceived Exertion Scale (RPE)

Score	Self-feelings	Fatigue Level
0	No exertion at all	
1	Extremely light	Fatigue Level 1
2	Very light	
3	Light	
4	Somewhat hard	Fatigue Level 2
5	Hard	
6		
7	Very hard	Fatigue Level 3
8		
9	Extremely hard	
10	Maximal exertion	Fatigue Level 4

3.2 Experiment Scheme Design

The experimental equipment: medical alcohol, Ag/AgCl gel electrodes, emery paste, 5 kg of dumbbells, stopwatches, multi-channels sEMG and near-infrared biological tissue oxygen collection platform, and the Borg subjective fatigue grade scale. The target muscles selected for the experiment are humerus biceps, ulnar wrist flexors, biceps brachii, and triceps brachii, because these four parts are more obviously contracted with human body movement and easier to achieve fatigue. The subject is 12 healthy young people who had slept enough for 24 h before the experiment and had a good mental state. Detailed information is shows in Table 2.

Table 2. Basic information of 12 volunteers

Volunteers	Sex	Age	Stature/cm	Weight/kg	BMI
Subject 1	man	23	174	70	23.1
Subject 2	man	22	175	74	23.9
Subject 3	man	24	178	69	21.8
Subject 4	man	25	180	75	23.1
Subject 5	man	26	176	77	24.8
Subject 6	man	24	179	72	22.5
Subject 7	man	27	178	78	24.6
Subject 8	man	25	174	73	24.1
Subject 9	woman	22	165	50	18.4
Subject 10	woman	24	166	53	19.2
Subject 11	woman	24	169	54	18.9
Subject 12	woman	28	174	57	18.8

Note: The Chinese standard for BMI is thin (BMI: <=18.4), normal (BMI: 18.5–23.9), overweight (BMI: 24.0 ~ 27.9), obese (BMI: >=28.0)

Before the experiment, the observer will inform the subjects about the usage of the RPE scale. Specifically, the subjects report their body condition and RPE table score to the observer according to their actual situation during the experiment, as shows in Fig. 2.

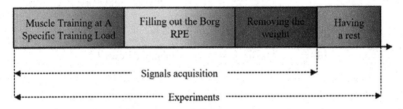

Fig. 2. The process of experiment

The experimental procedures: after the system was turned on for 10 min, the observer pressed the stopwatch, and the device started to collect the sEMG signal and hemoglobin concentration change data without load for 35 s. The dumbbell was placed in the hand of the subject to induce fatigue, and the subject's arm remained in its original state. Then the observer filled in the Borg score according to the subject's feedback, and record the corresponding time. During the experiment, when the subject feel that he was exhausted and could not continue to support, the observer took the dumbbell from the subject's hand, then continued to collect data for 45 s, and finally the above processes were repeated for several times.

4 Results

4.1 The Characteristics of Signals Analysis

sEMG signals and blood oxygen signals of the subject 4 were selected from the samples, the biceps brachii was took as an example, the analysis process of other muscle groups was the same. As shows in Fig. 3(b) and (c), the time domain characteristic parameters iEMG and RMS of the sEMG signals have an obvious trend of increasing during muscle fatigue. The reason is that the MU of muscle fibers in space is activated, the potential difference generated by each motor unit is gradually strengthen, making the iEMG and RMS characteristics of sEMG signals show an increasing trend. Figure 3(d) and (e) are the frequency domain characteristic parameters of sEMG. With the aggravation of muscle fatigue, the MF and MPF of sEMG signals shows a trend of moving in the low frequency direction. The reason is that in the process of fatigue, the volume conductor composed of various tissues would produce low-pass filter effect, which is specifically manifested in the attenuation of the activity of high-frequency units and the excitation of the activity of low-frequency units, making the spectral characteristics of sEMG move toward the low-frequency direction. At the same time, as shows in Fig. 3(f), sEMG is an assembly composed of a large number of nonlinear coupling motion units, in the process of muscle fatigue, the complexity of the time series of sEMG signals tend to decrease significantly.

As shown in Fig. 4, in the process of muscle fatigue, ΔHbO_2 shows a downward trend and ΔHb shows an upward trend. After reaching a certain threshold, they basically remain unchanged. The reason is that muscle contraction causes the increase of blood pressure, the rate of blood oxygen metabolism consuming is higher than that of fresh blood supplement, and the oxygen content provide by oxyhemoglobin in blood is limited, which is quickly consumed. Due to the lag of the supply of oxyhemoglobin, the concentration of oxyhemoglobin in local muscle tissue quickly enter the decline stage, and after reaching a certain threshold, they basically remain unchanged. However, deoxyhemoglobin continued to rise because of the consumption of oxygen from oxyhemoglobin, and finally remained unchanged after reaching a certain threshold almost at the same time with oxyhemoglobin. When the weight is removed from the hands of the subjects, local muscle fatigue gradually disappear, blood circulation and oxygen consumption in the blood return to normal, the concentration of the two hemoglobin gradually are similar to the initial weight-free state.

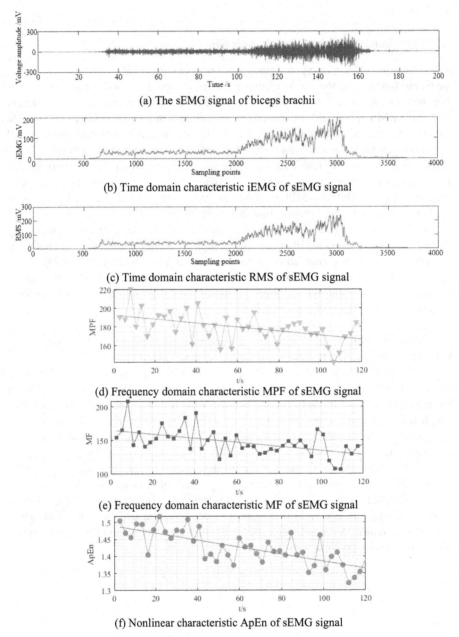

(a) The sEMG signal of biceps brachii

(b) Time domain characteristic iEMG of sEMG signal

(c) Time domain characteristic RMS of sEMG signal

(d) Frequency domain characteristic MPF of sEMG signal

(e) Frequency domain characteristic MF of sEMG signal

(f) Nonlinear characteristic ApEn of sEMG signal

Fig. 3. Characteristics analysis of sEMG signal

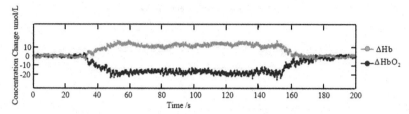

Fig. 4. Changes of two hemoglobin concentrations during muscle fatigue

4.2 Performance Comparison of Different Algorithms

BP neural network and the GA optimization BP neural network were used to classify muscle state. The "sample set 1" represented the combination of five characteristic parameters of four-channels sEMG and two hemoglobin characteristic parameters. Taking the GA optimization BP neural network as an example, the "sample set 1" was input into the GA-BP neural network.

The fitness change curve of the genetic algorithm is shows in Fig. 5. It can be seen that it start to converge after about 32 iterations. As shows in Fig. 6, the optimized neural network training has reached the set error requirements after 18 times, and the model has a good learning performance.

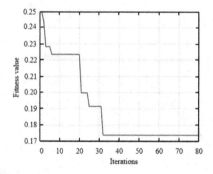

Fig. 5. The fitness curve of genetic algorithm

As shows in Fig. 7 the correlation analysis results of the training set, validation set, test set and overall of the neural network optimized by the GA are 0.99285, 0.99116, 0.99436 and 0.99279 respectively. the Fit curve is highly consistent with the Y = T curve. It can be concluded that the muscle fatigue model constructed by optimizing the weight and threshold of BP neural network through the GA has a satisfactory training, validation and testing effect with relatively high accuracy.

Table 3 shows the comparison of fatigue classification and recognition performance of the two classifiers when the data set used "sample set 1". It can be found from the table that under the same sample set, the classification effect of BP neural network optimized by the GA is better. The classification accuracy of the algorithm is 90.4%, which is 10.2% higher than that of BP neural network, and the running time of GA-BP neural network is 3.41 s shorter.

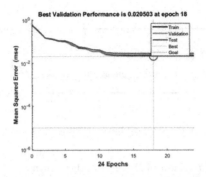

Fig. 6. The curve of each mean square error with training times

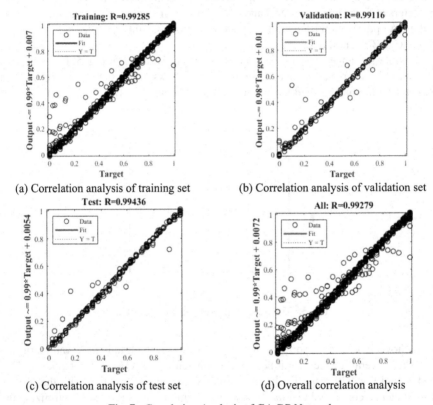

(a) Correlation analysis of training set

(b) Correlation analysis of validation set

(c) Correlation analysis of test set

(d) Overall correlation analysis

Fig. 7. Correlation Analysis of GA-BP Network

Table 3. Comparison of recognition results of two classification algorithms

Classification Algorithm	Fatigue Level 1	Fatigue Level 2	Fatigue Level 3	Fatigue Level 4	Running Time
BP neural network	80.2%	73.1%	72.4%	78.3%	20.51 s
GA-BP neural network	90.4%	84.8%	85.2%	87.7%	17.10 s

5   Conclusion

The GA could span the gap of BP neural network in global search capability. Localized muscle fatigue experiments has shown that compared to BP neural networks, the GA completed the initialization of population parameters configuration and design of fitness functions, and output the optimal weight and threshold contained by individuals that meet the conditions to BP neural networks. It could significantly reduce the problems caused by randomness in BP neural networks, and the accuracy of classification of multiple parameter muscle fatigue is significantly improved. The precision and efficiency of simulation are both better than traditional BP neural network. The highest recognition rate of GA-BP neural networks classification is 90.4%, and the running time of the algorithm is 3.41 s.

References

1. Wang, J., Sun, Y., Sun, S.: Recognition of muscle fatigue status based on improved wavelet threshold and CNN-SVM. IEEE Access **8**, 207914–207922 (2020)
2. Veiga, J., Faria, R.C., Esteves, G.P., et al.: Approximate entropy as a measure of the airflow pattern complexity in asthma. Annu. Int. Conf. IEEE Eng. Med. Biol. Soc. **2010**, 2463–2466 (2010)
3. Pincus, S.M.: Approximate entropy as a measure of system complexity. Proc. Natl. Acad. Sci. U S A. **88**(6), 2297–2301 (1991)
4. Li, H., Wang, Q., Liu, J., Zhao, D.: A prediction model of human resources recruitment demand based on convolutional collaborative BP neural network. Comput. Intell. Neurosci. **24**(2022), 3620312 (2022)
5. Moniri, A., Terracina, D., Rodriguez-Manzano, J., et al.: Real-time forecasting of sEMG features for trunk muscle fatigue using machine learning. IEEE Trans. Biomed. Eng. **68**(2), 718–727 (2021)
6. Zhao, G., Shi, H., Wang, J.: A grey BP neural network-based model for prediction of court decision service rate. Comput. Intell. Neurosci. **14**, 7364375 (2022)
7. Zhou, L., Wang, C.: Innovation of platform economy business model driven by BP neural network and artificial intelligence technology. Comput. Intell. Neurosci. **9**(2022), 3467773 (2022)
8. Wang, Z., Wu, J., Wang, H., Wang, H., Hao, Y.: Optimal underwater acoustic warfare strategy based on a three-layer GA-BP neural network. Sensors (Basel) **22**(24), 9701 (2022)

9. Ning, Y., Jin, Y., Peng, Y., Yan, J.: Small obstacle size prediction based on a GA-BP neural network. Appl. Opt. **61**(1), 177–187 (2022)
10. Wang, L., Qiu, K., Li, W.: Sports action recognition based on GB-BP neural network and big data analysis. Comput. Intell. Neurosci. **2**(2021), 1678123 (2021)

Data Technology and Network Security

Research on Typical Scenario Generation Based on Distribution Network Data Mining and Improved Policy Clustering

Jinhu Wang[1], Tongzhou Zhang[1], Ming Chen[1], Wei Han[1], Mingze Ji[2(✉)], and Yuzhuo Zhang[2]

[1] Huai'an Power Supply Branch, State Grid Jiangsu Electric Power Co., Ltd., Huai'an 223001, Jiangsu, China
[2] School of Electric Power Engineering, Nanjing Institute of Technology, Nanjing 211167, Jiangsu, China
jmzwork@126.com

Abstract. As the construction of the new type of power system, the high proportion of the distributed power grid, the electric car charging load is increased, make the distribution network scenarios cannot adapt to the current operation mode, in view of the current distribution network scenarios cannot adjust to the problems in operation mode, put forward an improved strategy based on multiple load evaluation model and the distribution network of clustering method to generate scenario. First, building the appraisal model of multiple load distribution network, through the model for regional assessment and scoring load, will score results using K-means clustering initial scenario, secondly, as the guidance, can use different way to design of initial scenario, can get different use type set in the middle of the scene, finally by improving strategy clustering method to analyze the middle scene set, The typical scenario set of distribution network is obtained. Simulation results show that the proposed method can effectively provide support for regional distribution network planning of new power systems with multi-type energy participation.

Keywords: load multivariate demand · Data mining · improved strategy clustering · planning scenario

1 The Introduction

In traditional distribution network planning, the most severe condition is generally taken as the typical scenario to carry out the design of planning scheme. For example, the electricity demand is aimed at meeting the maximum predicted load value. But as for the construction of the new type of power system development, renewable energy generation accounted for more and more high, the energy coupling is more and more closely, the load becomes more and more active, power grid to run more and more uncertainty factors, if still in the most severe conditions as scenario planning, will cause the investment cost is high, the electric grids and capacity utilization rate is low, It is difficult to control the fault risk and other negative consequences, which may become obstacles to the low-carbon development of power grid. Therefore, it is of great significance to construct typical scenarios of distribution network to adapt to the new development mode [1, 2].

Scenario building methods there are many kinds of distribution network, in the reference [3], put forward the thinking of new energy, electricity, heat, cooling load uncertainty integrated energy system equipment and distribution substation capacity more collaborative planning scenario planning method, considering the load can use comprehensive and coupling, making effective programmes to contain integrated energy system of power distribution network. In reference [4], a multi-dimensional typical scenario generation method for distribution network based on load clustering and network equivalence is proposed. Considering the different characteristics of load and the different types of distributed power supply, it is suitable for the scenarios requiring voltage evaluation.

Considering multiple load demand is a density clustering based on improved strategy of distribution network scenario generation method, first of all, build multivariate distribution network load model, through the model for the load area evaluation score, score result using the K – means clustering initial scenario, secondly, as the guidance, can use different way to design of initial scenario, The intermediate scene sets of different energy use types are obtained. Finally, the intermediate scene sets are analyzed by improved policy clustering method, and the typical scene sets of distribution network are obtained [5, 6]. Simulation results show that the proposed method can effectively provide support for regional distribution network planning of new power systems with multi-type energy participation [7, 8].

2   The Initial Scenario is Divided Based on the Multivariate Load Evaluation Model

In view of the planning area, multiple load build of the combination of evaluation model, using expert scoring method of evaluation based on two-level index contains factors, to evaluate the overall evaluation of regional scale score, and calculate the total score of each regional income, will score data K – means cluster analysis, the clustering result is the initial scenario.

2.1   To Construct the Multivariate Evaluation Model of Distribution Network Load

Firstly, To construct the multivariate evaluation model of distribution network load.

Step 1: Determine the evaluation object the evaluation objects of the multiple load evaluation model of distribution network are determined as the power load region or the load region of power coupled with comprehensive energy.

Step 2: The factors related to the load zone pole are screened and divided based on PEST analysis method

PEST analysis method is a macro factor analysis method from the macro perspective, taking politics, economy, society and technology as the entry point. With reference to

PEST analysis, the highly relevant factors affecting the distribution network planning scenario are comprehensively mined and analyzed, and the analysis matrix is formed, as shown in Table 1.

Table 1. PEST Analysis matrix for typical scenarios of distribution network

political	economic	social	technology
Regional orientation Territorial space planning	Level of economic development	Type and percentage of load users	Load density Load characteristic Load supply level Load supply quality

Step 3: To determine the indicators

Then according to the scientific principle, the principle of non-overlapping and organic combination, the principle of the combination of qualitative indicators and quantitative indicators, the principle of operability, the principle of stability and dynamic combination, through the relevant industry experts to screen the evaluation index. The evaluation indexes are shown in Table 2.

Table 2. Evaluation indicators

Head indicators	The secondary indicators
Policy indicators	The proportion of different land types
	The proportion of different industry types
Load indicators	Proportion of different load densities
	Load proportion of different characteristics
	Proportion of different load classes
The power supply indicator	Proportion of different voltage fluctuation range requirements

The land use types include content are as follows: wetland, garden land, forest land, grass, green space and open space land, cultivated land, construction land of agricultural facilities, land for residential land, public management and public service, land for public facilities, land for business services, industrial and mining land, warehousing, transportation, land use, special land, land for white space.

"Industry type" includes the following contents: Animal husbandry fishery, mining, manufacturing, electricity, heating gas and water production and supply industry, construction, wholesale and retail trade, transportation, warehousing and postal service, accommodation and catering industry, information transmission software and information technology services, finance, international organizations, real estate, leasing and business services, scientific research and technical services, water environment and public facilities management, Residential services, repair and other services, education, health and social work, culture, sports and recreation, public administration of social security and social organizations.

The calculation formula of load density is:

$$A = \frac{\text{The total load}}{\text{The area occupied by the total load}} W/m^2 \tag{1}$$

Characteristic loads include: three-peak and two-valley load, inverted U-shaped load, one-word load, shallow U-shaped load, two-peak and three-valley load, etc.

Load levels include: level 1 load, level 2 load, level 3 load.

The formula for calculating the voltage fluctuation range is:

$$B = \frac{|\text{The actual voltage} - \text{The rated voltage}|}{\text{The rated voltage}} \tag{2}$$

Step 4: Indicator Weight Setting

Considering that analytic hierarchy process (AHP) combines qualitative and quantitative analysis, can reduce subjective influence and is a hierarchical analysis method, AHP is adopted to weight each evaluation index. Its main steps are as follows:

Firstly, the hierarchy structure is constructed, then the judgment matrix is constructed, then the single hierarchy ranking and its consistency check, and finally the total hierarchy ranking and its consistency check.

Step 5: Expert scoring

The selected area was evaluated based on multiple load evaluation model and expert scoring method.

2.2 The Initial Scene is Generated Based on K-means Clustering Method

The obtained evaluation results are sorted out and analyzed by k-means clustering method, and each class of clusters obtained is an initial scene.

3 Design the Intermediate Scene Set Based on Different Ways of Energy Use

The scenario design is oriented to the energy consumption demand of users, and the design is carried out according to the energy consumption structure with different loads in each initial scenario, and two types of "single power supply demand" and "power and other energy supply demand" are obtained.

3.1 "Single Power Supply" Requirement

If there is only a single power supply demand in the area, the power source should consider the superior power supply and the distributed power supply. In the traditional distribution network scenario, the superior power supply is considered as the main power supply, and the distributed power supply is supplemented. In some distribution network reform areas and demonstration areas, the distributed resources are considered, and the distributed power supply is the main supply and the superior power supply is the auxiliary supply. According to different output ratios of distributed power supply, the initial scenario with only "single power supply" demand is divided into various intermediate scenarios, and the intermediate scenario set of "single power supply" is composed.

3.2 "Electricity and Other Energy Supply" Demand

In the region with electricity and other energy supply demand, two cases of integrated energy station supply and electricity supply are mainly considered. Among them, the traditional distribution network scenarios mainly focus on electric power supply, supplemented by energy conversion from a small number of comprehensive energy stations. Some new distribution network scenarios mainly consider energy supply in the form of integrated energy stations. According to the output proportion of different comprehensive energy stations, the initial scenarios with power and other energy supply demands are divided into various intermediate scenarios, and the intermediate scenario set of "power and other energy supply" is formed.

4   The Final Scene is Generated by the Density Clustering Method Based on the Improved Strategy

Data such as "regional load density", "peak-valley difference", "regional distributed power supply output ratio" and "regional comprehensive energy station output ratio" of many intermediate scenes were input. Cluster analysis was carried out using the density clustering method of improved strategy, and the final typical scenario was planned according to the clustering results.

4.1   Improved Density Clustering Method

Density clustering firstly selects the densest data in the data set as the first initial cluster center, and then selects the densest data that is relatively far from the first initial cluster center as the second center, and so on to determine all the initial cluster centers.

On this basis, the importance of Euclidean distance and local density calculated by each data set is weighted, and the weight of the more important factor is higher. Then, the Euclidean distance and local density are normalized, so that the calculation results are closer to the actual scenario planning requirements.

The distance between data points in the sample is calculated, namely, the Euclidean distance of "load density", "load peak-valley difference", "distributed power supply output ratio" and "integrated energy station output ratio" d_1, d_2, d_3, d_4, The expression is:

$$d_u(x_i, x_j) = \left[\sum_{k=1}^{m} (x_i^k - x_j^k)^2 \right]^{1/2} \quad (u = 1, 2, 3, 4) \tag{3}$$

$$\alpha = \frac{1}{\ln(\text{random}(\tau) + \max(d_u))} \quad \tau \in (1, 1.05) \tag{4}$$

$$\beta, \chi, \delta = (1 - \alpha)/3 \tag{5}$$

Random (τ) is a random function, Any value in the range of τ.
The normalized Euclidean distance D is:

$$d = \chi * d_1 + \beta * d_2 + \alpha * d_3 + \delta * d_4 \tag{6}$$

Set the threshold distance dt, and calculate the local load density within the distance threshold ρ_{1i}, Peak to valley load difference ρ_{2i}, Output density of distributed power supply ρ_{3i}, Output density of comprehensive energy station ρ_{4i} the expression is:

$$\rho_{vi} = \sum_{i \neq j, 1 \leq j \leq n} \exp\left\{-[d(x_i, x_j)/d_t]^2\right\} \quad (v = 1, 2, 3, 4) \tag{7}$$

The normalized local density is ρ:

$$\varepsilon = \frac{1}{\ln(random(\upsilon) + \max(d_u))} (\upsilon \in (1, 1.05)) \tag{8}$$

$$\phi, \varphi, \gamma = (1 - \varepsilon)/3 \tag{9}$$

$$\rho = \gamma * \rho_{1i} + \phi * \rho_{2i} + \varphi * \rho_{3i} + \varepsilon * \rho_{4i} \tag{10}$$

According to the idea of density clustering, the data point with the highest density is selected as the first initial clustering center m_1. According to the Euclidean distance, the most distant and dense point from m_1 is selected as the second initial cluster center m_2, which is successively calculated as follows:

$$\begin{cases} d_1(x_n, x_1), d_1(x_n, x_2)... \\ d_2(x_n, x_1), d_2(x_n, x_2)... \\ d_3(x_n, x_1), d_3(x_n, x_2)... \\ d_4(x_n, x_1), d_4(x_n, x_2)... \end{cases} \tag{11}$$

$$\begin{cases} \max[d_1(x_n, x_1), d_1(x_n, x_2)...] \\ \max[d_2(x_n, x_1), d_2(x_n, x_2)...] \\ \max[d_3(x_n, x_1), d_3(x_n, x_2)...] \\ \max[d_4(x_n, x_1), d_4(x_n, x_2)...] \end{cases} \tag{12}$$

Choose the formula obtained from eq. (12)

$$\max\left[\sum_{i=1}^{k-1} (\gamma * d_1(x_n, m_i) + \varphi * d_2(x_n, m_i) + \phi * d_3(x_n, m_i) + \varepsilon * d_4(x_n, m_i))\right] \tag{13}$$

The corresponding data point is selected as the third initial cluster center m_3, and so on,

$$m_k = \max\left[\sum_{i=1}^{k-1} (\chi * d_1(x_n, m_i) + \beta * d_2(x_n, m_i) + \alpha * d_3(x_n, m_i) + \delta * d_3(x_n, m_i))\right] \tag{14}$$

K initial cluster centers can be obtained.

The mixed evaluation function is constructed by comprehensively considering the differences within and between clusters. In a given sample set $X = \{x_1, x_2... x_n\}$, divide N data into k cluster classes $(C_1, C_2... C_k)$, and the initial cluster center $(M_1, M_2... M_k)$.

Intra-cluster difference represents clustering compactness, which is represented by the average distance between each data and its initial cluster center:

$$D_{in} = \left[\sum_{i=1}^{k} \sum_{j=1}^{n} \sqrt{(x_j - m_i)^2} \right] / n \tag{15}$$

The difference between clusters represents the distance between different classes, which is represented by the minimum distance between the center points of the initial cluster:

$$D_{out} = \min d(m_i, m_j) \tag{16}$$

The mixed evaluation function is defined as:

$$M(k) = \frac{D_{out} - D_{in}}{D_{out} + D_{in}} \tag{17}$$

As can be seen from the above formula, the value range of the function is $[-1, 1]$. The closer $M(k)$ is to 1, the difference within clusters can be ignored compared with between classes, and the better clustering effect will be. The closer $M(k)$ is to -1, the difference between clusters is negligible compared with that within clusters, and the worse clustering effect is. In order to gather within the cluster as much as possible, the classes should be separated as much as possible; When $M(k)$ is maximum, the clustering result is optimal, and the corresponding k is the optimal number of clusters k.

4.2 The Final Typical Scene is Generated According to the Clustering Results

5 Example Analysis

200 regions of a distribution network are selected. Firstly, the selected regions are evaluated and scored through the multiple evaluation model of distribution network load. Then, K-means clustering method is used to cluster and analyze all the scores to get the initial scene set. Finally, according to the data of "regional load density", "load peak-valley difference", "regional distributed power supply output ratio", "regional comprehensive energy station output ratio" and other data of the intermediate scene set, the typical scene set of the distribution network is obtained through the improved strategy of density clustering analysis.

5.1   Construct Multivariate Load Evaluation Model

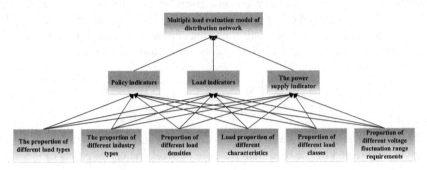

Fig. 1. Evaluation index hierarchy model

According to the evaluation indexes selected above, the analytic hierarchy process is used to build the evaluation index hierarchy model, as shown in Fig. 1.

Table 3. Indicators and weights at all levels

Head indicators	The weight	The secondary indicators	The weight
Policy indicators	0.6555	The proportion of different land types	0.4672
		The proportion of different industry types	0.2515
Load indicators	0.2648	Proportion of different load densities	0.0994
		Load proportion of different characteristics	0.082
		Proportion of different load classes	0.0641
The power supply indicator	0.0796	Proportion of different voltage fluctuation range requirements	0.0358

Indicators and weights at all levels are shown in Table 3.

5.2 K-means Clustering Analysis

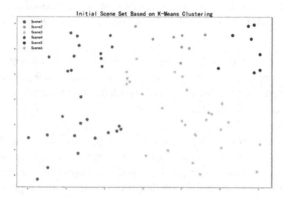

Fig. 2. Initial scene set based on K-means clustering

As can be seen from the figure, based on the distribution network conforming to the multivariate evaluation model, the scores of these 200 regions are obtained by k-means clustering analysis, and each cluster is an initial scene set, which is named according to the nature of land use and industry type (Fig. 2).

5.3 Density Clustering of Improved Strategies

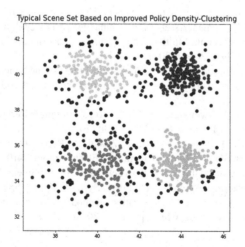

Fig. 3. Typical Scene Set Based on Improved Policy Density-Clustering

According to the intermediate scenario data designed for different energy demand scenarios, four class clusters as shown in the figure can be obtained through the improved policy density clustering method, and each class cluster is a typical scenario set of the distribution network (Fig. 3).

6 Conclusion

A typical scenario generation method for distribution network based on multivariate load evaluation model and improved strategy clustering is proposed. The main conclusions are as follows:

1) Construct the multiple load evaluation model of the distribution network and evaluate the load area to obtain the connection between the load area of the distribution network and the data. Analyze the evaluation score result through K-means clustering method, and each cluster is a kind of scene set to obtain the connection between the data and the scene.
2) Based on the different energy consumption requirements of the distribution network area, the scene design realizes different energy consumption division, which is conducive to the planning and design of the distribution network in the future.
3) The density clustering method with improved strategy is adopted to analyze the intermediate scenarios after energy-using design and obtain the typical scenarios of the distribution network, which improves the planning efficiency of the distribution network and has obvious advantages compared with the traditional planning method.

References

1. Wang, C., Wang, R., Yu, H., Song, Y., Yu, L., Li, P.: Problems and challenges of coordination planning under the evolution of distribution network morphology. Proc. CSEE **40**(08), 2385–2396 (2020)
2. Yu, X.: Research on Comprehensive performance Index System and risk Evaluation Model of distribution network Equipment Assets. North China Electric Power University, Beijing (2021)
3. Hu, Y., Xue, S., Yang, S., et al.: Multi-scenario planning of distribution network in the context of integrated energy. China Power (2021)
4. Bo, L., Sun, J., Yu, P., Zha, X., Wang, C., Xu, F.: Multi-dimensional typical scenario generation method for distribution network based on load clustering and network equivalence. Proc. CSEE **41**(08), 2661–2671 (2021)
5. Song, X., Liu, Y.: Wind power generation scenario partitioning based on improved k-means clustering. Power Gener. Technol. **41**(06), 625–630 (2020)
6. Xu, J., Chen, G., Yuan, F., Dai, Y., Zhang, W., Zhang, H.: Research on multi-attribute station clustering based on IBBO and K-Means++ fusion. Electr. Autom. **44**(01), 44–46 (222)
7. Wang, J., Zhang, S.: Abnormal power pattern detection based on linear discriminant Analysis and density peak clustering. Autom. Electr. Power Syst. **46**(05), 87–98 (222)
8. Liu, K., et al.: User power theft identification method based on transfer entropy density clustering. In: Proceedings of the CSEE, pp. 1–12, 30 Aug 2022

A Data-Driven and Deep Learning-Based Economic Evaluation Method for New Power System Distribution Grid

Yunzhao Wu[1][(✉)], Jialei Zhang[2], Qing Duan[1], Guanglin Sha[1], and Yao Zhang[1]

[1] China Electric Power Research Institute, Beijing 100192, China
zhoulq@njit.edu.cn
[2] State Grid Corporation of China, Beijing 100031, China

Abstract. In the future construction of new power system, in order to provide support and guidance for distribution grid planning, it is necessary to understand the economy of distribution grid. Therefore, this paper uses the multi-level fuzzy comprehensive evaluation method base on indicators to evaluate the technical economy of distribution grid. Then, a deep learning model is built, trained by a large amount of evaluation data, makes the network get the evaluation thought of each expert. Using this method can reduce the subjectivity in the process of evaluation, and can increase the rate of fault tolerance, the example analysis shows that using the evaluation results of this method is feasible and has practical significance.

Keywords: Distribution grid · Fuzzy evaluation · Neural Network · ANN

1 Introduction

Nowadays, under the influence of global warming, the use of green and clean energy is becoming more and more widespread. In the long-term planning, the new power system will adapt to the large-scale access of new energy with a high proportion. Therefore, the future distribution network structure will also change accordingly. In order to reasonably plan the shape of the future new power system, maximize the construction benefit, and guide the structural optimization of the future distribution grid, it is necessary to have a sufficient understanding of the power distribution grid economy. At present, economic evaluation has been widely used in power grid development planning [1] and power technology projects [2]. However, there are few articles about economic evaluation of distribution grid.

For the economic evaluation work, the commonly used method is to establish an economic index system. Reference [4] points out the benefits of establishing a scientific evaluation system. Reference [5] designed an economic evaluation index system for distribution network planning, and obtained similar results with traditional financial evaluation. Reference [6] establishes a multi-index comprehensive evaluation system for the economy of smart distribution network and applies it to the evaluation of smart distribution network planning effect of power supply companies, good results were obtained.

The traditional comprehensive evaluation method is to determine the index weight through the subjective and objective weight analysis method. Each evaluation needs to adopt the form of questionnaire, and the experts in the field are used to evaluate and score, which is not only complicated, but also introduces great subjectivity, and cannot carry out large-scale evaluation. With the development of deep learning and artificial intelligence in recent years, neural networks with self-learning, self-adaptation and self-organization functions have been widely used in the establishment of models. Reference [7] puts forward the research of science and technology evaluation method based on big data, and points out the advantages of this method. The combination of traditional evaluation method and deep learning can greatly simplify the process of traditional evaluation method. A large amount of comprehensive evaluation data is used to train the neural network model, and the idea of expert evaluation is endowed to the network, so that the evaluation process of experts can be simulated. Using this method can avoid the human error in the evaluation process, and can be directly used to deal with similar evaluation problems, avoiding the cumbersome scoring process. Reference [8] proposed the combination of Back Propagation Neural Network (BPNN) and multi-index evaluation model to achieve the purpose of accurate evaluation and optimal decision. In Reference [9], a comprehensive evaluation model of Radial Basis Function Neural Network (RBFNN) was established and used in the evaluation of comprehensive benefits of investment in refining and petrochemical projects.

In order to evaluate the economy of the distribution grid of the new power system, this paper establishes a total of 12 evaluation indexes from three perspectives of "construction economy, operation economy and social economy", determines the weight of the indexes by combination weighting method, and conducts comprehensive evaluation based on multi-level fuzzy analysis. After that, the Deep Belief Network (DBN) model is established, and a large amount of evaluation data is used to train the network and learn the evaluation ideas of experts. The deep learning algorithm is combined with the traditional comprehensive evaluation method to establish a universal economic evaluation model.

2 Multi-index for Economic Evaluation

Under normal circumstances, the economic evaluation of electric power technology mainly includes two aspects, on the one hand, the explicit benefits that can be directly measured by the form of monetary units, and on the other hand, the implicit benefits that cannot be directly measured by the value of money. In the construction process of actual projects, there are both explicit benefits and implicit benefits. Therefore, this paper constructs evaluation indexes from two aspects.

The evaluation indicators should be universal and can evaluate the technical economy of new power system distribution grid. A three-level index system is established, as shown in Fig. 1.

The explicit benefit index consists of construction economy and operation economy. "The total return on investment, investment payback period, annual asset utilization and annual electricity supply per unit of asset" are selected as basic indicators for construction economy. Operating economy chooses "net present value rate, internal rate of return, composite line loss rate, energy utilization efficiency, economic benefit cost ratio" as the basic index.

Choose social economy aspect as invisible benefit, and considering the new power system is connected by large scale and high proportion of new energy. "The proportion

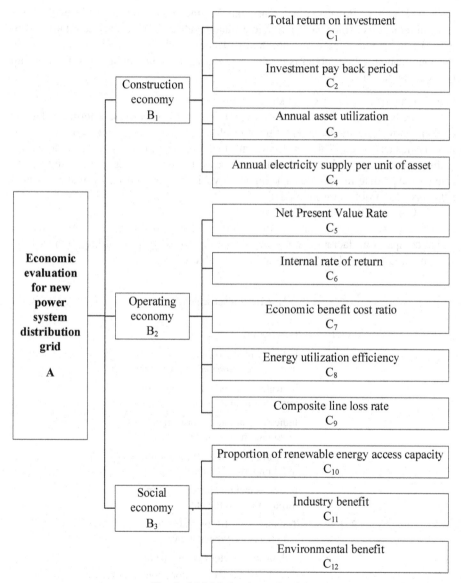

Fig. 1. Multi-index for evaluation

of access capacity of renewable energy, industry benefit and environmental benefit" are used as basic indicators.

3 Multi-level Fuzzy Comprehensive Evaluation Method

3.1 Calculate Subjective Weight with AHP

Analytic Hierarchy Process (AHP) is an analytical method to evaluate the level of importance of indicators, which can be used to evaluate both qualitative and quantitative problems. In this method, the target problem is decomposed into several factors, and then the analytical structure model is established according to the hierarchical relationship between the factors.

Step 1: Establish the hierarchical structure model.

On the basis of the constructed evaluation index, the objectives, criteria and factors of decision-making are divided into three levels according to the correlation. The lowest layer is the factor layer, which is also the sub-factor of the middle layer. The middle layer is the criterion layer, which is the main factor of decision-making and the key link to achieve the predetermined goal. The highest level is the goal of decision-making, which is to solve the problem through AHP.

Step 2: Construct the judgment matrix.

The method used to construct the judgment matrix is consistent matrix method, which compares all factors in pairs and selects the index scale according to the 9-level scale method proposed by Saaty, as shown in Table 1.

Table 1. AHP 9-level scale method.

Level	Description
1	Indicates that two factors are of equal importance compared to each other
3	Indicates that one factor is slightly more important than the other
5	Indicates that one factor is more important than the other
7	Indicates that one factor is significantly more important than the other
9	Indicates that one factor is **far more important** than the other
2, 4, 6, 8	The median of the two adjacent judgments mentioned above
Reciprocal	Judgment of factor i compared to j is a_{ij}, then the judgment of factor j compared to factor i is $a_{ji} = 1/a_{ij}$

The pairwise comparison matrix is to compare the relative importance of all factors in this layer against one factor (criterion or goal) in the next layer. The matrix element a_{ij} represents the comparison result of the factor i with the factor j. The scale value of each index is selected by experts and construct the judgment matrix as $A = [a_{ij}]_{m \times n}$.

Step3: Hierarchical single ordering and its consistency test.

Firstly, the established judgment matrix A is normalized, denoted as W, and the calculation formula is as follows:

$$W_i = \sqrt[n]{\prod_{i=1}^{n} \alpha_{ij}} \quad (n = 1, 2, 3 \ldots) \tag{1}$$

where, the element of W is the ranking weight of the same element to the relative importance of a factor at the next level, which is called hierarchical single ranking.

Then, the maximum eigenvalue $\lambda_{\max}$ of the judgment matrix is calculated as follows:

$$\lambda_{\max} = \sum_{i=1}^{n} \frac{(AW)_i}{nW_i} \quad (n = 1, 2, 3 \ldots) \tag{2}$$

Finally, the consistency test is conducted, and the calculation formula is as follows:

$$CR = CI/RI \tag{3}$$

where, RI is the average random consistency indicator, which can be identified according to the standard table. CI is the consistency index, which can be calculated by the following formula:

$$CI = \frac{\lambda_{\max} - n}{n - 1} \tag{4}$$

When $CR < 0.1$, it means that the judgment matrix meets the consistency check; otherwise, we need to readjust the judgment matrix and perform consistency check again.

Step4: Hierarchical total ordering and its consistency test.

Calculating the weight of the relative importance of all factors at a certain level to the highest level (the overall goal), which is called hierarchical total ranking, After that we can get the weights of each index.

3.2 Calculate Objective Weight with EWM

Entropy Weight Method (EWM) is an objective weight method, that is, the information entropy value of indicators is used to obtain the weight. In information theory, Shannon proposed to measure the disorder degree of the system by entropy value, which comes from abstract uncertain information. The objective information of each index needs to be analyzed first, and then the weight of the index is calculated according to the information entropy level in the index information. Because the calculation uses the objective information of the data, the entropy weight method has strong objectivity. The specific steps of the method are as follows:

Step 1: The original data are standardized, and the calculation formula is:

$$Y_{ij} = \frac{x_{ij} - \min(x_j)}{\max(x_j) - \min(x_j)} \tag{5}$$

where, x_{ij} represents the original data of the jth index of the ith sample.

Step 2: Calculate the proportion of the ith sample under the jth index and regard it as the probability used in the calculation of relative entropy:

$$p_{ij} = Y_{ij} \bigg/ \sum_{i=1}^{n} Y_{ij} \tag{6}$$

Step 3: Calculate the entropy value of the jth index:

$$e_j = -\frac{1}{\ln n} \sum_{i=1}^{n} p_{ij} \ln(p_{ij}) \tag{7}$$

Step 4: Define the information utility value:

$$d_j = 1 - e_j \tag{8}$$

Step 5: Normalize the information utility value and calculate the weight of each indicator:

$$\gamma_j = d_j \bigg/ \sum_{j=1}^{m} d_j \tag{9}$$

3.3 Calculate the Combined Weight

In order to make the obtained weight more reliable, through the combination evaluation method, EWM and AHP were used to integrate the index weights, the subjective weight and objective weight are combined to get the combined weight as the final index weight value. The combined formula is shown in Eq. (10).

$$\lambda_j = \frac{w_j \gamma_j}{\sum_{j=1}^{m} w_j \gamma_j} \tag{10}$$

where λ_j represents the combined weight, γ_j represents the objective weight determined by entropy value method, w_j represents the subjective weight determined by analytic hierarchy process, and m is the total number of indicators.

3.4 Multi-level Fuzzy Comprehensive Evaluation Method

Fuzzy Comprehension Evaluation method (FCE) is a method of transforming qualitative Evaluation into quantitative Evaluation according to the membership degree theory of Fuzzy mathematics. The specific evaluation steps are as follows:

Step 1: Determine the factor set and weight vector.

Factor set is a common set composed of various factors that affect the evaluation object, usually represented by $U = \{u_1, u_2, u_3, ..., u_m\}$. The element u_i represents the ith factor affecting the evaluation object.

Step 2: Establish a set of comments for comprehensive evaluation.

The comment set is a set composed of various possible evaluation results of the evaluation object by the evaluator, usually represented by $V = \{v_1, v_2, v_3, ..., v_n\}$. The element v_j represents the jth evaluation result.

Step 3: Carry out the single factor fuzzy evaluation to obtain the evaluation matrix.

The result of single factor evaluation of the ith element in factor set U is expressed by fuzzy set as: $R_i = \{r_{i1}, r_{i2}, r_{i3}, ..., r_{in}\}$. A matrix composed of m single factor evaluation sets $R_{n \times m}$, which is called fuzzy comprehensive evaluation matrix.

Step 4: Establish a comprehensive evaluation model.

After the single-factor fuzzy evaluation matrix R and factor weight vector A are determined, the fuzzy vector A on U is transformed into the fuzzy vector B on V through fuzzy change, that is $B = A_{1 \times m} \cdot R_{m \times n}$, the comprehensive evaluation score of each factor is calculated according to the evaluation situation at last.

4 DBN Model

Deep Belief Network is an energy model that integrates machine learning method and massive training data method. The work of machine learning method is to distribute information features and lay the foundation for information integration. DBN is essentially neural network models, which is composed of multiple Restricted Boltzmann Machines (RBM). RBM is used to input information need to be integrated, the characteristics of the neural network storage database all the information and its own characteristics, some information may exist multiple characteristics. DBN can be used in both supervised and unsupervised learning.

RBM is a stochastic generative neural network structure, the structure of DBN is limited to two layers: visible layer and hidden layer. There are connections between layers, but there are no connections between units within layers. The specific DBN network structure is shown in the following Fig. 2.

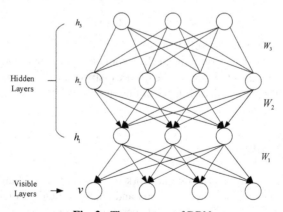

Fig. 2. The structure of DBN

The training process of RBM can be trained in a greedy hierarchical manner, and the weights of abstract hierarchical features extracted from the original input data can be fine-tuned. In addition, conditional probability distributions of input data can be determined and abstract features that are robust and invariant to transformation can be learned.

The process of training DBN is carried out layer by layer. In each layer, the data vector is used to infer the hidden layer, and this hidden layer is treated as the data vector of the next layer (higher layer). That is, several RBMS are "connected in series" to form a DBN, where the hidden layer of the previous RBM is the explicit layer of the next RBM, and the output of the previous RBM is the input of the next RBM. In the training process, the RBM of the current layer can only be trained after the RBM of the previous layer is fully trained until the last layer.

Information feature vectors need to be integrated in the first RBM layer to determine the hidden layer of information, and then the information feature vectors of the hidden layer are used as the data vectors of the next layer. The energy function of information data between layers is:

$$E(v, h|\theta) = -\sum_{i=1}^{n} n_i v_i - \sum_{i=1}^{m} b_i h_i - \sum_{i=1}^{nm} v_i w_{ij} h \tag{11}$$

where, n and m are the number of neurons in visible layer and hidden layer respectively; n_i and v_i are the bias of neurons in visible layer and hidden layer respectively; b_i is the connection weight of neurons in visible layer i and neurons in hidden layer j; θ is the set of model parameters; h_i represents the hidden layer, whose value is usually 0 or 1, following Bernoulli distribution; w_{ij} represents the visible layer; h represents the input layer nerve, and its value range is binary variable and real value.

According to the function, the information distribution probability of hidden layer and visible layer can be calculated with Eq. (12)

$$p(v, h|\theta) = \frac{e^{E(v,h|\theta)}}{z(\theta)} \tag{12}$$

where, $z(\theta)$ is the normalized coefficient.

The key of information retrieval in the deep confidence network model is the value of about θ. Its decision needs to integrate the feature distribution of information, determine the distribution probability of each layer in the model, and ensure the accuracy of the model calculation results.

5   Example Analysis

This paper takes a county distribution network in Huai'an City of Jiangsu Province as an example to conduct economic evaluation and analysis. Statistics required financial information, grid structure information and operation data information as the basic data. Then, a comprehensive evaluation questionnaire was designed and evaluated by experts in the field. A total of 50 questionnaires were distributed and 42 were recovered, of which 40 were valid.

Firstly, the index weight is calculated. According to the AHP-9 scale method, the ranking of the importance of indicators by experts is counted and integrated. Table 2 shows the importance scale of criterion layer B_1–B_3, and Table 3 shows the index scale of the 4 corresponding factor layers of B_1.

Table 2. Judgment matrix of criterion layer $B_1 \sim B_3$.

A	B_1	B_2	B_3
B_1	1	1/5	1/2
B_2	5	1	3
B_3	4	1/3	1

Table 3. Judgment matrix of factor layer $C_1 \sim C_4$.

B_1	C_1	C_2	C_3	C_4
C_1	1	1/3	5	2
C_2	3	1	5	4
C_3	1/5	1/5	1	3
C_4	1/2	1/4	1/3	1

Secondly, the combined weight of the index is calculated according to the statistical data, as shown in Table 4.

After that, experts' ratings are counted and processed. The elements of criterion layers and factor layers built by AHP are integrated into the factor set for FCE. The comments set is constructed according to the indicators, $Q = \{q_1, q_2, q_3, q_4, q_5\}$ and its elements are respectively "excellent (q_1), good (q_2), average (q_3), poor (q_4) and very poor (q_5)". The corresponding score of each comment is $\{1.0, 0.8, 0.6, 0.4, 0.2\}$. FCE was used to calculate the economic evaluation score, as shown in Table 5. The final calculation result is 0.70907777.

Finally, the evaluation data of 40 experts are collected and used as the learning data of neural network. 70% of the data is used as the training set and 30% of the data is used as the test set. The input layer is the evaluation value of each influencing factor, and a total of 12 input neurons are set. The output layer is the evaluation score, and the score interval is [0, 1]. The fitting effect of the trained model on the test set is shown in Fig. 3.

It can be seen from the test results of test set data that the fitting effect of the model is good. Using processed expert evaluation data as input, the model output is 0.69844631. Compared with the data calculated by the multi-level fuzzy analysis method, the data error is less, which can be used in the economic evaluation of distribution grid.

Table 4. Combined weight of index.

Criterion layer	Weight	Factors layer	Weight
B1	0.12202019	C1	0.27536462
		C2	0.5145836
		C3	0.12172673
		C4	0.08832506
B2	0.64832901	C5	0.51358596
		C6	0.24784722
		C7	0.11229177
		C8	0.09187944
		C9	0.03439561
B3	0.22965079	C10	0.33131291
		C11	0.28942849
		C12	0.37925861

Table 5. Score of each index.

Criterion layer	Score	Factors layer	Score
B1	0.090693607	C1	0.236813573
		C2	0.349916848
		C3	0.087643246
		C4	0.068893547
B2	0.461396443	C5	0.338966734
		C6	0.20323472
		C7	0.080850074
		C8	0.062478019
		C9	0.026140664
B3	0.156987721	C10	0.225292779
		C11	0.185234234
		C12	0.273066199

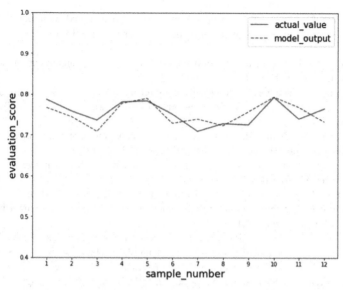

Fig. 3. Model fitting curve

6 Conclusion

In this paper, the multi-level fuzzy comprehensive evaluation method based on indicators is used to evaluate the economy of distribution grid. According to the characteristics of economic evaluation, the evaluation index system is used for comprehensive evaluation from three perspectives of "construction economy, operation economy and social economy". Then, a DBN model is constructed. A large amount of evaluation data is used to train the network, so that the network can learn the evaluation ideas of experts. The neural network model is used to reduce the subjectivity in the evaluation process and improve the fault tolerance rate. The example analysis shows that the learning effect of network is good, and it can learn the evaluation ideas of experts. The evaluation results of this method are in line with expectations, and the evaluation workload can be reduced to a certain extent. Through the economic evaluation of the distribution grid, we can understand the current planning of the distribution grid and analyze the optimization direction of the distribution grid in the scenario of new power systems in the future. So it can provide support for the evolution of power grid shape.

Acknowledgments. This work was funded by the Science and Technology Project of State Grid Corporation of China "Research on construction technology of distribution network form and management and control system supporting high proportion of distributed resources" (project number: 5100-202155291A-0-0-00).

References

1. Liu, M.: Technical and economic analysis and application in distribution network planning and design. Policy Res. Explor. **645**(03), 61 (2020)

2. Liu, T., Wu, G., Ge, H., et al.: Analysis on economic benefit and economic evaluation of electric power technology transformation project. China Manag. Informationization **23**(22), 124–125 (2020)
3. Xu, T., Qu, H., Zhao, S., et al.: Research on post-evaluation of researching programs of power industry. J. Xiangtan Univ. **40**(06), 109–114 (2018)
4. Tang, X., Sun, H., Wang, H., et al.: A fuzzy comprehensive evaluation method for distribution network economy based on combined weights. Electr. Power Technol. Econ. **02**, 141–142 (2019)
5. Xue, Y., Ma, L., Zheng, R., et al.: Research on economic evaluation method of smart distribution network. Hebei Electr. Power **37**(02), 18–21 (2018)
6. Wang, L.: Study on comprehensive evaluation of smart distribution network economy. J. Electr. Power **32**(05), 414–420 (2017)
7. Zhang, Q.: BP Neural Network Based Comprehensive Evaluation System of Government Response to Online Public Opinion: Construction and Analysis. Huazhong University of Science & Technology (2020)
8. Liu, W., Fu, X., Wu, J., et al.: Research on comprehensive operation benefit analysis of power grid enterprisies based on DEA-RBFNN. Shandong Electric Power **48**(10), 33–39+59 (2021)
9. Feng, K.: Research on Comprehensive Benefit Evaluation of Refining and Chemical Project Investment Based on RBF Neural Network. Dalian University of Technology (2019)
10. Lin, L.: Full cycle Economic Evaluation of Distribution Network Infrastructure Projects from the Perspective of Financial Management. Finance and Accounting for International Commerce (2021)
11. Zhan, X.: Fuzzy Comprehensive Evaluation of Distribution Network Operation Economy based on Analytic Hierarchy Process. Yanshan University (2013)
12. Li, X., Wang, L., Yan, N., et al.: Economic dispatch of distribution network with distributed energy storage and PV power stations. In: 2020 IEEE International Conference on Applied Superconductivity and Electromagnetic Devices (ASEMD), pp. 1–2 (2020)
13. He, L., Su, S., Wang, W., et al.: Economy evaluation of distribution networks with distributed generation based on cost-benefit method. In: 2017 4th International Conference on Industrial Economics System and Industrial Security Engineering (IEIS), pp. 1–6 (2017)

Study on Random Generation of Virtual Avatars Based on Big Data

Jian Zhao[1,2(✉)], Mo Peng[1], Bo-Lin Zhu[1], and Ling-Ling Li[1]

[1] School of Computer Engineering, Nanjing Institute of Technology, No. 1, Hongjing Road, Nanjing 211167, Jiangsu, China
zj616@hotmail.com
[2] SuXin Vision Technologies Co. Ltd., No. 2888, Dongwu Road, Suzhou 215000, Jiangsu, China

Abstract. With big data growing rapidly in importance over the past few years, Virtual Reality (VR) display technology has gained widespread attention. Especially, virtual avatars with unique identification are becoming increasingly important. Traditional generation methods are complicated, time consuming and low image quality. To improve the quality and rendering speed of generated virtual avatars, we present a set of optimized parameters of GAN based on deep learning. The experimental results showed that the best image quality is achieved in the case of ADAM (Optimization Function), BCE (Loss Function), l-r = 0.00075 (Learning Rate), the epoch = 200. The questionnaire survey showed that the recognition accuracy could be up to 84.29%. The conclusion of the questionnaire survey is consistent with our experimental results.

Keywords: Deep learning · Generative Adversarial Network · Image generation

1 Introduction

With the rapid development of big data technology, virtual reality display technology is gaining traction. Virtual avatars with unique recognition capabilities are coming into focus. Traditional image generation relies on four main aspects: namely the determination of visibility, the hierarchical models of detail, predictive computing, and offline computing. However, the generation speed is usually limited and the quality of the generated images is low, which does not match the requirements of the big data era. The advent of GAN has greatly accelerated the speed and the quality of the generated images. Unsupervised learning GAN was first presented in Generative Adversarial Networks by Ian J. Goodfellow. [1] Henceforth, the deep research and optimization improvement of GAN are gradually expanding. CGANS [2] proposes to improve the Unstable GAN training by adding the input of the category tag. StackGAN [3] introduces text information through a text vector and extracts some visual features. The DCGAN [4] achieved GAN by using CNN, this improvement is of great significance, and many GAN frameworks later will be based on this. The width and depth of the development of GAN have been well developed. P Isola [5] implements image conversion with PatchGAN model, but the data sets used under image-to-image must be paired, and such pairs of data sets are difficult to find. CycleGAN [6] was presented to solves this problem in their next paper. The data sets for both fields need to be prepared in CycleGAN. The proposal of ProGAN [7] and StyleGAN [8] also had excellent application value on high resolution images.

In GAN, generate model and discriminator model were trained at the same time. The labeling of the training sets can be completed efficiently by itself. GAN is a generative model that uses only reverse propagation and does not require complex Markov chains compared to other generation models [9], such as the Boltzmann machine and GSNs. Because GAN is trained in an unsupervised learning style, it can be widely used in the areas of unsupervised learning and semi-supervised learning. Compared to VAE [10], GAN does not change the nether bound. GAN is progressively consistent, but VAE is biased. To sum up, the application range of GAN is large with broad prospects and great potential.

This paper is organized as follows. In Methods, Sect. 2.1 describes the optimization of data sets, and Sect. 2.2 describes the construction of GAN. Section 2.3 describes the optimization function and the loss function. Afterwards we show the results and conclusions, respectively.

2 Methods

The main process has two modules: Data set optimization and GAN processing. Data set optimization is the basis for GAN training. The process of data set part mainly focuses on the interception of face image, the transformation of data format and the classification of images, which provide the best data image for GAN training. According to the logical structure, the specific principles and methods of the above three modules are described in detail. The flowchart is shown in Fig. 1.

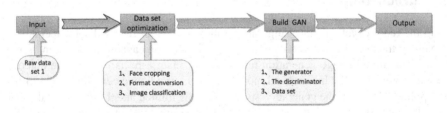

Fig. 1. Work structure

2.1 Data Set Optimization

There are three main processes for data set optimization, as shown in the following Fig. 2.

Fig. 2. Data set optimization architecture

The generation of virtual avatars is the ultimate goal. However, the original training sets contains multiple types of images, which will negatively affect the experimental results. So the original training sets need to be pre-processed by OpenCV [11]. After pre-processed, 96 × 96 face images were set as the original data set. Pre-processing is mainly to filter out images with face features using the LBP feature description operator. After the face is detected, the coordinate area of the current face needs to be recorded.

Due to the large number of datasets, it is not efficient to use the commonly image format for model training. Because HDF5 is a cross-platform data storage file that can store large amounts of data with the ability of high-speed reading. Therefore, the HDF5 format was used to improve the speed and efficiency of data reading [12].

At the same time, the classification of the image is carried out. The mean hash algorithm and hemming distance are used to classify the image [13, 14], mainly by compressing the image to reduce other small detail interference. The mean hashing algorithm is a class of hashing algorithms, which is generally used to search for similar images. The hash value of each image is calculated, and the image is classified by comparing the size of the Hemming distance between the hash values. The comparison standard adopted in this experiment is 3. In other words, the Hamming distance under 3 images can be divided into a category. To remove the effect of color on image similarity, the image needs to be converted to grayscale when compressing the image. This is also beneficial for improving the speeds of reading and writing.

After the above pre-processing, the images were used as the final training dataset.

2.2 Build GAN

2.2.1 The Discriminator

The data size in the training set is 96 × 96, the color channel is RGB. So the resolution of each image is 96 × 96 × 3 with 27,648 pixels. The image was first converted to a one-dimensional column matrix and then fed into the discriminator. In this case, 27,648 input nodes are required in the discriminator class. This basic model includes 27,648 input nodes, 100 intermediate layer and one output node in turn. The LeakyReLU [15] activation function and layer standardization are used between the intermediate layer The Sigmoid activation function [16] is applied to the output result. The model diagram of the discriminator is shown in Fig. 3.

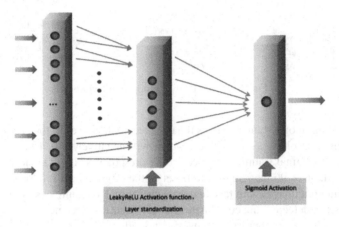

Fig. 3. The discriminator structure

2.2.2 The Generator

The generator is similar to the neural network structure of the discriminator. By training the models, the discriminator determines that the sample from the generator is false, and the generator will continue to generate samples that will allow the discriminator to be judged to be true. In the end, those could be got a balance. The figure generated by the generator can spoof the discriminator, so that the discriminator is determined to be true. The number of nodes of the output layer of the generator needs to be equal to the number of input nodes. Firstly, the size of the middle layer should be enough for the generator to learn and also to match the speed of the discriminator. Since we do not want one of the two models to be too far ahead of the other in the GAN training process. The generator model is shown in the following Fig. 4.

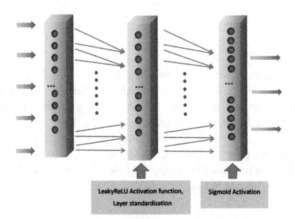

Fig. 4. The generator structure

The intermediate layer is connected to the output layer based on the LeakyReLU activation function and a layer standardization. The Sigmoid function is used as the output layer. The tensor needs to be reshaped before the result output, because the one-dimensional tensor is used in the model training process. But the generator should generate a three-dimensional tensor, so the one-dimensional tensor is reshaped into a three-dimensional tensor to the judge. This is different from the differential model. The subsequent work is similar to the above-mentioned discriminator, but the part of the creation of the loss function is removed. Because the losses used in accordance with the output of the discriminator in the cycle training of GAN, and the generator update is the error gradient calculated by the discriminator loss value.

2.2.3 Data Set

Data sets mainly contain with constructor, length functions, search functions, and check functions. The constructor is used to filter the data set to form the final training set. The data set length function is mainly used to check the size difference between the training set and the data set. The inspection function is used to detect whether the data is complete.

The Data Set class is a base class which is loaded in the image data set in Pytorch, so we must rewrite it to load our own data set. According to the classification of the aforementioned data sets, it is known that the data set in dataset.h5py has been classified and stored in the data.h5py file by class. Therefore, the initialization function cannot be read directly from the data in the entire file.

2.3 The Optimization Function and the Loss Function

The optimization function is used to transfer the loss value from the outermost layer of the neural network to the innermost layer. The mainstream optimization functions include SGD, RMSPROP and ADAM optimization functions.

- **SGD** (Stochastic Gradient Descent), which selects one sample parameter at random, so the processing speed is very fast and it can be updated online [17].
- **RMSProp** (root mean square prop), which is an improved algorithm based on AdapRAD (adaptive gradient algorithm). Adagrad has a very efficient performance in theory, however, the effect is poor in actual operation. The root cause of poor practical results is that the learning rate decreases too quickly as the training cycle increases. The RMSPROP introduces the attenuation factor based on the adjustment of the superior parameters. RMSProp's actual effect is more remarkable [18].
- **ADAM** (Adaptive momentum optimization), which is essentially RMSProp with momentum. It utilizes a gradient of moment estimate to dynamically adjust the learning rate of each parameter based on the second-order moment estimate.

The advantage of ADAM is that each iterative learning rate has a certain range after the offset correction, which makes the parameters smooth. ADAM combines the advantages of Adagrad's ability of handle sparse gradients and RMSprop's ability of handle non-stable targets [19].

The loss function uses MSE (Mean Square Error) and BCE (Binary Cross Entropy).

As for MSE, it is the difference between the value generated by the output node and the expected target value. The mean square error is the average of these square errors. Each node of the output layer of the length is **n**, the actual output is **o**, the expected target is **t**, the loss value loss, resulting in the formula [1]

$$loss = \frac{1}{n} \Sigma (t - 0)^2 \tag{1}$$

When the discriminator cannot distinguish between real data and generate data, the system does not output 1 or 0. Because it cannot be confident whether the data is true or confident data is generated. So, the discriminator will output 0.5 and the determination is kept neutral.

The target output of the neural network is the probability distribution, and the actual output is also a probability distribution. The difference between them is very high, and the cross entropy will be relatively high. If they are similar, the cross entropy will be lower. After the cross entropy is lost, the reverse propagation of the reverse propagation is no longer associated with the derivative of the Sigmoid function, which avoids the gradient disappearance to some extent. The difference between cross entropy and MSE is mainly the cross entropy contains logarithm, which is much larger than 1.0. Calculation of binary cross entropy losses is based on probability and uncertainty. BCE is used to calculate the binary cross entropy loss between the predicted value and the actual value.

Binary cross entropy is a cross entropy used in the case of only two categories, which is also facing the discriminator, the real data is 1.0 and the generated data is 0.0. When a balance is reached, the discriminator is equally good to the classification effect of the two data, so the output is always 0.5. Its specific formula is shown in [2] below.

$$loss = -\frac{1}{N} \sum\nolimits_{i=1}^{N} y_i \cdot \log(P(y_i)) + (1 - y_i) \cdot \log(1 - p(y_i)) \tag{2}$$

3   Results

The exploration of GAN contains four main parameters: the optimization function, the loss function, the epoch and the learning rate. Optimization functions include SGD, RMSPROP, and Adam. loss functions are MSE and BCE. After the first three variables are determined, the learning rate is slightly subdivided.

First, the following results were obtained according to the parameters in Table 1. It can be seen from the resulting image that all the images generated are noise. In subsequent training, the loss value changes slightly until the gradient gradually disappears after the epoch = 200 (Figs. 5 and 6).

Table 1. Results generated by SGD and MSE

Optimization Function/Loss Function	Epoch (based on l-r = 0.001)						
	1	20	50	100	200	300	400
SGD/MSE							

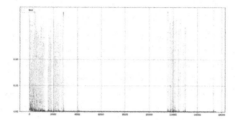

Fig. 5. D loss

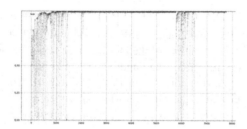

Fig. 6. G loss

In summary, it is found that the loss value of D will be reduced to 0 quickly, and the loss value of G will rise to 1 quickly. The combination of the optimization function SGD and the loss function MSE is shown, the gradient disappears after training, and the generator does not progress. So, we consider replacing the loss function (Figs. 7 and 8).

Table 2. Results generated by SGD and BCE

Optimization Function/Loss Function	Epoch (based on l-r = 0.001)						
	1	20	50	100	200	300	400
SGD/BCE							

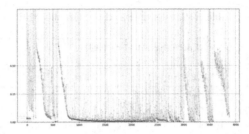

Fig. 7. D loss

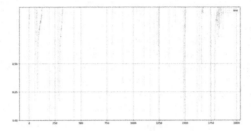

Fig. 8. G loss

Control other variables unchanged, MSE replaced with BCE, the results are shown as Table 2. It is clear that the outline of the face has been revealed by epoch = 100 with the use of the BCE loss function. The hundreds of subsequent training sessions have had a noticeable effect. At this point we mark this as Model1. Compare the loss value D with the loss value G again. The situation when the epoch = 100 tended to be similar to that when the epoch = 200 or more, and the situation was worse when the epoch was smaller.

After the selection of the loss function BCE and epoch = 100, the outline of the face gradually appears. But the loss value is more volatile, there is some progress, but not much. Overall, the effect is significantly better than the first scenario. It can be judged that under this data set, the effect of loss function BCE is significantly better than that of loss function MSE.

The replacement optimization function is RMSPROP, the other variables remain unchanged, and the training results are obtained as shown Table 3. Compared to using SGD, the effect is significantly improved when using the optimization function RMSprop. However, it is worth noting that at epoch equals 20 to 100, the effect begins to deteriorate, noting the impact of the number of training sessions, and subsequent optimization improvements.

The loss function is changed to BCE, and the result is as shown Table 4. When epoch = 200, the advantage is obvious. In the case of using the optimization function RMSprop, loss function BCE and l-r = 0.001, after many trainings, it can be found that the image quality of epoch = 200 is relatively good. As the BCE increases relative to the MSE, the outline noise of the image appears later as the epoch grows.

It can be concluded that the effect of the loss function BCE is still better than that of MSE when the optimization function RMSprop is selected, and it can be found that the effect of epoch is 100 or less has been poor, consider increasing the initial epoch. The replacement optimization function is Adam, the loss function is MSE, and the other variables remain unchanged. The result is as shown Table 5.

Table 3. Results generated by RMSProp and MSE

Optimization Function/Loss Function	Epoch (based on l-r = 0.001)						
	1	20	50	100	200	300	400
RMSProp/MSE							

Table 4. Results generated by RMSProp and BCE

Optimization Function/Loss Function	Epoch (based on l-r = 0.001)						
	1	20	50	100	200	300	400
RMSProp/BCE							

Table 5. Results generated by Adam and MSE

Optimization Function/Loss Function	Epoch (based on l-r = 0.001)		
	200	300	400
Adam/MSE			

The loss function is replaced by BCE, increasing the starting epoch, and the result is as shown Table 6. By comparing the above experimental results, the optimization effect of the optimization function ADAM is better than RMSPROP and SGD. Because, no matter which loss function is used after many trainings, the image quality under ADAM is better. They don't become noise. At the same time, it can also be found that the quality of the figure obtained at epoch = 200 will also be significantly better than the results obtained by epoch = 400, and it is better than the selected 175, 225, 250, 275, 300, and the like. Under the same conditions, the effect of using the loss function BCE is better than using the loss function MSE. In summary, under the framework of this neural network, the combination of the optimization function ADAM and the loss function BCE is optimal when using this training set to train GAN.

Table 6. Results generated by Adam and BCE

Optimization Function/Loss Function	Epoch (based on l-r = 0.001)						
	175	200	225	250	275	300	400
Adam/BCE							

In the case of determining the optimization function ADAM and the loss function BCE, we should start to think about the selection of learning rate.

Keep the optimization function is ADAM, the loss function is BCE, epoch = 200, only change the learning rate l-r. The results of Table 7 as follows.

Table 7. Results generated by different sets of learning rates

Vector/l-r							
0.000500	0.000625	0.000675	0.000700	0.000725	0.000750	0.000760	0.000775

After the image comparison, it can be seen more apparent that the effect of l-r = 0.00075 is more effective, and the quality of the image is higher.

Based on objective experimental analysis, we still carried out subjective experimental analysis. We use the form of online questionnaire survey. The number of participants in this questionnaire a total of 140 people. The images generated under the six models above are marked in order. The results are shown in the Table 8.

As shown in the figure, the final survey data for the six models reflect the optimism of our experiments. All of the best proportion have been more than 50% positive to justify the conclusions we have reached in each model. From Model 1 to Model 5, we determined that the optimization function ADAM is the best in this experiment, the loss function BCE is better, and the effect is better when the epoch is 200 by comparison. In the last Model 6, we fine-tuned the learning rate, and finally got l-r = 0.00075 is

Table 8. Subjective questionnaire survey results

Model 1	1	2	3	4	5	6	7	
Proportion	2.14%	0%	0%	1.43%	78.57%	11.43%	6.43%	

Model 2	1	2	3	4	5	6	7	
Proportion	0.71%	12.86%	15.71%	1.43%	10%	58.57%	0.71%	

Model 3	1	2	3	4	5	6	7	
Proportion	4.29%	0.71%	7.86%	2.14%	84.29%	0.71%	0%	

Model 4	1	2	3					
Proportion	55.71%	38.57%	5.71%					

Model 5	1	2	3	4	5	6	7	
Proportion	22.86%	72.14%	0.71%	0.71%	1.43%	1.43%	0.71%	

Model 6	1	2	3	4	5	6	7	8
Proportion	0.71%	2.86%	9.29%	12.14%	5%	60.71%	1.43%	7.86%

relatively better. This also validates our conclusion that the resulting image quality is optimal when the optimization function is ADAM, the loss function is BCE, epoch is 200, and l-r is 0.00075.

4 Conclusion

A novel and generalizable methodology and framework was proposed based on GAN which will greatly improve the quality of virtual human face image generation. The quality of the data set was improved by using face cropping, format conversion and classification of the dataset, which will greatly shorten the training time. The parameters of the loss function, the optimization function, epoch and learning rates are strictly designed and tested. Finally, a set of the best parameters when the image quality is optimal was found: Adam optimization function, BCE loss function, epoch = 200, lr-0.00075. Furthermore, subjective experimental results from a random sample of 140 people showed that the results of simulation are same as the results of the survey.

Acknowledgements. The authors gratefully acknowledge the participants in the user study and the anonymous reviewers for their constructive comments.

Funding. Funding by Basic Science (Natural Science) research project of Jiangsu Province(21KJB520038), the Scientific Research Foundation for Advanced Talents, Nanjing Institute of Technology (YKJ201979), and Natural Science Foundation of Jiangsu Province, China (Grant No. BK20201468).

References

1. Goodfellow, I., et al.: Generative adversarial nets. Adv. Neural Inform. Process. Syst. 27 (2014)
2. Mirza, M., Osindero, S.: Conditional generative adversarial nets. arXiv preprint arXiv:1411. 1784 (2014)
3. Radford, A., Metz, L., Chintala, S.: Unsupervised representation learning with deep convolutional generative adversarial networks. arXiv preprint arXiv:1511.06434 (2015)
4. Zhang, H., et al.: Stackgan: Text to photo-realistic image synthesis with stacked generative adversarial networks. In: Proceedings of the IEEE international conference on computer vision, pp. 5907–5915 (2017)
5. Isola, P., Zhu, J. Y., Zhou, T., Efros, A.A.: Image-to-image translation with conditional adversarial networks. In: Proceedings of the IEEE conference on computer vision and pattern recognition, pp. 1125–1134 (2017)
6. Zhu, J.Y., Park, T., Isola, P., Efros, A.A.: Unpaired image-to-image translation using cycle-consistent adversarial networks. In: Proceedings of the IEEE international conference on computer vision, pp. 2223–2232 (2017)
7. Mahalingaiah, K., Matichuk, B.: ProDeblurGAN: progressive growing of GANs for blind motion deblurring in face recognition. In: McDaniel, T., Berretti, S., Curcio, I.D.D., Basu, A. (eds.) Smart Multimedia: Second International Conference, ICSM 2019, San Diego, CA, USA, December 16–18, 2019, Revised Selected Papers, pp. 439–450. Springer International Publishing, Cham (2020). https://doi.org/10.1007/978-3-030-54407-2_37
8. Karras, T., Laine, S., Aittala, M., Hellsten, J., Lehtinen, J., Aila, T.: Analyzing and improving the image quality of stylegan. In: Proceedings of the IEEE/CVF Conference on Computer Vision and Pattern Recognition, pp. 8110–8119 (2020)

9. Zhou, W., Anastasio, M.A.: Markov-chain monte carlo approximation of the ideal observer using generative adversarial networks. In: Medical Imaging 2020: Image Perception, Observer Performance, and Technology Assessment, vol. 11316, p. 113160D. International Society for Optics and Photonics (2020)

10. Xian, Y., Sharma, S., Schiele, B., Akata, Z.: f-vaegan-d2: A feature generating framework for any-shot learning. In: Proceedings of the IEEE/CVF Conference on Computer Vision and Pattern Recognition, pp. 10275–10284 (2019)

11. Khan, M., Chakraborty, S., Astya, R., Khepra, S.: Face detection and recognition using openCV. In: 2019 International Conference on Computing, Communication, and Intelligent Systems (ICCCIS), pp. 116–119. IEEE (2019)

12. Koranne, S.: Hierarchical data format 5: HDF5. In: Koranne, S. (ed.) Handbook of open source tools, pp. 191–200. Springer US, Boston, MA (2011). https://doi.org/10.1007/978-1-4419-7719-9_10

13. Zhai, D., Liu, X., Chang, H., Zhen, Y., Chen, X., Guo, M., Gao, W.: Parametric local ultiview hamming distance metric learning. Pattern Recognition **75**, 250–262 (2018)

14. Li, B., Ming, D., Yan, W., Sun, X., Tian, T., Tian, J.: Image matching based on two-column histogram hashing and improved RANSAC. IEEE Geosci. Remote Sens. Lett. **11**(8), 1433–1437 (2014)

15. Dubey, A.K., Jain, V.: Comparative study of convolution neural network's relu and leaky-relu activation functions. In: Mishra, S., Sood, Y.R., Tomar, A. (eds.) Applications of Computing, Automation and Wireless Systems in Electrical Engineering: Proceedings of MARC 2018, pp. 873–880. Springer Singapore, Singapore (2019). https://doi.org/10.1007/978-981-13-6772-4_76

16. Pratiwi, H., et al.: Sigmoid activation function in selecting the best model of artificial neural networks. J. Phys.: Conf. Ser. **1471**(1), 012010 (2020)

17. Ruder, S.: An overview of gradient descent optimization algorithms. arXiv preprint arXiv: 1609.04747 (2016)

18. Kurbiel, T., Khaleghian, S.: Training of deep neural networks based on distance measures using RMSProp. arXiv preprint arXiv:1708.01911 (2017)

19. Kingma, D.P., Ba, J.: Adam: A method for stochastic optimization. arXiv preprint arXiv: 1412.6980 (2014)

Ordering, Pricing, and Coordination of a Closed-Loop Supply Chain with Risk Preference

Ronghua Lu[✉], Yisheng Wu, and Feng Xu

School of Economics and Management, Nanjing Institute of Technology, Nanjing, People's Republic of China
lrhlrx@163.com

Abstract. This paper considers the ordering, pricing, and coordination for a closed-loop supply chain (CLSC) made up of a risk-neutral manufacturer, a risk-neutral third-party collector, and a risk-preference retailer. We introduce the M-CVaR criterion depending on two parameters to describe the retailer's risk-preference behavior. The optimal order quantity, wholesale price, and acquisition price of decentralized and centralized decision conditions are found using the backward induction approach and the influences of the risk-averse and pessimistic coefficients on the optimal solutions are investigated using numerical simulations. The findings demonstrate that the optimal order quantity goes up with the risk-averse coefficient and falls down with the pessimistic coefficient in both centralized and decentralized conditions. The more risk-averse the retailer, the higher the manufacturer's wholesale price. The retailer's increased risk-taking and risk aversion tendencies could lead to the market exit. The manufacturer prefers the retailer who is more risk-taking. In the case of risk-taking, the CLSC's expected profit under the centralized condition may be smaller than under the decentralized condition, but in the case of risk-neutrality, the expected profit under the centralized condition is always bigger than that under the decentralized condition. The CLSC can achieve the expected profit under centralized conditions with risk neutrality through revenue-sharing and cost-sharing (RS&CS) contracts.

Keywords: Closed-loop supply chain · Risk preference · M-CVaR · Coordination · Revenue-sharing and cost-sharing contract

1 Introduction

Due to growing concerns about environmental, legal, social, and economic factors, more and more enterprises are engaged in recycling and remanufacturing of used products, resulting in CLSCs (Zheng et al., 2019). By implementing CLSC management, enterprises can gain a competitive advantage and sustainable development (Savaskan and Van Wassenhove, 2006). Therefore, CLSC has been used in a variety of industries, including those related to electronics, tires, engine oil, and general industry (Ebrahimi and Bagheri, 2022), as well as receiving wide concern by the academic circle.

© The Author(s), under exclusive license to Springer Nature Singapore Pte Ltd. 2023
Y. Tian et al. (Eds.): ICBDS 2022, CCIS 1796, pp. 368–390, 2023.
https://doi.org/10.1007/978-981-99-3300-6_27

When studying the ordering, pricing, and coordination strategies of the SCs, scholars mostly assume that decision-makers are risk-neutral. (Wu et al., 2014). However, supply chains (SCs) are increasingly susceptible to risks in the dynamic and competitive world of today. Therefore, more and more SC members take risk aversion in their decisions of marketing strategies (Li et al., 2016). Survey data from McKinsey also shows that over 40% of business managers think that their companies take risks, which has an important influence on business decisions (Feng et al., 2013). Hence, researchers have introduced many methods to assess decision makers' risk aversion in SC management, including downside risk (Yao et al., 2016), loss-averse (Shen et al., 2011), mean-variance (MV) (Kouvelis et al., 2013), value-at-risk (VaR) (Wu et al., 2013), conditional value-at-risk (CVaR) (Li and Ou, 2022; Fan et al., 2020), etc. However, most of these researches considered risk-averse rather than risk-taking behavior. But the empirical research has demonstrated that under uncertain conditions, decision-makers may also engage in risk-taking behavior (Bostian et al., 2008). In order to also simulate risk-taking behavior, Jammernegg and Kischka (2009, 2007) presented the mean conditional value-at-risk (M-CVaR) method. Based on the M-CVaR method, Xie et al. (2018) investigated how the wholesale price contract, buy-back contract, and revenue-sharing contract coordinate the SC respectively. The research based on the M-CVaR method in the SCs mainly focuses on ordering strategies and contract coordination with risk preference. However, there are few types of research considering the wholesale price and coordination strategies in the CLSC with risk preference.

Motivated by the above literature, this study investigates the order quantity, wholesale price, and acquisition price strategies and coordination mechanism of a CLSC with one risk-neutral manufacturer, one risk-sensitive retailer, and one risk-neutral third-party collector. We intend to provide answers to these questions: (i) What are the optimal selections for order quantity, wholesale price, and acquisition price? And how are they affected by the risk-averse coefficient and pessimistic coefficient? (ii) As the leader, what types of risk retailers do the manufacturer prefer to cooperate with? (iii) Could RS&CS contracts coordinate CLSC with risk preference?

These are the paper's primary contributions: First, we introduce the M-CVaR criterion depending on two parameters into CLSC to describe the retailer's three kinds of risk preference and get the optimal order quantity, wholesale price, and acquisition price. Xie et al. (2018) only studied the optimal order quantity and coordination strategies in a forward SC. Second, we look at the manufacturer's optimal wholesale price under the assumption that he/she is the CLSC's leader. Chen et al. (2017) similarly explored the optimal wholesale price but they assumed in the case of risk aversion. Our research shows that the manufacturer will assign a higher wholesale price when the retailer is more risk-averse and prefers to engage with the retailer who is more risk-taking. Third, we make the assumption that the centralized CLSC is also risk-sensitive which is distinct from the earlier research by Xie et al., 2018, Chen et al., 2017, etc., and we get some interesting results. For example, if the centralized CLSC is risk-taking, its expected profit may be smaller than that of the decentralized CLSC. The CLSC's expected profit is greatest when the centralized CLSC is risk-neutral. Through RS&CS contracts, the decentralized CLSC can reach the expected profit of the centralized CLSC with risk neutrality.

The remaining portions of this paper are split into five sections. A short overview of relevant literature on risk aversion, pricing, and coordination in CLSC is provided in Sect. 2. In Sect. 3 we outline the problem and notations associated with it. Section 4 proposes the CLSC model on the basis of the M-CVaR criterion and arrive at the optimal solutions and the coordination strategy. In Sect. 5, some numerical examples are used to demonstrate how risk parameters affect the optimal solutions and the coordination strategy. Section 6 outlined the main conclusions of this research.

2 Literature Review

Our paper is associated with the following two aspects: risk aversion in CLSC and pricing and coordination strategies in CLSC.

Many scholars have examined the operational decisions of CLSC under different risk-averse methods to measure and avoid the risks brought by uncertainty. MV is often used in measuring the members' risk-averse attitude in CLSC. Sun et al. (2017) proposed a CLSC model with financial hedging under the MV framework and got the conclusion that high (low) risk-averse remanufacturers will produce more new (remanufactured) products. Xing et al. (2020) considered three emission reduction models assuming every CLSC member is risk-averse. They found that the RS&CS contracts have only a negligible effect on manufacturers' low-carbon production. Zhang et al (2021) investigated the pricing strategy in the retailer and the third-party collection models when manufacturers are risk-averse toward unpredictability in production costs. One of the conclusions is that SC revenue and manufacturers' risk aversion are inversely correlated and that the retailer recycling is better than the third-party recycling. Xia and Nan (2022) adopted the MV criterion to measure the utility of distributors in their study of pricing decisions and financing options for undercapitalized remanufacturing CLSC. However, the MV method has some limitations because it only considers the increment of profit, but not the decrease of profit. VaR has also received much attention as a measure of downside risk (Alexander and Baptista, 2004). But VaR cannot serve as a reliable risk criterion because it neglects the upward profit and does not adhere to subadditivity (Artzner et al., 1999). CVaR method overcomes these defects and is easy to calculate, so CVaR has been widely used. For example, CVaR is used as a risk measure when studying operational efficiency improvement of the reverse SC network design under uncertainty (Das et al., 2022; Golpîra and Javanmardan, 2021, 2022) To overcome the defect that the CVaR criterion only measures the conditional mean of the certain percent of worst-case values of a continuous random variable (Eskandarzadeh et al., 2016), which makes the goal of decision-makers low, Jammernegg and Kischka (2007) proposed M-CVaR criterion in which the whole distribution of profit is taken into account and then all types of risk can be described. Chen et al. (2017) examined the optimal order quantity, wholesale price, and acquisition price under the M-CVaR criterion, but they assumed risk aversion.

Another related stream is the pricing and coordination strategies in CLSC. Numerous studies have examined pricing and coordination strategies in CLSC under the assumption of deterministic demand, including those by Savaskan et al. (2004), Ferguson et al. (2006), Sarkar and Bhala (2021), Liu et al. (2021), etc. Early work under uncertainty generally assumes risk neutrality of the decision maker, including Chuang et al. (2014),

Lu and Li (2016), etc. Recently, risk aversion has been introduced to the area of pricing and coordination in CLSC, such by Xing et al. (2020), Zhang et al (2021), Xia and Nan (2022), Chen et al. (2017) which we have mentioned before. Ke et al. (2018) studied a pricing issue in CLSC involving one risk-neutral manufacturer and two competitive risk-averse retailers. The risk aversion of either of the two retailers will be beneficial to the manufacturer. Gong and Zhang (2022) studied the pricing and reverse logistics network problem and proposed a distributed robust risk aversion model to handle high uncertainty in the quality of returns. They found that risk-averse policymakers always favor lower pricing strategies to steer clear of extreme risks rather than raising acquisition prices to promote higher-quality returns.

From the above all, we find that the application of the M-CVaR criterion in CLSC mainly focuses on operational efficiency improvement of the reverse SC network design under uncertainty and most research focused on pricing and coordination strategies in CLSC are based on risk neutrality or risk aversion, with little consideration of risk-taking. Based on this, our paper explores the ordering, pricing, and coordination problem in a CLSC with a risk-sensitive retailer using the M-CVaR criterion.

3   Problem Clarification and Basic Assumptions

This paper examines a CLSC system composed of a risk-neutral manufacturer, a risk-neutral third-party collector, and a retailer with risk preference, as shown in Fig. 1.

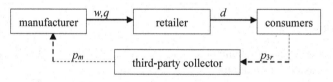

Fig. 1. The CLSC system

(1) The manufacturer can purchase raw materials from suppliers or recycle used products from third-party collectors to produce single-period products. The unit manufacturing cost is c_m, the unit remanufacturing cost is c_r, and the unit cost saved through remanufacturing is $\Delta = c_m - c_r > 0$ (Savaskan et al., 2004).

(2) New and remanufactured products are sold to the retailer at the same unit wholesale price w.

(3) The retailer orders goods from the manufacturer in quantities of q, and sells them at the unit retail price p.

(4) The retailer is faced with an uncertain sales market. The random demand d is a continuous non-negative variable having the probability density function $f(x)$ and probability distribution function $F(x)$. We assume that the probability distribution function is strictly monotone increasing and continuous (Jammernegg and Kischka, 2007).

(5) The third-party collector specifies the acquisition price p_{3r} of used products and acquires them from final consumers. We construct the quantity of used products R as a linear function of the acquisition price p_{3r}, and we have $R = a + bp_{3r}$ (Karakayali

et al., 2007), where $a > 0$ represents consumers' environmental awareness and $b > 0$ represents their sensitivity to the acquisition price.

(6) The manufacturer pays the transfer price p_m ($p_{3r} \leq p_m \leq \Delta$) to buy used products from the third-party collector.

According to the above assumptions, revenue functions of each CLSC member can be respectively formulated:

$$\pi_R(q) = (p - w)q - p\max(q - x, 0) \tag{1}$$

$$\pi_M(w, p_m) = (w - c_m)q + (\Delta - p_m)R \tag{2}$$

$$\pi_{3r}(p_{3r}) = (p_m - p_{3r})R \tag{3}$$

The superscripts D, C, and R represent the optimal solution under decentralized, centralized, and coordinated states respectively. π_x^y represents the expected profit or profit of x under the y strategy, where $x \in (R, M, 3r, SC)$ represents the retailer, the manufacturer, the third-party collector, and the CLSC respectively, and $y \in (D, C, R)$ represents the decentralized decision (DD), centralized decision (CD), and coordinated strategy respectively. For example, π_R^D represents the retailer's expected profit under the decentralized decision.

4   CLSC Model Under the M-CVaR Criterion

4.1   M-CVaR Model

Referring to the studies of Jammernegg and Kischka (2007, 2009) and Cai and Sun (2020), the measure formulation of M-CVaR is:

$$M\text{-}CVaR_\eta(\pi(x, y)) = \lambda E[\pi(x, y)|\pi(x, y) \leq z_\eta(\pi(x, y))]$$
$$+ (1 - \lambda)E[\pi(x, y)|\pi(x, y) \geq z_\eta(\pi(x, y))] \tag{4}$$

where E denotes the expected value of the objective function, $\pi(x, y)$ denotes the revenue function of decision makers, z_η denotes the η-quantile of the distribution of decision makers' benefit function, $\lambda \in [0, 1]$ denotes the pessimistic coefficient of decision makers, and a greater value of λ represents a higher level of risk aversion of decision makers.

According to Rockafellar and Uryasev (2002), CVaR is expressed as:

$$CVaR_\eta(\pi(x, y)) = E[\pi(x, y)|\pi(x, y) \leq z_\eta(\pi(x, y))]$$
$$= \frac{1}{\eta} \int_{\pi(x,y) \leq z_\eta} \pi(x, y)f(x)dx \tag{5}$$

where, $\eta \in (0, 1]$ represents decision makers' risk-averse coefficient, and a smaller value of η represents a higher level of risk aversion of decision makers.

Referring to (5), (1) can also be expressed as:

$$M-CVaR_\eta(\pi(x,y)) = \frac{\lambda}{\eta}\int_{\pi(x,y)\leq z_\eta}\pi(x,y)f(x)dx + \frac{1-\lambda}{1-\eta}\int_{\pi(x,y)\geq z_\eta}\pi(x,y)f(x)dx$$

(6)

From (6), it is clear that the decision makers' risk attribute is based on the value of the pessimistic coefficient λ and risk-averse coefficient η. When $\lambda=\eta$, the model at this time turns to the traditional model, which seeks to maximize the decision makers' expected profit while they are risk-neutral; When $\lambda > \eta$, the decision makers are more concerned about the part of the profit less than the quantile, and they are risk-averse, in particular, when $1 = \lambda > \eta$, the M-CVaR criterion changes to CVaR criterion; When $\lambda < \eta$, the decision makers are more concerned about the part of the profit greater than the quantile, and now they are risk-taking.

(6) can also be expressed as

$$M-CVaR_\eta(\pi(x,y)) = \int_0^\eta \frac{\lambda}{\eta}VaR_\theta[\pi(x,y)]d\theta + \int_\eta^1 \frac{1-\lambda}{1-\eta}VaR_\theta[\pi(x,y)]d\theta$$

(7)

where, VaR_θ represents the quantile at the confidence level of $(1-\theta)$.

Let

$$\varphi(\theta) = \begin{cases} \frac{\lambda}{\eta}, 0 \leq \theta \leq \eta \\ \frac{1-\lambda}{1-\eta}, \eta < \theta \leq 1 \end{cases}$$

(8)

Let $\Phi(\theta) = \int_0^\theta \varphi(x)dx$, then

$$\Phi(\theta) = \begin{cases} \frac{\lambda}{\eta}\theta, 0 \leq \theta \leq \eta \\ \lambda + \frac{1-\lambda}{1-\eta}(\theta - \eta), \eta < \theta \leq 1 \end{cases}$$

(9)

Therefore, (7) is also able to be written as

$$M-CVaR_\eta(\pi(x,y)) = \int_0^1 \varphi(\theta)VaR_\theta[\pi(x,y)]d\theta$$

(10)

4.2 Decentralized Decision (DD) Model

In this model, the decision sequence is presented as below: the manufacturer first determines the optimal wholesale price w and optimal transfer price p_m, after which the retailer and the third-party collector decide on the optimal order quantity q and the optimal acquisition price p_{3r}, respectively.

4.2.1 The Retailer's Optimal Decision

Depending on (1), the retailer's profit function is also stated as

$$\pi_R(q)=\begin{cases} px - wq, x \le q \\ (p - w)q, x > q \end{cases} \tag{11}$$

Therefore, the quantile of the retailer's profit at the confidence level of $(1 - \theta)$ is

$$VaR_\theta(\pi(q)) = \begin{cases} pF^{-1}(\theta) - wq, \theta \le F(q) \\ (p - w)q, \theta > F(q) \end{cases} \tag{12}$$

Substitute (12) into (10) to obtain the retailer's decision function under the M-CVaR criterion:

$$M\text{ - }CVaR_\eta(\pi(q)) = \int_0^{F(q)} (pF^{-1}(\theta) - wq)\varphi(\theta)d\theta + \int_{F(q)}^1 (p - w)q\varphi(\theta)d\theta$$

$$= \int_0^{F(q)} (pF^{-1}(\theta) - wq)\varphi(\theta)d\theta + (p - w)q(1 - \Phi(F(q))) \tag{13}$$

Let $\theta = F(t)$, then (13) can be simplified as

$$M - CVaR_\eta(\pi(q)) = \int_0^q (pt - wq)\varphi(F(t))dF(t) + (p - w)q(1 - \Phi(F(q))) \tag{14}$$

Therefore, the retailer needs to maximize (14) to calculate the optimal order quantity.

Proposition 1. Under the DD condition, the retailer's optimal order quantity $q^*(w)$ is.

$$q^*(w) = \begin{cases} F^{-1}(1 - \frac{1-\eta}{1-\lambda}\frac{w}{p}), w \le p(1 - \lambda) \\ F^{-1}(\frac{\eta}{\lambda}\frac{p-w}{p}), w > p(1 - \lambda) \end{cases} \tag{15}$$

Proof. (1) when $F(q) \ge \eta$, that is, when $q \ge F^{-1}(\eta)$, (14) becomes

$$M\text{ - }CVaR_\eta(\pi(q)) = \int_0^{F^{-1}(\eta)} (pt - wq)\frac{\lambda}{\eta}dF(t) + \int_{F^{-1}(\eta)}^q (pt - wq)\frac{1-\lambda}{1-\eta}dF(t)$$

$$+ (p - w)q(1 - (\lambda + \frac{1-\lambda}{1-\eta}(F(q) - \eta))) \tag{16}$$

The first derivative of (16) for q is

$$\frac{dM - CVaR_\eta(\pi(q))}{dq} = \frac{1-\lambda}{1-\eta}(p - w)(1 - F(q)) - w \tag{17}$$

The second derivative of (16) for q is $\frac{d^2M - CVaR_\eta(\pi(q))}{dq^2} = -\frac{1-\lambda}{1-\eta}(p - w)f(q) < 0$, so the optimal solution exists.

Let (17) equal 0, we get $F(q^*(w)) = 1 - \frac{1-\eta}{1-\lambda}\frac{w}{p}$, i.e., $q^*(w) = F^{-1}(1 - \frac{1-\eta}{1-\lambda}\frac{w}{p})$. For the condition $F(q) \ge \eta$ to be true, $F(q^*(w)) = 1 - \frac{1-\eta}{1-\lambda}\frac{w}{p} \ge \eta$, i.e., $w \le p(1 - \lambda)$ must be guaranteed.

(2) when $F(q) < \eta$, that is, when $q < F^{-1}(\eta)$, (14) becomes

$$M - CVaR_\eta(\pi(q)) = \int_0^q (pt - wq)\frac{\lambda}{\eta}dF(t) + (p - w)q(1 - \frac{\lambda}{\eta}F(q)) \qquad (18)$$

The first derivative of (18) for q is

$$\frac{dM - CVaR_\eta(\pi(q))}{dq} = (p - w) - \frac{\lambda}{\eta}pF(q) \qquad (19)$$

The second derivative of (18) for q is $\frac{d^2 M - CVaR_\eta(\pi(q))}{dq^2} = -\frac{\lambda}{\eta}pf(q) < 0$, so the optimal solution exists.

Let (19) equal 0, we get $F(q^*(w)) = \frac{\eta}{\lambda}\frac{p-w}{p}$, i.e., $q^*(w) = F^{-1}(\frac{\eta}{\lambda}\frac{p-w}{p})$. For $F(q) < \eta$ to be true, $F(q^*(w)) = \frac{\eta}{\lambda}\frac{p-w}{p} < \eta$, i.e., $w > p(1 - \lambda)$ must be guaranteed. Proposition 1 is proved.

It can be known from (15), when $w \leq p(1 - \lambda)$, $F(q^*(w)) = 1 - \frac{1-\eta}{1-\lambda}\frac{w}{p}$; when $w > p(1 - \lambda)$, $F(q^*(w)) = \frac{\eta}{\lambda}\frac{p-w}{p}$. $F(q^*(w))$ decreases with the increase of w, that is, when the manufacturer raises his/her wholesale price, the retailer will reduce his/her order quantity, and the corresponding probability distribution value will also decrease.

4.2.2 The Third-Party Collector and Manufacturer's Optimal Decisions

Proposition 2. Under the DD condition, the third-party collector's optimal acquisition price is $p_{3r}^D = \frac{b\Delta - 3a}{4b}$, the manufacturer's optimal transfer price is $p_m^D = \frac{b\Delta - a}{2b}$, and his/her optimal wholesale price is: (1) when $q^D \geq F^{-1}(\eta)$, if $c_m \leq w < (1 - \lambda)p$, then $w^D = c_m + \frac{1-\lambda}{1-\eta}pF^{-1}(1 - \frac{1-\eta}{1-\lambda}\frac{w^D}{p})f(1 - \frac{1-\eta}{1-\lambda}\frac{w^D}{p})$, otherwise $w^D = (1 - \lambda)p$; (2) when $q^D < F^{-1}(\eta)$, if $(1 - \lambda)p < w < p$, then $w^D = c_m + \frac{\lambda}{\eta}pF^{-1}(\frac{\eta}{\lambda}\frac{p-w^D}{p})f(\frac{\eta}{\lambda}\frac{p-w^D}{p})$, otherwise $w^D = p$.

Proof. By substituting $R = a + bp_{3r}$ into (3), the third-party collector's profit function becomes

$$\pi_{3r}(p_{3r}) = (p_m - p_{3r})(a + bp_{3r}) \qquad (20)$$

Taking the derivative of (20) and making its first derivative equal to 0, we can get

$$p_{3r}^* = \frac{bp_m - a}{2b} \qquad (21)$$

The manufacturer's profit function can be obtained by substituting (21) into (2).

$$\pi_M(w, p_m) = (w - c_m)q + (\Delta - p_m)\frac{a + bp_m}{2} \qquad (22)$$

The optimal transfer price can be determined by taking the derivative of (22) for p_m and setting its first derivative to 0:

$$p_m^D = \frac{b\Delta - a}{2b} \qquad (23)$$

Substituting (23) into (21), the optimal acquisition price can be obtained as shown below

$$p_{3r}^D = \frac{b\Delta - 3a}{4b} \tag{24}$$

Substituting (15) and (23) into (22), we get the manufacturer's profit function

$$\pi_M(w) = (w - c_m)q^*(w) + \frac{(a + b\Delta)^2}{8b} \tag{25}$$

Find the second derivative of w from (25):
(1) when $w \le p(1 - \lambda)$

$$\frac{d^2\pi_M(w)}{dw^2} = -\frac{1 - \eta}{p(1 - \lambda)f(1 - \frac{w(1-\eta)}{p(1-\lambda)})}(2 + \frac{(1 - \eta)(w - c_m)f'(1 - \frac{w(1-\eta)}{p(1-\lambda)})}{p(1 - \lambda)f(1 - \frac{w(1-\eta)}{p(1-\lambda)})}) < 0 \tag{26}$$

(2) when $w > p(1 - \lambda)$

$$\frac{d^2\pi_M(w)}{dw^2} = \frac{-\eta}{p\lambda f(\frac{\eta}{\lambda}\frac{p-w}{p})}(2 + \frac{\eta(w - c_m)f'(\frac{\eta}{\lambda}\frac{p-w}{p})}{p\lambda f(\frac{\eta}{\lambda}\frac{p-w}{p})}) < 0 \tag{27}$$

Therefore, there is an optimal solution which is classified and discussed below.

(1) when $w \le (1 - \lambda)p$, $\pi_M(w) = (w - c_m)F^{-1}(1 - \frac{1-\eta}{1-\lambda}\frac{w}{p}) + \frac{(a+b\Delta)^2}{8b}$. At this point, solving the optimal wholesale price is transformed into solving

$$\underset{w}{Max}(w - c_m)F^{-1}(1 - \frac{1 - \eta}{1 - \lambda}\frac{w}{p}) + \frac{(a + b\Delta)^2}{8b}$$
$$s.t.\ c_m \le w \le (1 - \lambda)p \tag{28}$$

Constructing the Lagrangean function of (26), and according to the Karush-Kuhn-Tucker conditions, it can be known that when $c_m \le w < (1 - \lambda)p$,

$$w^D = c_m + \frac{1 - \lambda}{1 - \eta}pF^{-1}(1 - \frac{1 - \eta}{1 - \lambda}\frac{w^D}{p})f(1 - \frac{1 - \eta}{1 - \lambda}\frac{w^D}{p}) \tag{29}$$

otherwise,

$$w^D = (1 - \lambda)p \tag{30}$$

(2) when $w > (1 - \lambda)p$, $\pi_M(w) = (w - c_m)F^{-1}(1 - \frac{\eta}{\lambda}\frac{p-w}{p}) + \frac{(a+b\Delta)^2}{8b}$. At this point, solving the optimal wholesale price is transformed into solving

$$\underset{w}{Max}(w - c_m)F^{-1}(1 - \frac{\eta}{\lambda}\frac{p - w}{p}) + \frac{(a + b\Delta)^2}{8b}$$
$$s.t.\ (1 - \lambda)p < w \le p \tag{31}$$

Constructing the Lagrangean function of (27), and according to the Karush-Kuhn-Tucker conditions, it can be known that when $(1 - \lambda)p < w < p$,

$$w^D = c_m + \frac{\lambda}{\eta} p F^{-1}(\frac{\eta}{\lambda} \frac{p - w^D}{p}) f(\frac{\eta}{\lambda} \frac{p - w^D}{p}) \tag{32}$$

otherwise,

$$w^D = p \tag{33}$$

Proposition 2 is proved.

The optimal order quantity can be derived by substituting the optimal wholesale price into (15).

$$q^D = \begin{cases} F^{-1}(1 - \frac{1-\eta}{1-\lambda} \frac{w^D}{p}), & w^D \le p(1 - \lambda) \\ F^{-1}(\frac{\eta}{\lambda} \frac{p-w^D}{p}), & w^D > p(1 - \lambda) \end{cases} \tag{34}$$

According to (1) ~ (3), (29), (30), and (32) ~ (34), the retailer's expected profit under DD is

$$E[\pi_R^D] = p \int_0^{q^D} x f(x) dx + (p - w^D) q^D - p q^D F(q^D) \tag{35}$$

The manufacturer's profit is

$$\pi_M^D = (w^D - c_m) q^D + \frac{(a + b\Delta)^2}{8b} \tag{36}$$

The third-party collector's profit is

$$\pi_{3r}^D = \frac{(a + b\Delta)^2}{16b} \tag{37}$$

The CLSC's total expected profit is

$$E[\pi_{SC}^D] = p \int_0^{q^D} x f(x) dx + (p - c_m) q^D - p q^D F(q^D) + \frac{3(a + b\Delta)^2}{16b} \tag{38}$$

Due to the complexity of w^D and q^D, it is difficult to obtain the effects of the retailer's risk characteristics on the optimal wholesale price, the optimal order quantity and the expected profit under the DD condition through the analytical method. Therefore, numerical simulation is used to help analyze in Sect. 5.

4.3 Centralized Decision (CD) Model

There is just one decision maker facing uncertain market demand under the CD model. The central planner's risk characteristics depend on the risk characteristics of the CLSC members. Since the risk characteristics of the manufacturer and the third-party collector are neutral, we assume the risk characteristic of the central planner is consistent with the retailer.

Under the M-CVaR criterion, the central planner optimizes

$$M\text{-}CVaR_\eta(\pi(q, p_{3r})) = \int_0^q (pt - c_m q)\varphi(F(t))dF(t)$$
$$+ (p - c_m)q(1 - \Phi(F(q))) + (\Delta - p_{3r})(a + bp_{3r}) \quad (39)$$

The optimal order quantity and acquisition price under the CD model is solved, and proposition 3 can be obtained.

Proposition 3. Under the CD condition, the CLSC's optimal order quantity is

$$q^C = \begin{cases} F^{-1}(1 - \frac{1-\eta}{1-\lambda}\frac{c_m}{p}), & c_m \le (1 - \lambda)p \\ F^{-1}(\frac{\eta}{\lambda}\frac{p-c_m}{p}), & c_m > (1 - \lambda)p \end{cases} \quad (40)$$

The CLSC's optimal acquisition price is

$$p_{3r}^C = \frac{b\Delta - a}{2b} \quad (41)$$

Proof. Refer to the proofs of propositions 1 and 2.

Corollary 1 can be obtained from (40).

Corollary 1. Under the CD condition, q^C increases with increasing risk-averse coefficient η and decreases with increasing pessimistic coefficient λ.

Proof. The partial derivative of (40) for η is (1) when $c_m \le (1-\lambda)p$, $\frac{\partial q^C}{\partial \eta} = \frac{c_m}{(1-\lambda)pf(x)} > 0$; (2) when $c_m > (1 - \lambda)p$, $\frac{\partial q^C}{\partial \eta} = \frac{p-c_m}{\lambda pf(x)} > 0$. Therefore, q^C increases with increasing risk-averse coefficient η. The partial derivative of (40) for λ is (1) when $c_m \le (1 - \lambda)p$, $\frac{\partial q^C}{\partial \lambda} = -\frac{(1-\eta)c_m}{(1-\lambda)^2 pf(x)} < 0$; (2) when $c_m > (1 - \lambda)p$, $\frac{\partial q^C}{\partial \lambda} = -\frac{\eta(p-c_m)}{\lambda^2 pf(x)} < 0$. Therefore, q^C decreases with increasing pessimistic coefficient λ.

The higher the η, the lower the risk-averse degree of the decision maker is. Therefore, the central planner increases his/her order quantity. The higher the pessimistic coefficient λ, the more the central planner is afraid of risks, so the central planner will reduce his/her order quantity.

The CLSC's expected profit under the CD condition is

$$E[\pi_{SC}^C] = p\int_0^{q^C} xf(x)dx + (p - c_m)q^C - pq^C F(q^C) + \frac{(a + b\Delta)^2}{4b} \quad (42)$$

In particular, when the central planner is risk-neutral, q^C under the centralized CLSC is

$$q^C = F^{-1}(\frac{p - c_m}{p}) \quad (43)$$

4.4 The Coordination Based on the M-CVaR Criterion

The SC is coordinated if the expected profit of the entire SC system is optimal (Zhao et al, 2013). In this part, we examine how to coordinate the CLSC with risk preference through an appropriate contract. According to the numerical analysis in Sect. 5, we discover that the expected profit of the centralized CLSC based on the M-CVaR criterion is not always greater than that under the decentralized CLSC unless the centralized CLSC is risk-neutral. Therefore, our purpose of CLSC coordination is to make the expected profit of the decentralized CLSC based on the M-CVaR criterion to reach the expected profit under the centralized CLSC with risk-neutrality.

According to Gan et al. (2011)'s SC contract coordination theory, to accomplish SC coordination, the decentralized SC system must match the performance of the centralized SC system. Therefore, the optimal order quantity and the optimal acquisition price under the DD system ought to be equivalent to those under the CD system, namely, $q^R = q^C$ and $p_{3r}^R = p_{3r}^C$. We use RS&CS contracts to coordinate the decentralized CLSC based on the M-CVaR criterion. RS&CS contracts specify that the manufacturer will take a specific portion of the retailer's sales revenue and that the manufacturer will also cover some of the third-party collector's collection costs. The coordinating procedure is: the manufacturer offers the retailer the RS contract (w^R, φ_1) and the third-party collector the CS contract (p_m^R, φ_2). The ratio of sales revenue retained by the retailer is $\varphi_1(\varphi_1 \in (0, 1))$ and the ratio of the collection cost borne by the third-party collector is $\varphi_2(\varphi_2 \in (0, 1))$. The RS&CS contracts provide that each CLSC member's profit is

$$E[\pi_R(q)] = (\varphi_1 p - w)q + \varphi_1 p \int_0^q tf(t)dt - \varphi_1 pq F(q) \tag{44}$$

$$\pi_M(w, p_m) = (w - c_m)q + (1 - \varphi_1)p[q + \int_0^q tf(t)dt - qF(q)]$$
$$+ (\Delta - p_m)(a + bp_{3r}) - (1 - \varphi_2)p_{3r}(a + bp_{3r}) \tag{45}$$

$$\pi_{3r}(p_{3r}) = (p_m - \varphi_2 p_{3r})(a + bp_{3r}) \tag{46}$$

Proposition 4 can be obtained.

Proposition 4. In the RS&CS contracts, namely, the CS contract (p_m^R, φ_2) and the RS contract (w^R, φ_1), the manufacturer's transfer price is $p_m^R = \varphi_2 \Delta$, and the whole-sale price is $w^R = \begin{cases} \frac{\varphi_1(1-\lambda)c_m}{1-\eta}, & c_m \leq (1-\eta)p \\ \varphi_1(p - \frac{\lambda}{\eta}(p - c_m)), & c_m > (1-\eta)p \end{cases}$. The third-party collector's profit is $\pi_{3r}^R = \frac{(a+b\Delta)^2\varphi_2}{4b}$. The retailer's expected profit is $E[\pi_R^R] = (\varphi_1 p - w^R)q^R + \varphi_1 p \int_0^{q^R} tf(t)dt - \varphi_1 pq^R F(q^R)$. The manufacturer's profit is $\pi_M^R = (w^R - c_m)q^R + (1 - \varphi_1)p[q^R + \int_0^{q^R} tf(t)dt - q^R F(q^R)] + \frac{(1-\varphi_2)(a+b\Delta)^2}{4b}$. And when $\pi_{3r}^R \geq \pi_{3r}^D$ (i.e., $1 > \varphi_2 \geq 0.25$), $E[\pi_R^R] \geq E[\pi_R^D]$ and $\pi_M^R \geq \pi_M^D$, the CLSC achieves the coordinated state.

Proof. Taking the derivative of (46) for p_{3r} and making its derivative equal to 0, we get $p_{3r}^R = \frac{bp_m - a\varphi_2}{2b\varphi_2}$. To make the SC coordination, $p_{3r}^R = p_{3r}^C = \frac{b\Delta - a}{2b}$ must be made. So

$p_m^R = \varphi_2 \Delta$. Substitute p_{3r}^R and p_m^R into (46) to obtain the third-party collector's profit $\pi_{3r}^R = \frac{(a+b\Delta)^2 \varphi_2}{4b}$.

Be similar the proof of Proposition 1, the retailer's optimal order quantity under the RS contract based on the M-CVaR criterion is $q^R = $
$$\begin{cases} F^{-1}(1 - \frac{1-\eta}{1-\lambda} \frac{w}{\varphi_1 p}), w \le \varphi_1 p(1-\lambda) \\ F^{-1}(\frac{\eta}{\lambda} \frac{\varphi_1 p - w}{\varphi_1 p}), w > \varphi_1 p(1-\lambda) \end{cases}$$
. To coordinate the SC, q^R must be equal to q^C under the risk-neutrality condition, that is $q^R = q^C = F^{-1}(\frac{p-c_m}{p})$. Therefore, when $w \le \varphi_1 p(1-\lambda)$, $F^{-1}(1 - \frac{1-\eta}{1-\lambda} \frac{w}{\varphi_1 p}) = F^{-1}(\frac{p-c_m}{p})$. We get $w^R = \frac{\varphi_1(1-\lambda)c_m}{1-\eta}$. For $w^R \le \varphi_1 p(1-\lambda)$ to be true, $c_m \le (1-\eta)p$ has to be guaranteed. When $w \le \varphi_1 p(1-\lambda)$, $F^{-1}(\frac{\eta}{\lambda} \frac{\varphi_1 p - w}{\varphi_1 p}) = F^{-1}(\frac{p-c_m}{p})$. We get $w^R = \varphi_1(p - \frac{\lambda}{\eta}(p - c_m))$. For $w^R > \varphi_1 p(1-\lambda)$ to be true, $c_m > (1-\eta)p$ has to be guaranteed.

Substituting q^R, w^R and p_m^R into (44) and (45) yields π_R^R and π_M^R. The CLSC would reach a coordinated state when φ_1 and φ_2 take suitable values such that $\pi_{3r}^R \ge \pi_{3r}^D$ (i.e., $1 > \varphi_2 \ge 0.25$), $E[\pi_R^R] \ge E[\pi_R^D]$ and $\pi_M^R \ge \pi_M^D$.

Due to $p_{3r}^R > p_{3r}^D$, the acquisition volume of third-party collectors in the coordinated state is greater than that in the DD state.

5 Numerical Examples

In this section, we investigate the effects of decision makers' risk-averse coefficient η and pessimistic coefficient λ on the optimal order quantity, wholesale price, and expected profit of CLSC members under CD and DD conditions, as well as the effects of these two coefficients on CLSC coordination through numerical simulation.

Referring to Chen et al. (2017), the market demand faced by decision-makers obeys a uniform distribution of [200,2000], and the other SC parameters are set as $p = 15$, $c_m = 7$, $c_r = 2$, $a = 100$, $b = 100$. D and C in brackets in Figs. 2, 3, 5, 6, 8, 9, 11 and 12 represent DD and CD decisions, respectively.

5.1 Effects of the Risk-Averse and Pessimistic Coefficients on Optimal Order Quantity

$q^D(q^C)$, w^*, and expected profit are obtained by substituting each parameter into each optimal solution under DD and CD when η and λ vary in the range of (0,1). The effects of η and λ on $q^D(q^C)$ under DD and CD are shown in Fig. 2 and Fig. 3, respectively. Figure 4 represents the effects of η and λ on $q^D(q^C)$ when they are varied simultaneously.

$q^D(q^C)$ increases with the increase of η in Fig. 2. The primary reason is that an increase in η implies a reduction in risk aversion, and when η increases further, with a constant λ, the decision maker's risk preference shifts from risk aversion to risk-taking. As a result, the decision maker will increase his/her order quantity. Specifically, under the DD, the retailer will leave the market since he/she cannot benefit from the SC when λ is little (e.g., $\lambda = 0.2$) and η is large (e.g., $\eta > 0.4$). In addition, q^C is larger than q^D for the same pessimistic coefficient.

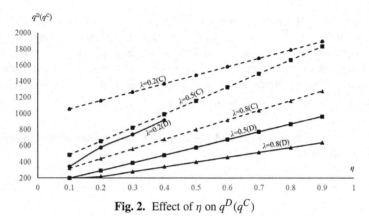

Fig. 2. Effect of η on $q^D(q^C)$

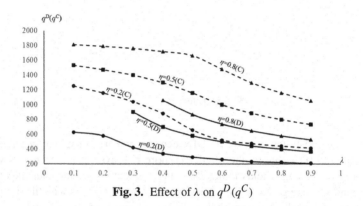

Fig. 3. Effect of λ on $q^D(q^C)$

The optimal order quantity under both decentralized and centralized CLSCs decreases with the increase of λ in Fig. 3. Under the same risk-averse coefficient, q^C is always larger than q^D. However, under the DD condition, when η takes a large value and λ is small, the retailer's risk-taking level is high and he/she at this time will exit the market.

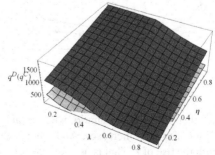

Fig. 4. Effect of simultaneous changes in λ and η on $q^D(q^C)$

In Fig. 4, the light-colored graph at the bottom represents the effects of concurrent changes in λ and η on q^D, and the dark-colored graph at the top represents the effects of concurrent changes in λ and η on q^C. From the graph, it is clear that the smaller (bigger) the λ and the larger (smaller) the η, the bigger (smaller) the $q^D(q^C)$. That is, the higher the risk-taking level, the more the $q^D(q^C)$, and the higher the risk-averse level, the less the $q^D(q^C)$. q^C is always larger than q^D.

5.2 Effects of the Risk-Averse and Pessimistic Coefficients on the Optimal Wholesale Price

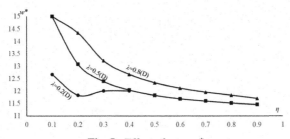

Fig. 5. Effect of η on w^*

Figure 5 demonstrates that, in the DD scenario, when λ takes larger values (e.g., $\lambda = 0.5$ and $\lambda = 0.8$), that is, the retailer is more risk-averse, w^* decreases with the increase of η, decreasing quickly in the early stages and slowly in the later stages. When λ takes a small value (e.g., $\lambda = 0.2$), w^* declines first and then rises with the rise of η and finally converges, at which time w^* takes the boundary value, i.e.,$w^* = 12$, and when η increases again, the retailer will exit the market because his/her expected profit is less than zero.

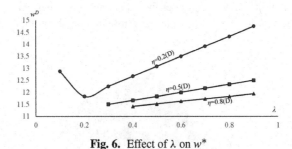

Fig. 6. Effect of λ on w^*

Figure 6 demonstrates that, in the DD scenario, when η takes larger values (e.g., $\eta = 0.5$ and $\eta = 0.8$), w^* increases as λ increases. And when η takes a small value, w^* declines and then rises with the rise of λ. That is, w^* decreases with λ when the retailer's risk-taking level is high and w^* increases with λ when the retailer's risk-taking level is low or the retailer is risk-averse.

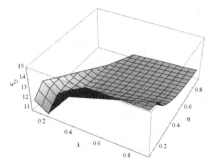

Fig. 7. Effect of simultaneous changes in λ and η on w^*

Figure 7 demonstrates the effects of simultaneous changes in λ and η on w^*. w^* is higher when λ takes a larger value and η takes a smaller value, that is, when the retailer's risk-averse level is high, the manufacturer will establish a high wholesale price. When the retailer's risk-averse level is high to a particular amount, such as $\eta = 0.1$ and $\lambda \geq 0.5$, the manufacturer's wholesale price will equal to the retail price, at which time the retailer will no further participate in the operation of the CLSC.

5.3 Effects of the Risk-Averse and Pessimistic Coefficients on the Expected Profit of Each CLSC Member

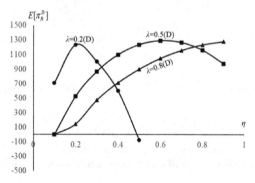

Fig. 8. Effect of η on the retailer's expected profit

Figure 8 demonstrates that when λ is larger, as η declines, the retailer's expected profit rises. In other cases, the retailer's expected profit rises and then declines as η rises. If λ is small, such as $\lambda = 0.2$, as η increases, i.e., the risk-taking degree becomes higher, the retailer's expected profit will be minus, and then the retailer will exit the market. The retailer's highest expected profit usually occurs when there is little difference between λ and η, i.e., it occurs near risk-neutral.

From Fig. 9, it is clear that as λ rises, the retailer's expected profit first rises and then falls. When η takes a moderate or big value and λ takes a small value, i.e., when

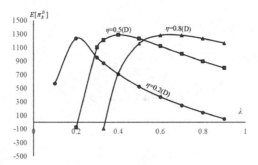

Fig. 9. Effect of λ on the retailer's expected profit

the retailer's risk-taking level is high, the retailer's expected profit will have a negative value.

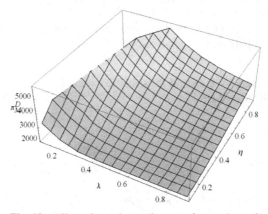

Fig. 10. Effect of λ and η on the manufacturer's profit

Figure 10 tells us that the manufacturer's profit declines with a rise in λ and rises with a rise in η in the scenario of the retailer entering the market. The manufacturer's profit rises with the retailer's level of risk-taking, while it declines with the retailer's risk aversion level.

Figure 11 demonstrates that with the retailer's entry into the market, the CLSC's expected profit rises with the rise of η under the DD condition. The expected profit of the CLSC rises and then drops as η rises under the CD condition. The CLSC's expected profit is at its highest when the decision-maker is risk-neutral under CD condition. The centralized CLSC's expected profit is not always greater than that of the decentralized CLSC. When λ is moderate or small and η is large, i.e., the decision-maker's risk-taking is strong, the CLSC's expected profit under the CD condition will be lower than that under the DD condition. This characteristic is primarily brought on by the decision-maker's risk attributes. However, the centralized CLSC's expected profit with risk neutrality is always higher than that of the decentralized CLSC with risk preference.

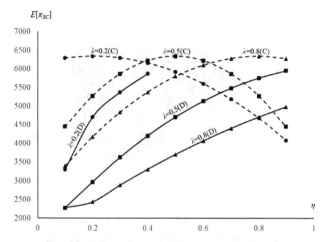

Fig. 11. Effect of η on the CLSC's expected profit

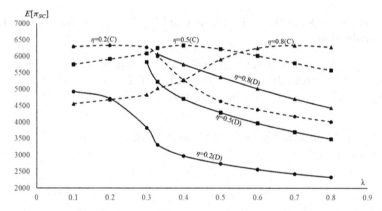

Fig. 12. Effect of λ on the CLSC's expected profit

Figure 12 illustrates how, in the DD state with the retailer entering the market, the CLSC's expected profit falls as the increase in λ. The CLSC's expected profit under the CD condition first rises and then falls as λ rises. The CLSC's expected profit is maximum when the decision-maker is risk neutral under the CD condition. When η has a larger value (e.g., $\eta=0.8$) and λ has a smaller value, i.e., the decision maker has a higher risk-taking degree, the CLSC's expected profit under the CD condition will be lower than that under the DD condition. From Fig. 12, it's also evident that the CLSC's expected profit with risk preference under the DD condition is always smaller than that under the CD condition with risk neutrality.

In Fig. 13, the light-colored graph depicts the CLSC's expected profit under the DD condition and the dark-colored graph depicts the CLSC's expected profit under the CD condition. When η takes a larger value and λ takes a smaller value, i.e., the decision

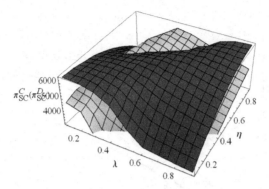

Fig. 13. Effect of λ and η on the CLSC's expected profit

maker has a higher risk-taking degree, the expected profit of the CLSC under the CD condition will be less than that under the DD condition.

5.4 Effects of the Risk-Averse Coefficient and Pessimistic Coefficient on CLSC Coordination

This section examines how η and λ affect CLSC coordination. The values of λ are 0.3, 0.5, 0.7, and 0.9 respectively, and the values of η are 0.2, 0.4, 0.6, and 0.8 respectively. The ranges of φ_1 and φ_2 for different λ and η are displayed in Table 1.

Table 1. The ranges of φ_1 and φ_2 for different λ and η

λ	η			
	0.3	0.5	0.7	0.9
0.2	$1 > \varphi_1 \geq 0.235$ $1 > \varphi_2 \geq 0.25$ $4.756\varphi_1 + \varphi_2 \leq 2.433$	$1 > \varphi_1 > 0$ $1 > \varphi_2 \geq 0.25$ $0.631\varphi_1 + \varphi_2 \leq 0.433$	-	-
0.4	$1 > \varphi_1 \geq 0.159$ $1 > \varphi_2 \geq 0.25$ $7.333\varphi_1 + \varphi_2 \leq 4.732$	$1 > \varphi_1 \geq 0.339$ $1 > \varphi_2 \geq 0.25$ $4.24\varphi_1 + \varphi_2 \leq 3.521$	$1 > \varphi_1 \geq 0.705$ $1 > \varphi_2 \geq 0.25$ $1.626\varphi_1 + \varphi_2 \leq 1.869$	$1 > \varphi_1 \geq 0.989$ $1 > \varphi_2 \geq 0.25$ $0.316\varphi_1 + \varphi_2 \leq 0.814$
0.6	$1 > \varphi_1 \geq 0.0798$ $1 > \varphi_2 \geq 0.25$ $9.911\varphi_1 + \varphi_2 \leq 4.403$	$1 > \varphi_1 \geq 0.159$ $1 > \varphi_2 \geq 0.25$ $7.849\varphi_1 + \varphi_2 \leq 3.767$	$1 > \varphi_1 \geq 0.313$ $1 > \varphi_2 \geq 0.25$ $4.571\varphi_1 + \varphi_2 \leq 3.088$	$1 > \varphi_1 \geq 0.521$ $1 > \varphi_2 \geq 0.25$ $2.608\varphi_1 + \varphi_2 \leq 2.393$
0.8	$1 > \varphi_1 \geq 0.0419$ $1 > \varphi_2 \geq 0.25$ $12.49\varphi_1 + \varphi_2 \leq 0.369$	$1 > \varphi_1 \geq 0.087$ $1 > \varphi_2 \geq 0.25$ $2.745\varphi_1 + \varphi_2 \leq 4.174$	$1 > \varphi_1 \geq 0.171$ $1 > \varphi_2 \geq 0.25$ $7.518\varphi_1 + \varphi_2 \leq 3.683$	$1 > \varphi_1 \geq 0.29$ $1 > \varphi_2 \geq 0.25$ $4.899\varphi_1 + \varphi_2 \leq 3.173$

The values of φ_1 and φ_2 are available in the range of $(0,1)$ as shown in Table 1, with the exception of when η takes larger values and λ takes smaller values, which is consistent with the traditional SC coordination. However, when η takes a large value and λ takes a small value, such as $\lambda = 0.2$, $\eta = 0.7$ and $\lambda = 0.2$, $\eta = 0.9$, the retailer's risk-taking level is high, and the expected profit under the DD looks to be negative, and the retailer will leave the market, thus the coordination strategy does not exist. The values of φ_1, φ_2 in the coordination process depend on the bargaining ability of the three members of CLSC.

6 Conclusion

This paper examined the ordering, pricing, and coordination strategies of the CLSC using the M-CVaR criterion to assess the retailer's risk preference. We also analyzed the effects of the risk-averse and pessimistic coefficients on the ordering, pricing, expected profit, and the coordination of CLSC. The work has contributed to the literature on CLSC management as: first, we proved that there is a unique optimal ordering and pricing strategy for both decentralized and centralized CLSCs involving a risk-preference retailer under the M-CVaR measure. Second, we found that risk preference strongly affects the ordering strategy, the pricing strategy, and the expected profits. The order quantity depends on how risk-averse or risk-taking the decision maker is. That is, the optimal order quantity rises as the risk-averse coefficient rises and falls as the pessimistic coefficient rises. The optimal order quantity under the CD is always higher than that under the DD. The more risk-averse the retailer, the higher the manufacturer's wholesale price. The retailer's greatest expected profit generally occurs close to his/her risk-neutrality in a DD system and the retailer's high level of risk-taking will benefit the manufacturer and the entire SC. With risk preference, the centralized CLSC's expected profit isn't always higher than the decentralized CLSC's. However, the centralized CLSC with risk neutrality is projected to make a higher profit than the decentralized CLSC, which is always the truth. Additionally, the retailer's enhanced risk-taking and risk aversion may both result in his/her exiting the market under the DD scenario. Finally, we develop a RS&CS contract which can coordinate the decentralized CLSC with risk preference to reach the expected profit of the centralized CLSC with risk-neutrality, with the exception of the retailer's withdrawal from the market as a result of his/her high risk-taking degree. Accordingly, the acquisition quantity of used products will increase under the coordinated condition, bringing greater reverse and environmental benefits.

The relevance to CLSC companies is that the wholesale price and the optimal order quantity will be significantly impacted by the retailer's risk attitude. Therefore, members of a CLSC must take the retailer's risk attitude into account. The retailer will gain the most by keeping his/her risk preference around risk-neutrality. Too much risk-taking will result in large losses for the retailer, while too much risk aversion may not bring profit. The manufacturer, on the other hand, prefers a risk-taking retailer, which will result in great profit for him/her and the entire SC, but in the case of an extremely risk-taking or risk-averse retailer, reduce wholesale price appropriately to make the retailer profitable and thus promote SC stability. All members should actively facilitate a coordinated contract for greater profitability.

Our analysis also might have some limitations. We considered the quantity of used products to be deterministic and correlated with the acquisition price. The likelihood of a random quantity of used products is very high, making it possible to further study the problem of a CLSC with risk preference in the scenario of a random demand for new items and a random quantity of old products. We just took the retailer's risk preference characteristics into consideration. This study can further address the issue of CLSC decision-making and coordination when all members have risk preferences by assuming that all SC members have risk preferences.

Acknowledgments. We are grateful for the Open Fund Project for Nanjing Institute of Technology (JGKB202003), the Research Project for Nanjing Institute of Technology (YKJ201923) and the Research Project for China Society of Logistics (2022CSLKT3–385).

References

Alexander, G.J., Baptista, A.M.: A comparison of VaR and CVaR constraints on portfolio selection with the mean-variance model. Manage. Sci. **50**(9), 1261–1273 (2004)

Artzner, P., Delbaen, F., Eber, J., Heath, D.: Coherent measures of risk. Math. Financ. **9**(3), 203–228 (1999)

Bostian, A.A., Holt, C.A., Smith, A.M.: Newsvendor "pull-to-center" effect: adaptive learning in a laboratory experiment. Manuf. Serv. Oper. Manag. **10**(4), 590–608 (2008)

Cai, S., Sun, J.: The supply chain option contract coordination model with bilateral risk preferences. J. Indus. Eng. Manage. **34**(6), 128–137 (2020)

Chen, Y., Xiong, L., Dong, J.: Closed-loop supply chain coordination mechanism based on mean-CVaR. Chinese J. Manage. Sci. **25**(2), 68–77 (2017)

Chuang, C., Wang, C.X., Zhao, Y.: Closed-loop supply chain models for a high-tech product under alternative reverse channel and collection cost structures. Int. J. Prod. Econ. **156**, 108–123 (2014)

Das, D., Verma, P., Tanksale, A.N.: Designing a closed-loop supply chain for reusable packaging materials: a risk-averse two-stage stochastic programming model using CVaR. Comput. Ind. Eng. **167**, 108004 (2022)

Ebrahimi, S.B., Bagheri, E.: A multi-objective formulation for the closed-loop plastic supply chain under uncertainty, Operational Research. 1–44 (2022)

Eskandarzadeh, S., Eshghi, K., Bahramgiri, M.: Risk shaping in production planning problem with pricing under random yield. Eur. J. Oper. Res. **253**(1), 108–120 (2016)

Fan, Y., Feng, Y., Shou, Y.: A risk-averse and buyer-led supply chain under option contract: CVaR minimization and channel coordination. Int. J. Prod. Econ. **219**, 66–81 (2020)

Feng, B., Yao, T., Jiang, B.: Analysis of the market-based adjustable outsourcing contract under uncertainties. Prod. Oper. Manag. **22**(1), 178–188 (2013)

Ferguson, M., Guide, V.D.R., Souza, G.C.: Supply chain coordination for false failure returns. Manuf. Serv. Oper. Manag. **8**(4), 376–393 (2006)

Golpîra, H., Javanmardan, A.: Decentralized decision system for closed-loop supply chain: a bi-level multi-objective risk-based robust optimization approach. Comput. Chem. Eng. **154**, 107472 (2021)

Golpîra, H., Javanmardan, A.: Robust optimization of sustainable closed-loop supply chain considering carbon emission schemes. Sustainable Production and Consumption **30**, 640–656 (2022)

Gong, H., Zhang, Z.: Benders decomposition for the distributionally robust optimization of pricing and reverse logistics network design in remanufacturing systems. Eur. J. Oper. Res. **297**(2), 496–510 (2022)

Jammernegg, W., Kischka, P.: Risk-averse and risk-taking newsvendors: a conditional expected value approach. RMS **1**(1), 93–110 (2007)

Jammernegg, W., Kischka, P.: Risk preferences and robust inventory decisions. Int. J. Prod. Econ. **118**(1), 269–274 (2009)

Karakayali, I., Emir Farinas, H., Akcali, E.: An analysis of decentralized collection and processing of end-of-life products. J. Oper. Manag. **25**(6), 1161–1183 (2007)

Ke, H., Wu, Y., Huang, H.: Competitive pricing and remanufacturing problem in an uncertain closed-loop supply chain with risk-sensitive retailers. Asia-Pacific J. Oper. Res. **35**(1), 1850003 (2018)

Kouvelis, P., Li, R., Ding, Q.: Managing storable commodity risks: the role of inventory and financial hedge. Manuf. Serv. Oper. Manag. **15**(3), 507–521 (2013)

Li, B., Hou, P., Chen, P., Li, Q.: Pricing strategy and coordination in a dual channel supply chain with a risk-averse retailer. Int. J. Prod. Econ. **178**, 154–168 (2016)

Li, Y., Ou, J.: Replenishment decisions for complementary components with supply capacity uncertainty under the CVaR criterion. Eur. J. Oper. Res. **297**(3), 904–916 (2022)

Liu, Z., Chen, J., Diallo, C., Venkatadri, U.: Pricing and production decisions in a dual-channel closed-loop supply chain with (re)manufacturing. Int. J. Prod. Econ. **232**, 107935 (2021)

Lu, R., & Li, N.: Take-back channel selection of closed-loop supply chain for an electronic product. Systems Engineering — Theory & Practice, 36(7), 1687–1695 (2016)

Rockafellar, R.T., Uryasev, S.: Conditional value-at-risk for general loss distributions. J. Bank. Finance **26**(7), 1443–1471 (2002)

Sarkar, S., Bhala, S.: Coordinating a closed loop supply chain with fairness concern by a constant wholesale price contract. Eur. J. Oper. Res. **295**(1), 140–156 (2021)

Savaskan, R.C., Bhattacharya, S., Van Wassenhove, L.N.: Closed-loop supply chain models with product remanufacturing. Manage. Sci. **50**(2), 239–252 (2004)

Savaskan, R.C., Van Wassenhove, L.N.: Reverse channel design: the case of competing retailers. Manage. Sci. **52**(1), 1–14 (2006)

Shen, H., Pang, Z., Cheng, T.C.E.: The component procurement problem for the loss-averse manufacturer with spot purchase. Int. J. Prod. Econ. **132**(1), 146–153 (2011)

Sun, H., Chen, W., Ren, Z., Liu, B.: Optimal policy in a hybrid manufacturing/remanufacturing system with financial hedging. Int. J. Prod. Res. **55**(19), 5728–5742 (2017)

Wu, M., Zhu, S.X., Teunter, R.H.: A risk-averse competitive newsvendor problem under the CVaR criterion. Int. J. Prod. Econ. **156**, 13–23 (2014)

Wu, M., Zhu, S.X., Teunter, R.H.: The risk-averse newsvendor problem with random capacity. Eur. J. Oper. Res. **231**(2), 328–336 (2013)

Xia, X., Nan, Y.: Pricing decision and financing approach selection of fund-deficient closed-loop supply chain under distributor's risk aversion. Mathematical Problems in Engineering, 1–23 (2022)

Xie, Y., Wang, H., Lu, H.: Coordination of supply chains with a retailer under the mean-CVaR criterion. IEEE Trans. Sys. Man, and Cybernetics: Systems **48**(7), 1039–1053 (2018)

Xing, E., Shi, C., Zhang, J., Cheng, S., Lin, J., Ni, S.: Double third-party recycling closed-loop supply chain decision under the perspective of carbon trading. J. Clean. Prod. **259**, 120651 (2020)

Yao, Z., Xu, X., Luan, J.: Impact of the downside risk of retailer on the supply chain coordination. Comput. Ind. Eng. **102**, 340–350 (2016)

Zhang, Q., Huang, Z., Zheng, R.: Risk-averse pricing decisions related to recyclables' quality in a closed-loop supply chain. Mathematical Problems in Engineering, 1–16 (2021)

Zhao, Y., Ma, L., Xie, G., Cheng, T.C.E.: Coordination of supply chains with bidirectional option contracts. Eur. J. Oper. Res. **229**(2), 375–381 (2013)

An Explainable Optimization Method for Assembly Process Parameter

Hongsong Peng[1](✉), Weiwei Yuan[1], Yimin Pu[2], Xiying Yang[2], Donghai Guan[1], and Ran Guo[3]

[1] College of Computer Science and Technology, Nanjing University of Aeronautics and Astronautics, Nanjing 210016, China
PengHongsong@nuaa.edu.cn
[2] Beijing Power Machinery Institute, Beijing 100074, China
[3] Cyberspace Institute Advanced Technology, Guangzhou University, Guangzhou 510006, China

Abstract. Vibration out-of-tolerance is a common condition of unqualified engine inspection, and the cause of vibration out-of-tolerance is closely related to the quality of the engine assembly. When the engine is found to vibrate out of tolerance, it needs to be reassembled. This process is very time-consuming and labor-intensive. In order to improve the assembly quality and reduce the vibration value during the engine assembly process. An explainable optimization algorithm is proposed, which combines LightGBM, SHAP and PSO. First, a vibration value prediction model is trained using the LightGBM algorithm. Second, SHAP is used to explain the vibration value prediction model, and obtain the importance order of each assembly process parameter, which is used as the subsequent optimization order. Finally, according to the optimization order, PSO algorithm is used to iteratively optimize the assembly process parameters and it uses the vibration prediction model as the fitness function. It has been verified by experiments that the optimized assembly process parameters can effectively reduce the vibration value of the engine, which has positive guiding significance for the assembly of the engine.

Keywords: explainable · SHAP · particle swarm optimization (PSO) · assembly process parameter optimization

1 Introduction

Vibration out of tolerance is one of the most common unqualified items in the engine inspection process, which is mainly caused by the imbalance of rotating parts. In addition to the amount of unbalance of the components themselves, the combination of components can lead to unbalanced rotating parts. Therefore, the quality of the engine assembly process will directly affect the overall vibration of the engine. When out-of-tolerance vibration occurs, technicians typically disassemble the engine, troubleshoot, and reassemble. This process is cumbersome, time-consuming and labor-intensive.

National Defense Basic Research Program (JCKY2020204C009).

In order to solve this problem, Shen Xianshao et al. [1] established a mapping relationship between assembly process parameters and the vibration value of the whole machine based on BP neural network, and used this to guide the assembly of the engine. However, they only predicted the assembly results of the engine through the BP neural network. And did not optimize the assembly process parameters of the engine with out-of-tolerance vibration. The optimization of assembly process parameters can give technicians some technical guidance and save a lot of time for engine assembly adjustment. Yang Aiping et al. [2] made improvements on this basis, using Pearson correlation analysis to select several assembly process parameters that are most correlated with the results, and using PSO to optimize these process parameters. But Pearson's correlation analysis is only valid when the two variables are simply linearly related. If two variables have a more complex correlation (non-simple linear correlation), the Pearson coefficient may be 0 even though they are highly correlated. Engine assembly is a complex process, the process parameters with the vibration values are not simply linearly related. The features analyzed by Pearson correlation may be very different from the real situation.

The explainable method SHAP is carried out on the model, which can solve the problem of nonlinear relationship between process parameters and vibration value. SHAP is an additive explanation model inspired by cooperative game theory. Considering all features as "contributors", the model produces a predicted value for each predicted sample. SHAP value is the value assigned to each feature in the sample, which reflects the contribution of each feature to the predictive ability of the entire model. The feature with a larger SHAP value is more important. In this paper, the vibration values are divided into three categories. The LightGBM algorithm is used to train the vibration prediction model, and SHAP is used to explain the model to obtain the contribution ranking of each feature. According to the ranking of the contribution of each feature, the heuristic optimization algorithm is used iteratively to optimize the assembly process parameters. Completed the optimization goal of "Optimal vibration values are achieved with minimal changes to process parameters".

2   Process Parameter Optimization Plan and Information Collection

2.1   Process Parameter Optimization Plan

This paper takes "to obtain the best optimization results under the premise of the minimum total optimization cost" as the optimization goal. By understanding the actual situation of the assembly workshop, it is found that each assembly process feature is optimized within the upper and lower limits given by the technical parameters of the process parameters, and the difficulty of optimization is roughly the same. The optimization objective can be translated into "to obtain the best optimization results under the premise of adjusting the minimum assembly process parameters". In order to realize the optimization goal, an iterative engine assembly process parameter optimization method is proposed. This method uses particle swarm optimization (PSO) as the core optimization algorithm of the iterative optimization method. The prediction model is trained by the LightGBM algorithm, and the model is used as the fitness function of the PSO algorithm.

The prediction model is explained by SHAP and the importance ranking of each feature is obtained. The iterative engine assembly process parameter optimization is based on the importance of each feature, and the PSO is used to optimize the assembly process parameters. One assembly process parameter is added for each optimization until the optimized vibration class reaches the optimal class, and the optimized assembly process parameters of each engine are output.

The flow of the overall plan for engine assembly process optimization is shown in, which includes the following main steps.

(1) Raw data acquisition: collect real engine assembly parameter data from the engine assembly workshop.
(2) Data preprocessing and feature selection: Check and process outliers and missing values in the original data to form a data format that can be recognized by machine learning algorithms. Combine expert knowledge and relevant methods of data selection, such as correlation analysis, F-Score method, etc. for feature selection
(3) Vibration value prediction model training: Use the LightGBM algorithm to train a vibration value prediction model.
(4) Prediction model interpretation: Use the SHAP interpretable method to explain the selected vibration value prediction model, and obtain the importance ranking of each feature.
(5) Iterative assembly process parameter optimization: At the beginning, the most important assembly process is the optimization object, and the vibration value prediction model is the fitness function, and the particle swarm algorithm is used to solve the optimal solution of the optimization object. Determine whether the vibration prediction value of the current optimal solution is qualified. If it is qualified, end the optimization and output the optimized assembly process. Otherwise, add the most important assembly process among the assembly processes of the current non-optimized object to the optimization object according to the order of importance. And re-run particle swarm optimization.

2.2 Data Collection of Engine Assembly Process Parameters

The iterative assembly process parameter optimization method uses the particle swarm optimization algorithm. The particle swarm optimization algorithm to solve the optimal process parameters depends on the vibration prediction model. The establishment of the vibration prediction model requires a training data set. In this paper, the assembly process parameter data of the engine is collected as the feature of the training data set, and the test vibration value of the engine is used as the label. At present, a total of 90 engines have been collected, and each engine has 240 assembly process data. The sample data of the test vibration value of some engines is shown in Table 1, and some assembly process data collected is shown in Table 2.

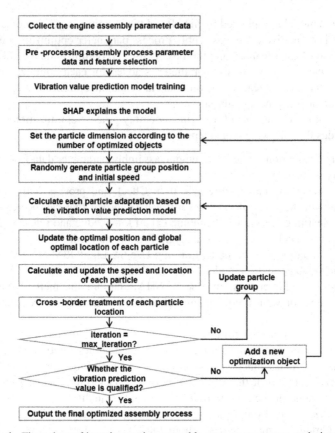

Fig. 1. Flow chart of iterative engine assembly process parameter optimization.

Table 1. Sample data of engine test run vibration values

Engine serial number	Test run vibration value/(g)	Whether the vibration is qualified	Engine serial number	Test run vibration value/(g)	Whether the vibration is qualified
1	23	NO	6	7	YES
2	12	YES	7	14	YES
3	15	YES	8	21	NO
4	4	YES	9	13	YES
5	13	YES	10	9	YES

Because the collected process parameter data is a high-dimensional and low-level feature, if all features are directly used for training, the accuracy of the trained prediction

Table 2. Part of the assembly process data collected

Engine serial number	Coaxiality of the three bearing holes/(mm)	A, B datum coaxiality/(mm)	Residual unbalance in plane I/(g·mm)	...	Great Wall Nut (left hand) tightening torque/((N·m)
1	0.046	0.0069	1.37	...	23
2	0.0399	0.012	1.54	...	12
3	0.128	0.0089	1.73	...	13
...	...	...	...	...	...
90	0.123	0.0076	0.72	...	17

model cannot meet the requirements for use. In order to improve the accuracy of model prediction, this paper combines expert knowledge and uses feature selection methods such as correlation analysis and F-Score method to perform feature selection on the collected process parameter data, and finally leaves 9 assembly processes. Because the amount of data is too small, the deviation of using the regression model is too large. In this paper, the classification model is used for training, and the vibration value of the engine is classified. Some classification results are shown in Table 3. Class 0 is the best and class 2 is the worst.

Table 3. Classification results of engine test vibration values

Engine serial number	Test run vibration value/(g)	Class (0/1/2)	Engine serial number	Test run vibration value/(g)	Class (0/1/2)
1	23	2	6	7	0
2	12	1	7	14	1
3	15	1	8	21	2
4	4	0	9	13	1
5	13	1	10	9	0

3 Vibration Prediction Model Training and Explanation

3.1 Vibration Prediction Model Training

LightGBM [3, 4] is a new classification model proposed in recent years, which is similar in principle to GBDT and XGBoost. Different from the traditional GBDT model, Light-GBM solves the problem of high time and space overhead of XGBoost from the following aspects, and accelerates the training speed of the GBDT model without compromising the accuracy.

(1) Decision tree algorithm based on Histogram.

(2) Gradient-based One-Side Sampling (GOSS): Using GOSS can reduce a large number of data instances with only small gradients, and only use data with high gradients to calculate information gain, which saves compared to XGBoost traversing all eigenvalues A lot of time and space overhead.
(3) Exclusive Feature Bundling (EFB): Using EFB, many mutually exclusive features can be bound into one feature, thus achieving the purpose of dimensionality reduction.
(4) Leaf-wise algorithm with depth limit: Leaf-wise is a more efficient strategy. From all the current leaves each time, find the one with the largest splitting gain, and then split, so cycle. Compared with the level-wise decision tree growth strategy of the traditional GBDT model, leaf-wise can reduce more errors and obtain better accuracy with the same number of splits.

In this paper, AUC is used as the evaluation index of the prediction model. Let the engine assembly process data be X (including data such as the coaxiality of each component), Y is the engine vibration value (unit is g), the data set, where. The dataset D is randomly assigned as training set and test set with a ratio of 7:3. The LightGBM algorithm is used to train the prediction model, and compared with the prediction model established by the decision tree algorithm, the random forest algorithm, the SVM algorithm, the XGBoost algorithm, and the single hidden layer neural network algorithm, all models use the Bayesian optimization algorithm to optimize the model parameters. Table 4 shows the AUC of each prediction model. From Table 4, it can be found that the AUC of the LightGBM algorithm is the highest, which is 0.895.

Table 4. Predictive model AUC trained by each algorithm

Decision tree	Random forest	SVM	LightGBM	XGBoost	Single hidden layer neural network
0.733	0.874	0.741	0.895	0.875	0.864

3.2 SHAP Explains Engine Vibration Value Prediction Model

SHAP (SHapley Additive exPlanation) [5–10] is an additive interpretation model built by Lunderg in 2017 inspired by cooperative game theory. Its core function is to calculate the SHAP value of each feature. All features are regarded as "contributors", and a prediction value is generated for each prediction sample model. SHAP value is the value assigned to each feature in the sample, reflecting the contribution of each feature to the prediction ability of the entire model. Spend. SHAP interprets the model's predictions as the sum of the attribution values (SHAP values) for each input feature, namely:

$$\widehat{y} = \vartheta_0 + \sum_{i=1}^{M} \vartheta_i \tag{1}$$

where $\widehat{y}$ is the predicted result of the model, ϑ_i is the attribution value of each feature, and ϑ_0 is the predicted mean of all training samples. This explanatory model eliminates explanatory differences caused by structural differences between models. ϑ_i in the formula is the difficulty of solving, if it is a linear model,

$$\widehat{f}(x) = \beta_0 + \beta_1 x_1 + \dots + \beta_M x_M \tag{2}$$

where β is the feature weight, and the prediction contribution of the i-th feature is defined as

$$\vartheta_i = \beta_i x_i - E(\beta_i X_i) = \beta_i x_i - \beta_i E(X_i) \tag{3}$$

where $E(\beta_j X_j)$ is the average impact estimate of feature j. Adding the contributions of all features of a sample, then:

$$\begin{aligned}
\sum_{i=1}^{M} \vartheta_i &= \sum_{i=1}^{M} (\beta_i x_i - E(\beta_i X_i)) \\
&= (\beta_0 + \sum_{i=1}^{M} \beta_i x_i) - (\beta_0 + \sum_{i=1}^{M} E(\beta_i X_i)) \\
&= \widehat{f}(x) - E(\widehat{f}(X))
\end{aligned} \tag{4}$$

That is to say, when the model is a linear model and the features are independent of each other, the sum of all feature contributions of the sample x is equal to the predicted value minus the average predicted value.

Through the SHAP explainable model, we will finally obtain the contribution of each feature of each sample. If a feature shows a consistent trend in most samples, then the additive model considers that the feature has an important positive or positive effect on the model's prediction. Negative effect.

The SHAP explainable method provides extremely powerful data visualization capabilities, which can well display the interpretation results of the model. Figure 2 shows the feature SHAP value of each sample, which plots the SHAP value of all its features for each sample, which reflects the positive and negative effects of each input feature on the model prediction. For example, the larger the value of feature ID223, the larger the predicted vibration value.

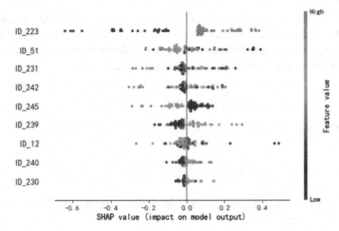

Fig. 2. The characteristic SHAP value of each sample.

SHAP can obtain the average contribution of each feature to the predicted vibration value by adding the SHAP value of each feature of each sample. The larger the average contribution, the greater the importance of the feature. The ranking of the average contribution of each feature is shown in. Feature ID223 has the greatest contribution to the predicted vibration value and is also the most important, followed by feature ID51.

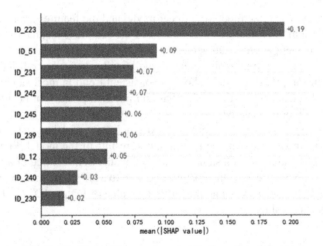

Fig. 3. Ranking of the average contribution of each feature.

The average contribution ranking of each feature is taken as the importance ranking of features. Through communication with technicians, it is confirmed that the feature importance ranking given by SHAP is consistent with the design scheme of actual engine assembly and the assembly experience of the assembly personnel. In general, the feature importance ranking obtained by SHAP is reliable. And the method of using the ranking to guide the optimization of engine assembly process parameters is also reliable.

4   Assembly Process Parameter Optimization Results

The optimization algorithm used in this paper for the optimization of engine assembly process parameters is PSO. PSO [11, 12] is a population-based stochastic optimization algorithm inspired by the predation action of flocks of birds. In the PSO algorithm, each possible solution in the solution space is imagined as a bird, called a "particle". At the beginning of the algorithm, a group of solutions is randomly generated in the solution space, called a "particle swarm", and each particle is A search entity whose current position is a candidate solution to the optimization problem. The flying speed of the particle is dynamically adjusted according to its current speed, the historical optimal position of the particle and the optimal position of all particles in the particle swarm. The particle swarm updates the speed and position of particles through continuous iteration. The update formula is as follows:

$$V_{id}(t+1) = wV_{id}(t) + C_1 * rand(0, 1) * (P_{id} - X_{id}) + C_2 * rand(0, 1) * (P_{gd} - X_{id})$$
(5)

$$X_{id}(t+1) = X_{id}(t) + V(t+1)$$
(6)

where V_{id} is the particle velocity, t is the number of iterations, w is the inertia weighting factor, P_{id} is the historical best position of the particle, P_{gd} is the best position of all particles in the particle swarm, X_{id} is the current position of the particle, and $C_1 \geq 0, C_2 \geq 0$ is the learning factor, indicating that the particle is affected by the historical best position and the degree of influence of the optimal position of the population.

In this paper, iteratively optimizes the assembly process parameters of engines with non-optimal vibration class. According to expert knowledge and process design, some assembly process parameters are not independent of each other. When one assembly process parameter of this type is adjusted in the iterative optimization process, another associated process parameter is also changed. According to the expert's engineering experience analysis of the engine assembly process. The relevant parameters of the assembly process parameters used by the vibration prediction model are: ID230 and ID231, ID239 and ID240. There is a linear relationship between the two sets of related features. In this paper, a linear regression function is used to fit the mapping relationship between them, and in the iterative process of optimization, only the most important assembly process features in the two groups are put into the optimization object. The eigenvalues with small importance in the medium and small change accordingly, and the changing values are obtained from the mapping relationship. The linear mapping relationship between ID230 and ID231, ID239 and ID240 is.

$$ID230 = 0.163 * ID231 + 0.898$$
(7)

$$ID240 = 0.141 * ID239 + 0.97$$
(8)

The solution of the particle swarm optimization algorithm contains all real numbers in the solution space. However, some solutions cannot be realized in the actual assembly process due to problems such as the accuracy of the test instrument during the assembly process. This part of the solution needs to be processed with precision to make it practical. In this paper, the rounding method is used for precision processing, and the precision of each assembly process parameter is shown in Table 5.

Table 5. Precision of each assembly process parameter

Assembly process parameter	Process accuracy	Assembly process parameter	Process accuracy
ID12	0.001	ID239	0.01
ID51	0.0005	ID240	0.01
ID223	1	ID242	0.01
ID230	0.01	ID245	0.001
ID231	0.01		

In the iterative optimization process, the initial dimension of each generation of particle swarm optimization algorithm is the number of optimization objects, and the initial population is the process parameter value of the optimization object; the vibration value prediction model trained by the LighttGBM algorithm is a classification model. In order to better adapt to the movement of particles, the classification probability of the optimal class predicted by the vibration value prediction model is used as the fitness function; the optimization goal is to reduce the vibration value of the engine (that is, to maximize the classification probability of the optimal class). The parameter settings of the particle swarm optimization algorithm are shown in Table 6. The technical indicators of each assembly process feature are used as the constraint conditions for particle movement. The technical indicators of each assembly process feature are shown in Table 7.

Table 6. Parameter setting of particle swarm optimization algorithm

Parameter	Parameter value
Dim	Number of optimization objects
Pn	30
C1,C2	2,2
W	0.6
generation	500

Table 7. Technical indicators of assembly process characteristics

Assembly process parameter	Technical indicators		
	upper limit	lower limit	unit
ID12	-0.01	0.01	mm
ID51	0	0.01	mm
ID223	55	75	N·m
ID230	0	2	g·mm
ID231	0	2	g·mm
ID239	0	2	g·mm
ID240	0	2	g·mm
ID242	0	2	g·mm
ID245	0.005	0.06	mm

The engine assembly process parameters with vibration classes divided into 1 and 2 are optimized respectively.Due for space reasons, this paper shows the specific optimization process of the assembly process parameters of an engine with vibration classes 1 and 2 respectively. The optimization process is shown in

Engine initial data with vibration class 1

ID_223	ID_51	ID_231	ID_242	ID_245	ID_239	ID_12	ID_240	ID_230	Vibration class
75	0.0085	1.05	0.83	0.01	0.96	0	0.48	0.85	1

optimization process:

For the first generation, only feature ID_223 is optimized, and the engine data after PSO optimization is:

ID_223	ID_51	ID_231	ID_242	ID_245	ID_239	ID_12	ID_240	ID_230	Vibration class
55	0.0085	1.05	0.83	0.01	0.96	0	0.48	0.85	1

The second generation, optimized features ID_223, ID_242,and the engine data after PSO optimization is:

ID_223	ID_51	ID_231	ID_242	ID_245	ID_239	ID_12	ID_240	ID_230	Vibration class
55	0.0005	1.05	0.83	0.01	0.96	0	0.48	0.85	1

The third generation, optimized features ID_223, ID_242,ID_231,and the engine data after PSO optimization is:

ID_223	ID_51	ID_231	ID_242	ID_245	ID_239	ID_12	ID_240	ID_230	Vibration class
55	0.0005	1.96	0.83	0.01	0.96	0	0.48	0.85	0

After optimization, the predicted vibration class is 0 (optimal class), the optimization is over, and the optimization results of the last generation are output.

Fig. 4. Specific optimization process of engine assembly process parameters with vibration class 1.

Table 8 and Table 9 show the optimization results of some engine assembly process parameters with vibration classes 1 and 2, and compared with the method of Yang Aiping et al.(PEARSON + PSO).

Engine initial data with vibration class 2

ID_223	ID_51	ID_231	ID_242	ID_245	ID_239	ID_12	ID_240	ID_230	Vibration class
75	0.0045	0.58	1.76	0.02	1.8	0.03	1.22	1.3	2

optimization process:

For the first generation, only feature ID_223 is optimized, and the engine data after PSO optimization is:

ID_223	ID_51	ID_231	ID_242	ID_245	ID_239	ID_12	ID_240	ID_230	Vibration class
55	0.0045	0.58	1.76	0.02	1.8	0.03	1.22	1.3	1

The second generation, optimized features ID_223, ID_242, and the engine data after PSO optimization is:

ID_223	ID_51	ID_231	ID_242	ID_245	ID_239	ID_12	ID_240	ID_230	Vibration class
55	0.0015	0.58	1.76	0.02	1.8	0.03	1.22	1.3	1

The third generation, optimized features ID_223, ID_242, ID_231, and the engine data after PSO optimization is:

ID_223	ID_51	ID_231	ID_242	ID_245	ID_239	ID_12	ID_240	ID_230	Vibration class
55	0.0050	1.98	1.76	0.02	1.8	0.03	1.22	1.3	0

After optimization, the predicted vibration class is 0 (optimal class), the optimization is over, and the optimization results of the last generation are output.

Fig. 5. Specific optimization process of engine assembly process parameters with vibration class 2.

Table 8. Engine optimization results with vibration class 1

Engine serial number with vibration class 1	SHAP + PSO		PEARSON + PSO	
	Number of adjusted process parameters	Optimized vibration class	Number of adjusted process parameters	Optimized vibration class
1	1	0	2	0
2	2	0	4	0
3	1	0	1	0
4	2	0	4	0
...	...	...	...	...
84	4	0	4	0
86	2	0	3	0
Average	2.81	0	3.36	0

Through experimental comparison, it can be seen that the feature importance ranking obtained by SHAP is more reliable than Pearson correlation analysis. And from Table 8 and Table 9, it can be seen that the average number of optimized processes for the engine with vibration class 2 is less than that of the engine with vibration class 1. Starting from the two directions of data and engineering experience, it is found that the assembly process of ID223 is particularly important. In terms of data, it is found that when the process is controlled to 55, there is an 85% probability that the engine vibration is less than 2. In terms of engineering experience, when the feature is 55, the vibration value will be greatly reduced. This is consistent with the SHAP's explanation of feature ID223. ID223 is the first feature to be optimized. After optimization, the engine with vibration class of 2 has a high probability of getting a better result, while the engine with feature class of 1 has mostly reached the optimal value.

Table 9. Engine optimization results with vibration class 2

Engine serial number with vibration class 2	SHAP + PSO		PEARSON + PSO	
	Number of adjusted process parameters	Optimized vibration class	Number of adjusted process parameters	Optimized vibration class
30	2	0	3	0
36	1	0	4	0
40	2	0	4	0
41	3	0	4	0
...	...	...	...	...
89	5	0	4	0
90	1	0	2	0
Average	2.43	0	3.4	0

5 Conclusion

By integrating LightGBM, SHAP and the particle swarm optimization algorithm (PSO), this paper proposes an iterative engine assembly process parameter optimization method. Different from Yang Aiping's parameter optimization method, this paper uses SHAP to obtain important assembly process parameters, avoiding the drawback that Pearson correlation analysis is only effective for simple linear relationships. Through the iterative optimization method, the solution with the least optimization cost is found, which further saves the assembly adjustment time of the assembly workers. The rationality and effectiveness of this method are also verified by the actual assembly test.

References

1. Shen, X., Fan, Q., Bai, S., Ai, Y.: Research on the influence of aero-engine assembly parameters on the vibration of the whole machine based on BP neural network. Aviation Maintenance & Engineering (01), 70–73 (2012)
2. Yang, A., et al.: Optimization of engine assembly process parameters based on neural network and PSO algorithm. Modern Manufacturing Engineering (02), 105–113 (2022)
3. Kim, J.Y., Lee, H.S., Oh, J.S.: Study on prediction of ship's power using light GBM and XGBoost. J. Adv. Marine Eng. Technol. **44**(2), 174–180 (2020)
4. Chen, X., Liu, Y., Li, Q., Li, W., Liu, Z., Guo, W.: Short-term photovoltaic power prediction based on LGBM-XGBoost. In: 2022 5th Asia Conference on Energy and Electrical Engineering (ACEEE), pp. 12–17. IEEE. (2022, July)
5. Liao, B., Wang, Z.,, Li, M., Sun, R.: XGBoost and SHAP model for football player value prediction and feature analysis. Computer Science (2022-04-13). Forthcoming
6. Xinnan, L., Lefan, L., Binqing, X., Honghai, Y.: Reexploring the default characteristics of small and micro enterprises: a machine learning model based on SHAP interpretation method. Chinese Journal of Management Science (2022-03-21). Forthcoming

7. Chen, X.K., Zuo, H.X., Liao, B., Sun, R.N.: Prediction and characteristic analysis model of coronary heart disease based on XGBoost and SHAP. Journal of Computer Applications (06) (2022)

8. Van den Broeck, G., Lykov, A., Schleich, M., Suciu, D.: On the tractability of SHAP explanations. Journal of Artificial Intelligence Research **74**, 851–886 (2022)

9. Liu, Y., Liu, Z., Luo, X., Zhao, H.: Diagnosis of Parkinson's disease based on SHAP value feature selection. Biocybernetics and Biomedical Engineering **42**(3), 856–869 (2022)

10. Lee, Y.G., Oh, J.Y., Kim, D., et al.: SHAP value-based feature importance analysis for short-term load forecasting. J. Electr. Eng. Technol. (2022)

11. Huang, J., He, L.: Application of improved PSO-BP neural network in customer churn warning. Procedia Computer Scoence **131**, 1238–1246 (2018)

12. Yand, W., Li, Q.: A survey of particle swarm optimization algorithms. Engineering Science **5**, 87–94 (2004)

A Correlational Strategy for the Prediction of High-Dimensional Stock Data by Neural Networks and Technical Indicators

Jingwei Hong[1,2] (ID), Ping Han[2], Abdur Rasool[2(✉)] (ID), Hui Chen[3,4],
Zhiling Hong[5], Zhong Tan[6], Fan Lin[6], Steven X. Wei[7],
and Qingshan Jiang[2(✉)] (ID)

[1] College of Mathematics and Information Science, Hebei University,
Baoding 071002, China
[2] Shenzhen Key Laboratory for High Performance Data Mining, Shenzhen Institute
of Advanced Technology, Chinese Academy of Sciences, Shenzhen 518055, China
{rasool,qs.jiang}@siat.ac.cn
[3] Shenzhen Polytechnic, Shenzhen 518055, Guangdong, China
[4] Institute of Applied Mathematics, Hebei Academy of Science, Hebei 050081, China
[5] Quanzhou Financial Holding Group Co. Ltd., Guangzhou, China
[6] Xiamen University, Xiamen 361005, China
[7] Hong Kong Polytechnic University, Hong Kong, China

Abstract. Stock price prediction generates interesting outputs for investors. In recent years, stock technical indicators (STI) have played an important role in stock price prediction. However, the current performance on high-dimensional data remains problematic due to the error rate in the correlational analysis. In this paper, we proposed a new correlational strategy to tackle such problems with STI and deep neural networks. We designed this strategy based on the Pearson correlation coefficient with a close index. we took eight companies's stock data for our analysis. The experimental results demonstrate that BiLSTM's performance (0.892% of R^2) outperformed GRU and LSTM in various factors for stock price prediction.

Keywords: Price prediction · High-dimensional stock data · Correlational strategy · Neural networks

1 Introduction

In the digital era, the economy of various countries depends on fluctuations in global economic conditions. For instance, the Russia-Ukraine war severely affected the stock market values of numerous companies [1]. Similarly, changes

Supported by The National Key Research and Development Program of China under Grant No. 2021YFF1200104, and Hebei Academy of Sciences under Grant No. 22602, and Research Centre for Quantitative Finance of The Hong Kong Polytechnic University under Grand No. P0042708.

Y. Tian et al. (Eds.): ICBDS 2022, CCIS 1796, pp. 405–419, 2023.
https://doi.org/10.1007/978-981-99-3300-6_29

in economic policies also affect the market level, which crucially affects investors and traders. Recently, various studies have been provided to predict the stock market with machine learning and deep learning neural networks. These methods are applied to predict high-dimensional data [2–5]. The key purpose of such work was to provide decision-making help to different stakeholders for future market investments.

Previously, a machine learning model with Bayesian methods has been widely adopted [3,6]. Recently, deep neural networks received great potential and attention from the research community for stock prediction with different models, long short-term memory (LSTM), gate recurrent unit (GRU), and other NN have higher prediction accuracy in stock time series data. For example, Saba (2021) presented LSTM for the stock market prediction for KSE100 index data. However, the reported variance of actual and predicated prices can be improved by comparing training and testing datasets [7]. The author [2] combined the GRU with an attention scheme to predict stock movements. However, it must be provided with challenging datasets. Similarly, the study [5] employed BiLSTM to improve the prediction by considering the SSE Shanghai index. However, the RMSE's magnitude was higher. To tackle these severe issues, authors have tried to introduce STI to improve the prediction ability of the model [4].

The STI output is received by particular mathematical formulas to analyze the stock data. This is currently an important analytical method to assess the stock market due to its constant variations [2,3,9]. For instance, Albahli S. [9] and [3] proposed an approach that analyzes the STI with machine learning and deep learning, and it provides the correlation of different stock market data. Similarly, the author [2] also efficiently utilized the relative strength index (RSI) to predict the stock movement by using GRU. However, these studies' performances were limited due to a lack of correlation between the stock movement and STI. Moreover, the DL model's performances are still seeking improvement for satisfactory trends between the actual and predicted prices.

This study proposes a correlational strategy to tackle the above-mentioned problems by employing DL networks to analyze the relationship between STI for stock market prediction. This strategy uses the Pearson coefficient to correlate the opening and closing prices with ten significant STIs, for which it extracts highly correlated STI as the input feature vector. These features are distributed in training and testing sets for the modeling of three deep neural networks, GRU, LSTM, and BiLSTM, to predict the future stock price in short intervals. The data for two years from 8 Chinese technology companies listed on the Hong Kong stock market is analyzed. Furthermore, the performance evaluation is reported based on 4 computational metrics, and the results are compared with prior studies. The following are the significant contributions of this study:

- A correlational strategy is proposed by employing 3 deep neural networks to analyze the relationship of STI with close prices for stock market prediction.
- The features are extracted from two years of stock data from 8 Chinese technology companies to predict the future stock price in short intervals.
- The proposed strategy's efficiency is evaluated with 4 metrics, and the results outperformed the prior works for price prediction.

2   Related Work

In recent years, the enormous public has participated in stock investment, and the stock market has to be closely watched by investors, economists and researchers. However, due to the volatility of stock prices and too many influencing factors, stock market forecasting is considered one of the most challenging issues in time series analysis [5]. Machine learning tools are generally used in stock price prediction and market analysis. Liang [6] proposed an ML-based method to deliver future stock price prediction. However, they suggested the proposed model should be estimated over a more complex and broader data set with other ML. In [3], different STIs were applied in training three classifiers, ANN, KNN, and SVM. This approach attained the best result in the SVM classifier. Unfortunately, the noise samples seriously influenced the prediction performances.

Besides ML, neural networks (NN) can build efficient learning models without constructing complex and specific feature engineering. The NN model can efficiently tackle stock data's nonlinear, uncertain, and volatile issues. A study proposed by [10] designed a new model by assembling the LSTM model with indicators to analyze the stock trends. However, they suggested improving the model with different parameters. Author [11] conducted experiments on LSTM with stock data and found 32.7% of MAE (Mean Absolute Error) and 54.1% of MSE (Mean Square Error). In the last few days, the Bidirectional LSTM (BiLSTM), a new variant of the LSTM, has been popularly implemented in the financial domain. The author [12] utilized another neural network, BiLSTM, to analyze the Amazon numeric data for price prediction. They provide the fitness of this neural network in this domain. Similarly, another study [13] brought a new advancement by using the LSTM-GRU network for the prediction of different stock data. This is a composite model in which the output of the LSTM layer is used as the input of the GRU layer to obtain the final result. The model attained an MSE value of 0.00098 in prediction precision. Recently, STIs are generally applied in training the LSTM structure to predict the stock trend. Nabipour [14] put forward an approach for stock price prediction. This method acquired the best outcome using the LSTM model, but since only 4 stocks have been evaluated, the model needs further improvement.

3   Preliminaries

3.1   Stock Technical Indicators (STIs)

The stock technical indicators (STIs) are relative to the primary analysis of stock price. They focus on analyzing the general economic situation, each company's operation, management status, industry dynamics, and other factors to measure the stock price. We use several stock technology indicators (given in Table 1) for our experiments to enhance stock price prediction [2,3,9].

3.2   Deep Neural Networks

LSTM: When we tackle the issues of time series, i.e., sequence data, natural language processing, or machine translation, previous deep neural networks are not efficient. LSTM is particularly applied to deal with these issues. Meanwhile, it avoids the vanishing gradient problem of long-term correlation with time series data. It incorporates the input gates, the forget gates, and the output gates to figure out the issues of gradient disappearance. As a result, LSTM can effectively deal with long-term dependence time series. The math equations of these gates are given in [7].

Table 1. The definition of STIs and their mathematical representation.

Stock Technology Indicators (STI)	Math Formula
BB_{Upper} can help shareholders effectively distinguish the time of oversold and overbought stock assets	$BB_{Upper} = MA + 2MD$
Exponential moving average (EMA) is a trend indicator for moving average weight by exponential decline	$EMA_n = \sum\limits_{i=0}^{n-1} w_i C_{t-i}$
Simple moving average (SMA) is the simplest statistical method to take the average of the prices in a specific period of time in the past	$SMA_n = \frac{1}{n} \sum\limits_{i=0}^{n-1} C_{t-i}$
Double exponential moving average (DEMA) is a smoother and faster-moving average to reduce the lag time of the general moving average	$DEMA = 2 \times EMA - EMA(EMA)$
Moving Average Convergence Divergence (MACD) is to judge the buying and selling opportunities by using the convergence and separation between the short-term and long-term index moving average	$MACD = 2 \times (DIF - DEA)$
Rate of Change (ROC) generally reflects the speed of changes in the stock market by comparing the price of the day with a certain day before	$ROC = AX - BX$
Average Directional Index (ADX) is used to show the market strength by studying of rise and fall process of stocks and using the change of long and short trends to find fluctuation of securities price changes	$ADX = SMA\left(\frac{DI^+ - DI^-}{DI^+ + DI^-}\right)$
Reversal of Average Direction Index (ADXR) finds the high position in downward indicates which often too late to really believe that ADX has turned its head downward, which causes trouble when applying ADX	$ADXR = \frac{ADX_i + ADX_{i-1}}{2}$

BiLSTM: The BiLSTM model is an altered framework of LSTM, which includes forward and backward LSTM layers. Similar to the LSTM calculation process, BiLSTM adds a reverse operation. It can be understood as reversing the input sequence and recalculating the output in the LSTM mode. The final result is a simple stack of forward LSTM results and reverse LSTM results. In this way, the model can be considered as context information. The formulas for the forward and backward layers can be found in [5].

GRU: GRU is a recurrent neural network (RNN). The traditional RNN can not deal with the long time series issues since the memory of RNN declines as the data sequence rises. In other words, RNN has gradient disappearance problems, and GRU can tackle the issues efficiently. GRU and LSTM are modified structures of simple RNN, and RNN replaces forget gate and input gate in LSTM with an update gate. GRU cell is the structure of neurons in a recurrent neural network, and the middle execution of the cell is provided in [2].

3.3 Performance Metrics (PM)

When the best model is trained, the testing data will be put into the trained model to calculate the predictive value. The predictive value of the test data and its matching real value are used for model evaluation. In this paper, we evaluate the results through four PMs (given in Table 2) [7–9].

Table 2. Four different performance metrics and their math terms.

Performance Metrics (PM)	Math Formula
Root mean squared error (RMSE) assesses the deviation between the observed value and real value. The smaller the RMSE, the better the prediction result	$RMSE = \sqrt{\frac{1}{n} \sum_{i=1}^{n} (y_i - \hat{y}_i)^2}$
Mean averaging error (MAE) is mainly used in machine learning and price prediction issues. It can balance and boost the confidence on the observed value	$MAE = \frac{1}{n} \sum_{i=1}^{n} |y_i - \hat{y}_i|$
Mean squared error (MSE) can evaluate the degree of change of data. The smaller the value of MSE, the better the accuracy of the prediction model	$MSE = \frac{1}{n} \sum_{i=1}^{n} (y_i - \hat{y}_i)^2$
R-squared (R^2) is a quantity to measure the fitting degree of the model. It is a proportional formula. The scale interval is [0,1]. The closer it is to 1, the higher the fitting degree of the model is	$R^2 = 1 - \frac{\sum_i (y_i - \hat{y}_i)^2}{\sum_i (y_i - \bar{y}_i)^2}$

4   Proposed Strategy

Our proposed strategy for stock prediction is based on the following stages. The systematics flow illustration is given in Fig. 1, in which rectangles show the main action process while the rounded rectangles indicate the input of the main process.

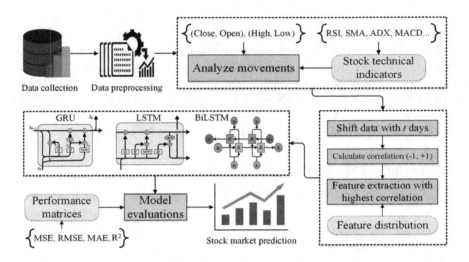

Fig. 1. The flow diagram of the proposed correlational strategy for the stock prediction.

4.1   Data Collection and Preprocessing

Since a publicly available dataset is fetched, it is crucial to understand the constraint of how the datasets were entered. However, we identified various gaps in the input data. It can cause the inadequate performance of the proposed strategy. Outlier, clustering, and normalization techniques have been recently applied to preprocess such data. However, our data is based on numeric data for which we applied the data transformation technique, a process to convert data from one format to another. In our datasets, some values are NaN, which affects the model performance and evaluation. We replaced such values by employing the Pandas $dropna()$ function, providing the final data on GitHub [19].

4.2   Stock Movements

The purpose of stock movement analysis is to design the proposed strategy for a different time interval of stock prediction. The overnight stock movement as positive or negative is calculated based on the opening price of the current trading day p_o^t and the closing price for the previous consecutive days p_c^{t-1}, by designing the Eq. 1.

$$\text{Movement} = \frac{\left(p_o^t - p_c^{t-1}\right)}{p_c^t} \tag{1}$$

As stock movement is volatile as usual, we deliberate the movements as 0.5 if it exceeds the positive and negative intervals of standard deviation. The correlation is reported with close price and various STI; the details are provided in Sect. 3.

4.3   Correlational Strategy

The close price is estimated as the significant influencer on the stock market prediction. As depicted in Fig. 2, we constructed a bar graph for the correlational strategy of different time intervals. Each bar comprises the last 14 days' intervals t, which is considered trading input based on the historical data. It delivers the output with $t + 1$ trading output for the next day's prediction. Identifying the dependencies between the different day intervals and stock technical indicators is critical. Each bar correlates to the next bar with one day difference by a particular correlation coefficient, the Pearson correlation coefficient r_{xy}. This coefficient provides an interesting correlation between the STI (x) and the closing price for the prediction (y).

$$r_{xy} = \frac{\sum_{i=0}^{n} (x_i - x)(y_i - y)}{\sqrt{\sum_{i=0}^{n} (x_i - x)^2 (y_i - y)^2}} \tag{2}$$

where n is the last numeric value of the stock data to calculate the prediction for the last interval.

By utilizing the cosine similarity [15], Eq. 2 can be further simplified as:

$$r_{xy} = \frac{\sum x_i \cdot y_i}{\sqrt{\sum (x_i^2) \cdot \sum (y_i^2)}} \tag{3}$$

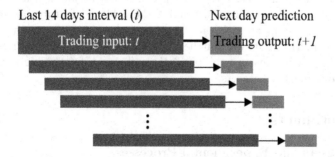

Fig. 2. Correlational strategy for stock prediction with different time intervals.

This correlation provides two values; positive (including 0) or negative. Thus, there will be two different correlations between each prediction bar depending on the closing price; positively correlated (correlation $\geq$ threshold) or negatively correlated (correlation $\leq$ threshold). As a result, there will be different correlations between the closing price and STI based on the last 14 days' stock intervals and the next day's prediction. These correlations will be fed to the deep neural networks for the actual 14 days' stock trends to predict the next day's trends based on training and testing datasets.

4.4   Neural Networks Implementation with STI

This work employed GRU, LSTM, and BiLSTM neural networks for stock prediction with STI (Sect. 3). The neurons of deep learning networks become activated for an input variable with suitable x and y weights. The correlational strategy provides rich information on correlation vectors to train the models with different feature sets. The $min - max$ scalar function is constructed for feature normalization of high-dimensional stock datasets. This function is critical to vary the values into a scaled form to reduce the gross impact on the dataset. It ignores the values which do not correlate with the log function $(0, 1]$ by the following formula:

$$z_i = \frac{x_i - \text{Min}(X)}{\text{Max}(X) - \text{Min}(X)} \tag{4}$$

where z_i indicates the normalized value, $\text{Min}(X)$ and $\text{Max}(X)$ present the minimum and maximum values of X, respectively. While x_i indicates the individual STI's data, $X = \{x_1, x_2, ..., x_n\}$ shows the dataset of all $x_i's$.

To implement the NN on the received feature vectors, we divided these vectors into 80% (training) and 20% (testing). The training sets are applied to each model, which is initialized by numerous hyperparameters based on the experiments and prior studies. Each neural network has different layers. For example, the dropout layer resolves the overfitting issue with a particular rate. It is recommended to experiment with the NN by varying and optimizing the hyperparameters to obtain adequate and effective outputs [16]. The detailed selection of these parameters is listed in Sect. 5. Optimal parameter selection is still a challenging task in training neural networks. Finally, the achieved features are utilized as input for the dense layer with the Adam optimizer to generate the prediction of the stock market dataset. Furthermore, four performance metrics (Sect. 3) are also adopted to measure the prediction efficiency for the high-dimensional Chinese stock market datasets.

5   Experiments

5.1   Datasets and Experimental Processes

In our experiment, we obtained the daily primary data of 8 Chinese companies listed in the Hong Kong stock market: (1) Tencent (1/7/2020 to 1/7/2022), (2)

Alibaba (1/7/2020 to 1/7/2022), (3) JD (1/7/2020 to 1/7/2022), (4) NetEase (1/7/2020 to 1/7/2022), (5) Meituan (1/7/2020 to 1/7/2022), (6) Xiaomi (1/7/20 20 to 1/7/2022), (7) China Mobile (CM) (1/7/2020 to 1/7/2022), (8) China Telecom (CT) (1/7/2020 to 1/7/2022). These data were crawled from the Sina Finance interface (https://finance.sina.com.cn). Our experiment only focuses on primary time series data (Date, Open, Close, High, Low, Volume). Table generated by Excel2LaTeX from sheet 'Sheet1'

For experiments, first, we preprocess the primary data of each company by calculating the required 10 STI by using $Ta-lib$ (http://ta-lib.org), then delete the rows with empty STI values. Second, we shift the data by 14 days and calculate the correlation between these STIs and the close price of the next day. Third, for these high-dimensional data, we choose the first 8 STIs with high correlation and close price for model training. Fourth, normalize these data and divide the dataset into train and test sets by 80% and 20% respectively. Finally, 3 NN are used on train sets. While to compare the three models' performances more intuitively and fairly, we use the same model parameters during training, i.e., Dimensionality of the output space = 512, Dropout rate = 0.2, Batch size = 32, Epochs = 200, Loss function = MAE, Optimizer = $Adam$ Activation function = $tanh$. Then, 4 PM is employed to measure the performance of the trained model on the test set. The experimental environment is given in Table 3.

Table 3. Experimental environment.

Name	Versions
System Information	Windows 10 64x, RAM 32 GB, GPU NVIDIA RTX 2080Ti, CPU Intel(R) 6240 2.60 GHz
Programming Environment	Python 3.6.13, IDE PyCharm 2022.1.3, Keras 2.10.0, Sklearn 0.24.2, TensorFlow 2.3.0

6   Results Evaluation

6.1   Movement Analysis of Hong Kong Stock

Many factors will directly lead to sharp fluctuations in stock prices, including policies, fundamentals, and industrial prosperity. Figure 3 shows the stock price trend of the Netease dataset. For a long time, the stock market trend has been the same as that of the fundamentals; if the fundamentals are good, the stock market as a whole will be good too. For example, at the beginning of 2021, the COVID-19 vaccine came out, and all industries resumed work, so the economic fundamentals were improved. Thus, the stock price in the corresponding period was higher than before, which can be found in the zoomed section of Fig. 3.

Investors can analyze individual stocks according to the changes in moving averages (MA) and close prices to make investment strategies. When the stock's

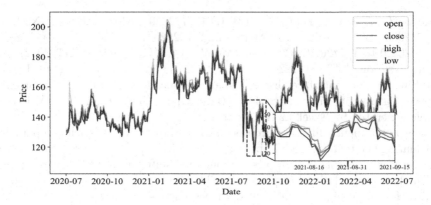

Fig. 3. The stock movement's trends of Netease from 1/7/2020 to 1/7/2022.

closing price stands above the 14-day MA, it supports individual stocks in the short term, and there is still room for an individual stock to rise, which is a buying signal, as shown in Fig. 4. The close price has been stable on the MA since January 2021; it rose rapidly in the short term.

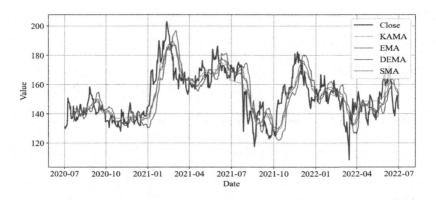

Fig. 4. The price trend between 4 STI and close index of the Netease company.

6.2   Correlation of Movement and STI

The Pearson coefficient [15] was adopted to calculate the correlation between the STI of the previous 14 days and the close price of the next day. We used seaborn (a Python visualization library based on Matplotlib) to draw a heatmap, as shown in Fig. 5. A value close to +1 indicates that X and Y have a strong positive correlation; on the contrary, a value close to 0 means no relationship between X and Y. As BB, SMA, EMA, DEMA, and KAMA all belong to the MA category, they have a strong positive correlation with each other. Although the close price is used in the calculation of RSI, ROC, ADX, and ADXR, the correlation with the next day's close price is one possible explanation: these apply to long-term prediction.

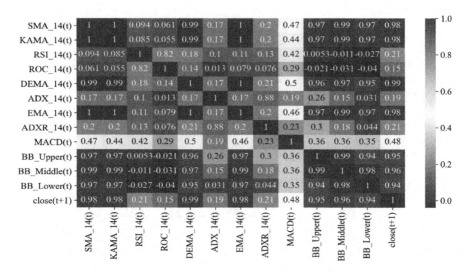

Fig. 5. A correlation results among 8 STI and the close price of Netease company.

6.3   Stock Prediction with NNs

This experiment compares the performance of different NN models. Then PMs are used to evaluate the performance of these models. Figure 6(a) demonstrates the actual closing price fitting curve with train and test data in the LSTM model. It presents that the training data between 1 July 2020 and 15 February 2022 fit well with the actual data, but the fitting performance between test data and actual data after April 2022 is not ideal. It indicates the LSTM's slightly poor performance on test data. Figure 6(b) illustrates that the testing data after 15 February 2022 fit well with the actual data, but the fitting effect between the training data and the actual data between January 2021 and July 2021 is not adequate, and the deviation between the two lines is a little critical in GRU.

Figure 6(c) reveals that the fitting effect of test data, training data, and actual data is more efficient than that of the LSTM and GRU models. The graph visually illustrates that the training and testing prediction results of the BiLSTM model are closer to the actual closing price, and the shape of the prediction line is more identical to the shape of the actual line. Thus, BiLSTM performed relatively more adequately for stock market prediction based on training and testing datasets. Meanwhile, according to the model prediction, we calculated the corresponding PMs (Table 4).

The Bi-LSTM model performs more effectively in the MSE, MAE, and R^2 evaluation categories. It achieves the best result with a 0.001 MSE value and a 0.031 MAE value in China Telecom's stock price forecast compared to the other models. Similarly, it acquires sufficient results in Xiaomi's stock with the R^2 matrix. In contrast, the GRU model obtains the best RMSE score in China Telecom's stock. In general, the Bi-LSTM model outperforms other models in most cases.

Fig. 6. Price predication trends among (a) LSTM, (b) GRU, and (c) BiLSTM.

Table 4. Comparison of PMs for different neural networks and datasets.

Models	PM	Tencent	Alibaba	CM	CT	JD	Meituan	Netease	Xiaomi
GRU	MSE	187.123	31.628	0.527	0.002	167.677	81.854	38.911	0.278
	RMSE	13.679	5.624	0.726	0.043	12.949	9.047	6.238	0.527
	MAE	10.099	4.411	0.553	0.032	9.732	6.773	4.684	0.415
	R2	0.818	0.661	0.805	0.817	0.768	0.837	0.564	0.889
LSTM	MSE	199.615	28.844	0.657	0.002	176.710	92.351	50.849	0.282
	RMSE	14.128	5.371	0.811	0.049	13.293	9.610	7.131	0.531
	MAE	10.391	4.267	0.611	0.037	10.165	7.177	5.481	0.412
	R2	0.807	0.773	0.742	0.727	0.732	0.813	0.517	0.861
BiLSTM	MSE	189.324	35.127	0.512	0.001	162.554	92.338	34.467	0.277
	RMSE	13.760	5.927	0.712	0.042	12.750	9.609	5.871	0.527
	MAE	10.707	4.528	0.549	0.031	9.673	7.224	4.616	0.392
	R2	0.816	0.693	0.811	0.820	0.770	0.809	0.621	0.892

6.4 Comparative Analysis

A comparative analysis of our proposed strategy's performance has also been conducted with existing work [5,11,17]. The results are compared in Table 5 by using performance metrics (PM) and various other datasets. The analysis demonstrates that our strategy received more effective outcomes than other work; it emphasizes the stock prediction with deep neural networks.

Table 5. Proposed work performance comparison with latest prior work.

Ref. – Year	Method/Model	Dataset	PM output
[17] – 2022	BiCuDNNLSTM-1dCNN	Global DAX index dataset	RMSE with GDAXI: 119.38; MAE with GDAXI: 86.13
[5] – 2022	BiLSTM	SSE Shanghai	RMSE: 98.35; MAE: 67.25
[11] – 2018	LSTM-based ModAugNet	S&P500; KOSPI200	MSE with S&P500: 0.54; MAE with KOSPI200: 0.32
Our work – 2022	Correlational strategy with GRU, LSTM, BiLSTM.	Hong Kong stock market dataset of 8 companies	MSE (BiLSTM with CT): **0.001**, RMSE (BiLSTM with CT): **0.042**, MAE (BiLSTM with CT): **0.031**, R^2 (BiLSTM with Xiaomi): **0.892**

7   Conclusion

The proposed strategy deals with the problem of correlational analysis between the STI and stock movement to report the actual and prediction prices of high-dimensional Chinese stock data. The results depicted in Figs. 3, 4, 5 reveal the correlated trends of STI with close index, which presents that these STIs have a strong influence on stock prediction. This prediction performance is validated through GRU, LSTM, and BiLSTM in Figs. 6, which concluded that the prediction performance of BiLSTM on train and test data was highly correlated to the actual close price. Furthermore, the metrics errors were also the least and most efficient than prior studies (Table 5), which signifies the outperformance of the proposed work.

In the future, diverse data mining techniques [18] and parameters can be applied to text and numeric data by constructing an attention mechanism of the neural networks to predict further correlations and comparisons them with baseline models. Meanwhile, it would be interesting to provide the performance confirmation of proposed methods or models on real-time or actual transaction stock datasets.

References

1. Ahmed, S., Hasan, M.M., Kamal, M.R.: Russia-Ukraine crisis: the effects on the European stock market. European Financial Management (2022)
2. Lee, M.C.: Research on the feasibility of applying GRU and attention mechanism combined with technical indicators in stock trading strategies. Appl. Sci. **12**(3), 1007 (2022). https://www.mdpi.com/2076-3417/12/3/1007
3. Shynkevich, Y., McGinnity, T.M., Coleman, S.A., Belatreche, A., Li, Y.: Forecasting price movements using technical indicators: investigating the impact of varying input window length. Neurocomputing **264**, 71–88 (2017). https://doi.org/10.1016/j.neucom.2016.11.095
4. Guo, J., Tuckfield, B.: News-based machine learning and deep learning methods for stock prediction. In: Journal of Physics: Conference Series, vol. 1642, no. 1, p. 012014. IOP Publishing (2020)
5. Liu, B., Yu, Z., Wang, Q., Du, P., Zhang, X.: Prediction of SSE Shanghai enterprises index based on bidirectional LSTM model of air pollutants. Expert Syst. Appl. **204**, 117600 (2022). https://doi.org/10.1016/j.eswa.2022.117600
6. Liang, D., Tsai, C.-F., Lu, H.Y.R., Chang, L.S.: Combining corporate governance indicators with stacking ensembles for financial distress prediction. J. Bus. Res. **120**, 137–146 (2020). https://doi.org/10.1016/j.jbusres.2020.07.052
7. Aslam, S., Rasool, A., Jiang, Q., Qu, Q.: LSTM based model for real-time stock market prediction on unexpected incidents. In: 2021 IEEE International Conference on Real-time Computing and Robotics (RCAR), 15–19 July 2021, pp. 1149–1153 (2021). https://doi.org/10.1109/RCAR52367.2021.9517625
8. Levi, S., Merlyn, S., Sudhanva, M.: Our Heritage an Empirical Study on Forecasting Price Movements Using Technical Indicators with Selected Equity Stock in Indian Stock Market (2021)

9. Albahli, S., Nazir, T., Mehmood, A., Irtaza, A., Alkhalifah, A., Albattah, W.: AEI-DNET: a novel densenet model with an autoencoder for the stock market predictions using stock technical indicators. Electronics, **11**(4), 611 (2022). https:// www.mdpi.com/2079-9292/11/4/611

10. Agrawal, M., Khan, A.U., Shukla, P.K.: Stock price prediction using technical indicators: a predictive model using optimal deep learning. Int. J. Recent Technol. Eng. **8**(2), 2297–2305 (2019). https://doi.org/10.35940/ijrteb3048.078219

11. Baek, Y., Kim, H.Y.: ModAugNet: a new forecasting framework for stock market index value with an overfitting prevention LSTM module and a prediction LSTM module. Expert Syst. Appl. **113**, 457–480 (2018). https://doi.org/10.1016/j.eswa. 2018.07.019

12. Kong, D., Liu, S., Pan, L.: Amazon spot instance price prediction with GRU network. In: 2021 IEEE 24th International Conference on Computer Supported Cooperative Work in Design (CSCWD), pp. 31–36 (2021). https://doi.org/10.1109/ CSCWD49262.2021.9437881

13. Hossain, M.A., Karim, R., Thulasiram, R., Bruce, N.D., Wang, Y.: Hybrid deep learning model for stock price prediction. In: 2018 IEEE Symposium Series on Computational Intelligence (SSCI), pp. 1837–1844 (2018)

14. Nabipour, M., Nayyeri, P., Jabani, H., Mosavi, A., Salwana, E, Shahab, S.: Deep learning for stock market prediction. Entropy, **22**(8), 840 (2020). https://www. mdpi.com/1099-4300/22/8/840

15. Rasool, A., Jiang, Q., Qu, Q., Kamyab, M., Huang, M.: HSMC: hybrid sentiment method for correlation to analyze COVID-19 tweets. In: Xie, Q., Zhao, L., Li, K., Yadav, A., Wang, L. (eds.) ICNC-FSKD 2021. LNDECT, vol. 89, pp. 991–999. Springer, Cham (2022). https://doi.org/10.1007/978-3-030-89698-0_101

16. Hong, W., Li, S., Hu, Z., Rasool, A., Jiang, Q., Weng, Y.: Improving relation extraction by knowledge representation learning. In: 2021 IEEE 33rd International Conference on Tools with Artificial Intelligence (ICTAI), pp. 1211–1215 (2021). https://doi.org/10.1109/ICTAI52525.2021.00191

17. Kanwal, A., Lau, M.F., Ng, S.P., Sim, K.Y., Chandrasekaran, S.: BiCuDNNLSTM-1dCNN - a hybrid deep learning-based predictive model for stock price prediction. Expert Syst. Appl. **202**, 117123 (2022). https://doi.org/10.1016/j.eswa.2022. 117123

18. Rasool, A., Bunterngchit, C., Tiejian, L., Islam, M.R., Qu, Q., Jiang, Q.: Improved machine learning-based predictive models for breast cancer diagnosis. Int. J. Environ. Res. Publ. Health **19**(6), 3211 (2022). https://www.mdpi.com/1660-4601/19/ 6/3211

19. Hong Kong Stock Market Dataset. https://github.com/abdul-rasool/Hong-Kong-Stock-Market-Dataset

Research on Attribute-Based Privacy-Preserving Computing Technologies

Shuo Qiu[1], Wenhui Ni[2], Yanfeng Shi[2(✉)], and Wanni Xu[3]

[1] School of Software Engineering, Jinling Institute of Technology, Nanjing 211169, China
[2] School of Computer Engineering, Nanjing Institute of Technology, Nanjing 211167, China
shiyf@njit.edu.cn
[3] School of Internet of Things Engineering, Hohai University, Changzhou 213022, China

Abstract. Privacy-preserving computing is an important topic in epidemic prevention, credit report and education resource sharing. Data analysis is the basis for realizing the overall speed increase of returning to work and production. This paper comprehensively summarizes the current academic research on privacy-preserving computing. In this work, we systematically summarize the four aspects of the related schemes on the attribute-based encryption schemes: keyword search, symmetric search, PSI, homomorphic encryption. We classify the schemes and compare the same-type schemes accordingly. Finally, we present the directions and challenges for our future work. This paper is intended to provide convenience for the subsequent research on privacy-preserving computing.

Keywords: Attribute based encryption (ABE) · Keyword Search · Symmetric search · PSI · Equality test · Homomorphic encryption

1 Introduction

Nowadays, the leakage of private information has caused great problems to everyday life of people. Personal privacy's protection is imminent. To prevent sensitive information leakage, each of us needs to strengthen the awareness of our own sensitive information protection. In addition, the academic circle has also launched quite a lot of specific research on this problem. This paper will present a detailed discussion on attribute-based privacy-preserving computing. It is suitable for epidemic data, credit data, educational data, and so on.

Privacy-preserving computing can be used without the data being publicly available. Sahai and Waters propose an attribute-based encryption algorithm [27]. Key policy and ciphertext policy are two fundamental categories among attribute-based encryption algorithms. The constructs of these two methods are different. In the CP-ABE, the ciphertext is decrypted only when the attributes satisfy the access control policy; In the KP-ABE scheme, the data is decrypted if the attributes in the ciphertext satisfy the key access control policy.

Y. Tian et al. (Eds.): ICBDS 2022, CCIS 1796, pp. 420–432, 2023.
https://doi.org/10.1007/978-981-99-3300-6_30

Under the premise of taking the attribute-based encryption algorithm as the basis element, combined with other encryption algorithms, scholars provide a variety of new encryption algorithms:

(1) Attribute-based encryption with keyword search: In the searchable keyword encryption, a token can be added to the encrypted data by the data owner, and users can search the encrypted data with the token. In attribute-based system, the corresponding retrieval is performed only if the data user meets the access control strategy set by the data encryptor. Zhang et.al, systematically describe the concept of searchable encryption [44]. Then, a good solution to the problem of multiple users is put forward, but the role of both solutions for multiple users in the solution is not the same [36, 45]. Also, a verifiable function to facilitate users to judge the search results' authenticity is proposed [17, 46] and revocable capabilities are provided [33, 41]. Extension of other functions will be detailed in the next section

(2) Attribute-based encryption with symmetric search: The searchable encryption algorithm was first proposed by [32].The scheme is an encryption algorithm where the client interacts with the server to obtain the search results. In this paper, several schemes combined with attribute-based encryption are studied. Also, SGX can be used to improve their performance [3, 4, 25].

(3) Attribute-based encryption with Private set intersection: In the PSI algorithm, the user can obtain the set intersection of the encrypted data without obtaining the private information. In addition, the equality test algorithm can provide users to detect whether the data is equal under different access control policies, and to classify the encrypted data.

(4) Attribute-based encryption with homomorphic encryption: Homomorphic encryption algorithm can realize the calculation of real encrypted data. The calculation of the data after the homomorphic encryption algorithm is no different from the original explicit calculation results. Combined with the attribute-based encryption algorithm, access control can be realized and the original function of the algorithm can be realized.

2 Schemes

2.1 Attribute-Based Encryption with Keyword Search

CP-ABE

Before outsourcing private data to a cloud server, the data owner encrypts it, affecting query efficiency and data sharing. In [35], Wang et al. provide a Ciphertext-policy attribute-based encryption scheme with keyword search function with bilinear pairings. When the scheme is implemented, the data owner encrypts the public private data on the basis of the access control policy and constructs the security index. The user decrypts the ciphertext only if the access control policy is met.

In [33], Sun et al., introduce the first attribute-based keyword search scheme with efficient user revocation. In this scheme, multiple data owners are supported to outsource encrypted data to the cloud, and users can search encrypted data independently. In addition, this scheme supports user revocation. During the revocation, the system update is handed over to the cloud server, reducing the system's computing burden. Meanwhile, for the multi-owners, the multi-user search scheme can give the verification of the results. Through verification, it resists the selected keyword attacks.

In [21], Lv et al. propose a multi-user Searchable Encryption with Efficient Access Control scheme. The scheme has the following contributions: 1. In view of the partial order relationship between ciphertexts, the cloud server builds an index based on this relationship, and users can search for the ciphertexts that can be decrypted from the index. 2. It can verify user attribute without disclosing user privacy. 3. Users outsource the decryption to improve efficiency and avoid data leakage.

Same as [21], the scheme proposed by [41] is also based on multiple senders and multiple users, namely: Attribute Based Searchable Encryption with synonym keyword search function.(SK-ABSE). The scheme mainly provides four functions: 1. No secret key sharing; 2. Semantic keyword search: the documents returned to the user contain synonym keywords; 3 Fine-grained search authorization; 4. User revocation.

In [14], Li et al. present an Outsourced Attribute -based Encryption with Keyword Search Function (KSF - OABE). It can outsource key issuance and decryption. The author generates a trapdoor for the keyword through encryption to ensure the user's privacy. Meanwhile, D-CSP is responsible for partial decryption in the absence of plaintext, which improves the security of the scheme greatly.

In [26], Qiu et al. introduce a novel scheme called hidden policy ciphertext-policy attribute-based encryption with keyword search (HP-CPABKS). When user attributes do not conform to the specified access control policies, privacy data and related access control structures cannot be searched, avoiding the risk of access control structures exposure.

In [19], Liu et al. proposed a verifiable attribute-based keyword search. This new scheme tags shared data to remove duplicate data in the cloud and supports verification of search results. To reduce the computational overhead, the authors moved attribute revocation to outsourcing.

In 2020, Lin et al. proposed a multi-user ciphertext policy attribute-based encryption scheme with keyword search for medical cloud system [16]. The scheme is suitable for multiple users and protects users' personal health records (PHR)on the cloud. In their proposed scheme, the system adopts an independent proxy server, which can effectively disconnect the customer from the cloud, so as to avoid a large number of computing and external attacks. Compared with other schemes, the architecture proposed by them possesses higher efficiency and shorter ciphertext length.

Gao et al. combine keyword search with ciphertext-based attribute encryption and apply it to e-mail encryption, allowing recipients to search for and filter out encrypted files. In this scheme, to ensure the scheme, the authors used dual system methodology and hidden policy to resist KGA, strengthening the protection function [11].

Traditional ABKS schemes are easy to leak ciphertext through peer decryption attacks. Meng et al. proposed an attribute-based encryption with dynamic keyword search [22]. It provides a new fog computing system to reduce the computational overhead. In the implementation of the scheme, users must provide at least one ciphertext keyword in order to prevent previous peer -decryption attacks. In addition, CPA and CKA have been confirmed to be no threatening to this protocol.

In the ABKS scheme, the cloud server undertakes complex computing work while being vulnerable to keyword guessing attack. Li et al. proposed the ABKS-SKGA scheme [15]. In the scheme, data owner's private key is signed before the cipher text of the key is generated, so as to prevent the entity from forging the keyword ciphertext.

Meng et al. introduce a ciphertext-policy attribute-based encryption with hidden sensitive policy from keyword search Techniques [23]. A novel security model is defined by authors, that is, chosen sensitive policy attack?(CSPA): a public access policy, a sensitive hidden access policy, simply means that only when users meet the public access policy, they have the opportunity to access the hidden attributes, and finally decrypt the ciphertext. In order to save cost, the authors also outsource the computing and encryption operations of the decryption part to the cloud platform, which makes the scheme more suitable for mobile devices.

At present, most schemes are based on the single-owner model. In [36], Wang et al. provided an Attribute-based Encrypted Search for Multi-owner and Multi-user Model.In the proposed scheme, the data owner can set the access control policy to encrypt the data, and the user can search the ciphertext through a single trapdoor to access the data set. It is important to note that users can only access data sets encrypted by the specified data owner. Compared with, both papers involve multi-owner encrypt the data, but the two schemes are different in their focus and solutions. In [45], multi- owners can encrypt cloud data, and users can obtain the right to decrypt only with the consent of multiple owners (Table 1).

Table 1. Property summary for CP-ABE with Keyword Search schemes

Schemes	Multi-user	Multi-owner	Verifiability	Revocation	Hidden-policy
[35]	×	×	×	×	×
[14]	×	×	×	×	×
[22]	×	×	×	×	×
[26]	×	×	×	×	√
[11]	×	×	×	×	√
[15]	×	×	√	×	×
[16]	√	×	×	×	×
[19]	×	×	√	√	×
[41]	×	√	×	√	×
[21]	√	×	√	×	×
[36]	√	√	×	×	×
[23]	√	×	√	×	√
[33]	√	√	√	√	×

KA-ABE

Zheng et al. puts forward a new method: verifiable attribute-based keyword search (VABKS) [46]. It has the ability to verify the cloud server's results. But it assumes an inappropriate secure channel in this scheme.

In order to avoid this hypothesis, Liu et al. put forward a novel Verifiable Public Key Encryption with Keyword Search Based on KP-ABE scheme (KP-ABKS),which is based on the VABKS scheme [17]. It can more effectively verify the correctness for the searched files. Moreover, it constructs public and private keys for the data owner and the cloud server, so the keywords and search tokens can be matched only on the cloud, and the offline guessing attack is resisted to a certain extent.

Yu et al. proposes a key-policy attribute-based Encryption With Keyword Search (KP-ABEKS) scheme [43], which has the ability to resist external Keyword guessing attacks and realize fine-grained access control just like [15]. This method can effectively resist external attacks. After the author's safety proof, the scheme can be safely and effectively used in practice (Table 2).

Table 2. Property summary for KP-ABE with Keyword Search schemes

Schemes	Multi-user	Multi-owner	Verifiability	Revocation	Hidden-policy
[43]	×	×	×	×	×
[46]	×	×	√	×	×
[17]	×	×	√	×	×

Blockchain

Generally, attribute-based encryption schemes are associated with a large amount of computational burden. Liu et al. proposed a blockchain-aided searchable attribute-based encryption (BC-SABE), which supports user revocation and predecryption [18]. The scheme uses blockchain to update revocation list and realize the user's revocation. In addition, blockchain helps users generate tokens to search the cloud by issuing a request to the CS. For the user in group G, the scheme can also search and decrypt the user, if the user only needs to require one exponentiation.

Multi-keyword Search

Cui et al. puts forward a searchable encryption technique attribute-based Multiple Keyword search (ABMKS) [7]. Different from other schemes, this scheme is proposed for the first time not to use exponentiation in keyword index generation, but to adopt multiplication calculation. Such algorithm makes keyword indexes cluster together, which has nothing to do with the number of keywords in the original data, and greatly reduces the cost consumption of keyword index generation.

Currently, Attribute-Based Keyword Searching (ABKS) schemes are mainly divided into two types, most schemes are based on a single-keyword search. Khan et al. first propose an Online/Offline-aided Attribute-Based Multi-keyword Search (OOABMS)

[13]. They add an additional online and offline functionality to the ABKS scheme. The redundant computational process, is completed in the offline phase, thus greatly improving the search efficiency. The continued experimental results also indicate its feasibility and efficiency in practice.

The existing CP-ABKS schemes have problems such as imprecision, high computational overhead, and wasted resources. In order to solve multiple issues, zhang et al. implement a multi-keyword searchable scheme based on ciphertext-Attribute-Based encryption[45]. This scheme differs from other multi-keyword search scheme, users can quickly locate to target results using multiple keywords.And a third -party is added to ensure verify the search results' accuracy. Futhermore, the scheme allows multiple data owners to encrypt cloud data and decrypts data only if the user has permission from multiple encryptors.

When a patient stores a Personal Health Record (PHR) in the cloud environment-personal privacy issues cannot be ignored. [29] proposed Multi Keyword Searchable Attribute Based Encryption (MK-SABE) schemes. Their scheme can remove redundant files and adopt multi-keyword search technology. To ensure the system security, the scheme also adds Dynamic Location Based ReEncryption and Location Based Encryption (LBE). The complexity, keyword search time, and performance of the proposed scheme have been significantly improved compared with other schemes (Table 3).

Table 3. Property summary for ABE with Multi-Keyword Search

Schemes	Multi-keyword	Multi-user	Multi-owner	Verifiability	KP/CP
[13]	✓	×	×	×	CP
[7]	✓	×	×	×	CP
[45]	✓	×	×	×	CP
[29]	✓	✓	✓	✓	CP

2.2 Attribute-Based Encryption with Symmetric Search

Both symmetric searchable encryption and attribute-based encryption are common privacy protection schemes with different advantages and disadvantages. Symmetric searchable encryption is able to avoid internal and external attacks, ABE can achieve user revocation, but the disadvantages are obvious. Michalas et al. propose a protocol that combines the two schemes, each taking advantage of its strengths [24]. With SSE scheme, users can search for the encrypted data they want, and CP-ABE is responsible for protecting the symmetric key.

Cloud storage security has always attached great importance to data privacy protection. Based on the function of SGX, Bakas et al. combined SSE and ABE proposed a completely independent ABE revocation mechanism [4].

Michalas et al. proposes a MicroSCOPE structure that combines SSE and ABE, and enhances the performance of the structure through the functionality provided by SGX [25].

Bakas et al. combing the functions provided by SGX, and combine SSE and ABE scheme, provided a revocation mechanism [3]. Access control in SSE occurs only in schemes with the public-key setting, ABE is used for encrypting symmetric keys. Security has been proven to withstand a variety of attacks.

2.3 Attribute-Based Encryption with Private Set Intersection

Cloud computing can reduce the computational overhead of outsourced data this method requires an encryption algorithm to ensure this process's security. But while ensuring its confidentiality, the data owner loses access control to the outsourced data set. Ali et al. proposes an attribute-based private set intersection scheme (AB-PSI), and provides users with fine-grained access control [1]. The scheme can support the data owner control the data set intersection calculation, and the data owner does not have to be online during the protocol.

Private set intersection(PSI) can calculate the set intersection in the case where the private information is not disclosed. Shi et al. proposed delegated key-policy attribute-based set intersection over outsourced encrypted data sets (KP-ABSI) scheme [31]. The cloud server in the scheme can calculate the set intersection. It also implements the fine-grained access authorization.

When users need to calculate the set intersection of outsourced encrypted data sets, the best way is to delegate the calculation to the cloud server and ensure the confidentiality of the set intersection. On this issue, Shi et al. introduce a Ciphertext-Policy Attribute-Based Encryption with Outsourced Set Intersection scheme [30], The scheme mainly supports fully outsourced encrypted storage, delegated computing processes to the cloud, and fine-grained authorization. Additionally, the data owner and the authority are independent (Table 4).

Table 4. Property summary for ABE with PSI

Schemes	[1]	[31]	[30]
KP/CP	cp	kp	cp
computation delegation	×	✓	✓
Multi-Elements Set	✓	✓	✓

Equality-Test

Classifying these enciphered data, which is encrypted by the data owner, is a worthwhile question. Cui et al. introduce a ciphertext-policy attribute based encryption with equality test(CP-ABEET) scheme. In the embodiment of the scheme, the label classification can be performed according to whether the encrypted data contains equal information [8].

Wang et al. introduced a combination of public key encryption and ABE scheme, puts forward a new type of encryption scheme CP-ABEET [37]. The cloud can test equivalence between two messages encrypted under different access policies, and the entrusted cloud server cannot get the ciphertext under the access policy.

Zhu et al. combining public-key Encryption with ABE scheme for the first time [47], a KP-ABE scheme with Equality Test function is realized: key-policy attribute based Encryption With Equality Test (KP-ABEwET). Compared with the above, the novelty of the scheme is that it can use fine-grained authorization without exposing the identity of the user. Besides, it can test whether there is the same information in the ciphertext encrypted by two different public keys. Moreover, a difficult computational problem Twin-Decision BDH problem (tDBDH) is proposed and its authorization security is proved.

In [8], CP-ABEET scheme, although it can classify the encrypted data, and test the equality of the two ciphertext without decryption but it is expensive to calculate. In [40], Yang et al. suggest outsourcing the computation to a third party, which greatly reduces the computational burden.

To protect the security of private data, Eltayieb et al. provided a fine-grained attribute-based encryption supporting equality test (FG-ABEET) scheme [10]. It suggests that ciphertext encrypted under the same or different access control strategies can be granted to cloud server execution. In addition, the cloud server can carry out equality tests without knowing the content of the ciphertext, strictly ensuring the security of sensitive data.

Wang et al. provide a keyword searchable attribute-based encryption scheme with equality test (KS-ABESwET) scheme [38], which combines an equality testing mechanism with an inverted index-based keyword search algorithm. Users can know whether ciphertexts contain the same plaintext without having to decrypt them, greatly reducing unnecessary consumption. In addition, the authors also outsource most of the calculations, reducing the computational burden of the scheme. The safety and reliability of the scheme have been proven.

In [28], Sakarkar et al. introduce a KP-ABEwET scheme that combines public-key encryption with equality testing and a KP-ABE scheme. The scheme can also provide ne-grained authorization to ciphertext without revealing user privacy. In addition, KP-ABEwET can also check whether there is constant data in the ciphertext encrypted by different public key while protecting the data security.

In 2020, Wang et al. introduce a novel CP-ABEET scheme The proposed scheme can test the ciphertext for equality and delete the duplicate data, which can reduce the waste of storage space [39]. In this scenario, an unauthorized adversary will be unable to distinguish between encrypted messages from the ciphertext. To reduce the computational burden, the authors also outsourced some complex calculations to third parties.

In Attribute-based encryption with equality test, the trapdoor can help us know if the encrypted ciphertext is the same. Akano et al. introduce a generic construction of CCA-secure attribute-based encryption with equality test based on identity encryption, the present scheme enables equality testing for hierarchical identity encryption. Compared with other schemes, the scheme proposed by [2] implements new functions such as adaptive security and various predicates (Table 5).

Table 5. Property summary for ABE with equality test

Schemes	CP/KP	Outsourced computing
[37]	CP	×
[8]	CP	×
[10]	CP	×
[47]	KP	×
[28]	KP	×
[40]	CP	√
[38]	CP	√
[39]	CP	√
[2]	CP/KP	×

2.4 Attribute-Based Encryption with Homomorphic Encryption

In [6], the authors propose a safe KP-ABFHE scheme based on LWE. The scheme can evaluate the infinite-depth circuits, but the input ciphertext is finite, but this drawback can be solved by setting the parameters.

A scheme combining ABE and FHE is proposed [5], in which homomorphic encryption can be performed across attributes. According to author's targeted homomorphic construction, the evaluator needs to know the target policy. In addition, the author also proposed a second scheme, the ciphertext increases as the number of the policies set in this scheme. The input to both schemes is independent of the number of properties.

Hiromasa et al. proposed the multi target homomorphic attribute-based encryption (MT-HABE) with dynamic homomorphic evaluation. When performing homomorphism calculations, any additional ciphertext can be input [12].

Ding et al. introduced a fully homomorphic encryption scheme combined with attribute encryption. It achieves fine-grained access policy and the desired data can be retrieved by the user. In addition, this scheme can also revoke user permissions, effectively resist traditional attacks, and reduce the computational cost [9].

In 2019, in order to conduct access control and homomorphic operation of the ciphertext with different attributes under multiple policy, and to dynamically add the ciphertext in the process of homomorphism operation, Yu et al. combined attribute-based encryption and multi-hop multi-key fully homomorphic encryption to develop the multi-hop multi-policy attributed-based fully homomorphic encryption scheme [42]. The multi-hop multi-key fully homomorphism encryption mechanism is mainly to solve the homomorphic encryption operation after the addition of the new ciphertext.

A fully homomorphic encryption scheme allows the encrypted data can be read without decryption. In current schemes that combine fully homomorphic encryption with attribute-based encryption, the ciphertext size changes with the number of system attributes. Liu et al. proposes an attribute-based fully homomorphic scheme with short ciphertext scheme based on lattice. This scheme classifies attributes and uses a special structure matrix to avoid ciphertext size changing [20].

While the popularity of big data, people also need to pay attention to the protection of privacy. In 2021, For the sake of strengthening the protection of big data security, the attribute-based adaptive homomorphic encryption (AAHE)was proposed[34]. Unlike other related scheme constructs, in this scheme, the authors adopt Oppositional Based Black Widow Optimization (OBWO) to select the optimal key parameters through AAHE. For the sake of evaluating the method proposed, enhance one way security in the aspect of the conjugacy examination issue. Non-abelian rings and the homomorphism process in ciphertext format was used by the authors. After verification, the present scheme is better than the other selected schemes.

3 Conclusions

In this paper, we summarized the four different privacy calculation schemes combined with attribute-based encryption: attribute-based encryption with keyword search, attribute-based encryption with symmetric search, attribute-based encryption with private set intersection, attribute-based encryption with homomorphic encryption. Besides, we have compared and classified the different schemes.

Through a summary of privacy computation schemes, we find that so far, most studies have been conducted with ciphertext-policy attribute-based encryption. In following studies, we can explore the relevant schemes of KP-ABE and propose new privacy computing schemes. In addition, the relevant research on multi-data owners and dynamic keywords is not diversified enough, which provides a research direction for our future work.

Acknowledgement. This research was funded by the Natural Science Foundation of Jiangsu Province (Grant No. BK20210928), the Philosophy and Social Science Foundation of the Jiangsu Higher Education Institutions of China "Research on Blockchain-based Intelligent Credit Information System and its Privacy Preservation Mechanism" (Grant No. 2021SJA0448), Beijing Key Laboratory of Security and Privacy in Intelligent Transportation, Scientific Research Foundation for Talented Scholars of Jinling Institute of Technology (JIT-B-201726), Natural Science Research Projects of Universities (19KJB520033), and the Higher Education Research Project of Nanjing Institute of Technology (Grant No. 2021ZC13).

References

1. Ali, M., Mohajeri, J., Sadeghi, M.R., Liu, X.: Attribute-based fine-grained access control for outscored private set intersection computation. Inf. Sci. **536**, 222–243 (2020)
2. Asano, K., Emura, K., Takayasu, A., Watanabe, Y.: A generic construction of cca- secure attribute-based encryption with equality test. Cryptology ePrint Archive (2021)
3. Bakas, A., Dang, H.V., Michalas, A., Zalitko, A.: The cloud we share: access control on symmetrically encrypted data in untrusted clouds. IEEE Access **8**, 210462210477 (2020)
4. Bakas, A., Michalas, A.: Modern family: A revocable hybrid encryption scheme based on attribute-based encryption, symmetric searchable encryption and sgx. In: International conference on security and privacy in communication systems. pp, 472–486. Springer (2019)
5. Brakerski, Z., Cash, D., Tsabary, R., Wee, H.: Targeted homomorphic attributebased encryption. In: Theory of Cryptography Conference, pp. 330–360. Springer (2016)

6. Clear, M., Goldrick, C.M.: Attribute-based fully homomorphic encryption with a bounded number of inputs. Int. J. Appl. Cryptogr. **3**(4), 363–376 (2017)
7. Cui, Y., Gao, F., Shi, Y., Yin, W., Panaousis, E., Liang, K.: An efficient attributebased multi-keyword search scheme in encrypted keyword generation. IEEE Access **8**, 99024–99036 (2020)
8. Cui, Y., Huang, Q., Huang, J., Li, H., Yang, G.: Ciphertext-policy attribute-based encrypted data equality test and classification. Comput. J. **62**(8), 1166–1177 (2019)
9. Ding, Y., Li, X.: Policy based on homomorphic encryption and retrieval scheme in cloud computing. In: 2017 IEEE International Conference on Computational Science and Engineering (CSE) and IEEE International Conference on Embedded and Ubiquitous Computing (EUC), vol. 1, pp. 568–571. IEEE (2017)
10. Eltayieb, N., Elhabob, R., Hassan, A., Li, F.: Fine-grained attribute-based encryption scheme supporting equality test. In: International Conference on Algorithms and Architectures for Parallel Processing, pp. 220–233. Springer (2018)
11. Gao, J., Zhou, F.: An encrypted cloud email searching and filtering scheme based on hidden policy ciphertext-policy attribute-based encryption with keyword search. IEEE Access **10**, 8184–8193 (2021)
12. Hiromasa, R., Kawai, Y.: Dynamic multi target homomorphic attribute-based encryption. In: IMA International Conference on Cryptography and Coding, p. 2543. Springer (2017)
13. Khan, S., Zareei, M., Khan, S., Alanazi, F., Alam, M., Waheed, A.: Oo- abms: Online/offline-aided attribute-based multi-keyword search. IEEE Access **9**, 114392–114406 (2021)
14. Li, J., Lin, X., Zhang, Y., Han, J.: Ksf-oabe: Outsourced attribute-based encryption with keyword search function for cloud storage. IEEE Trans. Serv. Comput. **10**(5), 715–725 (2016)
15. Li, J., Wang, M., Lu, Y., Zhang, Y., Wang, H.: Abks-skga: Attribute-based keyword search secure against keyword guessing attack. Computer Standards & Interfaces **74**, 103471 (2021)
16. Lin, H.Y., Jiang, Y.R.: A multi-user ciphertext policy attribute-based encryption scheme with keyword search for medical cloud system. Appl. Sci. **11**(1), 63 (2020)
17. Liu, P., Wang, J., Ma, H., Nie, H.: Efficient verifiable public key encryption with keyword search based on kp-abe. In: 2014 Ninth International Conference on Broadband and Wireless Computing, Communication and Applications, pp. 584–589. IEEE (2014)
18. Liu, S., Yu, J., Xiao, Y., Wan, Z., Wang, S., Yan, B.: Bc-sabe: Blockchain-aided searchable attribute-based encryption for cloud-iot. IEEE Internet Things J. **7**(9), 7851–7867 (2020)
19. Liu, X., Lu, T., He, X., Yang, X., Niu, S.: Verifiable attribute-based keyword search over encrypted cloud data supporting data deduplication. IEEE Access **8**, 5206252074 (2020)
20. Liu, Y., Pan, Y., Gu, L., Zhang, Y., An, D.: Attribute-based fully homomorphic encryption scheme from lattices with short ciphertext. Mathematical Problems in Engineering **2021** (2021)
21. Lv, Z., Zhang, M., Feng, D.: Multi-user searchable encryption with efficient access control for cloud storage. In: 2014 IEEE 6th International Conference on Cloud Computing Technology and Science, pp. 366–373. IEEE (2014)
22. Meng, F., Cheng, L., Wang, M.: Abdks: attribute-based encryption with dynamic keyword search in fog computing. Front. Comp. Sci. **15**(5), 1–9 (2021)
23. Meng, F., Cheng, L., Wang, M.: Ciphertext-policy attribute-based encryption with hidden sensitive policy from keyword search techniques in smart city. EURASIP J. Wirel. Commun. Netw. **2021**(1), 1–22 (2021). https://doi.org/10.1186/s13638-020-01875-2
24. Michalas, A.: The lord of the shares: Combining attribute-based encryption and searchable encryption for flexible data sharing. In: Proceedings of the 34th ACM/SIGAPP Symposium on Applied Computing, pp. 146–155 (2019)
25. Michalas, A., Bakas, A., Dang, H.V., Zalitko, A.: Microscope: enabling access control in searchable encryption with the use of attribute-based encryption and sgx. In: Nordic conference on secure IT systems, pp. 254–270. Springer (2019)

26. Qiu, S., Liu, J., Shi, Y., Zhang, R.: SCIENCE CHINA Inf. Sci. **60**(5), 1–12 (2016). https://doi.org/10.1007/s11432-015-5449-9
27. Sahai, A., Waters, B.: Fuzzy identity-based encryption. In: Annual international conference on the theory and applications of cryptographic techniques, p. 457473. Springer (2005)
28. Sakarkar, G., Rohad, M.P., Gupta, R.A.: Attribute-based encryption with equality test in cloud computing using key-policy. Inf. Technol. J. **5**(2), 2456–3307 (2019)
29. Sangeetha, D., Chakkaravarthy, S.S., Satapathy, S.C., Vaidehi, V., Cruz, M.V.: Multi keyword searchable attribute based encryption for efficient retrieval of health records in cloud. Multimedia Tools and Applications **81**(16), 22065–22085 (2022)
30. Shi, Y., Qiu, S.: Ciphertext-policy attribute-based encryption with outsourced set intersection in multimedia cloud computing. Electronics **10**(21), 2685 (2021)
31. Shi, Y., Qiu, S.: Delegated key-policy attribute-based set intersection over outsourced encrypted data sets for cloudiot. Security and Communication Networks **2021** (2021)
32. Song, D.X., Wagner, D., Perrig, A.: Practical techniques for searches on encrypted data. In: Proceeding 2000 IEEE symposium on security and privacy. S&P 2000, pp. 44–55. IEEE (2000)
33. Sun, W., Yu, S., Lou, W., Hou, Y.T., Li, H.: Protecting your right: verifiable attribute-based keyword search with fine-grained owner-enforced search authorization in the cloud. IEEE Trans. Parallel Distrib. Syst. **27**(4), 1187–1198 (2014)
34. Thenmozhi, R., et al.: Attribute-based adaptive homomorphic encryption for big data security. Big Data (2021)
35. Wang, C., Li, W., Li, Y., Xu, X.: A ciphertext-policy attribute-based encryption scheme supporting keyword search function. In: International Symposium on Cyberspace Safety and Security, pp. 377–386. Springer (2013)
36. Wang, M., Miao, Y., Guo, Y., Wang, C., Huang, H., Jia, X.: Attribute-based encrypted search for multi-owner and multi-user model. In: ICC 2021-IEEE International Conference on Communications, pp. 1–7. IEEE (2021)
37. Wang, Q., Peng, L., Xiong, H., Sun, J., Qin, Z.: Ciphertext-policy attribute-based encryption with delegated equality test in cloud computing. IEEE Access **6**, 760–771 (2017)
38. Wang, S., Yao, L., Chen, J., Zhang, Y.: Ks-abeswet: A keyword searchable attribute-based encryption scheme with equality test in the internet of things. IEEE Access **7**, 80675–80696 (2019)
39. Wang, Y., Cui, Y., Huang, Q., Li, H., Huang, J., Yang, G.: Attribute-based equality test over encrypted data without random oracles. IEEE Access **8**, 32891–32903 (2020)
40. Yang, G.: Outsourced ciphertext-policy attribute-based encryption with equality test. In: Information Security and Cryptology: 14th International Conference, In- scrypt 2018, Fuzhou, China, December 14–17, 2018, Revised Selected Papers, vol. 11449, p. 448. Springer (2019)
41. Yang, Y.: Attribute-based data retrieval with semantic keyword search for e-health cloud. Journal of Cloud Computing **4**(1), 1–6 (2015). https://doi.org/10.1186/s13677-015-0034-8
42. Yu, Q., Tu, G., Li, N., Zhou, T.: Multi-hop multi-policy attributed-based fully homomorphic encryption scheme. Journal of Computer Applications **39**(8), 2326 (2019)
43. Yu, Y., Shi, J., Li, H., Li, Y., Du, X., Guizani, M.: Key-policy attribute-based encryption with keyword search in virtualized environments. IEEE J. Sel. Areas Commun. **38**(6), 1242–1251 (2020)
44. Zhang, R., Xue, R., Liu, L.: Searchable encryption for healthcare clouds: a survey. IEEE Trans. Serv. Comput. **11**(6), 978–996 (2017)
45. Zhang, Y., Zhu, T., Guo, R., Xu, S., Cui, H., Cao, J.: Multi-keyword searchable and verifiable attribute-based encryption over cloud data. IEEE Transactions on Cloud Computing (2021)

46. Zheng, Q., Xu, S., Ateniese, G.: Vabks: Verifiable attribute-based keyword search over outsourced encrypted data. In: IEEE INFOCOM 2014-IEEE conference on computer communications, pp. 522–530. IEEE (2014)
47. Zhu, H., Wang, L., Ahmad, H., Niu, X.: Key-policy attribute-based encryption with equality test in cloud computing. IEEE Access **5**, 20428–20439 (2017)

Research on BIM Modeling Technology from the Perspective of Power Big Data Security

Yan Li[⊠]

Network Security Office of IOE Research Center, State Grid Jiangsu Electric Power Co., Ltd.,
Research Institute, Nanjing 211103, China
516587615@qq.com

Abstract. With the development of power digitization, BIM based modeling has been widely used in the process of power construction, and the challenges of privacy and big data security have also become an increasing trend. According to the requirements of digital management of power safety production, the big data security technology in the process of digital management modeling of power safety production is studied based on BIM Technology. Firstly, the adaptability of BIM in power safety production management and the basic model of big data safety analysis are introduced, including BIM data acquisition and visualization methods, as well as evaluation methods. Among them, the accuracy and effectiveness of big data security are further improved through the combination of high-precision positioning data based on satellite positioning and BIM data. Secondly, the modeling method and examples based on BIM big data security technology are analyzed from four aspects: risk identification, safety plan, safety inspection and safety training. Finally, through a group of practical applications, the verification results show that the proposed scheme is feasible.

Keywords: safety · big data · BIM Technology · Safety production management · power grid

1 Introduction

The safe production of electric power plays an important role in ensuring the sustainable, stable and coordinated development of economic construction [1–3]. Based on various advanced information and communication technologies, digital modeling of power construction process has great practical value in safety production. As the construction of power engineering and the maintenance of power equipment have the particularity of complex construction environment, high requirements for construction timeliness, many cross operations and high labor intensity of construction personnel, and power energy is a kind of high-risk energy, which is dangerous in itself. Improper operation can easily lead to personal electric shock accidents, which makes the safety management of power grid production full of uncertainty and challenges, Power BIM big data security not only has the importance of information security itself, but also has the significance of construction security [4, 5].

On one hand, power grid production safety management is a complex system engineering. In order to further improve the efficiency of safety management, it is necessary to study advanced digital safety management technologies and methods, build a perfect data center based on advanced safety management theoretical model, improve the management ability and automation level of safety big data, and reduce power casualties, power safety accidents Establish a long-term mechanism to continuously improve the management level of power grid safety production [4, 6]. On the other hand, the big data information security of power construction management based on BIM is a prerequisite to further ensure the effective and safe use of data, which is of great significance [7].

However, the research on BIM big data security is relatively few at present. Most of the research is based on how to improve the security management ability of BIM big data under the premise of data security [8].The essence of BIM Technology is to integrate a variety of information in the construction process through three-dimensional data model, so as to realize the functions of fast and accurate design guidance, schedule control, safety plan and so on. BIM big data can also greatly improve the management effect by using dynamic evolution visualization through simulation. The security attributes of BIM big data also have the requirements of privacy, authentication, integrity and consistency [9].

Thus, due to the lack of effective security management model and efficient information support, the implementation effect can not reach the expectation. Because BIM Technology has the characteristics of excellent visualization, strong coordination, high simulation and good coherence [10], this paper constructs a safety model based on BIM Technology, which compares it with satellite positioning data from the aspects of power production risk identification and simulation, improvement of safety awareness and operation skill training of construction personnel, safety guarantee of construction site, safety supervision and so on, Through the safety production management system and information technology means, jointly strengthen the standardization and safety of construction operation, eliminate potential safety hazards and prevent safety accidents. Study BIM big data modeling methods and safety characteristics to ensure the effectiveness of safety management. Combined with satellite positioning precision positioning technology, use various information and data of the model for safety detection. Relevant personnel can carry out safety control on the construction site based on comprehensive BIM data information and design reasonable management scheme [11].

2   Introduction to BIM Technology

BIM (building information modeling) technology, based on three-dimensional digital technology, is an engineering data model that integrates various information describing construction projects from the whole life cycle of building design, construction, operation and maintenance [12, 13]. The sharing and transmission of these information in the whole life cycle enables engineers to correctly understand and efficiently deal with all kinds of engineering information. BIM is a digital expression of the physical and functional characteristics of a facility. It is a process that provides a basis for decision-making by sharing the knowledge resources of the facility. Different stakeholders can extract, modify and update information at different stages of the facility to realize collaborative operation. BIM Technology is no longer a modeling technology in a narrow sense, but has become a new concept [14–16], which is applied in the fields of construction, engineering design, safety management and so on [17]. BIM Technology has the following characteristics:

(1) Visualization. Including design visualization, construction visualization, safety risk source and checkpoint visualization, and equipment operability visualization.
(2) Integration. BIM Technology can carry out the integrated management of the whole life cycle of engineering projects from design, construction to operation supervision.
(3) Big data features. BIM digital model grasps all the information of the project and can simulate the performance, construction scheme and progress, operation and maintenance monitoring and management, safety patrol, safety regulation training and emergency disposal of the project. Various data fusion and summary have big data attributes, and their definition, storage, use and safety protection are no different from conventional big data.
(4) Information completeness. It can integrate the data information of all links in the whole life cycle of the project, and describe the 3D geometric information and topological relationship of the engineering project.

By constructing BIM informatization model, reproducing the power production process by digital means, and deploying safety risk sources and checkpoints to carry out all-round safety control and management, safety problems can be found in advance or safety risks can be avoided [18, 19]. At the same time, through the integration and sharing of digital information based on BIM, it can ensure that the owner, designer, constructor and supplier have a unified safety view, and all participants can obtain comprehensive and accurate information of the project in time, so as to avoid decision-making errors caused by errors or loss in the process of information transmission [20–23].

3   BIM Based Security Modeling

3.1   Basic Model of Safety Management

The basic guarantee of power safety production is the combination of information technology and standardized and scientific management means. Therefore, we need to learn from advanced technology and management means to establish a security model of power production and comprehensively improve the security capability. Herbert William Heinrich, an American safety engineer, proposed the 1:29:300 rule, also known as the Heinrich rule, to clarify the various causes of casualty accidents and the relationship between accidents. Heinrich described the occurrence and development process of industrial injury accidents as a chain process of events with certain causality. The relationship of 1:29:300 in the ratio clearly shows the relationship between relevant accident levels. At the same time, it also reveals that to control the loss of accidents, we must find and start work from a larger and broader basic level, that is, danger and event reports, Therefore, in the safety management, all dangerous situations and property damage events should be reported, investigated and managed, especially the comprehensive and thorough investigation of small accidents such as dangerous situations, so as to fundamentally reduce the occurrence of accidents. Further, Heinrich describes the occurrence and development process of industrial injury accidents as a chain of events with certain causality, which is called Heinrich dominoes theory, and also provides a theoretical basis for power safety management.

On the basis of Heinrich accident causal chain, Bode put forward the accident causal chain which reflects the modern safety view. Bode believes that although the unsafe behavior of people and the unsafe state of goods are important causes of accidents, the most fundamental reason is management mistakes, including the management of people and things. Brid and Loftus further revised Heinrich's Domino model from the perspective of management theory and loss control, which is called "loss cause model". In this model, each domino shows one step of the accident link: lack of control, basic cause, direct cause, accident and loss. The comprehensive analysis method of safety risk is bowtie model, as shown in Fig. 1. In this model, a one to many list threatening events and consequences is established for each hazard, a suggestion list is developed to determine the barrier corresponding to the weakness, control and remedial measures are determined by carefully evaluating the sudden drop of hazard release, and safety events are prevented or event losses are reduced through HSSE key activities.

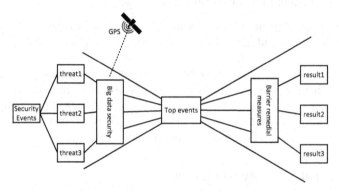

Fig. 1. BowTie model

Combined with the basic theory of safety production management, combining the safety specifications and risk information of power production with the traditional BIM model, assisted by safety patrol, authority management and reward and punishment mechanism, it can timely warn the safety problems in power production, and effectively combine the safety technology, safety strategy, safety management and safe operation by optimizing the construction safety plan and visual safety education and training, Fully consider the power grid, people, technology and operation, complement and cooperate with each other to form a complete and unified system to jointly ensure the safety of the power grid.

3.2 Data Security Fusion and Integration

BIM is an information technology that dynamically manages the whole life cycle data of power construction process. It can realize the organic integration of data model, location model and image model, and build holographic digital twin goals. Among them, security runs through the three model data, which is of great significance for data fusion and sharing. The whole process big data security management can give play to the credibility and data quality of the integration and integration of the three, and then has obvious advantages in modeling quality, simulation accuracy, decision-making efficiency, rendering expression and so on.

BIM big data security model in power application scenario is shown in the figure below (Fig. 2).

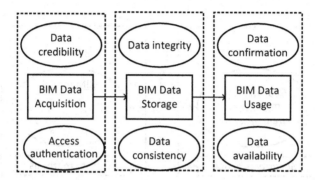

Fig. 2. BIM big data model

BIM big data security model aims at large-scale spatial data to realize the security protection of the whole process of data acquisition, storage and application. Among them, authentication algorithm and data source credibility evaluation method are used to ensure the credibility of BIM big data during data collection. In the data storage stage, data integrity and consistency are realized based on hash function or authentication code. In the data use stage, data confirmation and availability are realized through data security algorithm. In the process of BIM data security protection, for large-scale spatial geographic data, BIM model data and Internet of things data, study the geometric differences and semantic information differences between GIS data and BIM data, realize the transformation and integration of BIM model and 3D GIS model through the transformation of geometric data, coordinate system and attribute information, and finally realize the integration and integration of GIS, BIM and IOT.

3.3 Secure Digital Twinning Mechanism

Digital twin is a digital system that runs parallel in the physical world by means of digital modeling and simulation. Big data modeling of power construction based on BIM describes the physical entities from the aspects of location, geometry, behavior and rules in the information space involved in the power construction process, establishes the dynamic link and real-time interaction between the physical space and the information space, and realizes the closed-loop of state perception, real-time analysis, scientific decision-making and accurate execution based on data flow.

In the specific implementation process, the spatial interaction and fusion relationship between real data and entity BIM model in three-dimensional geospatial space is established to simulate the safety risks under various working conditions, environments and parameters, and generate identification schemes and response schemes to ensure the safety of information and engineering. The comprehensive perception, information inter-action, in-depth analysis and scientific decision-making based on the twin system can improve the organization and decision-making ability of power construction projects, realize the optimal allocation of overall resources, the unified scheduling of various functional modules, and improve the cooperation efficiency of the twin platform. The safety digital twin model is shown in Fig. 3.

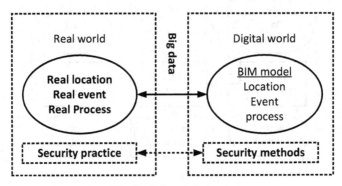

Fig. 3. Safety digital twin

3.4 Safety Risk Identification

BIM model is adopted to manage the risk sources in the process of power production, focusing on the identification and evaluation of risk points, and a visual safety checklist based on BIM is established to realize the whole process risk identification in advance, during and after the event. The specific process is shown in Fig. 4.

In the specific operation, the possible risks of the project are analyzed according to the safety management system and reflected in the BIM model. Through the simulation and deduction of the project process, the possible risk links are dynamically displayed and associated with the corresponding avoidance measures.

The risk source identification based on BIM model can help managers and technicians grasp the site situation in a visual way. It is not easy to miss items in hazard source identification, and it is easy to store, find and manage. On this basis, the hazard sources in BIM model can be identified, analyzed and evaluated automatically through fuzor and other safety analysis software, so as to quickly find out the construction points with hazard sources on site, and carry out identification and statistics, At the same time, output the safety analysis report, and finally effectively control the safety risk.

3.5 BIM Based Power Production Safety Plan

By establishing BIM model and combining the characteristics of the project in different construction stages, prepare detailed safety management planning scheme, formulate

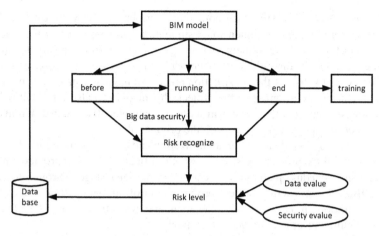

Fig. 4. Process of identification risk

practical safety management objectives according to the actual situation of the project, decompose the objectives and implement them to the person in charge. The specific process is shown in Fig. 5.

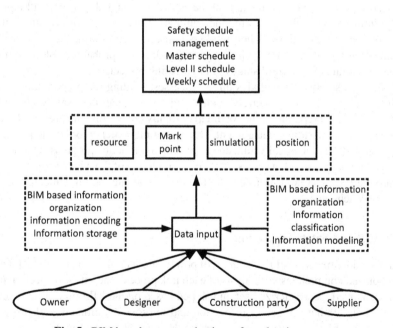

Fig. 5. BIM based power production safety planning process

The application of Bim in safety plan control covers the whole process of project implementation stage, and guides the planning, promotion, inspection, deviation correction and evaluation of project safety progress through virtual construction. The specific methods are as follows: firstly, each component and professional information model are constructed through three-dimensional simulation software; Then make a detailed schedule according to the requirements of project resources and total construction period; Then, by connecting the three-dimensional model and progress information, a 4D model is formed to visually display the construction process of the whole project from the time dimension. During the progress of the project, this model can also represent different project progress states (built, under construction and completed) through different colors and transparency, and compare them with the original plan.

Finally, the progress, data, personnel utilization and other reports are used to evaluate the progress of the project and store relevant information, so as to provide reference information for schedule planning and control in the later stage. Through the application of Bim in construction project progress control, the simulation of the project and the preparation, implementation, adjustment and evaluation of the schedule can be completed intuitively, efficiently and interactively.

Based on BIM, assist the safety production plan, improve the rationality of power production safety plan through safety simulation, and locate the dangerous links, areas and periods in power production in advance, so as to carry out power production activities in a safe and orderly manner. Through the spatial information positioning of BIM, the power production site is segmented and displayed in the form of area, layer or user-defined, and various safety information is displayed in batches on the BIM model. The BIM security management platform shall be established, and all parties shall input and edit the information in the platform, and summarize the security information into the BIM model at the first time. When workers consult the platform, they get the latest real-time security information. This can greatly reduce the probability of safety events in some potential safety hazard stages of engineering projects.

BIM based safety plan includes three processes: guiding the preparation of safety schedule, real-time in-process safety control and post evaluation of safety schedule. In the process of plan preparation, the roadmap of finally completing the project objectives on time through milestone management. During the implementation of the project, the safety plan shall be dynamically adjusted according to the actual progress, and the safety progress shall be measured in stages. After the completion of the whole project, the BIM software platform can be used to comprehensively evaluate the implementation effect of the safety schedule.

3.6   BIM Based Safety Inspection

Through the identification of risk sources of power safety production, combined with the simulation and comprehensive analysis of each link process, the safety inspection points can be visualized, parameterized set and shared based on the BIM platform, which can be used as an auxiliary of safety inspection and improve the efficiency of inspection. The workflow of BIM security rule inspection design is shown in Fig. 6.

The inspection process includes four stages: BIM model establishment, safety system description, rule implementation and feedback. Each safety checkpoint and inspection item are established in the process of the project. Through BIM visual display, the inspectors can easily carry out the inspection work and closed-loop situation.

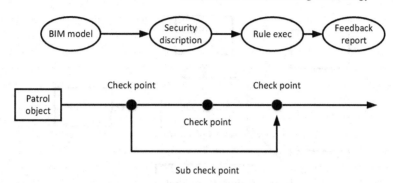

Fig. 6. BIM based safety inspection process

After dynamic simulation with BIM, the inspectors are further familiar with the characteristics of the project and possible safety problems, which is conducive to refining the safety management work, accurately finding out the potential safety hazards of the project and putting forward corresponding treatment schemes for the potential safety hazards. At the same time, the BIM model integrating the safety management system can facilitate baseline comparison, obtain the inspection results, generate the inspection report and support problem feedback and closed-loop.

3.7 BIM Based Safety Training

Safety training is an important guarantee for power safety production and the key content of safety work. Establish the safety system and project site simulation based on BIM, and present the simulated images in the project to the employees with animation as the carrier, which has good intuition and is a vivid embodiment of the safety system. The trained objects can be personally aware of the existence of work hazards, so as to achieve good training results. For example, the safety personnel introduce the potential safety hazards of the project to the operators entering the construction site, and point out what they should pay attention to. The BIM based safety training framework is shown in Fig. 7.

Carry out safety education and method dissemination based on BIM method to improve the safety awareness of on-site construction personnel. BIM based safety training materials are shown in Fig. 9, where green is the safe route and yellow is the dangerous route. In addition, with the help of BIM's emergency evacuation simulation model, the self-organizing behavior and dynamic whole process of personnel evacuation in emergency can be simulated, so as to optimize the emergency evacuation scheme. The BIM model generates 3D walking animation and perspective view, which can communicate the emergency plan with workers in real time.

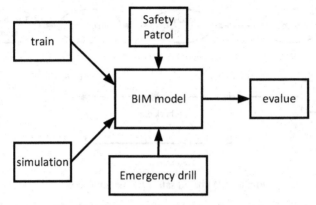

Fig. 7. BIM based safety training framework

4 Security Model

4.1 Satellite Positioning Data Comparison

BIM can establish the data of the construction itself and its life cycle, and assist decision-making through complete internal information [24]. However, due to the lack of absolute spatial positioning information such as positioning and trajectory, it is easy to cause the risk of data inconsistency or tampering. At present, the system for spatial positioning and trajectory tracking is GIS system. Through high-precision positioning technology, accurate space-time positioning can be realized, but it can not go deep into the internal space of the building. Therefore, through the big data fusion and integration of BIM information and GIS positioning information, on the one hand, the integration of BIM micro and GIS macro information can be realized, the acquisition and processing of all digital twin elements can be realized, and the problem of big data security can be further solved. The data fusion process is shown in the figure below (Fig. 8).

BIM model data can be collected in many ways. These relative data are combined with satellite positioning data, and the safety and credibility of BIM data can be determined by the deviation of the same observation point. In order to achieve accurate location, it is necessary to establish a correct and reasonable function model and random model. The function model describes the mapping relationship between the observed values and the parameters to be estimated, while the random model reflects the statistical characteristics of the observed values. In the conventional measurement, the most commonly used are the carrier phase and code pseudorange observations, and their non difference and non combination observation equations can be expressed as follows:

$$P_{rj}^s = \rho_r^s - ct^s + ct_r + (d_{r,j} - d_j^s) - (V_{ion})_j - (V_{trop})_j + \delta\rho_j + (\delta\rho_{mul})_j + \varepsilon_j$$

$$\varphi_{rj}^s \lambda_j = \rho_r^s - N\lambda_j - ct^s + ct_r + \lambda_j(d_{r,j} - d_j^s) + (V_{ion})_j - (V_{trop})_j + \delta\rho_j + (\delta\rho_{mul})_j + \varepsilon_j$$

In the above formula, subscript j is frequency; P_{rj}^s is the pseudo range observation value; φ_{rj}^s is the carrier phase observation value; Superscript s indicates the satellite number;

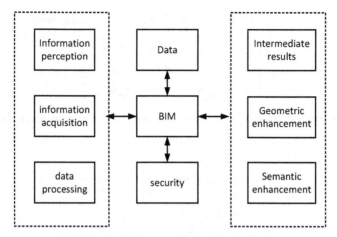

Fig. 8. Multidimensional data fusion model

Subscript r indicates the receiver number; ρ_r^s is the geometric distance term; t_r is the receiver clock error; t^s is the satellite clock error; $d_{r,j}$ and d_j^s are the pseudo range hardware delay of receiver and carrier respectively; $b_{r,j}$ and b_j^s are carrier hardware delays of receiver and satellite respectively; V_{ion} is the ionospheric delay error; V_{trop} is the tropospheric delay error; $\delta\rho_j$ is the distance error of the precise ephemeris in the signal propagation direction; $\delta\rho_{mul}$ is multipath effect; ε_j is the measurement noise.

Because the accuracy of the existing ionospheric delay model is not high, and it is difficult to establish the parameter estimation of the function model, the carrier and pseudo range observations with different frequencies are generally used for the first-order ionospheric combination, and the new carrier and pseudo range combined observations are used as the function model. Because it eliminates most of the influence of ionospheric delay and has a simple model, it is widely used in various orbit determination, positioning systems or software. However, the measurement noise of this combined observation value increases by three times, and the ambiguity also loses its whole cycle characteristics, which will lead to the increase of ambiguity convergence time. The pseudo range and carrier phase combined observations of the first-order ionospheric combination can be expressed as follows:

$$P_c = \frac{1}{f_1^2 - f_2^2}(f_1^2 P_1 - f_2^2 P_2)$$

$$\varphi_c = \frac{f_1^2}{f_1^2 - f_2^2}\varphi_1 - \frac{f_1 f_2}{f_1^2 - f_2^2}\varphi_2$$

In the above formula, P_c is the pseudo range combined observation value of eliminating the first-order ionosphere, φ_c is the carrier combined observation value of eliminating the first-order ionosphere, P_1 and P_2 are the pseudo range observation values of f_1 and f_2 frequencies respectively, and φ_1 and φ_2 are the carrier observation values of f_1 and f_2 frequencies respectively.

In data comparison, the coordinates of satellite positioning and navigation system and space rectangular coordinates need to be converted. Convert satellite positioning and navigation coordinates (L, B, H) into space rectangular coordinates:

$$\begin{bmatrix} X \\ Y \\ Z \end{bmatrix} = \begin{bmatrix} (N + H) \cos B \cos L \\ (N + H) \cos B \sin L \\ N(1 - e^2) + H] \sin B \end{bmatrix}$$

Convert Cartesian coordinates (x, y, z) into positioning coordinates (L, B, H):

$$\begin{bmatrix} L \\ B \\ H \end{bmatrix} = \begin{bmatrix} \arctan(y/x) \\ \arctan(\dfrac{z + e^2 b \sin^3 \theta}{\sqrt{x^2 + y^2} - e^2 a \cos^3 \theta}) \\ \dfrac{\sqrt{x^2 + y^2}}{\cos B} - N \end{bmatrix}$$

In the above formula, N is the radius of curvature of the earth's circle and e is the eccentricity of the earth, which satisfies

$$N = \frac{a}{\sqrt{1 - e^2 \sin^2 B}}, e^2 = a^{-2}(a^2 - b^2)$$

$$\theta = \arctan(\frac{zd \cdot a}{\sqrt{x^2 + y^2} \cdot b})$$

The semiaxis of the earth, where a is the major axis and b is the minor axis.

4.2 Hazard Identification Technology

Based on the stride model, this paper presents a method to determine threats, that is, threats are divided into six categories, and then consider whether each category of threats will affect the security of the system. However, when considering the security solution of the system, it is not enough to only refer to the six types of threats of stride model, because the classification of threats in this model is one-dimensional. Obviously, the attacks of the same type of threats may occur in multiple locations of the system. Therefore, the limitation of stride model is that this one-dimensional threat classification method is not specific enough, and the context of threat occurrence needs to be considered.

Since it is necessary to consider the location of the threat and the category of the threat at the same time, the dimension can be added to the original stride model, which is improved from the original one-dimensional dimension, that is, a single threat category dimension, to a model with two dimensions: threat category and the context in which the threat occurs. By adding the dimension of the context in which the threat occurs, we can get a hierarchical security threat model.

According to the improved stride model, when analyzing the threats faced by the system, firstly, based on the location of the threat, the threats are divided into three categories: threats at the core of the system, threats at the boundary of the system and threats outside the system. Then, the threat classification method of stride model is used as the classification criterion on each branch of the tree structure.

Data flow anomaly monitoring and analysis technology based on network flow order is the basis of monitoring and analysis supporting heterogeneous data source environment, which is often used for large-scale network communication monitoring. Based on this idea, this paper regards all kinds of information in BIM big data model as network input data flow for security analysis. The flow anomaly analysis technology takes the flow record of ipfix as the input. Through the monitoring based on entropy and data mining method, it finds the specific target, event type and specific service affected, and completes the alarm.

(1) Data anomaly classification
  1) Fault and performance abnormality. Fault abnormality refers to the abnormality of data flow due to equipment failure.
  2) The data behavior is abnormal, the data change rate suddenly increases, and the performance of the whole BIM system decreases. It may be related to social reasons such as rest days and major social activities, or it may be caused by natural factors, such as surface activities, mountain torrents, tsunamis, etc.
  3) Malicious attack exception: the traffic exception caused by a malicious attack on a terminal in the network. For example, DoS attack, worm attack or other man-made attacks cause abnormal data flow information.
(2) Data model establishment

After determining that the detection object of network anomaly is the network flow data, the anomaly detection of network data can be carried out after the entropy description and index calculation of the data. The traffic anomaly needs to be compared with the current window network flow data and the conventional traffic model to complete the anomaly detection. Therefore, it is very important to establish a normal data model. If the established model is unreliable, it will have an immeasurable negative impact on the detection stage. In recent years, many scholars use clustering analysis to establish normal data model, but many traditional clustering algorithms have the problem of low algorithm efficiency. Therefore, this project will analyze and improve the traditional clustering analysis algorithm to establish a normal data model efficiently.

The traditional artificial intelligence method K-means is easily affected by the selection of initial points. It has weak resolution in classified data. It is affected by abnormal data and the size of density variance of different categories. The solution is to use the dichotomous K-means process. Bisection k-means algorithm is an improved algorithm of K-means clustering algorithm. Its idea is: in order to divide the sample data into K clusters, first use k-means algorithm to divide all the sample data into two clusters, select a cluster with large sample data in these two clusters, and repeat the bisection operation of K-means algorithm to get k clusters. The steps of bisection k-means algorithm are as follows:

a) Initialize cluster set v. cluster set V contains only one cluster s containing all samples, and the number of clusters $km = 1$;
b) Take out a largest cluster N_i from cluster set V;
c) K-means clustering algorithm is used to perform Q-quadratic clustering operation on cluster N_i;
d) Calculate the SSE size of this q pair of sub clusters, select the pair of sub clusters with the lowest SSE value and add it to V, km++;
e) If km = k, the algorithm terminates. Otherwise, go to step b).

Sum of squares of error SSE is the evaluation function of clustering, as shown in the following formula:

$$SSE = \sum_{x_i \in N_1} ||x_i - Q_1^*||^2 + \sum_{x_j \in N_2} ||x_j - Q_2 * ||^2$$

5 Application Example

Figure 9 shows the risk point distribution model of a project in a specific stage. Using the three-dimensional visualization ability of BIM, users can arbitrarily select risk sources for analysis, simulated disposal and avoidance.

Fig. 9. BIM model of risk source identification

An example of BIM based power production safety plan is shown in Fig. 10. The upper part is the plan node of BIM system information production.

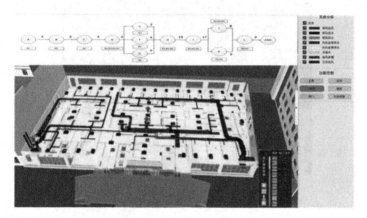

Fig. 10. Example of safety production plan

Figure 11 shows the distribution of checkpoints in BIM model.

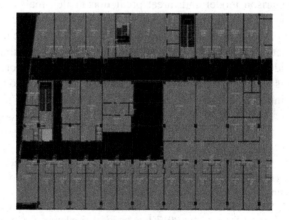

Fig. 11. Checkpoint distribution

Figure 12 is the schematic diagram of safety training.

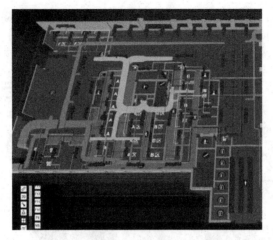

Fig. 12. Safety training material model

6 Conclusion

Based on BIM and big data security technology, model and simulate the location and state of safety elements on the power production site. Through the establishment of location information comparison model and threat prediction model, realize scientific safety management, help to better complete hazard identification, safety plan tracking, patrol work support, safety training and emergency drill, and greatly reduce unsafe behaviors and states in power production, Reduce potential accidents, reduce human and property losses, and provide strong support for power production safety informatization. The further research is to improve the intelligence and automation of model operation, as well as the real-time calculation.

References

1. Mahamadu, A., Mahdjoubi, L., Booth, C.: Challenges to BIM-cloud integration: implication of security issues on secure collaboration. In: 2013 IEEE 5th International Conference on Cloud Computing Technology and Science, pp. 209–214 (2013)
2. Smirnova, O.V., Smirnov, K.V.: Creating automation tools with BIM-programs for designing elements of metal bridges. In: 2017 International Conference "Quality Management, Transport and Information Security, Information Technologies" (IT&QM&IS), pp. 773–775 (2017)
3. Boyes, H.: Security, privacy, and the built environment. IT Prof. **17**, 25–31 (2015)
4. Wenpeng, D., Maoxuan, Q., Xiaofeng, F., Yixuan, W.: Safety monitoring platform for deep excavation based on BIM and big data technology. In: 2020 International Conference on Robots & Intelligent System (ICRIS), pp. 537–540 (2020)
5. Luo, J., Liu, P., Liu, L., Liu, Z.: Research on intelligent management and control technology of power grid engineering based on BIM. In: 2021 International Conference on Intelligent Transportation, Big Data & Smart City (ICITBS), pp. 141–144 (2021)
6. Ge, S.: Exploring the application of BIM engineering in multi-project main body collaborative management platform. In: 2019 4th International Conference on Mechanical, Control and Computer Engineering (ICMCCE), pp. 730–7303 (2019)

7. Kokorus, M., Eyrich, W., Zacharias, R.: Innovative approach to the substation design using Building Information Modeling (BIM) technology. In: 2016 IEEE/PES Transmission and Distribution Conference and Exposition (T&D), pp. 1–5 (2016)
8. Nguyen, T., Hoang, V., Tran, T.: A wireless physical layer security method based on binary Exclusive-Or jamming message and CSI alignment. In: 2019 International Conference on System Science and Engineering (ICSSE), pp. 291–296 (2019)
9. Jacomini, R.V., França, A.P., Bim, E.: Simulation and experimental studies on double-fed induction generator power control at subsynchronous operating speed. In: 2009 International Conference on Power Electronics and Drive Systems (PEDS), pp. 1421–1424 (2009)
10. Peijun, Q., Tao, Y., Xiaofei, Z., Shaoen, J., Yanbo, C.: Emergency evacuation simulation based on BIM technology for scientific facility. In: 2020 International Signal Processing, Communications and Engineering Management Conference (ISPCEM), pp. 210–213 (2020)
11. Kanak, A., Arif, İ., Kumaş, O., Ergün, S.: Extending BIM to urban semantic context for data-driven crisis preparedness. In: 2020 IEEE International Conference on Systems, Man, and Cybernetics (SMC), pp. 3813–3818 (2020)
12. Boyes, H.A., Isbell, R., Norris, P., Watson, T.: Enabling intelligent cities through cyber security of building information and building systems. In: IET Conference on Future Intelligent Cities, pp. 1–6
13. Wall, A., Butzin, B., Golatowski, F., Rethfeldt, M., Timmermann, D.: Software-defined security architecture for smart buildings using the building information model. In: 2019 IEEE Global Conference on Internet of Things (GCIoT), pp. 1–5 (2019)
14. Wang, L., He, Y., Han, Y.: Research on power engineering construction management based on BIM technology. In: 2018 International Conference on Robots & Intelligent System (ICRIS), pp. 107–109 (2018)
15. Marchi, R., Dainez, P., Zuben, F.V., Bim, E.: A multilayer perceptron controller applied to the direct power control of a doubly fed induction generator. In: 2015 IEEE Power & Energy Society General Meeting, p. 1 (2015)
16. Zhao, Q.: BIM design for reconstruction of old factory building based on sustainable perspective. In: 2020 IEEE 20th International Conference on Software Quality, Reliability and Security Companion (QRS-C), pp. 522–526 (2020)
17. Tan, T., Porter, S., Tan, T., West, G.: Computational Red Teaming for physical security assessment. In: The 4th Annual IEEE International Conference on Cyber Technology in Automation, Control and Intelligent, pp. 258–263
18. Wang, J.: Public building BIM safety early warning algorithm based on improved cyclic wavelet neural network. In: 2021 Fifth International Conference on I-SMAC (IoT in Social, Mobile, Analytics and Cloud) (I-SMAC), pp. 857–860 (2021)
19. Zaimen, K., Brahmia, M.E.-A., Dollinger, J.F., Moalic, L., Abouaissa, A., Idoumghar, L.: A overview on WSN deployment and a novel conceptual BIM-based approach in smart buildings. In: 2020 7th International Conference on Internet of Things: Systems, Management and Security (IOTSMS), pp. 1–6 (2020)
20. Kirstein, P.T., Ruiz-Zafra, A.: Use of templates and the handle for large-scale provision of security and IoT in the built environment. In: Living in the Internet of Things: Cybersecurity of the IoT - 2018, pp. 1–10 (2018)
21. Musgrove, J., Cukic, B., Cortellessa, V.: Proactive model-based performance analysis and security tradeoffs in a complex system. In: 2014 IEEE 15th International Symposium on High-Assurance Systems Engineering, pp. 211–215 (2014)
22. Zhao, Q., Li, Y., Hei, X., Wang, X.: Toward automatic calculation of construction quantity based on building information modeling. In: 2015 11th International Conference on Computational Intelligence and Security (CIS), pp. 482–485 (2015)

23. Zhao, Q., Tian, Q., Hei, X., Li, Y., Ma, Z.: Toward automatic review of bridge template turnover based on building information modeling. In: 2017 13th International Conference on Computational Intelligence and Security (CIS), pp. 376–380 (2017)
24. Lingling, Y., Haiyan, S., Yalong, X., Yulong, L., Zhihua, W., Qingbo, C.: Research and application of key technologies of BIM+GIS virtual-reality interaction for high-speed railway integration test. In: 2021 IEEE 5th Information Technology, Networking, Electronic and Automation Control Conference (ITNEC), pp. 204–209 (2021)

Security Risk Management of the Internet of Things Based on 5G Technology

Wei Cao, Yang Hu, Shuang Yang, Xue-yang Zhu, and Jia Yu[✉]

NARI Group Corporation/State Grid Electric Power Research Institute, Nanjing, China
401945335@qq.com

Abstract. The Internet of Things brings security issues as well as high connectivity. This paper proposes a security risk decision based on the bounded rationality of users, aiming at the security problems of power Internet of things. First of all, a sparse node cognitive network is constructed for each user. Based on this simplified cognitive network, each user establishes his own security decision by minimizing his own security cost in the real world. These two stages constitute a game-to-game framework. Then the concept of a structured Nash equilibrium (GNE) solution is proposed to solve the game decisions of users in security management under this bounded rationality. At the same time, an iterative algorithm based on the nearest point is designed to calculate GNE. Finally, we analyze the case of intelligent power station in the Internet of Things, and the results show that this algorithm can successfully identify key users. Other users need to consider the decisions of these key users in the security decision-making process, and their own security decisions also reduce each other's security management costs.

Keywords: Big data · Internet of things security · Bounded rational decision making · Cognitive network · Key users

1 Introduction

As an important infrastructure in urban and rural areas, the distribution network is a platform to support the grid connection of distributed power supply and carry the flexible adjustment of resources on the user side. The distribution network has become an important position to serve the double-carbon goal and build a new power system. The future development of the distribution network will face a new situation, new changes and new demand.

In addition to providing higher bandwidth services, 5G also introduces new application scenarios for ultra-reliable, low-latency communication (URLLC) to meet the diverse needs of data transmission. At the same time, the service diversity puts forward the higher requirements for the service index and the communication system. In order to provide millisecond ultra-low delay and flexible and choreographed communication services, and meet the explosive communication needs of power terminals, power grid equipment and users in 5G scenarios, the end-to-end low-delay jitter control, network slice dispatching, intelligent collaboration and other technologies are of

© The Author(s), under exclusive license to Springer Nature Singapore Pte Ltd. 2023
Y. Tian et al. (Eds.): ICBDS 2022, CCIS 1796, pp. 451–461, 2023.
https://doi.org/10.1007/978-981-99-3300-6_32

practical significance. The power production control business requires high delay, the precision load control service requires communication delay less than 50 ms, and the distribution network protection service requires communication delay less than 20 ms. 5G public wireless network congestion increases. The control service requires the fixed path of transmission network, the objective phenomenon of wireless channel decline and the error retransmission mechanism of public wireless network lead to delay jitter. At present, wireless communication bearer distribution network protection services lack relevant data in product design, engineering planning and operation and maintenance optimization, so relevant existing network applications need to be carried out.

2 Internet of Things Technology

2.1 Basic Knowledge

Taking the intelligent power station system in the power Internet of Things in Fig. 1 as an example, a sparse node cognitive network of users is built, in which each set of intelligent power station and its interconnections are modeled as nodes and links respectively. Since different smart power stations have different devices, namely, the security management of the Internet of Things is essentially decentralized.

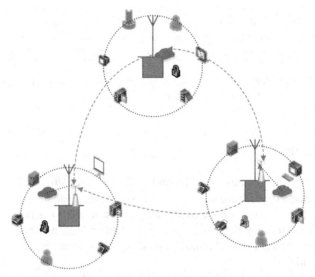

Fig. 1. Architecture diagram of the intelligent power station system based on the Internet of Things

Taking the distribution network differential protection service as an example, each protection terminal sends the electrical measurement data of the local end to the opposite end through the communication channel. At the same time, the data sent by the opposite end is received and compared to determine whether the fault position is within the protection range, and decides whether to start and remove the fault. The typical acquisition frequency of the protected terminal is 1200 Hz. The data is sent every 0.833 ms, the single data volume is 245 byte, and the communication bandwidth requirement is 2.36 Mbps. Because the failure of distribution network is random, the differential protection of distribution network requires continuous real-time communication transmission data to judge and detect whether the line is faulty, so it has a demand for continuous uplink bandwidth traffic, and a high requirement for bandwidth resource guarantee. In addition, continuous communication will also generate a large amount of network traffic, a single terminal is about 886 GB, high network traffic carrying capacity requirements.

2.2 Network Security Management Game

In a network of Iot users, there are nodes $N := \{1, 2, \ldots, N\}$, Each node can be viewed as a participant. Each node is a participant to making decisions ne $U := \{u_1, \ldots, u_N\}$ as the set of decisions for all participants. The security investment of participant i. $u_{-i} := U \backslash \{u_i\}$ is a set of secure investment decisions excluding participants in the network. For participant $i \in N$, the goal is to strategically minimize its security risks by taking costly action-decision u_i. We define $F_1^i : R_+ \to R_+$ as the cost of participant i security management efforts, which is an increasing function about u_i. Due to the interconnection in the Iot of Things, the risk of participants also depends on the users it is connected to. Therefore, we represent the impact of the participants' connected users on their security with a function $F_3^i : R_+ \times R_+^{N-1} \to R_+$. For security decisions, Internet of Things is a strategic complementary approach. That is, assuming that participant j is the connection node of participant i, when the security investment of participant i is large, it also indirectly reduces the network risk of participant i. Therefore, the cost function of participant i can be expressed

$$J^i(u_i, u_{-i}) = F_1^i(u_i) - F_2^i(u_i) - F_3^i(u_i, u_{-i})$$

$$F_1^i(u_i) = \frac{1}{2} R_{ii}^i u_i^2 \quad F_2^i(u_i) = r_i u_i \quad F_3^i(u_i, u_{-i}) = \sum_{j \neq i, j \in N} R_{ij}^i u_i u_j$$

It can be described as

$$J^i(u_i, u_{-i}) = \frac{1}{2} R_{ii}^i u_i^2 - r_i u_i - \sum_{j \neq i, j \in N} R_{ij}^i u_i u_j$$

where R_{ii}^i is the safety investment cost factor of participant i, r_i is the unit return of the security investment of participant i, and R_{ij}^i is the safety investment impact factor of participant j on participant i. $R_{ii}^i > 0$, $r_i > 0$, $\forall i$, $R_{ij}^i \geq 0$, $\forall j \neq i$, $i \in N$ The first item $\frac{1}{2} R_{ii}^i u_i^2$ in the formula is the safety management cost of increasing marginal income. The second item $r_i u_i$ indicates the corresponding return of safety management. The last item $\sum_{j \neq i, j=1} R_{ij}^i u_i u_j$ are users of the participants. Specifically, the structure of F_3^i indicates that the risk measure of the participant i, J^i decreases linearly with the action of the user j. Therefore, the larger investment of users in the established models helps to reduce the impact of network risk in a linear manner. We have the following assumptions on the safety impact parameters.

$$R_{ii}^i > \sum_{j \neq i, j \in N} R_{ij}^i \ \forall i \in N$$

In IoT networks, user security is\y determined by strategy, is not by the decisions of its associated users. At the same time, the characteristics of hypothesis 1 also influence the network, there is a coupling between their cost functions

$$R_{ii}^i u_i - \sum_{j \neq i, j \in N} R_{ij}^i - r_i = 0 \ \forall i \in N$$

Putting into the matrix form produces the

$$\begin{bmatrix} R_{11}^1 & -R_{12}^1 & \cdots & -R_{1N}^1 \\ -R_{21}^2 & R_{22}^2 & \cdots & -R_{2N}^2 \\ \cdots & & & \\ -R_{N1}^N & -R_{N2}^N & \cdots & R_{NN}^N \end{bmatrix} \begin{bmatrix} u_1 \\ u_2 \\ \cdots \\ u_N \end{bmatrix} = \begin{bmatrix} r_1 \\ r_2 \\ \cdots \\ r_N \end{bmatrix} \Leftrightarrow Ru = r$$

2.3 Limited and Rational Safety Management Game

In the actual network, because each user is rational, Specifically, participants' limited rationality a can be characterized with a vector $\vec{m^i} = [m_j^i], m_j^i \in [0, 1]$ Attention network established on behalf of participant i. When $m_j^i = 0$, user i does not follow the behavior of user j; when $m_j^i = 1$, user i observes the true value of the security management of user j. Thus, the decision of participant j perceived by participant i becomes a. Therefore, for participant i, considering its finite rationality, the cost function becomes

$$J^i(u_i, u_{-i}^{c_i}, m^i) = \frac{1}{2} R_{ii}^i u_i^2 - r_i u_i - \sum_{j \neq i, j \in N} m_j^i R_{ij}^i u_i u_j$$

$$= \frac{1}{2} R_{ii}^i u_i^2 - r_i u_i - \sum_{j \neq i, j \in N} R_{ij}^i u_i u_j^{c_i}$$

The first-order optimal condition of the equation is

$$\begin{bmatrix} R_{11}^1 & -m_2^1 R_{12}^1 & \cdots & -m_N^1 R_{1N}^1 \\ -m_1^2 R_{21}^2 & R_{22}^2 & \cdots & -m_N^2 R_{2N}^2 \\ \cdots & & & \\ -m_1^N R_{N1}^N & -m_2^N R_{N2}^N & \cdots & R_{NN}^N \end{bmatrix} \begin{bmatrix} u_1 \\ u_2 \\ \cdots \\ u_N \end{bmatrix} = \begin{bmatrix} r_1 \\ r_2 \\ \cdots \\ r_N \end{bmatrix} \Leftrightarrow R^s u = r$$

The participants' limited and rational optimal response becomes

$$u_i = BR^i(u_{-i}^{c_i}) = \frac{1}{R_{ii}^i}(u_i = BR^i(u_{-i}^{c_i}) = \frac{1}{R_{ii}^i}(\sum_{j \neq i, j \in N} R_{ii}^i u_j^{c_i} + r_i)$$

We denote the participants' limited and rational safety management game with ψ. In contrast to the notion ne of the game b solution, the notion of the game solution is extended.

2.4 Limited and Rational Safety Management Game

Because of the large connections in the Iot of Things, for this reason, given the limited rationality, the actual cost of the user i becomes

$$
\begin{aligned}
J^i(BR^i(u^{Ci}_{-j}), u_{-i}) &= \frac{1}{2R^i_{ii}}(\sum_{j\neq i, j\in N} R^i_{ii}u^{Ci}_j + r_i)^2 \\
&- \sum_{k\neq i, k\in N}[\frac{1}{R^i_{ii}}R^i_{ik}u_k(\sum_{j\neq i, j\in N} R^i_{ii}u^{Ci}_j + r_i)] - \frac{r_i}{R^i_{ii}}(\sum_{j\neq i, j\in N} R^i_{ii}u^{Ci}_j + r_i) \\
&= \frac{1}{2}\sum_{j\neq i, j\in N}\sum_{k\neq i, k\in N}\frac{1}{R^i_{ii}}R^i_{ij}R^i_{ik}u^{Ci}_j u^{Ci}_k - \frac{1}{2R^i_{ii}}(r_i)^2 \\
&- \sum_{k\neq i, k\in N}(\sum_{j\neq i, j\in N} R^i_{ii}u^{Ci}_j)\frac{1}{R^i_{ii}}R^i_{ik}u_k - \sum_{k\neq i, k\in N}\frac{1}{R^i_{ii}}r_i R^i_{ik}u_k
\end{aligned}
$$

Using the cognitive vector m^i to represent the actual cost to the participant, then

$$
\begin{aligned}
&J^i(BR^i(u^{Ci}_{-j}), u_{-i}) = \\
&\frac{1}{2}\sum_{j\neq i, j\in N}\sum_{k\neq i, k\in N} m^i_j \frac{1}{R^i_{ii}}R^i_{ij}R^i_{ik}u^{Ci}_j u^{Ci}_k - \frac{1}{2R^i_{ii}}(r_i)^2 \\
&-\frac{1}{2}\sum_{j\neq i, j\in N}\sum_{k\neq i, k\in N} m^i_j \frac{1}{R^i_{ii}}R^i_{ij}R^i_{ik}u^{Ci}_j u^{Ci}_k - \sum_{k\neq i, k\in N}[\frac{1}{R^i_{ii}}r_i R^i_{ik}u_k]
\end{aligned}
$$

The participants' cognitive network formation problem can be formulated as the cognitive vector corresponding to the actual cost minimization, i.e.

$$
\begin{aligned}
m^{i*} &= \arg\min J^i(BR^i(u^{Ci}_{-j}), u_{-i}) + \alpha_i\|m^i\| \\
&= \arg\min \frac{1}{2}\sum_{j\neq i, j\in N}\sum_{k\neq i, k\in N}\frac{1}{R^i_{ii}}R^i_{ij}R^i_{ik}u^{Ci}_j u^{Ci}_k m^i_j m^i_k \\
&- \sum_{j\neq i, j\in N}\frac{1}{R^i_{ii}}R^i_{ij}R^i_{ik}u^{Ci}_j u^{Ci}_k m^i_j + \alpha_i\|m^i\| \\
&= \arg\min \frac{1}{2}m^{iT}\Lambda^i m^i - e^T_{N-1}\Lambda^i m^i + \alpha_i\|m^i\|
\end{aligned}
$$

Therefore, for the participants, we need to address the following constraint optimization problem

$$
\begin{aligned}
&\min \frac{1}{2}m^{iT}\Lambda^i m^i - e^T_{N-1}\Lambda^i m^i + \alpha_i\|m^i\| \\
&0 \leq m^i_j \leq 1, j \neq i, j \in N
\end{aligned}
$$

where the constraints $m^i_j \in [0, 1]$, indicate the user's risk perception

$$
\begin{aligned}
&\min \frac{1}{2}m^{iT}\Lambda^i m^i - e^T_{N-1}\Lambda^i m^i \\
&0 \leq m^i_j \leq 1, j \neq i, j \in N \\
&\|m^i\| = \beta_i
\end{aligned}
$$

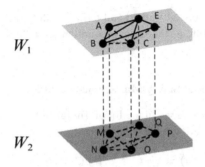

Fig. 2. Network relationship diagram of the user network and cognition of the Internet of Things

2.5 Format Tower Nash Equilibrium

Security management also has a game structure under finite rational problems. Figure 2 shows the relationship between the two very well.

Figure 2 shows that users determine their own cognitive network while making strategic security management decisions in the Internet of Things. The security management game of the layer W_1 and the cognitive network of the layer W_2 form the game interdependence, forming the game to the game framework.

The tower Nash equilibrium is a combination, as follows

$$J^i(u_i^*, u_{-i}^*, m^{i*}) \leq J^i(u_i^*, u_{-i}^*, m^i)$$

3   The Design of the Algorithm

3.1   Rewrite the Constraint Optimization Formula

We can rewrite the constraint optimization formula as

$$\min Q_i(m^i) = \tfrac{1}{2} m^{iT} \Lambda^i m^i - e_{N-1}^T \Lambda^i m^i + \alpha_i \|m^i\| + l_C(m^i)$$
$$l_C(x) = \begin{cases} 0, & \text{if } x \in C \\ +\infty, & \text{otherwise} \end{cases}$$

For convenience, we decompose the function into the following three sections

$$f_1^i(m^i) = \tfrac{1}{2} m^{iT} \Lambda^i m^i - e_{N-1}^T \Lambda^i m^i + \alpha_i \|m^i\| + l_C(m^i)$$
$$f_2^i(m^i) = \alpha_i \|m^i\|$$
$$f_3^i(m^i) = l_C(m^i)$$

The optimization problem is very challenging to solve. First, note that the convexity of f_i^i depends on the eigenvalue of the matrix Λ^i Especially for f_1^i, when the timing Λ^i is positive, f_1^i is convex in m^i. When Λ^i is not explicit, solving quadratic programs is an NP-hard problem. Second, the norm-based functions and the indicator functions, although convex, are non-smooth and nondifferentiable. Traditional gradient-based optimization tools are not sufficient to deal with such optimization problems. To this end, we designed an approximate algorithm to solve this problem.

3.2   End-To-End Time-Delay Jitter Analysis Model

Modeling the service flow according to the characteristics of distribution network protection service, and then analyzes the end-to-end delay jitter of distribution network protection service

$$P\{A(s, s+t) - \alpha(t) > x\} \leq f(x)$$

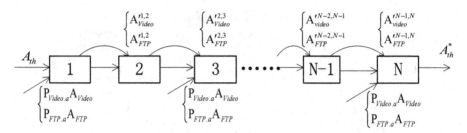

Fig. 3.   End to end time-delay jitter analysis model

On the other hand, the service model used to describe the random lower bound of the system service capability is usually expressed by the weak random service curve:

$$P\{A(t) \otimes \beta(t) - D(t) > x\} \leq g(x)$$

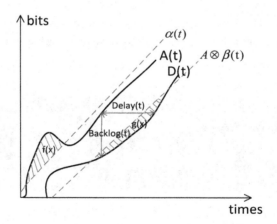

Fig. 4.   Time delay jitter calculus based on random networks

Based on the stochastic network calculus theory, the end-to-end delay jitter of the distribution network protection service is analyzed. By establishing the traffic model and service model corresponding to the current data flow and network nodes, and combining the minimum plus algebraic operation, the optimization results are close to the actual performance boundary.

3.3   End-To-End Time-Lapse Analysis

The system uses the ofdm signal to transmit data. In order to ensure the orthogonality of the ofdm signal, there must be a certain interval between each symbol. As shown in the figure above, the lte transmission time interval (tti) is at least 1 ms (Fig. 7).

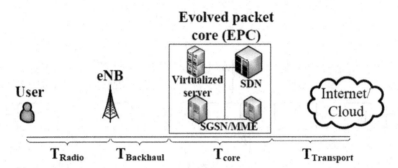

Fig. 5. Schematic diagram of the end-to-end time delay analysis

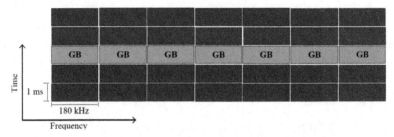

Fig. 6. Schematic representation of the ofdm frame package structure

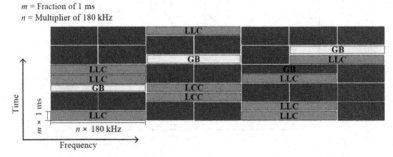

Fig. 7. A Schematic representation of the LTE transport structure

Transmission time interval is a major influencing factor of wireless delay, the greater the TTI, the greater the delay. Since tti is mainly from the OFDM frame protection interval, it is understandable that tti changes with the frame parameters. Therefore, an important step in 5G is the introduction of variable frame parameters and frame structure to adapt to the delay requirements in different scenarios.

4   Results of the Case Analysis

We use the case study of the intelligent power station system supporting the Internet of Things shown in Fig. 1 to confirm the designed algorithm, and show in this part that limited rationality can only be the security management of agents. We study a smart power station system that consists of two sets represented by G_1 and G_2, respectively. $\beta = \|m^i\| = 3$. G_1 consists of 6 agents $G_1 = \{1, 2, 3, 4, 5, 6\}$, G_2 consists of 4 agents, $G_2 = \{7, 8, 9, 10\}$. The same parameter settings of both power stations are as follows.

The simulation result diagram is shown in Figs. 3, 4, 5 and 6, where the step represents the number of iterative steps between the two components of the cognitive network formation and the security management strategy (Fig. 9).

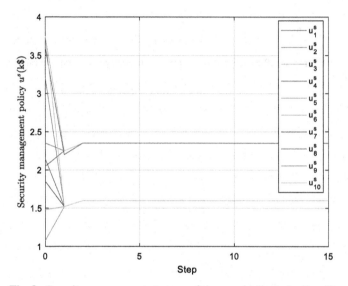

Fig. 8. Security management strategy of users under limited rationality

Figure 8 shows the security management strategy of users under limited rationality. As can be seen from the figure, the cost of participants in group G_1 is lower, which is also in line with the actual situation. For group G_1, r_i is large, that is, the return of security management is greater, so the security cost of the corresponding users is also reduced.

Figure 4 compares the difference between the cost of the users under the limited rationality and the complete rationality. The results show that the security risk of the users increases under the limited rationality model, and the difference in group G_1 is small (Fig. 10).

In Fig. 5, the two groups form their overall sparse cognitive network, depicting their cognitive vectors, as well as their cognitive resource allocation, respectively. Thus, in limited cognitive situations, all agents focus only on the safety decisions made by group G_1. Figure 5 also verifies the phenomenon that all agents allocate only cognitive resources to group G_1 of them, either in group G_1 or in group G_2 (6 agents in group G_1).

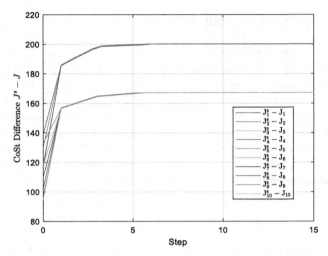

Fig. 9. User cost difference between limited rationality and complete rationality

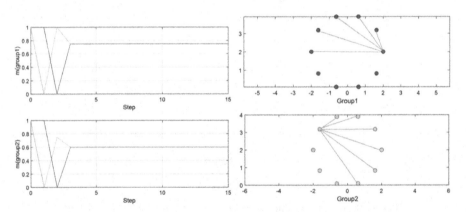

Fig. 10. Cognitive network-and cognitive resource allocation for each group

5   Conclusion

This paper designs a security management scheme based on a two-layer architecture under finite rational users. The two-layer architecture is the game to game architecture of cognitive network formation and security management decision, respectively, and the two-layer architectures are dependent on each other. We propose a concept of GNE solution to solve the problem of finite rational security risk management game. Through the simulation of the case, we found that with good cognitive ability of users can make mature decisions to reduce the network risk, so the network security risk management depends on these users, that is, the key users, other users in security decisions need to consider the key user decision-making, mutual decision between users each other to help each other to reduce the security risk.

Acknowledgments. The authors would like to thank the anonymous reviewers and editor for their comments that improved the quality of this paper. This work is supported by scientific project under Grant NO. 5246DR220010, the name of the project is research and application of the key technology of power 5G lightweight module and management platform.

References

1. Jia, Y., Peng, Z.: The analysis and simulation of communication network in Iridium system based on OPNET. In: The 2nd IEEE International Conference on Information Management and Engineering, Chengdu, China, 16–18 April (2010)
2. Ding, K., Chan, F.T.S., Zhang, X., et al.: Defining a Digital Twin-based Cyber-Physical Production System for autonomous manufacturing in smart shop floors. Int. J. Prod. Res. **57**(20), 6315–6334 (2019)
3. Zhuang, C., Liu, J., Xiong, H.: Digital twin-based smart production management and control framework for the complex product assembly shop-floor. Int. J. Adv. Manuf. Technol. **96**, 1149–1163 (2018)
4. Tao, F., Cheng, J., Qi, Q., et al.: Digital twin-driven product design, manufacturing and service with big data. Int. J. Adv. Manuf. Technol. **94**, 3563–3576 (2018)
5. Liu, Q., Zhang, H., Leng, J., et al.: Digital twin-driven rapid individualised designing of automated flow-shop manufacturing system. Int. J. Prod. Res. **57**(12), 3903–3919 (2019)
6. Mittal, S., Khan, M.A., Romero, D., et al.: Smart manufacturing: characteristics, technologies and enabling factors. Inst. Mech. Eng. **233**(5), 1342–1361 (2017)
7. Huang, S., Wang, G., Yan, Y., et al.: Blockchain-based data management for digital twin of product. J. Manuf. Syst. **54**, 361–371 (2019)
8. Rosen, R., Wichert, G., Lo, G., et al.: About the importance of autonomy and digital twins for the future of manufacturing. IFAC-Papers OnLine **48**(3), 567–572 (2015)
9. Wang, X., Zong, P., Yu, J.: Link analyzing and simulation of TDRSS based on OPNET. In: The International Conference on Communications and Mobile Computing, Shenzhen, China, 12–14 April (2010)
10. He, X., Ai, Q., Qiu, R.C., et al.: A big data architecture design for smart grids based on random matrix theory. IEEE Trans. Smart Grid **8**(2), 674–686 (2015)
11. Gray, J.: Jim gray on escience: a transformed scientific method. In: The Fourth Paradigm: Data-Intensive Scientific Discovery, pp. xvii–xxxi (2009)
12. Hong, T., Chen, C., Huang, J., et al.: Guest editorial big data analytics for grid modernization. IEEE Trans. Smart Grid **7**(5), 2395–2396 (2016)
13. Burges, C., Shaked, T., Renshaw, E., et al.: Learning to rank using gradient descent. In: Proceedings of the 22nd International Conference on Machine learning (ICML-05), pp. 89–96 (2005)
14. Yuan, Y., Ardakanian, O., Low, S., et al.: On the inverse power flow problem. arXiv preprint arXiv:1610.06631 (2016)
15. Chen, Y.C., Wang, J., Domínguez-García, A.D., et al.: Measurement-based estimation of the power flow Jacobian matrix. IEEE Trans. Smart Grid **7**(5), 2507–2515 (2015)
16. Kelly, J., Knottenbelt, W.: Neural nilm: deep neural networks applied to energy disaggregation. In: Proceedings of the 2nd ACM International Conference on Embedded Systems for Energy-Efficient Built Environments, pp. 55–64. ACM (2015)
17. Xu, S., Qiu, C., Zhang, D., et al.: A deep learning approach for fault type identification of transmission line. Proc. CSEE **39**(1), 65–74 (2019)
18. Boschert, S., Rosen, R.: Digital twin—The simulation aspect. In: Hehenberger, P., Bradley, D. (eds.) Mechatronic Futures, pp. 59–74. Springer, Cham (2016). https://doi.org/10.1007/978-3-319-32156-1_5

Multi Slice SLA Collaboration and Optimization of Power 5G Big Data Security Business

Daohua Zhu[1(✉)], Yajuan Guo[1], Lei Wei[2], Yunxiao Sun[1], and Wei Liu[1]

[1] State Grid Jiangsu Electric Power Co., Ltd., Research Institute, Nanjing 211103, China
zhu_dh@163.com
[2] State Grid Jiangsu Electric Power Co., Nanjing 211100, China

Abstract. 5G has become an important driving force for the digital transformation of the power industry. Especially today, with the increasing security risk of big data, the safe and available power 5G business plays an important role in improving power business innovation and user experience. This paper analyzes the demand level differences of different businesses for big data security in the application scenario of power 5G business, and establishes the SLA classification and classification model. On this basis, the power 5G business objective is divided into three processes: business perception, business execution and business SLA evaluation, which are assigned to the corresponding slices respectively. A power 5G slice perception collaborative optimization model is proposed and solved iteratively by multi-objective particle swarm optimization algorithm. Simulation experiments show that compared with the traditional 5G application mode, the proposed scheme can search and optimize the network resource allocation through the cooperation between slices, effectively schedule the slice resources and improve the operation efficiency and performance of power 5G service.

Keywords: Big Data Security · Power 5G Business · 5G Slice · SLA · Particle Swarm Optimization

1 Introduction

5G is an important part of the national new infrastructure strategy [1–3]. As a new information and communication technology, 5G has the network characteristics of high transmission bandwidth, large channel capacity, low end-to-end delay and supporting massive concurrency [4, 5]. It can support massive real-time data acquisition and form power grid big data. It plays a vital role in power grid safe production, enterprise digitization and intelligent transformation, but it also brings security challenges [6, 7].

The big data security challenges in the power 5G environment are mainly reflected in the following aspects:

(1) 5G edge computing reduces the centralized security protection ability of the system. After the calculation and processing sink to the edge, the data is transformed from centralized management to distributed management, resulting in more sensitive information exposure risks [8, 9].

(2) 5G supports massive concurrent data perception, which leads to a wider range of attacks on the system. In particular, the slicing technology opens more network permissions, resulting in more security risks faced by the system [10, 11].

(3) The service isolation of 5G slice is poor, especially in order to meet the better vertical application SLA quality, it often sacrifices the isolation security, which is easy to lead to sensitive data leakage in the process of big data processing [12].

At present, the power system is driven by the "double carbon" goal, distributed renewable energy and energy Internet are developing rapidly, and the multiple interaction and business collaboration of "source, network, load and storage" in the power industry have put forward higher requirements for network communication [13]. In order to support the explosive growth of business data in the power field and the construction of user-centered ecological chain, the power communication network urgently needs to change from a simple data transmission channel to an intelligent, digital and integrated development mode with the characteristics of power business [14, 15].

Compared with 4G communication network, 5G communication system has more abundant network resources, which can provide peak 20 gbps bandwidth, air interface delay of about 1ms and connection density of 1 million per square kilometer. Therefore, it has been widely used in power services involving a large number of data transmission and ultra-low delay requirements, such as power differential protection, accurate load control, UAV patrol, video interaction, etc. However, in the current application of power 5G, security guarantee is not fully considered, so it is difficult to give full play to the communication advantages of 5G. These advantages are: first, the cloud and sliced deployment of communication resources makes it possible to adopt more and more effective security protection means; Second, SLA differentiation requirements in the whole scene communication of power Internet of things provide a practical carrier for a variety of security protocols; Third, personalized services such as immersive experience and situational awareness provide room to improve the intelligent level of network security. In essence, the improvement of power 5G network big data security requires reasonable security control and allocation of massive network resources to realize vertical industry application customization and security slicing business collaboration [16].

Network slicing is one of the important technical features of 5G network [17, 18]. Its essence is a way of network resource virtualization. Network operators can allocate network resources for services sharing the same infrastructure through slicing. The power 5G network slice is divided into multiple sub domains such as management plane, control plane and user plane. Each sub domain can be regarded as multiple dedicated, isolated and customized security domains. Through the big data perception and demand prediction of power business, using slice resources to accurately match and dynamically respond to the security needs of different application scenarios can greatly give play to the performance of 5G network, meet new services such as energy Internet, and improve the system security service level [19, 20].

Based on the comprehensive analysis of 5G technology system and its energy Internet service, this paper studies the security perception, trusted collaboration and optimization method of power big data service based on 5G slice, extracts and quantifies the demand characteristics of power service, and establishes the objective optimization model of power 5G multi slice dynamic arrangement and optimal configuration from the perspective of power service SLA adaptation awareness and collaborative security guarantee, It is solved by particle swarm optimization algorithm, so as to provide the network service ability of deterministic indicators, and improve the efficiency of energy Internet information communication and the level of intelligent decision-making [21]. The main contributions of this paper are as follows:

(1) The established power 5G big data security SLA classification model;
(2) Based on the above model, an optimization model of security slicing arrangement of power 5G big data is proposed;
(3) Based on particle swarm optimization algorithm, the proposed model is solved and the optimization scheme is obtained.

2 Related Work

Accurate service perception is the key to optimize resource scheduling and realize multi service cooperation in power 5G network. In the traditional network architecture, service perception mainly depends on the analysis of traffic, protocol and other elements by the core network. However, this method is suitable for the field of network management and control, not for the perception of user services. The above business perception methods are only aimed at improving network performance and accurate fault location. The perception of big data security features is not involved and can not cope with more and more security risks [22, 23].

In the evolution process of 5G standard, the standardization organization 3GPP began to respond to differentiated service requirements through flexible network slicing from R15. R17 began to establish a periodic awareness interface between 5G and applications, and enhance service awareness through slicing remapping, fallback and data forwarding. At present, 5G standardization and application practice mainly realize the improvement of slot scheduling flexibility, scheduling efficiency and scheduling delay through service perception. However, for the association perception (such as the association between control data flow and feedback data flow) in the actual business scenario of energy Internet, especially the perception and optimization of power service level, two-way cooperation between network and service, etc., Further research is needed [24, 25].

5G network slicing is a collection of logical network functions used to support specific wireless configuration and transmission configuration. It is the main technical means to deal with the increasing difficulty of resource allocation due to the increasing complexity of the services carried on the premise of abundant network resources. In the energy Internet, a large number of distributed energy collection devices, distributed energy storage devices and various types of loads give birth to the business requirements of new power communication networks. Power 5G slices must be used to form the optimal configuration of multiple end-to-end logical networks to realize the scheduling and effective utilization of resources [26].

5G network has flexible slicing mode, which can be vertically divided into core network slicing, transmission network slicing and radio access network (RAN) slicing to realize end-to-end transmission management and control; Horizontal can be divided into eMBB (enhance mobile broadband) slice, mMTC (massive machine type communication) slice and uRLLC (ultra re liable & low latency communication) slice according to different bearer services to meet the QoS (quality of service) and SLA (service level agreement) requirements of different types of services. The core network slicing in the 3GPP technical standard has defined a virtualization architecture that separates the control plane from the user plane [27], which ensures the slicing ability based on Virtualization in the 5G underlying network.

At the level of transmission network and ran, user and service-oriented slice resource scheduling has become a research hotspot. It supports the real-time feedback of the whole research life cycle through the creation and adjustment of different slicing strategies, so as to maximize the performance of the whole research life cycle. In addition, resource optimization methods based on business performance requirements and the maximum utilization of network infrastructure have also become the focus of research, such as innovating slices on demand through tenant demand [28], dynamically allocating resources according to share proportion [29], solving the matching of link bandwidth and service capacity by binary linear programming [30], and the deployment of end-to-end 5G slices [31].

In the power 5G application scenario, 5G power communication network often carries multiple service flows at the same time. However, the research on 5G slice and its service perception mostly focuses on the optimization of slice one-way resource adaptation, ignoring the association and collaboration between services and the security protection of big data in collaboration. In terms of end-to-end network collaboration, the existing research only involves slice optimization selection, arrangement, mapping and automatic operation and maintenance, and does not involve business security collaboration at ran or UPF (user plane function). In the 5G application scenario of energy Internet, multi slice Association and cooperation for security protection is becoming more and more important. For example, in the application of precise load control, the safety certification and real-time control response of fast load control should be realized respectively according to different safety requirements. Therefore, through the security analysis of deterministic and periodic business characteristics, the slice resources required by the business are calculated in advance, and then the big data security pre scheduling is carried out to realize the feedback and synchronization between the security business and the network, which can greatly reduce the big data security problems caused by multi business concurrency and improve the reliability and user experience of the business [32].

3 Security Model for Power 5G Network Slice

3.1 Big Data Security SLA Analysis of Power 5G Service

At this stage, the power 5G infrastructure has been improved day by day, but there is still room for improvement in the security relationship between 5G power business scenario and 5G network slice. Therefore, on the one hand, it is necessary to fully analyze the demand characteristics of big data security of power 5G business under the background of energy Internet, on the other hand, it is necessary to release the ability of power 5G slice in networking flexibility and security, so as to meet the customization needs of diversified and differentiated power business. The combination of the two is to establish and improve the SLA big data security classification and classification system of power 5G, so as to achieve a consistent understanding of the business needs of power 5G users and the slicing capacity of power 5G.

At present, the commonly used network communication SLA indicators mainly include bandwidth, delay, reliability, isolation, etc. However, for the security requirements of power 5G business, in addition to meeting the basic communication requirements, it also needs to meet the high-level requirements such as authentication, security and integrity.

In terms of basic communication requirements, as the control mode of the new power business represented by the energy Internet has changed from centralized control to distributed control, the requirements for low delay and high reliability of the network have been enhanced, and it has the characteristics of deterministic network and time sensitive network. For example, in the accurate load control business, the delay from the beginning of fault information collection to the completion of terminal jump is no more than 650 ms, and the delay from the SGI interface of the core network to the terminal interface is less than 50 ms, The packet loss rate shall not exceed 10^{-4}.

According to the different security requirements of bearer services, 5G application scenarios are divided into three typical types: enhanced mobile broadband (eMBB), high reliability and low delay communication (uRLLC) and large-scale machine type communication (mMTC). Among them, eMBB mainly focuses on the peak rate, channel capacity, spectrum efficiency, network energy efficiency and other indicators of traditional 3G or 4G networks, which can carry common power information communication services; mMTC mainly supports the business requirements for concurrent access of massive power IOT terminals. It has relatively low requirements for communication delay and bandwidth, but has the highest requirements for the order of access terminals; uRLLC mainly supports high reliability, time sensitivity and deterministic power business applications, such as distribution automation, accurate load control, etc., which have high requirements for communication delay, bandwidth and reliability. The three types of businesses form complementary advantages of big data security through different emphasis on indicators according to different business needs. For example, eMBB can support the communication requirements of security algorithms such as encryption in the big data interaction environment. uRLLC can support the timeliness requirements of security algorithms, especially for high-precision timestamp synchronization. mMTC slice can support session processing in the process of massive concurrent authentication.

From the perspective of power business, power 5G can be applied to power generation, transmission, distribution, power consumption, dispatching, emergency communication and other power production and operation links. From the perspective of business interaction mode, it can be divided into control type, acquisition type, inspection type, multimedia business and new power grid business. Different service types have different requirements for communication performance. For example, the typical characteristics of control services are low delay and high availability. The bandwidth requirement is generally less than 10 Mbps. According to different scenarios, the average is about 2 Mbps, and the maximum delay cannot exceed 50 ms; The characteristics of acquisition services are that there are many points and a wide range, the bandwidth requirement is less than 2 Mbps, and the delay requirement is at the second level; The traffic volume of patrol service is large, but the bandwidth requirement is generally no more than 150 Mbps, the multimedia transmission delay is less than 200 ms, and the control information delay is less than 100 ms; New grid services such as edge computing and multi station integration have higher performance requirements. The bandwidth is no less than 100 Mbps, even 1 Gbps, and the delay is no more than 20 ms.

Based on the above analysis, the SLA requirements of power 5G business are divided into two types and multiple levels. Class I is the basic communication requirements, including bandwidth (B), delay (T), packet loss rate/bit error rate (L); Category II is security business requirements, including big data consistency (R), security (S), authentication (C) and security connection density (D). Each category can be divided into different levels according to different index intervals.

According to the above big data security classification and grading standards, SLAs for determining specific power 5G services can be classified and defined, so as to achieve the same understanding of communication performance at the business layer and network layer. For example, the SLA classification of power 5G precise load control service can be expressed as B1-T5-L2-R5-S3-C2-D3.

Based on the big data security demand characteristics and SLA analysis of power 5G, it can support the security and adaptive ability of power 5G channel, and break through the limitations of traditional application mode based on communication pipeline and hierarchical information and communication technology. By improving the adaptability of slice resources and applications in the power industry, the advantages of 5G communication can be brought into full play.

This paper determines the SLA type and level interval of different business characteristics under the security requirements of big data, establishes the security perception and collaborative optimization model of business big data, uses intelligent algorithm for evaluation, and finds the balance point between 5G network and power business SLA big data security requirements, so as to maximize the application value of power 5G communication.

3.2 Power Business Big Data Security Perception Collaborative Optimization Model

5G network slicing can realize the end-to-end secure network communication environment customized on demand in the power application scenario. By using the virtualization network function, it can provide programmable logic isolated security subnet for different users, and form a slicing model and deployment template with optimized configuration for rapid deployment.

The power 5G communication network adopts SDN mode to realize programmable, flexible and customizable virtual network services. Each logical subnet can be tailored into a network slice to meet specific business requirements, providing personalized security SLA guarantee for different power services and users. Network slice can be a kind of security subnet with end-to-end logical isolation. There is resource sharing or competition between different slices.

Power 5G end-to-end slice operation and management are mainly completed by communication service management function (CSMF), network slice management function

(NSMF), network slice subnet management function (NSSMF) and other components. Among them, CSMF maps the power business objectives and requirements into end-to-end network slice requirements and transmits them to NSMF. NSMF designs end-to-end slices according to the capabilities of each subnet, generates slice instances and arranges and manages them, decomposes the SLA of the whole network slice into SLAs of different slice subnets (such as core network slice subnet, wireless network slice subnet and bearer network slice subnet), and transmits the subnet deployment requirements to NSSMF. The core network, transmission network and wireless network have their own NSSMF, which mainly realizes the slice deployment, operation and monitoring in the subnet.

Each slice has specific network resources, and multiple slices cooperate to complete specific 5G power services. In the process of end-to-end slice deployment, SLA can be divided into three types of parameters, and the splitting relationship is shown in Table 1.

Table 1. Power 5G slice SLA splitting parameters

Type	Content	SLA Class
QoS parameter	Delay, bandwidth, lost rate, jitter	B, T, L
Channel capacity parameters	Number of users, active users and concurrent users	D
Safety parameters	Reliability, coverage area, reliability, safety isolation, customizability	R, S, C

By defining the SLA security mechanism of 5G service slice, the mapping and management of demand input to security slice deployment can be easily realized. Through the big data correlation analysis of service type, operation data, cloud resource characteristics, configuration parameters and measured data, the optimal SLA splitting and resource deployment suggestions can be obtained, so as to maximize the matching of customer needs while ensuring the resource utilization efficiency. For 5G service, the efficiency of two-way transmission network should be improved. That is, on the one hand, according to the SLA indicators of different services, we can perceive the security requirements of power business and realize the mapping from security business model to network model. On the other hand, through the 5G network interface, the communication resource consumption corresponding to the security service is monitored, and the communication flow, delay, packet loss rate and delay jitter of the end-to-end network slice are accurately measured, so as to realize the multi-dimensional portrait and intelligent analysis and prediction of the power 5G service, so as to obtain the response ability of the current 5G slice task arrangement to the SLA index, and further feedback and optimization. The specific process of intelligent dispatching and guarantee of power 5G slice is shown in Fig. 1.

The security service optimization model of power 5G slice is divided into three relatively independent and interrelated processes: Security big data perception, slice optimization collaborative scheduling and security SLA monitoring feedback. In modeling, 5G power slicing service security perception and collaborative optimization are

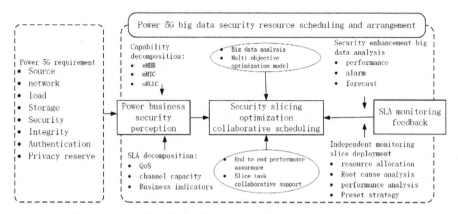

Fig. 1. Power 5G chip intelligent dispatching and guarantee process

transformed into multi-objective optimization problems. Multiple objectives such as power 5G service completion index and service security SLA adaptation are optimized at the same time, and multi-objective discrete particle swarm optimization algorithm is used to solve them.

The model can be expressed as a quad $\langle S, G, T, C \rangle$, where $S = \{S_s, S_e, S_v\}$ is a set of slices. Considering that there are multiple interrelated slices in the power 5G application scenario to cooperate to complete multiple tasks with different security levels, the power 5G slices are divided into three categories: big data perception slice $S_s = \{S_1^{(s)}, S_2^{(s)}, \cdots, S_i^{(s)}\}$, security service execution slice $S_e = \{S_1^{(e)}, S_2^{(e)}, \cdots, S_j^{(e)}\}$ and security SLA evaluation slice $S_v = \{S_1^{(v)}, S_2^{(v)}, \cdots, S_k^{(v)}\}$ to complete the tasks of service perception, service execution and service collaboration respectively. G is the target set to be achieved by power services, that is, the set of deterministic power 5G services. For example, 5G differential protection service can be regarded as an element in the target set. T is the set of security tasks decomposed on all targets, which is divided into perception tasks T_s, execution tasks T_e and SLA evaluation tasks T_v. For any 5G power business, the effective coordination and linkage of the above three types of slices are required. C is a set of constraints. For each kind of slice, the realization of its function needs to consume some resources and time. For the service execution slice, because it represents the service support capability of 5G network, the network resources consumed are equivalent to the network resources that the slice can provide when carrying power 5G service. Since the total communication resources of the system are fixed and the power 5G business needs to be completed in sequence within a certain time, there are resource constraints and time order coordination constraints.

The task allocation model of 5G power security slice is shown in Fig. 2:

For the deterministic power 5G service security goal g, it can be divided into a specific sequence arrangement set of three types of tasks: big data perception task T_s, security protection execution task T_e and SLA security evaluation task T_v. This set contains the task list, slice list and its occupied network resources. The overall task goal is completed by the three types of slices according to the task arrangement. $X \in \{0, 1\}$ is the task assignment variable. If the value is 1, it means that the corresponding task is assigned

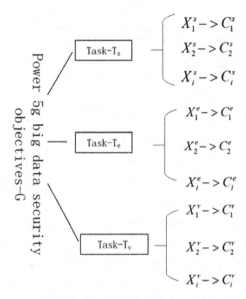

Fig. 2. Slice task allocation model

to the corresponding slice. C is the resource vector, including the resources required for the execution of the corresponding task, such as bandwidth, delay tolerance, maximum execution time, etc. For example, $X_i^s \rightarrow C_i^s$ at that time, it means that the power sensing service is assigned to slice i, and the consumed network resources are C_i^s.

- Model constraints

- Slice execution capacity limit

The amount of tasks assigned to each power 5G execution slice is less than its design value $init_l$. If this limit is not met, the slice will collapse and affect the operation of the whole power business. Based on this, for a specific single slice L, if the task assignment vector and resource consumption vector are X_l^m and C_l^m ($1 \leq m \leq j$) respectively, the capacity limit of a single slice can be obtained as follows:

$$\sum_{m=1}^{j} X_l^m C_l^m \leq init_l$$

- Slice type constraints.

When assigning power 5G slice tasks, it is necessary to assign them in strict accordance with the type of slice, that is, the corresponding slices in Service Perception slice, service execution slice and service SLA evaluation slice perform the tasks of service perception, service execution and service collaboration respectively. The 0–1 variable indicates that task m is assigned to the L-th slice, so there are:

$$X_l^m = \begin{cases} 1 & (S_s \rightarrow T_s) \cup (S_e \rightarrow T_e) \cup (S_v \rightarrow T_v) \\ 0 & otherwise \end{cases}$$

where $S_s \rightarrow T_s$ means tasks in T_s are assigned to slices in S_s. The same means include $S_e \rightarrow T_e$ and $S_v \rightarrow T_v$.

- Slice collaboration constraints

In the energy Internet with intelligent perception, the completion of 5G power business often requires multiple types of slice collaboration. Collaboration is divided into collaboration on the time axis and collaboration in the spatial dimension.

Among them, the collaboration on the time axis is reflected in the timing relationship of different slice execution tasks, that is, after the perception task is completed, the execution slice can schedule resources for business execution according to the perception results. After the execution is completed, the SLA evaluation slice can evaluate and feed back the completion quality of the execution process and user satisfaction, which is used to guide the next perception execution SLA evaluation cycle. Therefore, the completion time of all perceived tasks should be earlier than the start time of any execution task, and the end time of all execution tasks should be earlier than the start time of any evaluation task. Namely:

$$t_s^{\max} \le t_e^{\min}$$

$$t_e^{\max} \le t_v^{\min}$$

Collaboration in the spatial dimension means that in order to ensure the smooth completion of power 5G business, at least one slice needs to be allocated to each type of task. If there are multiple slices performing similar tasks at the same time, the task segmentation needs to have a clear boundary and the relationship between resource sharing and data exchange. Namely:

$$\sum_{l=1}^{i} X_l^s \ge 1$$

$$\sum_{l=1}^{j} X_l^e \ge 1$$

$$\sum_{l=1}^{k} X_l^v \ge 1$$

- Task requirements constraints

The task allocation of all 5G power slices shall meet the smooth development of supporting services, that is, the implementation of all slice functions shall meet the bandwidth, delay and bit error rate requirements of power services.

Let the resource vector required by the specific power 5G service t be C, and the specific indicators in C include the resource requirements specified in the SLA, such as bandwidth, delay, bit error rate, etc., then the corresponding task demand constraints can be expressed as:

$$\sum_{l=1}^{i} X_l^T C_l^T + \sum_{l=1}^{j} X_l^T C_l^T + \sum_{l=1}^{k} X_l^T C_l^T \ge opt(C)$$

Among them, $opt(C)$ is the minimum satisfaction value of each resource element in the resource vector. For example, the communication bandwidth is no less than B BPs, the end-to-end service delay is no more than D MS, and the bit error rate is no more than E.

- Objective function

The goal of power 5G slice collaborative optimization is to intelligently perceive and effectively support the secure power business carried by the upper layer, and meet the security index requirements of power business SLA. Therefore, the optimization model constructed in this paper considers two optimization indexes: the minimum task completion time and the minimum number of slices.

The task completion time includes the sum of the time required to complete the perception task, execution task and SLA evaluation task in turn in the same power 5G application business. In each task, the time required to complete the task is the longest completion time of the corresponding slice. Therefore, objective function 1 can be described as follows:

$$F_1(X) = \max(t_k^s + t_k^e + t_k^v)$$

where k is the total number of tasks required to complete a specific power 5G application.

In order to improve the satisfaction of business operation, the business capability realized by power 5G slice needs to be close to the business SLA requirements as much as possible, that is, all 5G chips The gap between the communication capability provided by the slice and the SLA index should be as small as possible. Therefore, objective function 2 can be described as follows:

$$F_2(X) = \min\{ \sqrt{\sum_{i=1}^{r}(C_i^v - C_i^{SLA})^2} \}$$

Among them, C_i^s is the current available communication resources measured by SLA evaluation slice, C_i^{SLA} is the communication requirements and indicators required by power 5G service, i is the resource type, and r is the total number of resource types.

It is worth noting that due to the abundant power 5G communication network resources, the minimum resource use can be used as a secondary optimization goal.

- Model solving

The model uses particle swarm optimization algorithm to solve the multi-objective optimization problem. Particle swarm optimization algorithm is a common algorithm for solving complex optimization problems. It has the advantages of fast convergence speed and good robustness. In the particle swarm optimization algorithm, the power 5G slice sensing and collaborative arrangement are regarded as the search and solution process of massless particles in the search space. Each feasible solution in the power 5G slice optimization problem domain is mapped into the position of the particle in the solution space, which is represented by x and the current velocity of the particle is represented by v. In this process, multiple particles in the feasible solution space can search separately and share the solution results with other particles. The model uses the information carried by the current optimal particle as the current stage optimal solution, updates all particles, and finally obtains the global optimal solution.

The flow of the algorithm is shown in Fig. 3.

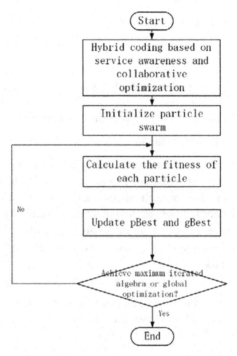

Fig. 3. Algorithm flow chart

The solution process includes three processes: business perception and collaborative optimization hybrid coding, initial feasible solution calculation and population update.

1) Hybrid coding method based on service awareness and collaborative optimization

The code is set according to the power 5G slice task arrangement. Each particle contains three elements, namely $P = \{T_u, S_u, C_u, t_u\}$, which are the task list T_u to be executed to complete the power business, the slice set S_u to execute this task list, the network resource collection C_u to be executed by the slice and the collaborative sequence t_u to be executed by the task. Particle code is shown in Table 2:

Each column in the table corresponds to a task assignment, including the task, the slice to execute the task, the required resources and the timing collaboration of task execution. A list of elements corresponding to each row in the table. SLA includes three categories: task perception and task execution; The slice set contains the slice arrangement corresponding to the three types of functions; The resource sets correspond to the resources required by the assigned slice to complete a specific task; The collaboration

Table 2. Particle Code Table

Task list-T_u	$T_u^{(1)}$	$T_u^{(2)}$	$T_u^{(3)}$	......	$T_u^{(N)}$
Slice set-S_u	S_1	S_2	S_3	......	S_N
Resource-C_u	C_1	C_2	C_3	......	C_N
Collaborative sequence-t_u	t_1	t_2	t_3	......	t_N

sequence represents the timing relationship that needs to be met according to the execution of different power 5G services. { $T_1, T_2, \cdots, T_N$} corresponds to an arrangement with sequential relationship in a specific application example.

2) Calculation of initial feasible solution

Using particle swarm optimization algorithm to solve the problem requires particle iteration from an initial feasible solution. The initial feasible solution can be randomly selected in the feasible solution space, the slices that meet the constraints can be assigned tasks, and the resource consumption and subsequent tasks can be updated.

The specific steps are to randomly select the qualified task $T_u^{(l)}$ from the task list T_u contained in the power 5G business, judge its task type, assign it to the appropriate power 5G slice S_l, update the task list $T_u' = T_u - T_u^{(l)}$ and slice list $S_u' = S_u - S_l$, update the resource consumption $C_u' = C_u - C_1$, and add t_l to the power 5G business collaboration sequence for collaborative arrangement, that is, $t_u' = t_u + t_l$. The elements in t_u' need to be arranged in order. Finally, a feasible solution of the optimization problem is obtained, that is, the initial particle $P^0 = \{T_u^0, S_u^0, C_u^0, T_u^0\}$.

3) Feasible solution optimization

After the initial feasible solution is obtained, the particles are updated through iteration, and finally the optimal solution is found. In each iteration, the particles are optimized and updated by tracking the value of the corresponding component in $P = \{T_u, S_u, C_u, t_u\}$. All updated particles are descendants of the initial particle $P^0 = \{T_u^0, S_u^0, C_u^0, T_u^0\}$.

Set the maximum iteration number, that is, the search length is s, the position of particle L in the search process is, the best historical position of particle L is $pBest = \{T_u^p, S_u^p, C_u^p, T_u^p\}$, the current best position of adjacent particles is $gBest = \{T_u^g, S_u^g, C_u^g, T_u^g\}$, and r_1, r_2 are random numbers, which are used to increase the randomness of particle search, and ω is the inertia coefficient, which is used to adjust the search range. Then the solution update formula of particle L in each dimension is:

$$x_l^k = x_l^{k-1} + v_l^{k-1}$$

where,

$$v_l^k = \omega v_l^{k-1} + c_1 r_1 (pBest - x_l^{k-1}) + c_2 r_2 (gBest - x_l^{k-1})$$

The four dimensions of task, slice, resource and collaboration in the model are substituted into the above formula to update, so as to obtain the new generation of best solutions that meet the constraints. If $k < s$ or two generations of optimal solutions is greater than the set threshold, it indicates that there is still room for updating. Update the values of *pBest* and *gBest* and enter the next round of iteration. Otherwise, determine the current solution as the optimal solution that meets the conditions.

4 Simulation

In order to verify the feasibility of the proposed scheme, experiments are carried out based on typical power 5G services. The verification is based on the 5G differential protection pilot project of a provincial power company. The comparison scheme 1 is the field test data of the 5G pilot project of another provincial power company, and the comparison scheme 2 is the field data of the pilot project in document.

Analyze and compare the performance of the scheme and the performance difference after using the 5G slice service aware collaborative optimization algorithm proposed in this paper, and verify the feasibility and progressiveness of the scheme proposed in this paper. Among them, the comparison scheme 1 only takes 5G as the upgrade scheme of traditional 4G network communication mode, and does not do slice aware collaborative optimization for service SLA.

In the experiment, 5G communication is used to realize accurate time synchronization and reliable connection between automation terminals and differential protection devices in distribution master station, substation and switching station. The application scenario of 110 kV substation is selected, the differential control device, protection device and CPE communication module are deployed in the ring network cabinet, the differential protection device is deployed at both ends of the line, and the timing system adopts the timing function based on Beidou satellite navigation and positioning system. In case of fault or abnormality, the differential control signal is transmitted through the power 5G slice, and the differential protection device completes the differential protection action to realize the effect of differential protection.

The experiment uses perception slice, differential control slice and SLA evaluation slice to realize the service function of differential control. The objective functions $F_1(X)$, $F_2(X)$ and four constraints of the perceptual collaborative optimization model are brought into the particle swarm optimization algorithm for operation. Since it is the maximum target, it is converted to the minimum target by solving $-F_1(X)$. In the particle swarm optimization algorithm, each particle represents a feasible solution of the model. Set the population size of 100 and the number of iterations of 100 for iteration. Figure 4 shows the convergence process of particle iteration. It can be seen that the optimal position of particle population tends to the same optimal solution with the increase of iteration times (see Fig. 4(f)).

The comparison curve between the corresponding differential control delay and the comparison scheme when the objective function value is optimized is shown in Fig. 5.

It can be seen that, compared with the comparison, the differential protection scheme using 5G slice aware cooperative optimization algorithm has significant advantages in time delay. This is because the perceptual cooperative optimization algorithm realizes the intelligent and accurate response to SLA through three kinds of slices, improves the processing efficiency of the network, and maximizes the use of the rich network resources of power 5G.

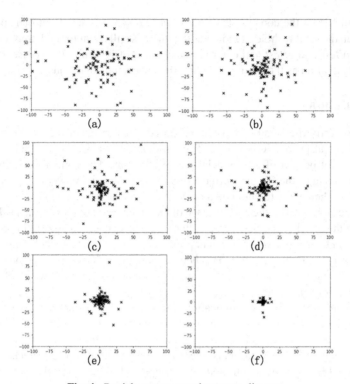

Fig. 4. Particle swarm search process diagram

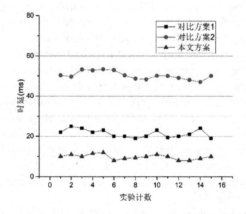

Fig. 5. Differential control service delay curve

The comparison of other key communication performance indicators is shown in Table 3.

Table 3. Communication network performance index

performance index	Comparison scheme 1	Comparison scheme 2	Proposed scheme
bandwidth (Mbps)	58	5.6	120
average delay (ms)	21	50	10
average jitter (ms)	0.57	0.1	0.1
Packet loss rate (%)	0.005	0.005	0.002
reliability (%)	100	100	100

It can be seen that the communication performance of power 5G service optimized by slicing is significantly improved compared with the existing schemes in terms of bandwidth, delay, jitter and packet loss rate.

5 Conclusion

The information communication technology represented by 5G not only provides support for the development of energy Internet, but also brings opportunities and challenges in big data security. The biggest advantage of power 5G is to provide services that meet differentiated SLAs to specific power services through slicing, so as to make full use of 5G massive network resources, realize the characteristics of optimal configuration, independent collaboration, security and credibility of power service carrying network, and finally provide customers with more agile, safer and reliable services. However, the traditional 5G application mode is only the continuation of 4G and lacks intelligent means, It is difficult to effectively deal with complex big data security situations. By analyzing the application scenarios of 5G power business, this study summarizes the SLA security requirements of many types of power 5G services such as control, acquisition and video inspection, designs the optimization model of collaborative operation of three types of slices: big data security perception, security service execution and SLA security evaluation, realizes the correlation perception between multiple slices, and obtains the optimal slice configuration scheme based on the solution of multi-objective optimization particle swarm optimization algorithm. The simulation results show that the power 5G service after slice sensing collaborative optimization makes full use of the advantages of 5G network, so it has better security performance. The further research direction is to popularize the model and realize the secure optimal resource scheduling and cooperation among multiple services.

Acknowledgement. This publication is supported by the science and technology project of State Grid Jiangsu Electric Power Co., Ltd. (Project No.: J2021125).

References

1. Jain, S., Gupta, S., Sreelakshmi, K.K., et al.: Fog computing in enabling 5G-driven emerging technologies for development of sustainable smart city infrastructures. Clust. Comput. **25**(2), 1111–1154 (2022)

2. Soleymani, S.A., Anisi, M.H., Abdullah, A.H., et al.: An authentication and plausibility model for big data analytic under LOS and NLOS conditions in 5G-VANET. Science China Inf. Sci. **63**(12), 220305 (2020)
3. Behrad, S., Bertin, E., Crespi, N.: A survey on authentication and access control for mobile networks: from 4G to 5G. Ann. Telecommun. **74**(9), 593–603 (2019)
4. Aggarwal, S., Kumar, N.: Fog computing for 5G-enabled tactile Internet: research issues, challenges, and future research directions. Mob. Netw. Appl. (2019)
5. Sankar, S.P., Subash, T.D., Vishwanath, N., et al.: Security improvement in block chain technique enabled peer to peer network for beyond 5G and Internet of Things. Peer-to-Peer Network. Appl. **14**(1), 392–402 (2021)
6. Chu, Y., Pan, L., Leng, K., et al.: Research on key technologies of service quality optimiza-tionfor industrial IoT 5G network for intelligent manufacturing. Int. J. Adv. Manuf. Technol. **107**(3), 1071–1080 (2020)
7. Benslimen, Y., Sedjelmaci, H., Manenti, A.-C.: Attacks and failures prediction framework for a collaborative 5G mobile network. Computing **103**(6), 1165–1181 (2021). https://doi.org/10.1007/s00607-020-00893-8
8. Lindgren, P., Wuropulos, K.: Secure persuasive business models and business model innovation in a world of 5G. Wirel. Pers. Commun. **96**(3), 3569–3583 (2017)
9. Ji, X., Huang, K., Jin, L., et al.: Overview of 5G security technology. Science China Inf. Sci. **61**(8), 081301 (2018)
10. Sharma, A., Jha, R.K.: A comprehensive survey on security issues in 5G wireless communi-cation network using beamforming approach. Wirel. Pers. Commun. **119**(4), 3447–3501 (2021)
11. Fourati, H., Maaloul, R., Chaari, L.: A survey of 5G network systems: challenges and machine learning approaches. Int. J. Mach. Learn. Cybern. **12**(2), 385–431 (2021)
12. Chochliouros, I.P., Spiliopoulou, A.S., Kostopoulos, A., et al.: Security threat analysis of the 5G ESSENCE platform. Wirel. Pers. Commun. **120**(3), 2409–2426 (2021)
13. Jorquera Valero, J.M., Sánchez Sánchez, P.M., Lekidis, A., et al.: Design of a security and trust framework for 5G multi-domain scenarios. J. Netw. Syst. Manag. **30**(1), 7 (2021)
14. AlQahtani, S.A., Alhomiqani, W.A.: A multi-stage analysis of network slicing architecture for 5G mobile networks. Telecommun. Syst. **73**(2), 205–221 (2020)
15. Luo, M., Wu, J., Li, X.: Cross-domain certificateless authenticated group key agreement protocol for 5G network slicings. Telecommun. Syst. **74**(4), 437–449 (2020)
16. Liu, T., Wu, F., Li, X., et al.: A new authentication and key agreement protocol for 5G wireless networks. Telecommun. Syst. **78**(3), 317–329 (2021)
17. De Dutta, S., Prasad, R.: Security for smart grid in 5G and beyond networks. Wirel. Pers. Commun. **106**(1), 261–273 (2019)
18. Nayak Manjeshwar, A., Jha, P., Karandikar, A., et al.: VirtRAN: an SDN/NFV-based framework for 5G RAN slicing. J. Indian Inst. Sci. **100**(2), 409–434 (2020)
19. Mumtaz, T., Muhammad, S., Aslam, M.I., et al.: Inter-slice resource management for 5G radio access network using markov decision process. Telecommun. Syst. **79**(4), 541–557 (2022)
20. Kotulski, Z., Nowak, T.W., Sepczuk, M., et al.: Towards constructive approach to end-to-end slice isolation in 5G networks. EURASIP J. Inf. Secur. **2018**(1), 2 (2018)
21. AlQahtani, S.A., Altamrah, A.S.: Supporting QoS requirements provisions on 5G network slices using an efficient priority-based polling technique. Wireless Netw. **25**(7), 3825–3838 (2019)
22. Maman, M., Calvanese-Strinati, E., Dinh, L.N., et al.: Beyond private 5G networks: appli-cations, architectures, operator models and technological enablers. EURASIP J. Wirel. Commun. Netw. **2021**(1), 195 (2021)

23. Mathew, A.: Network slicing in 5G and the security concerns. In: Proceedings of the 2020 Fourth International Conference on Computing Methodologies and Communication (ICCMC), F 11–13 March 2020 (2020)
24. Sattar, D., Matrawy, A.: Towards secure slicing: using slice isolation to mitigate DDoS attacks on 5G core network slices. In: Proceedings of the 2019 IEEE Conference on Communications and Network Security (CNS), F 10–12 June 2019 (2019)
25. Kapassa, E., Touloupou, M., Stavrianos, P., et al.: Dynamic 5G slices for IoT applications with diverse requirements. In: Proceedings of the 2018 Fifth International Conference on Internet of Things: Systems, Management and Security, F 15–18 October 2018 (2018)
26. Grønsund, P., Gonzalez, A., Mahmood, K., et al.: 5G service and slice implementation for a military use case. In: Proceedings of the 2020 IEEE International Conference on Communications Workshops (ICC Workshops), F 7–11 June 2020 (2020)
27. Mahmood, K., Mahmoodi, T., Trivisonno, R., et al.: On the integration of verticals through 5G control plane. In: Proceedings of the 2017 European Conference on Networks and Communications (EuCNC), F 12–15 June 2017 (2017)
28. Bega, D., Gramaglia, M., Banchs, A., et al.: Optimising 5G infrastructure markets: the business of network slicing. In: Proceedings of the IEEE Infocom-IEEE Conference on Computer Communications, F (2017)
29. Caballero, P., Banchs, A., Veciana, G.D., et al.: Network slicing games: enabling customization in multi-tenant mobile networks. IEEE/ACM Trans. Network. 27(2), 662–675 (2019)
30. Zhang, N., Liu, Y.F., Farmanbar, H., et al.: Network slicing for service-oriented networks under resource constraints. IEEE J. Sel. Areas Commun. 35(11), 2512–2521 (2017)
31. Guan, W., Wen, X., Wang, L., et al.: A service-oriented deployment policy of end-to-end network slicing based on complex network theory. IEEE Access 6(19), 691–701 (2018)
32. Kotulski Z, Nowak T, Sepczuk M, et al.: On end-to-end approach for slice isolation in 5G networks. Fundamental challenges. In: Proceedings of the 2017 Federated Conference on Computer Science and Information Systems (FedCSIS), F 3–6 September 2017 (2017)

Virtualized Network Functions Placement Scheme in Cloud Network Collaborative Operation Platform

Youjun Hu[1], Lan Gan[1], E. Longhui[1]($\boxtimes$), Fangcheng Chu[1], Yang Lu[1], Xifan Nie[2], and Fei Zhao[2]

[1] Nari Group Corporation State Grid Electric Power Research Institute, Nanjing, China
elonghui@sgepri.sgcc.com.cn
[2] State Grid Beijing Electric Power Company, Beijing, China

Abstract. As the cloud network collaborative operation platform becomes the start and end point of network traffic and the number of service types carried by the data center increases, traffic interaction between data centers (east-west traffic) increases gradually. In this paper, a virtualized network functions placement scheme is proposed to meet the demand of large bandwidth, low delay and differentiated load for the increasing east-west traffic, which mainly carries east-west traffic between data centers in different geographical locations. The proposed scheme provides fast, automatic, diversified and differentiated carrying service for the above traffic. The proposed scheme mainly includes three parts: 1) L3 virtual private network services, namely the cloud network backbone for customers in different network room or L3 virtual private network services cloud pool of resources, ensure data security; 2) differentiation bandwidth service, i.e. the cloud network backbone network according to the different quality of service requirements of different customers and money demand reserved link bandwidth resources; 3) self-service automation, choreographer and controller as the cloud network backbone to achieve business automation opened and deployment, administrators through management portal implementation business rapid deployment and adjustment, the customer can realize self-help resources through services portal application and business plan. Evaluation results have validated the effectiveness of the proposed method and show its advantages over counterparts.

Keywords: Virtualized Network Functions Placement · Latency Minimization · Network Services · Cloud Network Collaborative Operation Platform

1 Introduction

The two technologies, "SDN" (software defined network) and "NFV" (network function virtualization), promote each other. SDN realizes the separation of control and forwarding and the capability opening on the centralized control. NFV realizes the decoupling of hardware and software and the virtualization of network functions at the NE level, and redefines the cloud network collaborative operation platform architecture.

Y. Tian et al. (Eds.): ICBDS 2022, CCIS 1796, pp. 480–492, 2023.
https://doi.org/10.1007/978-981-99-3300-6_34

Network reconstruction combines cloud and SDN technologies to transform the infrastructure layer of traditional telecommunication network and form a new infrastructure of cloud network integration. After network reconstruction, IaaS (telecommunications cloud, public cloud, and private cloud) capabilities are enabled for the infrastructure of cloud network convergence.

Service reconstruction focuses on the implementation of VNF under the NFV framework, how to further structure and fusion of various VNF, how to accept the management of VNFM to achieve one-click deployment and elastic scaling, and how to realize the openness of VNF capabilities. After the network reconstruction, the NFVI layer under the NFV architecture is formed at the infrastructure level, and the service reconstruction is mainly based on the flexible deployment of various VNF services and third-party applications. Including the necessary communication services in the operator network (such as vEPC, vIMS, vBNG, vCPE, etc.), corresponding to the VNFaaS capability; It also includes the overlay of featured PaaS platform on IaaS to provide the industry and operators with the basic functional environment suitable for telecom application development and related communication basic protocol components, so as to facilitate the third party to participate in innovative business development in the telecom field.

Network reconstruction and service reconstruction will complete the transformation of the front-end system of the telecommunication network, while operation reconstruction focuses on the transformation of the back end operation system. Including the operation and management of the new virtual network, seamless connection with the traditional network, to achieve end-to-end closed-loop automation. The goal of operational refactoring is to create an intelligent operational architecture based on cloud services.

Network reconfiguration and service reconfiguration are the enablement layers of IaaS, PaaS, and SaaS respectively. Operation reconfiguration implements operational features such as cloud capability presentation, subscription, and billing. After operation reconstruction, telecom network will become the cloud service as the main model, to achieve everything: XaaS.

In this paper, a virtualized network functions placement framework is proposed, wherein a software-definable elastic network built with layered centralized control and unified management by introducing cloud technology, big data and openness. As a key component of elastic network, is built on the DC based on the NFV framework to provide virtual network functions for various networks. MANO is introduced to manage the whole life cycle of cloud service and automate deployment, operation and maintenance. Combined with unified orchestration, automatic deployment of E2E NFV services and capability opening of the whole network can be implemented. The optimal policies can be adopted according to user requirements and whole network resources to realize rapid deployment of services and maximize utilization of resources, quickly build customized networks, and effectively reduce network construction costs.

The rest of this article is organized as follows. Literature review is briefly reviewed in Sect. 2. In Sect. 3, we present the system model of virtualized network functions placement method in cloud network collaborative operation platform. In Sect. 4, we describe the management scheme. The validity of the method is presented through experimental evaluations in Sect. 5, and finally we conclude the entire paper in Sect. 6.

2 Related Work

Since the virtualized network functions placement technology was proposed, it has become the focus of attention of all parties in the industrial chain and the goal of joint efforts of operators, cloud service providers, hardware/software providers and customers, hoping to develop together with SDN/NFV and cloud. The international standard organizations cooperated with the open source organizations to build the theoretical system and develop the product prototype of virtualized network functions placement. The efficient cooperation between the two organizations promoted the rapid molding and implementation of the virtualized network functions placement standard, also known as service function chain (SFC) deployment.

Standard organizations such as IETF and BBF put forward their requirements from the aspects of SFC scenario, deployment, operation and management, and conducted POC experiments of SFC scenarios in combination with open source organization products. In terms of theoretical research, IETF is the leader. It defines the framework, process, protocol and package format of SFC, and conducts in-depth discussions on the details of traffic optimization and operation and maintenance management.

2.1 The IETF Standard

IETF is the base camp of SFC technology. The principle, architecture, implementation mechanism, optimization and operation and maintenance management of SFC are comprehensively and deeply reviewed and discussed, so as to prototype, productize and further present SFC. The network deployment provides a theoretical basis and has a very high reference value. However, IETF pays more attention to the solution of detailed technical problems, while the end-to-end deployment and implementation of SFC in the live network lacks multi-dimensional and macro to micro discussion, which requires the input of relevant documents. The IETF SFC Group has officially released two RFCS (Requests For Comments), covering the architecture, components, protocol mechanisms, and functions of the SFC Capability, management, diagnosis, design analysis and security model are studied in depth. The Draft focuses on SFC solutions for data centers, mobile networks, broadband networks, vCPE and high-traffic scenarios.

For IETF, the main research contents focus on the following aspects:

1) Research on business chain architecture [1]: Hierarchical SFC architecture, in which cross-domain and hierarchical forwarding mechanism become research hotspots.
2) Research on control plane technology [2]: There are many disputes on the selection of control protocol in SFC, and there is no unified solution for now. Whether to use an extension of the traditional Protocol or a newly created protocol, such as SF instance Resource Discovery Protocol Off-path Signaling Protocol (OSP), you need to deploy the field based on the SFC view, scale and maturity of the product.
3) Research on data plane technology: The working group innovatively proposed NSH (Network Service Header encapsulation) [3], which provides packet matching information to SFF by carrying Service Path ID (SPID) and Service ID (SID). The working group has conducted in-depth and detailed research on NSH, including NSH TLV, NSH service forwarding process, NSH radius attribute definition, DHCP attribute of

NSH, NSH based on UDP, NSH based on IPv6 extension, and so on. It has become the mainstream de facto standard of SFC forwarding surface protocol. In the application, the classifier maintains the NSH mapping table, which greatly improves the efficiency of SFF by matching SPID and SID, and solves the problem that traditional SF needs to match the quintuple or other parameters to identify the characteristic traffic, and the SF mapping table is too large in the case of various parameter combinations. In addition, the NSH can carry metadata, flexibly passing more personalized message processing instructions and operation and maintenance parameters. At the same time, the working group also focused on a supplementary scheme to carry SFC information through extended headers such as LISP/PCEP/BGP LS/IPv6 to provide technical reference for the existing network upgrade.

4) Study on traffic/path optimization scenarios: Multiple deployment modes of SFC components lead to potential problems such as traffic rotation and complicated paths. SFC traffic is forwarded from SFF to SF and back to SFF in a roundabout way, which directly leads to bandwidth waste and delay jitter increase. To solve this problem, the working group proposed two solutions: SF bypass and SF flow offloading. SFC traffic unloading offloads the traffic that SF is not interested in to SFF for processing by means of instructions. The discussion of this scheme is relatively active in the group. In addition, strategy-based path optimization, load balancing problem analysis, SFC dynamic path selection and so on have attracted more attention. These optimization schemes focus on the elaboration of methodology and process, but lack the application introduction based on specific network business scenarios.

2.2 The BBF Standard

BBF is an operator-led standards organization that pays more attention to application scenarios and cases, and generally focuses on requirements and solution framework for operational problems. However, most specific technologies refer to IETF achievements through notification, which is therefore subject to the progress of IETF SFC group. From the perspective of operators, BBF provides comprehensive comparison and selection suggestions for different application scenarios and corresponding different solutions, and provides feasible suggestions for guiding operators to deploy SFC.

Research project SD326 [4] studied the market demand and application scenario of Flexible Service Chaining (Flexible Business chain) in FSC, and built a "Flexible Service Chaining network architecture". The hierarchical BNG defined by TR-178 is regarded by SD326 as the service chain application scenario of SFC at the edge of MAN, and on this basis, six application modes are extended. These scenarios include CGNAT and Web Filtering, access and parental control, DPI and Lawful Intercept, DPI and URL filtering, host security and strict SLAs, flexibility and redundancy of service chains in physical and virtual networks. For the deployment requirements of operators, BBF focuses on the following three aspects of research:

1) Complex service chain related issues include open loop and closed loop service chain, dynamic service chain deployment, dynamic path change, symmetric and asymmetric forwarding, cross-CO/POP/DC service chain, cross-carrier service chain, and interface address movement in virtual migration scenarios.

2) Operation-level business chain related issues include QoS deployment and guarantee based on session/user business chain, and service chain SLA formulation based on bandwidth/delay/OAM and other factors.

3) Automatic configuration in cross-domain scenarios includes user-aware session authentication and accounting, dynamic load balancing, high reliability, and on-demand flexible bandwidth allocation.

2.3 The ETSI Standard

As a standard organization led by European operators and equipment vendors, ETSI (European Electric Union) is the maker and leader of NFV. It proposes to adopt NFVFG mode to realize the service chain in NFV environment, and organizes the industrial chain to carry out the corresponding scenario pilot, so as to provide technical reference for the deployment of operators. ETSI's research on the business chain is scattered and distributed in various research documents. GS NFV 001 proposed an application case of NFVFG [5], focusing on NFVFG framework and implementation mode, mapping between virtualization functions and physical entities, collaboration between virtualization functions and dedicated devices, etc. Carriers can flexibly deploy service functions anywhere on the network based on the performance of the whole network service functions. GS NFV-EVE 005 focuses on the implementation relationship among SFC, SDN and NFV [6], discusses the introduction of SDN controller based on IETF SFC architecture, and proposes the multi-tenant implementation scheme of carrier and the cross-NFVI implementation model under the NFVI environment. GSNFV-MAN 001 standardizes the NFVFG information unit [7], develops the metadata content of vnffgd and vnffgr, and provides the basic information model for NFVFG application.

2.4 The ITU-T Standard

ITU-T (International Telecommunication Union-Telecommunication Standards Authority) is a branch of the International Telecommunication Union (ITU) that develops telecommunications standards. It focuses on the deployment model of service chains in the network, the protocol interaction between various entities, and the end-to-end testing methodology. In addition, ITU-T Y-series Recommendations - Supplement 41 studied the service chain deployment framework and functional requirements [8], proposed three service chain deployment modes such as linear, recursive and branch, and further studied the service path selection strategy under direct and indirect interconnection scenarios. ITU-T Y.3512 [9], from the perspective of cloud computing NaaS, puts forward the necessary conditions for the realization of service chain, including the requirements of service chain application and the security isolation requirements of NaaS for multi-tenant service chain. The research project Q.CO focuses on the signaling requirements for the realization of the service chain in the scenario of the end office, pursuing the easier realization of the interaction between multiple systems and improving the flexibility of deployment [10].

3   System Model

As shown in Fig. 1, to meet the requirements of cloud data centers, the SDN vDC solution uses a TECS+ cloud management platform and a SDN controller. Overlay and end-to-end SDN control networks are flexibly adopted based on requirements. In Overlay networking scenario, virtual switch is recommended as the VTEP for the virtualization server. For bare-metal servers and VNF clusters with demanding performance and delay requirements, 5960 ToR physical switch is recommended as the VTEP, which supports SR-IOV access. The proposed placement scheme supports the hybrid networking solution of vSwitch, physical switch, and SR-IOV, and adopts the distributed routing solution. In this way, cross-subnet traffic does not need to be forwarded by devices in a centralized manner, effectively reducing traffic dedirection and network delay. For outgoing DC traffic, the southbound traffic and east-west traffic are uniformly diverted through the VxLAN GW network, simplifying external networking and reducing the need for IP addresses for devices to communicate with each other.

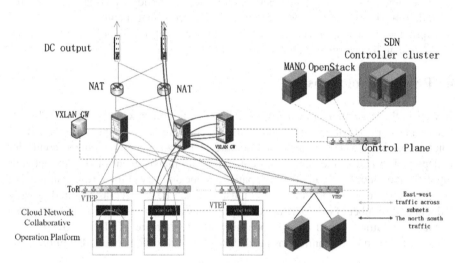

Fig. 1. Network virtualization solution model for the cloud network collaborative operation platform

In addition, we provide a variety of VxLAN gateway solutions according to the network scale and northbound traffic characteristics. For large private clouds, 9900 is recommended as VxLAN GW, which has the lowest unit traffic cost. For small private clouds, 5960 is recommended as VxLAN GW to reduce network construction costs. For large public clouds, M6000-S is recommended as the VxLAN GW, which supports tenants with more than 64 KB to ensure the expansion of public cloud services. In addition, M6000-S supports the all-in-one NAT deployment, which greatly improves the device integration.

For L4-L7 services in vDC, we provide self-developed hardware IPSecVPN devices and virtual IPSecVPN devices, as well as third-party hardware and software firewalls and load balancers. In addition, we can also integrate third-party L4-L7 services based on customer requirements. It defines a service link port based on the OpenStack Neutron model. Traffic paths are delivered by the SDN controller without special forwarding surface processing by L4-L7 devices. Therefore, virtual devices can be easily integrated into the overall vDC solution.

The advantage of the proposed model:

- The SDN controller has a global network topology, as well as the network dynamic published, and on the basis of the overlay network diagnostic tool, which can realize fault location analysis, realized the efficient operations of the network.
- The unity based controller can realize entire network optimization and real-time scheduling, thus achieve energy-saving optimization of network level.
- The vDC controller supports clustering, the biggest can support 128 controller node cluster, can significantly improve the system reliability and capacity, meet the needs of large-scale commercial data center.
- The layout is used to control and manage VNF with interaction at the bottom of the computation, storage, and network resources, provides a visualization of the underlying infrastructure management and resource management.
- It provides vSwitch project, and can be combined with DPDK and smart card, can provide high performance ability of forwards.

4 Proposed Solutions

In view of the large number of IPRAN network nodes, complex network protocols, difficulty and workload of operation and maintenance, it creatively proposed SDN IPRAN solution based on SDN technical architecture. An independent centralized controller is deployed to realize the centralized collection and management of IPRAN network topology, the centralized calculation of paths, and the delivery of forwarding paths using standard interfaces. In addition, virtual clustering can be realized as required, greatly reducing the number of logical nodes on the network and simplifying the network architecture. In addition, based on the open network architecture of SDN, corresponding network apps can be customized as needed to achieve flexible network definition.

4.1 SDN IPRAN Solution

The proposed SDN IPRAN's key advantages and values:

- SDN based virtual cluster is achieved, management control and access the IPRAN network virtualization, massive IPRAN access equipment is virtual as gathering the far side of the card. Tens or hundreds of nes on the network can be virtualized into a logical NE, greatly simplifying the network architecture.
- network topology obtaining, calculation and selection of the path, the establishment of the business channels are completed by SDN controller, need not run on IPRAN equipment complex IP/MPLS protocol, reducing the professional and technical requirements;
- IPRAN business one-click deployment, configuration of a single business time more than 15 min;

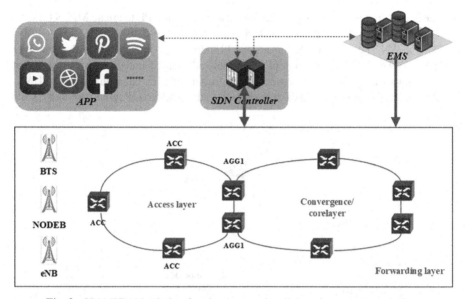

Fig. 2. SDN IPRAN solution for cloud network collaborative operation platform

- provides network elastic scalability should the APP, can quickly realize the flexible adjustment of the network (Fig. 2).

As the data center becomes the start and end point of network traffic and the number of service types carried by the data center increases, traffic interaction between data centers (east-west traffic) increases gradually. DCI scheme is proposed to meet the demand of large bandwidth, low delay and differentiated load for the increasing east-west traffic, which mainly carries east-west traffic between data centers in different geographical locations. DCI backbone network provides fast, automatic, diversified and differentiated carrying service for the above traffic. At present, DCI schemes are divided into two types: one is loosely coupled scheme in which the DCI network can sense tenant traffic, and the other is uncoupled scheme in which the DCI network cannot sense tenant traffic.

4.2 Loose Coupling Scheme

- Tenant networks in DC use the VxLAN + openflow scheme. That is, the data plane uses VxLAN packets to encapsulate packets. The control plane uses the centralized openflow controller to learn virtual machine arp, create and deliver the MAC forwarding table of the VTEP, and the distributed routing forwarding table.
- VxLAN GW is configured in the DC. Southbound traffic and EW-bound traffic are uniformly diverted through the VxLAN GW to relieve the EW-bound routing pressure of the VTEP. VxLAN GW creates VRF instances for each tenant to isolate routes between tenants. Create a VxLAN VNI for each tenant subnet. The VxLAN VNI is terminated from the tenant VRF instance at Layer 3 to isolate the routes of tenant subnets.

- The access router on the DCI backbone network acts as a PE to create MPLS L3VPN for tenants between the PE access devices.
- DC VxLAN The GW and DCI backbone PE networks communicate with each other in VxLAN + EVPN mode to implement route advertising and data forwarding. That is, the forwarding plane between the DC controller and PE is encapsulated by VxLAN. The control plane learns and exchanges MAC addresses and IP routes through EVPN (Fig. 3).

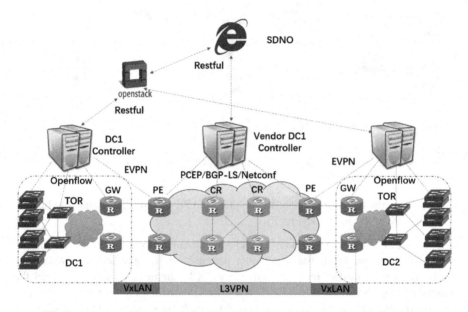

Fig. 3. Loose coupling scheme for cloud network collaborative operation platform

In the loosely coupled scheme, the choreographer mainly coordinates the network parameters between the data center and the DCI to realize the end-to-end connection of computing resources of different data center tenants. In the loosely coupled scheme, the VRF between the tenant's VNI and the L3VPN is 1:1. VPNS are set up based on the number of VNIS, that is, the tenant granularity. Therefore, the DCI network can sense the traffic information of each tenant. The advantage of this scheme is that the DCI network can implement fine-grained traffic scheduling and bandwidth adjustment for tenants, which can guarantee the SLAs of tenants more precisely.

4.3 No Coupling Scheme

- The cloud tenant network in DC uses the VxLAN + openflow solution, and the dedicated VxLAN GW is configured.
- The access router on the DCI backbone network acts as a PE and establishes an MPLS L3VPN underlay route between all pes to carry all VxLAN GW of DC.

- VxLAN GW of different DCS use vxlan-EVPN to implement end-to-end interconnection of tenant VRFS. That is, the control plane implements route advertising by enabling EVPN among DC controllers, and the data plane constructs an end-to-end VxLAN tunnel between GW.

In the no-coupling scheme, the DCI backbone network establishes MPLS L3VPN for DC GW to transparently transmit VxLAN data packets. The DCI network cannot detect tenant-granularity traffic, and the DC GW implements tenant subnet isolation. The no-coupling solution has low requirements on devices and does not require devices to support EVPN and VxLAN protocols.

Key benefits and values of the proposed SDN DCI:

- The SDN based open architecture achieved across different geographical location data center end-to-end business network and backbone network deployment, meet the needs of DC interconnection.
- It is based on VXLAN encapsulation and control, meet the needs of different tenants business isolation, facilitate business development and provide.
- The backbone network and data center together, making the backbone network can provide differentiated services for different tenants, which can effectively increase the network operating income, promoting the value of the network.
- It provides self-service, administrators through management portal implementation business rapid deployment and adjustment, the customer can realize self-help resources through services portal application and business plan.

4.4 Solutions for SDON

Driven by new business types and new business models such as mobile Internet, Internet of Things, high-definition video and cloud computing, optical transmission network not only needs to meet the demand of 0 massive bandwidth growth, but also needs to meet the challenges of dynamic business changes, cost reduction and network function increment. The software-defined optical network SDON solutions help operators build intelligent, resilient, efficient and open optical networks, transforming from traditional closed infrastructure to IT-oriented software (Fig. 4).

The transmission plane adopts the programmable optical network equipment with large cross-capacity, good transmission performance, all service types, and for 100G and over 100G. The programmable characteristics of optical transmission plane mainly include three levels: component programmable, node programmable, network programmable. Component programmability is reflected in software-definable optical interfaces and components, node programmability is reflected in switching granularity, optical path resources, and node scale, and network programmability is reflected in service connectivity and protection and recovery capabilities.

Control plane to transfer plane programmable optical network equipment transfer and exchange ability for centralized control, have business route computation, the allocation of resources and connection control functions, has a global network view, forwarding state, utilization rate of network information resources and information, and will be open after transmission resource virtualization to upper applications. The hierarchical controller design (single-domain controller + multi-domain controller) facilitates the

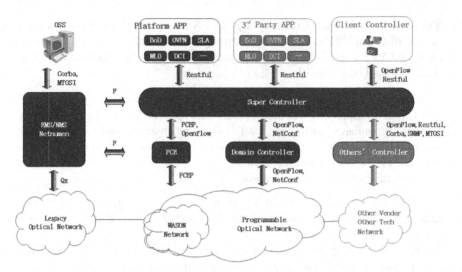

Fig. 4. Solutions for SDON of cloud network collaborative operation platform

integration with the carrier's network and can be flexibly expanded according to the scale of the network. The interface between the controller and APP or the upper-layer controller is the northbound CVNI interface, which can be OpenFlow or Restful. The interface between the controller and the device is the southbound interface CDPI and uses the OpenFlow extension protocol. The NBI will support NetConf in the future.

Application plane Provides service application clouds for carriers, leased customers, and partners to meet maintenance, operation, and value-added service requirements. SDON solutions are committed to building an open platform and promoting business innovation. Customers can choose to provide them with a variety of application services, and can also easily develop the required applications and quickly deploy them according to the open API interface provided by SDON controller, realizing revenue and efficiency.

5   Evaluation and Discussions

This section focuses on discussing the performance of the proposed VNF placement method. As shown in Figs. 5 and 6 by adopting the proposed method, the memory and CPU occupancy rates are largely reduced, showing that with network function being defined as a relatively independent can be invoked by flexible service module, requires each NF components to a smaller granularity resources, on-demand mixed deployment in virtual machine, virtual machine, bare metal containers, container to realize cross-platform deployment, the greatest degree to achieve resource sharing, saves the cost of investment in infrastructure. This provides a good foundation for leveraging artificial intelligence and machine learning techniques to adapt VNF (and even microservice components) of network services to dynamic changes in end-user requirements, environmental conditions, and business goals. With the continuous development of VM, container, bare metal, Real-time OS, macro kernel and other technologies, there are more diverse technology combinations and possibilities centering on the business goals of low latency and high reliability, which has room to play.

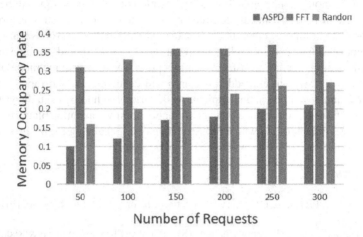

Fig. 5. The VNF placement performance (the memory occupancy rate) with respect to different number of requests

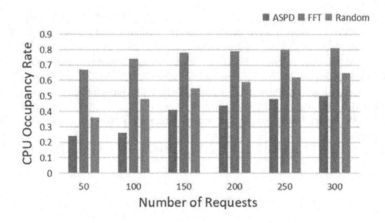

Fig. 6. The CPU occupancy with respect to number of requests

6   Conclusion

This paper introduces the basic architecture and functional components of virtualized network functions placement in cloud network collaborative operation platform, and summarizes and analyzes the research progress of virtualized network functions placement technology in various standard in the industry. On this basis, it discusses the evolution trend of virtualized network functions placement technology and the key research directions in the future. In summary, the virtualized network functions placement will bring a new breaking point of the Internet industry, which has been recognized and input by all parties and has huge market potential. With the development and introduction of SDN/NFV technology, the application and promotion of new technology will be limited to a large extent if the technical requirements of virtualization system are carried out according to the traditional operation mode. In the new IP field, the proposed framework will become one of the core of intelligent operation. Operators should combine their own business development and reconstruct business processes to realize the mode of breaking one by one, carry out embedded research and development, and rapidly promote the research and development and application of various technologies in the virtualized network functions placement in cloud network collaborative operation platform, so as to drive the development of the whole industry chain while realizing the business growth.

References

1. Halpern, E.J., Pignataro, E.C.: Service Function Chaining (SFC) Architecture [EB/OL], 14 April 2017
2. Boucadair, M.: Service Function Chaining (SFC) Control Plane Components & Requirements [EB/OL], 14 April 2017
3. Quinn, P., Elzur, U.: Network Service Header [EB/OL], 14 April 2017
4. Broadband Forum SD326: Flexible Service Chaining [EB/OL], 14 April 2017. http://www.broadband-forum.org/
5. GS NFV 001: Network Functions Virtualisation Use Case [EB/OL], 14 April 2017
6. GS NFV-EVE 005: Report on SDN Usage in NFV Architectural Framework [EB/OL], 14 April 2017
7. GS NFV-MAN 001: Network Functions Virtualisation Management and Orchestration [EB/OL], 14 April 2017
8. ITU-T Y-series Recommendations–Supplement 41: Deployment models of service function chaining [EB/OL], 14 April 2017
9. ITU-T Y 3512: Cloud computing–Functional requirements of Network as a Service [EB/OL], 14 April 2017
10. ONF TS-027: L4-L7 Service Function Chaining Solution Architecture [EB/OL], 14 April 2017

Grounded Theory-Driven Knowledge Production Features Mining: One Empirical Study Based on Big Data Technology

Hao Xu[1,2]([✉]) [iD], Yiyang Li[3], Mulan Wang[1] [iD], Yufang Peng[1] [iD], Qinwei Chen[1],
Pengcheng Liu[1] [iD], and Yijing Li[1] [iD]

[1] School of Economics and Management, Nanjing Institute of Technology, Nanjing 211167,
Jiangsu, China
xhnjit@njit.edu.cn
[2] School of Information Management, Nanjing University, Nanjing 210023, Jiangsu, China
[3] Nanjing University of Information Technology, Nanjing 210044, Jiangsu, China

Abstract. Grounded theory can help scholars solve complex management problems and build a link between practice and theory and has received much attention in recent years. This paper takes CNKI as primary data source, constructs professional retrieval strategy, realizes initial collection of academic papers related to grounded theory, and then combines content analysis methods to manually annotate 2358 papers from titles, keywords, abstracts, and full texts. To realize whether one paper uses grounded theory approach to conduct research. Using the scientific knowledge graph drawing tool CiteSpace, combined with information visualization analysis and social network analysis methods, to identify characteristics of knowledge production driven by grounded theory as a knowledge carrier. The research indicates: In terms of research focus, related research focuses on the multidisciplinary application of grounded theoretical analysis methods and their integration with qualitative research, mixed research, case study and other methods, and focuses on revealing influencing factors of various research issues; in terms of time, grounded theory became the central node of complex networks in 2004, and began to focus on the integration and application of various research tools in 2006, with apparent characteristics of temporal changes; in terms of the features of scientific research collaboration, the grounded theory-driven scientific research collaboration process has formed multiple research sub-networks oriented to the fields of management and education. In the institutional cooperation network, it is found that the large-scale institutional cooperation network driven by the grounded theoretical analysis method has not yet formed and the formed ones were driven by grounded theory can be well used in key links such as innovation management, management consulting decision making, etc.

Keywords: Grounded Theory · Big Data Analysis Methods · Discipline Introduced Features Recognition · Research Collaboration Pattern Recognition · Research Priorities Identification

Y. Tian et al. (Eds.): ICBDS 2022, CCIS 1796, pp. 493–511, 2023.
https://doi.org/10.1007/978-981-99-3300-6_35

1 Introduction

Since the grounded theory was put forward by Glass and Strauss in 1967, it has significantly impacted the social science research community [1]. Grounded theory requires researchers to keep an open mind before starting the research and avoid the influence of the existing theory on the research process. Therefore, the grounded theory approach produces ideas derived from empirical material [2, 3]. With the advent of the information age and the popularization of big data technology, quantitative research based on massive data has become one of the main paradigms of research because grounded theoretical analysis methods can construct new concepts and generate new theories based on empirical data, and refine ideas based on data, so multidisciplinary fields favor it. As of March 2, 2020, the number of academic papers related to grounded theory in CNKI database (China national knowledge infrastructure) has reached to 28,509. The interdisciplinary knowledge production and diffusion characteristics driven by it are gradually revealed, and they play a pivotal role in the process of knowledge production.

Knowledge diffusion can promote the generation of innovative results, which has become a consensus in academia and has gradually become an important research topic in the fields of information science, library and information science, and knowledge management [4, 5]. The methodological knowledge in academic literature is a fine-grained knowledge storage unit and is the knowledge carrier in academic literature which is similar to scholarly literature, it can promote the exchange and diffusion of knowledge. So, what research hotspots have formed in the process of driving knowledge production by grounded theory? Does it drive collaboration among researchers, and what are the characteristics of collaborative networks? What are the features of the time distribution? Whether it can be revealed based on extensive data analysis and visual analysis technology to identify the knowledge production features driven by grounded theory and to promote the rational and standardized use of the method and the generation of innovative results.

This research takes grounded theory as the unit of knowledge storage, takes the knowledge production results driven by the grounded theory in CNKI as the research object, and uses the content analysis method to identify academic papers that carry out empirical research with the grounded theory. Using the big data visualization analysis tool CiteSpace [6] to identify its key features in the process of driving knowledge production based on big data analysis technology, mainly including research focus, features of the author's scientific research collaboration network, attributes of the institutional collaboration network, etc., and It is expected that analysis methods and technologies based on big data will help the standardized use of grounded theory and ensure the accuracy of relevant academic achievements.

2 Related Work

In the past ten years, qualitative research has been paid more and more attention in the field of domestic management research. As a kind of methodological knowledge, grounded theory can help scholars solve complex management problems, better understand the nature and characteristics of problems, and build new theories to explain future issues. It is widely used in management, education, psychology, sociology, nursing, and other disciplines [7, 8]. Chen Xiangming [1]explained the related concepts of grounded theory, introduced the basic operation steps and methods of grounded theory and discussed the significance and limitation of this method to Chinese educational research and the possibility of localization innovation through one classroom teaching example. Fei Xiaodong [9] introduced several versions of the grounded theory and elaborated on the elements of methodological knowledge, research procedures, and evaluation criteria. Wang Han et al. [10] adopted grounded theory and conducted semi-structured interviews to study the perception of flipped classroom for students majoring in library, information and archives and obtained a flipped classroom construction model; Jhony ChoonYeongNg et al. [11] used grounded theory to conduct in-depth interviews with 38 college students, professionals at different stages, and retirees to study and analyze the specific production process and impact of procrastination and the evolution of procrastination at various locations. One first-level, eight second-level, and three third-level codes were concluded and the corresponding solutions are proposed for the third-level coding. Wang Gang [12] used grounded theory to study the characteristics and formation mechanism of marine environmental risks, extracted 49 concepts related to the formation of maritime ecological threats, and condensed 11 categories, which were summarized into natural factors, psychological factors, and social factors. The three main categories have reference significance for an in-depth discussion of marine environmental risks and marine environmental governance.

Existing studies have shown that, as an important methodological knowledge, grounded theory has been researched based on data or data extraction theory. Tools for knowledge production and theoretical refinement. Knowledge Diffusion Theory provides a new idea to study the characteristics of grounded theory-driven knowledge production from the perspective of disciplinary introduction characteristics. Our research is expanding in this area, based on the theory of knowledge diffusion, grounded theory is used as one kind of knowledge carrier. With the help of big data analysis and mining technology, it identifies the characteristics of its introduction of disciplines in the process of driving knowledge production, and uses the scientific knowledge graph drawing tool CiteSpace software to reveal the research hotspots and scientific research collaboration network characteristics driven by rooted theory.

3   Data Sources and Methods

The methods used in this paper mainly include information visualization, social network, and content analysis methods. Information visualization method, that is, this paper uses the scientific knowledge graph drawing tool CiteSpace to materialize and visualize the collected and processed data and display it graphically; the social network analysis method is to analyze and interpret the scientific knowledge map drawn by CiteSpace with the help of social network analysis method; While the content analysis method is mainly embodied in the process of defining whether the academic literature is carried out by the grounded theory analysis method.

3.1 Data Collection

The basic data of this paper was extracted from CNKI database preliminary. CNKI includes 8 first-level disciplines, including basic science, engineering science and technology, agricultural science and technology, medical and health science and technology, philosophy and humanities, social sciences, information technology, and economics and management science, covering a wide, comprehensive and complete range. It is one of the important basic data sources for Chinese bibliometric research [13].

The author used "grounded theory" or "qualitative research" as the search term to conduct an advanced search in the full text and as of March 2, 2020, a total of 28,509 related literatures were obtained. With the help of knowledge service function of CNKI, we found 2139 literatures were directly related to "grounded theory", and 4468 literatures were directly related to "qualitative research", and there was a certain correlation between the two preliminary. In order to ensure the recall rate and precision rate of the data at the same time, the author adjusted the search method to "grounded theory" and included "qualitative research", with the goal of identifying "academic papers that use grounded theory methods to carry out qualitative research". A total of 3686 related literatures were obtained. Combined with the content analysis method, 2358 papers were manually identified and the academic papers that were actually researched by the grounded theoretical analysis method. Relevant papers cover 8 major disciplines involved in CNKI (for statistical convenience, the author merges the Engineering Science and Technology Series I and II listed in CNKI into Engineering Science and Technology, and the Social Science Series I and II into Social Science). The research design and data collection process based on this study is shown in Fig. 1.

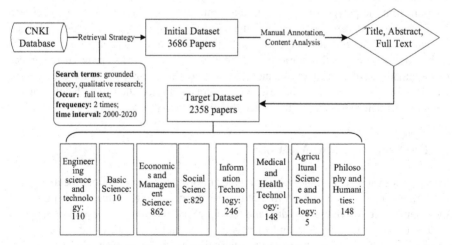

Fig. 1. Data acquisition and processing flow chart

3.2 Data Preprocessing

The purpose of data preprocessing is to start from the title, abstract, and full text of the literature related to the initially collected data, to determine whether the literature uses grounded theory to conduct research, and to assess the role of "grounded theory" in knowledge production. The author used the collected 3686 relevant documents as the initial data, used the bibliographic analysis tool SATI [14] for manual processing, checked the titles, abstracts, and full-text information one by one, and finally obtained 2358 relevant documents.

3.3 Data Set Storage

For the convenience of secondary statistics, in this study, the bibliographic information of the academic literature that "practically adopts the grounded theoretical analysis method to carry out research" is structured with the help of SATI software and stored in the MySQL database. It should be noted that records in MySQL database need to be uniquely identified by encoding, so the subject data names are converted, and the corresponding relationship is shown in Table 1.

Table 1. Subject code conversion

NO.	Subject	Id Code	NO.	Subject	Id Code
1	Engineering Technology	gckj	5	Social Science	shkx
2	basic science	jckx	6	Social Science	xxkj
3	Economics and Management Science	jjgl	7	Medical and Health Technology	yyws
4	Agricultural Science and Technology	nykj	8	Philosophy and Humanities	zxrw

By converting subject name into ID code, the data can be imported into the database, and the unique identification for academic literature and its related information can be completed by coding.

4 Research Focus Mining Driven by Grounded Theory

Identifying keyword co-occurrence and its clustering characteristics based on social network analysis and clustering analysis methods can reveal the research focus of a specific research field. From 2001 to 2020, 2,358 knowledge production results driven by grounded theory methods contained a total of 4,134 distinct keywords, totaling 7,718 times. The keyword co-occurrence knowledge map based on CiteSpace contains 10,758 pairs of co-occurrence relationships, the complex network density is 0.0013, the complexity of the formed complex network is high, and it is impossible to carry out keyword clustering analysis to reveal the research focus in this field. Therefore, based on the threshold adjustment function provided by CiteSpace k = 25 in g-index is set, and the network is simplified based on the pathfinder pruning algorithm. With one year as the time period, the keyword clustering knowledge driven by the grounded theory is drawn respectively. The graph (Fig. 2) and its timeline view (Fig. 3), and at the same time to identify the key mutational features in the development of the field, the 2001–2020 keyword mutation knowledge graph (Fig. 4) is also presented (Table 2).

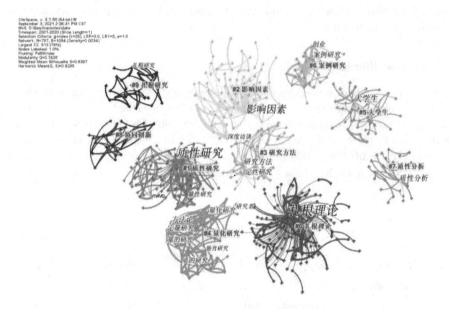

Fig. 2. Keyword Clustering Knowledge Graph Driven by Grounded Theory

Figure 2 is the keyword clustering map of the knowledge generation results driven by grounded theoretical knowledge in the 20 years from 2001 to 2020. Our work selected the first ten clustering results to reveal. Judging from the two values of modularity = 0.7425 and weighted mean silhouette S = 0.9397, the scientific knowledge graph has achieved a good clustering effect, and the research focus in this field can be further analyzed based on this result. A total of 10 clusters are formed in Fig. 2 and the cluster names are #0 grounded theory, #1 Qualitative Research, #2 Influencing Factors, #3 Research Methods, #4 Quantitative Research, #5 College Students, #6 Case Study, #7 Qualitative Analysis, #8 Collaborative Innovation, #9 Grounded Research. The 10 clusters formed can be further divided into three categories:

1. The reasons for forming the four categories #0, #1, #7, and #9 are relatively similar, focusing on the multi-field application of grounded theory or qualitative research methods. By further analyzing the keyword node information and related literature within the cluster, #0 and #9 can be combined into one category, using grounded theory to analyze policy texts and conduct research on strategic frameworks, social governance capabilities and performance. The representative papers include "Governance Function and Dimension Construction of Technology Innovation Network

Table 2. High-frequency keywords driven by grounded theory

NO	KeyWords	First Appearance	Word Frequency	NO	KeyWords	First Appearance	Word Frequency
1	Grounded Theory	2004	1064	8	Empirical Research	2007	20
2	Qualitative Research	2001	374	9	Scale Development	2011	16
3	Influencing Factor	2006	191	10	Quantitative Study	2004	15
4	College Students	2009	65	11	Depth Interview	2005	14
5	Case Study	2010	37	12	Teenager	2004	14
6	Research Method	2006	36	13	Driving Factor	2017	14
7	Methodology	2004	23				

Practices," "E-Government Governance System, Governance Capability and Governance Performance - Exploratory Research Based on Grounded Theory," etc.; #1 contains a total of 92 nodes, which first appeared in 2011. And the formation method of this cluster is a qualitative research on psychological problems in colleges and universities driven by grounded theory. The primary papers include "A Qualitative Research on the Interpersonal Conflict Patterns of Post-95s College Students", "An Analysis of Psychological Resilience and Protective Factors of Outstanding Poor College Students," etc. #7 is the related application of grounded theory in human resources, which is mainly used for the informal training of human capital, human resources, and the impact of economic transformation on human resources.

2. The second largest category includes three subcategories #3 Research methods, #4 Quantitative research, and #6 Case stud. The reasons for forming these three clusters are the combination of grounded theory me or qualitative research methods and other types of methods. Use is manifested as the knowledge production driven by this multi-type method. Further research found that these three types focus on the integration of grounded theoretical analysis methods with qualitative research, quantitative research, case studies, mixed research methods, content analysis methods, in-depth interviews, and other research methods, and focus more on enterprise development, innovation and entrepreneurship, and research. Management consulting, etc. The representative papers are the research on grounded theoretical thought logic and action learning in management consulting published in 2017. Published in 2013, the role and behavior of local leaders in the process of enterprise development and the process model of the entrepreneurial platform, entrepreneur and consumer value co-creation: taking Xiaomi as an example, etc.

3. The third category includes three subcategories: #2 Influencing factors, #5 College students, and #8 Collaborative innovation. It mainly focuses on the relevant research

on identifying influencing factors driven by grounded theory. Among them, there are more topics about college students and collaborative innovation. Through further investigation, it is found that the total number of articles used for the identification of influencing factors by the grounded theory is 162, while the number of articles focusing on the topic selection of college students is 65, and the annual distribution of knowledge production is relatively uniform. It lasts for a long time, mainly focusing on College students' career development, Entrepreneurial motivation, Learning behavior, Green consumption, Course participation, etc.

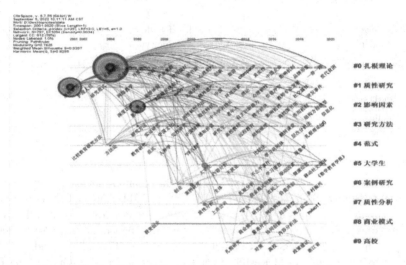

Fig. 3. Timeline View of Grounded Theory-Driven Research Outcomes

Combined with Fig. 3, the distribution characteristics of clustering subnets in time can be found:

1. The related research on the qualitative research of clustering #1 is earlier, and in 2004, there were related researches with grounded theory as the central node. These two clusters are distributed over the 20 years from 2001 to 2020; in 2006, related research on identifying influencing factors driven by grounded theory began to appear and gradually became the primary research paradigm in the field.
2. In the process of knowledge production driven by grounded theoretical analysis methods, since 2006, the integration of various research methods has been gradually emphasized, such as case studies, social network analysis, qualitative and quantitative integration, content analysis, scale development, case study, etc. the software used, in addition to the commonly used software nvivo for grounded theoretical analysis, also pays attention to the integrated use of the scientific knowledge map drawing tool CiteSpace to achieve cross-development.
3. In terms of research topics, since 2006, this research field has begun to focus on fission entrepreneurship, business models, entrepreneurial entrepreneurship, collaborative innovation, and other issues. In 2010, it attached great importance to the

relevant research on employment issues, study intentions and behaviors of college students; since 2012, the research topic has added relevant research on policy recommendations for the development of colleges and universities. Further enriching the research objects, increasing the number of college teachers, researchers and other groups.

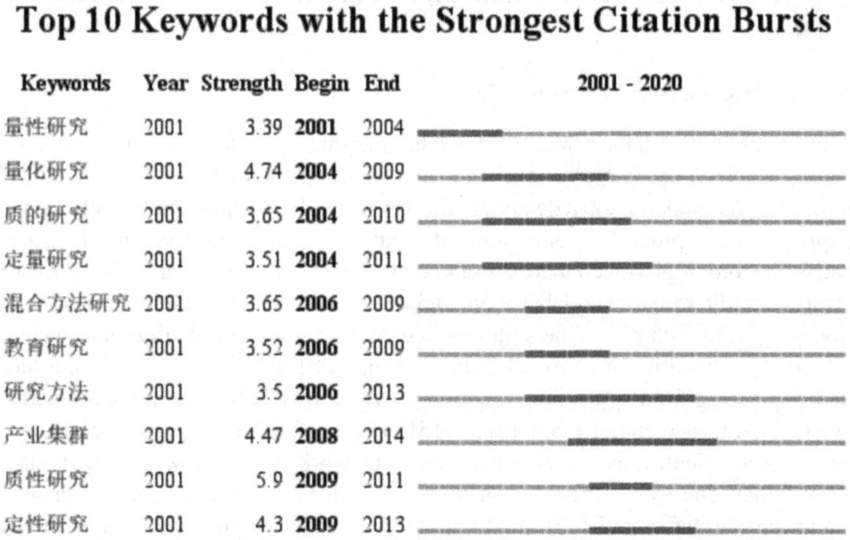

Top 10 Keywords with the Strongest Citation Bursts

Keywords	Year	Strength	Begin	End	2001 - 2020
量性研究	2001	3.39	2001	2004	
量化研究	2001	4.74	2004	2009	
质的研究	2001	3.65	2004	2010	
定量研究	2001	3.51	2004	2011	
混合方法研究	2001	3.65	2006	2009	
教育研究	2001	3.52	2006	2009	
研究方法	2001	3.5	2006	2013	
产业集群	2001	4.47	2008	2014	
质性研究	2001	5.9	2009	2011	
定性研究	2001	4.3	2009	2013	

Fig. 4. Keyword Mutation Map Driven by Grounded Theory

Figure 4 shows the mutation of the keywords marked by authors in the process of knowledge production which were driven by grounded theory analysis method from 2001 to 2020. It can be found that it is relatively novel to combine grounded theory and quantitative research to carry out knowledge production in the span of 2001–2011, embodied in the emergence of quantitative research, quantitative research and quantitative research. The earliest academic paper that integrates grounded theoretical analysis and quantitative research within the sample range of this study is the research on the concept and components of psychological quality of middle school students; In 2006, the field began to pay attention to the analysis of mixed methods in the process of driving knowledge production by grounded theory, with a period time of 2006–2009, and a similar educational research had a duration of 2006–2009. The duration of industrial clusters is 2008–2014, and the mutation period time of qualitative research is 2009–2013. The changes of emergent words indicate that the field of knowledge production research driven by grounded theory is kept dynamic and updated, not unchanging and it pays more attention to the common use and common driving of multidisciplinary theoretical analysis methods.

The key characteristics of the knowledge production results driven by comprehensive grounded theory can be summarized as follows: in terms of research objects, it focuses on college students, college teachers, scientific researchers, entrepreneurs, nurses, etc.; In terms of research topics, it focuses on education research, enterprise development research and other fields; in terms of research methods, it pays attention to the integration of multi-disciplinary methods, such as in-depth interviews, case analysis, social network analysis and other methods.

5 Scientific Research Collaboration Pattern Driven by Grounded Theory

5.1 Author Collaboration Networks

Scientific research collaboration is one of the important paradigms of knowledge production, which can promote the exchange and sharing of knowledge. In the era of big science, this method of knowledge production is particularly important when faced with complex interdisciplinary, cross-regional, difficult, and large-scale problems. In order to identify the role of grounded theory as a knowledge production factor in the process of driving scientific research collaboration, and to identify the scientific research collaboration network driven by it. The author collected the author information of knowledge production results driven by grounded theory from 2001 to 2020, set k = 25 in g-index based on the threshold adjustment function provided by CiteSpace, and simplified the network based on pathfinder algorithm [15]. The knowledge graph of the grounded theory-driven scientific research collaboration network is shown in Fig. 5. It should be noted that, due to the existence of duplicate names in Chinese, during our work, the authors who have published more than 5 times were searched one by one through

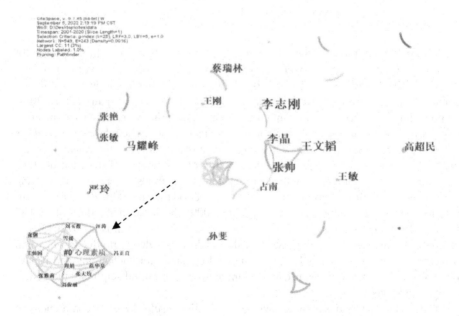

Fig. 5. Author collaboration network driven by grounded theory

the author's publishing institution and scientific research resume. After verification and consolidation, the results are shown in Table 3.

Figure 5 contains 549 author nodes and 243 pairs of scientific research collaborations. The largest sub-network formed includes 11 nodes, and the overall density of the formed author collaboration network is 0.0016, Indicates that the large-scale collaborative network of authors driven by grounded theory as a factor of knowledge production has not yet formed. Combining the Fig. 5, Table 3 and the bibliographic information of articles, we can further find:

1. In the author scientific research collaboration network driven by grounded theory, the largest subnet has 11 nodes, and the authors who published more than 1 article in this subnet are Feng Zhengzhi from the Mental Health Education Center of the Third Military Medical University, Zhang Dajun from the Teaching Institute of Southwest Normal University, and Zhang Li from the Psychology Teaching and Research Office of the Nursing Department of the Third Military Medical University, and the three authors are the core authors of this subnet, and the scientific research collaboration network structure formed by them tends to be a complete network. With the help of grounded theoretical analysis, the research collaboration network focuses on the psychological quality of middle school students [16], nurses [17] and other groups and the competence of nurses to carry out research [18]. In terms of time, this sub-network was first formed in 2001, focusing on the research on the concept and components of psychological quality of middle school students, and then expanded to nurses in the research group.

2. Zhigang Li and Shining He from the School of Management of Ocean University of China, Jingwei Zhang from the School of Economics and Management of Yan Shan University, and Zhen Liu from the School of Business of Qingdao University of Technology formed a relatively close institutional cooperation network and in which Zhigang Li is the central node of the network. Further research found that Zhigang Li's team mainly focused on strategic and entrepreneurial management and has formed 11 high-quality academic literature in the field. Combined with the resume analysis method [19], Zhigang Li's resume [20] was analyzed and found that he obtained a doctorate in management from Nankai University Business School in 2006. In 2006, he published 2 papers based on the grounded theory. Since 2006, he has worked in the School of Management of Ocean University of China. The grounded theory continues to carry out research and gradually deepens. It can be seen that the research method has a certain continuity in the process of driving knowledge production and can be extended to other scientific research groups.

3. One organization cooperation network driven by grounded theory is Wentao Wang, Jing Li, Shuai Zhang from the School of Management of Anhui University, and the organization is Nanzhan of the School of Management of Henan University of Science and Technology. In the scientific research collaboration subnet formed by the school of management, Henan University of Science and Technology, the number of publications is more than 4 times, including 4 people, the publication cycle from 2016 to 2020, the subject area is the field of information technology, and the research topics focus on research on user information behavior [21], academic social networks [22], and virtual health communities [23, 24] based on grounded theory.

Table 3. High frequency authors driven by grounded theory

NO.	Name	Number of published	First published	Institutional Information	Same Author or not
1	Zhigang Li	11	2006	2006 Nankai University 2007–2019 Ocean University of China	Yes
2	Wentao Wang	8	2017	2017–2020 Anhui university 8	Yes
3	Jing Li	8	2017	SuZhou University, 1, 2019 GuangZhou university, 1, Anhui university, 2017–2019, 6	No
4	Shuai Zhang	8	2017	Anhui university, 2017–2019, 8	Yes
5	Yaofeng Ma	7	2010	Shaanxi Normal University	Yes
6	Ling Yan	7	2014	Tianjin University of Technology	Yes
7	Ruilin Cai	7	2014	Changshu Institute of Technology, 2, Nanjing University of Aeronautics and Astronautics, 5	Yes
8	Min Wang	6	2019	Anyang College, 2 South China Normal University 1 Civil Aviation Flight Academy of China, 2 Jinan University 1	No

(*continued*)

Table 3. (*continued*)

NO.	Name	Number of published	First published	Institutional Information	Same Author or not
9	Chaomin Gao	6	2016	Baise College, 6	Yes
10	Gang Wang	5	2015	Ocean University of China 4, Shanxi Art Vocational College 1	Yes
11	Nan Zhan	5	2016	Henan University of Science and Technology, 5	Yes
12	Yan Zhang	5	2019	Chinese Academy of Sciences University, 5	Yes
13	Min Zhang	5	2019	Wuhan University, 5	Yes
14	Fei Sun	5	2015	Lanzhou University, 5	Yes

4. In the field of education, a scientific research collaboration sub-network has been formed for athletes and college students. Driven by grounded theory, the sub-network is mainly based in the School of Education, Soochow University. The core authors include Liyan Liu and Dianzhi Liu. Further research found that in the process of the formation of grounded theory-driven author research collaboration network, the diffusion of the grounded theory method among institutions was further diffusion. For example, the members in this sub-network are further expanded to the Basic College of Zhejiang Wanli University, the School of Foreign Languages of Soochow University, the School of Education and Public Administration of Suzhou University of Science and Technology, and Lijiang Normal College etc.

The analysis of the characteristics of the scientific research collaboration network driven by the grounded theory method shows that grounded theory, as a knowledge production factor, can promote the diffusion of knowledge among institutions, within the academic community, and within disciplines. In some disciplinary fields, it has formed an interdisciplinary collaboration network. In order to further identify the research topic focus of the research collaboration network driven by the grounded theory method, we draws a timeline view, as shown in Fig. 6.

Combining with Fig. 6 it can be intuitively found that the changes in the selection of scientific research topics driven by grounded theory, the application of grounded theory analysis methods from 2001 to 2006 focused on Zhengzhi Feng's research team at Third Military Medical University, focusing on research in psychology; After 2006, the research team of Zhigang Li (PhD from Nankai University) of Ocean University of China applied the grounded theory to the related research in the field of management, especially strategic management; In 2015, Dianzhi Liu from the School of Education, Soochow University, etc. applied it to the area of education research; In 2017, a research team with Wentao Wang of Anhui University as the core applied it to the research on user information behavior. With the passage of time, the driving role of grounded theory in academic research has continued to expand, promoting the common development of multidisciplinary fields.

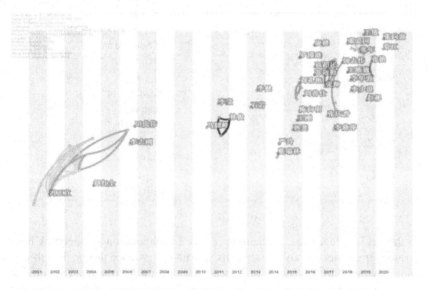

Fig. 6. Timeline View of Author Collaboration Driven by Grounded Theory

5.2 Institutional Collaborative Network

Grounded theory that exists as a means of knowledge production can drive not only scientific research collaboration among authors but also scientific research collaboration among institutions to maximize the generation of methodological knowledge-driven innovative results. According to statistics, from 2001 to 2021, a total of 194 institutions published at least two papers with the help of grounded theory analysis methods to carry out knowledge production activities. In order to identify the characteristics of institutional scientific research collaboration network driven by grounded theory, the author also used CiteSpace software to carry out the characteristics of scientific research collaboration network driven by grounded theory analysis method, set the node type as institution, the graph complexity filter value g-index in k = 25, and based on the pathfinder pruning algorithm to achieve the streamlining of the network, it is revealed by 5 years as a time division, the generated institutional scientific research collaboration network The map is shown in Fig. 7, and its corresponding timeline view is Fig. 8.

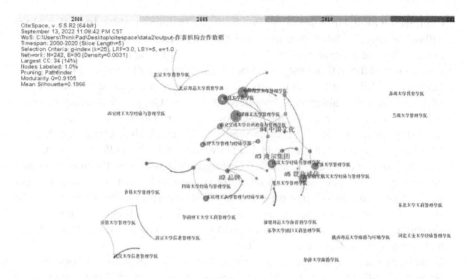

Fig. 7. Institutional Co-authorship Network Diagram Driven by grounded theory

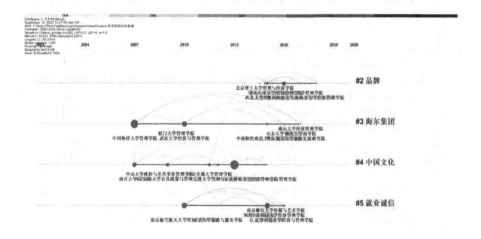

Fig. 8. Timeline View of Institutional Co-authorship Network Diagram Driven by grounded theory

Combining with Figs. 7 and 8, it can be intuitively found that:

1. Figure 7 has 242 nodes and 90 pairs of institutional cooperation relationships. The overall density of the complex network is 0.0031, which means that the institutional cooperation network driven by the grounded theory analysis method is relatively sparse, and the large-scale institutional collaboration network has not yet formed.

2. Combined with the timeline view (Fig. 8), it can be found that the formation of the author's research collaboration network driven by grounded theory can be traced back to the School of Management at Ocean University of China in 2007. In this institution, grounded theoretical analysis methods have driven Li Zhigang, Cai Libin, Wang Shuilian, Cai Libin and others to carry out academic research, and spread this knowledge to Shandong University School of Management, Qingdao University Business School, Nankai University Business School and other institutions. According to the clustering characteristics, Ocean University of China, Wuhan University, Xiamen University, Shandong University, Hubei University, and other colleges and universities have conducted related research on enterprise innovation and entrepreneurship, innovation management, and other fields. The research objects mainly include Haier Group, fission incubation enterprises, State-owned enterprises, etc., emphasizing the support of grounded theoretical analysis methods in institutional entrepreneurship strategies, which has well promoted the diffusion of grounded theoretical analysis methods among colleges and universities.

3. There are ten universities in the inter-university scientific research collaboration subnetwork with the Department of Management and Economics of Dalian University of Technology, the School of Economics and Management of Northwest University, and the Business School of Renmin University of China as the core, which mainly focus on brand development such as brand equity, customer interaction, and influencing factors.

4. The subnet with Tianjin University of Technology School of Management, Nankai University Business School, and Xi'an Jiaotong University School of Public Policy and Management as the core contains nine institutional nodes. The reason for the formation of this clustering is the work among the universities in the subnet around the development of quantitative scales, brand fit, and research on planned behavior. The core authors mainly include Zhao Bin, Yan Ling, Du Ya, etc.

5. The university scientific research collaboration subnet with Jiangsu University School of Management, Nankai University School of Tourism and Service, and Tianjin University of Science and Technology School of Economics and Management as the core contains six institutional nodes. The institutional network mainly focuses on social media, competitive intelligence, innovation, and entrepreneurship. Research on employment integrity, etc.

It can be seen that the main reason for the formation of the scientific research collaboration network driven by the grounded theory is that the method can be well used in key links such as innovation management and management consulting decision-making. However, the large-scale collaborative network of pedagogical colleges and universities it drives has not yet formed, and this phenomenon should attract enough attention in related fields.

6 Summary and Outlook

This paper mainly uses the knowledge diffusion analysis theory and the scientific knowledge graph drawing software CiteSpace to identify the changes in research priorities and research collaboration network driven by grounded theory. The research data source comes from CNKI database, which is collected manually by constructing a professional retrieval method, combined with the content analysis method, from the perspective of title, abstract, keyword, and even full text, and manually annotate research results related to knowledge production using grounded theory approaches. The data analysis results based on a large sample show that the related research on grounded theory focuses on the multidisciplinary application of grounded theory analysis methods and their integration with qualitative research, mixed research methods, case study methods, and other methods, and special attention is paid to revealing the influencing factors of various research issues; in terms of research objects, it focuses on college students, university teachers, scientific researchers, entrepreneurs, nurses, etc.; in terms of research topics, this field focuses on education research, enterprise development research, and other fields; In terms of research methods, focus on the integration of multi-disciplinary methods, such as in-depth interviews, case analysis, social network analysis and other methods. In terms of time, in 2004, Grounded Theory became the central node of the complex network. In 2006, it began to focus on integrating and applying various research tools, which have apparent characteristics of time change. In terms of the characteristics of scientific research collaboration, the grounded theory-driven scientific research collaboration process has formed multiple research sub-networks oriented to the fields of management and education. In the institutional cooperation network, it is found that the large-scale institutional cooperation network driven by the grounded theoretical analysis method has not yet formed, and the formation of the related institutional cooperation network that has been created is because the grounded theoretical analysis method can be well established. The main reason for the formation of the scientific research collaboration network driven by the grounded theory analysis method is that the grounded theory analysis method can be well used in key links such as innovation management and management consulting decision making, however, the large-scale collaborative network of research in the field of pedagogy that it drives has not yet formed, and this phenomenon should attract enough attention in related fields.

The shortcomings of this study are: in terms of data sources, the primary data source of this paper is Chinese, which can only reflect the introduction of domestic grounded theory disciplines, and whether the relevant research results are universal needs further verification; In the process of identifying academic literature that uses grounded theory for knowledge production, it mainly relies on content analysis methods to carry out, manual annotation and screening of large amounts of data and high time costs. In the later research, try to integrate rule-based and machine learning technology to assist in order to save time and cost. These two directions also constitute the main research direction of the research team.

Acknowledgments. The research was supported by JIANGSU PROVINCIAL SOCIAL SCIENCE FOUNDATION YOUTH PROJECT: Grant number 21TQC003; the INNOVATION FUND GENERAL PROJECT I OF NANJING INSTITUTE OF TECHNOLOGY, Grant number CKJB202003; MAJOR PROJECTS OF PHILOSOPHY AND SOCIAL SCIENCE RESEARCH IN UNIVERSITIES OF JIANGSU PROVINCE, Grant number 2021SJZDA178; OPEN RESEARCH FUND OF NJIT INSTITUTE OF INDUSTRIAL ECONOMY AND INNOVATION MANAGEMENT, Grant number JGKA202202; The TEACHING REFORM AND

CONSTRUCTION PROJECT OF NANJING INSTITUTE OF TECHNOLOGY, Grant number JXGG2021031; and JIANGSU PROVINCE EDUCATION SCIENCE "14TH FIVE-YEAR PLAN" 2021 ANNUAL PROJECT, Grant number C-c/2021/01/62. PRACTICE AND INNOVATION TRAINING PROGRAM FOR COLLEGE STUDENTS OF NANJING INSTITUTE OF TECHNOLOGY (Grant number 202211276090Y).

References

1. Chen, X.: The application of grounded theory in Chinese education research. Peking Univ. Educ. Rev. **13**(01), 2–15, 188 (2015). (in Chinese)
2. Glaser, B.G., Strauss, A.L., Strutzel, E.: The discovery of grounded theory; strategies for qualitative research. Nurs. Res. **17**(4), 555 (1968)
3. Glaser, B.G., Holton, J.: Remodeling grounded theory. Hist. Soc. Res. – Suppl. **4**(1), 47–68 (2007)
4. Liu, Y., Rousseau, R.: Towards are presentation of diffusion and interaction of scientific ideas: the case of fiberoptics communication. Inf. Process. Manag. **48**(4), 791–801 (2012)
5. Ge, S.: Research on the diffusion process of academic innovation. Chin. Libr. J. **41**(1), 62–75 (2015). (in Chinese)
6. Chen, C.: Science mapping: a systematic review of the literature. JDIS **2**(2), 1–40 (2017)
7. Glaser, B.G.: Grounded Theory: 1984–1994. Sociology Press, Mill Valley (1995)
8. Glaser, B.G.: Doing Formal Grounded Theory: A Proposal. Sociology Press, Mill Valley (2007)
9. Fei, X.: Grounded theory research methodology: elements, research procedures and judgment criteria. Rev. Public Adm. **03**, 23–43+197 (2008). (in Chinese)
10. Wang, H., Cui, X.: Research on the flipped classroom based on the perception of students majoring in graphic files. Libr. Res. Work **11**, 72–77 (2019). (in Chinese)
11. Ng, J.C.Y., Shan, Z., Tan, Q.: Research on the evolution process of procrastination at different ages: based on the classical grounded theory. J. Shijiazhuang Univ. **21**(05), 29–39 (2019). (in Chinese)
12. Wang, G.: Characteristics and formation mechanism of marine environmental risks: analysis based on grounded theory. China Popul. Resour. Environ. **26**(04), 22–29 (2016). (in Chinese)
13. Hu, C.P., Hu, J.M., Gao, Y., et al.: A journal co-citation analysis of library and information science in China. Scientometrics **86**(3), 657–670 (2011). (in Chinese)
14. Liu, Q., Ye, Y.: The technical method of bibliographic information mining and the realization of its software SATI—Taking Chinese and foreign library and information science as an example. J. Inf. Resour. Manag. **01**, 50–58 (2012). (in Chinese)
15. Chen, C., et al.: The structure and dynamics of co-citation clusters: a multiple-perspective co-citation analysis. JASIST **61**(7), 1386–1409 (2010)
16. Feng, Z., Zhang, D., Fan, H.: A preliminary study on the characteristics of middle school students' psychological quality. Psychol. Sci. **04**, 890–895 (2004). (in Chinese)
17. Zhang, L., Wang, X., Feng, Z., et al.: Qualitative and quantitative research on the concept and components of nurses' psychological quality. J. Nurs. **06**, 406–407 (2003). (in Chinese)
18. Liu, J., Zhang, L., Feng, Z., Wang, T.: Concept and component analysis of nurse competency characteristics. J. Fourth Mil. Med. Univ. **10**, 941–944 (2006). (in Chinese)
19. Tian, R., Yao, C., Yuan, J., Pan, Y.: Research progress on the mobility of scientific and technological talents based on scientific research experience. Books Inf. **05**, 119–125 (2013). (in Chinese)
20. Introduction to Zhigang Li [EB/OL]. http://ibs.ouc.edu.cn/2020/0325/c7073a283147/page.htm

21. Li, J., Zhang, S., Wang, W.: Exploration on the antecedent motivation of users' academic social insufficiency in scientific research social networks: a qualitative research perspective. Mod. Inf. **39**(02), 121–127+144 (2019). (in Chinese)
22. Zhang, S., Li, J., Wang, W.: The influence mechanism of insufficient social networking of academic social networking site users: an exploration based on qualitative methods. Libr. Inf. Serv. **62**(04), 81–88 (2018). (in Chinese)
23. Wang, W., Xie, Y., Liu, K.: Research on user willingness to use virtual health community based on grounded theory. Inf. Doc. Serv. **03**, 75–82 (2017). (in Chinese)
24. Wang, W., Zhang, Z., Li, S., Wu, Z., Xie, Y.: Construction of user online health information acceptance-driven situation model based on system evaluation method. Mod. Intell. **39**(09), 74–83, 108 (2019). (in Chinese)

Research on Digital Twin Technology of Main Equipment for Power Transmission and Transformation Based on Big Data

Yu Chen[✉], Ziqian Zhang, and Ning Tang

NARI Group Corporation/State Grid Electric Power Research Institute, Nanjing, China
401945335@qq.com

Abstract. This paper faces the typical application scenarios of power grid equipment operation and maintenance, maintenance management, emergency disposal, etc., and establishes the array camera spatial deployment strategy of under the constraint condition of the number of acquisition terminals. The automatic fitting and three-dimensional correlation of real scene images are proposed to meet the requirements of single data association and real scene visualization service configuration capability of the power grid equipment model. The selected digital twin technology must conform to the demand characteristics of economic, compatibility, efficient, safe and sustainable development of the current power grid equipment management. The research results of this paper promote the development of DT technology and the application of data science in engineering.

Keywords: Digital twin · Big data · Power system · Image synthesis technique · Multi-visual image

1 Introduction

State Grid Corporation is an asset-heavy, high-risk and service-oriented enterprise, bearing important political, economic and social responsibilities [1–3]. Equipment is an important basis to ensure the safe operation of the power grid, ensuring the reliable supply of power, improving the company's operation performance, and supporting the construction of international leading energy Internet enterprises with Chinese characteristics [4–7] In recent years, the company has vigorously promoted the transformation of the power grid development mode and the transformation of the company's development mode. The power grid equipment scale has increased significantly, the equipment technology level has been significantly improved, the equipment management foundation has been continuously consolidated, the equipment reliability has been greatly improved, and the equipment control capacity and lean level have been continuously improved [7, 8]. As our economy and society has entered the stage of high-quality development, the comprehensive deepening of reform in depth, equipment management in the management concept, methods, means, capabilities and other aspects of the development requirements of the company and the power grid [9].

Y. Tian et al. (Eds.): ICBDS 2022, CCIS 1796, pp. 512–523, 2023.
https://doi.org/10.1007/978-981-99-3300-6_36

In terms of the accumulation of 3 D model data, State Grid Corporation of China currently has a large number of 3 D data resources, including the self-built power transmission and transformation model of the equipment Department, the digital design results of the UHV power transmission and transformation project, the digital design results of the power transmission and transformation project of the Ministry of Infrastructure, and the laser point cloud data of the overhead transmission lines of the General Aviation Company [10]. The digital twin technology based on the main equipment of power transmission and transformation improves the ability of time dimension, data dimension and service dimension based on the original three-dimension. However, not any digital twin technology is suitable for the management of current power grid equipment. However, not any digital twin technology is suitable for the management of current power grid equipment. The selected digital twin technology must conform to the demand characteristics of economic, compatibility, efficient, safe and sustainable development of the current power grid equipment management [11].

2 Research on Technology

2.1 Geometric Information Measurement Technology Based on Multi-visual Image

When an image is taken at two (the same object or more) locations, the rays composed of the photography center and the object pass through the corresponding object point, that is, each ray should intersect at the object point [12]. This principle can be used to rendezvous and locate space points, referred to as line-line intersection, which is the basic principle of measuring three-dimensional intersection and positioning of multivisual image geometric information [13]. Therefore, precise determination of rays composed of image points and photographic centers is key for multivisual image geometric measurements [14]. To do this, it is necessary to solve two key problems, one is to accurately calculate the internal and external orientation parameters of the photography imaging system, such as the photography center, focal length, and the other is to accurately extract the image coordinates of the corresponding image point of the target object on each image (Fig. 1).

In the three-dimensional data collection based on multi-visual images, most non-measuring cameras are used, whose internal orientation parameters are unknown, and the images have large lens geometric distortion [15]. Therefore, it is necessary to check the camera to obtain the precise internal orientation parameters and the camera distortion parameters, and then correct the geometric distortion in the image. The content of camera inspection generally includes the following aspects, determination of the main point position and camera focal length, determination of image geometric distortion parameters, and determination of focal length change after focusing; determination of geometric distortion difference change after focusing. At present, the inspection methods of ordinary non-measuring cameras are roughly divided into three categories, traditional inspection methods based on control field and self-inspection methods based on active vision. The control field-based inspection method performs the camera inspection based on the scene information by accurately giving the control point or the control line of the spatial coordinate. The inspection method based on active vision requires controlling

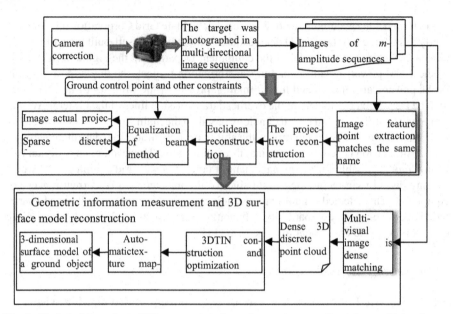

Fig. 1. Technical flow chart of 3D geometric information measurement based on multiview image

the camera to do some special motion and using the camera motion information for checking.

2.2 Real-Time Target Detection and Tracking Technology Based on Real-Scene Video

Real-time detection, recognition and tracking of target images are very important for security monitoring. Background subtraction has the advantage of being simple and fast, but it is affected by shading, shadows, light changes or camera jitter. In practice, the tracking target may be blocked, and it is difficult for the simple background subtraction result to correctly segment the tracked target object [16]. Background subtraction, on the other hand, is difficult to deal with sudden changes in light. Another method is based on the tracking and clustering of the feature points. This method first extracts and tracks the angles, and then clusters according to the position of the corners and the movement trajectory. The clustered classes are used to represent the target object. Compared with background subtraction, the angular clustering method can better deal with the occlusion of the target object, but the actual target due to different sizes, clustering is difficult to achieve a stable effect. In order to use real-scene video for real-time object detection, identification and image tracking, the method of combining background estimation and feature tracking is a more feasible method [17]. The basic idea is shown in Fig. 2. First take some video samples, extract feature points from the target object to be tracked and learn and train. For fixed cameras, a video is collected at regular intervals, and a reliable background image can be estimated by median filtering based on a certain number of video frames collected. This background also requires dynamic updates, given that light conditions can change over time. Compare the current video frame with the background image to detect the object area to be tracked. A global optimization can be used to mitigate the effects of local light changes or noise, resulting in more robust detection of target objects. According to the tracked feature points are classified through the learned classifier, so as to identify which category of objects the tracked target object belongs to.

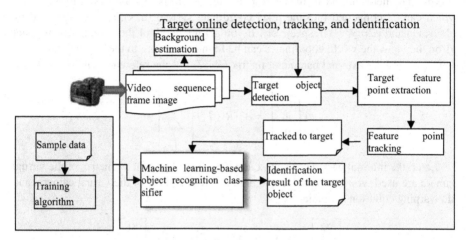

Fig. 2. Technical flow chart of real-time detection and tracking of targets in real-scene video

3   Image Synthesis Technique from a Free Perspective

3.1   Free-Perspective Image Synthesis Based on Depth Information

Image fusion based on a multi-angle camera array is used to solve the fusion deformation problem of intermediate viewpoints under a discrete camera, and the best perspective viewpoint image can be synthesized with the help of surrounding reference camera viewpoints. The overall process of integration is as follows (Fig. 3).

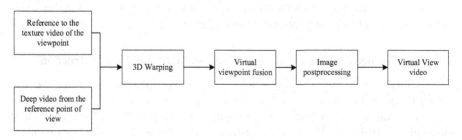

Fig. 3. The overall process of integration

For each pixel on the reference viewpoint, its corresponding depth information and the parameter matrix can be projected into 3D space using the reference camera. Then, the points in the 3D space are projected onto the plane of the virtual camera according to the parameter matrix of the virtual camera, and the process is called 3D-Warping. In the 3D-Warping process, the transformation of multiple spatial coordinate systems is mainly involved. A particular point $P(X_w, Y_w, Z_w)$ in world space uses the camera's external parameter matrix (R, T) to convert into the camera coordinate frame (X_c, Y_c, Z_c). The internal parameter matrix of the corresponding camera is then projected to the plane, which can be converted into the pixel coordinate system (u, v), and is expressed by $p1(u_1, v_1)$ and $p2(u_2, v_2)$, respectively. If you get the depth of the pixel z_1 at any point $p1$ on the view, the world coordinates can be found according to the internal parameter matrix A_1 and the external parameter matrix (R_1, T_1) of the reference camera [18].

$$z_1 \begin{bmatrix} u_1 \\ v_1 \\ 1 \end{bmatrix} = A_1(R_1, T_1) \begin{bmatrix} X_w \\ Y_w \\ Z_w \\ 1 \end{bmatrix}$$

Later, the internal parameter matrix and the external parameter matrix of the virtual camera are used, you can reproject the points onto the plane of the virtual camera, and 3D warping equation is obtained.

$$z_2 \begin{bmatrix} u_2 \\ v_2 \\ 1 \end{bmatrix} = z_1 A_2(R_2, T_2)(R_1, T_1)^{-1} A_1^{-1} \begin{bmatrix} u_1 \\ v_1 \\ 1 \end{bmatrix}$$

After the projected virtual viewpoint, emptiness, artifacts and overlap need further post-processing. There are three solutions to the empty problem. One is the depth map preprocessing. By filtering the depth map and smoothing the depth map, it can reduce the hole on the virtual viewpoint image to a certain extent, but also cause the image distortion to a certain extent. The second is to merge multiple reference viewpoints. In order to compensate for the insufficient scene information of single reference viewpoints, we can consider mapping and merging multiple reference viewpoints. Generally, two reference viewpoints are combined to generate an intermediate virtual viewpoint image. Multi-reference viewpoint combination can not only eliminate most of the voids due to object occlusion, but also be very effective for boundary voids. Finally, the cavity post-treatment. For cavity regions that still exhibit after the forward mapping of the reference viewpoint, only a final cavity treatment can be performed.

3.2   Free-Perspective Image Synthesis Based on Light-Field Reconstruction

This method only requires taking a few photos from different angles for the free perspective image synthesis through body drawing.

First by taking several photos at different angles on the object, the scene is then modeled by a differentiable drawing formula. The color of the light is approximated by integrating multiple samples collected along the rays, as described in the following equation [12].

$$C(r) = \sum_{i=1}^{N} T_i(1 - \exp(-\sigma_i \delta_i))c_i$$

$$T_i = \exp\left(-\sum_{j=1}^{i-1} \sigma_j \delta_j\right)$$

T_i represents the amount of light transmitted, $1 - \exp(-\sigma_i \delta_i)$ indicates how much light is contributed to the sample i, σ_i represents opacity, c_i represents sample color, and δi represents distance. To accelerate the process and to improve the display quality, it is optimized from the following aspects. First by reconstructing a sparse table of voxels, each occupied voxel having opacity and spherical harmonic coefficient. The spherical harmonic function is a set of orthogonal bases defined on a sphere, where low harmonic codes can represent smooth color changes and higher frequency color changes, represented using a quadratic spherical harmonic function. The opacity and color at an arbitrary position and observed direction are determined by trilinear interpolation of the values stored on adjacent voxels and the spherical harmonics calculated in the appropriate observed direction. The opacity and spherical harmonic coefficient of the voxels were optimized by minimizing the mean squared error (MSE) of the rendered pixels, and the TV regularization was used to help eliminate the noise, as described below.

$$\zeta = \zeta_{recon} + \lambda_{TV}\zeta_{TV}$$

$$\zeta_{recon} = \frac{1}{|R|}\sum_{r\in R}\|C(r) - C(r)\|_2^2$$

$$\zeta_{TV} = \frac{1}{|V|}\sum_{v\in V}\sqrt{\Delta_x^2(v,d) + \Delta_y^2(v,d) + \Delta_z^2(v,d)}$$

3.3 Camera Array Building Strategy

The optimization goal of the ring camera array construction strategy is to cover the target area with a minimum number of cameras and to synthesize arbitrary free view images. For simplification, it is assumed that the position of the free perspective virtual camera is also in the annular space, and the free perspective image can be synthesized when the adjacent camera image overlap rate exceeds a certain threshold.

For all removable camera collections in the circular space $\mathbb{C} = \{C_1, C_2, \ldots, C_n\}$, n indicates the number of removable cameras, any camera C_j ($C_j \in \mathbb{C}$) can be indicated by $C_j[location(X_j, Y_j, H_j), posture(P_j, T_j), inner(Size_j, f_j)]$. Assuming that the internal parameters are already known, it is determined by five parameters. The camera parameter space is a continuous five-dimensional space, and this topic will sample the collection of candidate cameras in this five-dimensional space $\mathbb{C}$. The target area contains numerous spatial points. To improve the optimization deployment efficiency, this topic samples the target area into a limited number of spatial points, forming the set $\mathbb{G} = \{G_1, G_2, \ldots, G_m\}$, where m is the number of sampled spatial points. In this subject, any point G_i ($G_i \in \mathbb{G}$) in the target area C_j is covered by the camera and recorded as $cover_{C_j}(G_i)$, while $cover_{c_j}$ represents the collection of points covered by the camera C_j. The total number of cameras is minimized with the guarantee that the overlap rate of adjacent camera images is greater than the threshold. Therefore, the ring array camera deployment optimization model can be expressed as the following expressions

$$\begin{cases} \min_{\mathbb{C}'} F(\mathbb{C}') = card(\mathbb{C}'), \ \mathbb{C}' \subseteq \mathbb{C} \\ s.t. \quad \forall G_i \in \mathbb{G}, \exists C_j \in \mathbb{C}', cover_{C_j}(G_i) = 1 \\ \quad \forall C_s, C_t \in \mathbb{C}', C_s.location \neq C_t.location \\ \quad \forall C_i \in \mathbb{C}', overlay(C_i, C_{i+1}) > \gamma \end{cases}$$

where, $F(\mathbb{C}')$ represents the target function, $card(*)$ represents the number of cameras (the same below), and $C_i.location$ represents the erection location of the camera. $overlay((C_i, C_j))$ indicates the overlap rate of the two cameras. According to the optimization model, the optimization process is to select a subset of the optimization from all the sets of candidate cameras, and this problem is the permutation and combination problem. It is obviously not feasible to enumerate the combinations, so the heuristic search method is used for deployment optimization. The heuristic search method algorithm can be used to construct the optimized graph structure, cost function and heuristic function.

3.4   Automatic Fusion and Matching of Images with 3D Models

Fusion matching of image with 3D geographic scenes determines the visible area of the camera perspective pixel by pixel and mapped to image and video textures. First, you need to get the camera coverage in the 3D scene. After determining the coverage, each pixel within the coverage is transformed into the camera space, calculating its image texture coordinates and sampling the image. For ordinary cameras, the virtual and real fusion of images and 3-dimensional scenes is based on the ideal pinhole imaging model, but due to various reasons, the images often produce certain nonlinear geometric distortion, which is mainly divided into radial distortion and tangential distortion. For more precise virtual and real fusion, nonlinear distortion parameters should be introduced in the pinhole linear model.

Suppose (u, v) is the ideal image pixel coordinates, the corresponding (u', v') is the truly obtained pixel coordinates, (x, y) is the ideal image physical coordinates, and (x, y) is the actually obtained image physical coordinates. Radial distortions are generally expressed as

$$\begin{cases} x' = x + x \left[k_1 (x^2 + y^2) + k_2 (x^2 + y^2)^2 \right] \\ y' = y + y \left[k_1 (x^2 + y^2) + k_2 (x^2 + y^2)^2 \right] \end{cases}$$

k_1, k_2 are known as the radial distortion parameter. The pixel coordinates added after the distortion correction are represented as

$$\begin{cases} u' = u + (u - u_0) \left[k_1 (x^2 + y^2) + k_2 (x^2 + y^2)^2 \right] \\ v' = v + (v - v_0) \left[k_1 (x^2 + y^2) + k_2 (x^2 + y^2)^2 \right] \end{cases}$$

The tangential distortion model is

$$\begin{cases} \delta_{xd} = 2p_1xy + p_2(r^2 + 2x^2) + \cdots \\ \delta_{yd} = 2p_1(r^2 + 2y^2) + 2p_2xy + \cdots \end{cases}$$
$$r^2 = x^2 + y^2.$$

The above distortion correction model is applied to the virtual and real fusion to correct the texture coordinates of the image to realize the accurate matching between the image and the 3D model. For wide-angle cameras, the perspective range is far larger than that of ordinary cameras. They introduce beneficial nonlinear distortion through the combination of several different lenses to achieve the purpose of very large field of view angle imaging. However, the resulting image has a large deformation, which needs to be corrected when the 3D scene is fused. Wide-angle camera models are mainly divided into four categories, isometric projection model, isostereoscopic angle projection model, orthogonal projection model and stereological projection model. To avoid the complexity of using different models for different wide-angle cameras, this study used isometric projection models to approximate and describe the distortion of various wide-angle cameras

$$r_d = f * \theta_d$$

where θ_d takes the first five terms of the Taylor expansion, while taking a single term of 1, so that sufficient degrees of freedom are guaranteed to approximate the wide-angle projection model.

$$\theta_d = 1 + k_1\theta^2 + k_2\theta^4 + k_3\theta^6 + k_4\theta^8$$

The model given in the above formula is a polynomial model of the general wide angle camera, which can obtain the distortion point in the wide angle camera through the distortion-free image point, and then correct the pixel template based on the pinhole model to obtain the corrected sampling coordinates.

4 Simulation and Implementation

Based on the basis of the digital twin research of power grid, the method of panoramic display and analyzing the big data of the operation state of power transmission and transformation equipment, and the basic technical route is shown in the figure (Figs. 4 and 5).

The modeling and implementation of the twin system are mainly based on the data. For the current flow equation, it can be regarded as a process of some known parameters solving other parameters, so the process can be modeled by deep learning. When the DT modeling and implementation are adopted, the mathematical tools selected by DT modeling and the corresponding required data types, data accuracy, and granularity all depend on the application scene and the engineering reality (Figs. 6, 7 and 8).

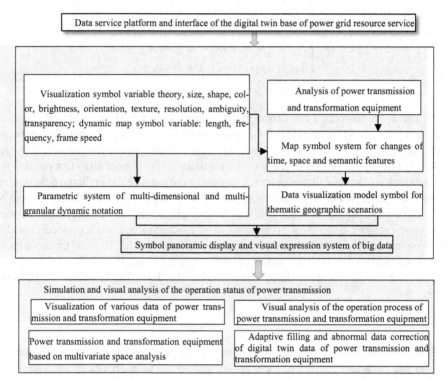

Fig. 4. Technical flow chart of big data panoramic display and analysis method of main power transmission and transformation equipment

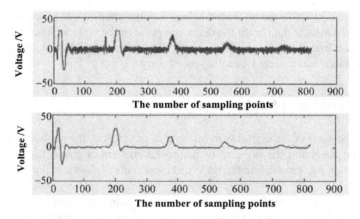

Fig. 5. Open-circuit waveform before and after noise reduction

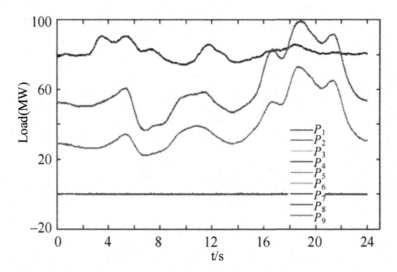

Fig. 6. Load active setting

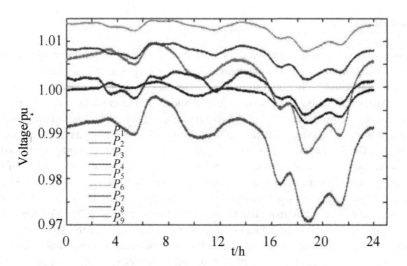

Fig. 7. The amplitude of the voltage

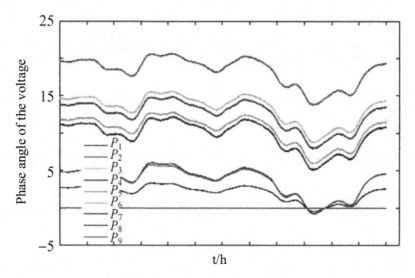

Fig. 8. Phase angle of the voltage

5 Conclusion

This paper faces the typical application scenarios of power grid equipment operation and maintenance, maintenance management, emergency disposal, etc., and establishes the array camera spatial deployment strategy of under the constraint condition of the number of acquisition terminals. The automatic fitting and three-dimensional correlation of real scene images are proposed to meet the requirements of single data association and real scene visualization service configuration capability of the power grid equipment model. To improve the 3D data management standard, build the integrated management system, and create the typical application of 3 D data, we need to improve the ability of time dimension, data dimension and service dimension on the basis of the original 3D, and realize the multi-dimensional fusion application of digital twin. In the time dimension, the real scene can be traced to realize the twin synchronization of 3 D model, real image, monitoring value and business data of the power transmission and transformation main equipment. In the data dimension, it can be fully interactive, and the digital twin base of the power grid resource business with the capability of index, display and interaction is built.

References

1. Yu, J., Zong, P.: The analysis and simulation of communication network in Iridium system based on OPNET. In: The 2nd IEEE International Conference on Information Management and Engineering, Chengdu, China, 16–18 April 2010
2. Ding, K., Chan, F.T.S., Zhang, X., et al.: Defining a digital twin-based cyber-physical production system for autonomous manufacturing in smart shop floors. Int. J. Prod. Res. **57**(20), 6315–6334 (2019)

3. Zhuang, C., Liu, J., Xiong, H.: Digital twin-based smart production management and control framework for the complex product assembly shop-floor. Int. J. Adv. Manuf. Technol. **96**(1–4), 1149–1163 (2018). https://doi.org/10.1007/s00170-018-1617-6

4. Tao, F., Cheng, J., Qi, Q., Zhang, M., Zhang, H., Sui, F.: Digital twin-driven product design, manufacturing and service with big data. Int. J. Adv. Manuf. Technol. **94**(9–12), 3563–3576 (2017). https://doi.org/10.1007/s00170-017-0233-1

5. Liu, Q., Zhang, H., Leng, J., et al.: Digital twin-driven rapid individualised designing of automated flow-shop manufacturing system. Int. J. Prod. Res. **57**(12), 3903–3919 (2019)

6. Mittal, S., Khan, M.A., Romero, D., et al.: Smart manufacturing: characteristics, technologies and enabling factors. Inst. Mech. Eng. **233**(5), 1342–1361 (2017)

7. Sihan, H., Guoxin, W., Yan, Y., et al.: Blockchain-based data management for digital twin of product. J. Manuf. Syst. **54**, 361–371 (2019)

8. Rosen, R., Wichert, G., Lo, G., et al.: About the importance of autonomy and digital twins for the future of manufacturing. IFAC-Papers OnLine **48**(3), 567–572 (2015)

9. Wang, X., Zong, P., Yu, J.: Link analyzing and simulation of TDRSS based on OPNET. In: The International Conference on Communications and Mobile Computing, Shenzhen, China, 12–14 April 2010

10. He, X., Ai, Q., Qiu, R.C., et al.: A big data architecture design for smart grids based on random matrix theory. IEEE Trans. Smart Grid **8**(2), 674–686 (2015)

11. Gray, J.: Jim gray on escience: a transformed scientific method. The fourth paradigm: Data-intensive scientific discovery, pp. xvii–xxxi (2009)

12. Hong, T., Chen, C., Huang, J., et al.: Guest editorial big data analytics for grid modernization. IEEE Trans. Smart Grid **7**(5), 2395–2396 (2016)

13. Burges, C., Shaked, T., Renshaw, E., et al.: Learning to rank using gradient descent. In: Proceedings of the 22nd International Conference on Machine Learning (ICML-05), pp. 89–96 (2005)

14. Yuan, Y., Ardakanian, O., Low, S., et al.: On the inverse power flow problem (2016). arXiv preprint arXiv: 1610.06631

15. Chen, Y.C., Wang, J., Domínguez-García, A.D., et al.: Measurement-based estimation of the power flow Jacobian matrix. IEEE Trans. Smart Grid **7**(5), 2507–2515 (2015)

16. Kelly, J., Knottenbelt, W.: Neural nilm: deep neural networks applied to energy disaggregation. In: Proceedings of the 2nd ACM International Conference on Embedded Systems for Energy-Efficient Built Environments, pp. 55–64. ACM, (2015)

17. Shuwei, X., Caiming, Q., Dongxia, Z., et al.: A deep learning approach for fault type identification of transmission line. Proc. CSEE **39**(1), 65–74 (2019)

18. Boschert, S., Rosen R.: Digital twin—the simulation aspect. In: Hehenberger, P., Bradley, D. (eds.) Mechatronic Futures, pp. 59–74. Springer, Cham (2016). https://doi.org/10.1007/978-3-319-32156-1_5

Efficient Spatiotemporal Big Data Indexing Algorithm with Loss Control

Ziyu Wang[1], Runda Guan[1], Xiaokang Pan[1], Biao Song[1(✉)], Xinchang Zhang[1], and Yuan Tian[2]

[1] Science & Technology (NUIST), Nanjing University of Information, Nanjing, China
bsong@nuist.edu.cn
[2] Nanjing Institute of Technology (NJIT), Nanjing, China

Abstract. Compression algorithm can drastically reduce the volume of spatiotemporal big data. However, lossy compression techniques are hardly suitable due to its inherently random nature. They often impose unpredictable damage to scientific data, making them unsuitable for data analysis and visualization that require certain precision. In this paper, we propose a tree-based indexing method using Hilbert curve. The key idea of this method is that it divides the space into minimum bounding rectangles according to the similarity of the data. Our algorithm is able to select appropriate minimum bounding rectangles according to the given maximum acceptable error and use the average value contained in each selected MBR to replace the original data to achieve data compression. We propose the corresponding tree construction algorithm and range query processing algorithm for the indexing structure mentioned above. Experimental results emphasize the superiority of our method over traditional quadrant-based minimum bounding rectangle tree.

Keywords: spatial-temporal data · lossy compression · data indexing

1 Introduction

With the development of big data technology, the sources of spatiotemporal data are becoming increasingly complex and diverse [25]. Because of this, storing and processing big data has become more and more difficult. Since the main reason for high communication bandwidth usage and high energy consumption is the transmission of large-scale data [1], it is necessary to compress large-scale data. Even though lossy compression can significantly reduce data volume, achieving a relatively good balance between the volume reduction and the information loss is still a difficult task.

Quadrant-based minimum bounding rectangle (QbMBR) tree is proposed in [2] and considered as a solution to this problem. It uses a method similar to quadtree to divide

The authors extend their appreciation to National Key Research and Development Program of China (International Technology Cooperation Project No.2021YFE014400) and National Science Foundation of China (No.42175194) for funding this work

the space and index the spatial data based on it. However, although QbMBR tree can compress data to a certain extent, it only simply divides the data in space, and does not consider the similarity of the data itself, nor can it bounds error rates [3].

Designing an efficient error-controlled lossy compressor which can effectively reduce the data scale with a relatively high compression ratio is very challenging [4, 24]. In order to cope with this problem, we propose a novel indexing method based on Hilbert curve. The main idea of this method is that it divides the space into minimum bounding rectangles according to the similarity of data value and construct an index tree on this basis. The main contributions of this paper are listed as below:

- We introduce an indexing structure using Hilbert curve, which takes full advantage of the feature that adjacent data values are similar. And it is easily to control error when making a range query.
- We propose the tree building processing algorithm and range query processing algorithm on the indexing structure mentioned above. We also propose an algorithm for merging MBRs with Hilbert curve, which is necessary for the tree building processing algorithm.
- We make an evaluation of the performance of proposed algorithms based on actual datasets. The results of the experiment show that our algorithms have excellent efficiency and stability, and achieve a relatively good balance between the volume reduction and the information loss.

The rest of this paper is organized as follows: in Sect. 2, we mainly provide a review of related works. In Sect. 3, our index structure and its corresponding algorithms are described. Section 4 shows experimental results, and the performance of our indexing methods is evaluated. Our final conclusions are given in Sect. 5.

2 Related Work

Lossy compression and error detection of spatial data has been extensively researched in recent years. With the development of Data acquisition techniques, Internet of Things and sensors account for a greater proportion of data in the network [5]. In this environment, traditional computing unable to cope with such a large data size. At present, the scale of data on the Internet are currently in the order of PB, and their scale is continuously rising [6, 7]. Lossy Compression of scientific data has become increasingly popular due to limitations in computer storage capacity, for example, supercomputers for data processing supercomputers are being seriously affected [8]. Therefore, due to the contradiction between the enormous amount of data that is difficult to stored and the need for detailed data analysis, it is necessary to perform error-controlled compression on the data, data compression provides an alternative solution for largescale experiments because it can significantly reduce the size of the data while maintaining key information. The compression factor of lossless compression makes it impossible to meet scientific experiments and simulations requirements [9]. Therefore, only customized error-controlled lossy compression can meet users' requirement in terms of data and speed [10, 11].

Traditional lossy compression and error detection was focused on discussing data features in each block in order to achieve the optimum compression quality, such as some adaptive compression frameworks. However, the source data compressed with these simple lossy compression methods cannot be easily expanded, and it is not feasible to maintain data compressed based on different error tolerant simultaneously.

According to the specific requests, we use R-tree to implement this requirement.

R-tree [12] is a outstanding tree data structure which can used for spatial access methods. The key idea of R-tree is to group nearby objects and represent them with their MBR (Minimum Bounding Rectangle). In the same way, The MBR in the child node is completely contained by the MBR of the parent node [13]. R-tree is also a balanced search tree, which means that all the leaf nodes are at the same depth. The data is organized in pages for convenience of reading and writing on disks and databases [14].

Although the traditional spatial data structure has spatial querying, retrieval indexing, and expandable key-value storage capabilities. However, on the one hand, it lacks scalability; on the other hand, it does not have the ability to handle multi-dimensional spatial data. To address this issue, we propose adding an extra layer of spatial index to the key-value style. We accomplish this by using a linearization method known as the Hilbert curve [14]. The path of a Hilbert space-filling curve gives the multi-dimensional grid points a one-dimensional linear order, which makes it easy to process the data in multi-dimensional space as in one-dimension space [15–18]. In this case, R-tree have excellent expansibility. Other parameters can be introduced as the basis for generating tree structure on the premise that MBR is not destroyed. In this paper, we try to add CUDR (Extrapolated population - maximum error rate) as new attribute of R-tree nodes in order to build efficient error query.

3 Proposed Methodology

3.1 System Model

In order to achieve lossy compression of spatial data according to given maximum error, we use MBRs (Minimum Bounding Rectangles) to partition the spatial data. An MBR contains data within a certain space range, as well as the information about the average value of these data and the maximum error of these data [3]. In the process of compression, we select appropriate MBRs according to the given maximum acceptable error and use the average value contained in each selected MBR to replace the original data.

In order to realize the above-mentioned selection process quickly, we construct an index tree for these MBRs. The structure of the index tree is similar to that of R-tree. Each node in the index tree contains an MBR. The MBR in the child node is completely contained by the MBR of the parent node. The maximum error value contained in nodes at the same layer in the index tree is the same. The maximum error value contained in the node in the deeper position in the tree is smaller than that of the node in the shallow position. Specially, the root node contains the entire spatial data and its maximum error value is the largest in the tree. An example of the structure of the index tree is shown in Fig. 1.

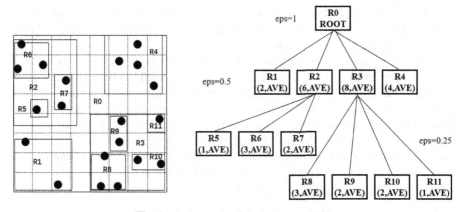

Fig. 1. An example of the index tree [18]

3.2 Construct MBRs with Hilbert Curve

In order to construct the index tree mentioned above, the key is to construct MBRs with larger maximum error value according to existing MBRs with smaller maximum error value. In this paper, we propose a heuristic method similar to the method used in Hilbert R-tree to realize it [18].

Hilbert curve is a kind of space filling curve, which can visit all the points in a k-dimensional grid exactly once and never crosses. As shown in the Fig. 2, the basic Hilbert curve also called the curve of order 1 is on a 2x2 grid denoted by H_1. The curve of order i is derived from four curves of order i-1 with different orientations. The second order and third order Hilbert curve are also shown in Fig. 2. When the order of a Hilbert curve gradually increases until it reaches infinity, the curve becomes fractal.

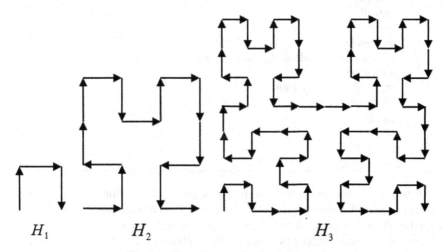

Fig. 2. Hilbert Curves of order 1, 2 and 3

The path of a Hilbert space-filling curve gives the multi-dimensional grid points a one-dimensional linear order, which makes it easy to process the data in multi-dimensional space as in one-dimension space [20, 21].

Next, we propose a method to construct MBRs with Hilbert curve. It is assumed that the maximum error value of the MBRs to be constructed has been given. First, we sort the existing MBRs according to their centers in the order of Hilbert curve. Second, scan backward from the first MBR until the nth MBR is scanned, and the maximum error value of the first n MBRs is just greater than the given maximum error value. Therefore, the first n-1 MBRs can be merged into a larger MBR whose error value is not larger than the given maximum error value. Then, repeat the above operation with the nth MBR as the first MBR until all the existing MBRs are processed. The specific algorithm pseudocode is shown in Algorithm 1.

Algorithm 1. Merge MBRs with Hilbert curve

Input: A set of MBRs with the same maximum error value p, maximum error of new MBRs to be obtained x

Output: A set of new MBRs with given maximum error value, inclusion relationship between new MBRs to be obtained and existing MBRs

$S \leftarrow \varnothing$

$R \leftarrow \varnothing$

sort p according to their centers with Hilbert curve

$i \leftarrow 0$

$j \leftarrow 0$

while $i < p$.size **do**

  while $j < p$.size **do**

    $y \leftarrow$ calculate maximum error of the MBR of $p_i, p_{i+1}, \ldots, p_j$

    if $y > x$ **then**

      break

    end if

    $j \leftarrow j+1$

  end while

  $m \leftarrow$ calculate the MBR of $p_i, p_{i+1}, \ldots, p_{j-1}$

  S.insert(m)

  for $k = i, i+1, \ldots, j-1$ **do**

    R.insert($p_k \subseteq m$)

  end for

  $i \leftarrow j$

end while

return (S, R)

Hilbert curves have good clustering properties, that is, they maintain locality between objects in a multidimensional space in a linear one-dimensional space [16]. Such good properties are very consistent with the requirements under the spatial data scenario.

The above is mainly about two-dimensional Hilbert curve. Hilbert curve can be conveniently extended to three dimension or higher dimensions. Three-dimensional Hilbert Curve is shown in Fig. 3. The extension method is described in detail in [21, 22].

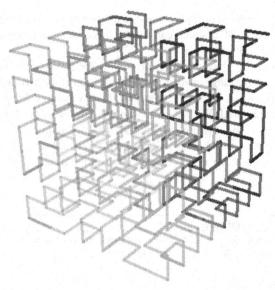

Fig. 3. Three-dimensional Hilbert Curve

3.3 Indexing Algorithm

Algorithm 2 presents the tree building algorithm for the index tree. In order to implement it, we use the bottom-up tree construction method. First, we regard spatiotemporal data as several 1x1 MBRs. Then Algorithm 1 is continuously used to merge MBR to the upper layer where the maximum error of each layer increases in the form of multiplication. At the same time, the relationship between the upper and lower layers is established. Until all MBRs are merged into one MBR, the MBR is the root node of the index tree.

Algorithm 2. Build the index tree
___

Input: spatial data D, maximum error of leaf nodes x
Output: the index tree
   $T \leftarrow \varnothing$
   $p \leftarrow$ transform D into MBRs whose size is 1x1 and maximum error is x
   T.addNode(p)
   while p.size > 1 **do**
   $x \leftarrow 2x$
   $(q, R) \leftarrow$ merge_MBR(p, x)   // Algorithm 1
   T.addNode(q)
   T.addEdge(R)
   $p \leftarrow q$
   end while
   return T

A range query receives a query rectangle range and maximum acceptable maximum error and return a set of MBRs who can fill the space of the rectangle range and meet the requirement of maximum error.

Algorithm 3 describes the range query algorithm. We mainly use recursive methods to realize error-controllable range query. I is the intersection of the MBR of the current node and the query range. When I is empty, there is no MBRs meeting the query requirement, so an empty set is returned. When I is not empty and *eps* of the MBR of the current node less than or equal to the given *eps*, I has satisfied the requirement, so I is returned. Specially, when the root node has no child, even if the error does not meet the condition, only I can be returned. After the above conditions are eliminated, recursion calling is required.

Algorithm 3. Range query

Input: the root node of a subtree *root*, rectangle range R, maximum error *eps*
Output: A set of MBRs contained in range R
  $S \leftarrow \varnothing$
  $I \leftarrow R \cap root.MBR$
  if $I = \varnothing$ **then**
   return $\varnothing$
  end if
  if *root.MBR.eps* $\leq$ *eps* or the root node has no child **then**
   return I
  end if
  for *ch* in all the children of *root* **do**
   $S \leftarrow S \cup$ range_query(*ch, R, eps*)   // recursive function call
  end for
  return S

---

4 Experimentation and Results

4.1 Experimental Setup

In order to assess the merit of our proposed index tree with Hilbert curve, we implemented and ran experiments on a two-dimensional space. The method was implemented in C++, under linux. We compared our method against the quadtree. The performance is measured by the number of nodes returned and the number of nodes traversed by the range query.

The hardware specification is listed as below:

- Processor: Intel(R) Core(TM) i7-10875H CPU @ 2.30GHz
- RAM: 16GB
- OS: Ubuntu 22.04

The test data set used in the experiment is the ocean current data measured by the sensor, and its data scale is about tens of thousands to hundreds of thousands.

4.2 Performance Evaluation for Range Query

The number of nodes returned by the range query reveals the actual effect of the compression algorithm, and the number of nodes traversed by the range query reveals the query speed of the algorithm. The curves of these data changing with the query area are shown in Fig. 4 and Fig. 5 when ε is 0.5.

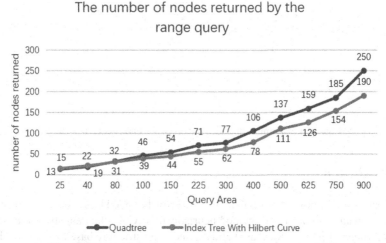

Fig. 4. The number of nodes returned vs. Query area(ε = 0.5)

It can be seen from Fig. 4 that the index tree with Hilbert curve is slightly better than the traditional quadtree in terms of the compression effect of the algorithm especially in the case of large data scale. In terms of speed, Fig. 5 reveals that on the whole the index tree with Hilbert curve slightly outperforms the quadtree.

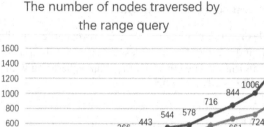

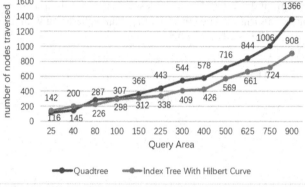

Fig. 5. The number of nodes traversed vs. Query area ($\varepsilon = 0.5$)

5 Conclusion

In this paper, we proposed a novel indexing and error-bounded lossy compression method for spatial data. The proposed method heuristically divides the data space into several MBRs through Hilbert curves, and builds an indexing structure based on this. Additionally, the clustering property of Hilbert curve used in our method is consistent with the characteristics of spatial data [26, 28]. The algorithms for range query using the index tree with Hilbert curve were also presented in this paper. The results of this experiment demonstrated that our proposed methods are better than the methods used in the quadtree. In the Internet of everything environment, it is often necessary to display the data [27]. For the efficiency of data display, it is often necessary to compress data. Our method can be used to effectively process the data in this kind of scenario.

References

1. Aekyeung, M., et al.: Lossy compression on IoT big data by exploiting spatiotemporal correlation. In: 2017 IEEE High Performance Extreme Computing Conference (HPEC). IEEE (2017)
2. Jo, B., Jung, S.: Quadrant-based minimum bounding rectangle-tree indexing method for similarity queries over big spatial data in HBase. Sensors **18**(9), 3032 (2018)
3. Jo, B, Jung, S.: Quadrant-based MBR-tree indexing technique for range query over HBase[C]. In: Proceedings of the 7th International Conference on Emerging Databases: Technologies, Applications, and Theory. Springer Singapore, 2018: 14–24. Liang, Xin, et al. "Error-controlled lossy compression optimized for high compression ratios of scientific datasets". 2018 IEEE International Conference on Big Data (Big Data). IEEE (2018)
4. Ainsworth, M., Tugluk, O., Whitney, B., Klasky, S.: Multilevel techniques for compression and reduction of scientific data—the univariate case. Comput. Vis. Sci. **19**(5–6), 65–76 (2018). https://doi.org/10.1007/s00791-018-00303-9

5. Lee, J.-G., Kang, M.: Geospatial big data: challenges and opportunities. Big Data Res. **2**(2), 74–81 (2015)
6. Ahmed, E., Mokbel, M.F.: The era of big spatial data: A survey. Found. Trends® Databases **6**(3–4), 163–273 (2016)
7. Eldawy, A.; Mokbel, M.F.: The era of big spatial data: a survey. In: Proceedings of the IEEE 31st International Conference on Data Engineering Workshops, Seoul, Korea, 13–17 April 2015, pp. 42–49
8. Ratanaworabhan, P., Ke, J., Burtscher, M.: Fast lossless compression of scientific floating-point data. In: DCC 2006, pp. 133–142 (2006)
9. Richard H., Steve D., Bruce T.: Parallel Pro-cessing Algorithms for GIS. Taylor & Francis Ltd, UK (1998)
10. Liu, H., Ma, H., El Zarki, M., et al.: Error control schemes for networks: an overview. Mob. Netw. Appl. **2**, 167–182 (1997)
11. Burton, H.O., Sullivan, D.D.: Errors and error control. Proc. IEEE **60**(11), 1293–1301 (1972)
12. Beckmann, N., Kriegel, H.-P., Schneider, R., Seeger, B.: The R*-tree: an efficient and robustaccess method for points and rectangles. In: ACM SIGMOD, pp. 322–331 (1990)
13. Jo, B., Jung, S.: Quadrant-based MBR-tree indexing technique for range query over HBase. In: Proceedings
14. Guttman, A.: R-trees: a dynamic index structure for spatial searching. In: Proceedings of the ACM STGMOD, pp. 47–57 (1984)
15. Hilbert, D.: Uber die stetige Abbildung einer Linie auf ein Flachenstuck. Math. Ann. **38**, 459–460 (1891)
16. Austin, E.: Advanced photon source. Synchrotron Radiat. News, **29**(2), 29–30 (2016)
17. Mandelbrot, B.: Fractal Geometry of Nature. W.H. Freeman, New York (1977)
18. Kamel, I., Faloutsos, C.: Hilbert R-Tree: An Improved R-Tree Using Fractals (1999)
19. Jagadish, H.V.: Linear clustering of objects with multiple attributes. In: Proceedings of the ACM SIGMOD Conference, pp. 332–342 (1990)
20. Kumar, A.A., Makur, A.: Lossy compression of encrypted image by compressive sensing technique. In: TENCON 2009–2009 IEEE Region 10 Conference, pp. 1–5 IEEE (2009)
21. Ochoa, I., Hernaez, M., Goldfeder, R., et al.: Effect of lossy compression of quality scores on variant calling. Brief. Bioinform. **18**(2), 183–194 (2017)
22. Griffiths, J.G.: An algorithm for displaying a class of space-filling curves. Softw.-Pract. Exp. **16**(5), 403–411 (1986)
23. Tao, D., Di, S., Chen, Z., Cappello, F.: Significantly improving lossy compression for scientific data sets based on multidimensional prediction and error-controlled quantization. In: IEEE International Parallel and Distributed Processing Symposium IPDPS2017, Orlando, Florida, USA, 29 May– 2 June, pp. 1129–1139 (2017)
24. Lindstrom, P.: Fixed-rate compressed floating-point arrays. IEEE Trans. Vis. Comput. Graph. **20**(12), 2674–2683 (2014)
25. Foster, I., et al.: Computing Just what you need: online data analysis and reduction at extreme scales. In: Rivera, F.F., Pena, T.F., Cabaleiro, J.C. (eds.) Euro-Par 2017. LNCS, vol. 10417, pp. 3–19. Springer, Cham (2017). https://doi.org/10.1007/978-3-319-64203-1_1
26. Tao, D., Di, S., Chen, Z., Cappello, F.: In-depth exploration of single-snapshot lossy compression techniques for N-body simulations. In: IEEE International Conference on Big Data (BigData17) (2017)
27. Baker, A.H., et al.: A methodology for evaluating the impact of data compression on climate simulation data. In: HPDC 2014, pp. 203–214 (2014)
28. Faloutsos, C.: Gray codes for partial match and range queries. IEEE Trans. Softw. Eng. **14**(10), 1381–1393 (1988). early version available as UMIACS-TR-87–4, also CS-TR-1796

Cybersecurity and Privacy

Privacy Measurement Based on Social Network Properties and Structure

YuHong Gong[1,2], Biao Jin[1,2,3], and ZhiQiang Yao[1,2,3]($\boxtimes$)

[1] College of Computer and Cyber Security, Fujian Normal University,
Fuzhou 350117, Fujian, China
jinbiao@fjnu.edu.cn, yzqfzfj@163.com
[2] Engineering Research Center of Big Data Analysis
and Application, Fujian Provincial University, Fuzhou 350117, Fujian, China
[3] Engineering Research Center for ICH Digitalization and Multi-source Information
Fusion, Fujian Provincial University, Fuqing 350300, Fujian, China

Abstract. The serious consequences of the leakage of personal privacy information spread in social networks have reached the point where we have to pay attention. Conventional research on social network privacy measurement usually measures the risk of user privacy leakage from different perspectives, such as personal data, privacy settings, information dissemination, etc. The factors that affect privacy risks considered in the research content are not comprehensive enough. This paper constructs an effective privacy measurement method based on the specific situation of measuring the risk of user information authorization behavior in the social network environment. To take full advantage of many factors to more accurately measure user privacy risk, We propose a new global privacy metric scheme to measure user privacy risk. The personal privacy risk is measured by the proposed Attribute Frequency Inverse User Frequency (AFIUF) algorithm, and then the importance of users in the social network is estimated according to the social network user importance algorithm. Finally, considering users' common privacy leakage, the global privacy score is calculated by combining the similarity between users. We apply our metric scheme to a large dataset of real Facebook social networks. Experimental results demonstrate the effectiveness and efficiency of our solution.

Keywords: Privacy Measurement · Attribute · Similarity · Social Network

1 Introduction

With the rapid development of science and technology, due to the low cost and convenience of online networks, as well as the impact of the global epidemic in recent years, the development of social networks has been catalyzed. When

Supported by the National Natural Science Foundation of China under Grant (61872090, 61872088, and 61972096), and the Open Fund of Fujian Provincial University Engineering Research Center (FJ-ICH201901).

people join social networks, they are asked to fill in personal information to create virtual characters. Since people expect a good social experience and personalized service, users are encouraged to use authentic information. This behavior may result in the disclosure of user private information, which may lead to users being subjected to various malicious attacks from the real world and cyberspace, including stalking, defamation, spam, phishing attacks, identity theft attacks and personal data cloning attacks, witchcraft attack etc. The low threshold of social networks is the main reason why many users lack understanding of social networks. They don't understand the potential risks that it might bring. Faced with such a complex and huge social network environment, it is difficult for users not to be disturbed and violated [12]. Due to the natural contradiction between online social behavior and privacy protection, how to protect users' personal privacy information is an important and challenging issue.

In the current network environment, social network privacy data security mainly relies on social network service providers to provide institutional guarantees for privacy protection. They have to do this to get stable users. In fact, personal information may be provided to third-party users for profit-making purposes, such as viral marketing, targeted advertising, etc. And Uber admitted in 2017 that it had been hacked to steal the personal information of more than 57 million customers and drivers at the same time. In the same year, Twitter publicly announced that it would abandon the DNT (Do not track) privacy protection standard. Therefore, service providers cannot also guarantee users' privacy. Even if we treat social network service providers as semi-honest and curious third parties, rather than as objects of defense, this would greatly limit users' social behavior. We need to understand the risk of our privacy leakage in this open social network to protect our own lives and property from being violated.

There are several ways to protect users' privacy. As the main body of social networks, it is an effective and direct method of improving user privacy awareness. People can easily understand physical and objective things, but it is difficult to grasp the subjective concept of privacy. Therefore, some literature proposes to measure the privacy leakage risk of social network users as a specific value and inform users to alert them. Take certain protective measures to improve awareness of prevention, to achieve the purpose of protecting user privacy. For example, [8] aims to increase users' awareness of social network data dissemination and management by collecting data on people with different social network profiles and conducting statistical evaluations on them. Pilton et al. [22] study found that individuals often do not expect privacy, by developing extensions to show that privacy-centric behavioral changes occur when individuals begin to consider the impact of privacy policies and expose how their data is used. This means that measuring the user's privacy risk status can indeed have a positive effect on the user's privacy protection. We do some effective research on how to accurately measure user privacy status. This paper makes several significant contributions, which are outlined below.

(1) We propose a method for computing social user privacy scores based on the Attribute Frequency Inverse User Frequency (AFIUF) algorithm and verify its effect on real datasets.

(2) We consider a method for computing global similarity scores between users in a disconnected graph using attribute similarity and structural similarity.
(3) We construct a method that effectively combines user attributes and social network structure to measure user privacy risk measurement model, which can more accurately evaluate user privacy in real datasets.

The remainder of the paper is structured as follows. Section 2 introduces the related work. Section 3 illustrates the usage scenarios in this paper and the notation used in this study. The fourth part is the specific privacy leakage risk measurement scheme. Section 5 is an introduction to the experimental dataset and the analysis and discussion of the experimental results. Finally, Sect. 6 presents our conclusions and possible future research directions.

2   Related Work

Preliminary work on the measurement of a single privacy indicator. For instance, prior research [10] has investigated the potential loss of user privacy resulting from the disclosure of age-related information. With the deepening of research, more and more researchers have begun to pay attention to more elements of users that may affect privacy risks. Maximilien et al. [18] discuss the concepts of attribute sensitivity and profile visibility and then use a Bayesian approach to evaluate these two values as a measure of privacy. Liu et al. [17] extended their research and proposed a mathematical model for generating privacy risk scores using profile attribute information, which is a relatively intuitive mathematical method based on item response theory (IRT) combining sensitivity and visibility. This work paved the way for many follow-up studies. Li et al. [15] considered accessibility, attribute extraction difficulty, reliability, and privacy awareness in the privacy scoring process, and then used sensitivity and visibility to calculate a user's final privacy risk score in multiple online social networks(OSNs). While [1] proposed a Privacy Disclosure Score (PDS) based on the information shared between multiple OSNs. Shi et al. [23] introduced a method for privacy measurement using the entropy of the network structure, one of the static characteristics of the network in complex networks, and defined a privacy measurement index (PMI) to measure the privacy protection capabilities of the graph structure. Pensa R G.et al. [19] proposed a theoretical framework to measure user privacy risks and alert users when their privacy is compromised, helping users customize their privacy settings semi-automatically by limiting the number of manual actions. Wang et al. [24] studied data from multiple sources with different characteristics to protect user privacy.

In recent years, some studies have also paid attention to the privacy of unstructured content, such as the privacy risks brought by the published text content [2,3,5,7]. Researchers have proposed several techniques and methods in the existing literature to measure the privacy risk of social networks, which usually consider user attributes, published text content, and the social environment [6,9,20]. The ideas of these studies are novel and yield some valuable conclusions, but the assessment of the overall privacy status of social network users is not accurate enough. Some researcher work [11, 25] on the privacy co-disclosure problem that may be caused by users' friends. Zeng et al. [26] believe that the degree of privacy disclosure of individuals will be affected by the degree of privacy protection of information released by public friends. Li et al. [14] argue that attackers can exploit the background knowledge of public neighbors to gain the privacy of target users. Alsarkal et al. [4] proposed an innovative measure to capture the actual privacy loss of individuals caused by self-disclosure and co-disclosure. Their research effectively proves that users' friends may bring privacy leaks to themselves, but they do not apply it to the user's global privacy assessment. Different from the existing research, this paper constructs a more reasonable social network privacy measurement scheme according to the information characteristics of the attributes and structure of the social network. The proposed privacy assessment scheme effectively measures the user's privacy leakage risk.

3   Privacy Guarantee Framework

In the scenarios envisaged in this paper, the risk of privacy leakage is mainly caused by OSN service providers sending user information to third-party applications. We assume that the hosting OSN service provider is completely reliable, but the third-party application is not. In addition, what is more worrying is that malicious attackers can disguise as normal applications and collect private information to harm the interests of users. Therefore, when users authorize third-party applications to access personal information on social networks, we must warn users of privacy risks. Our privacy disclosure risk algorithm should be implemented on the server of the OSN service provider.

Table 1 presents the fundamental notations that are commonly employed in our research.

Table 1. Notation

Notation	Explanation
$G(V, E, A)$	Social network graph
V	Set of Users
E	Set of Edges
v, v'	Users $\in V$
$e(v, v')$	An edge between v and v'
n	Number of users
p	Number of attributes
R	An $n \times p$ User attribute matrix
T	An $n \times k$ User attribute class matrix
I	User Importance Vector
θ	Attribute sensitivity vector
β	Attribute Class Sensitivity Vector

4   Privacy Risk Calculation Methods

The risk of privacy leakage refers to the possibility that attackers will notice users on the current social network and collect information to cause users losses. Therefore, our scheme first considers the risk of leakage of users' personal information in social networks and then considers the importance of users in social networks. We understand that online social networks are mirrors of real society. From the perspective of the attacker, the most profitable attack outcomes would likely target users who hold influential positions within the social network. We are inspired by the PageRank algorithm to calculate the importance value of users. To comprehensively consider the possible joint leakage caused by users' friends, we try to find the most similar friends of the target user and take into account their privacy leakage.

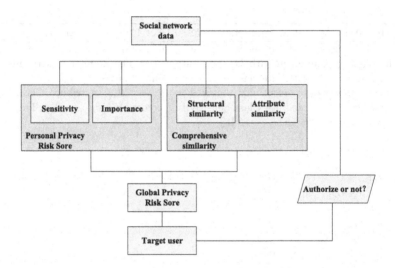

Fig. 1. Privacy Risk Control Flowchart.

Figure 1 illustrates the specific techniques and procedures utilized by the privacy risk calculation module. The user's global privacy risk score is obtained by combining their individual privacy risk score with the global similarity score, thereby enabling the evaluation of the user's privacy risk level and providing supplementary authorization judgment information.

4.1   Individual Privacy Risk Score

This section aims to compute a privacy risk score for each user based on their profile information and level of importance within the network.

AFIUF Algorithm. Because the relationship between various attributes is not equal, we propose this algorithm to better describe the sensitivity of attributes to users. For example, attributes such as high school and college can be divided into education attributes. We use attributes and attribute classes to process data. Inspired by the term frequency inverse document frequency (TFIDF) algorithm, considering users as documents and the corresponding attributes to terms, we construct the AFIUF algorithm applied to the calculation of user privacy leakage in the field of social networks. Using IUF means that a certain attribute appears more frequently in different user profiles, indicating that more users have a low privacy sensitivity to this attribute, so most people are willing to fill in such an attribute. AF indicates that when the same type of attribute has multiple descriptions in users' profile, we believe that this type of attribute has a higher descriptive effect on users' characteristics and will also reveal more personal privacy information from users. Enter the parameters of the social network dataset to get the privacy score of level 1, denoted by $S1$. The specific steps are presented in Algorithm 1.

Algorithm 1. Attribute Frequency Inverse User Frequency Algorithm.

Input: The number of attribute class k; The number of users i with the ath attribute; The number of users m with kth attribute class ; The number of attributes contained in the kth attribute class m; User attribute matrix $R_{(n \times p)}$.

Output: Sub-attribute sensitivity vector $\theta = (\theta_1, \cdots, \theta_n)$; Attribute Class Weight Matrix $W_{(n \times k)}$; Attribute Class Sensitivity Vector $\beta = (\beta_1, \cdots, \beta_k)$; The Level 1 Privacy Score $S1 = (S1_1, \cdots, S1_n)$;

1: for $a = 0$ to n do
2:     if $i = 0$
3:         $c = log(n/0.8)$
4:     else
5:         $c = log(n/b)$;
6:     $\theta_a = c$
7: for $a = 0$ to n do
8:     for $b = 0$ to k do
9:         for $c = 0$ to m do
10:             $W_{a,b} = W_{a,b} + \theta$
11: The matrix $R_{(n \times p)}$ is converted to matrix $T_{(n \times k)}$
12: for $a = 0$ to k do
13:     repeat step 2-5
14:     $\beta_a = c$
15: for $a = 0$ to n do
16:     for $b = 0$ to k do
17:         $c = c + W_{a,b} \times T_{a,b} \times \beta_b$
18:     $S1_a = c$
19: return $\theta, W_{(n \times k)}, \beta, S1$

Pagerank Algorithm. A typical social network can be abstracted as a mesh structure consisting of edges and nodes. In the context of this study, the nodes correspond to individual users, while the edges signify the presence or absence of a connection between them. Inferring from the reality, the more important users in social networks are, the more likely they are to have higher visibility and thus be noticed by attackers. In addition, from the attacker's perspective, the confidential information of users who hold a more prominent position within the social network possesses a greater degree of exploitative value. To measure the importance of users in social networks, the existing Pagerank algorithm maps users to web pages to obtain the user's importance value. Pensa et al. [21] consider the network topology properties and propose a center-based privacy score according to the PageRank algorithm to measure the privacy state of users, which demonstrates the efficacy of the proposed methodology.

Algorithm 2. Social Network User Importance Algorithm.

Input: Transition probability matrix T; Damping coefficient q; The number of all
   users n; Acceptable Error ε.
Output: Social network user importance vector I;
1: set $X = (1/n \cdots, 1/n, \cdots, 1/n)_n$;
2: set $S = ((1 - q)/n, \cdots, (1 - q)/n, \cdots, (1 - q)/n)_n$;
3: $I = S + q \cdot T^{\mathrm{T}} \cdot X$;
4: while $\|I - X\|_2 > \varepsilon$ do
5:       $X = I$;
6:       $I = S + q \cdot T^{\mathrm{T}} \cdot X$;
7: return I;

In our scheme, the importance of users is proportional to the risk of privacy leakage, and according to the privacy score of level 1 and the value of user importance, we get the privacy score of level 2, denoted by S2. An elevated privacy score corresponds to an increased level of privacy risk. First, user importance values are normalized. Second, considering that even if the user exists alone in the social network and has no relationship with other users, the risk of privacy leakage will be low, we set the I value to a minimum of 0.1.

$$S2 = S1 \cdot \sigma \cdot I. \tag{1}$$

In formula 1, σ is the degree of influence of user importance. Here, set $\sigma = 1$, where I is the value after normalization. Through formula 1, the privacy of level 2 is calculated.

4.2   Similarity Calculation Method

To fully consider the impact of the social network environment on the leakage of personal privacy, we start from two perspectives, one is to consider the structure of the network and the other is to consider the content of the attributes. In our scheme, the dataset is collected by the social network service provider, regardless of the privacy rights set by the user, all the collected data are uniformly considered to be visible so that the attribute similarity between users can be calculated. Based on the graph structure formed between social network users, we can calculate the corresponding structural similarity. Combining the two to get the overall similarity between users, and then according to the personal privacy disclosure score, we can get the privacy leakage risk value in the network environment. This privacy value is provided to the user so that the user can intuitively understand the risk of privacy leakage and then make a decision on whether to adjust personal privacy information and disclose related privacy.

Structural Similarity. For the social network dataset, in the graph structure composed of social network users, we filter the users who are closely related to a specific user by comparing the similarity between nodes. After investigation and research, to account for the unique structural properties of social networks, we have selected the Simrank algorithm as our primary analytical tool. The Simrank algorithm is a topological information algorithm that operates on graphs and is utilized to evaluate the similarity between two objects. The algorithm functions on the premise that two objects can be regarded as similar if they are referenced by similar objects in a comparable manner.

$$R_{k+1}(v_a, v_b) = \frac{C}{|D(v_a)||D(v_a)|} \sum_{i=1}^{|D(v_a)|} \sum_{j=1}^{|D(v_b)|} R_k(D_i(v_a), D_j(v_b))$$

$$R_0(v_a, v_b) = \begin{cases} 0, & v_a \neq v_b \\ 1, & v_a = v_b \end{cases}, \tag{2}$$

As in the original algorithm, the value of C was set to 0.8. C represents the damping coefficient. $D(v_a)$ denotes the set of nodes that have incoming edges to node a, when $D(v_a) = 0, D(v_b) = 0, R(v_a, v_b) = 0$.

Attribute Similarity. When people use social networks, they mostly fill in their data in fixed options, which contain a lot of private information. As for the content of different sensitive attributes that can be filled in, even if some users are not very aware of privacy, few people will fill in all of them. They know to protect their sensitive and overly private information. In the collected user data, we process all occurrences of attribute values into a series of n columns, and all users use an n-dimensional 0–1 bit string of equal length to describe personal data. This facilitates efficient attribute similarity calculation for all users.

$$A(v_a, v_b) = \|F(v_a) * F(v_b)\| \cdot \theta. \tag{3}$$

where $F(v_a)$ and $F(v_b)$ are vectors that describe the attribute content of user a and user b. $F(v_a) * F(v_b)$ do the AND operation of the two vectors to get the attribute vector with the same attribute content. Since this is an attribute of one-hot vector encoding, the sensitivity vector of the attribute class needs to be expanded by the corresponding number of digits and then perform the quantity product operation of two vectors of the same dimension to obtain the attribute similarity between user a and user b.

Global Similarity. After filtering out the graph structure similarity of the targeted user sets, the user's most similar friends are selected and combined with attribute similarity to derive the global similarity score, as illustrated in Eq. 3.

The researcher [16] uses Eq. 3 to calculate the user global similarity in the directed graph. In our scheme, the social structure graph is a disconnected graph. We argue that even real-world friends do not guarantee the existence of edges that represent friend relationships on social networks. Similarly, the existence of edges between users in the social network does not mean that two people must be connected in the real world. Therefore, we have improved Eq. 3 to be more in line with the actual application scenarios.

$$S(v_a, v_b) = \frac{R(v_a, v_b)(1 - e^{-\lambda \| 10 * A(v_a, v_b) \|})}{R'(v_a, v_b)}, \tag{4}$$

where $e(v_a, v_b) = 1$, $v_a \in N_b$ and $v_b \in N_a$

$$R'(v_a, v_b) = \sum_{v_x \in N_a} R(v_a, v_x) + \sum_{v_y \in N_b} R(v_b, v_y) - R(v_a, v_b). \tag{5}$$

where $e(v_a, v_b) = 0$, $v_a \notin N_b$ and $v_b \notin N_a$

$$R'(v_a, v_b) = \sum_{v_x \in N_a} R(v_a, v_x) + \sum_{v_y \in N_b} R(v_b, v_y) + R(v_a, v_b). \tag{6}$$

The constructed global similarity calculation formula is used to average the privacy scores of multiple users. In order to ensure the stability of the value, we need to ensure that the denominator part is not 0, and $R(v_a, v_b)/R'(v_a, v_b) <= 1$. If $e(v_a, v_b) = 0$ and $R'(v_a, v_b) = 0$, set

$$S(v_a, v_b) = 0.1 * (1 - e^{-\lambda \| 10 * A(v_a, v_b) \|}). \tag{7}$$

N_a and N_b represent the sets of neighboring nodes of v_a and v_b, respectively. λ represents the influencing factors of attribute similarity, and is employed to modulate the extent of influence.

By integrating both relationship and attribute information, Eq. 4 enables the identification of users with the highest degree of similarity to the target user. These user relationships are easily exploited by malicious attackers for link reasoning and attribute reasoning to obtain undisclosed private information from target users. Analysis of formula 4 shows that when the value of the attribute similarity is high and close to 1, the molecule tends to be structurally similar. When attribute similarity is minimal, the value of this item is in close proximity to zero, and the global similarity is also close to 0. In actuality, if the structural similarity between two users is substantial, the resulting privacy breach of the target user will likely encompass similar attribute information as their friends. Nonetheless, when the structural similarity between users is significant, but the attribute information varies, it implies that the confidential information of the target user has not been compromised.

4.3   Global Privacy Risk Score

We combine the previously calculated level 2 privacy score with the global similarity for the next step and finally get the users' global privacy risk in the entire network structure. That is the privacy score of level 3, which is represented by S3 for convenience of expression.

$$Score(p_a) = \eta(v_a) + \sum_{v_b \subseteq Max_n(S(v_a,v_b))} S(v_a, v_b)\eta(v_b), \tag{8}$$

where $Max_n(S(v_a, v_b))$ represents the set of the top n friends with the highest similarity of user a, and $\eta(v_b)$ represents the level 2 privacy score of the target user. By utilizing global similarity, we screen out the most probable acquaintances that may unintentionally disclose confidential information of the target user, and subsequently compute the comprehensive privacy leakage risk of the user. This procedure is based on the assumption that the majority of privacy violations are caused by shared privacy breaches among users and their acquaintances. We draw the conclusion that users with elevated privacy scores are at a higher risk of privacy breach compared to those with lower privacy scores.

5   Experimental Results

In order to assess the efficacy of the proposed approach, we conducted several empirical experiments on real social network datasets and performed a thorough analysis of the obtained results.

5.1   Dataset

There are very few publicly available social network datasets, even for research purposes, and few researchers publish the datasets they collect because the data contain a lot of sensitive information about users. This is a difficulty and a challenge for privacy measurement research in the field of social networks. To validate the efficacy of the proposed approach, we apply our algorithm to the ego network dataset from the Stanford Network Analysis Project (SNAP) [13], The Facebook dataset comprises 4,039 users and 88,234 social connections. Each user profile is composed of 11 categories, such as gender, birthday, location, hometown, work, and education. Some categories also have subcategories, such as job title and employer belonging to the job category.

5.2   Individual Privacy Risk Score

Our scheme improves previous studies. Most existing privacy scores are calculated based on the visibility and sensitivity of privacy attributes. In our consideration, visibility is divided into two levels. The first level of visibility is how much the attackers collect users' private information through social networks, and the second level of visibility is that users are noticed by malicious attackers in the network. In actual social network applications, users can set privacy permissions on their social homepages, but in our envisaged scenario, users directly grant information to third-party applications through social network service providers, so first-level visibility means whether the user has filled in some information. It is represented by an attribute matrix consisting of 0 and 1 during the calculation.

We first obtain the sensitivity of each subattribute through the IUF algorithm and then convert the user-subattribute matrix into a user-attribute class matrix. According to the visibility of sub-attributes in each attribute class, AF accumulates the corresponding sensitivity as the weight of the attribute class. Then the sensitivities of the attribute class are calculated again using the IUF algorithm. The user's privacy score is the sum of the product of the sensitivity of each attribute class and its weight, represented by $S1$, which is the level 1 privacy score.

Table 2. Attribute Class Sensitivity.

Attribute	Sensitivity	Attribute	Sensitivity
birthday	3.384	education	0.414
gender	0.034	hometown	3.384
languages	1.775	name	2.691
locale	0.052	location	1.88
political	4.088	work	0.819

As can be seen from Table 2, the target user group has the lowest sensitivity to the two attributes of locale and gender and higher sensitivity to education and work. In ascending order of sensitivity, language, location and name are more sensitive, followed by birthday and hometown, and the most sensitive attribute is political.

5.3   User Importance Analysis

The damping coefficient $q = 0.85$, and the acceptable error $e = 10^{-4}$ are set experimentally. In the selected ego social network dataset, a transition matrix T is constructed according to the friendship relationship between users, and the value of user importance is obtained using the social network user importance algorithm.

Sort user importance values from small to large, as shown in Fig. 2. Since the social network graph is weakly connected, there are results where the user value is 0 in the algorithm. According to Fig. 2, it can be seen that users with high and low importance indices on the social network belonging to a minority. The importance index of most user groups is average.

5.4   Global Similarity Score

Literature [16] improved the simrank algorithm to calculate the similarity between microblog users. The relationship between users of social platforms such

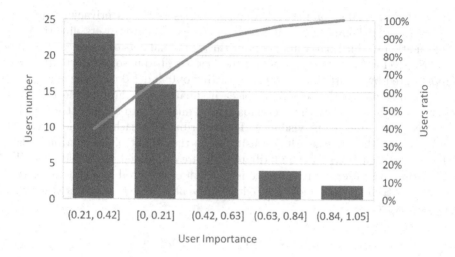

Fig. 2. User Importance Index.

as Weibo has a unilateral follow-up relationship, which is similar to Instagram. The content studied in this paper is a social network with a disconnected graph structure such as Facebook. The basic simrank algorithm can get the results. At the same time, in a social network that forms a mutual friend relationship, the relationship between users will be closer than the relationship between following and being followed. Therefore, the structural similarity occupies more weight when calculating the final global similarity. We adjust the value of λ to 0.2 to reduce the influence of attribute similarity.

5.5   Global Privacy Risk Score

In our scheme, in order to reasonably filter out the most similar friends of users, the value of global similarity is obtained according to attribute similarity and structural similarity. In the final user global privacy risk score, that is the level 3 privacy score, the friend with the highest global similarity value is selected to calculate the final score. As shown in Eq. 4, Max_n is an adjustable parameter, and We can customize the parameter settings based on the specific dataset and usage scenarios to achieve more precise outcomes. In this study, we compute the global privacy score and set the value of n as 1.

As shown in Fig. 3, the privacy score of level 2 is reduced to different degrees compared with level 1. It is unreasonable to use only numerical values to compare user privacy status because the numerical values obtained by the privacy measurement methods using different indicators are necessarily different. What we can observe is the relative magnitude of user privacy in the user privacy profile. For example, in the privacy score of level 1, the privacy risk of user 12 is significantly greater than that of user 7, but in the privacy score of level 2, the privacy risk of user 12 is smaller than that of user 7. This is because user 7 is more important in the social network than user 12, giving user 7 a higher visibil-

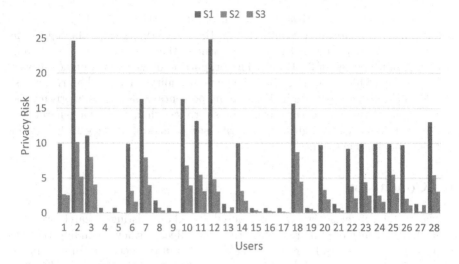

Fig. 3. Privacy Score Comparison.

ity in the network, which leads to the reversed risk after considering the degree of user importance. It can be found that when most users switch from level 2 to level 3, the changes in privacy scores are uncertain. According to formula 4, in the figure User 13 and User 27 have a significant increase, indicating that the most similar users among their friends have high privacy scores and high global similarity. User 1's privacy score is lower than both User 6 and User 14 if the privacy co-disclosure of the user's friends are not considered. However according to the privacy score comparison results of level 3, user 6 and user 14 have higher privacy risk scores with their most similar friends.

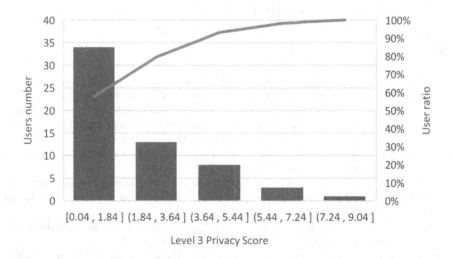

Fig. 4. Privacy Risk Index Analysis.

Analyzing the final privacy score we obtained, the broken line represents the cumulative frequency percentage, and the larger the change, the higher the percentage. As depicted in Fig. 4, it is evident that the privacy risk of most people is in the range of 0.04–1.84. The proportion of users with higher privacy risks is small, which is in line with the general reality. Finally, the privacy risk result sent to the user should be the ranking percentage of the user's privacy risk in the social network structure. It can be set to less than 60% as a general risk, and more than 60% as a high risk, to assist users in making privacy authorization decision-making behaviors.

6 Conclusion

In the content of the scheme we considered, based on existing research, we comprehensively considered more factors that can affect privacy, including the sensitivity of attributes and the importance of users in the network. In our understanding, this can also be used as a second layer of attribute visibility. For malicious third-party applications, the first layer of attribute visibility does not consider the user's personalized privacy settings on the website, but only considers the difference between filled and unfilled. Finally, we discuss possible privacy leaks caused by user friends. Measure common privacy disclosures to obtain the final result of privacy risk assessment. Our experiments on real social network datasets show that users' privacy leakage risks can be effectively assessed, which can help users improve privacy protection awareness and strengthen privacy protection behaviors.

In the future research direction, we will further consider the common value of risk and utility brought by personal attributes to users, and comprehensively affect the impact of user privacy assessment results. Thinking about risk blindly is not the purpose of a privacy assessment. The utility of attributes can better assist users in implementing online social behaviors.

References

1. Aghasian, E., Garg, S., Gao, L., Yu, S., Montgomery, J.: Scoring users' privacy disclosure across multiple online social networks. IEEE Access (2017)
2. Aghasian, E., Garg, S., Montgomery, J.: An automated model to score the privacy of unstructured information-social media case. Comput. Secur. (2020)
3. Al-Asmari, H.A., Saleh, M.S.: A conceptual framework for measuring personal privacy risks in Facebook online social network. In: International Conference on Computer and Information Sciences (2019)
4. Alsarkal, Y., Zhang, N., Xu, H.: Your privacy is your friend's privacy: examining interdependent information disclosure on online social networks. In: Hawaii International Conference on System Sciences (2018)
5. Baocun, C., Zhu, N., He, J., He, P., Shuting, J., Shijia, P.: A semantic inference based method for privacy measurement. IEEE Access (2020)
6. Bioglio, L., Pensa, R.G.: Impact of neighbors on the privacy of individuals in online social networks. In: International Conference on Computational Science (2017)

7. Bioglio, L., Pensa, R.G.: Analysis and classification of privacy-sensitive content in social media posts. EPJ Data Sci. (2022)
8. Cirillo, S., Desiato, D., Polese, G.: Social network data analysis to highlight privacy threats in sharing data. J. Big Data (2022)
9. Coban, O., Inan, A., Ozel, S.A.: Inverse document frequency-based sensitivity scoring for privacy analysis. SIViP **16**(3), 735–743 (2022)
10. Dey, R., Tang, C., Ross, K.W., Saxena, N.: Estimating age privacy leakage in online social networks. In: International Conference on Computer Communications (2012)
11. Han, X., Wang, L., Wu, J., Yang, Y.: Large-scale privacy-preserving network embedding against private link inference attacks (2022)
12. Khazaei, T., Xiao, L., Mercer, R.E., Khan, A.: Understanding privacy dichotomy in twitter. In: ACM Conference on Hypertext (2018)
13. Leskovec, J., Krevl, A.: SNAP Datasets: Stanford large network dataset collection, June 2014. https://snap.stanford.edu/data
14. Li, M., Liu, Z., Dong, K.: Privacy preservation in social network against public neighborhood attacks. In: Trust Security and Privacy in Computing and Communications (2016)
15. Li, X., Yang, Y., Chen, Y., Niu, X.X.: A privacy measurement framework for multiple online social networks against social identity linkage. Appl. Sci. (2018)
16. Li, X., Zhao, C., Tian, K.: Privacy measurement method using a graph structure on online social networks. ETRI J. **43**(5), 812–824 (2021)
17. Liu, K., Terzi, E.: A framework for computing the privacy scores of users in online social networks. ACM Trans. Knowl. Discov. From Data (2009)
18. Maximilien, E.M., Grandison, T., Sun, T., Richardson, D., Guo, S., Liu, K.: Privacy-as-a-service: models, algorithms, and results on the Facebook platform. In: Proceedings of Web, vol. 2 (2009)
19. Pensa, R.G., Blasi, G.D.: A privacy self-assessment framework for online social networks. Expert Syst. With Appl. (2017)
20. Pensa, R.G., Di Blasi, G., Bioglio, L.: Network-aware privacy risk estimation in online social networks. Soc. Netw. Anal. Min. **9**(1), 1–15 (2019). https://doi.org/10.1007/s13278-019-0558-x
21. Pensa, R.G., Di Blasi, G.: A centrality-based measure of user privacy in online social networks. In: 2016 IEEE/ACM International Conference on Advances in Social Networks Analysis and Mining (ASONAM), pp. 1438–1439. IEEE (2016)
22. Pilton, C., Faily, S., Henriksen-Bulmer, J.: Evaluating privacy: determining user privacy expectations on the web. Comput. Secur. (2021)
23. Shi, W., Hu, J., Yan, J., Wu, Z., Lu, L.: A privacy measurement method using network structure entropy. In: International Conference on Networking (2017)
24. Wang, C., Tianqing, Z., Xiong, P., Ren, W., Choo, K.K.R.: A privacy preservation method for multiple-source unstructured data in online social networks. Comput. Secur. (2021)
25. Yang, R., Ma, J., Miao, Y., Ma, X.: Privacy-preserving generative framework against membership inference attacks (2022)
26. Zeng, Y., Sun, Y., Xing, L., Vokkarane, V.M.: Trust-aware privacy evaluation in online social networks. In: International Conference on Communications (2014)

Research on 5G-Based Zero Trust Network Security Platform

Zaojian Dai[1,2(✉)], Jidong Zhang[3], Yong Li[1,2], Xinyi Li[3], Ziang Lu[1,2], and Wengao Fang[1,2]

[1] Grid Digitizing Technology Department, State Grid Smart Grid Research Institute Co., Ltd, Nanjing 210003, China
daizaojian@geiri.sgcc.com.cn
[2] State Grid Key Laboratory of Information & Network Security, Nanjing 210003, China
[3] State Grid Jibei Electric Power Company Limited Information & Communication Dispatch, Beijing 100053, China

Abstract. The number and types of network access devices and functions in the cloud computing and big data environments are continuously increasing, so the ability to actively expand network services is needed to ensure that the security and privacy protection needs of network practices are met on a continuous basis. The traditional physical isolation network security protection architecture is facing challenges in new technology scenarios such as big data and mobile Internet, and urgently needs to be changed. Based on this, this paper proposes a 5G-based zero-trust network security platform to better adapt and serve the dynamic network application environment. The security architecture and model are firstly studied to provide security principles of the proposed platform. The implementation scheme of proposed platform is then further analyzed where security algorithms are suggested. The results show that the proposed platform demonstrates better performance in identity, program, configuration and behavior detection. Therefor, it is expected to better deal with the network risks under the new technology scenarios.

Keywords: Zero Trust · Network Security · 5G Technology · Security Platform

1 Introduction

The deepening of intelligent network applications represented by IoT (Internet of Things) has greatly facilitated the relevant users to carry out business while bringing new challenges to the network security of the relevant nodes [1]. The current network security model is more of an isolation model, which isolates the internal network of the network user from the external network and establishes a physically isolated network security protection architecture [2]. The applicability and security of this protection architecture in new technology fields such as big data and mobile Internet are insufficient, and it cannot effectively meet the security protection needs in the current network environment [3]. On the other hand, the mobile information technology represented by 5G technology has made significant progress and development, especially the network security model built by combining 5G and zero-trust architecture can greatly avoid the occurrence of network security incidents [4].

The 5G-based zero-trust network security architecture ensures continuous access to the network in a trusted state by controlling the trustworthiness of network visitors and continuously verifying their identities [5]. In view of the typical characteristics of the number and types of network access devices and the continuous diversification of functions in the cloud computing and big data environment, as well as the actual demand for real-time intensive network services, it needs to actively expand the ability of network services while ensuring that the security and privacy protection needs are met [6]. In this context, building a 5G-based zero-trust network security guard is an important part of implementing network security applications [7]. A new type of network security application solution is established with the 5G zero-trust network security platform to achieve an effective balance between business functions and network security [8].

In addition, compared to the traditional physical isolation model of network security protection, the 5G-based zero-trust network security platform not only better secures access to physical objects, but also better adapts and serves the cloud application environment with dynamic data storage [9]. The 5G-based zero-trust network security platform assumes that that the nodes in the internal network (including clients, personnel, etc.) are untrusted, and targeted protection measures and levels need to be set to better prevent vulnerabilities [10]. Therefore, the research on 5G-based zero-trust network security platform has important practical value for dealing with network security risks in the new situation.

2 Requirement Analysis

The 5G network security risks include several aspects such as business terminals and interfaces. In the aspect of network application terminal, it will be indirectly affected by the network architecture [11]. Unreasonable architecture design will make some terminal devices vulnerable to attack, resulting in data leakage or tampering. The 5G network's high bandwidth characteristics also bring greater difficulties and challenges to its network protect [12]. At the interface security level, the main concern is the privacy of the communication protocol, which can only be effectively and securely verified through enhanced authentication. For example, attackers can analyze the number of times TMSI (Temporary Mobile Station Identifier) occurs in the paging information as a basis for analyzing the presence or absence of the attacked terminal device. In serious cases, attackers can map the user's mobile phone to TMSI through weak anonymity and determine the user's location [13]. Due to the plaintext window, 5G network is vulnerable to attacks, which may lead to the theft of privacy information of devices implanted with Trojans.

The NFV (Network Function Virtualization) and SDN (Software Defined Networking) technology features of 5G networks enable effective performance upgrades while also leading to increased security threats, mainly in the virtual network aspect, as well as in the hardware and software system aspect [14]. Connected internal and external edge computing devices will also lead to increased risks, making the network more vulnerable to attacks and exploitation.

In response to the threats and risks faced by 5G networks, targeted initiatives need to be developed to improve the availability and security of the network. The zero-trust network security platform is expected to effectively verify the identity of systems and users accessing the network and to restrict their privileges [15].

3 Security Model

The mobile Internet represented by 5G has strongly promoted high-speed interconnection between various fields, and typical scenarios such as intelligent assistance, autonomous driving, and high-precision map navigation are getting closer to people's life practice applications with the support of 5G network. In these environments requiring low latency, high bandwidth, and high speed mobile network applications, the security of 5G technology becomes a crucial indicator that will not only directly relate to the popularity of 5G technology, but also have a direct impact on the secure and stable operation in many scenarios [16]. Therefore, in the typical application scenarios of 5G technology, a complete, feasible, reasonable and reliable security target should be established first of all. Hence, the research and development objectives of a 5G-based zero-trust network security platform include identity verification, latency indicators, privacy protection, and so on. The security platform needs to be developed under standardized security verification architecture to guarantee the implementation of the functional metrics of the zero-trust network security platform.

3.1 Security Architecture

As the boundary protection architecture needs to isolate the industry's internal and external networks and set up isolation firewalls and other facilities to better achieve network security protection [17]. The traditional boundary protection model for internal and external networks is difficult to meet the security needs of the industry in decentralized and dynamic scenarios such as cloud computing and big data in terms of its functionality and performance [18]. In response to the limitations of the boundary protection model, the security platform is built to achieve dynamic configuration and deployment of security protection and to guide the integration of network security and network applications. The architecture design of the security platform focuses on breaking the limitations of the boundary protection model, and its architecture is shown in Fig. 1, in which all network traffic needs to be recorded and inspected to ensure the security of network resources.

In addition, the security architecture includes several aspects such as network security access, network domain security, authentication and key security, security service, and security visualization. In the aspect of network security access, the core network authentication ID is set by the control system to correlate the data between the wireless access side and the core network to guarantee the comprehensiveness of data protection. In the aspect of network domain setting, it mainly includes the setting of network core nodes, service environment and shared architecture. In addition, in the authentication and key management, data authentication is adapted according to the specific application scenarios of 5G mobile networks, thus guaranteeing the integration and availability of security credentials. Security services and security visualization are the basis of 5G network and service protection. They need to be set flexibly according to the specific needs of security protection, and effectively ensure the secure usage and provision of mobile network services.

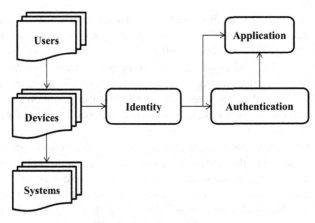

Fig. 1. Security architecture

3.2 Security Model

In the boundary protection model, the authentication and interaction of data between the inner and outer networks are implemented by setting isolated authentication zones as shown in Fig. 2. Due to the full trust between the network modules of the intranet part of the boundary protection model, once the internal and external network isolation part is damaged, the data of the intranet will be leaked in a large area. Therefore, the model architecture has high security risks and hidden dangers [19].

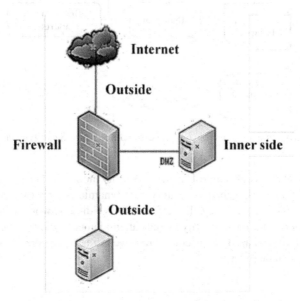

Fig. 2. The boundary protection model

The basic principles of the 5G-based zero-trust security model include protecting the legitimacy and authenticity of the identity of network users by authenticating users, implementing the network service of authorized users with the lowest authority by restricting access rights, and ensuring the legitimacy and security of 5G network terminals connecting to devices through device authentication. In addition, the 5G-based zero-trust security model can synthesize the interaction information of each terminal and personnel, and adaptively develop and adjust network access control policies to maximize network security.

The dynamic trust assessment process architecture of zero-trust security model is shown in Fig. 3, and these information flows and data flows together constitute the overall architecture of the security guard model. In the 5G-based zero-trust security model, all information connection requests are untrustworthy by default. And for each request, the model performs a case-by-case review and judgment [20]. Compared with the boundary protection model, the 5G-based zero-trust cyber security model has significant feature advantages in the aspects of authentication, dynamic access control and variable trust management. In particular, at the authentication level, the security model additionally verifies user permissions and behavioral characteristics, and analyzes user information in a comprehensive manner to enhance the trustworthiness of access verification.

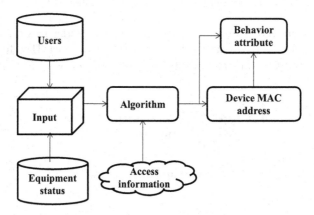

Fig. 3. Dynamic trust assessment process architecture of Security Guard model

In addition, at the access control level, the security model can better achieve real-time verification of the access subject's identity and dynamic control of access rights with its dynamic access control policy, thus effectively avoiding network security threats. In the trust management aspect, security model can implement the diversified allocation of different visitor rights based on the comprehensive rating of visitors, thus achieving the dynamic management of trust.

4 Security Platform

4.1 System Architecture

In order to protect the normal applications of 5G network, a network security platform based on zero-trust architecture is expected to effectively reduce 5G network security threats and attack events. In the zero-trust security architecture, ACL (Access Control List), IPS (Intrusion Prevention System), WAF (Web Application Firewall), etc. are more dependent on the granularity of ID for access, and no longer in the boundary-based configuration. Therefore, the zero-trust security architecture can guarantee the effective security protection of 5G network in the context of continuous blurring of network boundaries. Among them, the dynamic authorization and evaluation function expands the openness and feasibility of application terminal access. Therefore, the zero-trust security architecture can effectively protect the core nodes of the 5G network system, such as servers and databases.

In the 5G network environment, the zero-trust security platform mainly includes several domains as shown in Fig. 4. At the level of security system, effective configuration management of the network system is required to establish a data security hierarchy control mechanism. Secondly, permission access control is performed on 5G network data to avoid over-authorization of data to non-relevant persons. In addition, baselines are set for the flow of data in the network domain and household domain, and intelligent algorithms are used to screen data transmission. In the application and service domains, an early warning architecture is built to ensure stable, reliable and secure network operation.

In addition, in order to solve the network vulnerabilities and network threats existing inside the 5G network, the zero-trust platform should implement the authorized flow, sharing and distribution of data in the network. Hence, the control module and the application module are needed. The control module can establish dynamic evaluation, analysis and processing of the flow of data resources inside the 5G network, and grant the corresponding network access rights to different application terminals. Based on the permissions distributed by the control module, the application module provides targeted data access to different nodes inside the network. The 5G application clients need correct authorization credentials to access network resources, and unauthorized and unauthenticated requests will be prohibited. Thus, it can achieve the rapid and secure transmission between network entities.

4.2 System Functions

Zero-trust network architecture enables enhanced authentication of network users, establishment of device trust, and encryption of authentication and review of access behavior. The enhanced access user authentication establishes an identity-centric access mechanism in 5G networks and becomes the basis of network access control. The enhanced means include various authentication passwords, biological and physical verification means, etc., thus greatly enhancing the security of access user identity. At the level of establishing device trust, a trust relationship between devices in a zero-trust network is a prerequisite for establishing effective device control. Through complete monitoring and analysis of the status of devices accessing the network, their security is audited and

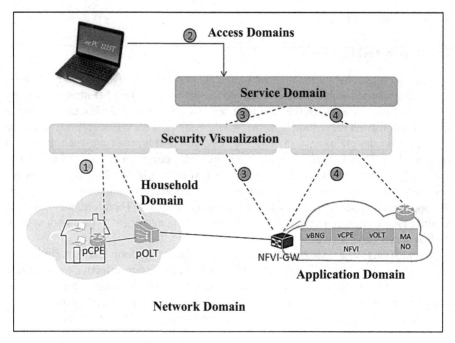

Fig. 4. Security system architecture

targeted connection privileges are granted based on the analysis results. In addition, in the encryption authentication aspect, data packets in the zero-trust network can only be transmitted and circulated through strict review, and the data circulating in the network are operated under controlled protection mechanisms to achieve encrypted data transmission. The review of access behavior is a strict review of all traffic in the network, and the traffic is classified, hierarchically controlled and defined based on the review results, thus providing decisions for its subsequent access control. 5G network traffic, users, and all behaviors of terminals are built up with mapping records to locate abnormal behaviors, data, and processes more accurately.

The 5G core network has its own typical advantages and features at the levels of two-way authentication, traffic security, inter-access control and API (Application Program Interface) protection. At the level of two-way authentication, the 5G core network can better guarantee the legitimacy of 5G access terminals through two-way authentication of users and networks. Mutual authentication of identities is achieved in the 5G core network using client-side and server-side certificates to ensure communication security. Secondly, in the traffic security and inter-access control aspect, SEPP (Security Edge Protection Proxies) and NRF (Network Repository Function) are used to achieve autonomous management of signalling traffic security and network function services, respectively. In addition, in the API protection aspect, the security of APIs and interfaces rely on NF (Network Function) and CAPIF (Common API Framework).

The 5G security protocols and zero-trust architecture have certain correlations at the levels of identity authentication, access authorization, traffic security and service set. Such correlations enable 5G zero-trust security platform to be better applied to many practical scenarios and achieve security protection level of authentication and verification. In addition, under the SPA (Single-Packet Authorization) mechanism, 5G-based zero-trust security platform achieves security protection, especially the enhanced protection against DDoS (Distributed Denial of Service) attacks with the help of SPA mechanism. As an important part of 5G network security protection, monitoring abnormal traffic in the network is the main way to sense the health status of 5G communication process and enhance security warning and health capability.

As important functions of the 5G-based zero-trust security platform, API security protection and network function scoring are important tools to prevent and resist API network attacks, limit API parameter tampering and calling, and dynamically evaluate the network environment to develop a comprehensive trust scoring mechanism. On the one hand, the security platform implements authorization based on user trust level through authorization verification. On the other hand, it can dynamically adjust the scope and level of authorization and whether it needs to revoke authorization according to the changes of 5G mobile network environment.

The security platform implements the restriction and control of access rights to devices, people, etc. with the help of dynamic authorization mechanism. By establishing authentication, authorization and evaluation between the access host and the client, a dynamic trust mechanism between them is constructed. Protected objects such as business applications and data are run using authentication and restrictions on the identity of the accessing subject, and authentication and permission control are achieved using agents deployed at the accessing object side and gateways deployed at the sever side.

In addition, the digital identity-based access control architecture enables the integration and packaging of different access subjects to carry out authentication more efficiently. The protection of business resources in the security platform is achieved based on mechanisms such as business permission minimization, traffic encryption, and dynamic authorization. With the help of trust assessment algorithms and models, identity verification and trust mechanisms are integrated to build a comprehensive assessment function of the security platform for access subjects.

In order to meet the need for dynamic verification of the access subject's identity under 5G network conditions and environment, the security platform is required to be able to dynamically adjust the trust assessment strategy. It uses the trust assessment algorithms to autonomously judge and sense the security of diverse mobile terminals in 5G networks, and integrates all the data to achieve effective evaluation and verification of the access subject's identity. Based on the evaluation results of the dynamic evaluation algorithms, the trust level and permission content of the access subject are dynamically controlled.

The application of 5G-based zero-trust security platform includes several aspects such as security compliance audit, security policy review, data security detection, operation behavior audit, and active security scanning. In the process of dynamic monitoring 5G network data security risks, a dynamic monitoring mechanism based on data flow is established to actively identify, warn and defend against security threats. The dynamic assessment mechanism of zero-trust security platform is shown in the Fig. 5.

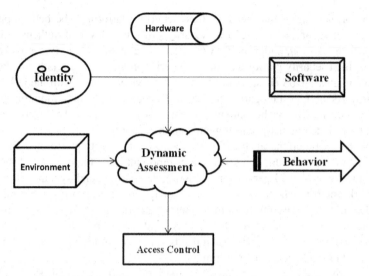

Fig. 5. The dynamic assessment mechanism of security platform

In addition, in the process of monitoring data security risks in the 5G network, the data flow is monitored and audited with the help of the tool collection to effectively identify potential threats. At the application and operation level of the security platform, the zero-trust architecture is integrated with the 5G operation network as a security protection architecture to assess, analyze and reveal the data security risk status of the business system. With the help of security logs, the security platform establishes an analysis model of abnormal behavior and conducts long-term, dynamic tracking and control, thus effectively strengthening network security.

5 Application Results and Discussion

5.1 Application Results

The 5G-based zero-trust security platform establishes its efficient protection architecture in many scenarios in the industries by means of trusted control and trusted access. In this paper, four types of accuracies of the 5G-based zero-trust security platform are tested and compared to the results of the traditional boundary model with IDS (Intrusion Detection System) as shown in Fig. 6. The tested accuracies include accuracy of detection abnormal identities (Accuracy #1), accuracy of detecting abnormal programs (Accuracy #2), accuracy of detecting abnormal configurations (Accuracy #3) and accuracy of detecting abnormal behaviors (Accuracy #4). It can be seen that the application of the security platform shows relatively high accuracy at the level of identity verification of the accessing subject as well as the configuration identification. In addition, it also demonstrates good performance at the level of program and behavior identification and monitoring.

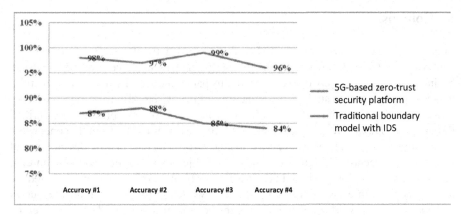

Fig. 6. Accuracy of the security platform

5.2 Discussion

The 5G-based zero-trust network security platform can be established in the self-built mode. The self-built mode mainly includes zero-trust controllers represented by private clouds and data center, clients represented by 5G NRs (New Radios), peripheral elements such as MEC (Multi-access Edge Computing) management centers represented by situational awareness, servers and resource arrangement, and core elements represented by MFP (Multi-Function Processor), edge NFVI (NFV Infrastructure) and so on. Although zero-trust network security platform for 5G under self-built mode is common, there is still much room for improvement in terms of construction cycle, cost, and maintainability.

The zero-trust security platform hides important resources in the 5G network and automatically and effectively eliminates network malicious requests and attacks while dynamically controlling and approving secure connections to legitimate clients. The 5G network and intranet connections make the network boundary more blurred. The SDP (Service Discovery Protocol) ID-based authorization access, rather than overly dependent on boundary protection, may be used to ensure that all clients can only access normally under authorization. By screening and encrypting the access process, it strongly guarantees that the core resources in the network can only be accessed after the trusted request is accessed.

In addition, during the 5G signal transition, the zero-trust platform effectively controls terminal access to core network nodes and opens the corresponding network service ports only after authorized authentication. As a mandatory authentication mode before connection, the zero-trust platform comprehensively evaluates the identity of the access requestor, the operating environment of the network, the behaviour of the visitor and the state of the terminal device. By evaluating and analysing various comprehensive factors, it finally controls the access status of traffic and automatically plans the access content, and only responds to authorized access with targeted services, thus meeting the demand for dynamic access.

6 Conclusion

In summary, the construction of 5G-based zero-trust network security platform as a new type of network security solution effectively achieves an effective balance between business functions and network security. In this paper, the security model and its architectural components are studied. The functions of the 5G-based zero-trust platform are analyzed through the study of its algorithms. The results of its application are verified through the comparative analysis of the 5G zero-trust security platform. In conclusion, the combination of 5G network security and the zero-trust concept provides an efficient integration of security designs such as access subject authorization and trust in core network functions. The 5G-based zero-trust security platform can significantly reduce network security threats and their adverse effects while controlling the limited resources of devices, and may work with other intelligent technologies to warn, identify and defend against attacks on 5G networks. In this paper, the research on independent security control and evaluation of 5G network all node zero trust network security protection needs to be further developed, and the analysis and discussion of subsequent topics need to be further refined.

References

1. Zuo, Y.: Research on the application of zero-trust architecture in critical information infrastructure security protection. Secrecy Sci. Technol. **11**, 33–38 (2019)
2. Zeng, L., Liu, X.: Security architecture based on zero trust. Commun. Technol. **53**(7), 1750–1754 (2020)
3. Ye, M.: Research on the application of zero-trust security model in the security management of central enterprises. Electron. World **11**, 164–165 (2019)
4. Liu, H., Yang, S., Liu, H.: Zero trust security architecture and application. Commun. Technol. **53**(7), 1745–1749 (2020)
5. Hong, T., Gong, W.: The method of trust evaluation based on fuzzy mathematics. Tech. Autom. Appl. **39**(2), 41–44 (2020)
6. Shen, C.: Building a firm cybersecurity defense with trusted computing v3.0. Inf. Commun. Technol. **11**(3), 4–6 (2017)
7. He, X., Yue, P., Lu, Q., Yin, Y.: Evolution and key technologies of 5G-oriented IP RAN. Telecommun. Sci. **36**(3), 125–135 (2020)
8. Ma, P., Wu, W., Zhang, W., Yang, G., Yang, F.: Key technologies and development of 5G bearer network. Telecommun. Sci. **36**(9), 122–130 (2020)
9. Wu, W., Zhang, W., Yang, G., Ma, P., Yang, F.: SRv6 +EVPN technology research and scale deployment of 5G bearer network. Telecommunications Science **36**(8), 43–52 (2020)
10. Feng, D., Liu, J., Qin, Y., Feng, W.: Trusted computing theory and technology in innovation-driven development. Sci. Sinica (Inf.) **50**(08), 1127–1147 (2020)
11. Yuan, J., Zhang, F., Yu, L., Zhang, H., Sang, Y.: Research of security of 5G-enabled Industrial Internet and Its Application. In: 2021 IEEE Conference on Telecommunications, Optics and Computer Science (TOCS), pp. 428–435 (2021)
12. Barth, D., Gilman, E.: Zero Trust Networks: Building Security Systems in Untrusted Networks. O'Reilly Media, Sebastopol, CA (2017)
13. Wylde, A.: Zero trust: never trust, always verify. In: 2021 International Conference on Cyber Situational Awareness, Data Analytics and Assessment (CyberSA), pp. 1–4 (2021)

14. Yan, W., Shu, Q., Gao, P.: Security risk prevention and control deployment for 5G private industrial networks. China Commun. **18**(9), 167–174 (2021)

15. He, C., Peng, B., Cui, M.: Research on the design of zero trust firewall based on single packet authorization. J. Southwest Minzu Univ. (Nat. Sci. Ed.) **47**(2), 181–186 (2021)

16. Dutta, A., Hammad, E.: 5G Security challenges and opportunities: a system approach. In: 2020 IEEE 3rd 5G World Forum (5GWF), pp. 109–114 (2020)

17. Zhang, D., Wang, J.: Research on security protection method of industrial control boundary network. In: 2021 IEEE Conference on Telecommunications, Optics and Computer Science (TOCS), pp. 560–563 (2021)

18. Zhang, B., Zhu, X., Sun, Y., Yu, Y.: Research on practice of big data security guide. Inf. Technol. Stand. **03**, 33–37 (2021)

19. Zhang, Y., Wang, Y., Xie, J.: Analysis on security of 5G network and suggestions for security scheme. Inf. Commun. Technol. Policy **4**, 47–53 (2020)

20. Singla, A., Hussain, S.R., Chowdhury, O., Bertino, E., Li, N.: Protecting the 4G and 5G cellular paging protocols against security and privacy attacks. Proc. Priv. Enhancing Technol. **1**, 126–142 (2020)

A Mobile Data Leakage Prevention System Based on Encryption Algorithms

Wen Shen[1]([envelope]) and Hongzhang Xiong[2]

[1] State Grid Smart Grid Research Institute Co., Ltd., Nanjing 210003, China
shenwen@geiri.sgcc.com.cn

[2] State Grid Jibei Marketing Service Center (Fund Intensive Control Center and Metrology Center), Beijing 100045, China

Abstract. Mobile Internet is an emerging field that is developing rapidly. However, the frequent data leakage events caused by the security problems of mobile Internet have brought great impact to enterprises and individuals. Cryptography is promising way for data security and is widely used in the industries such as power systems. How to effectively use data encryption algorithms in the field of mobile Internet to meet the security requirements of data sharing is a problem to be solved. Therefore, this paper proposes a mobile data leakage prevention system that adopts the encryption algorithms SM3 and SM4 that are approved by the State Cryptography Administration of China. The cipher-text retrieval model is proposed for secure data sharing between data owner and data user via cloud servers. The system model that is built based on the studied encryption algorithms and models is describe. Additional functions are also designed for mobile data leakage prevention such as data security management and security data analysis. The proposed system is expected protect the data transmission, storage and sharing between data owner, data user and cloud server, providing an architecture to build a security mechanism to lower the risks from data theft, eavesdropping and tampering.

Keywords: Mobile Internet · Encryption algorithms · Data leakage prevention

1 Introduction

Mobile data refers to information that can be transmitted through radio communication technology or other wireless means. Mobile data transmission is not affected by geographical environment, space and other factors, and can be transmitted on the mobile Internet or mobile terminals [1]. At present, with the popularization of intelligent terminals and the arrival of 5G network era, mobile data analysis occupies an increasingly high position in various business applications, and has become a topic that cannot be ignored in the information age [2]. With the acceleration of wireless network construction, mobile applications have been widely used in the government and enterprises, and the number of intelligent terminal users has increased rapidly. Therefore, how to effectively prevent data from being eavesdropped and tampered with is one of the security problems of mobile data, and encryption technology is one of the important means to ensure the secure transmission of mobile data.

© The Author(s), under exclusive license to Springer Nature Singapore Pte Ltd. 2023
Y. Tian et al. (Eds.): ICBDS 2022, CCIS 1796, pp. 564–574, 2023.
https://doi.org/10.1007/978-981-99-3300-6_40

The symmetric encryption algorithms such as DES (Data Encryption Standard), AES (Advanced Encryption Standard) are a data encryption technologies based on the encryption domain. They can encrypt the plaintext with the key by bit calculation, substitution, row or column shifting, so as to achieve information security. The algorithms have the function of key management that establishes a complete secret matrix through cryptographic method, and encrypt and decrypt data using symmetric keys to achieve the functions of data confidentiality [3]. SMS4 algorithm is a symmetric encryption algorithm that is adopted by State Cryptography Administration of China as SM4 algorithm standard. It has been widely used in the field of data leakage prevention for wireless communications, which uses a key generation system to provide different keys for each encryption and decryption round [4].

The asymmetric encryption algorithms such as RSA (Rivest, Shamir, Adleman) use the key pair of public key and private key for encryption and decryption [5]. The key pairs are generated by a key management server and the public key can be used for digital certificate issued by a CA (Certificate Authority). The cryptographic hash functions such as SHA-256 (Secure Hash Algorithm 256), SM3 (Hash algorithm standard approved by State Cryptography Administration of China) covert the original message to a fixed-length digest while the original message can hardly be obtained by analyzing the digest [6].

As mentioned above, the purpose of this paper is to explore the adjusted application of encryption algorithms in the mobile data leakage prevention filed so that the security of data storage, data transmission and data utilization is improved. The organization of our paper is as follows. Section 2 describes the principle of adopted encryption algorithms in the proposed system. The architecture and functions of the proposed system are described in Sect. 3. Conclusions are drawn in Sect. 4.

2 Mobile Data Encryption Methods

2.1 SM4 Encryption Algorithm

SM4 symmetric encryption algorithm adopts symmetric block encryption structure similar to other symmetric encryption algorithms, such as DES and AES, and adopts multi round nonlinear iteration method to perform data operation. Each round of iteration operation will have corresponding round key participation. Hence, the primary components in SM4 include the encryption module and the key module. The process of SM4 encryption module is shown in Fig. 1.

It can be seen from Fig. 1 that the input plaintext $P = \{x_0, x_1, x_2, x_3\}$ and the output cipher-text $C = \{y_0, y_1, y_2, y_3\}$, the encryption process is shown in Eq. (1), where $F(\cdot)$ denotes the round function and rk_i denotes the round key.

$$x_{i+4} = F(x_i, x_{i+1}, x_{i+2}, x_{i+3}, rk_i), i = 0, 1, 2..., 31 \tag{1}$$

The round function $F(\cdot)$ is used to implement XOR calculation, nonlinear substitution and linear transformation, in which the nonlinear substitution is an important function as shown in Fig. 2, where the input bits and output bits are in the finite field

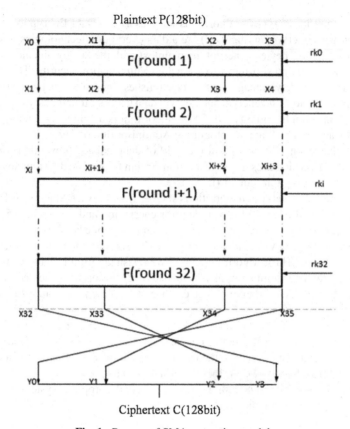

Fig. 1. Process of SM4 encryption module

of 2^8, and *Sbox*($\cdot$) is a mapping table that receives the input bits as the coordinates and outputs the value in the corresponding cell.

While applying SM4 in the mobile data encryption scenarios, the performance and power consumption need to be considered since the mobile terminals usually have limited computation capability and battery life. Hence, the lightweight SM4 can be designed for energy efficient secure communications [7]. It uses a long-term keystream for parallel encryption and decryption processes on the multi-processor platform and the session key is updated periodically to resist the leakage of the long-term keystream. In addition, the security of SM4 can be further improved while the performance is considered. The lookup tables for encoding and decoding data in each round can be introduced to improve the security of SM4 [8]. Meanwhile, some of the lookup tables can be reused so as to decrease the memory consumption of the mobile terminals that usually have limited memories.

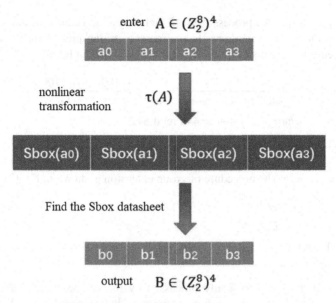

Fig. 2. Nonlinear substitution in round function

2.2 SM3 Hash Function

SM3 hash function is widely used in the information security fields such as message integrity verification, digital signature verification and message authentication data generation. Its process is shown in Fig. 3.

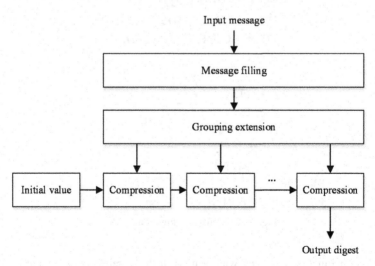

Fig. 3. Process of SM3

It can be seen that the process of SM3 include the procedures of message filling, group extension and compressions. In the message filling procedure, the message is pre-processed by filling the data with several bits as shown in Eq. (2).

$$\underbrace{\cdots\cdots\cdots\cdots\cdots\cdots\cdots\cdots}_{original\ message\ l\ bits}\ \underbrace{1}_{1\ bit}\ \underbrace{0\cdots0}_{n\ bit}\ \underbrace{0\cdots0011000}_{64\ bit}$$

(2)

$$where,\ l + 1 + n \equiv 448 \ mod \ 512$$

The filled message is then divided into groups of 512 bits which is separated as 16 words $w_0, ...w_{15}$. The output of the group extension is composed of 132 words as $w_0, ...w_{67}, w_0^*, ...w_{63}^*$. The procedure of group extension is shown in Eq. (3).

$$w_i = EF(w_{i-16} \oplus w_{i-9} \oplus (w_{i-3} <<< 15)) \oplus (w_{i-13} <<< 7) \oplus w_{i-6}, i = 16, 17, ..., 67$$
$$w_i^* = w_i \oplus w_{i+4}, i = 0, 1..., 63$$
$$where\ EF(x) = x \oplus (x <<< 15) \oplus (x <<< 23)$$

(3)

The extended words are finally processed by the compression function to output a 256-bit digest as shown in Fig. 4, where $V^{(0)}$ denotes the initial value, $V^{(n)}$ denotes the compressed result, A, B, C, D, E, F, G are registers of compression function, $SS1, SS2, TT1, TT2$ are intermediate variables.

```
ABCDEFGH ← V⁽ⁱ⁾
FOR j = 0 TO 63
            SS1 ← (A<<<12)+E+(Tⱼ<<<(j mod 32)<<<7)
            SS2 ← SS1⊕(A<<<12)
            TT1 ← FFⱼ(A,B,C)+D+SS2+W'ⱼ
            TT2 ← GGⱼ(E,F,G)+H+SS1+Wⱼ
            D ← C
            B ← A
            A ← TT1
            H ← G
            G ← F<<<19
            F ← E
            E ← P₀(TT2)
ENDFOR
V⁽ⁱ⁺¹⁾ ← ABCDEFGH ⊕ V⁽ⁱ⁾
```

Fig. 4. Compression function of SM3

SM3 hash function has been widely used in the wireless communications or IoT (Internet of Things) scenarios in power systems [9, 10]. The performance of SM3 can be improved by hardware and software design by optimizing critical path and adding parallel operations [11, 12].

2.3   Cipher-Text Retrieval Model

Since the mobile data is usually encrypted by the intelligent terminals and the storage server, the cipher-text retrieval becomes difficult. The efficiency of the cipher-text retrieval should be considered while the retrieval algorithm plays an important role. The cipher-text retrieval model is proposed as shown in Fig. 5.

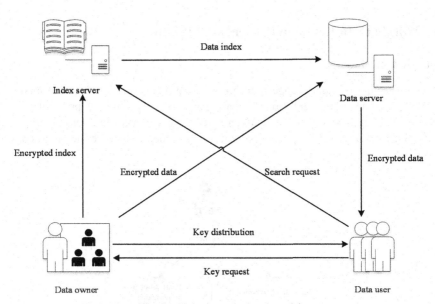

Fig. 5. Cipher-text retrieval model

It can be seen that the cipher-text retrieval model includes data owner, data user, index server and data server. The data owner who might be a person or an organization is concerned with the data privacy protection of his uploaded data. Hence, the data owner encrypted his original data and index file before uploading it to data server and index server respectively so that the user data is not disclosed to the server in the cloud service platform.

While the data user request for data in the cloud server, he has to ask for permission from the data owner, which means the key for the encrypted data. Once the data user is authorized, he will use the key form a search request to the index server which will then sends the related data identifiers to the data server. The data server searches the required data according to the data identifiers without decrypting the data and sends the ordered encrypted data to the data user who can obtain the original data by decrypting the data with authorized key. The index structure for cipher-text is shown in Eq. (4), where ck_i denotes the cipher-text keyword, dp_i denotes the data pointer and ap_i denotes the data address pointer.

$$\{ck_i, dp_i\} \rightarrow \{dp_i, ap_i\} \tag{4}$$

The improvement of cipher-text retrieval can be achieved by extending the supporting heterogeneous databases and data sets where a cross-platform and cross-database cipher-text retrieval system is designed [13]. The efficiency of cipher-text retrieval method can also be improved by supporting multiple data owners [14]. The process of that method is similar to the proposed model while the index server and data server are separated in the proposed model.

3 Mobile Data Leakage Prevention System

3.1 System Model

The architecture of data leakage prevention system is composed of several modules, and each module achieves information sharing and encryption through protocols, which ensures the integrity of the system. Data encryption algorithm is a multilateral computing technology based on cryptography and information theory. Its core idea is to convert

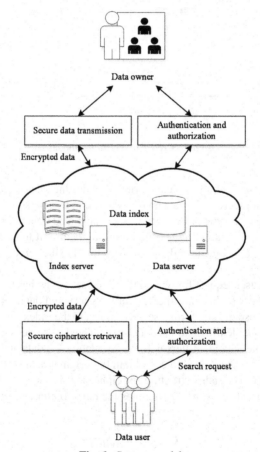

Fig. 6. System model

secret information into ciphertext so that it will not be disclosed to a certain extent, so as to realize the protection of data security and privacy. The system model of the mobile data leakage prevention system is shown in Fig. 6.

It can be seen that the data user has to obtain the permission from the data owner and is approved to access the cloud server before requesting for the data. The authorized data owner uploads his data via secure data transmission module while the authorized data user may obtain the requested encrypted data via cipher-text retrieval module.

3.2 Functions Design

As mentioned in the system model, the primary modules in the proposed system include secure data transmission module, secure cipher-text retrieval module and authentication and authorization module. The secure data transmission process is shown in Fig. 7.

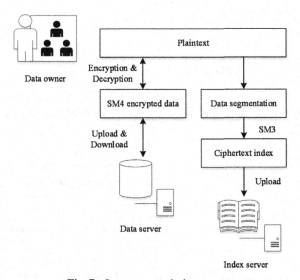

Fig. 7. Secure transmission process

It can be seen that the SM4 algorithm is used to encrypt and decrypt the original data while the encrypted data is uploaded and stored in the data server. The cipher-text index is generated by combining the random number generated by upload time and the digest data generated by using SM3 to data segments and data owner identifier.

The secure cipher-text retrieval process is shown in Fig. 8. It can be seen that the data user uploads the encrypted search keyword to the index server that subsequently calculate the similar data identifiers, according to which the data server returns the corresponding encrypted data. The data user decrypted the cipher-text using authorized key to obtain the original data.

Finally, the authentication and authorization module is used to authenticate the identities of data owner and data user, and give the appropriate authorization for data operatons.

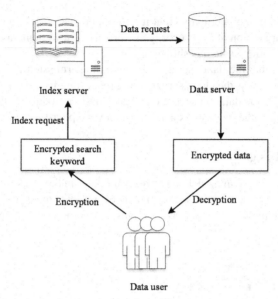

Fig. 8. Secure cipher-text retrieval

In addition, various functions are designed for mobile data leakage prevention as shown in Fig. 9.

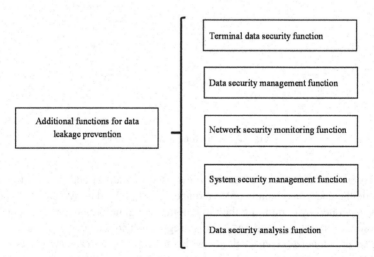

Fig. 9. Additional functions for mobile data leakage prevention

The terminal data security function is to ensure the security of mobile terminal data. Sensitive information identification and data encryption algorithms can be used to protect important information such as mobile terminal user identity. The data security management function is to manage the data security function configuration and ensure the correct configuration and operation of the data security functions of the server and the user. Network security monitoring function is to monitor the process of network data collection, storage and transmission. The server security management function is to manage and maintain the server data. If the data is tampered or destroyed during the operation of the system, the database file shall be restored to normal within a certain time. The data security analysis function performs security analysis according to the collected monitoring data to determine whether the system has potential data leakage.

4 Conclusion

At present, people have begun to protect the security of various types of data through encryption technology, but there are still many problems in the field of mobile data encryption technology. For example, there is no effective cooperation mechanism for data encryption between service providers and mobile users. The development of data encryption technology is an important and challenging topic. Some traditional encryption methods are limited in the field of mobile applications due to their operating efficiency and energy consumption, which will cause attackers to steal or destroy data through mobile networks or terminals. Therefore, a data leakage prevention system is proposed for applications in mobile scenarios where encryption algorithms are adopted. The main purpose of the proposed system is to ensure data security during data sharing via the cloud servers. The future research may include the design of the efficient cipher-text retrieval algorithm and the performance improvement of the mobile data leakage prevention methods.

Acknowledgments. The research in this paper was financially supported by science and technology project of State Grid Corporation of China under Grant No. 5700-202153172A-0-0-00.

References

1. Cheng, X., Fang, L., Yang, L., Cui, S.: Mobile big data: the fuel for data-driven wireless. IEEE Internet Things J. **4**(5), 1489–1516 (2017)
2. Yin, X., He, J., Gao, Y., Li, J.: Multi-source data analysis method of exhibition site based on mobile internet. Int. Wireless Commun. Mobile Comput. (IWCMC) **2021**, 41–44 (2021)
3. Zhang, Q.: An overview and analysis of hybrid encryption: the combination of symmetric encryption and asymmetric encryption. In: 2021 2nd International Conference on Computing and Data Science (CDS), pp. 616–622 (2021)
4. Zheng, X., Xu, C., Hu, X., Zhang, Y., Xiong, X.: The software/hardware co-design and implementation of SM2/3/4 encryption/decryption and digital signature System. IEEE Trans. Comput. Aided Des. Integr. Circuits Syst. **39**(10), 2055–2066 (2020)
5. Atmaja, I.M.A.D.S., Astawa, I.N.G.A., Wisswani, N.W., Nugroho, I.M.R.A., Sunu, P.W., Wiratama, I.K.: Document encryption through asymmetric RSA cryptography. Int. Conf. Appl. Sci. Technol. (iCAST) **2020**, 46–49 (2020)
6. Rajeshwaran, K., Kumar, K.A.: Cellular automata based hashing algorithm (cabha) for strong cryptographic hash function. In: 2019 IEEE International Conference on Electrical, Computer and Communication Technologies (ICECCT), pp. 1–6 (2019)

7. Li, T., et al.: Energy-efficient and secure communication toward UAV networks. IEEE Internet Things J. **9**(12), 10061–10076 (2022)

8. Jin, C., Zeng, Z., Miao, W., Bao, Z., Zhang, R.: A nonlinear white-box SM4 implementation applied to edge IoT agents. In: 2021 IEEE 5th Conference on Energy Internet and Energy System Integration (EI2), pp. 3358–3363 (2021)

9. Liu, D., Wang, R., Zhang, H., Chen, J., Liu, X., Ma, L.: Research on terminal security technology of ubiquitous power internet of things based on PUF and SM3. In: 2019 IEEE 3rd Conference on Energy Internet and Energy System Integration (EI2), pp. 910–915 (2019)

10. Wang, T., et al.: The research of the SM2, SM3 and SM4 Algorithms in WLAN of transformer substation. In: 2019 3rd International Conference on Electronic Information Technology and Computer Engineering (EITCE), pp. 276–283 (2019)

11. Zang, S., et al.: IEEE 5th advanced information technology. Electron. Autom. Control Conf. (IAEAC) **2021**, 915–919 (2021)

12. Liu, Y., Zhao, R., Han, L., Xie, J.: Research and implementation of parallel optimization of SM3 algorithm based on multithread. In: 2022 7th International Conference on Intelligent Computing and Signal Processing (ICSP), pp. 330–33 (2022)

13. Feng, X., Ma, J., Liu, S., Miao, Y., Liu, X., Choo, K.-K.R.: Transparent ciphertext retrieval system supporting integration of encrypted heterogeneous database in cloud-assisted IoT. IEEE Internet Things J. **9**(5), 3784–3798 (2022)

14. He, H., Chen, R., Liu, C., Feng, K., Zhou, X.: An efficient ciphertext retrieval scheme based on homomorphic encryption for multiple data owners in hybrid cloud. IEEE Access **9**, 168547–168557 (2021)

Research on Data Security Access Control Mechanism in Cloud Computing Environment

Chen Luo[1], Yang Li[1], and Qianxuan Wang[2(✉)]

[1] State Grid XinJiang Electric Power Co., Ltd., Urumchi 830000, China
[2] State Grid XinJiang Electric Power Co, Ltd. Marketing Service Center (Capital Intensive Center, Metering Center), Urumchi 830000, China
413744709@qq.com

Abstract. Cloud computing is an Internet-based virtualization application model that has been in development for these years. Cloud computing technology provides users with a large number of virtualized computing and storage resources. As a continuously developing emerging technology, some theoretical and technical systems have been formed in countries all over the world. However, the data security in the virtualization environment of cloud service providers has attracted extensive attentions of users over the years. In the cloud computing environment, data access control mainly includes two aspects: one is the safe transmission of required information resources in the network, and the other is the reasonable control of user permissions. In this paper, we analyze the cloud computing platform based on OpenStack and the related data security access control model is proposed. The data access control process is studied where trust of the cloud user is evaluated. An access control system based on the studied model is then designed whose architecture and its components are described. The proposed model and system is expected to provide a new technical method for data security protection so as to lower the risks of data leakage.

Keywords: Cloud computing · Data security · Access control

1 Introduction

Cloud computing is an application based on the Internet. With the development of network technology, its scale is constantly expanding. In this context, a large number of emerging fields such as information management, data storage, and cloud services have emerged, which have brought great convenience to people's life and work. However, this information also faces some security challenges. In the process of data storage and transmission, a large amount of sensitive information will be generated. In order to better protect the sensitive information and user privacy from being leaked, corresponding measures can be taken for encryption [1]. Therefore, how to design and implement a safe and reliable cloud computing data security control platform that can bring great benefits to enterprises is now an urgent problem.

Cloud computing technology is a new computing mode that takes large-scale network as the core, provides services to users through management, storage and analysis of

Y. Tian et al. (Eds.): ICBDS 2022, CCIS 1796, pp. 575–585, 2023.
https://doi.org/10.1007/978-981-99-3300-6_41

resources, and implements information sharing, data processing and service provision. The cloud computing environment has seen tremendous progress in computer technology, but there are also some problems in its development process. In traditional computer applications, hardware devices are usually installed in a software environment, but with the advent of the Internet era, a new model called "virtualization" has emerged [2, 3]. The computer itself is widely used because of its freedom of operational functions, which makes the network an open system platform to meet the needs of users. However, the openness of the network and the unlimited operating environment lead to many risks in the application of computer technology in cloud computing [4]. Therefore, there is a need to protect the sensitive data using data security access control mechanism, which not only ensures the security of users' information but also reduces the risks that exist in cloud computing applications.

The data security access control mechanism refers to an access control strategy implemented by using various security technical means to protect sensitive data [5]. At present, the data resources in cloud computing environment have the characteristics of large capacity and complex applications, which makes the traditional user management methods cannot meet the needs. The service model built on the infrastructure based on virtualized storage and distributed query mode can better solve the above problems, so as to implement the management and control of data resources in the cloud computing environment [6]. This paper mainly studies the algorithms of establishing security mechanism in cloud computing environment. These algorithms can make the system run more stably and efficiently, and maximize the value of data resources [7].

2 Cloud Computing OpenStack Platform

The main function of the cloud computing platform is to analyze and process user needs through data warehouse, virtualization technology and service applications. It can provide complete information services for users to access data in the process of use, so as to realize virtualization, automation and intelligent management. At present, the cloud computing OpenStack platform is widely used in industries, which is an embedded server-side platform based on the Page architecture and the VLSI (Very Large Scale Integration) framework. The OpenStack platform architecture is shown in Fig. 1. The main function of the platform is to implement virtualization through the access to the server, and use the user ID for access control to protect its core information from damage [8]. However, there are many uncertain factors in the cloud computing deployment environment, which makes the embedded service providers based on this architecture and VLSI framework unable to meet the security demand.

3 Data Security Access Control Model

Data security access control model mainly refers to the management of information resources to ensure that user data is effectively protected, so as to avoid unnecessary losses. The data security access control process is shown in Fig. 2, where the access reinforcement is supported by the decision service via the interface and policy management and attribute service are connected to decision service. For database application

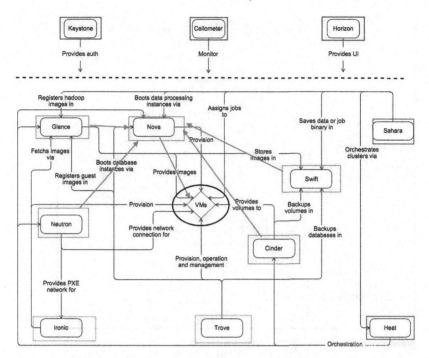

Fig. 1. OpenStack platform architecture

systems, data encryption, authentication and authorization in the cloud computing environment require the establishment of corresponding security mechanisms to prevent data leakage and thus achieve effective protection for users. In order to achieve this purpose, cloud service providers should provide reliable, controllable and secure cloud services. In addition, they should also ensure that users can have a reasonable degree of access control policies to ensure the security of user data. In the cloud computing environment, information resources are very large and expanding. In order to ensure that they can be used and developed reasonably, it is necessary to strengthen the research and design of data access control strategies and technologies [9, 10].

The current commonly used security access control algorithm is mainly through the fuzzy hierarchical analysis method to first calculate the direct trust value of user data in the cloud environment, and the first step before the specific calculation is set the initial judgment matrix, as shown in Eq. (1), where n indicates that the user behavior is divided into n features, and m is used to describe the maximum number of items in the feature.

$$E_Q = (eq_{ij})_{n \times m} \tag{1}$$

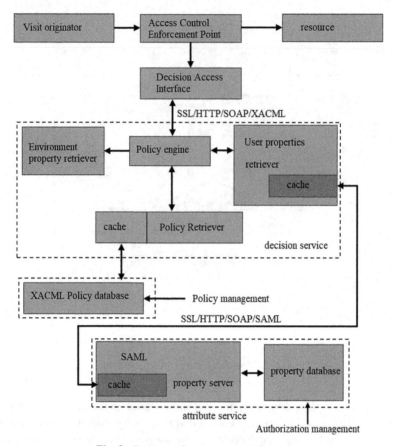

Fig. 2. Data security access control process

eq_{ij} is the binary comparison of the importance of e_i and e_j that are the evidences of each feature as shown in Eq. (2), and the initial judgment matrix E_Q is changed into a fuzzy consistency matrix Q as shown in Eq. (3).

$$eq_{ij} \begin{cases} 0, e_i < e_j \\ 0.5, e_i = e_j \\ 1, e_i > e_j \end{cases} \tag{2}$$

$$Q = (q_{ij})_{n \times m}$$
$$\begin{cases} q_{ij} = (q_i - q_j)/(2m) + 0.5 \\ q_i = \sum_{k=1}^{m} eq_{ik} \end{cases} \tag{3}$$

The weight vector W of m evidences of a feature and the matrix F of characteristic evaluation values can be obtained by the above calculation, as shown in Eqs. (4) and (5). The final obtained direct trust value of user behavior T_{a1} is calculated as shown in

Eq. (6).

$$W = (w_1, w_2, \cdots, w_m)^T$$

$$where, \; w_i = \frac{1}{m(m-1)/2}(\sum_{k=1}^{m} q_{ik} - 0.5) \tag{4}$$

$$F = (f_1, f_2, \cdots, f_n) \tag{5}$$

$$T_{a1} = 1 - F \times W_f^T = 1 - \sum_{i=1}^{n} f_i w_i \tag{6}$$

Based on the above calculation analysis, the integrated user trust value in the cloud environment is calculated as shown in Eq. (7), where T_{a1} and T_{a2} are trust values of user behaviors, a and b are the parameters of corresponding behavior.

$$T_{A(u_i)} = aT_{a1} + bT_{a2} \tag{7}$$

Data access control process is mainly to verify the identity of the user. In the cloud computing environment, if login or registration information is illegally intercepted, the whole system will not work normally, or even the system will be paralyzed. Therefore, the access control of data in the cloud computing environment needs to take measures such as access rights setting, identity verification and security management [11]. The specific data access control procedure is shown in Fig. 3, and the process of implementing the access control algorithm for user data security in the cloud environment is as follows.

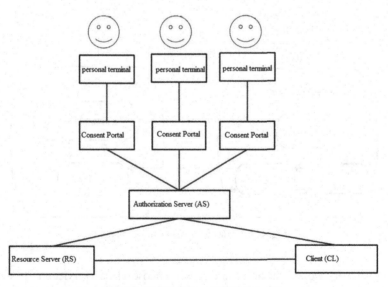

Fig. 3. Data access control program

Firstly, the user enters the cloud computing virtualization system and requests access to the resources. The system collects the trust evidence of the user, the user confirms the access request to the resources, and returns the result to the virtualization system. Secondly, different trust evidences are classified and analyzed to get the results of trust and response time, so as to get the service quality and trust evidences of the cloud computing virtualization system. The trust value of user data is then derived and the model of trust evidence is established. The results are analyzed to derive the quality of service of the cloud computing virtualization system and there is a correlation between the trust and response time [12]. Finally, the user data trust value is compared with the established threshold value, and if the user data trust value exceeds the threshold value, it means that the user has a trust relationship, and the user data trust level is determined, and the user authority is judged based on the trust level. On the contrary, it means that the user does not have a trust relationship, and access requests are denied.

There are four main types of traditional access control: mandatory access control, discretionary access control, role-based access control and attribute-based access control [13].

Mandatory access control is based on user identification. In the cloud computing environment, user identification and access control are the most basic and important functions in the cloud computing environment. The illegal behaviors will affect the whole database management system. Therefore, cloud computing technology is needed to deal with illegal access to data. In the cloud computing environment, data storage, management and application are the functions provided by the system control mechanism that is the key to secure data access control in the cloud computing environment. The mandatory access control model is shown in Fig. 4, where the secure sever stores the security access policies and the object manager controls the access of objects.

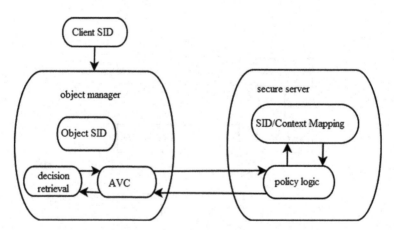

Fig. 4. Mandatory access control model

Discretionary access control means that users choose relevant services on the network according to their needs and let these services execute. Currently, data encryption in the cloud computing environment mainly relies on the internal server structure and external interface design of the system to achieve confidentiality of relevant information content [14]. Discretionary access control model is shown in Fig. 5, where the access right and the corresponding access path are decided by the user who owned the objects. In the discretionary access control model, the owner decides whether to grant his own object access or part of the access to other subjects.

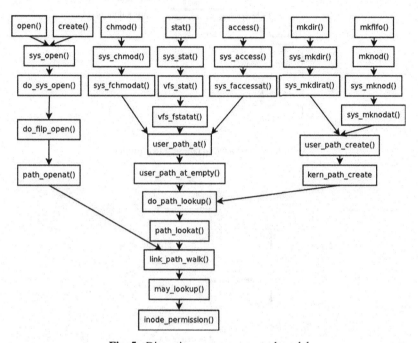

Fig. 5. Discretionary access control model

Role-based access control is that in the data security management, a user is assigned a role in the application system and the permitted access rights are defined in this role as shown in Fig. 6. The role can be considered as the collection of access rights for the specific user to complete his tasks. The roles in the system are usually defined according to the work responsibilities such security manager, database administrator and so on.

Attribute-based access control mainly refers to the management of user information security requirements to achieve data storage security and stability. A large number of private resources and applications are stored in the cloud computing environment, and these applications exist in various computer devices. Therefore, it is necessary to establish a system with the characteristics of high reliability and strong scalability to meet its requirements. In addition, reasonable and feasible security mechanisms and access control strategies should be designed according to its own system structure, so as to achieve data security and stability [15]. The attribute-based access control model is shown in Fig. 7. The PEP (Policy Execution Point) is responsible to query attributes from AA (Attribute Authority) and to send the attribute-based request to PDP (Policy Decision Point). PDP receives the policies from PAP (Policy Administration Point) so as to decide whether to permit the access request.

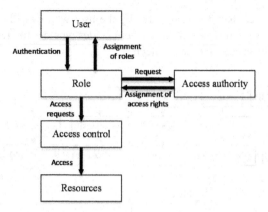

Fig. 6. Role-based access control model

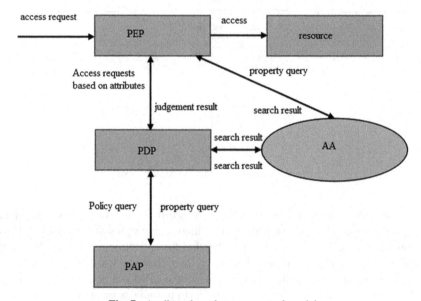

Fig. 7. Attribute-based access control model

4   Access Control System Based on OpenStack

Data security access control mechanism is an important part of a system. In the cloud computing environment, users need to access the required resources and perform the corresponding operations, which has certain requirements for users' access rights. Data encryption technology is a very important element, and its main purpose is to safeguard information resources from illegal attacks. Therefore, a network architecture-based data encryption system is needed to improve the security in the whole database application, which is the main direction of implementing data security technology at present. In order to ensure that the data storage process is not damaged, it is necessary to provide backup files and record logs on each node. In addition, it also needs to use firewall technology and intrusion detection technology to control user access and monitor illegal behaviors so as to realize the security of data storage process and user identification. In this paper, we mainly use the access control system based on cloud computing platform to study the data security access control mechanism in the cloud computing environment. The system architecture is shown in Fig. 8.

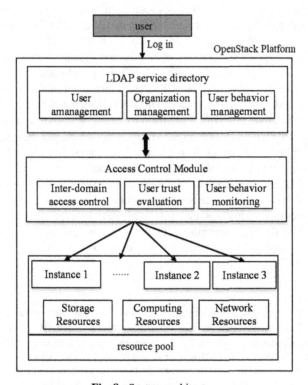

Fig. 8. System architecture

The LDAP (Lightweight Directory Access Protocol) service directory and access control module are implemented based on the OpenStack platform. The LDAP provides the basis for the access control that implements the user identity management, user relationship management, user behavior management, organization information management and so on. The access control module is designed to implement the user behavioral monitoring, user trust evaluation and inter-domain access control. As mentioned above, the user behaviors in the cloud environment are collected and analyzed so as to obtain the corresponding trust values. The integrated trust value of each user in the cloud environment is then calculated via comprehensive evaluation of his behaviors. The access to the instances and resources in the resource pool is controlled and monitored via the proposed system.

5 Conclusion

In summary, cloud computing has become a popular field today, and its development prospects are very promising. In the cloud computing environment, the data access control mechanism also needs to be continuously improved with the development of technology and applications. It has very important applications in the Internet, enterprises and other industries, and is also an indispensable part of the current social development. However, due to the particularity of cloud computing technology and users in the cloud computing environment, there are still many deficiencies in data access control mechanisms. For example, illegal intruders use computers or other storage devices to destroy the integrity and confidentiality of cloud computing platforms, resulting in data loss. In the case of illegal intrusion, the lack of timely and effective technical means of security monitoring and protection will cause a large area of data leakage. In modern network environment, it is necessary to improve the data access control mechanism so as to protect the cloud computing platform users and system resources. In addition, since the traditional network management system is not sound and the constraints of the system vulnerabilities, it may result in the inability to protect the cloud service effectively. In order to better protect data security, this paper analyzes the cloud computing environment based on OpenStack architecture. A data security access control model is proposed, based on which an access control system is designed. The proposal in this paper is expected to provide a framework to implement an improved access mechanism so as to lower the risks of compromise of cloud service platforms. The algorithms in the proposed system need to be further designed in the future research.

References

1. Reddy, Y.: Big data processing and access controls in cloud environment. In: 2018 IEEE 4th International Conference on Big Data Security on Cloud (BigDataSecurity), IEEE International Conference on High Performance and Smart Computing, (HPSC) and IEEE International Conference on Intelligent Data and Security (IDS), 2018, pp. 25–33 (2018)
2. Mirajkar, S.B., Khatawkar, S.D.: A provenance-based access control model for securely storing data in cloud. In: 2017 2nd International Conference for Convergence in Technology (I2CT), 2017, pp. 906–909 (2017)
3. Wang, F., Wang, H., Xue, L.: Research on data security in big data cloud computing environment. In: 2021 IEEE 5th Advanced Information Technology, Electronic and Automation Control Conference (IAEAC), 2021, pp. 1446–1450 (2021)
4. Bertolissi, C., Boucelma, O., Uttha, W.: Enhancing security in the cloud: when traceability meets access control. In: 2017 12th International Conference for Internet Technology and Secured Transactions (ICITST), 2017, pp. 365–366 (2017)
5. Time and attribute based dual access control and data integrity verifiable scheme in cloud computing applications. IEEE Access **7**, 137594–137607 (2019)
6. Gao, L., Yan, Z., Yang, L.T.: Game theoretical analysis on acceptance of a cloud data access control system based on reputation. IEEE Trans. Cloud Comput. **8**(4), 1003–1017 (2020)
7. Celiktas, B., Celikbilek, I., Ozdemir, E.: A higher-level security scheme for key access on cloud computing. IEEE Access **9**, 107347–107359 (2021)
8. Wang, Y., Sun, Q., Ma, Y., Zhang, J., Liu, Z., Xue, J.: Security enhanced cloud storage access control system based on attribute based encryption. In: 2018 International Conference on Big Data and Artificial Intelligence (BDAI), 2018, pp. 52–57 (2018)

9. More, P.: Cloud data security using attribute-based key-aggregate cryptosystem. In: 2018 International Conference on Research in Intelligent and Computing in Engineering (RICE), 2018, pp. 1–6 (2018)
10. Wang, J., Ye, C., Ou, Y.: Dynamic data access control for multi-authority cloud storage. In: 2019 IEEE 21st International Conference on High Performance Computing and Communications; IEEE 17th International Conference on Smart City; IEEE 5th International Conference on Data Science and Systems (HPCC/SmartCity/DSS), 2019, pp. 599–608 (2019)
11. Varma, A., Saxena, K., Khatri, S.K.: Preventive measures to secure issues in cloud computing. In: 2019 International Conference on Intelligent Computing and Control Systems (ICCS), 2019, pp. 504–508 (2019)
12. Cloud-trust—a security assessment model for infrastructure as a service (IaaS) clouds. IEEE Trans. Cloud Comput. 5(3), 523–536 (2017)
13. Soni, K., Kumar, S.: Comparison of RBAC and ABAC security models for private cloud. In: 2019 International Conference on Machine Learning, Big Data, Cloud and Parallel Computing (COMITCon), 2019, pp. 584–587 (2019)
14. Belguith, S., Kaaniche, N., Russello, G.: PU-ABE: lightweight attribute-based encryption supporting access policy update for cloud assisted IoT. In: 2018 IEEE 11th International Conference on Cloud Computing (CLOUD), 2018, pp. 924–927 (2018)
15. Li, Q., Tian, Y., Zhang, Y., Shen, L., Guo, J.: Efficient privacy-preserving access control of mobile multimedia data in cloud computing. IEEE Access 7, 131534–131542 (2019)

Research on Data Security Storage System Based on Distributed Database

Bo Liu[1], Lan Zhang[2], and Jinke Wang[2(✉)]

[1] State Grid Henan Electric Power Co., Ltd., Zhengzhou 450000, China
[2] State Grid Henan Marketing Service Centre, Zhengzhou 450000, China
hndl-lb@foxmail.com

Abstract. Data security storage technology is an important part of information management. The security of data storage is the key to user information security, system operation efficiency and economic benefits. The implementation of data security storage technology plays an important role in improving the efficiency of data management and reducing the operating costs of enterprises. Due to the data leakage caused by intentional or unintentional wrong operation, which infringes the user's personal privacy, the traditional data storage methods face greater risks in the operation process. These disadvantages affect the use effect of the system, and even lead to system paralysis and data loss in serious cases. Distributed database has the characteristics of high degree of structure, good openness and small storage space requirements, and plays an important role in data management. In this paper, a data security storage model is studied combining the symmetric encryption algorithm, asymmetric encryption algorithm and the hash algorithm. A data security storage system is then proposed based on distributed storage while its functional composition, data transmission framework and database design are described. The proposed system in this paper is expected improve the data storage security so as to reduce the risks of information leakage.

Keywords: Data security · Distributed storage · Data encryption

1 Introduction

Data storage management, commonly known as mass storage management, is one of the most important aspects of database management technology. It is related to users' information security, access security and data availability. Large-scale database technology has the following advantages in data storage. First of all, it can realize the classification, retrieval and backup of a large amount of complex and massive information, effectively improve the efficiency of data storage management, reduce the information loss caused by human errors, and thus reduce the risks that enterprises need to bear in daily business [1]. Secondly, by classifying and searching massive databases, users can achieve secure access to data, which can effectively prevent malicious access and improve the efficiency of data storage management. Finally, large-scale database technology can provide a powerful, complete and reliable protection mechanism to avoid some unnecessary losses or information leakage caused by hacker attacks. Distributed data security storage

© The Author(s), under exclusive license to Springer Nature Singapore Pte Ltd. 2023
Y. Tian et al. (Eds.): ICBDS 2022, CCIS 1796, pp. 586–596, 2023.
https://doi.org/10.1007/978-981-99-3300-6_42

is an effective way to store a large amount of data, which can improve the operation, maintenance efficiency and security of network systems. It is easier for enterprises to maintain data security in their daily business [2, 3].

Data security storage based on distributed database occupies an important position in the era of big data. The research and application of data security storage technology is of great significance to improve the application of large databases in the field of social life. Large capacity storage and high-speed computing speed make cloud storage become the mainstream, and data security encryption technology based on distributed storage mode has become a research hotspot. Data security storage is that in a large capacity computing environment, users manage a large amount of information through certain means and convert it into available resources. It can improve the operation efficiency of the database system, reduce the risk caused by network load, and ensure the information security of users [4]. The data security storage technology based on distributed database has the characteristics of high efficiency, real-time and flexibility, which provides a reliable guarantee for data security and provides a technical basis for data security storage [5]. At the same time, it also helps to achieve the security control measures and privacy protection objectives in the data storage platform, and can also ensure the implementation, maintenance and use of database application software. The research of data security storage technology is of great significance to improve the operation efficiency of database system and provide important guarantee for user information management [6].

2 Data Security Storage Model

Data security storage technology is a computer-based database system. Its main goal is to ensure the storage security of various types of files, graphic documents, etc. The data storage structure is shown in Fig. 1, where the logical data storage structure may include table space, part, area and data block while the physical data storage may include files and block. The data security storage method based on distribution is very different from the traditional database storage method. Its storage method is to store the data in the form of cipher-text on the database server by encrypting the data, so as to ensure that users can safely access and query the content they want to access anytime and anywhere [7]. Distributed file system has strong and stable access performance and scalability, so that the data storage of distributed database system could have good security capability. However, since the distributed file system is formed by the characteristics of server centered, user oriented and application environment, the security of data storage also faces some security risks, and the data encryption and access control of distributed database are necessary. The common encryption algorithms can be divided into three categories: symmetric encryption algorithm, asymmetric encryption algorithm and hash algorithm.

Symmetric encryption algorithm is a method to maintain data confidentiality whose principle is shown in Fig. 2. As shown in Fig. 2, in the process of a traditional symmetric algorithm 3DES (Triple Data Encryption Algorithm), the DES are executed three times and the keys are identical in each encryption-decryption procedure. The selection of keys including K1, K2 and K3 will decide the security of the algorithm. The longer

Logical and Physical Database Structure

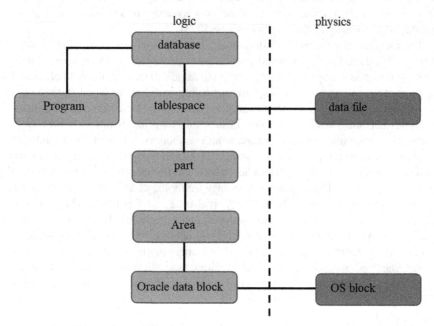

Fig. 1. Data storage structure

the symmetric encryption key, the more secure the encryption. However, there are some drawbacks of this technique. The key must be transmitted in a secure way to ensure that it cannot be obtained by any unauthorized person. If the key is leaked, the encrypted data will be threatened. If anyone finds the key and knows the symmetric encryption algorithm, all data encrypted with this key can be stolen. Hence, the symmetric encryption algorithm should be sufficient to resist the decoding of known plaintext types, which means even if the decipherer has some cipher-text and plaintext that generates the cipher-text, he cannot translate the cipher-text or crack the key [8–10].

Symmetric encryption algorithm usually adopts the method of block encryption, that is, the plaintext is divided into several groups, and then encrypted through the key and algorithm. The inputs of symmetric encryption algorithm include the plaintext that may be divided into fixed-length blocks and the key that should be stored in a secure place. The process of a typical symmetric encryption algorithm is shown in Fig. 3. It can be seen that the plaintext is divided into 64-bit blocks and each block is processed with the encryption key for 16 rounds to produce a 64-bit cipher-text.

In order to improve the security and reduce the data leakage risks, a cipher-text storage algorithm based on distributed database is designed, the main idea of which is to divide the security levels to be achieved in the encryption and decryption process into different levels. The encryption process is to encrypt the plaintext information through the data encryption algorithm to obtain the cipher-text, and then sparse the relevant attributes of the plaintext, and store the cipher-text data in the corresponding file according to different attribute levels. This method may reduce the number of interactions between

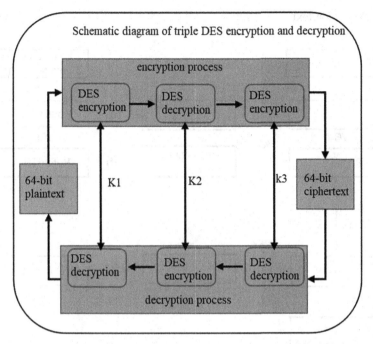

Fig. 2. Principle of symmetric encryption algorithm

the storage server side and the database client and reduce the security threats caused by network attacks [11]. The process is shown in Eqs. (1) and (2), where P denotes the plaintext, C denotes the cipher-text, K1, K2 and K3 represent the keys for encryption and decryption, $D_{K1}(\bullet)$ denotes the decryption function using K1, $E_{K3}(\bullet)$ denotes the encryption function using K3.

$$P = D_{K1}(E_{K2}(D_{K3}(C))) \tag{1}$$

$$C = E_{K3}(D_{K2}(E_{K1}(P))) \tag{2}$$

Asymmetric encryption algorithm refers to the algorithm that converts information into cipher-text to store information through cipher-text conversion rather than plaintext encryption in the transmission process. This method has good confidentiality, which can improve the security in the process of data transmission, reduce the loss caused by information leakage, and reduce the operating cost of the system. The principle of asymmetric encryption algorithm is shown in Fig. 4. It can be seen that the client and server hold their keys of "13" and "15" respectively. The real information of "10" will not be known even if the public data of "6" and "12" transmitted in the network are intercepted by a third party. And the real information can be restored at both sides by using their keys. However, there are still some shortcomings in the practical application. For example, data security storage technology requires the encryption of a large number of confidential files and sensitive content, and the encryption and decryption efficiency of asymmetric encryption algorithm is facing great performance challenges. In addition, for the security

64-bit plaintext

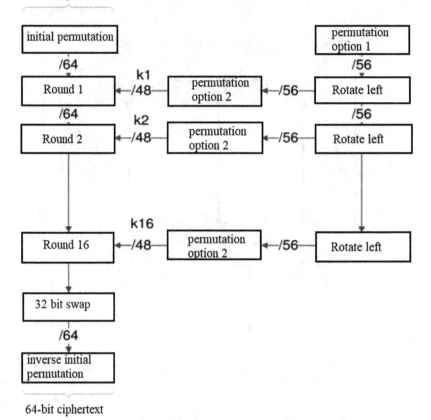

Fig. 3. Process of a typical symmetric encryption algorithm

management of sensitive information stored in data warehouse, distributed database technology needs to be used. However, due to the different characteristics of distributed database, heterogeneous distributed databases limits their efficient applications [12].

RSA (Rivest, Shamirh, Adleman) encryption algorithm is a typical asymmetric encryption algorithm that is based on hash method. Its basic idea is to use the key pair of public key and private key to encrypt and decrypt the data. The data encrypted with public key can only be decrypted with the corresponding private key. Similarly, the data encrypted with private key can only be decrypted with the corresponding public key. The model takes RSA as the basic theory, adopts the distributed storage method, realizes the information security leakage in the process of ciphertext conversion through mathematical modeling and analysis, and realizes the encryption and decryption of data at the same time [13]. The encryption and decryption in the data transmission process between A and B are shown in Fig. 5 and Fig. 6.

It can be seen from Fig. 5 that A encrypts the data with its private key and sends the encrypted data to B. B then decrypts the data with the public key of A so as to confirm

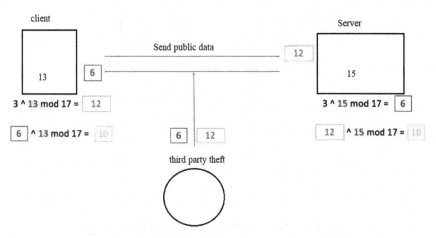

Fig. 4. Principle of asymmetric encryption algorithm

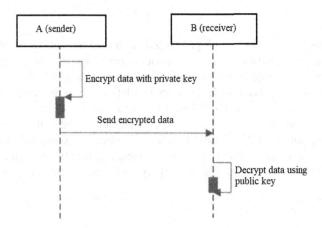

Fig. 5. A sends encrypted data to B for authentication

that the message is sent by A. The asymmetric encryption algorithm used in Fig. 5 is to authenticate the message sender since only the public key of A can be used to decrypt the data successfully.

It can be seen from Fig. 6 that B encrypts the data with the public key of A and sends the encrypted data to A. A decrypts the data with its private key to obtain the original data. The asymmetric encryption algorithm used in Fig. 6 is to protect the confidentiality of the data since only the private key of A can be used to decrypt the data while only A holds it private key.

In the RSA encryption algorithm, the ciphertext can be processed without entering the password when the data is encrypted on the computer. The encryption formula is shown in Eq. (3) and the decryption formula is shown in Eq. (4), where C denotes the cipher-text, P denotes the plaintext, (b, N) and (d, N) are public key and private key.

$$C = P^b \bmod N \tag{3}$$

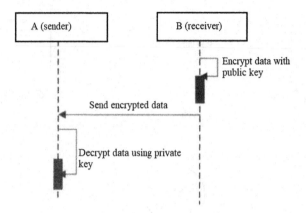

Fig. 6. B sends encrypted data to A for confidentiality

$$P = C^d \bmod N \tag{4}$$

Hash algorithm (as shown in Fig. 7) is a data storage method based on probability and mathematical statistics, which can provide a mapping of some complex, random information to other objects through its intrinsic connection, and decide the type and security level of data according to the mapping relationship. If the result of the original data is to be stored in the database, then the data security storage can be based on probability and mathematical statistics. First, determine whether the keyword has the corresponding function relationship formula, then select its corresponding output value and storage location according to the known rules, and finally determine the security level of the input data, so as to achieve the purpose of safe storage of database data.

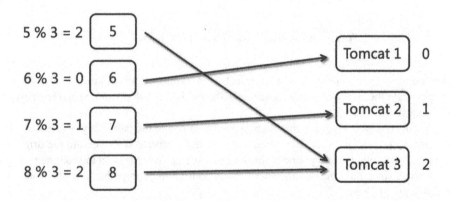

hash(ip) % node_counts = index

Fig. 7. Hashing algorithm

Hash algorithm maps input data of any length into a fixed-length hash code through a hash function. The core idea is to concentrate all the values of the data set into the same function. In this way, any set can have the same or similar degree, thereby improving the efficiency of the algorithm. The space of hash code is much smaller than that of the original data, so it can reduce the storage space constraints and improve the performance of the algorithm. However, when the amount of data is too large, it will lead to problems such as slow calculation speed and insufficient memory. If it is too small, it may not be possible to implement functional modules that have high requirements on storage space and protection capabilities in the process of fast and accurate search. Therefore, this paper takes distributed database as the research object, analyzes its data security storage process, and designs and implements data protection based on distribution [14]. Commonly used hashing algorithms include: Spectral Hashing (SH), Iterative Quantized Hashing (ITQ), Kernel-based Supervised Hashing (KSH), Fast Supervised Hashing (FastH), Convolutional Neural Network Hashing (CNNH), Deep Regular Similarity Hashing (DRSCH), etc.

3   Data Security Storage System Based on Distributed Storage

The data transmission framework is composed of the bottom layer and the supporting layer. It connects the middle and lower layer users through the network to realize the storage of massive and high-capacity formats. The database stores various file types and their corresponding access control rule information, which is stored in a fixed form on the distributed server, and can be encrypted or provided with security services by using protocols as needed in the application environment. The data transmission framework is composed of a client/server and a support layer that physically connects the underlying network to the users. The functional composition of the data security storage system is shown in Fig. 8.

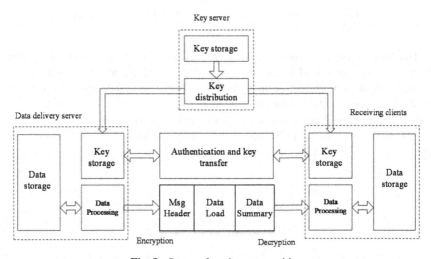

Fig. 8. System function composition

The proposed system comprises a key server, a data delivery server and several receiving clients. The key server is responsible for key storage and distribution to data server and clients. The data is distributed stored in the data server and clients. The framework of data transmission of distributed data storage is shown in Fig. 9.

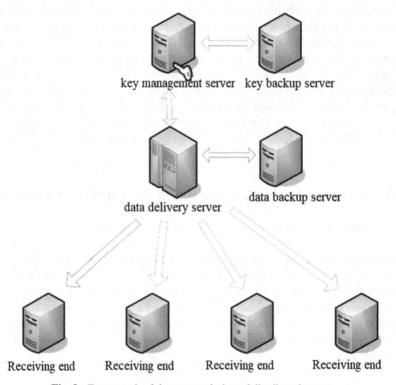

key management server   key backup server

data backup server

data delivery server

Receiving end   Receiving end   Receiving end   Receiving end

Fig. 9. Framework of data transmission of distributed storage

The design of secure data storage aims to solve the problems existing in distributed databases, which may lead to important information leakage and improper access. A security analysis is proposed for the important information in the secure storage of data based on the distributed database structure model and SQL statement engine technology implementation. The demonstrative design of database tables of the system is shown in Fig. 10, where the tables can be designed for files, file logs, domains, servers, public keys, private keys and master key, etc.

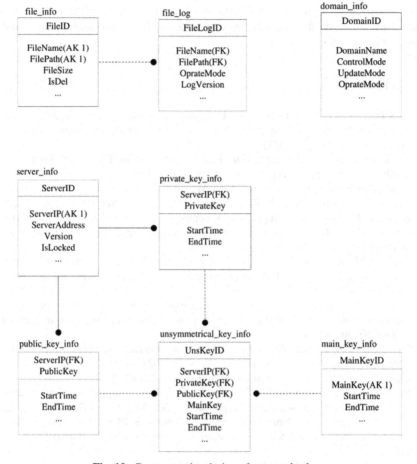

Fig. 10. Demonstrative design of system database

4 Conclusion

Data security storage is a new way of database information management. It is a comprehensive upgrade of traditional database technology. It realizes the three-tier architecture of data storage to improve its operation efficiency, and has become the mainstream of today's industry. However, with the continuous development of the network application environment and the renewal of computer systems, the data security storage technology faces great challenges. Traditional databases have the problems such as slow server-side operation, low security, slow data update, frequent SQL injection, and easy to be illegally modified or deleted. In the era of cloud computing, a method of data security storage and management based on distributed platform is proposed, which realizes the distributed database structure design and access control, improves the efficiency of server operation, and reduces the network risk. Through the studies on the principle of data security storage, based on the characteristics of distributed database structure, a set of stable, reliable, versatile and complete protection scheme suitable for various application scenarios is established. However, the performance optimization of the proposed system could be examined in the future research.

References

1. Al-Sakran, A., Qattous, H., Hijjawi, M.: A proposed performance evaluation of NoSQL databases in the field of IoT. In: 2018 8th International Conference on Computer Science and Information Technology (CSIT), pp. 32–37 (2018)
2. Xu, J., et al.: Healthchain: a blockchain-based privacy preserving scheme for large-scale health data. IEEE Internet Things J. 6(5), 8770–8781 (2019)
3. Ovando-Leon, G., Veas-Castillo, L., Marin, M., Gil-Costa, V.: A simulation tool for a large-scale NoSQL database. In: 2019 Spring Simulation Conference (SpringSim), pp. 1–12 (2019)
4. Zhang, J.: Research on the application of computer big data technology in cloud storage security. In: 2021 IEEE International Conference on Data Science and Computer Application (ICDSCA), pp. 405–409 (2021)
5. Shuvo, A.M., Amin, M.S., Haque, P.: Storage efficient data security model for distributed cloud storage. In: 2020 IEEE 8th R10 Humanitarian Technology Conference (R10-HTC), pp. 1–6 (2020)
6. Syed, A., Purushotham, K., Shidaganti, G.: Cloud storage security risks, practices and measures: a review. In: 2020 IEEE International Conference for Innovation in Technology (INOCON), pp. 1–4 (2020)
7. Zhang, X., Yu, Z., Chen, J., Zhu, G., Wang, J., Feng, H.: Research on secure storage of network information resources based on data sensitivity. In: 2021 6th International Conference on Smart Grid and Electrical Automation (ICSGEA), pp. 422–426 (2021)
8. Halak, B., Yilmaz, Y., Shiu, D.: Comparative analysis of energy costs of asymmetric vs symmetric encryption-based security applications. IEEE Access 10, 76707–76719 (2022)
9. Spasova, G., Karova, M.: A new secure image encryption model based on symmetric key. In: 2021 International Conference on Biomedical Innovations and Applications (BIA), pp. 107–110 (2022)
10. Cho, H.-H., Tsai, M.-Y., Tseng, F.-H., Wu, H.-T., Chen, C.-Y.: Improving randomness of symmetric encryption for consumer privacy using metaheuristic-based framework. IEEE Consum. Electron. Mag. 11(1), 42–49 (2022)
11. Niu, S., Chen, L., Liu, W.: Attribute-based keyword search encryption scheme with verifiable ciphertext via blockchains. In: 2020 IEEE 9th Joint International Information Technology and Artificial Intelligence Conference (ITAIC), pp. 849–853 (2020)
12. Xu, H., Chen, G., Zhang, C., Zhou, J., Wei, H., Gao, X.: Key technologies of distributed transactional database storage engine. In: 2020 IEEE International Conference on Industrial Application of Artificial Intelligence (IAAI), pp. 106–112 (2020)
13. Radhakrishnan, S., Akila, A.: Securing distributed database using elongated RSA algorithm. In: 2021 7th International Conference on Advanced Computing and Communication Systems (ICACCS), pp. 1931–1936 (2021)
14. Dattana, V., Gupta, K., Kush, A.: A probability based model for big data security in smart city. In: 2019 4th MEC International Conference on Big Data and Smart City (ICBDSC), pp. 1–6 (2019)

Design of an Active Data Watermark Detection System

Lan Zhang[✉], Xiangyang Zhang, and Tiejun Yang

State Grid Henan Marketing Service Centre, Zhengzhou 450000, China
zhanglan@163.com

Abstract. Nowadays, with the rapid development of network technology and the rapid increase of information, the importance of data is becoming more and more obvious, and the requirements of data security are also improving. Using the detection and tracking technology based on data watermarking can quickly and effectively obtain the information of data watermarking, and trace the source of possible attacks, so as to improve the security of data. The traditional passive data watermarking detection and tracking technology has some limitations in the real-time tracking of possible attacks. Therefore, this paper proposed an active data watermark detection system. The related watermark embedding and detection technologies are firstly studied. The system architecture is proposed where primary modules and submodules are described. The proposed system is designed to be integrated into the network nodes and servers in order to embed and detect the watermark information in real time. In addition, the watermarking parameters can be adjusted according to the sensed network environment. The proposed system can be implemented in the industrial departments that own a large amount of sensitive data so that the data transmission can be monitored and traced.

Keywords: Data watermarking · Watermark detection · Data security

1 Introduction

Nowadays, information security has become an increasingly important issue, and data has gradually received attention. In order to protect data security, digital watermarking technology has been used to protect data. Digital watermarking technology is a method based on embedded database retrieval, which has good robustness, reliability and scalability, and can extract and track data information at anytime and anywhere. It also has features such as real-time detection of watermark and timely update of data, which can effectively protect data and improve the security of watermark information [1]. Therefore, it is widely used in the fields of digital image processing, multimedia retrieval and visual analysis technology. With the continuous progress of technology and the increasing development of network communication, various data encryption algorithms have emerged, such as digital signature method, which can effectively solve the security problem of watermark information, so that the data can be found in time after being illegally tampered, so as to protect information security from infringement [2, 3].

This paper mainly studies a data watermarking algorithm based on active sniffing to realize watermark detection. Combined with the method based on motion experience and classical algorithm, the implementation method of watermark tracking is designed according to the system requirements [4].

The active watermark tracking method is to extract the concerned part of the data from the original data, and then extract this part of the data to find some rules in the watermark data, so as to ensure the continuity of the original data. It means that to find the location of the watermark and the change rules in the original data, so as to find the change rules in time in the watermark data tracking. Active sniffing is a new watermark tracking technology which is called "active watermarking". It is a time-domain analysis method based on the observation of features in the original data to obtain information before finding the data source and extracting the data set. Passive sniffing is to detect the surface information of the target object or detect itself, and then extract the acquired data information to obtain the attributes of the target object [5]. In practical applications, a combination of image processing and digital signal analysis can be used to determine whether there are active tracking aliases and whether there are potential intrusion objects, so that the target object can be monitored to ensure the accuracy in watermark information extraction [6]. Stealth attack detection can also be used, that is, to find and track the watermark traces hidden in the target object itself, so as to ensure the authenticity and accuracy of the data, which can also provide some technical support for the extraction of watermark information [7].

2 Data Watermark Detection Technology

Data watermark tracing mainly uses advanced embedded technology and data processing technology to acquire and extract the original data information and analyze the historical sequence. Data watermarking technology is a kind of embedded watermarking algorithm with digital image as the carrier. The framework of data watermarking technology is shown in Fig. 1. It can be seen that the features are embedded in the data that are monitored during the process of data transmission and usage. The data features are extracted and compared to the original data features to detect the violations of data usage rules. This method requires a series of preprocessing operations on the data to obtain the image of the data object to be tracked, so this method needs a certain degree of robustness and can meet the accuracy requirements in practical applications [8]. Commonly used data watermarking techniques are time-based data watermarking technique, stream time-slot segmentation feature-based data watermarking technique, and stream rate-based data watermarking technique.

Time-based data watermarking technology that is a basic technology in the data watermark tracking system uses the change of time to determine the watermark information, where data can effectively use various resources in the process of continuous transformation and update. The framework of time-based data watermarking technology is shown in Fig. 2. It can be seen that the framework comprises system performance module, prediction model training module, data feature extraction module, time series forecasting module and watermark distribution module. The data features are extracted from the original data source according to the trained rules and are transmitted to the time

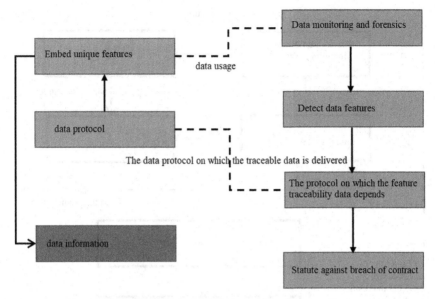

Fig. 1. Data watermarking technology framework

series forecasting module. Based on the time series forecasting results, the watermarks are generated and distributed. In addition, the performance of the system is continuously monitored so that the data feature training could be adapted.

Dynamic image processing with high real-time requirements requires fast, accurate and complete extraction of relevant information to obtain watermark related information. For those different time and different levels of information, the watermark tracing system is required to carry out corresponding retrieval, analysis and other processing [9]. In the data watermarking method based on the time characteristics of the data stream, the data acquisition is based on network information, and the watermark tracking depends on image processing and retrieval technology. The watermark information can be embedded by adding a certain degree of delay to the selected target data stream. A simple delayed watermark embedding scheme can be represented by Eq. (1), where $\tau_{i,j}^b$ represents the watermark embedded data, $\Delta_{i,j}$ denotes the time delay that depends on b that denotes watermark information bit, $\vec{x}$ that denotes deterministic parameter and $\vec{r}$ that denotes the probability parameter.

$$\tau_{i,j}^b = \tau_{i,j} + \Delta_{i,j}(b, \vec{x}, \vec{r}) \tag{1}$$

The IPD (Inter-Packets Delays)-based data watermarking algorithm uses the embedded data structure to find the source of the imprint in the network and embed it into the original data that is stored in historical database. The process of watermark embedding is shown in Fig. 3. Equations (2) is used to complete the embedding of watermark information, where ipd denotes the inter-packet delay, w denotes the watermark information and s denotes the quantization step size. Equation (3) is used at the watermark detection end

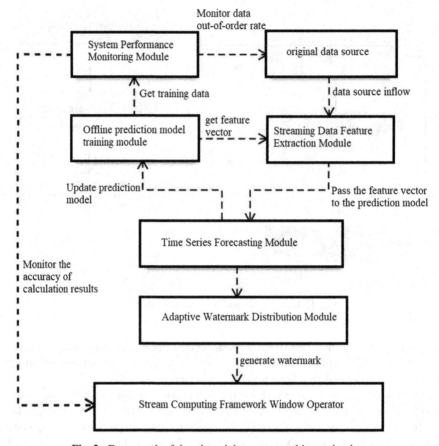

Fig. 2. Framework of time-based data watermarking technology

to extract the watermark information $DE(ipd^w, s)$ to be compared and analyzed. Finally, a complete network data is obtained so as to achieve embedding into the database.

$$ipd^w = EM(ipd, w, s) = [round(ipd + \frac{s}{2}, s) + \Delta] \cdot s \qquad (2)$$

$$where, \ \Delta = (w_i - (round(ipd + \frac{s}{2}, s) \bmod 2) + 2) \bmod 2$$

$$DE(ipd^w, s) = round(ipd^w, s) \bmod 2 \qquad (3)$$

RAINBOW (Robust And Invisible Non-Blind Watermark)-based data watermarking strategy is an embedded dynamic interactive closed mode and self-checking technology based on data watermarking. It can extract the original data information based on the real-time analysis and decision [10]. The watermark embedding and extraction process based on RAINBOW is shown in Fig. 4, where the IPDs are calculated, stored in the IPD database and used for embedded watermark information.

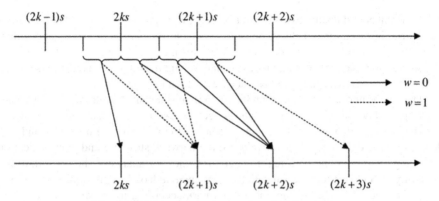

Fig. 3. IPD-based data watermark embedding process

The mean balance approach can be used to watermark data for traceability. The implementation of mean balanced watermark tracking technology not only realizes the data extraction in the case of network quality changes, but also analyzes the information such as the trajectory and time of the data watermark, so as to provide real-time data watermark tracking and network quality change prediction.

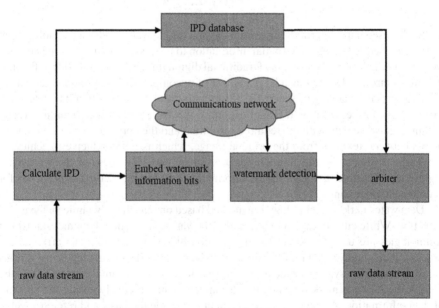

Fig. 4. RAINBOW-based watermark embedding and extraction process

The extraction of data watermarking requires geometric transformation of the original carrier to obtain the newly extracted information. While the stream time-slot segmentation feature-based technology can achieve this function, data watermark tracking is based on embedded feature extraction technology, which uses sensors to obtain the original carrier information to achieve detection and control analysis of the target position, size and other important attributes in the data. This method can well solve the problem that the original data processing process cannot obtain the effective data volume, and it can effectively improve the speed and accuracy of data analysis [11].

The data watermarking algorithm based on time slot center is a dynamic watermark tracking method based on data set, and its center $Cent(I_i)$ is calculated as shown in Eq. (6), where I_i denotes the time slot, n_i denotes the number of time delays and Δt_{ij} denotes a time delay. It can effectively use the network structure and communication technology and combine with real-time control rules for analysis. The algorithm first randomly selects the time interval with the segment length of T as the similarity measure of the data, decides whether there is a watermark according to the similarity between the feature points, and then infers the information of the tracked object by using the similarity function. At this time, the watermark information bits can be embedded by changing the number of packets in the adjacent time slot pairs I_i and I_{i+1}, as shown in Fig. 5. The length of the embedded time slot is determined by the information bits of the data set, and the tracked object will change its position within a certain range after embedding.

$$Cent(I_i) = \frac{1}{n_i} \sum_{j=0}^{n_i-1} \Delta t_{ij} \tag{4}$$

Scale based data watermarking technology is a digital watermarking technology that uses the embedded large-scale spatial information to process, extract, analyze and track the watermark data. In the process of traditional digital image processing, due to the limitations of threshold selection, a large number of uncompressible regions are generated, which affects the tracking of watermark information, and makes it difficult to detect and extract in the process of practical application. At the same time, it is difficult to directly obtain large-scale data with the required resolution and the correlation between feature points between textures from the original image, which is not conducive to achieving the goals of improving the computational accuracy and robustness of the watermark algorithm. Therefore, the scale-based information embedding method is proposed for deep image processing.

Data watermarking technology is a method based on real-time dynamic analysis and detection. While embedding the watermark data, various real-time dynamic acquisition technologies are used to extract the information hidden in the original carrier in the process. It can analyze data information after the watermark is extracted using various algorithms, and the system can determine the existence of the original carrier [12]. In the field of digital watermark tracking, this technology can effectively ensure the security of data information. At the same time, it can also provide the basis and reference value for the verification of the subsequent simulation, thus providing technical support for the tracking of data watermark. The architecture of watermark embedding and detection module is shown in Fig. 6. In the specific watermarking process, the original signal is preprocessed to reduce the impact of noise. Filtering methods are usually used to eliminate low-frequency drift and other problems, and effective information is extracted. Then the watermarking algorithm based on multi-granularity distance transform model

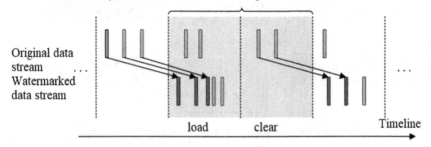

Watermark embedded information bit '0'

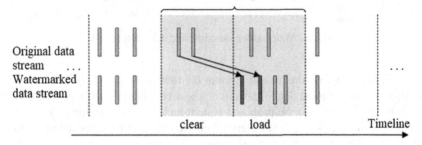

Watermark embedded information bit '1'

Fig. 5. Embedding of watermark information bitmap

is used for experimental verification and analysis. Secondly, it is necessary to convert the digital quantization format obtained by sampling into a standard sinusoidal component as the output value using the multiscale transform, and establish a certain quantity ratio relationship (i.e., mapping function) with the original signal, so as to obtain the useful parameters contained in the watermarked data. The method introduces the direct-sequence spreading mechanism used in wireless communication systems into the network watermarking method. By preprocessing the data watermark and simulating it in the network, it can effectively ensure the authenticity and reliability of the parameters contained in the original signal.

3   Active Data Watermark Detection System

Data watermarking is based on data processing methods to extract information from the original carrier (such as paper, film, table) and then analyze it to extract the required data and perform the corresponding operations, so as to achieve the purpose of protecting data information. With the increasing availability of resources, data watermarking

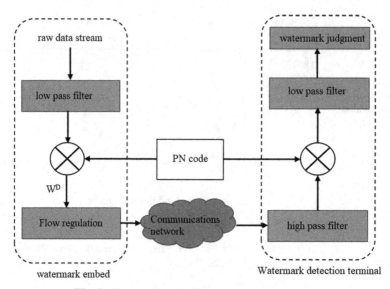

raw data stream

low pass filter

W^D

Flow regulation

PN code

Communications network

watermark embed

watermark judgment

low pass filter

high pass filter

Watermark detection terminal

Fig. 6. Watermark embedding and detection module

technology is being used more and more in the field of digital image processing, and it is also receiving a great deal of attention. The architecture of the system is shown in Fig. 7. It can be seen that the proposed system includes three primary models, which are active sniffing module, data watermarking module that is composed of watermark embedding submodule, watermark detection submodule and adaptive service submodule, and auxiliary traceability module that comprises packet mark tracing submodule and stream abstract tracing submodule.

The active sniffing module uses the traffic analysis technology to detect the springboard node in the network, and analyzes the delay of the springboard node to the data flow and the delay between traffic packets. The data watermarking module is used to generate and detect data watermarks based on IPD method mention in the Sect. 2. The auxiliary tracing module is used to assist the data watermarking module for data tracing.

The data watermark embedding submodule is deployed on the routing node, which is called the watermark embedding node, and its watermark embedding module framework is shown in Fig. 8. The data watermark submodule is deployed in the FORWARD component to intercept the data packets that are not to be transmitted to the local host. The NFQUEUE component is used to put intercepted data packets in a queue, waiting for the data watermarking process.

The watermark detection submodule is also deployed on the routing node, and its main function is to perform feature analysis on the data, so that it can get the source location and the target object being attacked that it wants to track out. The watermark detection node mainly uses the tcpdump tool to capture packets and store them in the local tcp.cap file, whose tcp.cap file structure is shown in Fig. 9.

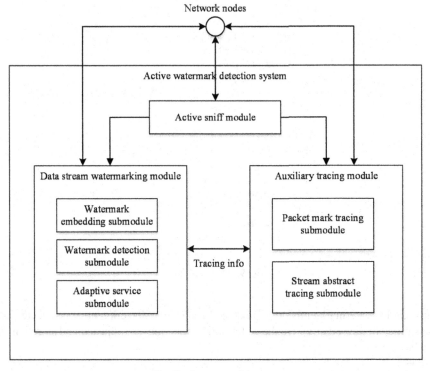

Fig. 7. System architecture

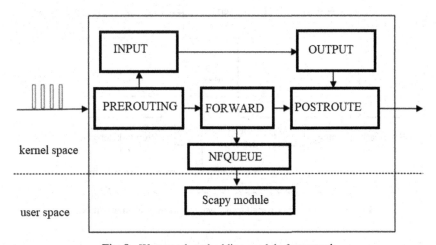

Fig. 8. Watermark embedding module framework

The adaptive parameter sub-module is used to adjust the watermark parameters according to the sensed network environment. The framework of the adaptive watermarking parameter module is shown in Fig. 10. It can be seen that the time delay

```
struct pcap_file_header {
bpf_u_int32 magic;
u_short version_major;
u_short version_minor;
bpf_int32 thiszone;
bpf_u_int32 sigfigs;
bpf_u_int32 snaplen;
bpf_u_int32 linktype;
};
struct pcap_pkthdr{
struct timeval ts;bpf_u_int32 caplen;
bpf_u_int32 len;
};
struct EthernetPacket{
char MacDst[6];
char MacSrc[6];
unsigned short PacketType;
};
```

Fig. 9. Data structure

between the watermark embedding node and watermark detection node is detected and transmitted to the server where the watermark parameters are adjusted and stored in the database.

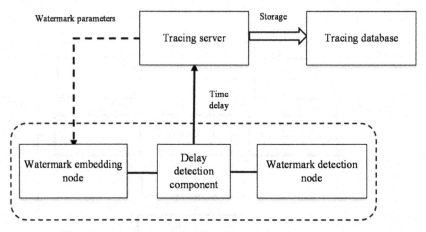

Fig. 10. Framework for adaptive watermarking parameter module

In the auxiliary tracing module, the packet tracing submodule is used to insert marks to the data packets so as to find out the source of the attacker while an attack is detected in a network host. In addition, the stream abstract tracing submodule is used to record the abstract information of the transmitting data packets in order to find out the source of the attacker.

4 Conclusion

In a word, watermark is an important digital information carrier, which plays a very important role in data security. Therefore, the detection and tracking of digital watermark plays a very important role in data security. With the continuous development of embedded technology, network communication and multimedia processing applications, data watermarking technology is also developing. Meanwhile, how to quickly and effectively detect and trace the source of extracted digital information in the network environment has been attracting attentions from researchers. In the networked system, the study of data quality has become an important issue in its development process. In order to ensure the normal operation of the system with high reliability and security, a complete and effective detection and tracing method is needed to achieve this goal. In this paper, the data watermark detection related technologies are studied, especially in the IPD-based data watermarking field. A data watermark detection system is proposed that makes use of studied technologies. The implementation and the performance analysis can be further studied in the future research.

References

1. Ding, W., Ming, Y., Cao, Z., Lin, C.-T.: A generalized deep neural network approach for digital watermarking analysis. IEEE Trans. Emerg. Top. Comput. Intell. **6**(3), 613–627 (2022)
2. Shankar, A., Kannammal, A.: A hybrid of watermark scheme with encryption to improve security of medical images. In: 2021 Third International Conference on Intelligent Communication Technologies and Virtual Mobile Networks (ICICV), pp. 226–233 (2021)
3. Chen, W., Zeng, B., Zheng, P.: A robust watermarking scheme for encrypted JPEG bitstreams with format-compliant encryption. In: 2019 18th IEEE International Conference on Trust, Security And Privacy In Computing And Communications/13th IEEE International Conference On Big Data Science And Engineering (TrustCom/BigDataSE), pp. 397–403 (2019)
4. Shen, X., Zhang, Y., Wang, T., Sun, Y.: Relational database watermarking for data tracing. In: 2020 International Conference on Cyber-Enabled Distributed Computing and Knowledge Discovery (CyberC), pp. 224–231 (2020)
5. Gavilanes, G.B.: Persons counter through Wi-Fi's passive sniffing for IoT. In: 2018 IEEE Third Ecuador Technical Chapters Meeting (ETCM), pp. 1–6 (2018)
6. Kim, W., Lee, K.: Digital watermarking for protecting audio classification datasets. In: ICASSP 2020 - 2020 IEEE International Conference on Acoustics, Speech and Signal Processing (ICASSP), pp. 2842–2846 (2020)
7. Kim, J., Ko, W.-H., Kumar, P.R.: Cyber-security through dynamic watermarking for 2-rotor aerial vehicle flight control systems. In: 2021 International Conference on Unmanned Aircraft Systems (ICUAS), pp. 1277–1283 (2021)
8. Ma, Z., Zhang, W., Fang, H., Dong, X., Geng, L., Yu, N.: Local geometric distortions resilient watermarking scheme based on symmetry. IEEE Trans. Circuits Syst. Video Technol. **31**(12), 4826–4839 (2021)
9. Haddad, S., Coatrieux, G., Moreau-Gaudry, A., Cozic, M.: Joint watermarking-encryption-JPEG-LS for medical image reliability control in encrypted and compressed domains. IEEE Trans. Inf. Forensics Secur. **15**, 2556–2569 (2020)
10. Houmansadr, A., Kiyavash, N., Borisov, N.: Non-blind watermarking of network flows. IEEE/ACM Trans. Netw. **22**(4), 1232–1244 (2014)

11. Azizian, B., Ghaemmaghami, S.: Tampering detection and restoration of compressed video. In: 2018 15th International ISC (Iranian Society of Cryptology) Conference on Information Security and Cryptology (ISCISC), pp. 1–5 (2018)
12. Rakhmawati, L., Wirawan, Suwadi: Image fragile watermarking with two authentication components for tamper detection and recovery. In: 2018 International Conference on Intelligent Autonomous Systems (ICoIAS), pp. 35–38 (2018)

Research on Privacy Protection Methods for Data Mining

Jindong He[1(✉)], Rongyan Cai[2], Shanshan Lei[1], and Dan Wu[1]

[1] State Grid Fujian Electric Power Research Institute, Fuzhou 350007, China
dky.he_jindong@fj.sgcc.com.cn
[2] State Grid Fujian Electric Power Co., Ltd., 350001 Fuzhou, China

Abstract. With the applications of big data and cloud computing technologies in industries, data mining technologies have been developing rapidly in these years. However, privacy issues have been attracting attentions for users and researchers since the laws and regulations of protecting personal information are issued. How to appropriately apply data mining technologies while meeting the privacy protection requirements become an important problem to address. In this paper, the privacy preserving data mining technologies are studied including K-means, Support Vector Machine, decision tree and association rule mining. In addition to their principles, the corresponding privacy protection methods for them are discussed. Furthermore, the commonly used privacy protection methods are studied including restricted release, searchable symmetric encryption, homomorphic encryption and digital envelope. Finally, the suggestions are given that the data processing algorithms need to be improved to obtain the better balance between data mining efficiency and privacy protection, and the system could be designed to provide privacy protection measures to meet personalized demands. The studies in this paper are expected to provide technical ideas to various service providers such as personal recommendation to implement privacy protection strategies.

Keywords: Privacy protection · Data mining · Privacy preserving methods

1 Introduction

In the age of big data, distributed data mining technology has attracted the attention of researchers in various fields. It is based on the analysis and processing of a large number of user behavior records and social relationship records in the database, extracts the data of user interaction, and stores data in the database in the form of rules, so as to realize the analysis and prediction of user behavior [1]. With the continuous development of computer technology and network communication industry as well as the increasingly extensive application of Internet, distributed data mining technology has been widely used in various fields [2]. However, in the Internet environment, data mining technology also faces problems such as information security and privacy leakage. Therefore, how to extract valuable and useful resources and services by analyzing user behavior features in distributed data while protecting the privacy is an urgent problem nowadays. This motivates us to study and analyze the user centric distributed data mining technology and its privacy protection methods [3, 4].

© The Author(s), under exclusive license to Springer Nature Singapore Pte Ltd. 2023
Y. Tian et al. (Eds.): ICBDS 2022, CCIS 1796, pp. 609–620, 2023.
https://doi.org/10.1007/978-981-99-3300-6_44

In distributed databases, data are stored in various ways, but from the user's point of view, some information is ignored, such as the privacy of the data itself, processing and analysis of sensitive events [5]. Therefore, the privacy protection of data is very important. In the distributed database, how to improve the security of user information and prevent the leakage and abuse of personal information also needs to be discussed. Since the traditional mining methods have different technical situations, different protection strategies can be adopted to achieve privacy security protection [6]. Among them, encryption technology can be used to protect the user's privacy information to prevent the user's personal information from being illegally stolen. How to improve the privacy security coefficient in the distributed database is a problem that needs to be focused on. From the research point of view, the security and confidentiality of data is put in a prominent position. In distributed databases, the security of data mainly refers to user information, personal privacy and other important contents [7]. The study of privacy protection in distributed databases mainly focuses on data security and confidentiality by analyzing the information security issues between different users and the various situations that may occur during the use of data. The study of data security and privacy protection raises the importance of information security issues and achieves the coordination between user privacy, personal information management, and other interests [8].

2 Privacy Preserving Data Mining Methods

Data mining algorithm is an algorithm that extracts potentially valuable information from massive databases, converts it into useful, available, effective and feasible rules, and then stores them in the database. Data privacy protection is an innovation of the traditional privacy management mode. Users cannot directly access the data they need. They can only apply for data requirements and the system will return the processed data to them. In the Internet era, users can use the network for various social activities, such as blog and online chat software. Therefore, personal privacy data involves a large amount of data and interactive information generated by data mining technology and distributed algorithms based on large sample statistical analysis [9]. With the continuous development of network technology and the expansion of computer applications, as well as the increasing number of intelligent terminals, there are more and more ways to obtain information from these massive data. Current data mining methods with privacy protection include clustering algorithms, classification algorithms, decision tree algorithms, and association rule mining algorithms.

2.1 Privacy Preserving K-Means Algorithm

Clustering algorithm is an effective data mining method which has an important role in solving massive and complex information sets. Currently, the main clustering technique commonly used in distributed databases is the K-means algorithm that uses the combination of nearest neighbor method and distance metric to deal with the original data set, and its algorithm complexity is low [10]. However, since there is a large amount of noise in the K-means method, it is easy to fall into local optimum when processing data, and the K-means algorithm is implemented as shown in Fig. 1.

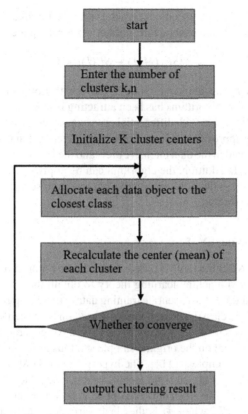

Fig. 1. K-means algorithm implementation

1. Given n data samples, set $I = 1$, randomly select K initial clustering centers $Z_j(I), j = 1, 2, 3...K$.
2. Solve the distance between each data sample x_i and the initial clustering center as shown in Eq. (1), and allocate x_i to its nearest clustering center as shown in Eq. (2).

$$D(x_i, Z_j(I)) = \left\| x_i - Z_j(I) \right\|^2, i = 1, 2, 3...n; j = 1, 2, 3...K; K < n \qquad (1)$$

$$D(x_i, Z_j(I)) = \min\{D(x_i, Z_j(I))\} \qquad (2)$$

3. Set $I = I + 1$, the new clustering center $Z_j(I + 1)$ is calculated as shown in Eq. (3), where n_j denotes number of data samples that belong to clustering center $Z_j(I)$, $x_i^{(j)}$ denotes the data samples that belong to clustering center $Z_j(I)$. The value of the error square criterion function is calculated as shown in Eq. (4).

$$Z_j(I + 1) = \frac{1}{n_j} \sum_{i=1}^{n_j} x_i^{(j)}, j = 1, 2, ..., K \qquad (3)$$

$$SE(I + 1) = \sum_{j=1}^{k} \sum_{k=1}^{n_j} \left\| x_k^{(j)} - Z_j(I + 1) \right\|^2 \qquad (4)$$

4. Finally, if the Eq. (5) is satisfied or it reaches the maximum cycle, the algorithm is terminated, where ξ is the change threshold of the error square value.

$$|SE(I+1) - SE(I)| < \xi \tag{5}$$

Improving the k-means algorithm with privacy protection methods such as differential privacy protection algorithms has been attracting researchers' attentions [11–13]. Improved k-means algorithm with differential privacy protection algorithm aims to solve problems such as the appropriate selection of initial clustering centers The initial clustering center can be located in the data intensive area, and the initial center point distribution is relatively uniform. In addition, the algorithm can be improved by optimizing the privacy budget allocation in the differential privacy protection so as to meet the minimum privacy budget requirements.

2.2 Privacy Preserving SVM

The Support Vector Machine (SVM) based classification algorithm is a combination of spatial tree module and machine learning theory to obtain the optimal combination of training sample set and the most accurate training data set, thus improving the robustness of SVM algorithm. The classification algorithm based on SVM can simplify the process of classifying data, which can effectively reduce the error generated when the classification algorithm is trained on the original sample set, thus reducing the error during the training of the original sample set [14]. The hyperplane of SVM based classification is shown in Eq. (6), where $\mathbf{x}$ denotes the feature vector, w denotes the normal vector of hyperplane and b denotes the intercept. The optimal classification function of nonlinear SVM is shown in Eq. (7), where ξ_i is the slack variable to introduce fault tolerance, C denotes the punishing parameter. The support vector machine algorithm principle is shown in Fig. 2.

$$\mathbf{x} \cdot w + b = 0 \tag{6}$$

$$\min_{w,b} \frac{1}{2}\|w\|^2 + C \sum_{i=1}^{N} \xi_i$$

$$\text{s.t. } y_i(\mathbf{x}_i \cdot w + b) \geq 1 - \xi_i \tag{7}$$

$$y_i \in \{-1, 1\}$$

$$\xi_i \geq 0, i = 0, 1, \dots, N$$

Privacy preserving SVM classification can be achieved via converting original data into negative database before using SVM functions for training and classification [15]. In addition, secure computation protocols based on cryptosystems can be used to achieve the privacy protection for SVM training while the data samples and training parameters are not disclosed to cloud servers [16, 17].

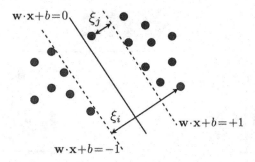

Fig. 2. Support vector machine algorithm principle

2.3 Privacy Preserving Decision Tree

The decision tree algorithm is a probabilistic and rule-based stochastic optimization method that can use data to determine unknown parameters and search without knowing the type of data. The basic idea of decision tree is to establish a functional relationship based on the obtained information, build a model with specific attributes in the existing sample set, and then apply the model to different fields to predict unknown data, thus making it one of the methods to achieve global optimization and local optimization.

The classification process of decision trees is the process of dividing the training set into smaller subsets, with a tree structure consisting of many interdependent and closely connected sets, each with specific information. In this process, the training set both provides accurate and valid data for decision makers and allows them to obtain useful information from a large number of different isolated points [18]. The classification model of the decision tree is shown in Fig. 3. It can be seen that the root node of the decision tress is the final decision node and each branch corresponds to a possible choice. Each path in decision tree including from leaf node to decision node may introduce a probability attribute value.

The decision tree algorithm can be improved in privacy protection by using cryptography such as lightweight secret sharing scheme that does not require a trusted third party [19]. Meanwhile, the secure decision tree algorithm can be implemented by using searchable encryption to protect the privacy of the data and classifier while achieve satisfactory classification efficiency [20].

2.4 Privacy Preserving Association Rule Mining

Association rule mining algorithm is an effective data processing method, which can classify new things when solving complex problems. Its main principle is to connect different objects to form a whole. In this process, we can find the connection between different objects and thus link them together. This method can make complex problems simple and solve the troubles encountered in data mining to some extent. As shown in Fig. 4, this technology can acquire and process the information of objects, and can represent these relationships in the data model, providing useful information for decision makers. The characteristic of this technology is that it can link data with different

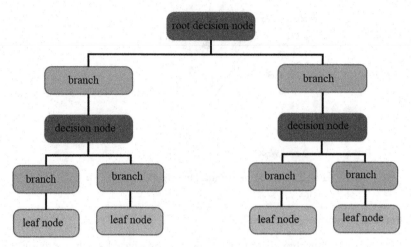

Fig. 3. Classification model of decision tree

objects, deal with more complex problems through association rule mining algorithm, and describe the relationship between data and objects in the data model, so as to deal with problems better, efficiently and accurately.

Privacy preserving association rule mining methods may include six categories including data obscure based methods that adds noises to the original data, heuristic based methods that are based on perturbation and blocking, reconstruction based methods where the released data is reconstructed from the knowledge base, high level heuristic based methods that uses intelligent algorithms such as Genetic Algorithm (GA) and Ant Colony algorithm (ACO), cryptography based methods that are usually used in the outsourced scenarios, Secure multiparty computation methods that do not reveal the data input to other parties [21].

3 Privacy Protection Methods for Data Mining

As mentioned in Sect. 2, privacy protection is an important part of distributed data mining. It can provide users with a more secure data environment, so that they can effectively protect their personal information. Commonly used privacy protection techniques include restricted publication, RSA public key encryption, homomorphic encryption and digital envelope.

3.1 Restricted Release

Restricted release technology mainly uses data anonymization to protect privacy, so as to prevent data miners from accessing the original data and attackers from hiding and attacking the original data. In distributed data mining, the process of encryption and decryption is to compress the original information, so as to reduce the chance of attackers stealing private data and improve the security of encryption and decryption

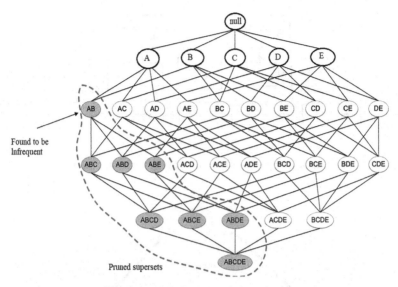

Fig. 4. Association rule mining principle

in data mining technology. The main means to implement the anonymization technology include two ways of suppression and generalization. The suppression method is mainly realized by encrypting the original data, while the generalization method uses fuzzy clustering algorithm and artificial neural network technology, and uses multi-layer distributed perceptron to disperse multiple objects in the data, which may have multiple uncertainties in different regions and different users. The generalization approach is mainly achieved by dividing the original data into different subsets and then classifying them using fuzzy logic techniques to achieve a description of the relationship between uncertainty information and sensitive topics.

3.2 Searchable Symmetric Encryption

The traditional symmetric encryption and decryption process is shown in Fig. 5. It can be seen that the original data is encrypted using Content Encryption Key (CEK) to achieve the confidentiality of the data while the CEK is encrypted using Key Encryption Key (KEK) to prevent the leakage of the CEK during its transmission in the network. At the receiving end, the KEK and CEK are the same as those of the sending end.

Searchable Symmetric Encryption (SSE) is a promising technology for protection privacy in various fields such as data mining and data outsourcing [22]. A demonstrative SSE service system is shown in Fig. 6.

It can be seen from the Fig. 6 that the entities in SSE service system include the data owner, the data user, the trusted authority and the cloud server. The data owner produces original data and uploads the encrypted data to the cloud server. The trusted authority is responsible for the search authority management and the distribution of the keys. If the search request sent by data user is approved by the trusted authority, the trusted authority forwards the request to the cloud server. The cloud server then returns the

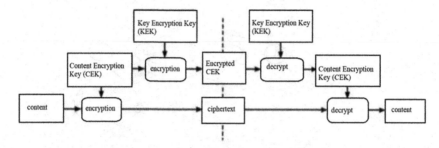

Fig. 5. The process of traditional symmetric encryption

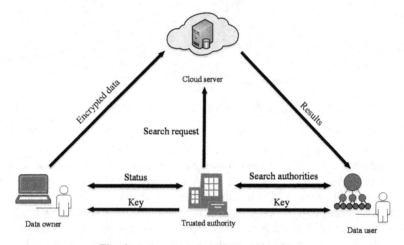

Fig. 6. A demonstrative SSE service system

searched results to the data user who verifies and decrypts the data. During this process, the original data is not disclosed to the cloud server and only authorized data user is allowed to search the data, so that the data privacy is protected.

3.3 Homomorphic Encryption

Homomorphic cryptography is also popular to protect the privacy in data mining to achieve secure outsourcing of data mining tasks [23]. Its essential feature is that it can be used to transmit and receive information directly without any encoding and decoding, and it can be used for confidential access to internal system files and to protect data privacy using the corresponding algorithms for cipher-text computation. Data encryption based on homomorphic cryptography is shown in Fig. 7, which is a cipher-tex based encryption technique that protects the information by analyzing the encryption instructions of the sender, which transmits the data to the receiver in an asynchronous way.

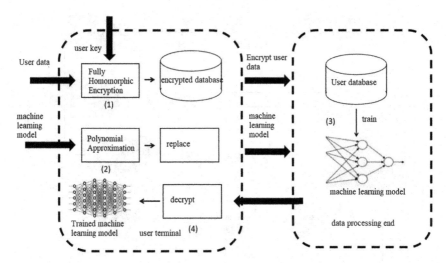

Fig. 7. Data encryption based on homomorphic encryption technology

3.4 Digital Envelope

Digital envelope technology is a computer-based processing and storage method that allows users to protect their privacy by using the network information provided by the user when accessing the data. The digital envelope process is shown in Fig. 8. It can be seen that the digital envelope is composed of the encrypted message using symmetric encryption and the encrypted receiver's public key using asymmetric encryption. While receiving the digital envelope, the receiver uses its private key for decryption to get the symmetric key that is used in the subsequent decryption to obtain the original message.

The core technology in digital envelope technology is digital certificate technology. This technology enables information to be transmitted among different users, and allows users to fully understand the resources they have and obtain corresponding resources through digital certificates. The digital certificate technology is shown in Fig. 9. It can be seen that the digital certificate technology is implemented based on PKI (Public Key Infrastructure) where a CA (Certificate Authority) is responsible to issue digital certificates to users. Hence, the digital certificate comprises the CA identification, certificate identification, user's public key and so on. The corresponding private key is kept by the user and cannot be disclosed to anyone else.

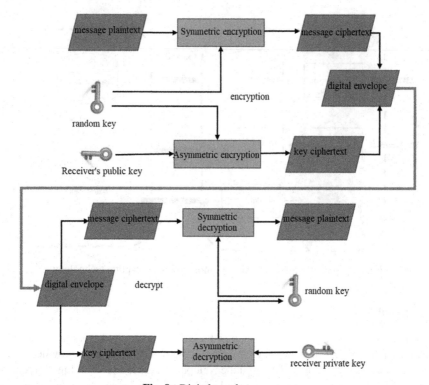

Fig. 8. Digital envelope process

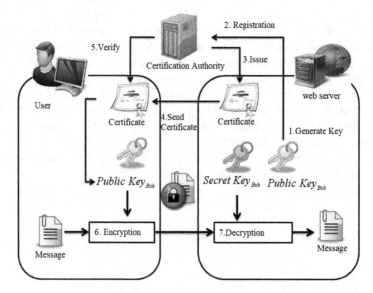

Fig. 9. Digital certificate process

4   Conclusion

In summary, this paper studies the privacy protection methods for distributed data mining technology, which may effectively solve the problems of users' personal privacy issues in the process of information services in data mining technology. The following suggestions are given. First of all, under the development trend of big data and cloud computing technology, the user information security and privacy protection strategies need to be studied so as to protect the user's data privacy while using data mining technology. Secondly, according to the user behavior theory and human-computer interaction experience, a system to meet personalized demands needs to be designed to provide users with privacy protection strategies based on personalized needs, and achieve effective classification, mining and processing of information data. Finally, the data processing algorithms that balance the performance of data mining and privacy protection need to be studied, so as to improve the effectiveness and efficiency of distributed mining and privacy protection, and provide decision support for enterprises.

References

1. Wu, X., Zhu, X., Wu, G.-Q., Ding, W.: Data mining with big data. IEEE Trans. Knowl. Data Eng. **26**(1), 97–107 (2014)
2. Mahmud, M.S., Huang, J.Z., Salloum, S., Emara, T.Z., Sadatdiynov, K.: A survey of data partitioning and sampling methods to support big data analysis. Big Data Min. Analytics **3**(2), 85–101 (2020)
3. Gan, H.: Research on data mining method based on privacy protection. In: 2020 3rd International Conference on Advanced Electronic Materials, Computers and Software Engineering (AEMCSE), pp. 502–506 (2020)
4. Su, X., Fan, K., Shi, W.: Privacy-preserving distributed data fusion based on attribute protection. IEEE Trans. Industr. Inf. **15**(10), 5765–5777 (2019)
5. Zigomitros, A., Casino, F., Solanas, A., Patsakis, C.: A survey on privacy properties for data publishing of relational data. IEEE Access **8**, 51071–51099 (2020)
6. Binjubeir, M., Ahmed, A.A., Ismail, M.A.B., Sadiq, A.S., Khan, M.K.: Comprehensive survey on big data privacy protection. IEEE Access **8**, 20067–20079 (2020)
7. Samaraweera, G.D., Chang, J.M.: Security and privacy implications on database systems in big data era: a survey. IEEE Trans. Knowl. Data Eng. **33**(1), 239–258 (2021)
8. Wang, X., Luo, W., Bai, X., Wang, Y. Research on big data security and privacy risk governance. In: 2021 International Conference on Big Data, Artificial Intelligence and Risk Management (ICBAR), pp. 15–18 (2021)
9. Lv, C. The Dilemma and Countermeasures of Personal Privacy Protection in the Era of Big Data. 2022 3rd International Conference on Electronic Communication and Artificial Intelligence (IWECAI), pp. 335–338 (2022)
10. Venkatachalam, K., Reddy, V.P., Amudhan, M., Raguraman, A., Mohan, E.: an implementation of k-means clustering for efficient image segmentation. In: 2021 10th IEEE International Conference on Communication Systems and Network Technologies (CSNT), pp. 224–229 (2021)
11. Xing, K., Hu, C., Yu, J., Cheng, X., Zhang, F.: Mutual privacy preserving k-means clustering in social participatory sensing. IEEE Trans. Industr. Inf. **13**(4), 2066–2076 (2017)
12. Lu, Z., Shen, H.: Differentially private k-means clustering with convergence guarantee. IEEE Trans. Dependable Secure Comput. **18**(4), 1541–1552 (2021)

13. Lv, Z., Wei, L., Chen, Y., Liu, Y., Li, C., Peng, D.: Differential privacy algorithm for integrated energy system based on improved k-means. In: 2021 6th International Conference on Power and Renewable Energy (ICPRE), pp. 1359–1363 (2021)
14. Mohan, L., Pant, J., Suyal, P., Kumar, A.: Support vector machine accuracy improvement with classification. In: 2020 12th International Conference on Computational Intelligence and Communication Networks (CICN), pp. 477–481 (2020)
15. Sun, X., Zhang, Z., Huang, W. Privacy-preserving SVM classification algorithm based on negative database. In: 2022 IEEE 25th International Conference on Computer Supported Cooperative Work in Design (CSCWD), pp. 1402–1407 (2022)
16. Wang, J., Wu, L., Wang, H., Choo, K.-K.R., He, D.: An efficient and privacy-preserving outsourced support vector machine training for internet of medical things. IEEE Internet Things J. 8(1), 458–473 (2021)
17. Chen, Y., Mao, Q., Wang, B., Duan, P., Zhang, B., Hong, Z.: Privacy-preserving multi-class support vector machine model on medical diagnosis. IEEE J. Biomed. Health Inform. 26(7), 3342–3353 (2022)
18. Yang, F.-J.: An extended idea about decision trees. In: 2019 International Conference on Computational Science and Computational Intelligence (CSCI), pp. 349–354 (2019)
19. Ding, S., Cao, Z., Dong, X.: Efficient privacy preserving decision tree inference service. In: 2020 IEEE International Conference on Advances in Electrical Engineering and Computer Applications(AEECA), pp. 512–516 (2020)
20. Liang, J., Qin, Z., Xiao, S., Ou, L., Lin, X.: Efficient and secure decision tree classification for cloud-assisted online diagnosis services. IEEE Trans. Dependable Secure Comput. 18(4), 1632–1644 (2021)
21. Zhang, L., Wang, W., Zhang, Y.: Privacy preserving association rule mining: taxonomy, techniques, and metrics. IEEE Access 7, 45032–45047 (2019)
22. Shi, Z., Fu, X., Li, X., Zhu, K.: ESVSSE: enabling efficient, secure, verifiable searchable symmetric encryption. IEEE Trans. Knowl. Data Eng. 34(7), 3241–3254 (2022)
23. Wu, J., Mu, N., Lei, X., Le, J., Zhang, D., Liao, X.: SecEDMO: enabling efficient data mining with strong privacy protection in cloud computing. IEEE Trans. Cloud Comput. 10(1), 691–705 (2022)

A Cluster-Based Facial Image Anonymization Method Using Variational Autoencoder

Yuanzhe Yang[1], Zhiyi Niu[1], Yuying Qiu[1], Biao Song[1(✉)], Xinchang Zhang[1], Yuan Tian[2], and Ran Guo[3]

[1] Nanjing University of Information Science and Technology (NUIST), Nanjing, China
bsong@nuist.edu.cn
[2] Nanjing Institute of Technology (NJIT), Nanjing, China
[3] Cyberspace Institute Advanced Technology, Guangzhou University, Guangzhou, China

Abstract. Existing methods for face de-identification often cause inevitable damage to the utility of facial information. The anonymized facial images can hardly be applied in practical applications. In this work, we propose a cluster-based generative model that conceals the identity of images while preserving the utility of facial images. We extract facial features in the first stage, then classify images into several clusters. Four naive protection methods, blindfold, mosaic, cartoon and mosaic, are adopted to form facial image inputs without private information. Along with the four de-identified images, a random facial image in the same cluster is also chosen as another input for better preservation of facial features. We train a novel model with multiple inputs, called Multi-stage Utility Maintenance-Variational AutoEncoder (MsUM-VAE), generating a facial image using the mentioned multi-inputs. The output of the model retains a large portion of the facial characteristics, but cannot be distinguished from the original image dataset, avoiding the disclosure of privacy. We perform numerous evaluations on the CelebA dataset to showcase the effectiveness of our model, and the findings indicate that the model surpasses conventional techniques for obscuring identity and maintaining the utility of images.

Keywords: face de-identification · facial features · privacy protection · deep learning

1 Introduction

Recently, with the rapid growth of technology, online transmission and sharing of personal images have become normal in modern social life. With the proliferation of cameras and facial recognition systems, facial recognition, and facial identification are becoming increasingly popular tools for identification and verification purposes, which has the potential to compromise our personal information security and have a major effect on almost every aspect of life. As a result, the matter of safeguarding personal facial information is becoming more and more crucial.

The authors extend their appreciation to National Key Research and Development Program of China (International Technology Cooperation Project No.2021YFE014400) and National Science Foundation of China (No.42175194) for funding this work.

The identification of individuals is dependent on the facial embeddings extracted from the image, and facial-related deep learning techniques utilize these features to accomplish specific tasks. When applying naïve de-identification methods like blurring or occlusion, although the identity of an individual is protected, fundamental traits that are not related to physical characteristics could disappear. As a result, after the process of removing identifying information, because of disrupted features, the availability of processed images will be influenced when applied in modern machine learning algorithms that utilize facial features for specific purposes. As a result, ensuring privacy protection while preserving data related to specific requirements of facial-related algorithms after deidentification becomes crucial. However specific facial features may involve privacy, and the boundary between them is vague. Therefore, it is a conundrum in facial deidentification how to achieve a balance between protecting privacy and retaining quality, ensuring processed images in the dataset are available for subsequent machine learning algorithms.

Much existing work maintains the usefulness of facial images while concealing identity information. Reference [2] utilized conditional generative adversarial networks to remove the identifying characteristics of faces and bodies and produce high-quality images and videos. Reference [3] it proposed an individualized and reversible method of de-identification using the deep generative model, introducing a user-customized password and a modifiable parameter that regulates the extent and manner of identity alterations. Reference [4] suggested a technique of image inpainting that combines facial landmarks generated from image context and facial landmark-conditioned head inpainting for generating realistic head inpainting in the photo. However, features will be weakened or blurred after processing by existing methods. There is no de-identification model that can preserve certain aspects of features for images in a dataset that can still be used in subsequent machine learning tasks (such as facial expressions) [5] so far. The importance of creating an efficient deep learning model for concealing identity in facial images cannot be emphasized enough.

In order to address these challenges, we propose a novel de-identification model called Multi-stage Utility Maintenance-Variational AutoEncoder (MsUM-VAE) in this paper, which builds upon prior research. The proposed generative model that is capable of producing utility-preserving de-identification images in facial datasets takes advantage of a powerful de-identification model Quality Maintenance-Variational AutoEncoder [1]. To generate deidentifying images contained in the dataset while maintaining features based on specific generation goals, for each image, the proposed strategy utilizes, on one side, corresponding privacy-concealed images processed by several typical protection methods and on the other side, considering features preserving, facial features extracted from other facial images that are similar to this image in the dataset. By incorporating approximate facial features, it is method guarantees that the output image preserves original characteristics and synthesized images are indistinguishable from the dataset, accomplishing the desired tradeoff between privacy and utility. We transformed face images into corresponding embeddings in the first stage, then classified images into several clusters based on embeddings. Subsequently, we employ four common privacy protection techniques, i.e., blindfolding, mosaicking, cartooning, and pixelating, to manipulate original faces, creating four groups of images that do not contain any sensitive information. Along with four de-identified images and a randomly chosen image in the same cluster as the input, to cater to the requirement of specific services, the loss function is tailored, creating a service quality evaluation function.

The structure of remaining sections of the article is organized as follows. Section 2 provides a review of prior research on face de-identification. Section 3 offers an in-depth explanation of our proposed model, MsUM-VAE. Section 4 entails quantitative evaluation experiments that were conducted to validate the efficacy of our proposed approach, and corresponding results are presented, showcasing the efficiency of proposed model. Finally, Sect. 5 offers a concise conclusion to our research.

2 Related Work

The family of algorithms that utilize k-anonymity concept [6–8], adopting the average face of similar faces in the whole image set to represent the resulting face provides a sequence of techniques with theoretical anonymity guarantees. Sweeney [9] was the first to introduce the k-anonymity idea and successfully implemented it in a relational database. The idea of k-anonymity subsequently gave rise to a set of k-same algorithms. To deal with this problem that generated de-identified images suffer from ghosting effects, Gross et al. proposed the k-Same-Model in [7]. The model adopts the idea of Active Appearance Models [15], which achieves better alignment between images, and synchronized images appear more realistic. Proposed by Sun et al. k-Diff-furthest [10] utilized a novel algorithm to address the issue that the generated de-identified facial image has minor difference. Reference [11] proposed k-Same-furthest-FST. It completes the goal of face confusion by morphing the identity-concealed face region and original background. What is more, this method has been proven to provide significant privacy protection in the context of the FERET database. [12]. Meden et al. [13] proposed the k-Same-Net scheme. It combines the k-anonymity algorithm and GNN architectures, achieving good results in visual. Reference [14] explores a novel model based on AAM. It divides the face space into two subspaces (identity and utility) and uses appropriate k-anonymity technique to process utility to achieve face de-identification. Although facial privacy is, to some extent, well protected by k-anonymity family algorithm, algorithm comes with substantial limitations, as each individual can only be represented once in the dataset. This may cause a decrease in identity diversity in the whole dataset.

Currently, generative models that synthesize synthetic but natural-looking images provide novel ideas for de-identification. The most famous model in all generative models is Generative Adversarial Networks [16] (GANs), providing a novel idea for research in the field of facial identity concealing [17–20]. It comprises two deep models that are in competition with each other: a model containing a generator and a discriminator network. Qi et al. [21] put forwards a novel Loss-Sensitive Generative Adversarial Network (LS-GAN). The approach incorporates the principles of specific regularization theory and algorithms and utilizes game theory, encouraging the generator to produce the most authentic samples. CGAN-based PPGAN is proposed by Wu et al. [22] that utilized a pre-trained discriminator to output a structurally similar image, using the extracted identity-associated feature space. Li et al. [23] have introduced the SF-GAN technique to improve the efficiency of de-identification. This method combines both a geometry synthesizer and an appearance synthesizer to construct various external mechanisms, achieving the goal of identity concealing. Reference [24] proposed a privacy protection technique based on auto-GAN, which decreases the number of dimension of features in data prepared for specific machine learning tasks. It generates deidentified data through confrontation. Reference [25] put forwards FPGAN, an end-to-end method. The method uses both enhanced U-Net architecture and two discriminators, and its loss function is devised dependent on the requirement of the specific scenario of service. Because of lacking the powerful grasping ability for facial features, each of the GAN-based methods has a common drawback in that details of the generated facial images are not perfect.

There are many categories of privacy-concealing technologies in machine learning tasks; the most famous kind is differential privacy. Dwork et al. [26] proposed it in 2006. The background of this technology is assumed that attackers will manipulate not only the target information but also all other information available. This approach provides a systematic and measurable way to quantify the risk of privacy disclosure. The idea of Differential Privacy (DP) [27] is commonly employed in numerous identity concealing technologies [28] for facial images. Reference [29] proposed a new model called PEEP. To prevent privacy attacks such as model memorization attacks [30] or membership inference [31], the model takes advantage of local differential privacy, adding noise to the characteristics of the facial distribution extracted from original images. The perturbed data is stored on third-party servers. In [22], Privacy-Preserving Adversarial Protector Network (PPAPNet) was developed. It generates artificial images by adding appropriate noise to the original face to resist inversion attacks [32]. Tackling the imbalanced distribution in the dataset, reference [33] proposes a method that is dependent on the quantity of data points in every partitioned grid to divide a single dataset into two levels, utilizing an adaptive partitioning strategy that satisfies the requirements of identity obfuscation. Reference [34] presents DP-GAN, which is for semantic-rich data. The framework utilized a deep generative model and trains the model with the differentially private manner of original data. Although this approach generates privacy-preserving facial images, it cannot be applied to some specific tasks of privacy protection. Reference [35] introduces a Privacy-Preserving Semi-Generative Adversarial Network (PPSGAN) as a solution to this issue. Adopting the mechanism of self-attention, the noise is added to the features that are independent of privacy preservation. It allows the generated images to match the original label. While differential privacy does de-identify privacy from identification, without taking into account the facial embedding contained in the image, the usability of generated images is degraded visually.

3   Proposed Methodology

3.1   System Model

With regard to preserving utility, concealing the identity of individuals is a complex task. Previous approaches do not take the possible loss of the utility of images into consideration in the process of removing identical information. As a result, for specific tasks, the quality of service will be far from expected. To address this issue, we propose a distinct generative model called MsUM-VAE with delicate designs of architecture and loss, making a tradeoff between identity hiding and utility preserving. Figure 1 represents a visual representation of the overall structure of our model.

Firstly, to all images in the dataset, we cropped faces from images and generated a 128-dimensional face feature vector(embedding) for each face through the network. Then, we classified images into 15 clusters according to the face embedding. For each image in the dataset, in the next stage, four naïve de-identification ways is applied, forming part of dataset. In the next stage, guided by the service loss function, the proposed model utilized the dataset to generate images that preserving related trait while concealing the identity. During the training process, the loss function incorporates an assessment of the usefulness of generated images in a service scenario. In maintaining service quality, backpropagation is a significant part that helps update the output continuously.

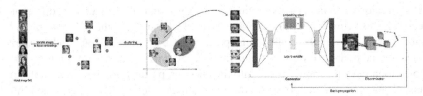

Fig. 1. The structure of MsUM-VAE

3.2 Architecture and Working

The target of our research is to establish a multi-stages generative model that makes use of several privacy-removed images to generate quality-maintained images. Taking a set of N different sample images, to reduce the influence of background information and effectively improve the reliability of facial features the pre-trained MTCNN model was used. It carries out bounding box regression, probability prediction of a real face, and localization of facial landmarks (like mouth, eyes, and nose) at the same time by applying several networks in a cascade. By detecting the geometric structure of the image, the boundary rectangle of the detected face was returned. According to the detected five facial points, the input face image was cropped from the rectangle. To perform face alignment, transformation, and normalization, which depend on the position of the located key landmark were made on cropped faces. After that faces were further resized to $48 \times 48 \times 3$ pixels, producing a set of N identified images $X = \{X_1, X_2, X_3, \ldots, X_n\}$. To extract 128-dimensional facial embedding from each face in X, FaceNet [36] that utilizes deep convolutional networks [37, 38] (DNNs) to map face images to a compact Euclidean space was applied, generating face features $V = \{V_1, V_2, V_3, \ldots, V_n\}$.

The principal goal of this stage is to divide V into 15 different categories such that features in one group are very similar while the difference among different groups is quite large. Firstly, we randomly selected 15 face features $V_\mu = \{V_{\mu 1}, V_{\mu 2}, \ldots, V_{\mu 15}\}$ from V as centroids. Then to assign other face features to the closest cluster, we calculated the square errors J between every element in V and every centroid. Facial features in the same cluster are more homogeneous when the value of J is lower. The Eq. (1) defines the objective function J.

$$J = \sum_{i=1}^{N} \sum_{k=1}^{15} \omega_{ik} \left\| v_i - v_{\mu_k} \right\|^2 \tag{1}$$

By controlling the value of ω_{ik}, we got the lowest square error based on the random centroids. And the belonging of different clusters of face embedding is defined by ω_{ik}. The next step is to update the centroid in each cluster by computing the average value among all face embeddings in the cluster. To get the global lowest variation within clusters, we kept iterating the above steps until there is no change to the centroids. The whole faces were then split into 15 clusters.

The next stage is inspired by QM-VAE [1], which is a novel model that uses several privacy-removed facial images as the input to generate images that fit different services. The inspiring framework contains three different parts: the mapping model, the generating model and the embedding space e. Concatenated by four tradition privacy protection method, covering eyes, blurring face, adding Laplace noise and transforming into cartoon face, the input i is fed into the encoder, producing $z_e(i)$. Instead of directly transporting $z_e(i)$ into the done like ordinary autoencoder, $z_e(i)$ is transformed into the new embedding vector e_i by searching for closest embedding. The Eq. (2) shows the one-hot defined form of posterior categorical distribution $q(z|i)$ probabilities.

$$q(z = k|i) = \begin{cases} 1 \text{ for } k = \text{argmin}_j \left\| z_e(i) - e_j \right\|_2, \\ 0 \text{ otherwise} \end{cases} \tag{2}$$

To realize the discretization process, the transformation of finding the closest element of $ze(i)$, which is transmitted to decoder as its own mapping is represented below in Eq. (3).

$$z_q(i) = e_k, \qquad \text{where} \quad k = \arg\min_j \left\| z_e(i) - e_j \right\|_2 \tag{3}$$

The loss function is divided into three parts. The first part L_q represents the specific machine learning task service quality loss. To be more specific, we concentrated on facial expression recognition. In each iteration of training, the expression of generated images is recorded. To ensure that the expression of generated image is similar to that of original image, L_q is set to 0 if detected expression of them are aligned otherwise the value is set to 1, shown in Eq. (4).

$$L_q = \begin{cases} 0, \text{ if } E(i) = E(z(i)) \\ 1, \text{ if } E(i) \neq E(z(i)) \end{cases} \tag{4}$$

Next part L_{ml} measures degree of resemblance between images produced and images corresponding included in the dataset. The first term describes the dissimilarity between the model's outputs and the original images that were used as input for the model. The subsequent element is intended to enhance and refine e, and consistently update the glossary throughout the entirety of the model's training process. The commitment loss, the third term, impose restrictions on the encoder's updates to maintain consistency with the latent embedding vector, and prevent abrupt deviations.

$$L_{m_1} = \log p(i|z_q(i)) + \|sg[z_e(i)] - e\|_2^2 + \beta_{m_1} \|z_e(i) - sg[e]\|_2^2 \qquad (5)$$

where sg represents the stop gradient, stopping the gradient flow from flowing through specific parts of the network and is defined as constant value in forward computing of the whole model. Changes in this parameter β_{m1}, ranging from 0.1 to 2.0, did not significantly affect the outcome.

Similar to L_{m1}, the third part L_{m2} shown in the Eq. (6) below measures the degree of likeness between images produced and facial images selected randomly from the same cluster.. The difference is that L_{m2} is used to describe the image reconstruction loss of the surrogate images and the model outputs.

$$L_{m_2} = \log p(i|f(i)) + \|sg[f(i)] - e\|_2^2 + \beta_{m_2} \|f(i) - sg[e]\|_2^2 \qquad (6)$$

The whole loss function L is defined below:

$$L = \alpha L_q + (1 - \alpha)(\beta L_{m_1} + (1 - \beta)L_{m_2}) \qquad (7)$$

where α is designed to assign the appropriate weight between degradation in the quality or performance of the service and the decline in the effectiveness of the morphing process; β is employed to determine the appropriate distribution of importance for original images and surrogate images. The value of both α and β ranges from 0 to 1.

3.3 Method Execution Process

Derived from the concept of concealing the identity of image and subsequently rebuilding it, we drew figure below to illustrate the whole process of our approach (Fig. 2).

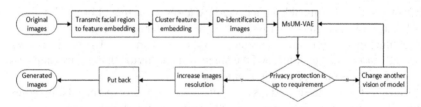

Fig. 2. The execution flow of MsUM-VAE.

In the beginning, we carry out the process of identification of facial regions on the original image in the dataset to crop out the face area. Then, the cropped face is transformed into facial embedding and classified into one cluster. And we utilize its corresponding centroid to synthesize surrogate images. The surrogate face and four de-identified cropped faces modified by four face methods (covering eyes, blurring face, adding Laplace noise and transforming into cartoon face) are fed into the MsUM-VAE to reconstruct the image that conceals identity while preserving utility.

The service utility estimator takes advantage of the difference in attributes within the serving scene earlier than and after processing to quantify service quality loss of images. It modifies the manner in which whole model is trained with the intention of the model generates facial images that fulfill the goal of privateness removal and utility renovation, supplying reliable and secure facial images that are suitable for use in scenarios that is related to specific services.

4 Experimentation and Results

4.1 Experimental Setup

The training dataset of our proposed model, MsUM-VAE, is CelebA [7] dataset, which is a publicly available dataset containing quite a few facial images utilized as the basis for facial dataset for various computer vision applications. We opted to use the first one thousand female images from the dataset as the dataset of the model. Three quarters of these images were used for training, and the remaining twenty percent were reserved for testing purposes. In order to verify the broad usefulness of our model, we categorized the datasets into six categories based on various facial expressions including: angry, fearful, happy, sad, surprised, and neutral.

The TensorFlow 1.9 and Keras 2 framework, created by Google, was utilized to develop the MsUM-VAE. The model was trained on an RTX 3070 GPU. Paper [39] validate that the result did not vary from values when β_{m1} in Eq. (5) and β_{m2} in Eq. (6) were set between 0.1 and 2.0. As a result, we set the value of β_{m1} and β_{m2} to 0.25 in all following experiments. During the stage of the model development, we employed the ADAM optimizer with a learning rate of 1×10^{-3}. Other parameters are listed in Table 1.

4.2 Privacy Preservation Evaluation

For the training of our model, we gathered a dataset consisting of original images, one facial image selected randomly from the identical cluster as the original image, and four de-identified images (blindfold, mosaic, Laplace, and cartoon). The batch size was set to 64, the learning rate to 0.001, and the number of epochs to 50. In the training process, we used Eq. (7) as our loss function with α set to 0.

In an effort to gain the lowest loss, we conducted multiple experiments. We adjust the value of parameter β, which controls the proportion assigned to the surrogate faces and original faces in the loss function after which we checked the maintenance quality loss to choose the most suitable percentage of β. The variation in the loss rate is illustrated in Fig. 4.

As Fig. 3 depicted, when β is about 0.4 the effort of the model is much better and after 50 rounds, the reduction in loss rate is significant, with a decrease to 0.08, which is lower than other ratios. Additionally, the loss rate is decreased by a minimum of 2.4%.

When β is 0.4, the de-identification success rate of generated images reached about 70%. The results result of images is shown in are shown in Fig. 4.

Table 1. The parameters of proposed method.

Parameter name	Function	Range of value
k	Allocate the relative weight between the image coordinates and the correspond centroid image coordinate	[0, 1]
t	Control proportional weight of the image region and the correspond centroid image region to synthesis surrogate image	[0, 1]
β_{m1}	Commitment loss in L_{m1}, making sure encoder part makes a commitment to the embedding	[0.1, 2]
β_{m2}	Commitment loss in L_{m2}, ensuring encoder part makes a commitment to the embedding	[0.1, 2]
α	Allocate the relevant weight of loss function used in the model combines the loss of specific requirements of scenario and the loss of morphing	[0, 1]
β	Control proportional weight of original images and surrogate images	[0, 1]

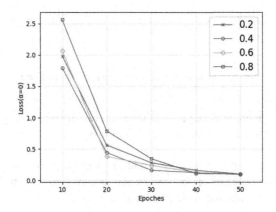

Fig. 3. The changing trend of the loss rate when $\alpha = 0$.

4.3 Image Utility Maintenance

We modified the value of α in Eq. (7) that determines the proportion of quality loss with β fixed to 0.4. To get the minimum loss rate to image quality after modifying the value of α, we also checked the model effect of quality maintenance to each value of α respectively. The downward trend of quality loss is depicted in the Fig. 5.

As the above result shows, when α is 0.4 the output is the best. After 50 epochs, the loss reduced to about 0.23, the lowest one compared with other four kinds of α percent. It reduced by at least 5.7% compared with the quality loss of the four protected images, demonstrating that our model is a significant preserving effect for face expressions. The

Fig. 4. The result image after using our model

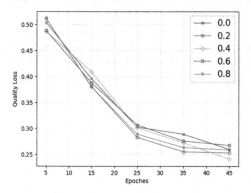

Fig. 5. The decreasing trend of expression loss rate

output of $\alpha = 0.4$ is more advantageous in terms of training rounds in general compared with naïve image fusion, showing that in overall loss function, expression loss is vital for preserving quality.

We analyze the output of the model that has undergone 50 rounds of training with a value of $\alpha = 0.4$. The loss rate of six types of expressions processed by various methods was measured, and the outcomes are presented in Table 2.

Table 2. Facial expression loss rate under different methods.

Loss Rate	Angry	Fear	Happy	Sad	Surprise	Neutral
Our Model	0.235	0.342	0.136	0.273	0.429	0.231
Blindfold	0.441	0.737	0.029	0.669	0.893	0.814
Cartoon	0.794	0.513	0.489	0.360	0.785	0.459
Laplace	0.911	0.895	0.665	0.756	0.964	0.702
Mosaic	0.294	0.302	0.299	0.361	0.321	0.169

5 Conclusion

This paper introduces a new framework for identity concealing and utility preserving called MsUM-VAE that incorporates several related protection methods. The concept of de-identification on datasets for machine learning while preserving service-related features is presented along with a novel generative model. The experiments validate that our model can quantitatively process a dataset that is available for subsequent machine learning. Our approach is the first to provide a general solution for identity concealing in facial datasets used in modern machine learning, offering great flexibility and efficiency.

We provided quantitative evidence of the effectiveness of MsUM-VAE in concealing identity information in datasets used for machine learning tasks. However, we did not have a way to determine the value the accuracy of the privacy information removal in our proposed model using a standardized method or metric. In the follow-up research, creating a proper quantitative model that can measure the extent of protected privacy is vital. Our future research, in the field of facial images, can be a breakthrough, at the same time, it can be applied to more tasks of modern machine learning.

References

1. Qiu, Y., Niu, Z., Song, B., Ma, T., Al-Dhelaan, A., Al-Dhelaan, M.: A novel generative model for face privacy protection in video surveillance with utility maintenance. Appl. Sci. **12**(14), 6962 (2022)
2. Maximov, M., Elezi, I., Leal-Taixé, L.: CIAGAN: conditional identity anonymization generative adversarial networks. In: Proceedings of the IEEE/CVF Conference on Computer Vision and Pattern Recognition, pp. 5447–5456 (2020)
3. Cao, J., Liu, B., Wen, Y., Xie, R., Song, L.: Personalized and invertible face de-identification by disentangled identity information manipulation. In: Proceedings of the IEEE/CVF International Conference on Computer Vision, pp. 3334–3342 (2021)
4. Sun, Q., Ma, L., Oh, S.J., Van Gool, L., Schiele, B., Fritz, M.: Natural and effective obfuscation by head inpainting. In: Proceedings of the IEEE Conference on Computer Vision and Pattern Recognition, pp. 5050–5059 (2018)
5. Chibelushi, C.C., Bourel, F.: Facial expression recognition: a brief tutorial overview. In: CVonline: On-Line Compendium of Computer Vision, vol. 9 (2003)
6. Gross, R., Airoldi, E., Malin, B., Sweeney, L.: Integrating utility into face de-identification. In: Danezis, G., Martin, D. (eds.) PET 2005. LNCS, vol. 3856, pp. 227–242. Springer, Heidelberg (2006). https://doi.org/10.1007/11767831_15
7. Gross, R., Sweeney, L., De la Torre, F., Baker, S.: Model-based face de-identification. In: 2006 Conference on Computer Vision and Pattern Recognition Workshop (CVPRW 2006), p. 161. IEEE (2006)
8. Samarzija, B., Ribaric, S.: An approach to the de-identification of faces in different poses. In: 2014 37th International Convention on Information and Communication Technology, Electronics and Microelectronics (MIPRO), pp. 1246–1251. IEEE (2014)
9. Sweeney, L.: k-anonymity: a model for protecting privacy. Int. J. Uncertain. Fuzziness Knowl.-Based Syst. **10**(05), 557–570 (2002)
10. Sun, Z., Meng, L., Ariyaeeinia, A.: Distinguishable de-identified faces. In: 2015 11th IEEE International Conference and Workshops on Automatic Face and Gesture Recognition (FG), vol. 4, pp. 1–6. IEEE (2015)

11. Meng, L., Sun, Z., Ariyaeeinia, A., Bennett, K.L.: Retaining expressions on de-identified faces. In: 2014 37th International Convention on Information and Communication Technology, Electronics and Microelectronics (MIPRO), pp. 1252–1257. IEEE (2014)

12. Phillips, P.J., Wechsler, H., Huang, J., Rauss, P.J.: The FERET database and evaluation procedure for face-recognition algorithms. Image Vis. Comput. **16**(5), 295–306 (1998)

13. Meden, B., Emeršič, Ž, Štruc, V., Peer, P.: k-Same-Net: k-Anonymity with generative deep neural networks for face deidentification. Entropy **20**(1), 60 (2018)

14. Liu., C., Wang, Y., Chi, H., Wang, S.: Utility preserved facial image de-identification using appearance subspace decomposition. Chin. J. Electron. **30**(3), 413–418 (2021)

15. Cootes, T.F., Edwards, G.J., Taylor, C.J.: Active appearance models. In: Burkhardt, H., Neumann, B. (eds.) ECCV 1998. LNCS, vol. 1407, pp. 484–498. Springer, Heidelberg (1998). https://doi.org/10.1007/BFb0054760

16. Ian, G., Pouget-Abadie, J., Mirza, M., Xu, B., Warde-Farley, D.: Generative adversarial nets. In: Advances in Neural Information Processing Systems, vol. 27, pp. 2672–2680 (2014)

17. Cai, Z., Xiong, Z., Xu, H., Wang, P., Li, W., Pan, Y.: Generative adversarial networks: a survey toward private and secure applications. ACM Comput. Surv. (CSUR) **54**(6), 1–38 (2021)

18. Han, C., Xue, R.: Differentially private GANs by adding noise to Discriminator's loss. Comput. Secur. **107**, 102322 (2021)

19. Yang, R., Ma, X., Bai, X., Su, X.: Differential privacy images protection based on generative adversarial network. In: 2020 IEEE 19th International Conference on Trust, Security and Privacy in Computing and Communications (TrustCom), pp. 1688–1695. IEEE (2020)

20. Hukkelås, H., Mester, R., Lindseth, F.: DeepPrivacy: a generative adversarial network for face anonymization. In: Bebis, G., et al. (eds.) ISVC 2019. LNCS, vol. 11844, pp. 565–578. Springer, Cham (2019). https://doi.org/10.1007/978-3-030-33720-9_44

21. Qi, G.: Loss-sensitive generative adversarial networks on lipschitz densities, CoRR abs/1701.06264. arXiv preprint arXiv:1701.06264 (2017)

22. Liu, Y., Peng, J., James, J.Q., Wu, Y.: PPGAN: privacy-preserving generative adversarial network. In: 2019 IEEE 25th International Conference on Parallel and Distributed Systems (ICPADS), pp. 985–989. IEEE (2019)

23. Li, Y., Lu, Q., Tao, Q., Zhao, X., Yu, Y.: SF-GAN: face de-identification method without losing facial attribute information. IEEE Signal Process. Lett. **28**, 1345–1349 (2021)

24. Nguyen, H., Zhuang, D., Wu, P.Y., Chang, M.: Autogan-based dimension reduction for privacy preservation. Neurocomputing **384**, 94–103 (2020)

25. Lin, J., Li, Y., Yang, G.: FPGAN: face de-identification method with generative adversarial networks for social robots. Neural Netw. **133**, 132–147 (2021)

26. Dwork, C.: Differential privacy: a survey of results. In: Agrawal, M., Du, D., Duan, Z., Li, A. (eds.) TAMC 2008. LNCS, vol. 4978, pp. 1–19. Springer, Heidelberg (2008). https://doi.org/10.1007/978-3-540-79228-4_1

27. Dwork, C., Roth, A.: The algorithmic foundations of differential privacy. Found. Trends® Theor. Comput. Sci. **9**(3–4), 211–407 (2014)

28. Yu, J., Xue, H., Liu, B., Wang, Y., Zhu, S., Ding, M.: GAN-based differential private image privacy protection framework for the internet of multimedia things. Sensors **21**(1), 58 (2020)

29. Chamikara, M.A.P., Bertok, P., Khalil, I., Liu, D., Camtepe, S.: Privacy preserving face recognition utilizing differential privacy. Comput. Secur. **97**, 101951 (2020)

30. Nasr, M., Shokri, R., Houmansadr, A.: Comprehensive privacy analysis of deep learning: passive and active white-box inference attacks against centralized and federated learning. In: 2019 IEEE Symposium on Security and Privacy (SP), pp. 739–753. IEEE (2019)

31. Shokri, R., Stronati, M., Song, C., Shmatikov, V.: Membership inference attacks against machine learning models. In: 2017 IEEE Symposium on Security and Privacy (SP), pp. 3–18. IEEE (2017)

32. Fredrikson, M., Jha, S., Ristenpart, T.: Model inversion attacks that exploit confidence information and basic countermeasures. In: Proceedings of the 22nd ACM SIGSAC Conference on Computer and Communications Security, pp. 1322–1333 (2015)
33. Qardaji, W., Yang, W., Li, N.: Differentially private grids for geospatial data. In: 2013 IEEE 29th International Conference on Data Engineering (ICDE), pp. 757–768. IEEE (2013)
34. Ho, S., Qu, Y., Gu, B., Gao, L., Li, J., Xiang, Y.: DP-GAN: differentially private consecutive data publishing using generative adversarial nets. J. Netw. Comput. Appl. **185**, 103066 (2021)
35. Kim, T., Yang, J.: Selective feature anonymization for privacy-preserving image data publishing. Electronics **9**(5), 874 (2020)
36. Schroff, F., Kalenichenko, D., Philbin, J.: FaceNet: a unified embedding for face recognition and clustering. In: Proceedings of the IEEE Conference on Computer Vision and Pattern Recognition, pp. 815–823 (2015)
37. LeCun, Y., et al.: Backpropagation applied to handwritten zip code recognition. Neural Comput. **1**(4), 541–551 (1989)
38. Rumelhart, D.E., Hinton, G.E., Williams, R.J.: Learning representations by back-propagating errors. Nature **323**(6088), 533–536 (1986)
39. Van Den Oord, A., Vinyals, O.: Neural discrete representation learning. In; Advances in Neural Information Processing Systems, vol. 30 (2017)

IoT Security

Research on the Security Diagnosis Platform for Partial Discharge of 10 kV Cables in Urban Distribution Networks

Xinping Wang, Guofei Guan(✉), Chunpeng Li, Hao Zhang, Chao Jiang,
and Qingwu Song

Jiangsu Frontier Electric Technology Co., Ltd., Nanjing 211106, China
guangf@js.sgcc.com.cn

Abstract. Cables in 10 kV distribution networks play a key function in ensuring the secure operation of distribution network systems. The traditional methods of diagnosing partial discharges in 10 kV cables need to be improved at the levels of cost, efficiency, diagnostic accuracy, and anti-interference capability. Therefore, this paper studies and designs a security diagnosis platform that can effectively extract, identify and diagnose the signal characteristics of cable discharge models. The architecture and diagnostic process of the proposed system are described in details. Through the security diagnostic verification of the partial discharge capability of 10 kV cables in distribution networks, the effectiveness and efficiency of the proposed platform is validated. The application results show its capability in quickly locating and eliminating hidden cable insulation problems in distribution networks. The proposed platform, through the integration of different modules, is expected to significantly improve the security and reliability of power system.

Keywords: Security Diagnostic · Partial Discharge · Distribution Networks

1 Introduction

As an important basic guarantee for urbanization, the urban distribution network is not only a key support for the normal operation of the city, but also an important component network for the intelligent and secure development of the city [1]. The 10 kV distribution network cables play a key role in ensuring the normal operation of the distribution system, but their partial discharge often leads to faults and errors in the distribution network, which needs to be effectively monitored and diagnosed [2]. With the accelerating urbanization process, the application and demand for distribution networks in various industries are also increasing. The application of increasing electrical devices in the distribution network makes the distribution network under greater operating pressure [3]. The partial discharge of cables in the distribution network is one of the important factors leading to the failure of the network operation that endangers the security of power grid. How to implement the efficient and low-cost security diagnosis of the partial discharge of cables in the urban distribution network has become the focus of attention and research in the power industry [4].

Y. Tian et al. (Eds.): ICBDS 2022, CCIS 1796, pp. 637–650, 2023.
https://doi.org/10.1007/978-981-99-3300-6_46

The traditional security diagnostic method for partial discharge of 10 kV cable has the shortage of requiring power outage operation, which will lead to serious impact on the operation efficiency of the distribution network while there is still much room for improvement in diagnostic accuracy and anti-interference ability [5]. For example, the current widely used TEV (Transient Earth Voltage) cable partial discharge security diagnosis method is difficult to effectively identify in the case of mild cable discharge, and it is difficult to filter in the case of environmental interference noise signals [6]. To address those problems, this paper studies and designs a platform that can effectively meet the needs of 10 kV cable partial discharge security diagnosis in urban distribution networks, which can effectively extract, identify and diagnose the signal characteristics of cable discharge models [7].

The primary goal of constructing a security diagnosis platform for 10 kV cable partial discharge in urban distribution network is to optimize the security diagnosis process to overcome the shortcomings of traditional methods, so as to improve the stability, security and reliability of the whole distribution network system [8]. The intelligent security diagnosis platform is used to accurately identify the partial discharge of 10 kV cables in urban distribution network without shutting down the power grid, so as to facilitate the maintenance of cable insulation and thus achieve the long-term economic operation of the distribution network [9]. The proposed platform in this paper is verified to meet the requirements of real-time, remote and power on security diagnosis and monitoring, and is expected to provide great value to the reliable operation of urban distribution networks.

2 Partial Discharge Model

The 10 kV cable in urban distribution network is affected by many factors in the production process, resulting in uneven composition of cable medium or certain impurities and holes inside [10]. Those impurities and holes may be broken down under the action of high-voltage electric field, resulting in cable partial discharge. Since the discharge phenomenon only occurs in the local area of the distribution network cable and will not lead to the voltage breakdown between the cable conductors, there is only an electrical discharge in the part of cable insulation layer. However, it will lead to the accelerated aging of the cable insulation layer which will greatly shorten its insulation life. Hence, it needs to be monitored timely and effectively, so as to avoid the failure of the distribution network system and to better guarantee the secure operation of the urban power system.

The partial discharge model of 10 kV cable in urban distribution network is mainly based on several types of internal discharge, tip discharge, surface discharge and suspension discharge. Among them, internal discharge is a discharge phenomenon inside the cable. The tip discharge is caused by the breakdown of the protruding edge of the conductive part of the cable under the action of uneven electric field [11]. Suspension discharge and surface discharge are caused by the structural defects of the distribution network cable such as the accumulation of dirt on the surface or the presence of condensation or foreign matter. For the 10 kV cable, the structural part where partial discharge occurs is shown in Fig. 1 below. Under the action of high voltage electromagnetic field, the impurity molecules in the distribution network cable are displaced and move to both ends of the cable according to the difference in polarity. With the expansion of impurity voids in the cable, they will eventually be broken under the high-voltage electric field and a stronger current will be released, resulting in the surface discharge.

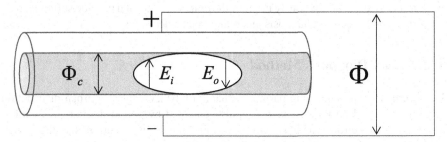

Fig. 1. Structural parts of 10 kV cable partial discharge

The role of 10 kV cable in urban distribution network is very important, which is the basic support to implement the power transmission of each power terminal. Under the high voltage of 10 kV, the electromagnetic field of the cables of the distribution network shows the characteristics of non-uniform distribution. The electromagnetic field strength of different areas inside the cable varies, so that partial discharge occurs in the area after the electric field length of the distribution network reaches the threshold value of the cable [12]. Partial discharge is an important parameter to measure the insulation performance of cable. If it is not monitored in time and allowed to develop freely, it will lead to insulation breakdown fault in distribution network system, which will have a greater negative impact on the security of urban power grid. For this reason, effective security diagnosis and control of partial discharges in 10 kV cables of distribution networks is necessary.

The proportion of cables in urban distribution network, especially in 10 kV and above high-voltage distribution network, is gradually increasing, which puts forward higher requirements for the stability of cables. On the other hand, it also poses a greater challenge to the security diagnosis of cable partial discharge [13]. Generally, the monitoring of high-voltage cables in urban distribution networks is mainly carried out by means of field tests, condition assessments and cable defect tests. With the continuous breakthrough of intelligent security diagnosis technology represented by oscillation wave diagnosis and monitoring, the application of this technology in the partial discharge is also gradually deepening. However, the security diagnosis of partial discharge of high-voltage cables usually requires power interruption that will bring great interference to the operation of urban distribution networks. Secondly, in the process of cable partial discharge security diagnosis, it will be interfered and influenced by various signals and data, which makes it difficult to control the diagnosis accuracy [14]. In addition, due to the large scale of urban distribution network, how to achieve effective partial discharge diagnosis of 10 kV cable at a small economic cost and obtain greater social benefits is the difficulty and key to build a partial discharge diagnosis platform.

To address the above problems, the partial discharge security diagnosis platform for 10 kV cables in urban distribution networks proposed in this paper is expected to effectively achieve a balance of accuracy, efficiency, cost, and anti-interference. The platform can not only effectively filter the interference signals existing in the diagnosis process, but also can continuously monitor the diagnosis data and provide sufficient data support for cable security diagnosis and maintenance decisions.

3 Security Diagnosis Method

The mechanism of diagnosing partial discharge of 10 kV cables in urban distribution networks is based on the discharge signals generated by partial discharge of cables, which include electromagnetic signals, ultrasonic signals, pulse current signals, as well as photoelectric and thermal signals [15]. The number of cables in urban high-voltage distribution networks, especially those above 10 kV, is large and the distribution is complex, so if the traditional outage diagnosis strategy is adopted, it will bring negative impact on the long-term operation of the distribution network. Therefore, this paper focuses on the characteristics of partial discharge of cables in urban 10 kV distribution network and makes targeted security diagnosis of cable partial discharge phenomenon.

The diagnosis technology of partial discharge of 10 kV cable in urban distribution network mainly includes several aspects such as UHF (Ultra High Frequency) diagnosis, HF (High Frequency) diagnosis and partial discharge localization. Among them, in the process of UHF diagnosis, it is mainly based on the fact that in the process of partial discharge, it is often accompanied by the release of high-intensity electric field and pulse current. Hence, by monitoring the excited high-frequency electromagnetic wave, it can effectively diagnose whether there is partial discharge phenomenon of the cable. Secondly, the diagnosis of HF partial discharge is mainly based on the acquisition of partial discharge signals by HF cable sensors. In addition, at the level of localization of the cable partial discharge signal, a time difference signal sensor is deployed outside the cable to detect the discharge location. In the cable local discharge signal sensor arrangement scheme shown in Fig. 2, sensors x and y are deployed in the insulation and outside of the cable, respectively, and the signal acquisition is oriented towards the cable and the external air medium. The location of the local discharge signal can be determined by making sensor y move around sensor x, based on the sequential relationship between the signals monitored by sensor x and sensor y.

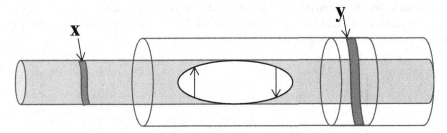

Fig. 2. Partial discharge monitoring sensor deployment

In the case that sensor x always precedes the signal monitored by sensor y, it can be indicated that the local discharge signal occurs inside the cable, otherwise it can be found that the signal is an external environmental interference noise signal. After locating the cable partial discharge signal inside the cable, it is necessary to locate its discharge location more precisely. In the deployment scheme for precise positioning of partial discharge in the cable shown in Fig. 3, the sensors x and y are deployed at the two ends of the cable insulation layer, and the detection of the precise location of partial discharge in the cable is calculated by the following Eqs. (1) and (2).

$$\delta t = \frac{d - w}{v} - \frac{w}{v} \tag{1}$$

$$w = \frac{d - v\delta t}{2} \tag{2}$$

where d is the distance between the two sensors, w is the distance between the point of partial discharge inside the cable and sensor x, δt is the time difference of the received signal between sensor y and sensor x, and v is propagation speed of the electromagnetic wave signal generated by the partial discharge.

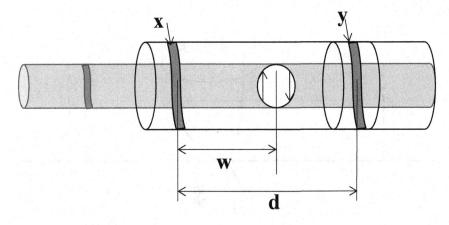

Fig. 3. Precise location detection sensor deployment

In addition, the acquisition of the time difference of the received signal between sensor y and sensor x is obtained by reading the oscilloscope data, and this time difference is acquired as shown in Fig. 4.

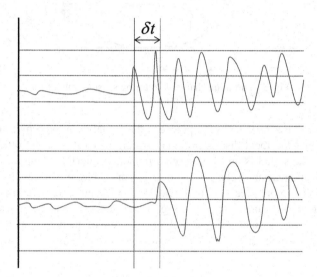

Fig. 4. Time difference of the signal received between sensor y and sensor x

In the case of weak local discharge signal of 10 kV cable, in order to quickly confirm the authenticity of the local discharge signal and screen out the interference signal, the rapid diagnosis strategy is selected [16]. The local discharge signal monitoring sensors are deployed in the outer layer of the cable and the grounding wire position respectively, so as to implement the rapid collection and identification of the local discharge signal of the cable and make a direct judgment on the severity of the local discharge. The deployment method is shown in Fig. 5 below.

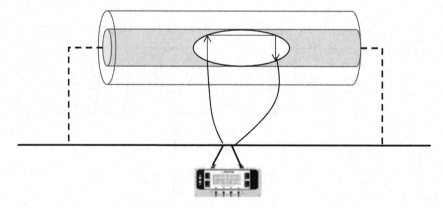

Fig. 5. The local discharge signal monitoring sensors deployment

After a quick detection of the partial discharge signal of 10 kV cable in urban distribution network, the level of the partial discharge signal needs to be further estimated. Intensive monitoring shall be carried out according to the location where partial discharge often occurs in 10 kV cable, such as the location of cable joint and the location with thin insulation layer. Partial discharge signal monitoring sensors are deployed on the surface layer of the cable, and then high-frequency signal acquisition is carried out and a data map of the partial discharge signal is established. By constructing a similar matching database, an estimate of the degree of partial discharge of the cable is implemented and the corresponding measures are automatically assembled. The application of the local discharge signal database greatly enhances the level of identification of the local discharge signal of 10 kV cables.

4   Security Diagnosis Platform

The architecture of the partial discharge security diagnosis platform for 10 kV cables in urban distribution networks proposed in this paper is shown in Fig. 6. The security diagnosis platform system mainly consists of local discharge signal transmitters, signal sensors, filtering devices, acquisition units and signal processing units. By deploying two sets of identical signal acquisition and processing units at both ends of the cable, the pulse current signals propagating along the cable are analyzed and processed. Firstly, by measuring the propagation of the pulse current in the cable of length D, the bi-directional propagation time t in the cable is recorded, and the propagation speed v is calculated as shown in Eq. (3) below.

$$v = \frac{2D}{T} \tag{3}$$

After monitoring the propagation speed of the pulse current on the 10 kV cable, the pulse location of the partial discharge needs to be further located. The pulse signal collected at the x end of the cable is plotted into a waveform and the position of the partial discharge in the cable is calculated by Eq. (4), where T_1 and T_2 are the times when the first and second pulses are received by sensor x, respectively, and d is the distance between the partial discharge location and the x end.

$$d = \frac{(T + T_1 - T_2)v}{2} \tag{4}$$

4.1   Hardware System of the Proposed Platform

The hardware system of partial discharge security diagnosis platform is mainly composed of signal acquisition sensor, transmission module, signal amplification and processing modules. Among them, the key component of the partial discharge signal transmitting module is the signal transmitting antenna, and its transmitted signal will be transmitted quickly along the cable during operation. In addition, the signal is conducted to the ground using the grounding wire, and the pulse signal in the position of the grounding wire is captured by the sensor and run in the circuit to complete the whole signal

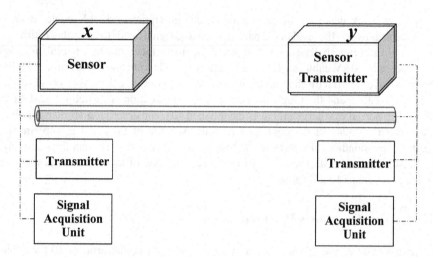

Fig. 6. Architecture of the proposed security diagnosis platform

transmission and acquisition process. In order to improve the filtering ability of the diagnostic platform for interference signals, the pulse circuit needs to be further optimized to improve the anti-interference ability of the whole circuit, and the architecture of this filtering circuit is shown in Fig. 7 below.

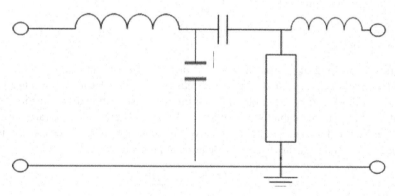

Fig. 7. Architecture of the filter circuit

4.2 Software System of the Proposed Platform

The software part design of the 10 kV cable partial discharge diagnosis platform for urban distribution networks is mainly carried out based on control language. The IPC chip is used to realize automatic sampling, fast screening and removal of abnormal signals as well as efficient transmission and processing. In addition, in order to build a threshold database, the collected signals need to be automatically compared and stored, and data such as characteristic patterns, noise categories and signal analysis are analyzed and stored through the software.

4.3 Security Diagnostic Process of the Proposed Platform

A diagnostic test of partial discharge of a 10 kV cable inlet in the urban distribution network is selected. After the abnormal partial discharge signal of cable is found, UHF current and time difference are used to phase and locate the discharge signal to determine the detailed data information of partial discharge cable. In the process of further diagnosis, the discharge signals could be monitored in multiple phases of the cable line. Since the UHF current diagnosis is more sensitive to interference signals, further detection of the local discharge signals is required. UHF discharge diagnosis is performed on the 10 kV cable to observe whether there is any abnormality in the obtained amplitude. In order to pinpoint in which phase of the 10 kV cable the local discharge signal occurs, the signal acquisition sensors are deployed according to the scheme shown in Fig. 8.

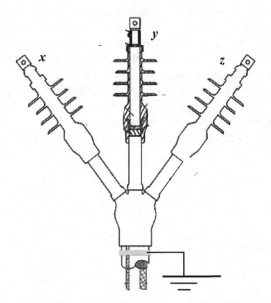

Fig. 8. Signal acquisition sensors at cable terminals

The waveforms of the x-phase, y-phase, and z-phase signals in the three-phase cable shown in Fig. 8 were detected, and the phase waveforms shown in Fig. 9 are obtained. From the obtained three-phase waveforms, it can be seen that the detection signal of phase x is different from that of the other two phases, so the location of the partial discharge signal can be determined to come from the x-phase cable. At this point, further confirmation of the partial discharge location of the x-phase cable is required, and further diagnosis of its ground wire is needed.

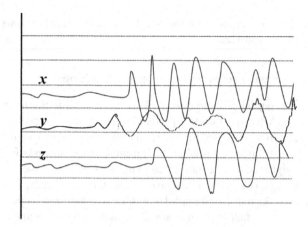

Fig. 9. Phase waveform of three-phase cable

The grounding line of the x-phase cable was diagnosed using the UHF current diagnostic method, and the diagnostic mapping shown in Fig. 10 is obtained. From this mapping, it can be seen that there is a time difference between the abnormal signals diagnosed by the upper and lower separately arranged sensors, where the partial discharge signal appears first at the upper sensor position. Thus, it can be found that the partial discharge appears at the upper part of the x-phase cable. Through the detailed diagnosis of the upper part of the positioned x-phase cable, obvious signs of partial discharge can be identified, which proves the accuracy and effectiveness of the diagnosis platform in detecting and locating the cable partial discharge signal.

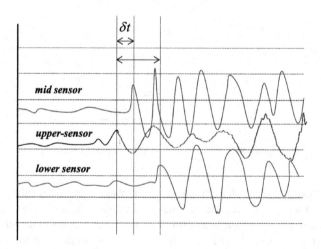

Fig. 10. Diagnostic mapping of x-phase cables

5   Application of the Security Diagnosis Platform

In order to further verify the performance of the security diagnostic platform for partial discharge of 10 kV cables in urban distribution networks proposed in this paper, a voltage field is applied to the distribution network cables and the data and spectrum of partial discharge of cables under the action of the voltage field are analyzed. Figure 11 shows the diagnostic results of the internal discharge of the cable. It can be seen that the distribution of the frequency component is more concentrated in the case of internal partial discharge of the 10 kV cable, but the amplitude and phase of the discharge are more dispersed and stable.

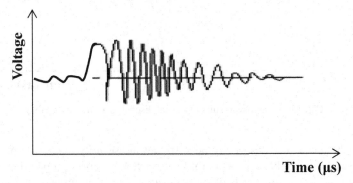

Fig. 11. Diagnostic results of internal cable discharge

The diagnostic results of partial surface discharge of 10 kV cable in urban distribution network are shown in Fig. 12 and the results show that the surface discharge of the cable is also more concentrated in the UHF signal, and the amplitude of its pulse discharge is more dispersed, but the time interval is more jumpy.

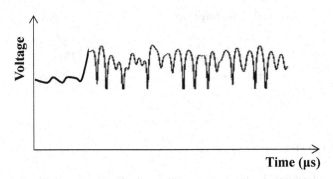

Fig. 12. Diagnosis results of cable partial surface discharge

The diagnosis results of local tip discharge of 10 kV cable in urban distribution network are shown in Fig. 13, which shows that the surface discharge of the cable is also more concentrated with high frequency signal and the sensitivity of diagnosis is low. However, the amplitude of the tip partial discharge of the cable is not dispersed and the stability of the time interval is high.

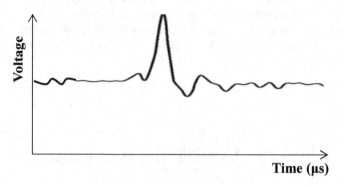

Fig. 13. Diagnosis results of partial discharge at the tip of cable

From the above analysis, it can be seen that the security diagnostic platform for partial discharge of 10 kV cables in urban distribution networks proposed in this paper can effectively detect the signals of surface partial discharge, tip partial discharge and internal partial discharge in cables, and produce a comprehensive analysis of their signal characteristics. The diagnostic sensitivity of the security diagnostic platform is shown in Table 1, which can meet the actual needs of power systems.

Table 1. Diagnostic sensitivity of partial discharge of 10 kV cable in distribution network

No.	Sensitivity	
	Partial discharge type	Results
1	Surface discharge	High
2	Internal discharge	High
3	Tip discharge	Medium

6   Conclusion

Cable partial discharge in distribution network is one of the important factors leading to power grid operation failure. The cable partial discharge security diagnosis platform proposed in this paper can implement the efficient and low-cost diagnosis of cable partial discharge in urban distribution network. The diagnosis platform can accurately identify partial discharge, meet the needs of power operation and maintenance department to diagnose cable partial discharge without shutdown, and ensure the maintenance of cable insulation performance, so as to realize the long-term economic operation of distribution network system. Through the verification of the effect of the security diagnosis platform, the results show that the platform can quickly locate and eliminate the hidden dangers of cable insulation, further improve the security and reliability of power system cables. In this paper, the research and combination of distribution network diagnosis platform and smart city integration level is not deepened enough, which needs to be expanded and analyzed in the future research.

References

1. Li, Y., Li, Q., Chen, Y., Zhang, S.: Research and application of calibration and comparison system for partial discharge live detection equipment. In: 2021 IEEE 5th Advanced Information Technology, Electronic and Automation Control Conference (IAEAC), pp. 435–438 (2021)
2. Deng, Z., Cai, M., Wang, H., Fan, R., Zheng, S., Hao, Y.: Partial discharge detection and structure optimization of a bushing of 10 kV switchgear cabinet. In: 2019 2nd International Conference on Electrical Materials and Power Equipment (ICEMPE), pp. 628–634 (2019)
3. Cheng, Y., et al.: Statistical analysis of partial discharge faults of HV cables. In: 2020 IEEE Electrical Insulation Conference (EIC), pp. 422–425 (2020)
4. Yamashita, K., Watanuki, S., Miyake, T., Sakoda, T., Kawano, W.: Development of on-line partial discharge locator for electric power cable. In: 2018 IEEE Electrical Insulation Conference (EIC), pp. 216–219 (2018)
5. Wen, W.: Analysis of 10 kV cable partial discharge on-line monitoring and positioning system based on urban distribution network. Big Technol. (25), 13–15 (2016)
6. Lin, S., Xie, C., Li, D., Fu, Y.: Load preprocessing method based on grey correlation and fuzzy cluster analysis. Electr. Meas. Instrum. **54**(11), 3642 (2017)
7. Kim, H., Marwah, M., Arlitt, M.F., et al.: Unsupervised disaggregation of low frequency power measurements. In: Eleventh Siam International conference on Data Mining, pp. 747–758 (2012)
8. Wang, L., Lv, H., Wang, Z., et al.: Application research on partial discharge detection and location technology of switchgear. Guangdong Electr. Power (4), 91–94 (2014)
9. Lv, F., Li, H., Wang, Z., et al.: Research on partial discharge detection and location of switchgear based on TEV and ultrasonic. Electr. Meas. Instrum. **50**(11), 73–78 (2013)
10. Liu, Y., Wang, H., Wang, J., et al.: Design and application of on-line monitoring system for partial discharge in high voltage switchgear. Comput. Digit. Eng. **49**(9): 1788–1792+1888 (2021)
11. Xie, R., Yang, C., Shen, Q., Li, S., Luo, Y., Yu, B.: Comparative study on the switchgear partial discharge characteristics based on transient earth voltage and pulse current detection methods. Electr. Power **55**(3), 37–47 (2022)
12. He, X., Xu, Z.: Study on insulating property detection and fault diagnosis technology for HV switchgear. Zhejiang Electr. Power (5): 6–10 (2010)
13. Wu, D., et al.: Partial discharge monitoring and characteristic parameters extraction for high-voltage switchboards based on ultra-high frequency method. Electr. Eng. (7), 14–16 (2021)
14. Qiu, S., Zheng, Y., Gao, D., Xu, X., Mao, S.: Research on realization of on-line monitoring system for 10 kV ring network cabinet. Electr. Power Equip. Manage. (5), 23–25 (2022)

15. Xiong, J., Wang, Y., Huang, H., et al.: Analysis of on-line PD detection technology on switchgears and its application to guangzhou distribution system. Mod. Electr. Power **27**(5), 25–29 (2010)
16. Tian, Y., Chen, W., Ning, X., Han, H., Bian, K., Zhou, L.: Review of non-contact on-line detection technology of outdoor overhead equipment in distribution network. High Volt. Eng. (8), 2495–2501 (2019)

Research on the Electromagnetic Sensor-Based Partial Discharge Security Monitoring System of Distribution Network

Xinping Wang[✉], Chunpeng Li, Xiaoping Yang, Feng Jiang, Qiqi Luan, and Yifan Wang

Jiangsu Frontier Electric Technology Co., Ltd., Nanjing 211106, China
wxp1995@hotmail.com

Abstract. The generation of partial discharges in distribution networks may have a significant negative impact on the secure and stable operation of the power grid. Therefore, it is of great practical value to design a security system that can monitor the partial discharge status of the distribution network in real time, remotely and online. The security monitoring system is expected to effectively diagnose the health status of the power grid system and predict the development of its status. Although the traditional distribution network security monitoring system is capable of monitoring partial discharge to an extent, there is still much room for improvement in terms of signal immunity, data transmission efficiency and intelligent identification of partial discharge patterns. Hence, this paper designs an electromagnetic sensor-based partial discharge security monitoring system to achieve rapid identification, filtering, transmission and processing of local discharge signals. The effect of the proposed security system is verified by applying it to distribution lines, the results show that the security monitoring system based on electromagnetic sensors proposed can effectively meet the actual monitoring requirements of the power grid.

Keywords: Security monitoring · Electromagnetic sensors · Partial discharge · Distribution network

1 Introduction

At present, various industries are increasingly dependent on the electric power system [1]. The functions and structures of widely deployed electric terminals are becoming more complex, putting forward higher requirements for the security and stability of the distribution network system [2]. The partial discharge phenomenon of distribution network will bring a big negative impact on the secure and stable operation of the network. For example, partial discharge can lead to a significant reduction in the functionality of electrical equipment in the distribution network, and even cause equipment failure and scrap [3]. Since partial discharges in the distribution network can be harmful to the whole network, it is necessary to monitor and prevent them effectively. Partial discharge monitoring of distribution network is an effective prerequisite for power grid troubleshooting. It can not only prevent the occurrence of power grid sudden problems, but also ensure that the power grid system can obtain greater social and economic benefits [4].

Y. Tian et al. (Eds.): ICBDS 2022, CCIS 1796, pp. 651–663, 2023.
https://doi.org/10.1007/978-981-99-3300-6_47

It is of great practical value to study and apply the system that can monitor the partial discharge status of distribution network in real-time, remotely and online [5]. On the one hand, the partial discharge security monitoring system can monitor the health of the system in real time; on the other hand, the system can effectively diagnose the health status of the power grid system and effectively predict the development of its status [6]. There are many problems and shortcomings in the traditional methods of partial discharge security monitoring of distribution network, mainly including insufficient filtering ability of external environmental interference signals, and weak automatic and intelligent identification ability of partial discharge mode [7]. Among them, the former problem is mainly solved by digital signal filtering technology represented by Fourier analysis, FIR (Finite Impulse Response) filter, IIR (Infinite Impulse Response) filter and signal correlation method and the latter problem is mainly solved with the aid of intelligent algorithms.

Although the traditional distribution network partial discharge security monitoring system is probably capable of local and remote monitoring, there is still much room for improvement in terms of signal anti-interference, efficient data transmission and intelligent identification of partial discharge patterns [8]. The current research methods for partial discharge security monitoring of distribution network mainly include ultrasonic monitoring method, infrared monitoring method, conventional electrical detection method, chemical monitoring method, optical monitoring method and monitoring method based on electromagnetic sensors [9]. Among them, the ultrasonic detection method is relatively sensitive to noise interference, and the monitoring signal is affected by the distance factor and other factors [10]. Infrared detection method is easy to be greatly disturbed when thermal faults are generated inside the distribution equipment. Chemical detection method is difficult to accurately determine the type of local discharge in distribution network. The pulse current method and optical detection method have poor adaptability to remote on-line monitoring [11]. Based on the above analysis, this paper designs an electromagnetic sensor-based partial discharge security monitoring system for distribution network, which is expected to provide rapid identification, filtering, transmission and processing of partial discharge signals with relatively high accuracy, and make intelligent processing decisions according to the severity of partial discharge.

2 Theory of Partial Discharge

2.1 Factors of Partial Discharge in Distribution Network

Circuits and various electrical devices in the distribution network system may generate various interactions under the action of electromagnetic field, especially in the case of high electric field in the distribution network, which will lead to partial discharge of electrical devices. Generally speaking, partial discharge does not cause breakdown of the insulation of the electrical system, but a flow of electrostatic charge [12]. There are various factors that lead to partial discharge in the distribution network, such as asymmetry of the electrode system of the electric device, asymmetric drop of the electrode system, uneven insulation media and impurities inside the insulation system. Among them, the electric field and electrical properties of the insulation layer inside the electric device play a crucial role. The weaker the electric field strength of the insulation layer, the easier it is for partial discharges to occur. The partial discharge of the distribution network will bring many hazards to the grid system, including the security, reliability and stability of the electrical equipment, corrosive discharge and insulation breakdown.

2.2 Security Monitoring Parameters of Partial Discharge

Since there are many factors affecting the partial discharge of the distribution network, the electrical equipment in the distribution network will inevitably produce various degrees of partial discharge [13]. In order to effectively control the partial discharge phenomenon, besides the security monitoring, the location and arrangement of electrical equipment in the distribution network need to be reasonably optimized to minimize the adverse effects of partial discharge. In order to effectively monitor the parameter values of partial discharge in the distribution network, it is necessary to determine the parameter characterization index of the level of partial discharge inside the electrical equipment [14]. The characterization parameters of partial discharge in the distribution network mainly include the relationship between the actual discharge and the apparent discharge, the discharge phase, the initial discharge and discharge extinguishing voltage, the repetition rate of discharge and the discharge power.

3 Security Monitoring Method of Partial Discharge

At present, with the continuous expansion of the power grid scale, the complexity of the distribution network and the internal and external operating environment of the equipment are more demanding, especially the partial discharge problem faced by electrical equipment operating continuously under high voltage and high electric field environment is becoming more and more prominent [15]. In order to ensure the secure, stable and reliable long-term operation of the distribution network system, it is necessary to carry out the monitoring of partial discharge. Currently, there are various methods to monitor the partial discharge of the distribution network, mainly based on the characteristic parameters of the partial discharge signal and the comprehensive analysis of the characteristic quantity data, so as to obtain the discharge status of the distribution network system. Table 1 below shows the comparison of the advantages and disadvantages of the existing distribution network partial discharge security monitoring methods.

Table 1. Comparison of existing security monitoring methods

Methods	Sensitivity	Anti-interference	Precision	Fault location
Ultrasonic detection method	High	Strong	High	Medium
Chemical detection method	Poor	High	Poor	High
Light detection method	Poor	High	Poor	Poor
UHF detection method	High	Medium	High	High
Pulse current	High	Poor	High	Poor
Electromagnetic sensors	High	Medium	High	High

From Table 1, it can be seen that the current common distribution network partial discharge monitoring methods have more or less certain problems or deficiencies, which make it difficult to achieve the expected level of monitoring efficiency and effectiveness of the partial discharge phenomenon. In comparison, electromagnetic sensors have relatively more advantages in monitoring sensitivity, accuracy and fault location and thus are adopted in our method.

3.1 Security Monitoring Based on Electromagnetic Sensing

In the case of partial discharge of electrical devices in the distribution network, pulse current will be generated and the current amplitude will increase significantly under the action of electromagnetic field. With the occurrence of partial discharge, the electric field force will gradually abate, thus making the current amplitude show periodic decay. The frequency of the pulse current generated by partial discharge of electrical devices can be calculated by the function shown in Eq. (1) below. Where, p, Q, T are the peak value, pulse duration and rise time of partial discharge pulse current respectively.

$$p(f) = \left| \frac{Q}{(i + fT)^2} \right| \tag{1}$$

The difference between T and Q at a particular discharge volume leads to different time-domain waveforms and amplitude-frequency characteristics as shown in Fig. 1 below. It can be seen the pulse amplitude, frequency spectrum and exhibited energy are negatively correlated with the rise time of the partial discharge pulse current.

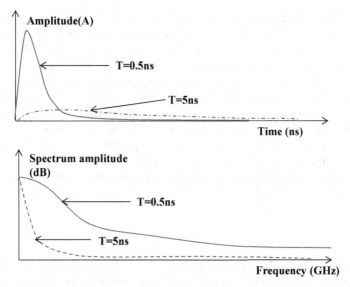

Fig. 1. Different time-domain waveforms and amplitude-frequency characteristics

3.2 Partial Discharge Electromagnetic Radiation Characteristics

Under the action of high-voltage electric field, it will produce oscillating current and further lead to partial discharge electromagnetic radiation whose intensity is positively correlated with the current intensity [16]. The following Eqs. (2) and (3) are the calculation of the electric field strength of the near-area field and the far-area field respectively, where M is the magnetic field strength, S is the electric field strength, Q is the current RMS (Root Mean Square) vector, Δd is the permeability of the medium, γ is the dielectric constant of the medium, e is the phase constant of the electromagnetic wave propagating in the medium, the angle between the directional diameter of the observation point and the antenna axis is α, κ is the length of the observation point from the center of the electric dipole, φ is the angular frequency of the electromagnetic wave.

$$\overline{M} = -i\frac{Q\Delta d \cos\alpha}{2\pi\gamma} - -i\frac{Q\Delta d \sin\alpha}{4\pi\gamma} \tag{2}$$

$$\overline{S} = i\frac{Q\Delta d \sin\alpha}{4\pi\kappa}e^{-r\varphi} \tag{3}$$

3.3 Local Discharge Signal Transmission Mechanism

In the process of partial discharge in the distribution network, discharge energy and electromagnetic waves will be generated, and the propagation direction of both is the same. Due to the difference in the complexity of the internal structure of different electrical devices, the transmission path of the partial discharge electromagnetic wave signal also differs, and the transmission process of the signal is also more complex. In addition, the transmission process of partial discharge signal will be interfered by various factors, including narrowband signal, random noise, pulse interference, space interference, ground network interference, and various electromagnetic and random interference, etc.

The key parameter indicators of electromagnetic waves released by local discharge in the propagation process include electromagnetic, magnetic field and current density. Those indicators show the regularity of transmission, while the attenuation rate is very fast and the intensity increases with the increase of conductor conductivity and magnetic permeability. The penetration depth of the electric and magnetic fields of UHF (Ultra High Frequency) electromagnetic waves propagating in a good conductor can be calculated by the function shown in Eq. (4) below. Where m and e are the magnetic and electrical permeability, respectively, and s is the depth of electromagnetic wave propagation.

$$s = \sqrt{\frac{1}{\varepsilon m e}} \tag{4}$$

Generally speaking, the metal casing of the electrical device will bring a large barrier to the electromagnetic signal, resulting in a large marketing of the partial discharge signal transmission. In order to better collect the electromagnetic signals generated by partial discharge of electrical devices, the electromagnetic sensors need to be reasonably arranged inside the electromagnetic devices of the distribution network.

4   Security Monitoring System of Discharge Signal

Aiming at the problems of poor anti-interference capability in the traditional distribution network partial discharge monitoring process, especially the insufficient recognition and suppression of interference signals, this paper designs an electromagnetic sensor-based partial discharge security monitoring system for distribution networks. The system implements the execution of multi-process and high-efficiency monitoring commands by integrating computer software and hardware algorithms. By deploying noise filtering, signal amplification and signal transmission modules in the security monitoring system, effective monitoring of the partial discharge process is realized. The electromagnetic (EM) sensor-based partial discharge signal security monitoring architecture is shown in Fig. 2 below, in which the data acquisition module contains the signal amplification function, which can further amplify the weak signal. The data de-noising module sets the filtering threshold by intelligent algorithm to implement the screening and retention of the signal. The feature extraction and pattern recognition module can locate the signal with high accuracy and help the remote monitoring system to implement automated data analysis and processing, reducing the arithmetic pressure of the system.

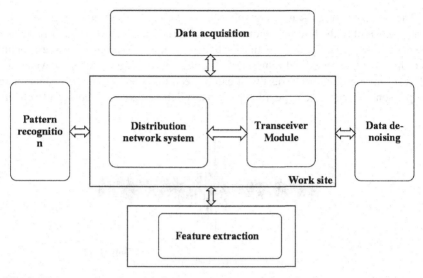

Fig. 2. EM sensor-based partial discharge signal security monitoring system architecture

4.1 Deployment of Electromagnetic Sensors

The electromagnetic sensors are deployed in a targeted manner according to the type of partial discharge signals in the distribution network. In particular, for local partial discharge cases, electromagnetic sensors are deployed in the housing of electrical devices to better collect and capture the partial discharge signals. For the case of cable partial discharge in the distribution network, since the generated partial discharge electromagnetic signal propagates along the cable discharge point to both ends, it is usually necessary to deploy electromagnetic sensors in the cable branch structure to better capture the discharge signal as shown in Fig. 3. The electromagnetic sensors will periodically analyze the collected discharge signals and periodically analyze the collected data.

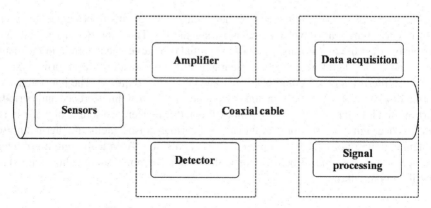

Fig. 3. Deployment of electromagnetic sensors

The electromagnetic sensor classifies and organizes the collected partial discharge signals and applies the filtering algorithm to make a comprehensive analysis and evaluation of the signals. The types of partial discharges in the distribution network are obtained according to the set threshold values as well as the filtering algorithm, as shown in Fig. 4 below. From the monitoring results, it can be seen that the monitoring results contain comparison patterns, discharge trend patterns, and these data are recorded effectively.

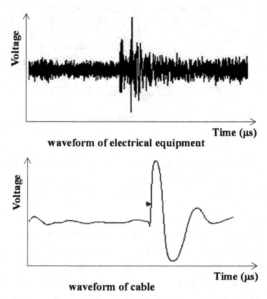

Fig. 4. The types of partial discharges in the distribution network

4.2   Interference Sources of Local Discharge Signals

In the process of security monitoring of the partial discharge, it will be subject to excess interference signals and environmental noise signals, etc. These interference signals will seriously affect the monitoring effect of the partial discharge phenomenon in the distribution network. Therefore, in order to guarantee the accuracy of the monitoring system, effective filtering and screening of the monitoring data is required. The interference of partial discharge signal mainly includes white noise, impulse interference and periodic narrowband interference and so on. Among them, the interference source of white noise interference signal is a random combination of various noises, including thermal noise, system coupling noise, scattered particle noise and so on. A typical white noise interference is shown in Fig. 5 below, which shows that the noise source shows a certain distribution regularity.

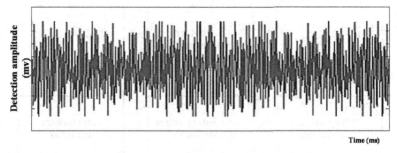

Fig. 5. Typical white noise interference

Periodic narrow-band interference and pulse-type interference have typical discrete characteristics and action impulsivity, respectively. The former mainly comes from various electrical devices in the distribution network system, while the latter includes both random and periodic types, and either type will produce greater interference to the monitoring of partial discharge.

4.3 Anti-interference Scheme for Security Monitoring

Security monitoring of distribution network based on electromagnetic sensors has more advantages than other monitoring schemes in terms of accuracy, efficiency and adaptability, but its anti-interference capability is more general. For this reason, a reasonable anti-interference scheme needs to be developed to improve the universality of the monitoring system. In order to make the whole monitoring system more effective, multiple monitoring measures are taken to improve the anti-interference ability of the system under multiple interference sources. In order to filter the interference noise, it is necessary to combine the interference filtering circuit with intelligent algorithm. For the interference of white noise on the partial discharge security monitoring, the noise filtering threshold is set using wavelet analysis algorithm to eliminate the noise while maximizing the retention of the effective signal transmission. For the interference of pulse-type signals, the process of interference noise removal is shown in Fig. 6 below, and the interference noise is filtered by a combination of hardware as well as software. For example, white noise is eliminated by wavelet changes, periodic impulse interference is identified using classification algorithms, etc.

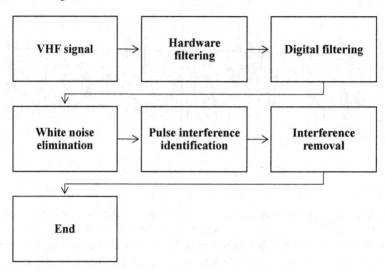

Fig. 6. The process of interference noise removal

In addition, for periodic noise disturbances, digital filtering algorithms with filter hardware are used to effectively suppress the periodic disturbance noise in the electrical installations of the distribution network.

5   Tests and Analysis

In order to verify the practical application effect of the electromagnetic sensor-based partial discharge security monitoring system for distribution networks, three actual distribution network lines operating in the network are selected for monitoring. During the application test of the monitoring system, the selected distribution network lines are monitored for partial discharge for a duration of one hour. The monitoring results of this system were compared and analyzed with the monitoring results of oscillatory wave partial discharge, and the results are shown in Table 2 below.

Table 2. Compared with the monitoring results of oscillatory wave partial discharge

Chanel	Voltage	Sensors	pC	Quantity	Partial discharge ratio
1	10 kV	RDFH-2020	257	51	17%
2	10 kV	RDFH-2020	65	9	2%
3	10 kV	RDFH-2020	156	121	10%

Through a comprehensive assessment of the monitoring results of partial discharge, the monitoring results obtained are shown in Fig. 7 below. It can be seen that among the selected distribution network lines, line 1 has more obvious partial discharge phenomenon. The interference signal of distribution network line 2 is weak, but the partial discharge characteristics are not obvious.

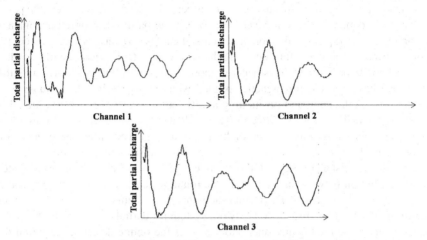

Fig. 7. The monitoring results of partial discharge

The amplitude accumulation of partial discharges in the distribution network is counted using security monitoring system and the results are obtained as shown in Fig. 8 below. It can be seen that in the process of conducting security monitoring of the distribution network based on electromagnetic sensors, the faults existing in the distribution network system are effectively screened using the threshold of the system. The distribution network line partial discharge is continuously monitored and compared with the oscillatory wave partial discharge detection test results, and it can be seen from the comparison results that the electromagnetic sensor-based security monitoring system proposed in this paper can produce effective test results.

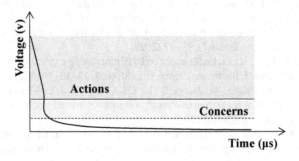

Fig. 8. The amplitude accumulation of partial discharges

6 Conclusion

The partial discharge phenomenon of the distribution network will have a great negative impact on the secure and stable operation of the power grid and will cause great harm to the whole power grid, so it is necessary to effectively monitor and prevent the partial discharge phenomenon. By effectively monitoring the partial discharge phenomenon, we can identify and prevent the potential faults of cables and various electrical devices in the distribution network, thus ensuring the secure and stable operation of the whole distribution network system. This paper proposes a partial discharge security monitoring system based on electromagnetic sensors, which not only has the advantages of high accuracy, efficiency and positioning ability, but also achieves a breakthrough in the level of anti-interference and can meet the demand of effective monitoring of the whole operation status of the system. In this paper, through a comprehensive analysis of the causes of the partial discharge phenomenon in the distribution network, combined with the characteristics of the partial discharge signal, the security monitoring system of the distribution network based on the electromagnetic sensor is constructed and its application effect is verified. The results show that the system can effectively meet the monitoring needs of the distribution network system for partial discharge. In this paper, the research on the intelligence and automation of the online detection of partial discharge in distribution network is still not deep enough, and the intelligent calibration of the discharge signal needs to be improved, which needs to be further studied in the future research.

References

1. Chen, C., Chen, Y., Liu, W., Gao, W.: Research on ground sensing method for online detection of partial discharge in transformers. Zhejiang Electr. Power (12), 21–25 (2014)
2. Di, C., Zhang, J., Bian, D., Cai, X., Liu, B.: Research on online monitoring method of transformer partial discharge. China High-Tech Enterprise (02), 154–155 (2015)
3. Yuan, W., Jia, M., Chen, W., Liu, X., Han, H.: Cable local discharge signal denoising method based on spectral subtraction and wavelet analysis. Mod. Electron. Tech. 44(19), 71–75 (2021)
4. Su, S., Zeng, L., Lin, Y., Yan, C., Meng, C.: Design of GIS partial discharge on-line monitoring system for substations. Electr. Saf. Technol. 23(09), 41–45 (2021)
5. Xia, Y.: Partial discharge detection method of distribution network cable based on UHF identification. Electron. Test (01), 93–97 (2022)
6. Liu, X., Zheng, W., Li, H., Li, L.: Research on UHF monitoring technology of partial discharge in power transformer. J. Shenyang Ligong Univ. 40(06), 27–30+35 (2021)
7. Wang, C., Tang, Z., Chang, W., Zheng, S., Li, C.: A method for anti-interference and multi-source discharge signal separation in ultra high-frequency partial discharge detection. Power Grid Technol. 36(03), 46–50 (2012)
8. Zhang, H.: Partial Discharge Detection and Location Based on Ultra-high Frequency and Ultra-sonic Method. Dissertation for the Master Degree. Hebei University of Science and Technology (2019)
9. Lü, F., Jin, H., Wang, Z., Zhang, B.: GIS partial discharge detection and identification based on combined kernel multi-feature fusion method. Trans. China Electrotechnical Soc. 29(10), 334–340 (2014)

10. Zhou, H., et al.: The anti-interference method of Michelson optical fiber interferometer for GIS partial discharge ultrasonic detection. In: 2019 IEEE Conference on Electrical Insulation and Dielectric Phenomena (CEIDP), pp. 283–286 (2019)
11. Jun, H., Si, W., Wang, S., et al.: Status and development of localization methods for partial discharge in power transformers. Transformer **44**(6), 40–43 (2017)
12. Wang, S., He, Y., Yin, B., Zeng, W., Deng, Y., Hu, Z.: A partial discharge localization method in transformers based on linear conversion and density peak clustering. IEEE Access **9**, 7447–7459 (2021)
13. Madhu, S., Bhavani, H., Sumathi, S., Vidya, H.: A novel algorithm for denoising of simulated partial discharge signals using adaptive wavelet thresholding methods. In: 2015 2nd International Conference on Electronics and Communication Systems (ICECS), pp. 1596–1602 (2015)
14. Jing, W.: Research and application of GIS partial discharge signal positioning based on UHF intelligent sensors. In: 2022 IEEE International Conference on Electrical Engineering, Big Data and Algorithms (EEBDA), pp. 1163–1167 (2022)
15. Zhang, S., Li, Y., Liu, Z., Chen, Q.: Performance detection and analysis of built-in UHF sensors for UHV GIS equipment. In: 2021 IEEE 5th Conference on Energy Internet and Energy System Integration (EI2), pp. 3364–3367 (2021)
16. Zhao, L., Ye, L., Yu, B., Lin, H., Yang, Y., Zheng, W.: Research on partial discharge localization in 252 kV GIS using ultrasonic associated with electromagnetic wave method. In: 2020 IEEE 5th International Conference on Integrated Circuits and Microsystems (ICICM), pp. 14–18 (2020)

Design of Ultrasonic-Based Remote Distribution Network Online Security Monitoring Device

Qiqi Luan[⊠], Feng Jiang, Xinping Wang, Qingwu Song, Tianze Zhu, and Jiangbin Wang

Jiangsu Frontier Electric Technology Co., Ltd., Nanjing 210000, China
704998432@qq.com

Abstract. The scale of the power grid and the degree of informationization and intelligence of the power equipment are increasing, and the end devices and users are becoming more diversified and complex, which makes higher requirements on the stability and security of the electrical system. On the other hand, the facilities of the power grid system are widely distributed, and the relevant equipment is deployed in a more dispersed manner, which puts forward higher requirements on the real-time and remote nature of the security monitoring means of the distribution network. In this paper, through the analysis of the components of ultrasonic-based online security monitoring system, especially based on the mechanism of partial discharge and the mechanism of action between partial discharge and ultrasonic waves, the online security monitoring device of partial discharge is designed. The system contains operation modules including acquisition, amplification, filtering and processing of partial discharge signals. The simulation results show that the proposed device may improve the identification efficiency and the anti-interference capability.

Keywords: Ultrasonic · Remote Distribution Network · Partial Discharge · Online Monitoring

1 Introduction

As an important part of modern society, the power system has a vital impact on all aspects of the social economy [1]. The current scale of the power grid and the degree of informationization and intelligence of the power equipment are constantly increasing, and the end devices and users are becoming more and more diversified and complex, making higher requirements for the stability and security of the electrical system [2]. As an important part of the entire power grid, the distribution system plays an important role in ensuring the effective operation of the entire power system [3]. During the operation of distribution grid devices, there are inevitably operations such as energy switching, and distribution grid faults represented by partial discharges will have a greater adverse impact and interference on the stable and secure operation of the power grid system. Hence, the effective monitoring and prevention of distribution grid partial discharges are needed [4].

Y. Tian et al. (Eds.): ICBDS 2022, CCIS 1796, pp. 664–676, 2023.
https://doi.org/10.1007/978-981-99-3300-6_48

Due to the wide distribution of power grid system facilities and the relatively scattered deployment of relevant equipment, higher requirements are put forward for the real-time remote monitoring of partial discharge in distribution network [5]. The traditional monitoring methods for partial discharge of distribution network mainly include regular inspection and maintenance, offline maintenance, etc. [6]. Those monitoring methods generally have relatively low efficiency, low precision and need to occupy large human resources. In this context, how to design and develop a device that can remotely monitor the status of distribution network devices in real time is of great importance for research and application [7]. With the development of technology, the monitoring of partial discharges in distribution networks has gradually developed in the direction of non-electrical, online monitoring, and has achieved more significant application effects.

The application of ultrasonic technology in the online security monitoring of partial discharge in the distribution network can effectively avoid the intrusion and damage to the state of the power grid system [8]. The ultrasonic technology can achieve effective monitoring of the state of the equipment by collecting the electronic collision signals existing in the electrical equipment under the partial discharge [9]. The technology is well adapted to the typical characteristics of decentralized deployment and remote interconnection of distribution network equipment, and can effectively monitor the discharge status of various decentralized terminals without affecting the reliability of power supply to the grid [10]. Based on this, this paper proposes an ultrasonic-based remote distribution network partial discharge online security monitoring device in hardware architecture and software implementation, which can collect, process, analyze, warn the partial discharge status data efficiently and effectively to guarantee the long-term stable and secure operation of the distribution network equipment.

2 Principles of Online Security Monitoring

2.1 Mechanism of Partial Discharge

The research on partial discharge mechanism of remote distribution network includes various types. According to different discharge environments, there are different discharge mechanisms, such as flow injection discharge and town transmission discharge [11]. The partial discharge of remote distribution network is usually caused by the lack of purity of the insulation medium of the distribution network cable, which contains various impurities that cause the change of the dielectric constant of the cable and the gathering of abnormal electric field under the action of the distribution network voltage [12]. When the abnormal electric field in the insulation medium of the distribution network cable gathers to a certain strength, it will produce ionization phenomenon, which will lead to partial discharge of the distribution network.

Remote distribution network partial discharge phenomenon is not necessarily caused entirely by the impurities present in the distribution network cable, the distribution network cable electric field distribution and other factors can lead to the generation of partial discharge phenomenon. In the remote distribution network cable shown in Fig. 1 below, the impurity z is surrounded by the insulating medium e of the cable. Under the effect of short-time discharge impulse signal and the influence of resistance value, the capacitance and resistance of impurities in dielectric and cable in distribution network can be ignored.

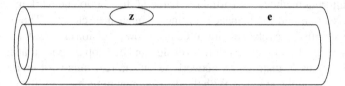

Fig. 1. Insulating medium containing bubbles

When the distribution network insulation medium is subjected to the action of applied voltage, the larger voltage impact will break the impurities in cable, which leads to the impurities discharge [13]. The discharge of the insulation medium will show the characteristics of periodic changes, as shown in Fig. 2 below. In general, the symmetrical distribution of the medium will cause the voltage load to change its direction continuously, so that the accumulated charge in the cable will accumulate continuously in the accumulation-release cycle. In the actual partial discharge process, the quadrant where the discharge is mainly concentrated differs according to the difference of the external voltage discharge phase.

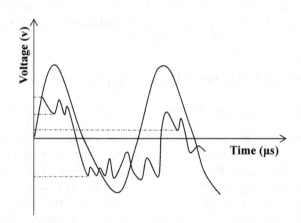

Fig. 2. The discharge of the insulation medium of the distribution network

2.2   Calculation of Partial Discharge

The partial discharge process in the remote distribution network can be constrained and influenced by a variety of factors, and therefore there are many discharge characterization parameters for partial discharge. In the case of partial discharge in the distribution network, the equivalent circuit of partial discharge in the remote distribution network is shown in Fig. 3 below.

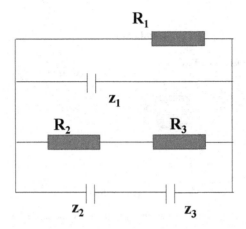

Fig. 3. The equivalent circuit of partial discharge in the remote distribution network

The actual amount of discharge in the distribution network is calculated as shown in Eq. (1) below, where D is the actual discharge of the distribution network, and ΔV is the voltage drop of impurity z in the distribution network cable. Since the actual discharge of the distribution network and the voltage drop of impurities in the cable are not easily obtained directly, the measurement of the voltage drop is usually obtained with the help of capacitors. In addition, since the single discharge of the distribution network often occurs instantaneously, the voltage drop of impurity z in the distribution network cable will be accompanied by the voltage change of impurities at different locations in the cable, as shown in Eq. (2) below, where ΔV_1, ΔV_3 are the voltage drops at impurities 1 and 3 in the cable, respectively.

$$D = \Delta V(z_3 + \frac{z_1 + z_2}{z_1 z_2}) \tag{1}$$

$$\Delta V_3 = \Delta V_1(\frac{z_1 + z_2}{z_1 z_2}) \tag{2}$$

The partial discharge of the distribution network is not only caused by the impurities inside the cable insulation layer, the characteristics of the cable insulation layer and the size and distribution of the impurities can lead to the generation of local internal discharge phenomenon. In fact, since there is inevitably a gap between the insulation layer and the conductive layer in the distribution network cable, as shown in Fig. 4 below, the discharge phenomenon will occur in the presence of AC (Alternating Current) voltage in the two dielectric layers.

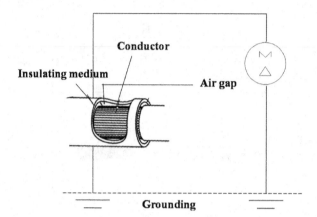

Fig. 4. Gap between the insulation layer and the conductive layer in the cable

From the above analysis, it can be seen that there is a certain difference in the electric field strength at different locations of the insulating medium and conducting medium in the remote distribution network, and this difference can lead to the generation of partial discharge phenomena. In general, the causes of partial discharge phenomena in distribution networks caused by insulating medium factors mainly include rated physical defects in the insulation layer of the power grid equipment, poor contact in the connecting part of the equipment, poor processing and assembly process, and free displacement of the electric field of metal particles [14].

As one of the manifestations of mechanical waves, ultrasound propagates by means of transverse and longitudinal oscillations. Due to its high frequency oscillation, ultrasonic waves can propagate through a wide range of media and have good penetration in solid and liquid phase media [15]. Therefore, sensors based on ultrasonic waves are often used for the detection of various substances. In addition, because ultrasonic waves also have the typical characteristics of concentrated energy and direction, long diffusion distance, and strong sense of interaction with the propagation carrier, various monitoring means based on ultrasonic waves have the double advantages of efficiency and accuracy.

2.3 Ultrasound and the Monitoring Mechanism

In a remote distribution system, if a partial discharge phenomenon occurs it is usually accompanied by an energy transformation that is caused by acoustic waves excited during the contraction and expansion of the medium in the cable under the action of voltage and electric field [16]. The application of ultrasonic technology in the remote distribution network includes several different modes, and its mechanism architecture is shown in Fig. 5 below. The sensor includes several main parts such as metal housing, socket, piezoelectric sheet, conductive medium and protective frame. The sensor achieves signal monitoring and positioning based on Doppler reflection theory. Among them, the metal protection frame can effectively shield the external electromagnetic interference signal, piezoelectric sheet and other structures can better enhance the friendliness of the monitoring environment and reduce the common mode electrical noise interference.

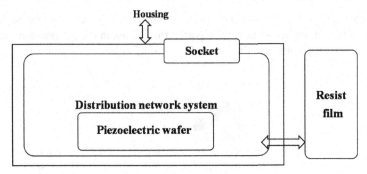

Fig. 5. Mechanism architecture of ultrasonic technology

2.4 Ultrasonic Determination Method of Partial Discharge

The determination of partial discharge of remote distribution network based on ultrasonic includes the judgment method based on the discharge characteristics of distribution network, such as the phase difference of discharge, and the judgment method of pulse current. The former method can effectively determine the partial discharge signal and the latter method has a high monitoring accuracy for the partial discharge inside the electrical equipment. Usually, in order to further improve the monitoring accuracy, the fusion of ultrasonic and pulse current is adopted to carry out the monitoring of partial discharge in remote distribution network, which can significantly eliminate the influence of internal and external interference factors, thus further improving the efficiency and accuracy of monitoring.

In addition, when monitoring the partial discharge of the remote distribution network, targeted countermeasures should be taken according to the difference of the collected monitoring signals to ensure the stable operation of the power grid. For example, if the discharge pulse interval is less than the set discharge threshold (usually less than 2.5 ms), it can be determined that the partial discharge intensity of the distribution network is large, and countermeasures need to be taken immediately to avoid larger losses. If the monitoring data feedback discharge pulse is much larger than the set threshold, it is necessary to further monitor and track the discharge status rather than deal with it.

3   Ultrasonic-Based Security Monitoring Device

3.1   Hardware Architecture

The hardware system architecture of the ultrasonic-based remote distribution network partial discharge online security monitoring device mainly consists of a remote online monitoring center, a remote data monitoring device, an industrial control computer, a data communication link, and various data concentration sensors, as shown in Fig. 6 below. Among them, all kinds of ultrasonic sensors represented by data concentration effectively collect the partial discharge signals of various electrical devices in the distribution network, and by comparing the captured signal with the monitoring threshold, the target is warned and disposal suggestions are given. The ultrasonic partial discharge data sensor establishes a direct connection with the control mechanism through a communication bus. Remote monitoring of partial discharges in the distribution network is implemented using digital monitoring and control software.

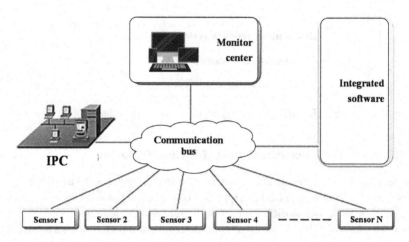

Fig. 6. The architecture of the ultrasonic-based remote monitoring device

In order to better guarantee the real-time and stability of the remote monitoring process of the partial discharge phenomenon in the distribution network, a comprehensive remote data transmission network architecture needs to be built, especially to ensure the low loss and high efficiency of the network communication process. To this end, a wireless communication architecture is established as shown in Fig. 7 below to achieve efficient interconnection of remote data in the distribution network. It mainly includes several parts, such as the information collection port for ultrasonic sensing, the data transmission port represented by wireless data transmission, and the centralized data processing port represented by the central control module. The data transmission network has good interfaces for upgrading and expansion between different ports, so the whole system is expected to has strong scenario applicability.

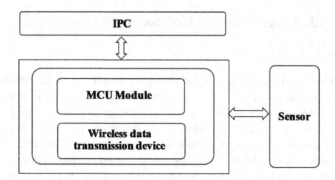

Fig. 7. The architecture of wireless communication

In the remote distribution network partial discharge online security monitoring system, ultrasonic sensors are used to convert the ultrasonic signal generated by the distribution network partial discharge into an electrical signal that can be better operated and processed. In order to guarantee the sensitivity of ultrasonic sensor data acquisition and achieve more accurate measurement of partial discharge, the sensitivity of ultrasonic sensor needs to be calculated and set specifically. The voltage sensitivity of the ultrasonic sensor is calculated as shown in Eq. (3) below, where P is the free sound field acoustic pressure of the ultrasonic wave with frequency φ and V is the voltage generated on the distribution network load.

$$S_\varphi = \frac{V(\varphi)}{P(\varphi)} \tag{3}$$

As another key indicator affecting the performance of ultrasonic sensors, the selection of the center frequency is crucial to the improvement of the sensor's data acquisition accuracy. In order to get a better center frequency, it is usually necessary to use the energy frequency of partial discharge occurring in the distribution network as the center frequency of the ultrasonic sensor according to the ultrasonic spectrum of partial discharge. In addition, the ultrasonic wireless sensor also includes pre-amplification circuit, filter circuit and MCU and wireless transmission module, which realize the functions of ultrasonic signal amplification processing, data signal selection and remote transmission and online monitoring of partial discharge data.

The structure of the ultrasonic data acquisition system includes the data acquisition chip, the main control board, and the power supply, clock, and display circuits of the system. In order to enhance the key indicators of the ultrasonic receiver part, such as the main resonant frequency, the main resonant bandwidth and the effective detection distance, and other aspects. The circuit of ultrasonic data acquisition system includes power management, data acquisition, signal processing and partial discharge alarm modules. Among them, the data acquisition circuit includes charge conversion, pre-amplification circuit and filtering circuit. With the help of these circuits, the data and signals with low frequency interference, including electromagnetic wave signals and background noise signals, can be effectively filtered out.

3.2 Software Implementation

The software part design of the ultrasonic-based remote distribution network partial discharge online security monitoring system includes the data diagnosis module and the data analysis module. Among them, the diagnostic module classifies the collected partial discharge information of the distribution network by analyzing the data, and classifies them into mild, moderate and severe discharges according to the degree of partial discharge. Mild partial discharges may not threaten the normal operation of the whole distribution network, so they can be left untreated for the time being. Moderate partial discharges require intensive monitoring and rapid response according to the development trend of partial discharges. Severe partial discharges require immediate maintenance and repair of electrical equipment to ensure the effective operation of the system. Based on the above principles, the software logic architecture of the whole ultrasonic remote distribution network partial discharge online monitoring system is designed.

The software is used to effectively compare and analyze the collected distribution network data with the data in the database, including the spectral amplitude and spectral characteristics of the ultrasonic signal, so as to automatically determine the type of data collection.

There are various kinds of interference and invalid data in the monitoring signal of remote distribution network. It is not enough to rely on the filtering circuit alone, but it is also necessary to identify and filter the interference data effectively with the help of software algorithms. The typical characteristics of the distribution network partial discharge data are further analyzed by using the transformation algorithm shown in Eq. (4) below, where STFT is the short-time Fourier transform and $g(v)$ is the change operation at time t.

$$STFT(t, s) = \int_{-\infty}^{+\infty} g(v)\alpha(v - t)e^{-2\pi sv}dv \qquad (4)$$

In addition, through monitoring, it is found that the distribution network partial discharge data has typical time-frequency characteristics. In the electrical signal waveform and amplitude patterns shown in Fig. 8 below, the amplitude of electrical signal is relatively concentrated and significant, with certain symmetrical distribution characteristics. After the processing of signal transformation algorithm, the local discharge signal of the distribution network is extracted and a comparison benchmark is established. Generally, the benchmark signal of partial discharge in the distribution network is mainly the time-frequency signal, which forms the basis for establishing the interference mechanism and judging the partial discharge situation in the system.

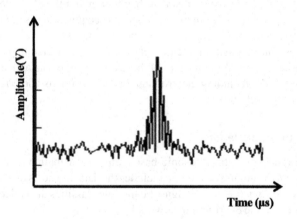

Fig. 8. The electrical signal amplitude patterns

After the partial discharge signal is collected by the ultrasonic-based online security monitoring device, the data will be stored in the system's database, and the monitored data will be processed and analyzed. The computer system will store and process the data regularly within a specific time period for later data recall and maintenance. In addition, at the level of implementation of the remote online warning algorithm for partial discharge, the system will compare the monitored signals with the set threshold signals in real time to determine whether the electrical devices in the distribution network system are in a partial discharge state and the discharge level they are in, and the logical architecture of the implemented algorithm is shown in Fig. 9 below.

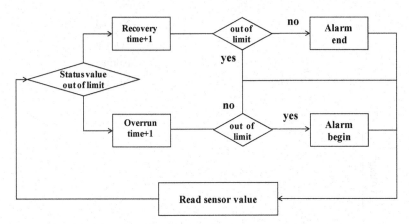

Fig. 9. Logical architecture of the implemented algorithm

4 Validation of the Effectiveness of Security Monitoring Device

In order to verify the practical use of the online security monitoring device and the stability and robustness of the whole monitoring system, a section of electrical devices in the distribution network is selected for partial discharge processing and the whole workflow of the ultrasonic monitoring system is simulated. Firstly, the remote and real-time performance of the ultrasonic sensor is verified. The positions of the partial discharge electrical device and the sensor in the distribution network are adjusted, so as to verify the monitoring effect of the sensor at different positions and distances, and the results are shown in Table 1 below. It can be seen that the sensor is still able to maintain effective monitoring of the partial discharge signal at a certain distance.

In order to verify the anti-interference performance of the monitoring device against noise signals, the effectiveness of the data acquisition and processing procedure of the monitoring system was tested under the condition of no partial discharge in the distribution network. The monitoring results of the online security monitoring device in the distribution network without partial discharge are shown in Fig. 10 below, and it can be seen from the results that the whole monitoring device did not have false alarms and has strong anti-interference capability.

In the case of partial discharge phenomenon, the feedback of monitoring results is shown in Fig. 11 below. It can be seen that the ultrasonic-based online security monitoring device can effectively monitor the partial discharge phenomenon and can eliminate the influence of invalid interference signals, which has strong practicality.

Table 1. The monitoring effect of the sensor at different position distances

No.	Distances	Results
1	1 m	Normal
2	2 m	Normal
3	3 m	Normal
4	4 m	Normal
5	5 m	Normal
6	6 m	Normal

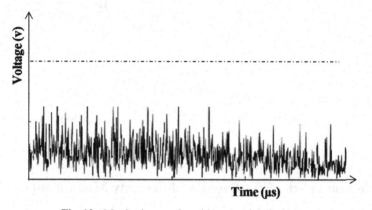

Fig. 10. Monitoring results without partial discharge

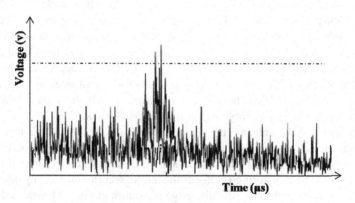

Fig. 11. Monitoring results with partial discharge

5 Conclusion

The ultrasonic-based online security monitoring device can assist power staff to effectively identify and warn the working condition of the distribution network, especially the partial discharge phenomenon. The data acquisition module of this system can greatly release the dependence on manual monitoring and identification, and improve the identification efficiency and effect of the whole system. In this paper, through the analysis of the primary components of the ultrasonic partial discharge online security monitoring system, especially based on the mechanism of partial discharge and the mechanism of action between partial discharge and ultrasonic waves, the online monitoring device of partial discharge is designed. The system includes operation modules such as acquisition, amplification, filtering and processing of partial discharge signals, and the software algorithm is used to further improve the anti-interference performance of the monitoring device. Finally, the effectiveness of the whole online security monitoring device is verified by setting up a simulated partial discharge phenomenon in the distribution network. The effectiveness of the system is verified by analyzing the performance of the ultrasonic sensor, the anti-interference capability of the monitoring device and the accuracy of the security monitoring. As the scale of the distribution network continues to expand and the complexity of the electrical devices increases, the monitoring system needs to be further improved at the level of intelligence of the system comparison threshold setting, which can be further optimized with the help of intelligent algorithms in the future research.

References

1. Li, S., Wang, S.: China southern agricultural machinery. China Southern Agric. Mach. **50**(20), 225 (2019)
2. Tan, D., Deng, S., Jiang, F., Liu, H.: Review on detection and signal denoising technology of partial discharge in electrical equipment. Electr. Wire Cable (4), 4–8 (2020)
3. Pan, H.: Analysis of causes and treatment of 35 kV indoor enclosed switchgear interval discharge. Sci. Technol. Innov. Herald **31**, 135–136 (2015)
4. Tian, T., et al.: Partial discharge characteristics of typical defects in oil paper insulation under AC and DC voltage. J. Electr. Power Sci. Technol. **36**(6), 40–46 (2021)
5. Liu, B., Jing, T., Gao, S.: Partial discharge detection technology of trench cable based on ultrasonic wave. Instrum. Tech. Sens. (5), 43–46+61 (2018)
6. Shin, J., Kim, S., Jo, H., Jung, J., Kim, E.: Partial discharge induction with X-rays to detect void defects in solid insulating materials. In: 2018 Condition Monitoring and Diagnosis (CMD), pp. 1–3 (2018)
7. Su, J., Guo, X., Zhang, M., Deng, N.: Design of partial discharge acquisition system in power transformer based on ARM. Instrum. Tech. Sensor (11), 89–91 (2011)
8. Liu, Y., Xiao, Y.: Self-assessment method for reliability of intelligent high-voltage switchgear. Power Syst. Technol. **39**(03), 862–866 (2015)
9. Haq, S., Thirugnanasam, M., Dickens, K., Tariq, H.: What should you know before acquiring partial discharge on high voltage motors and generators. In: 2021 IEEE IAS Petroleum and Chemical Industry Technical Conference (PCIC), pp. 247–256 (2021)
10. Du, S.: Classic Application Examples of Integrated Operational Amplifier. Electronic Industry Press, Beijing (2015)

11. Liu, Y., Tian, Y., Wang, F.: Circuit design and waveform analysis of partial discharge ultrasonic sensor based on parallel systems. In: 2021 IEEE 1st International Conference on Digital Twins and Parallel Intelligence (DTPI), pp. 1–4 (2021)

12. Liang, C., et al.: Partial discharge characteristics of 10 kV power cable defects under very low frequency voltage and oscillating wave voltage. In: 2021 IEEE 4th International Electrical and Energy Conference (CIEEC), pp. 1–5 (2021)

13. Pan, Y., Chen, J., Lin, J., Jin, J.: Cause analysis and treatment on discharging of 40.5 kV switch cabinet. Zhejiang Electr. Power **33**(3), 35–37+62 (2014)

14. Gao, H., Lv, C.: Research on partial discharge detection technology based on distribution high voltage switchgear. Electr. Power Syst. Equip. (2), 36–38 (2022)

15. Jin, X.: Common fault analysis and quality control of 10 kV switchgear. Mech. Electr. Inf. (20), 54–55 (2020)

16. Mao, Y., Ding, Y., Wu, J., Chen J.: Research on partial discharge detection technology for power transformers. In: 2020 IEEE 4th Conference on Energy Internet and Energy System Integration (EI2), pp. 3956–3959 (2020)

An Intelligent IoT Terminal Detection System Based on Data Sniffing

Tao Chen[1], Can Cao[2(✉)], and Pengcheng Ni[2]

[1] State Grid Xinjiang Electric Power Co., Ltd., Urumqi 830017, China
[2] Anhui Jiyuan Software Co. Ltd., Hefei 230088, China
caocan@sgitg.sgcc.com.cn

Abstract. Millions of intelligent terminals are connected in the IoT (Internet of Things) networks providing services for industrial applications around the world. The distributed deployment of terminals increases the exposure to cyber attackers. The detection of intelligent IoT terminals is the prerequisite for effective terminal security protections. Traditional detection methods have shortcomings such as low accuracy and difficult to detect heterogeneous terminals. Hence, a detection system for intelligent IoT terminals from the aspect of information security is proposed in this paper. Critical methods in the proposed system including comprehensive detection model and IoT protocol analysis method are studied. The system architecture including functional modules is introduced. The proposed system may operate in terminal mode and access point mode and work flows of both modes are described. Finally, the IoT terminal security is discussed from the levels of system security hardware, terminal file system and IoT network security. The proposed system is expected to detect terminals including hidden terminals in the networks of targeted area so as to effectively monitor and protect the terminals in target area.

Keywords: IoT Terminal · Terminal Detection · Security Scanning

1 Introduction

IoT (Internet of Things) technologies have been applied in several industrial scenarios where thousands of intelligent terminals are connected to provide value-added services [1]. Since the complex and heterogeneous connectivity of intelligent IoT terminals, the reliability of the IoT network is considered and community structure based method can be used to achieve better ordering of entire IoT network [2]. The IoT security challenges and countermeasures have been attracting researches in these years. The IoT security challenges may include data-related security, communication-related security and security for end applications where the and the data generated by IoT end nodes should be authentic and confidential [3]. However, a large number of distributed intelligent IoT terminals are accessed through heterogeneous networks, increasing the entry point for network attacks. Intelligent IoT terminal security plays an importing role in ensuring the security of the entire IoT infrastructure.

© The Author(s), under exclusive license to Springer Nature Singapore Pte Ltd. 2023
Y. Tian et al. (Eds.): ICBDS 2022, CCIS 1796, pp. 677–688, 2023.
https://doi.org/10.1007/978-981-99-3300-6_49

Security reinforcement of IoT terminals can be implemented via security detection, security protocol, security hardware design and so on. The security detection of terminal firmware can use the firmware code analysis, classification and code feature description to obtain better matching results [4, 5]. Abnormal behaviors of wireless IoT terminals can be detected using double HMM (Hidden Markov Model) where multiple individual abnormal behaviors can be used to analyze a longer span attack [6]. Additionally, as a prerequisite of security detection, the IoT traffic data analysis can be done where the fingerprint model is established and the fingerprint features are extracted [7]. Secure protocols can also be designed to strengthen the IoT terminal security. Handover security protocol for mobile IoT terminals supporting adaptive and periodic key updates can secure the exchange data between terminals via hubs [8]. Finally, the trust of remote IoT terminal can be verified while the sensitive data is sealed in the enclave page cache (EPC) using security hardware tools provided by Intel [9].

Hidden terminal emulation (HTE) attack in IoT is found recently where a hidden terminal can interfere with transmissions [10]. The behaviors of HTE attacks can be captured, analyzed and modelled for security detection of IoT terminals [11]. However, the traditional IoT terminal detection methods have the shortcomings such as low efficiency and difficult to detect heterogeneous terminals. Hence, to facilitate the security detection of intelligent IoT terminals, we are motivated to study the intelligent IoT detection methods and system to provide a clear overview of the access terminals in the IoT scenario. The IoT architecture in smart grid is taken as the typical IoT architecture that is described in Sect. 2. Intelligent IoT terminal detection methods including active detection and protocol analysis are proposed in Sect. 3. Based on the detection methods, a detection system is proposed in Sect. 4. Section 5 discusses the security applications for IoT terminals and Sect. 6 gives the final conclusion.

2 Typical IoT Architecture

IoT technologies have been applied in the scenarios such as smart grid, smart city and smart factory. In this section, IoT application in smart grid is taken as the typical IoT architecture as shown in Fig. 1. According to the access level, the access of power IoT terminals can be divided into network layer access and perception layer access. Network layer access refers to the connection of an access node (such as an edge IoT agent) to the main station business system or IoT management platform. Perception layer access refers to the connection of a sensing terminal or an aggregation node to an access node (such as an edge IoT agent).

The perception layer is composed of four parts including field acquisition component, intelligent business terminal, local communication access and edge IoT agent. Micro-electro Mechanical System (MEMS) and integrated energy collection technology are adopted for the field acquisition components to realize low power consumption and long standby operation of the field acquisition components. Intelligent business terminals are deployed in the whole process of power grid operation, customer service and enterprise operation to realize the whole process observable and measurable. Emerging businesses are deployed according to the actual needs of expansion and develop iteratively. In local communication access, the access of power IoT terminal can be divided into wired mode and wireless mode. Wired mode includes optical fiber, twisted pair, serial port, etc. while wireless mode includes power wireless private network, WiFi, ZigBee, LoRa, etc. The edge IoT agent is an edge processing device under the ubiquitous power IoT Cloud Architecture. It has the functions of communication protocol adaptation, edge computing, unified data model, virtual exchange, security protection, etc. to realize the calculation and storage of data at the edge, improve the response speed, and relieve the pressure of cloud centralized processing on servers and network resources.

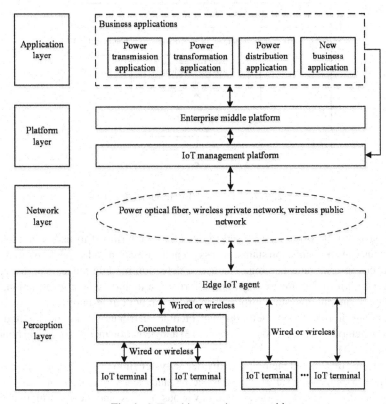

Fig. 1. IoT architecture in smart grid

3 Intelligent IoT Terminal Detection Methods

3.1 Comprehensive Detection Model

The comprehensive detection model combining active detection method with passive detection method is proposed to improve the accuracy and efficiency of IoT terminal detection as shown in Fig. 2.

It can be seen that the proposed model is composed of active detection module, passive detection module, detection analysis module and detection knowledge database.

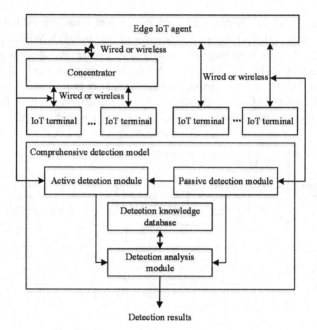

Detection results

Fig. 2. Comprehensive IoT terminal detection

The passive detection module is used to detection the terminal information including ports status, data transmission status, access point information and so on with timestamps via packet capturing and parsing. The active detection module makes use of network scanning toolkit to acquire IoT terminal information including host information, ports information, operating system information and so on with timestamps.

Scanning and detection methods may include distributed scanning method [12], detection method based on evidence theory [13] and detection method based on honeypot technology [14].

Firstly, the distributed method is to divide the system into two parts for targeted scanning. The sensor uses the state detection method, and the analyzer uses the classification analysis method. Sensors are distributed in various subnets, and the abnormalities in the subnets are scanned. By summarizing and analyzing the data of each subnet on the network, the scanning status on the network can be inferred by the analyzer. Secondly, the main principle of the Dempsey-Schaefer (DS) theoretical scanning method is to analyze and integrate the port information obtained by various port scanning methods, and then the status of the port can be inferred based on evidence. This method may reduce the alarm error rate while maintaining a high detection rate. Finally, honeypot technology is used to create virtual systems and their operating environments where interactions are recorded. The attacks observed by honeypot and darknet can be correlated and analyzed. This method also effectively improves the scanning and detection rate.

The detection analysis module receives the detected terminal information and process the information by combination and ordering with timestamps. The detection knowledge database stores the predefined rules for terminal detection in business categories e.g.

power transformation service acquisition terminal, power transmission service acquisition terminal. Each rule may contain ports information, operating system information, upload intervals, etc. The detection analysis module compares the obtained records to the rules in the database to output the detection results of the terminal. The rules in the knowledge database can be updated periodically to include new emerging business terminals.

The proposed model is computational efficiency so that the detection efficiency is expected to be improved while the accuracy may be slightly enhanced due to the combination of active detection and passive detection.

3.2 IoT Protocol Analysis

To improve the accuracy of the IoT terminal, the protocol packet parsing and analysis can be used. As mentioned in Sect. 3, the wireless communications in smart grid IoT architecture includes power wireless private network, WiFi, ZigBee, LoRa, etc. The applications of LoRa (Long Range Radio) technology in smart grid and IoT have been studied while LoRa is considered as a promising way to enable dynamic network and to solve the scalability issues [15]. The integration of LoRa into 5G IoT in smart grid may achieve better resource utilization and improve network scalability and energy efficiency [16]. In this section, the LoRa and LoRaWAN (LoRa Wide Area Network) protocols are taken for IoT protocol analysis The LoRa modulation frame structure is shown in Fig. 3.

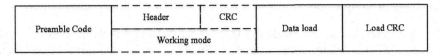

Fig. 3. LoRa modulation frame structure

It can be seen that the first part of the frame is a preamble code, which is used to synchronize the receiver and the arriving data stream. The preamble code can be customized according to different application scenarios. The longer the preamble, the more likely the receiver will detect the signal, but the transmission time will increase correspondingly. The LoRa frame has two working modes. The first is the explicit mode, that is, the header uses the maximum error correction code rate for transmission and has its own independent CRC (Cyclic Redundancy Check). The second is the implicit mode, that is, when the receiver and the transmitter have known the load length, coding rate and whether to use the check code, the header is removed to reduce the time consumption.

LoRaWAN is the protocol based on LoRa, which uses star network topology. The gateway is the central node of the whole network. The data interaction between each terminal and the network server can only be through the gateway. Its protocol stack is shown in Fig. 4, where FHDR includes device address (DevAddr), frame control (FCtrl), frame counter (FCnt) and frame options (Fopts).

It can be seen that in the LoRaWAN protocol, three classes of terminals are defined. Class A terminal is in sleep mode most of the time and initiate uplink when necessary. After each uplink data transfer, the class A terminal will have two short downlink

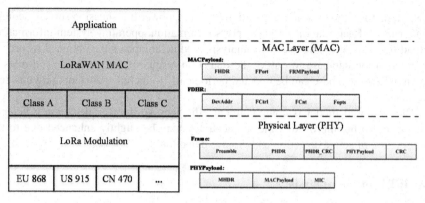

Fig. 4. LoRaWAN protocol stack

receiving windows waiting for downlink data. Class B terminal has guaranteed receiving windows while the receiving window of class C equipment remains open. Thus, class C terminal has the highest energy consumption and lowest data transmission time among three class terminals.

4 Intelligent IoT Terminal Detection System

4.1 System Architecture

The system architecture is shown in Fig. 5. It can be seen that the proposed system is composed of simulated terminal module, simulated access point module, detection module, protocol analysis module, data analysis module, learning module, knowledge data base and terminal database. The simulated terminal module is connected with simulated access point module and detection module while both of data analysis module and protocol analysis module are connected with detection module, knowledge database and terminal database.

In the proposed system, the simulated terminal module should support the simulation of different types of IoT terminals in the target area and the simulated access point needs to support the simulation of the concentrator in the target area. The detection module is used to execute the active and passive scanning and detection tasks and the data analysis module is used to process the scanning results as mentioned in Sect. 3.1. Protocol analysis module can parse and analyzed the target protocol data packet such as LoRa in Sect. 3.2. Various classification algorithms are integrated into the learning module which is used to assist the feature pattern recognition in knowledge database. While a terminal in the target area is successfully detected, the record is stored in the terminal database.

4.2 System Workflow

The proposed system can operate in two modes including terminal mode and access mode. The work flow of the proposed system in terminal mode is shown in Fig. 6.

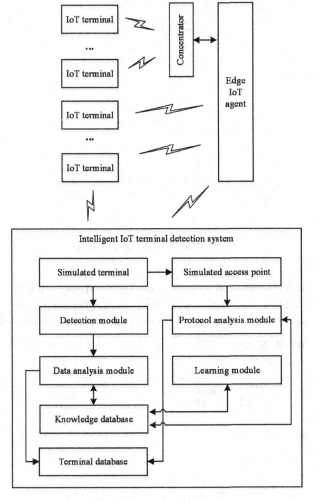

Fig. 5. System architecture

It can be seen that the work flow in terminal mode includes the following steps:

1. The simulated terminal initiates the detection process by scanning and detecting the existing networks in the target area. The proposed system then accesses to the target network as a normal terminal.
2. The detection module completes the passive scanning and active scanning tasks as proposed in Sect. 3.1. The scanning results are transmitted to the data analysis module.
3. The data analysis module processes the scanning results by combination and ordering with timestamps in data and compares the data with the terminal features in the knowledge database. If matching is successful, go to step 5. Otherwise, go to step 4.
4. The data analysis module transmits the processed data to the learning module for classification. The learning module supports the classification algorithms such as DNN

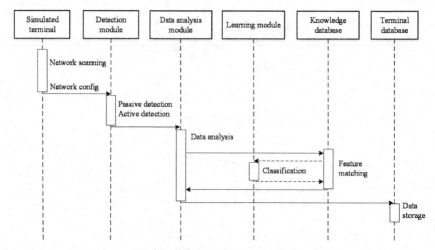

Fig. 6. Work flow in terminal mode

(Deep Neural Networks) and RFA (Random Forests Algorithms). The classification results are used to update the feature patterns in knowledge database.

5. The data analysis module transmits the matching results to the terminal database.

The workflow of the proposed system in access mode is shown in Fig. 7.

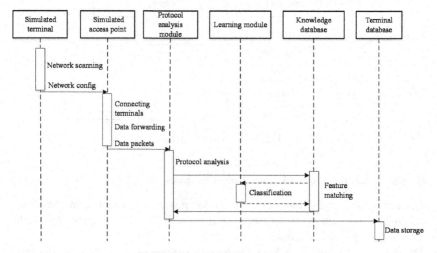

Fig. 7. Work flow in access mode

It can be seen that the work flow in access mode includes the following steps.

1. The simulated terminal scans and detects the existing networks in the target area to acquire the network configurations that are transmitted to the simulated access point.

2. The simulated access point disguises itself as an access point in the target network and entices terminals to connect. It forwards the data stream to the network server to keep connected terminals working normally. Meanwhile, it forwards the intercepted data packets to the protocol analysis module.
3. The protocol analysis module supports the protocol parsing and analysis and the analysis results are compared with the terminal features in the knowledge database. If matching is successful, go to step 5. Otherwise, go to step 4.
4. The protocol analysis module transmits the analysis results to learning module for classification. The classification results are used to update the feature patterns in knowledge database.
5. The protocol analysis module transmits the matching results to the terminal database.

5 Discussion on IoT Terminal Security

The detection of intelligent IoT terminals is the prerequisite for terminal security management. First of all, the misuse of equipment should be avoided. Secondly, when the programs are installed in terminals, the corresponding security review system should be installed. Finally, we should have an effective security review mechanism to prevent major businesses from being affected or interrupted. In addition, the terminal needs to strictly control the ports that enable related services and the correspondingly configured network security policies, so as to prevent attacks from outside the terminal.

System-level security includes chip security and system startup security. The basic chip-level security is mainly guaranteed by the chip manufacturer, and it is based on the security chip. It mainly verifies the initial security of the system, which consists of the following parts: OTP (One Time Programmable) security storage area, key derivation module, hierarchical key generation module, decoding module and master control model, as shown in Fig. 8.

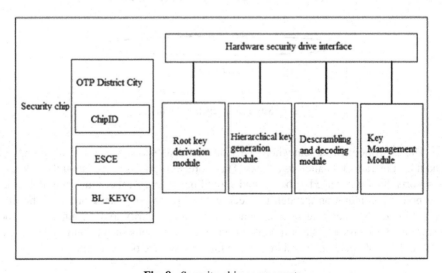

Fig. 8. Security chip components

The OTP security storage area is used to store important information embedded in the chip such as ChiP_ID (Chip storage ID), ESCK (Security Chip Key), BL_KEYO (Public and private key), etc.

If the terminal file system is more secure, users can safely store files, data, and applications on the system equipment. The security policy of the terminal file system can effectively ensure that user information is not leaked. It can also prevent unauthorized intrusion code execution, and the data will be stored in the database after four layers of encryption when the data is saved through the application, and the database has its own security technology. Figure 9 shows the multi-layer encryption of data.

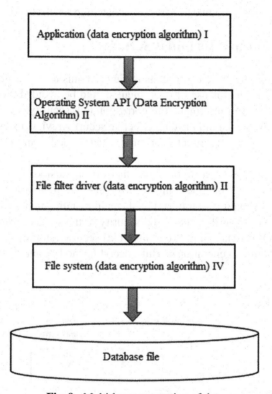

Fig. 9. Multi-layer encryption of data

The network environment where the smart terminal is located is relatively complex, and it is vulnerable to malicious attacks. Therefore, unneeded services should be closed, and ports that do not need to be opened should be closed. At the same time, the security policy configuration through the secure network protocol stack provides the first protection of the operating system, which can ensure security to a certain extent. The secure network protocol stack module provides the functions such as anti-DOS attack, anti-ARP spoofing, IP address black and white list, service port control.

6   Conclusion

With the development of IoT technologies, the application of intelligent terminal security detection systems has become more extensive. This paper studies the advanced detection methods for intelligent IoT terminals. A detection system is proposed for detection of IoT terminals in a target area. In addition, the IoT terminal security is discussed where multi-layer encryption is used to effectively protect the user's information. However, the algorithms design such as classification algorithms in the proposed system need to be further studied in the future research.

Acknowledgments. This work is supported by Science and Technology Project of State Grid Corporation of China (No. 5700-202124182A-0-0-00).

References

1. Hwang, J., Nkenyereye, L., Sung, N., Kim, J., Song, J.: IoT service slicing and task offloading for edge computing. IEEE Internet Things J. **8**(14), 11526–11547 (2021)
2. Mo, Y., Xing, L., Guo, W., Cai, S., Zhang, Z., Jiang, J.: Reliability analysis of IoT networks with community structures. IEEE Trans. Netw. Sci. Eng. **7**(1), 304–315 (2020)
3. Iqbal, W., Abbas, H., Daneshmand, M., Rauf, B., Bangash, Y.A.: An in-depth analysis of IoT security requirements, challenges, and their countermeasures via software-defined security. IEEE Internet Things J. **7**(10), 10250–10276 (2020)
4. Zhu, X., Li, Q., Chen, Z., Zhang, G., Shan, P.: Research on security detection technology for internet of things terminal based on firmware code genes. IEEE Access **8**, 150226–150241 (2020)
5. Zhu, X., Li, Q., Zhang, P., Chen, Z.: A firmware code gene extraction technology for IoT terminal. IEEE Access **7**, 179591–179604 (2019)
6. Wu, K., Li, J., Zhang, B.: Abnormal detection of wireless power terminals in untrusted environment based on double hidden Markov model. IEEE Access **9**, 18682–18691 (2021)
7. He, X., Yang, Y., Zhou, W., Wang, W., Liu, P., Zhang, Y.: Fingerprinting mainstream IoT platforms using traffic analysis. IEEE Internet Things J. **9**(3), 2083–2093 (2022)
8. Kim, J., Astillo, P.V., Sharma, V., Guizani, N., You, I.: MoTH: mobile terminal handover security protocol for HUB switching based on 5G and beyond (5GB) P2MP backhaul environment. IEEE Internet Things J. **9**(16), 14667–14684 (2022)
9. Wang, J., Hong, Z., Zhang, Y., Jin, Y.: Enabling security-enhanced attestation with Intel SGX for remote terminal and IoT. IEEE Trans. Comput. Aided Des. Integr. Circuits Syst. **37**(1), 88–96 (2018)
10. Hossain, M., Xie, J.: Hidden terminal emulation: an attack in dense IoT networks in the shared spectrum operation. In: 2019 IEEE Global Communications Conference (GLOBECOM), pp. 1–6 (2019)
11. Hossain, M., Xie, J.: Third eye: context-aware detection for hidden terminal emulation attacks in cognitive radio-enabled IoT networks. IEEE Trans. Cogn. Commun. Netw. **6**(1), 214–228 (2020)
12. Sanz, I.J., Lopez, M.A., Menezes Ferrazani Mattos, D., Muniz Bandeira Duarte, O.C.: A cooperation-aware virtual network function for proactive detection of distributed port scanning. In: 2017 1st Cyber Security in Networking Conference (CSNet), pp. 1–8 (2017)

13. Aparicio-Navarro, F.J., Kyriakopoulos, K.G., Gong, Y., Parish, D.J., Chambers, J.A.: Using pattern-of-life as contextual information for anomaly-based intrusion detection systems. IEEE Access **5**, 22177–22193 (2017)
14. Akiyoshi, R., Kotani, D., Okabe, Y.: Detecting emerging large-scale vulnerability scanning activities by correlating low-interaction honeypots with darknet. In: 2018 IEEE 42nd Annual Computer Software and Applications Conference (COMPSAC), pp. 658–663 (2018)
15. Gallardo, J.L., Ahmed, M.A., Jara, N.: LoRa IoT-based architecture for advanced metering infrastructure in residential smart grid. IEEE Access **9**, 124295–124312 (2021)
16. Wu, J., et al.: Energy efficient 5G LoRa ad-hoc network for smart grid communication. In: 2021 IEEE 11th International Conference on Electronics Information and Emergency Communication (ICEIEC), pp. 1–4 (2021)

Intelligent IoT Terminal Software Identification System Based on Behavior Features

Zhiyuan Ye[1,2], Cen Chen[3], Nuannuan Li[3], Wen Yang[3], Zheng Zhang[3], and Can Cao[1,2(✉)]

[1] State Grid Information and Telecommunication Group Co., Ltd, Beijing 102200, China
caocan@sgitg.sgcc.com.cn
[2] Anhui Jiyuan Software Co. Ltd, Hefei 230088, China
[3] State Grid Henan Electric Power Research Institute, Zhengzhou 450000, China

Abstract. Intelligent IoT (Internet of Things) terminals are widely deployed in IoT systems and complete tasks such as data collection, data processing and analysis. The intelligent services provided by IoT systems are implemented based on various application software installed in terminal side and server side. Hence, the behaviors of intelligent IoT terminals depend largely on the interactive behaviors of application software. It is necessary to monitor and identify IoT terminal behaviors so as to achieve security state awareness and abnormal detection. The identification system in the environment of limited hardware configuration should not affect the performance of the target system. Therefore, non-invasive instruction and data tracing method is studied in this paper where the supported tools are described. Based on the studied method, an intelligent IoT terminal software identification system is proposed and the functional modules are designed. The proposed system can operate in offline training mode and online identification mode. The processes of both modes are described in details. Finally, the terminal identification technology based on multi-source information is discussed. The proposed system is expect to identify the software and even the terminal in the IoT system so that the security mechanism can be strengthened.

Keywords: IoT terminal · Terminal identification · IoT security

1 Introduction

The Internet of Things (IoT) system with mobile and intelligent terminals is widely applied in industrial scenarios such as healthcare and security management, providing services that improves efficiency of the corresponding business processes [1, 2]. The intelligent IoT terminal usually uses embedded operating system and energy-efficient application software due to its limited hardware configuration. Intelligent IoT terminals may include different types of sensors or edge devices that can capture and preprocess data in a timely and effective manner. The stable and reliable data transmission provided by the intelligent IoT terminal makes more industries and individuals start considering its applications. However, due to its interactivity and intelligence in system control

© The Author(s), under exclusive license to Springer Nature Singapore Pte Ltd. 2023
Y. Tian et al. (Eds.): ICBDS 2022, CCIS 1796, pp. 689–700, 2023.
https://doi.org/10.1007/978-981-99-3300-6_50

and management functions, it also faces more risks than that of traditional functional terminals [3]. The IoT terminal security reinforcement methods in recent years include terminal identification, terminal security threat assessment, terminal security access and terminal security detection, etc. as shown in Fig. 1.

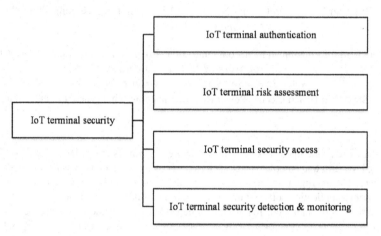

Fig. 1. The current method of intelligent Internet of Things terminal identification technology

Firstly, IoT terminal authentication can be achieved through establishing fingerprints such as RF (Radio Frequency) fingerprints and firmware fingerprints of IoT devices, while efforts are made to improve the terminal identification accuracy [4–6]. Secondly, risks of IoT terminals can be evaluated via risk graph or knowledge graph where the terminal data such as vulnerabilities, threats, asset information are collected and fused [7, 8]. Thirdly, secure access protocols or algorithms can be designed and implemented to ensure that the terminal access has capability of resisting network attacks such as tampering, eavesdropping and counterfeit [9, 10]. Finally, the abnormal detection or intrusion detection in IoT system may monitor the terminal behaviors and provide security protection for terminals. In order to reduce the computational complexity, double-layer abnormal behavior detection model can be established where lower-layer detects single network abnormal event and upper-layer obtains period attack behaviors [11]. In addition, the device security state awareness model can be established so that the security state of the device can be evaluated and state transition relationships can be obtained [12].

Since the IoT terminals usually have limited hardware configurations, the security mechanism need to adapt to the operating environment of end devices. The existing security detection and monitoring methods are effective in observing some terminal behaviors. However, the efficiency and performance can be improved. Thus, we are motivated to study an IoT terminal software identification system while the performance of terminals is not affected. The identification methods are described in Sect. 2. The proposed system is described in Sect. 3. Sections 4 and 5 give the discussion and conclusion, respectively.

2 IoT Terminal Software Behavior Detection

2.1 Software Architecture of Intelligent IoT Terminal

Taking the power intelligent IoT terminal as an example, its software architecture is composed of operating system, container platform and business application as shown in Fig. 2 [13].

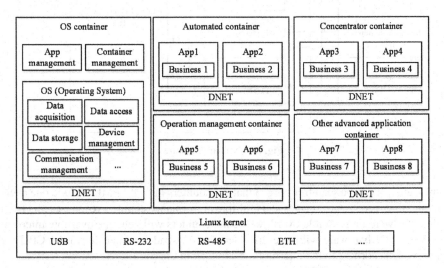

Fig. 2. Software architecture of power intelligent IoT terminal

It can be seen that the software architecture of power intelligent IoT terminal includes the OS container, concentrator container, operation management container, reserved containers and Linux kernel that supports the multi-source data access interfaces. The communications between containers are through DNET (DeviceNet) that is based on CAN (Controller Area Network). The business containers initiates data request via integrated interface to DNET. The data interface in OS container responds to the request and sends the data to the request application in business container via DNET.

2.2 Non-invasive Instruction and Data Tracing

Since the common hardware architecture in IoT terminals is based on ARM architecture, the non-invasive instruction and data tracing methods are studied. Non-invasive tracing components can access memory, trace data and instructions when the program is running, and can also perform performance analysis. It will not interrupt the CPU during work and will not affect CPU performance. PMU (Performance Monitoring Unit) is such a component provided in ARM whose architecture is shown in Fig. 3.

PMU is used to track and count some underlying hardware events in the system, such as events related to CPU (number of instructions executed, number of exceptions captured, number of clock cycles, etc.), events related to cache (cache access times, miss

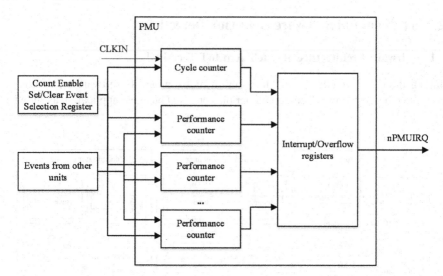

Fig. 3. PMU architecture

times, etc.). It can be seen from Fig. 3 that the counters in ARM PMU include one cycle counter that records CUP cycles and multiple performance counters receive events from other hardware units. While overflow occurs, counters will generate overflow interrupt and the PMU hardware will determine whether to send the interrupt to the CPU for processing according to the interrupt mask bit set in the control register.

The registers for PMU may include three functional categories including registers used to describe/control PMU resources such as PMCR_EL0 (Performance Monitors Control Register), registers used to configure counting events such as PMEVCNTR<n>_EL0, registers for configuring interrupt status such as PMINTENSET_EL1.

PMU events are recorded, e.g. SW_INCR (Software increment), L1I_CACHE_REFILL (L1 instruction cache refill), L1D_CACHE (L1 data cache access), MEM_ACCESS (Data memory access), MEM_ACCESS_RD (Data memory access, read), L1D_CACHE_RD (L1 data cache access, read), L1D_CACHE_WR (L1 data cache access, write), L2D_CACHE (L2 unified cache access), BUS_ACCESS (Bus access).

ETM (Embedded Trace Macrocell) is another non-invasive tracing component provided by ARM. Its architecture includes core interface module, trace generation module, filtering and triggering resources, FIFO memory and trace out module, as shown in Fig. 4.

The behaviors of core are monitored by the core interface module and trace packets are generated by trace generation module. The trace data generation can be limited to a defined range or condition by filtering and the trigger can be generated to stop trace capturing. FIFO provides a buffer to output traces to ATB (Advanced Trace Bus). The ETM trace registers can be programmed and read via Debug APB (Advanced Peripheral Bus) interface.

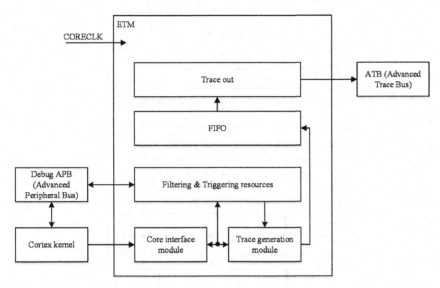

Fig. 4. ETM architecture

ETM event resources include memory access resources, instrumentation resources, derived resources and external inputs. For example, single address comparators in memory access resources compare the instruction or data address to a programmed value. Each comparator can be configured to match conditions such as instruction executed, data load and data store.

3 IoT Terminal Software Identification System

3.1 System Architecture

The system architecture is shown in Fig. 5. The proposed system is composed of support module that includes the supporting data capturing tools and interfaces, data acquisition module, configuration model that is used to set parameters of data acquisition module and data capturing tools, data storage module that is used to store captured data and feature data, and user interface module that provides graphic user interfaces.

3.2 System Processes

The proposed system can operate in offline training mode and online identification mode. The process of offline training mode is shown in Fig. 6. First of all, the applications in sample intelligent IoT terminals are executed in experimental environment. The executed instructions and associated data are collected by the data acquisition module to produce data samples for training and testing, which are store in the data storage module. Part of data samples are read by the feature classification module for model training. The classification results are then tested using the rest of data samples. If the classification accuracy reaches the satisfactory threshold, the trained model is stored in the classification model as a ready model. Otherwise, the training process will keep going.

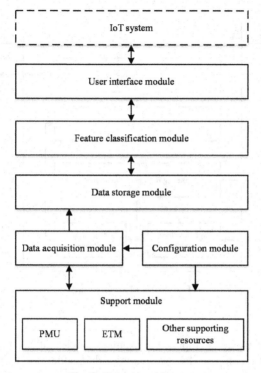

Fig. 5. System architecture

The training process adopts supervised learning algorithms where the executed instructions and associated data of an application is automatically added by a software mark. In addition, the business type of a terminal is predefined and the behavioral data of applications running in that terminal is marked by a business terminal tag.

The process in online identification mode is shown in Fig. 7. While the system is operating in the online identification mode, it monitors the behavioral data of applications running in IoT terminals. The executed instructions and data are captured as data samples to be classified. The classification module may give the classification results online. If the results belong to the predefined types of applications and terminals, which means the condition is normal, the identities of software and terminals are transmitted to user interface for situational awareness and the process will continue. Otherwise, the warning information is transmitted to the user interface for final decision on whether there is a security risk. If the warning application is a new normal application, the user interface begins the retraining process and the corresponding model is updated.

The data capturing process in the proposed system adopts the non-invasive methods proposed in Sect. 2. The example events collected are shown in Table 1. The collected events may include CPU information, branch execution, bus access, L1 and L2 cache access, data memory access, etc.

The data acquisition process is shown in Fig. 8. The perf_event_open in Linux is used for data capturing. First of all, the structure of perf_event_attr is defined to state

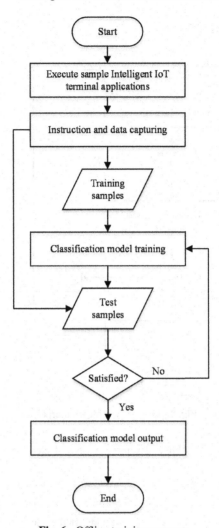

Fig. 6. Offline training process

the events to be tracked, procedure ID to be tracked and so on. The read format then is defined in order to read multiple events in the returned data groups. The event counters are enabled and initiated while the definition tasks are completed. If the initialization fails, check the log and determine whether the event data can be captured. If yes, recheck the configuration parameters and correct them. If not, end the event feature collection. While the initialization successes, the counters star capturing the predefined events. The capture tool will trigger an interrupt and stores data in buffer when the counters overflow. Finally, the data can be read from buffer via memory mapping mechanism.

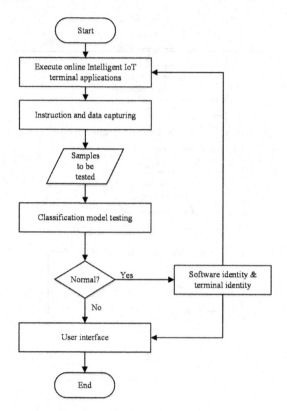

Fig. 7. Online identification process

Table 1. Example events collected

Event	Event description
SW_INCR	Software increment
BR_MIS_PRED	Mispredicted branch executed
BR_PRED	Predictable branch executed
CPU_CYCLES	CPU cycle
BUS_ACCESS	Bus access
L1D_CACHE_RD	L1 data cache read
L1D_CACHE_WR	L1 data cache write
CACHE_ACCESS_RD	L2 unified cache read
CACHE_ACCESS_WR	L2 unified cache write
MEM_ACCESS_RD	Data memory read
MEM_ACCESS_WR	Data memory write

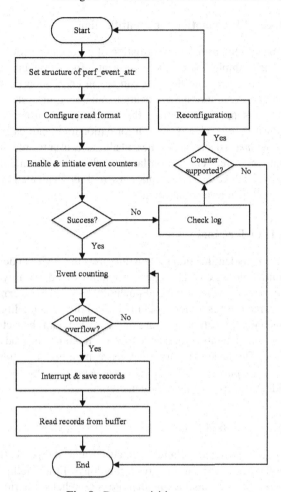

Fig. 8. Data acquisition process

4 Discussion

The accuracy of intelligent IoT terminal software identification technology is beneficial to the development and optimization of intelligent IoT terminal in many industries such as power industry. Using diversified and organized information to identify intelligent Internet of things terminals can solve the problem of singularity and concealment of terminal system identification code. Compared with the traditional identification technology, the high accuracy identification technology can implement identification and detection in more information levels. More information can be screened through perception points, such as user's time-domain usage information, terminal system usage, identity key, etc., so that more real-time information can be obtained for the improvement of identification technology. Through the perception points, we can monitor the current terminal's information through identity information detection, so as to determine whether it can be correctly connected.

4.1   Use Multifaceted Information for Identification

In the identification system, different information of users can be collected in the application software. For example, the user's fingerprint information and facial recognition information can be collected, and the user can set an encryption password separately to protect the user's terminal through application and operating system layers. The system background data is analyzed to obtain the data frequently used by users in normal operation. Once the user uses other types of information for identification, the intelligent terminal system can make a decision in time and allow the user to enter the lower encryption layer through the current encryption layer. In this way, the intelligent terminal is closely protected by the three-layer encryption method supplemented by the information judgment of the intelligent terminal system.

4.2   Use a Variety of Terminal Codes

The traditional terminal identification system only uses the device code set by the development end to identify the system. Its singleness increases the possibility that the terminal system is invaded, so the new terminal equipment codes need to be explored to identify the system. The characteristics, usage and functions of different intelligent IoT terminal operating systems and application software are analyzed, and their characteristics are taken as the new terminal identification code to make it unique, instead of the single and regular device code. The code generation process can be based on the actual needs of users, through the encryption algorithm to generate a set of codes for users, so that the terminal can be identified by a variety of characteristics.

4.3   Use Multiple Perceptual Points

Diversified information is screened and detected through the perception layer, which is used to realize the accurate identification technology of the intelligent IoT terminal system. Diversified sensing points can obtain more comprehensive terminal information. Its functional characteristics can not only help the system to identify information, but also to analyze the abnormal situation when identifying the terminal. If the user information is not correctly identified, the identification system of the intelligent IoT terminal can identify the device information in time to ensure the security of the terminal information.

For the upgrading and optimization of the accurate identification technology of the intelligent IoT terminal application software, the research on intelligent risk matching verification technology can also be carried out in combination with the information characteristics of different versions of terminal operating systems and application software, as well as the vulnerability information of different versions.

5   Conclusion

With continuous development of intelligent IoT terminals, they will spread in all walks of life with the continuous expansion of the network, thus affecting industries and even the society. The operating system, processing system and application software in the intelligent IoT terminal will also be developed and optimized accordingly. Therefore, the terminal software identification and authentication and other security measures should be improved in time. The accurate identification technology of the intelligent IoT terminal application software is an effective security monitoring method. However, the current method is insufficient to effectively implement information monitoring and identification in the environment of limited computing resources, leading to certain security risks. Due to the interactivity of intelligent Internet of things terminals, it is necessary to pay attention to the diversity and privacy of information, modular processing, multi-dimensional system information identification, and private information encryption of applications in the process of exploring accurate identification technology. Based on the introduction of non-invasive data tracing methods that do not affect the terminal performance, an intelligent IoT terminal software identification system is proposed. The future research may focus on the optimization of behavior feature classification so that the online identification performance can be improved.

Acknowledgement. This work is supported by Science and Technology Project of State Grid Corporation of China (No. 5700-202124182A-0-0-00).

References

1. Xu, X., Zhang, L., Sotiriadis, S., Asimakopoulou, E., Li, M., Bessis, N.: CLOTHO: a large-scale internet of things-based crowd evacuation planning system for disaster management. IEEE Internet Things J. **5**(5), 3559–3568 (2018)
2. Liu, L., Xu, J., Huan, Y., Zou, Z., Yeh, S.-C., Zheng, L.-R.: A smart dental health-IoT platform based on intelligent hardware, deep learning, and mobile terminal. IEEE J. Biomed. Health Inform. **24**(3), 898–906 (2020)
3. Zhang, P., Wang, Y., Kumar, N., Jiang, C., Shi, G.: A security- and privacy-preserving approach based on data disturbance for collaborative edge computing in social IoT systems. IEEE Trans. Comput. Soc. Syst. **9**(1), 97–108 (2022)
4. Peng, L., Zhang, J., Liu, M., Hu, A.: Deep learning based RF fingerprint identification using differential constellation trace figure. IEEE Trans. Veh. Technol. **69**(1), 1091–1095 (2020)
5. Wu, W., Hu, S., Lin, D., Liu, Z.: DSLN: securing internet of things through RF fingerprint recognition in low-SNR settings. IEEE Internet Things J. **9**(5), 3838–3849 (2022)
6. Zhu, X., Li, Q., Zhang, P., Chen, Z.: A firmware code gene extraction technology for IoT terminal. IEEE Access **7**, 179591–179604 (2019)
7. Xu, A., et al.: Terminal security reinforcement method based on graph and potential function. In: 2021 International Conference on Intelligent Computing, Automation and Applications (ICAA), 2021, pp. 307–313 (2021)
8. Pang, T., Song, Y., Shen, Q.: Research on security threat assessment for power IOT terminal based on knowledge graph. In: 2021 IEEE 5th Information Technology, Networking, Electronic and Automation Control Conference (ITNEC), 2021, pp. 1717–1721 (2021)
9. Giuliano, R., Mazzenga, F., Neri, A., Vegni, A.M.: Security access protocols in IoT capillary networks. IEEE Internet Things J. **4**(3), 645–657 (2017)
10. Kim, J., Astillo, P.V., Sharma, V., Guizani, N., You, I.: MoTH: mobile terminal handover security protocol for HUB switching based on 5G and beyond (5GB) P2MP backhaul environment. IEEE Internet Things J. **9**(16), 14667–14684 (2022)

11. Wu, K., Li, J., Zhang, B.: Abnormal detection of wireless power terminals in untrusted environment based on double hidden Markov model. IEEE Access **9**, 18682–18691 (2021)
12. Lei, W., Wen, H., Hou, W., Xu, X.: New security state awareness model for IoT devices with edge intelligence. IEEE Access **9**, 69756–69765 (2021)
13. Chen, W., et al.: Software architecture and implementation mechanism of integrated intelligent terminal for marketing and power distribution based on container technology. Electr. Eng. **03**, 149–152 (2022)

Research on the Identification Model of Power Terminal

Wenbo Shang[✉], Xin Jin, Biying Sun, Xiaoqin Liu, and Chunhui Du

State Grid Gansu Information and Telecommunication Company, Lanzhou 730050, China
275965618@qq.com

Abstract. The continuous access to various intelligent terminals in the power system has greatly improved the functionality and intelligence of the system, while also affecting the security of the whole system to a large extent. Through designing the identification model of power terminals from the aspects of security, convenience, applicability and efficiency, and verifying the identity of the terminals connected to the power system, it is an important premise and guarantee to effectively prevent malicious terminal access from causing damage to the whole system. In this paper, an identity identification model of power terminals is proposed and the discrete feature coding is optimized. The implementation of the proposed model in the power information network is then suggested. Experiments including training data sets, verification data sets and interaction environment are established. The results show the advantages of the proposed model in the aspects of feature selection, abnormal identity identification and identity classification of terminals.

Keywords: Identification Model · Power Terminal · Internet of Things · Power System · Network Security

1 Introduction

At present, the pace of information technology continues to accelerate, and intelligent interconnection and big data have become key applications in related industries represented by power industry [1]. As an important pillar industry related to the country's livelihood, the electric power system plays a vital function and influence on the stability and development of society [2]. For example, the types and numbers of terminal devices in the power system are growing continuously. On the other hand, the power system is constantly connected to various intelligent terminal devices, which greatly enhances the functionality and intelligence of the system while also makes the security of the whole system affected to a greater extent [3]. In order to ensure the efficient and effective operation of the whole power system, it is necessary to identify and verify the identity of the terminal devices connected to the power system [4].

The power terminal itself has typical features such as wide distribution, various types, complex functions and different means of communication, which makes the identification of power terminal identity more difficult and challenging [5]. The wide range, deep level and multiple kinds of security threats faced by the power system make the identification of power terminal identity of high urgency. In order to guarantee the privacy, security and integrity of the operating data of the power terminal without affecting the original function of the power terminal, it is necessary to verify the identity of the terminal accessing the power system and prevent the security and stability of the whole system from being damaged due to the access of malicious terminals [6]. In the big data environment, the identification of power terminal identity needs to adopt specific means to improve the accuracy and efficiency of identification and enhance the usability of the identification system [7].

In addition, in the process of power terminal identity identification, the traditional password identification and verification means, although effective, still have many shortcomings, specifically in terms of easy to crack, not easy to save, and low verification efficiency and many other aspects [8]. Under the trend of exponential growth of intelligent terminals in power system, the identity of terminals needs to be systematically unified in order to identify and manage various terminal applications more conveniently [9]. By designing the identification model of power terminal identity in many dimensions, such as security, convenience, applicability and efficiency, it could verify and evaluate the effectiveness of the identification of power terminals and improve the usability of the identification model in response to the security threat environment and trends faced by the power system [10].

In this paper, the logic flow of access, identification, verification and management is used to reduce the cost of data acquisition and computing power in the process of power terminal identification, and improve the anti-cracking performance of the system. Based on the principle of improving the security performance of power system, an intelligent power terminal identity authentication model is established, and with the help of intelligent algorithm, the accuracy, efficiency and practicality of the model for power terminal identity authentication are improved [11]. Finally, the efficiency of the power terminal identification model is quantitatively analyzed by setting the effect verification parameters. The results show that the model can effectively ensure the efficient and stable operation of the whole power system, so it has important application and promotion value.

2   Power Terminal Identification Technology Analysis

Identification of power terminals is a verification of the legitimacy, security and authenticity of the terminal devices or applications accessed by the power system. Since there are large differences in the types, functions and complexity of terminals in the power system, it is necessary to carry out differentiated identification and management according to the differences in the identity of the devices [12]. In addition, the power terminal identity identification system also needs to be able to adopt different verification strategies for terminals of different levels, so as to ensure that the identification model is easy to implement. Generally, for terminals with higher security level, the requirements for identity identification system will be higher, so as to guarantee the system's unforgeability and impenetrability [13].

Identification of the power terminal is the basis and prerequisite for achieving the security and stability of the power system, and the identification and verification of the identity of the power terminal mainly includes certificates, passwords and other ways to carry out [14]. The identification technology of electric power terminal is usually based on the architecture of electric power industrial control system, and the security environment state of the terminal is judged with the help of identity communication authentication. The terminal identity identification represented by digital certificate and trusted computing establishes a reliable and stable communication system environment under the grant communication protocol [15].

2.1 Principle of Power Terminal Identification Technology

The implementation of power terminal identification technology mainly includes two dimensions: connection and communication between terminals and the main system. Among them, in the connection dimension, the access state detection is used to achieve two-way identity authentication and establish a trusted environment for terminals. In the communication dimension of both sides, the state of the power terminal relying on the communication key is analyzed and verified to protect the security of the communication process. The authentication and protection of the power terminal's identity, privacy, and trusted state together build the power terminal identity identification framework. In the 5G communication environment, communication protocols and wireless communication technologies are used to securely connect the control hub of the cable system to the power terminal. In addition, the authentication of the power terminal identity is obtained with the joint support of encryption algorithms and communication protocols, and the communication protocols are exchanged, the process of which is shown in Fig. 1 below.

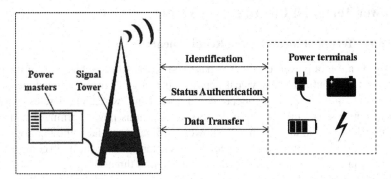

Fig. 1. Power terminal identity communication protocol exchange process

2.2 Comparison of Power Terminal Identification Technologies

The identification mode of power terminal usually includes several typical forms such as digital certificate authentication, algorithm authentication and key authentication. Among them, digital certificate authentication, as an asymmetric authentication mode, is mainly used for identity authentication and communication between communication modules and gateways. Secondly, algorithmic identity authentication, as a symmetric authentication method, is mainly used for interactive authentication after certificate authentication is established between communication and gateway, and thus has advantages in terms of high efficiency and small arithmetic power occupation. In addition, at the level of key identity authentication, in contrast to algorithmic authentication, the gateway and communication module need to perform certificate authentication after interactive authentication.

Communication module is an important support for mutual authentication between power terminals and business front-end. Software programs such as algorithms and hardware such as chips together constitute an important framework for the system to identify power terminals, implement communication information sharing, transmission and protocol distribution. The overall power terminal identity identification technology includes several ways based on user knowledge and user characteristics. The former is easy to implement and economical, so it is widely used, but its security factor is low, which is easy to lead to identity forgery, information leakage and other risk events. The latter has high application advantages in the security level, but the economy is poor, so its applicability is limited. Specifically, in the field of power system, more attention needs to be paid to the security performance of power terminal identification technology because the identity of power system terminals can threaten the security of the entire power grid, which in turn leads to greater risks and losses. The identification architecture of power systems usually includes multiple layers and multiple-identification of power terminals, and intelligent algorithms are used to achieve identification between the terminals in the system.

3   Power Terminal Identification Model

3.1   Power Terminal Identification Requirements

The identification of power terminals is based on the network architecture of the power system, and the identification device is deployed in a targeted manner. It includes servers for identity identification data collection and processing, wired and wireless networks for data transmission, identification devices, and various power terminals and power users. For the external attacks that the power terminals may face, the topology of the network needs to be optimized to connect the power terminals to the main control system for security protection to better defend against external threats.

The identification device of power terminal is usually deployed near of the power terminal in a bypass way, so as to monitor the traffic data, access protocol and security status used by the power terminal. Secondly, at the level of model construction for identification of power terminals, it is necessary to make targeted adaptations based on the possible threats faced by the terminals, so as to identify the power terminals more accurately and efficiently. The terminal threats faced by the power system can be broadly classified into several typical types such as vulnerability attacks, identity forgery and information theft, fuzzy attacks, etc. Therefore, in the process of their identification, the protocols and port data of the power terminals are fully utilized for their effective identification. In addition, because of the typical characteristics of widely distributed and various types of power terminals, the security identification module deployed is also more scattered and targeted in order to guarantee the efficiency, applicability and economy of power terminal identification.

3.2 Power Terminal Identification Model

The architecture of the power terminal identification model is shown in Fig. 2. The identification model classifies and encodes the data by pre-processing the collected data and selects the data according to its characteristics. The data pre-processing process effectively reduces the arithmetic power requirement of the system calculation and improves the processing efficiency, accuracy and the classification effect of the identity of the power terminal.

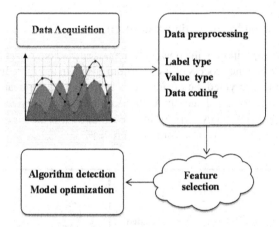

Fig. 2. Architecture of power terminal identification model

Secondly, during the pre-processing of data in the identification model, the encoding of data needs to be obtained using the mapping method shown in Eq. (1), where, a is the data feature values, b is target columns, V is coded values, Y is the total number of samples corresponding to a, and H is the indicator function.

$$V_k = \frac{1}{Y} \sum_{j=1}^{Y} B_j + \frac{1}{Y_k} \sum_{j=1}^{Y} B_j \cdot H\{a_j = a_k\} \tag{1}$$

The correspondence between a and Y is calculated as shown in Eq. (2).

$$Y_k = \sum_{j=1}^{Y} H\{a_j = a_k\} \tag{2}$$

The pre-processing process for the collected power terminal identity data is shown in Fig. 3, which mainly includes data initialization, loop iteration and coding mapping, so as to complete the training of the data coding set.

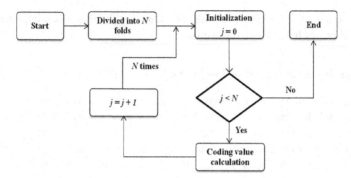

Fig. 3. Preprocessing of power terminal identity data

3.3 Power Terminal Identification Algorithm

The identification algorithm of the power terminal is carried out based on an asymmetric public key cipher, and the process of its algorithm is shown in Fig. 4. In this case, during the transmission of encrypted data from user x to user y, the application of key pair y_1 and y_2 are used to encrypt and decrypt the transmitted data respectively. In addition, the encryption and decryption keys cannot infer each other's value, thus guaranteeing the security and privacy of the data transmission process.

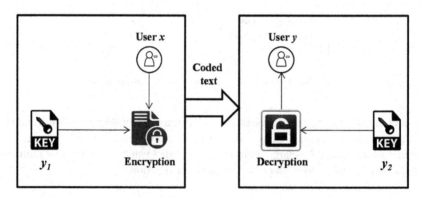

Fig. 4. Identity authentication algorithm decryption process

The data transmission process of power terminal uses digital signature algorithm and Hash operation to compare the data at the sending and receiving ends, thus enhancing the privacy, security and non-repudiation of data transmission. The application of digital certificate in the process of power terminal identification can enhance the judgment of terminal identity legitimacy. The terminal identity is digitally signed to the public key of the power terminal through the registration and authentication of the digital certificate, and the digital certificate is applied to verify the public key of the power terminal. In addition, the legitimacy of the received power terminal identity data is verified with the help of the data server in the power system.

Decision trees are introduced in the power terminal identification algorithm to classify, iterate and train the collected terminal data, thus obtaining a model with more balanced efficiency and accuracy. Secondly, in order to reduce the excessive requirements of the terminal identification algorithm on the system arithmetic power, the depth production of the decision tree is limited so as to prevent the training efficiency from the overfitting of the data.

4 Implementation of the Identification Model

The implementation of the identification model for power terminals needs to be based on the current security situation and future development plan of the power system, and designed in terms of the security, stability, economy, applicability and feasibility of the system. At the level of model construction, it needs to fully absorb the advantages of existing identification algorithms and technologies, and also need to comprehensively consider the technical maturity and the cost economy of large-scale application of power system.

The main function of the identification model of the power terminal is to verify the trustworthiness of the terminal identity, and manage and control the access of the power terminal. Secondly, the identification model is used for the control of communication protocols between terminals to guarantee the security and privacy of authentication and data transmission between terminal devices and between terminals and the master station. The implementation architecture in the identification model is shown in Fig. 5, and the granted terminals are connected to the communication network of power system using data encryption algorithm.

The data security transmission gateway is deployed between the firewall and the power management servers to realize the data communication of the master station while guaranteeing the security of data access and interaction. The security module

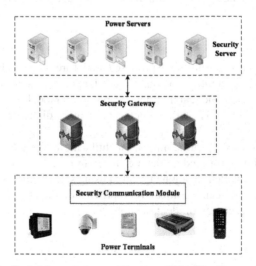

Fig. 5. Implementation architecture of identification model

is deployed between the power terminal and the communication equipment to realize the secure access and secure communication of the power terminal. And deploying the security module inside the power terminal can further supervise the data transmission of the terminals and realize the authorized access of the terminal identity.

5 Experiment and Results Analysis

In order to verify the application effect of the power terminal identification model, the model needs to be verified and analyzed in the usage environment. In order to reduce the cost of result verification and improve the efficiency and accuracy of result analysis, it is necessary to build a test scenario that fits the actual usage environment. Firstly, a collection of power terminal test samples with disorderly discrete characteristics, high redundancy and large data volume is established. Secondly, analyze and eliminate duplicate records and redundant data in the test samples while retain the samples with abnormal identities.

In the Internet of things environment, in order to effectively screen the abnormal identity data of power terminals, it is necessary to filter the application layer protocol data in the power system terminal network environment to better adapt to the actual deployment and operation scenarios of power system. The establishment of the identification environment for power terminals also requires effective simulation of data transmission and interaction between terminals. Thus, it is necessary to retain the common protocol data in the power system.

In order to verify the effectiveness of the power terminal identification model proposed in this paper, the accuracy evaluation indicators, including the correct recognition rate, error recognition rate and other indicators, are set to reflect the training ability and identity authentication accuracy of the model. The calculation of accuracy A is shown in Eq. (3), where TE represents the number of identity samples that are correctly recognized and FP represents the number of terminal identities that are incorrectly authenticated.

$$A = \frac{TE}{TE + FP} \tag{3}$$

The feature selection results of the proposed model are shown in Fig. 6 after multiple terminal identification operations. It can be seen that compared to the traditional identification method using static feature rules, the proposed model improves the efficiency of training and identification while reducing the feature dimensions and maintaining identification accuracy.

Secondly, in terms of abnormal identity identification of power terminals, the identification results of the proposed model are shown in Fig. 7, where "Other" represents the traditional terminal identification algorithm using static feature rules. It can be seen that the proposed model can significantly improve the efficiency of identification and slightly enhance the accuracy of identification.

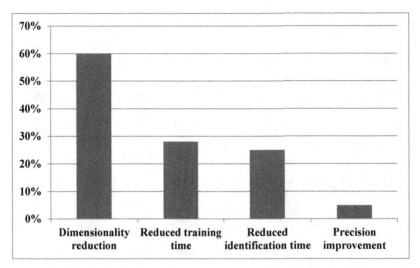

Fig. 6. Results of feature selection for terminal identification model

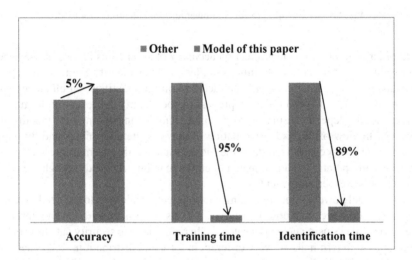

Fig. 7. Power terminal abnormal identity identification results

In addition, in the identity classification dimension of power terminals, the classification results of the proposed model are shown in Fig. 8. It can be seen that the proposed model has high identification accuracy for the abnormal identity of power terminals, which can meet the screening and filtering requirements of the power system for abnormal data terminals. However, the accuracy of identification is closely related to the number of training samples, and as the number of training samples decreases, the identification of abnormal identity by the model will have a higher probability of missing.

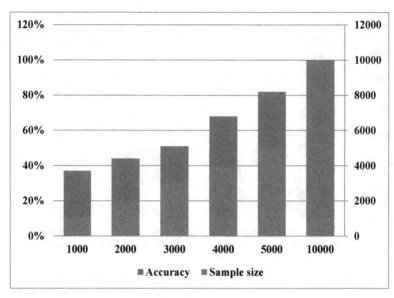

Fig. 8. Classification results of power terminal identification model

In order to improve the identification accuracy of anomalous identities, we need to ensure a sufficient number of training samples to better identify the identity types of terminals, but this leads to a significant decrease in the identification efficiency and a large use of computing power. By pre-processing the identity data of power terminals, it could reduce the dependence of model on training samples and optimize the identification efficiency. In view of the wide distribution of power system terminals and the typical characteristics of decentralized data, the model's adaptability to multiple scenarios of power system operation and automated operation can be improved through the feature selection of power terminal identity.

In the actual power system operating environment, in addition to the need to identify the identity of the accessed power terminals, it is also necessary to defend against possible external attacks using network protocols. In particular, the security data threats faced by power system terminals are very different in form and distribution, so it is necessary to classify the terminal identity data set to deal with these threats. In conclusion, the proposed model shows high application advantages in feature selection, terminal abnormal identity identification and terminal identity classification, and is able to meet the demand for high-precision and high-efficiency power terminal identity identification in the power network environment.

6   Conclusion

In summary, in this paper, a terminal identification model for typical services of modern power grids is developed for the current and future development needs of security management of widely distributed power terminals. In the model architecture designed in this paper, the terminal identity data collection, analysis and authentication control processes enable end-to-end data communication, identity identification and authorization in power systems. In view of the actual characteristics and application scenarios of large number and scattered distribution of power terminal identities, this paper optimizes the discrete feature coding so that the efficiency of feature selection and dimensionality reduction of power terminal identity data can be significantly improved. Although the proposed identification model shows typical advantages in the dimensions of feature selection, terminal abnormal identity identification and terminal identity classification, there is still much room for improvement in the identification effect of the model for rare or specific types of power terminal identity, which needs to be further analyzed and optimized in the future research.

Acknowledgments. The research in this paper is supported by science and technology project of State Grid Gansu Electric Power Company (Grant No.: 522723220008).

References

1. Wang, J.: Application of the unified identity authentication and user management platform in electric group enterprise. Netinfo Secur. (12), 81–85 (2016)
2. Zhang, D., Xue, Z., Liao, G., He, Y., Fu, C.: Design and application of expert identification system for bidding base of power enterprises. Digit. Technol. Appl. (8), 171–172 (2017)
3. Fei, J., Pei, P., Zhang, M., Sun, J.: Hierarchical association analysis method in industrial control cyber attack scenario of power grid. J. Nanjing Univ. Sci. Technol. **44**(6), 715–723 (2020)
4. Zhang, C., Ma, Z., Zhang, Q., Liu, M. An authentication solution of distributed file system of power enterprises. Tech. Autom. Appl. **36**(3):23–26+31 (2017)
5. Zhang, X., et al.: Overview of power industry control system penetration attack technology. Electr. Power Inf. Commun. Technol. **19**(3), 49–59 (2021)
6. Kwon, Y., Kim, H.K., Lim, Y.H., Lim, J.I.: A behavior-based intrusion detection technique for smart grid infrastructure. In: 2015 IEEE Eindhoven PowerTech, pp. 1–6 (2015)
7. Li, T., Wang, G., Liu, Y., Yang, Z., Ren, S., Shang, W.: Information security risk analysis of intelligent terminal in distribution network. Smart Power **48**(9), 118–122 (2020)
8. Liu, Y., Wang, H., Fang, X., Wang, J. Research on client side terminal security detection technology for smart grid. In: 2021 International Conference on Wireless Communications and Smart Grid (ICWCSG), pp. 468–472 (2021)
9. Huang, H., Chen, X.: Power mobile terminal identity authentication mechanism based on blockchain. In: 2020 International Wireless Communications and Mobile Computing (IWCMC), pp. 195–198 (2020)
10. Li, W., Li, R., Wu, K., Cheng, R., Su, L., Cui, W.: Design and implementation of an SM2-based security authentication scheme with the key agreement for smart grid communications. IEEE Access **6**, 71194–71207 (2018)
11. Liu, D., Wang, R., Zhang, H., Chen, J., Liu, X., Ma, L.: Research on terminal security technology of ubiquitous power internet of things based on PUF and SM3. In: 2019 IEEE 3rd Conference on Energy Internet and Energy System Integration (EI2), pp. 910–915 (2019)
12. Wang, H., Yu, H., Zheng, H., Wang, G., Wang, C., Li, B.: A secure and efficient data transmission scheme for edge devices in smart grids. In: 2020 IEEE International Conference on Progress in Informatics and Computing (PIC), pp. 323–327 (2020)
13. Zhao, B., Wang, Z., Wang, S.: Research and application of trusted identity authentication technology in power terminals. Cybersp. Secur. **9**(7), 15–18 (2018)

14. Liu, R., Zhao, G., Li, Y., Liu, J., Huang, J., Miao, W.: The protectable privacy preserving authentication for IoT devices access. In: 2020 IEEE 9th Joint International Information Technology and Artificial Intelligence Conference (ITAIC), pp. 511–516 (2020)
15. Feng, W.: A lightweight anonymous authentication protocol for smart grid. In: 2021 13th International Conference on Intelligent Human-Machine Systems and Cybernetics (IHMSC), pp. 87–90 (2021)

Research on Firmware Vulnerability Mining Model of Power Internet of Things

Chao Zhou[(⊠)], Ziying Wang, Jing Guo, Yajuan Guo, Haitao Jiang, Zhimin Gu, and Wei Huang

Electric Power Science Research Institute, State Grid Jiangsu Electric Power Co., Ltd., Nanjing 211103, China
userrr@qq.com

Abstract. Power IoT (Internet of Things) has been developing for a few years where various types of terminals are deployed. Since the power IoT devices need to be connected to the public network, the security situation is more severe, and it is imperative to develop an efficient and reliable vulnerability mining model for the device firmware in the power IoT field. Based on this, this paper analyzes the common mining means of power IoT device firmware vulnerabilities including static and dynamic analysis methods. By comparing the characteristics of different mining techniques and their applicability, an IoT device firmware vulnerability mining model applicable to the power system environment is proposed and its process and associated methods are designed. Finally, a test system is established to verify the effectiveness of the proposed model compared to the common static and dynamic analysis tools. The test results show that the proposed model demonstrates better performance in terms of execution time and code coverage efficiency.

Keywords: Firmware Security · Vulnerability Mining · Internet of Things · Power System

1 Introduction

The dependence of all sectors of society on the power system is increasing, and the functionality and complexity of power system equipment is also increasing. In this context, power IoT (Internet of Things) has gained rapid application and development [1]. However, the characteristics of IoT determine that it inevitably has vulnerabilities and is easy to be attacked and cracked. If a security incident occurs, the power Internet of things will often lead to more serious consequences, so it needs to be carefully designed and built to ensure the stable operation of the whole system [2]. At present, in the network environment, the security problem of the power IoT is becoming more and more prominent and serious, especially the particularity of the operating environment of the power IoT makes the firmware of the power IoT integrated into the system equipment in an embedded manner [3]. In a relatively closed environment, the security protection level of power terminal firmware has a great relationship with the hardware settings, so it is particularly important to mine its firmware vulnerabilities.

The diversity, intelligence and embeddedness of power IoT terminals make it difficult for traditional vulnerability mining technologies or means to achieve the expected application effect [4]. On the one hand, relying on manual firmware mining method is not only inefficient, but also unable to meet the security needs of massive data and devices in the Internet of things environment. On the other hand, the software automated vulnerability mining technology in the environment of power Internet of things has great limitations and is difficult to implement effectively. IoT terminal firmware vulnerability mining techniques mainly include static and dynamic methods [5]. Static firmware vulnerability mining is based on the unpackaging analysis of the firmware file format, so as to get the vulnerability status of the firmware at the level of data flow, control flow, etc. Common static analysis methods for firmware vulnerabilities include angr framework, taint-style, etc. [6]. These analysis techniques are highly effective, but there are usually problems of lack of compatibility and low efficiency.

The dynamic analysis methods include firmware emulation, fuzzy testing and so on. The firmware emulation technology as an open technology in the field of IoT firmware has significant application advantages, commonly used software including QEMU, Avatar, etc. [7]. The firmware emulation technology can emulate simple IoT device firmware, but its applicability is not enough for more complex device firmware [8]. Fuzzy testing technology has high application advantages at the scalability level, but the random variability of the algorithm and the applicability level of the research scenario are still insufficient. In the field of power system, the investment of power Internet of things in hardware is high, but the protection ability of the system is relatively weak [9]. While the power IoT is connected to the public network, the security situation it faces is more severe, and it is urgent to research and develop an efficient and reliable vulnerability mining system for the firmware in the power IoT.

In conclusion, the openness and compatibility of IoT makes it inevitable that unpredictable and unknown vulnerabilities in the terminal firmware may seriously threaten the secure, stable and reliable operation of power systems [10]. Therefore, this paper researches and develops effective firmware vulnerability mining methods based on the current state of power IoT firmware vulnerability to overcome the shortages of vulnerability mining techniques under common platforms, and to meet the actual application needs of power systems [11]. Based on the analysis of the traditional firmware vulnerability mining technology of the IoT, combined with the characteristics of the power IoT and the reasons for the existence of firmware vulnerabilities in it, this paper makes an in-depth research and analysis on the firmware mining methods from the aspects of improving the mining efficiency, security, accuracy and scalability, so as to improve the security level of the power IoT.

2 Power IoT Terminal Firmware

2.1 Architecture of Power IoT

In order to effectively detect the power IoT firmware vulnerabilities, the architecture of the whole system needs to be analyzed. A typical IoT system architecture is shown in Fig. 1, which mainly includes the application side, the service side, and the device side. While in the technical aspect, the layers of IoT mainly include three levels of perception, network and application. The application side is mainly composed of network protocols, which enables effective management of the device side [12]. The server side is mainly used for the management of IoT devices, and provides firmware upgrade services to the application side for data preservation and management. Due to the complexity of the power Internet of things system, the characteristics and functions of the terminal firmware of different layers are different, which makes the firmware vulnerability mining technology also need to be targeted.

The architecture of power IoT devices is divided into different aspects such as firmware and hardware. The hardware architecture tends to vary widely depending on the function of its device. Typically, the hardware architecture includes SoC (System on Chip), JTAG (Joint Test Action Group) interface, UART (Universal Asynchronous Receiver/Transmitter) and so on [13]. Due to the particularity of the IoT device instruction architecture, its computing instruction architecture is relatively lean, so the vulnerability mining and security protection technologies developed for servers are often difficult to effectively match on IoT devices [14]. The power IoT device firmware architecture, as a program to achieve device functionality, mainly includes various application systems and software. For example, the operating system, file system, and various application software are used to realize the connection between hardware and software, the processing of files, and device functions, respectively.

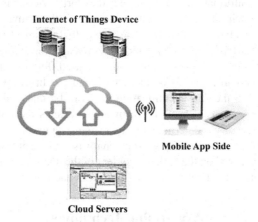

Fig. 1. Typical IoT system architecture

2.2 Acquisition of Terminal Firmware

Power IoT terminal firmware acquisition is an important prerequisite for achieving firmware vulnerability mining, and its acquisition methods mainly include serial port reading, debug interface reading, device vendor acquisition, programmer reading, and network upgrade. Among them, the most direct and easy way is to obtain from the device hardware manufacturer [15].

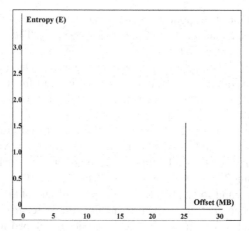

Fig. 2. Display status of unencrypted device firmware

In the network upgrade process, the use of man-in-the-middle attack to intercept IoT firmware information is an effective means of obtaining firmware without certificate verification on the server side. UART serial port and JTAG debug interface reading are used to obtain debug information of the device and export device firmware, respectively. In addition, with the help of the programmer, the code in the firmware can be obtained and the data can be effectively read and written. Power IoT terminal firmware acquisition establishes an effective basis for carrying out extraction and unpacking of firmware files. Since the types of firmware file system in terminals are different and the identification is unique, the file system needs to be extracted from the firmware with the help of authorization tools and the data identification needs to be matched for unpacking. If a power IoT device vendor encrypts its firmware, it affects the process of firmware unpacking, so it is necessary to determine whether it is encrypted or not before unpacking. The device firmware is analyzed using entropy analysis, and the encryption status of the firmware can be seen based on the realistic content of the analysis result curve. Figure 2 above shows the status of a device firmware that is not encrypted.

3 Firmware Vulnerability Mining Techniques

The main reason for power IoT firmware vulnerabilities is mostly due to code vulnerabilities in the underlying operating system. Due to the huge increase in both the number and complexity of IoT devices, this makes their firmware vulnerabilities often have more serious consequences. Power IoT device vulnerabilities mainly include stack overflow, heap overflow, integer overflow, and reuse after release, formatted strings, and so on. Among them, stack overflow vulnerability may cause code and commands to be tampered with and arbitrarily executed. Heap overflow vulnerability is that the executable file is easy to be hijacked due to insufficient data length. Post-release reuse vulnerability, as a special form of heap vulnerability, is data contamination by released heap blocks, which can also lead to hijacking of executable programs. In addition, the integer overflow vulnerability in power IoT terminal firmware itself has little impact on the whole system, but once it is exploited as a whole with other vulnerabilities, it will produce a series of chain reactions. The formatted string vulnerability is directly related to formatted output, and the vulnerability not only leads to data leakage, but also allows confidential data to be tampered with or overwritten.

Terminal firmware vulnerability mining in power IoT is mainly carried out around source code or binary files. The former uses more static analysis for firmware vulnerability mining, through disassembly, de-compilation, taint analysis, symbolic execution, and other detection processes to complete the entire mining process. The latter can take many forms of coding analysis, such as dynamic, static, and a combination of both. In addition, static analysis and dynamic analysis are based on binary code conversion and fuzzy detection techniques to test for vulnerabilities, respectively.

The traditional IoT firmware vulnerability mining techniques usually focus on monitoring the program outside the device. However, it is difficult to arrange the analysis module in the power IoT device, and the limitation of the arithmetic power of the computing module in the device makes it difficult to carry out dynamic analysis, so that only static analysis can be used to monitor the program. Meanwhile, the heterogeneous and complex firmware and code privacy of power IoT devices make it difficult to use general computing instruction compilation to implement static analysis schemes. The privacy of the code and documentation makes it difficult to use the source code to analyze the firmware of the device, leading to difficulties in carrying out vulnerability mining of the power IoT firmware.

In addition, the inherent properties of the power IoT device firmware make it challenging to conduct vulnerability mining on it as well. The rich interactivity of power IoT, the reusability of component code and the open source code of third-party libraries enable power IoT to interact with power end devices, servers, etc. In this context, dynamic analysis can be used to synthesize the interaction architecture outside the system. Meanwhile, power IoT may introduce vulnerabilities in third-party components as it may use third-party libraries to reduce the cost of building. To effectively uncover such firmware vulnerabilities, the use of static analysis allows the type and source of vulnerabilities to be analyzed. In addition, the vulnerabilities of power IoT may be categorized into a few common types. For these vulnerabilities in power IoT device firmware, static, dynamic, or a combination of both schemes can be used to detect common vulnerability types.

3.1 Static Analysis Techniques

The application of static analysis techniques in IoT systems is an effective measure to deal with cases where code and documentation are not provided by external vendors. As a software system in power IoT, the device firmware represented by system programs such as operating system and file system can control the underlying logic of the system as a whole. Static analysis technology obtains the vulnerability model of firmware based on reverse engineering, and excavates and analyzes vulnerabilities through a specific process. The static analysis vulnerability mining method of power IoT firmware can effectively cope with the increasing complexity of devices in the power system, and its analysis process is shown in Fig. 3. Among them, the firmware format is analyzed with the help of the firmware program and the target program is extracted using the execution information reply technique. Vulnerability analysis rules are used to further validate the suspected vulnerabilities so that the real firmware vulnerabilities are finally found.

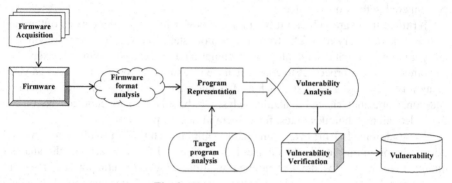

Fig. 3. Static analysis process

3.2 Fuzzy Testing Techniques

As an important means of software vulnerability mining mainly for IoT systems, the dynamic mining process of firmware vulnerabilities for fuzzy testing is shown in Fig. 4. The test samples are generated as the data input, and the test target is monitored for anomalies. Through feeding the monitoring results to the samples, to achieve continuous iteration, and finally get the final results of the test samples.

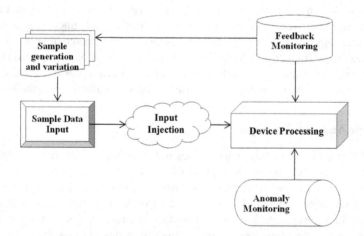

Fig. 4. Dynamic mining process of firmware vulnerabilities

In order to further optimize the efficiency and accuracy of fuzzy testing for firmware vulnerability mining, the fuzzy test architecture flow is designed to analyze the target program in depth. Compared with the dynamic mining process, this process further enhances the design of fuzzy test components, including sample generation and state detection components that can improve test performance, as well as peripheral analysis system, monitoring and simulation components. Based on the inherent properties of the protocol communication method of power IoT devices, the fuzzy test method also needs to be continuously updated and iterated. The internal and external monitoring modules such as guidance and monitoring are added to achieve real-time recording of the program execution effect. The external analysis system prevents the loss of test samples through the extraction of protocol interaction data and realizes the in-depth analysis of the tested program.

4 Firmware Vulnerability Mining Model

By analyzing the challenges of the firmware vulnerability mining techniques in power IoT as well as technical features, it can be seen that most of the existing IoT device firmware vulnerability mining techniques need to be improved in aspects of efficiency, accuracy or difficulty in offline firmware simulation. Hence, this paper constructs intelligent firmware interaction for effective mining and verification of power IoT device firmware vulnerabilities. In addition, to address the problem that the target program of power IoT device firmware cannot fully resist to external input data, conditional branches are processed to establish model conditional constraints so as to improve the effectiveness of vulnerability mining.

4.1 Firmware Vulnerability Mining Process

The vulnerability mining process based on the power IoT device firmware requires first collecting the device's files and getting the desired power IoT device firmware information based on the obtained device files. Secondly, after obtaining the IoT device firmware information, the symbolic data of the firmware is extracted from it and the function address of the power IoT system is obtained with the help of the vulnerability search script. In addition, after getting the function address of the power IoT system, the function code is also obtained by using the vulnerability search script. The function code is used as an important criterion to determine whether the function has injection risk, and the target vulnerability information can be confirmed based on the injection risk of the referenced function. The vulnerability mining process for the power IoT device firmware is shown in Fig. 5.

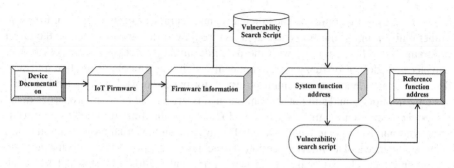

Fig. 5. Vulnerability mining process for power IoT device firmware

4.2   Firmware Sample Selection Method

In the process of power IoT device firmware vulnerability mining, if there are changes in program control flow in the feedback data of variant samples, further sampling and sample generation are required to expand the size of variant sample queue and further enhance the coverage of vulnerability mining code. In order to effectively determine the indicator data for firmware vulnerability mining, the indicator parameter variable P_v is defined as shown in Eq. (1), where E_d denotes the number of execution jumps of external data and E_b denotes the number of branch jumps affected.

$$P_v = \frac{E_d}{E_b} \times 100\% \tag{1}$$

The firmware vulnerability mining model built in this paper uses shared files to obtain the feedback data after the execution of the target program. By reading and analyzing the samples and shared files, the status of the feedback data is judged. In the calculation of the sample weight value Q_v shown in Eq. (2), EA_v and EB_v denote the number of execution array and the number of conditional branch jumps, respectively.

$$Q_v = \sum_{v=1}^{k} \left(\frac{EA_v}{EB_v} \times 1000 \right) \tag{2}$$

The larger value of Q_v means that the sample performs more jumps. By covering more code and branch hops, a deeper mining of firmware vulnerabilities in power IoT is performed.

4.3   Firmware Status Detection

Power IoT device firmware state detection is an important tool for vulnerability mining, and the state of the firmware is determined by judging the process state of the executing program. Power IoT device firmware state detection includes detection of hardware devices and emulation platforms. Among them, the detection of hardware devices is performed with the help of UPD (User Datagram Protocol), TCP (Transmission Control Protocol) and other protocols for survivability detection. The detection for the emulation platform is furthermore analyzed with the help of system memory. Moreover, the detection strategies for UDP and TCP protocols also differ significantly. The former uses the service connection state to determine, and the latter is based on the running state of the terminal program. Differences in system platforms may make the types of vulnerabilities more significantly different. For different types of power IoT device firmware vulnerabilities, specific mining detection schemes need to be established, especially using a combination of schemes to achieve effective mining of vulnerabilities.

5   Tests and Results Analysis

In order to verify the effectiveness of power IoT device firmware vulnerability mining techniques, a test system needs to be designed. On the other hand, the reliability, accuracy, and efficiency of the power IoT device firmware vulnerability mining system will be greatly affected by the test platform settings, so it is necessary to first configure the software and hardware and other facilities in the test environment, including physical machines, virtual machines, and the software environment and operating environment, and the configuration of the test system environment is shown in Table 1 below.

Table 1. The configuration of the test system environment

No.	Environment	Configuration	
1	Operation system	Microsoft Windows 10	
2	Hardware	CPU	Intel i7-9750h
		Memory	32GB DDR4
		Hard Disk	1T SSD
3	Software	Fusion Pro 15	
4	Virtual machine	CPU	3 Core
		Memory	16G
		Hard Disk	500G SSD

In the process of testing the power IoT device firmware vulnerability mining method, the effectiveness of the mining method is verified by comparing the mining effect of the test system with common analysis systems. The execution time comparison between static and dynamic analysis in programs using dynamic instrumentation tools represented by DynamoRIO, Pintools, the method proposed in this paper called PIoT, and Dyninst that supports static and dynamic instrumentation is shown in Fig. 6, where four types of firmware are extracted from electronic key terminal (Firmware #1), intelligent locker (Firmware #2), power data acquisition terminal (Firmware #3) and temperature sensor (Firmware #4).

From the comparative analysis of the execution time of the instrumentation under different program operations in Fig. 6, it can be seen that the proposed method demonstrates better at the program execution time level. The execution time of static instrumentation

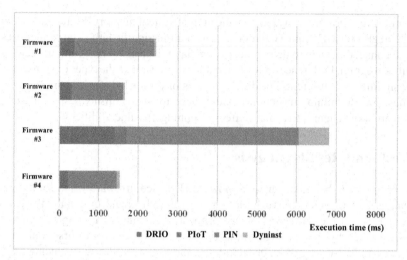

Fig. 6. Comparison of execution times in the program

is relatively shorter because of the reduced program interaction steps. In contrast, the execution time of dynamic instrumentation increases significantly due to the presence of the program interaction process.

In the aspect of code coverage efficiency of power IoT device firmware vulnerability mining, the execution results are shown in Fig. 7. It can be seen that the faster the code coverage per unit time, the higher the efficiency of program execution, the stronger the effect of firmware vulnerability mining.

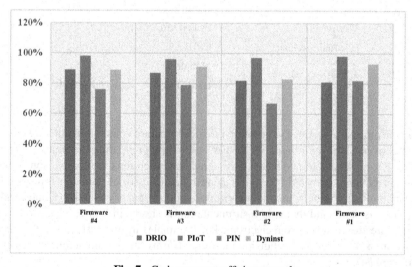

Fig. 7. Code coverage efficiency results

The comprehensive results show that the power IoT device firmware vulnerability mining model constructed in this paper has advantages in the aspects of execution time and code coverage efficiency. Therefore, the power IoT device firmware vulnerability mining model proposed in this paper can be effectively applied to the application process of firmware vulnerability mining in power IoT, taking into account applicability, practicality and efficiency.

6 Conclusion

In summary, based on the current research and application status of power IoT device firmware vulnerability mining technology, this paper proposes an effective firmware vulnerability mining model for the practical application requirements of power system. By analyzing the architecture of power IoT systems, the process of power IoT firmware acquisition and unpackaging is analyzed. Secondly, the generic vulnerability mining techniques for IoT firmware are studied, and the characteristics of different mining techniques and their applicability are compared to establish the basis for building the firmware vulnerability mining model in this paper. In addition, the study of the power IoT device firmware vulnerability mining process analyzes the theoretical basis of the mining algorithm and establishes the power IoT device firmware state detection method. Finally, this paper establishes a test platform for the power IoT device firmware vulnerability mining environment to compare and test the performance of different firmware vulnerability mining methods, and the test results show the effectiveness and applicability of the power IoT device firmware vulnerability mining model proposed. However, the research in this paper is not deep enough at the level of automated security analysis of power IoT device firmware, and the vulnerability search script optimization is needed in the future research.

Acknowledgments. The research in this paper is supported by the science and technology project of State Grid Jiangsu Electric Power Co., Ltd. under Grant No. J2021154.

References

1. Ren, Y., Zhang, Y., Ai, C.: Survey on taint analysis technology. Comput. Appl. **39**(8), 2302–2309 (2019)
2. Wang, L., Li, F., Li, L., Feng, X.: Principle and practice of taint analysis. J. Softw. **28**(04), 860–882 (2017)
3. Wu, Z., Chen, X., Yang, Z., Du, X.: Survey on information flow control. J. Softw. **28**(1), 135–159 (2017)
4. Zhang, X., Zhang, K., Sang, H., Zhang, H., Wei, P., Zhou, H.: IoT security annual report. Inf. Secur. Commun. Priv. **2020**(01), 45–62 (2019)
5. Zheng, Y., Davanian, A., Yin, H.: FIRM-AFL: high-throughput grey box fuzzing of IoT firmware via augmented process emulation. In: Proceedings of the 28th USENIX Conference on Security Symposium (SEC 2019), pp. 1099–1114 (2019)
6. Pereira, J.D.: Techniques and tools for advanced software vulnerability detection. In: 2020 IEEE International Symposium on Software Reliability Engineering Workshops (ISSREW), pp. 123–126 (2020)

7. Mera, A., Feng, B., Lu, L., Kirda, E. DICE: automatic emulation of DMA input channels for dynamic firmware analysis. In: 2021 IEEE Symposium on Security and Privacy (SP), pp. 1938–1954 (2021)

8. Wang, Y., Shen, J., Lin, J., Lou, R.: Staged method of code similarity analysis for firmware vulnerability detection. IEEE Access 7, 14171–14185 (2019)

9. Sun, Y., Sun, L., Shi, Z., Yu, W., Ying, H.: Vulnerability finding and firmware association in power grid. In: 2019 Fifth Conference on Mobile and Secure Services (MobiSecServ), pp. 1–5 (2019)

10. Zhang, B., Xi, Z., Gao, K.: Fuzzy test guidance technology for power internet of things firmware vulnerability detection. In: 2021 IEEE International Conference on Energy Internet (ICEI), pp. 157–163 (2021)

11. Zhang, H., Zhou, A., Jia, P., Liu, L., Ma, J., Liu, L.: InsFuzz: fuzzing binaries with location sensitivity. IEEE Access 7, 22434–22444 (2019)

12. Böhme, M., Pham, V., Roychoudhury, A.: Coverage-based greybox fuzzing as Markov chain. IEEE Trans. Softw. Eng. 45(5), 489–506 (2019)

13. Cheng, K., et al.: DTaint: detecting the taint-style vulnerability in embedded device firmware. In: 2018 48th Annual IEEE/IFIP International Conference on Dependable Systems and Networks (DSN), pp. 430–441 (2018)

14. Nicho, M., Girija, S.: IoTVT model: a model mapping IoT sensors to IoT vulnerabilities and threats. In: 2021 20th International Conference on Ubiquitous Computing and Communications (IUCC/CIT/DSCI/SmartCNS), pp. 123–129 (2021)

15. Chen, Y., Tao, Y., Zhai, S., Sui, S.: Design and implementation of a universal offline reading system for embedded device firmware. In: 2022 7th International Conference on Intelligent Computing and Signal Processing (ICSP), pp. 1307–1310 (2022)

How Can Social Workers Participate in Big Data Governance? The Third-Party Perspective on Big Data Governance

Di Zhao[⊠]

Department of Social Work, School of Economics and Management, Nanjing Institute of Technology, Nanjing, China
sociology2017@163.com

Abstract. The existing research on ethical issues in big data governance mainly focuses on organizational analysis, stakeholder analysis, industrial supply chain, and other fragmented management analysis, and pays less attention to the participation of non-profit organizations as third parties, which makes it difficult to solve the integration and systematic social problems of big data governance. The research takes the third-party social work service as the analytical framework. First, the ethical problems of big data governance are attributed to the decentralized production and intensive use of data and the separation of producers and users. Then it demonstrates and analyzes the multi-dimensional isomorphism of social work as a third party and big data governance in regards to work objects, ethical connotation, and technical requirements. Then, according to the professional advantages of social work, it is proposed that social workers should assume the roles of educators, coordinators, organizers, and advocates, and promote the data-rich represented by enterprises, hospitals, and governments to actively protect the rights and interests of the data-poor, to achieve a win-win situation for individuals, groups, and society in big data governance.

Keywords: big data · ethics · governance · social work

1 Introduction

Big data has become an existence that cannot be ignored in the information age. Computer-related technical experts use data mining and algorithms to obtain valuable data and improve the efficiency and convenience of our work and life. We have smartphones, accurate Internet recommendations, ubiquitous monitoring, GPS positioning, ubiquitous social media, Internet hospitals, and various merged large databases for scientific research. While big data brings us convenience, the accompanying breach of privacy and violation of individual dignity have attracted the attention of scholars and the general public worldwide (Novak and Pavlicek 2021; Murtagh et al. 2018).

The existing studies mostly discuss the ethical principles of big data governance from the organizational level (Janssen et al. 2020), industrial supply chain (Martin 2015), and stakeholders (Someh et al. 2019; 15), and seldom discuss the involvement of third parties other than the government and the market, especially the participation of non-profit organizations. They only discuss the management of platform companies and the governance of different links of the industrial chain, which cannot systematically integrate multiple forces to solve the problem of data governance. Therefore, this paper plans to take social work as the third party as an example to explore the logic and action mechanism of non-profit organizations' involvement in big data governance.

This paper believes that the essence of big data related technologies and the resulting ethical problems is a social problem caused by the separation of decentralized production and intensive use of data. Therefore, in discussing the ethics and social governance of big data, we need to define the social discussion related to big data as a social problem, not a problem that can be solved only from the technical level, organization management, and industrial norms. The social issues of ethics and governance of big data as the existence that affects the well-being of individuals, groups, and the general public, naturally enter the disciplinary vision of social work which focuses on solving social problems. Therefore, this paper plans to analyze the ethics and governance of big data in the theoretical framework of social work participation as third-party non-profit organizations, to provide a new analytical perspective and integrated problem-solving ideas for the discussion of big data, and also extend new space for the development and practical application of social work discipline.

2   Literature Review and Analytical Framework

The relevant research on big data governance has increased recently in the past 10 years, and the concern about ethical issues in big data governance has become a research hotspot. Researchers mostly analyze and reveal the principles and frameworks that big data governance should adopt from the perspective of the organization and management of big data governance such as data platform companies, stakeholders, and the industry supply chain.

2.1   Platform Organization-Level Analysis of Big Data Governance

The research on the platform organization level of big data governance mainly discusses the ethical issues of data governance and their solutions from the perspective of algorithm governance and organization management. As early as 2016, some scholars outlined six possible problems of big data algorithms from the perspective of big data algorithm governance, which are inconclusive evidence, unidentified evidence, misguided evidence, unfair results, transformation effect, and traceability (Mittelstadt et al. 2016). These epistemological and normative concerns will directly lead to unconvincing actions, opacity, unwanted bias, autonomy, privacy protection, and moral responsibility, thus providing feasible guidance for the design, development, and deployment of algorithms (Tsamados et al. 2021). This analysis mainly focuses on how the internal management of big data platform companies can achieve the social and economic effects and ethical values of algorithms and pays less attention to data subjects (the general public), government departments, research institutions, and other stakeholders outside profit-making organizations.

2.2 Stakeholder Analysis of Big Data Governance

The stakeholder framework is a common framework for ethical analysis in big data governance. The researchers used the Delphi method to seek experts to identify and rank the core concerns of individuals, organizations, and society in data governance and found that privacy and trust are the two most important ethical concerns of individuals, and data trading and ethical governance are the most important core concerns of organizations, and power imbalance and principles are the most concerned topics at the society level (Someh et al. 2019). The researchers used the ethical analysis framework of stakeholders to outline the different interests of stakeholders and then described how the internal governance institutions and external management institutions of the organization cooperate to close the alignment gap between different subjects (Nair 2020). The above research mainly analyzes the ethics and problem-solving of big data governance from the horizontal combination and interaction of different stakeholders. Although this analysis method of different levels and elements is clear, it cannot better link and integrate various elements to solve the practical problem in data governance.

2.3 Industry Supply Chain Analysis of Big Data Governance

In addition to the element analysis of horizontal stakeholders, some researchers believe that big data governance should not only be regarded as a social problem arising from technology, but also as an ethical problem faced by the data industry. They believe that the big data industry includes the generation of personalized data, the tracking, and aggregation of data, advertising marketing, and consumers. They analyze the ethical requirements of different links from the upstream source, intermediate manufacturing, and downstream use of the big data industry, and regard downstream consumers as supervisors of the industrial chain (Martin 2015). The analytic thinking of the industrial supply chain is basically a copy of economics and management. Although it has some inspiration for the systematic development of data governance, it has not paid enough attention to the uniqueness of the big data industry. As a common asset, big data has strong ethical attributes, which makes simple economic management thinking inadequate.

2.4 An Analytical Framework of Big Data Governance: The Third Party of Social Work Service

Whether it is organization analysis, stakeholder analysis, or industrial supply chain analysis, it is mainly limited to profit-making economics and management thinking. In recent years, data governance has been more and more regarded as social data governance, and more attention has been paid to the exploration of its social ethical value and framework within and outside the academic community. However, as a non-profit organization, the participation of the third party has not received due attention except in a few studies. In a study on obesity, researchers mentioned that experts repeatedly called for the participation of third parties to provide reports, clarify ethical requirements for data governance, provide corresponding skills training, and promote data sharing (Vogel et al. 2019). Existing researchers have analyzed data governance from the perspective of social science and summarized four models from practice, namely, data sharing pool, data cooperative, public data trust, and personal data sovereignty. They introduced civil society and public institutions into data governance to balance the unbalanced power relations in data governance, safeguard public interests and promote economic development (Micheli et al. 2020).

Although these existing studies have highlighted the important value of civil society forces such as public institutions in realizing democratic data governance and balancing the unbalanced power relations among them, they have not provided a general analytical framework and solutions. Therefore, this paper hopes to explore the logic of the participation of the third party (non-profit organization) represented by social work in big data governance and how they could participate.

Big data has attracted the attention of scholars in many disciplines, including those in social work. However, researchers in social work regard big data as a method and tool to empower social services and improve service efficiency. They also believe that social work can play a more efficient role in using big data to diagnose, evaluate, predict and deal with problems of service recipients. They also only mentioned the importance of data security and privacy in the research implication, advocating that social workers should not only take advantage of the convenience of big data but also advocate the fair and just use of big data (Zetino and Mendoza 2019).

Social work is not an ordinary subject, since social work has not only a professional theoretical system and methodology but also a unique ethical value system. Social work aims at solving the problems of individuals, groups, and society and improving their well-being, and promoting social justice. It is a professional helping discipline and occupation. The ethical value pursuit permeated in this discipline is the soul that distinguishes the discipline from other disciplines. Therefore, in the face of big data governance, big data should not be used only as a tool to empower social work practice and research, just like big data empowers work in any other field. The sensitivity of social work to social issues and the continuous attention of social work to ethical values make social work a suitable perspective for analyzing big data governance.

The basic assumption of this paper is that the development of information technology has brought big data, and also led to the separation of the data rich and the data poor. The asymmetry of relations and the imbalance of rights in the use of big data lead to the damage to the rights and interests of the general public. As a relatively neutral third party, social workers who aim to achieve social justice and increase social welfare can play a role as a bridge to unite the parties separated by information technology and weaken the asymmetric and unbalanced relationship between the parties, to protect the privacy rights, self-determination rights, consent rights and interests of the general public, also the data poor. In this process, social workers hold a balanced position, trying to coordinate between the strong stakeholders such as enterprises and the weak masses, to promote all parties to reach consensus and seek win-win results.

3   Retrospective Analysis of Ethical Issues in Big Data Governance

To learn the generation of ethical problems of big data, we need to trace the birth process of big data. In the traditional era, the transmission of data was mainly through letters, books, newspapers, and the discovery of electricity in the second industrial revolution, which enabled mankind to have long-distance transmission beyond time and space, such as telegraph, telephone, television, and radio. In the era before the computer came into being, people could only record data and related archives with paper and pen. The arrival and widespread of the internet made everyone become we media, data producers, and disseminators. Big data is the massive data gathered based on the internet technology platform. Therefore, the production and use of data before the computer age are scattered, with limited total data and limited dissemination capacity. However, the data in the computer age is widely distributed and used in a relatively centralized manner. There is a great imbalance between the producers and users of data. This asymmetry is not only the asymmetry of data ownership but also the asymmetry of influence. The general public, as the data poor, powerful enterprises, governments, and other data-rich people form an antagonistic situation, as shown in Fig. 1. Massive data are gathered on social media operating platforms, hospitals, schools, banks, corporates, and governments. The combination of computing methods and databases in the internet era makes it possible to merge data from different institutions and fields into larger databases, thus providing important information for interested parties with data to study the needs and preferences of the public. The analysis results of these data are used for profit-making activities in marketing and other aspects, also for social welfare undertakings. Yet these data are not available to the general public. The contradiction caused by the separation of data generation and data use has damaged the public's right to privacy, informed consent, and self-determination.

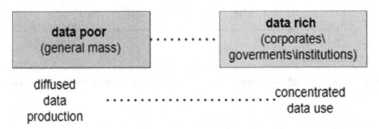

Fig. 1. The Logic of Big Data Governance

According to the professional ethical values of social work, respect, privacy protection, informed consent, and self-determination of service recipients are the most cherished value principles of social work. The contradiction between decentralized production and intensive use of big data has led to the deprivation of privacy, respect, informed consent, and self-determination, making the public the most vulnerable group. The governance of big data needs to overcome the contradiction between the decentralized production and intensive use of data and the separation of producers and users. It needs to combine the production and use of data again and alleviate the contradiction between decentralized production and intensive use of data. For this reason, the public, as decentralized data producers, needs to have more rights to informed consent, participate in decision-making, protect privacy, and be respected in the use and governance of data. These contents are isomorphic with the ethical value creed of social work. Therefore, we believe that the ethical connotation of big data should be defined as respect, informed consent, privacy protection, and participation in independent decision-making, both theoretically and practically. In the face of strong big data owners, that is, operators of network platforms, huge social institutions, and organizations such as governments, enterprises, hospitals, etc., the power of individuals and groups is negligible. However, in the face of the contradiction between the data-rich and the data poor, social workers can act as a bridge between the data-rich and the data poor through their professional knowledge, methods, and ethical value creeds, effectively prevent and resolve the risks in data governance, to protect the interests of individuals, groups and the general public (see Fig. 2).

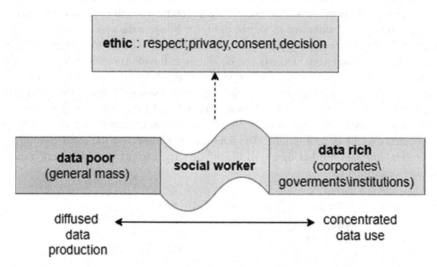

Fig. 2. How Social Work Mitigates the Divide Between Data Poor and Data Rich

4   Multidimensional Isomorphism of Third-Party Social Work Services and Big Data Governance

4.1   Work Object Isomorphism

The service objects of social work and the multiple subjects of data governance are isomorphic. Social work is a discipline and profession committed to improving the well-being of individuals, groups, communities, and society, and promoting social fairness and justice. Social work organizations are also important representatives of non-profit third parties around the world. Social work organizations serve a variety of fields and objects, including enterprise social work, medical social work, school social work, etc. According to the different levels of individuals, groups, communities, and society they serve, social workers can adopt different working methods, such as casework, group work, community work, social administration, and integrated methods. Big data governance is also a process that includes multiple subjects. The meaning of governance increasingly focuses on the interaction and participation of multiple subjects, including data subjects, data platform companies, researchers, data users, government departments, etc. (Micheli et al. 2020; Vogel et al. 2019). Therefore how linking these subjects in different fields to solve problems around common topics requires a relatively neutral third party. The diversity of service subjects of social work makes it isomorphic with the service subjects of big data governance, which makes it easy to carry out work.

4.2 Isomorphism of Ethical Connotation

The professional ethics of social work and the ethical connotation of big data governance have the same structure. The American National Association of social workers stipulates that the ethical principles of social work include social justice, service, dignity and value, the importance of human relations and competence, etc. At the same time, social work also defines its ethical standards for clients such as commitment to clients, self-determination, informed consent, competence, privacy and confidentiality, participation, etc. These are consistent with the ethics of big data governance. Although there is no consensus on the ethical connotation of big data governance at present, many studies believe that privacy protection, informed consent, transparency, self-determination, and participation are important and indispensable contents (Ballantyne and Stewart 2019; Mittelstadt 2019; Favaretto et al. 2020). These ethical requirements are almost the same as the professional ethical requirements of social work, so this isomorphism helps social work organizations, as a third party, to participate in it and follow their professional ethics to achieve good governance of big data.

4.3 Technical Requirement Isomorphism

The development of global social work is influenced by evidence-based medicine, and more and more attention is paid to evidence-based interventions and services. Its emphasis on evidence is the same as the technical logic of big data governance. Evidence-based social work has gradually become an important paradigm in social work. The evidence of evidence-based social work is exactly the existing research findings from various channels (Zetino and Mendoza 2019). The value of big data itself lies in providing scientific decision-making evidence for social and economic actions through the analysis and calculation of large-scale data (Price and Cohen 2019; Vayena et al. 2018). In this sense, social work must intervene in big data governance, and it is also conducive to the common development of evidence-based social work and big data governance (see Fig. 3).

The isomorphic characteristics of social work and big data governance in terms of ethical connotation, service objects and technical requirements enable social workers to better participate in providing services. Social workers themselves do not pursue the interests of their own small groups. As a third party, they pay more attention to how to protect the interests of service objects and improve the welfare of enterprises and the public by improving their professional abilities. They adhere to the principle of giving priority to the interests of service objects, so they can better maintain neutrality in solving the ethical dilemma of big data governance. Their belief in fairness and justice within the society can ensure that they will not simply favor the public or the

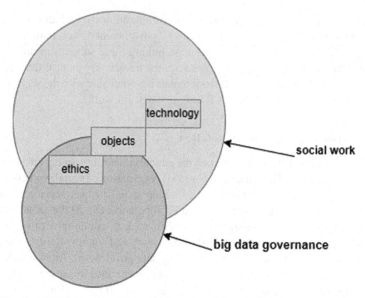

Fig. 3. Multidimensional isomorphism of social work and big data governance

powerful enterprises. In regards of competence, social workers are more systematically and professionally trained than practitioners of general non-profit organizations. They have unique advantages both in theory and method. Therefore, these make social workers the best choice to participate in the big data governance of third parties.

5   How Third-Party Social Work Participates in Big Data Governance

From the perspective of social work discipline, big data governance is not only a tool for empowering all fields but also the object and field of social workers' services. Social work mainly plays the role of educator, coordinator, organizer, and advocate in the governance of big data. Social workers carry out their work by conducting corresponding education to big data stakeholders, coordinating the relations of stakeholders, organizing and carrying out multi-party participation in decision-making activities, and providing policy advice to the government and relevant departments. We take the three common big data-rich parties of hospitals, enterprises, and governments as examples for analysis.

First, social workers should assume the role of educators in big data governance. Social workers have professional theoretical knowledge and value ethics belief. When service objects in different fields encounter big data governance problems, they should first play the role of educators, and through independent communication with stakeholders, make them understand the ethical issues in the use of big data, such as the privacy protection of patient's health information, the protection of consumers' privacy information by enterprises, and the respect of government departments for the public's right to participate in decision-making. With the educational activities of social workers in relevant departments, they play an important role in fulfilling the social responsibilities of enterprises and protecting the interests and dignity of patients.

Second, social workers should play the role of coordinator in big data governance. In the face of specific contradictions and conflicts in big data governance, social workers can use their advantages of communication and coordination to play a bridge role, so that both parties can understand each other's goals and demands, eliminate misunderstandings, strive for the greatest consensus, and protect the interests of the vulnerable party in big data conflicts. Specifically, it is to protect the basic interests of patients, consumers, and ordinary people and help them convey their demands, enable strong data-rich people to reflect and restrict their actions, protect the informed consent rights of data-poor people, and achieve a win-win situation for individuals, groups, and society. The coordinator not only undertakes the coordination of relations among stakeholders but also conducts the coordination of social resources such as relevant data scientists, professionals, and researchers by social workers, to help the vulnerable data poor to better safeguard their basic interests and rights.

Thirdly, social workers should play the role of organizers in big data governance. To solve the ethical problems related to big data in enterprises, medical systems, government departments, and other fields, social workers often need to play the role of organizers, and organize multi-stakeholders of big data to carry out face-to-face discussions or exchange activities by using case, group or community work methods, to build a platform for communication between both parties, promote the exchange and communication of stakeholders, and then make them reach a consensus. This can solve the dilemma that vulnerable data-poor individuals or groups lack the opportunity to talk with powerful data-rich people. The platform built by social workers is of great value to attract representatives of the data-poor to participate in the decision-making of big data use and governance.

Finally, social workers should play the role of advocates in big data governance. As owners of big data, non-profit departments such as the government often face different problems in the use and governance of data. Although the government's use of big data is basically to serve the interests of the public, the governance of big data is more likely to be technology-driven anticipatory governance and social classification, leading to the neglect of special social groups and the deviation of expected governance from the basic demands of the public. Indeed, the government's use of big data may also face data leakage, and deprivation of the social masses of the data-poor of the right to participate, decision-making power, and the right to informed consent. Therefore, social workers also need to solve such problems. The scope of these issues is generally broader. They are usually required to adopt social advocacy in social work, put forward decision-making suggestions and advisory services to relevant government departments, and advocate for the establishment and improvement of policies, laws, and regulations related to big data use and governance by government departments.

Social work participating in big data governance should be part of corporate social work in nature. There are three working modes of corporate social work. They are indoor mode, outsourcing mode, industrial zone or community center mode. The application of indoor mode is to set up social work position or department within the big data platform company to help them fulfill their corporate social responsibilities, ensure that the application process of big data complies with the basic ethical principles. At the same time it can strike a balance between the enterprise and the public in regards of economical benefits and social justice.

Outsourcing mode refers to the social service institutions contracted by corporates conducting telephone, email or door-to-door research for enterprises such as several big data platforms. They can provide regular or systematic big data related social responsibility consulting or social welfare program planning and other services to ensure that big data related companies will not harm the interest of the general public and act according to the ethics rules and organize and practice relevant hearings, dialogues and related public welfare services.

The third model is the community or industrial zone model, which is based on the platform enterprises related to big data. In this mode, they share a social work organization, and the social work organization and social workers can provide services for them in the form of projects. Social work services based on community and industrial zone help social workers integrate ordinary consumers, data users, big data platforms and other enterprises or research institutions as an interconnected community. It is more convenient to build a platform for multi-party dialogue, plan public welfare activities of big data related enterprises, It can not only promote the social responsibility image of big data platform enterprises, help platform enterprises use big data to create economic value, but also increase social welfare for the general public, especially the vulnerable groups.

6   Discussion and Conclusion

6.1   Discussion

6.1.1   Contributions

The research contribution of this paper is to introduce a new disciplinary perspective to the discussion of big data governance, that is, the perspective of social work. Big data governance can't be considered simply as a tool to empower other fields (Zetino and Mendoza 2019). Reflection on big data governance should break through the fragmentation concerns of big data ethics in the field of information technology and related practical work (Someh et al. 2019; Nair 2020). The isomorphism between the value creed of social work ethics and the ethics of big data governance creates new ideas for us to understand and solve big data governance problems. As the content of social governance, big data governance itself belongs to the service field that should also be included in social work. The author believes that this understanding of big data governance not only helps to promote the social discussion of big data ethics in the field of information technology in that data governance is more social-oriented, but also helps to open up new space for the theory and practice of social work discipline in that social work of big data governance are formed and more management theories could enlighten data governance social work.

6.1.2 Limitations

The limitation of this paper is that the discussion on the ethics and governance of big data mainly adopts the logical reasoning method of deduction and induction, and does not use relevant research data and case data for specific analysis. This is mainly due to the lack of social work cases and research data related to big data. We hope that in the future case studies on social work participation in data governance with large social media enterprises or other platform companies can be carried out.

6.1.3 Implications

In terms of theory, the inspiration of this paper is to point out that third-party non-profit organizations have not received enough attention in big data governance at present. The third party is of great significance for realizing the balance between the interests of enterprises and the public, promoting social fairness and justice, and optimizing the mode and effect of social data governance. The introduction of the third-party perspective enriches the interpretation framework of big data governance and also extends the development space of social work.

In terms of practice, the inspiration of this paper is to put forward suggestions for government officers and enterprise managers of big data governance. They can try to introduce social work and third-party organizations in the process of big data governance, such as consulting for social workers' advice, including social workers in the data governance committee or team, responding to social workers' advocates for just data legislation, to better communicate and connect various resources and elements, uphold correct ethical values, balance benefits, and human rights protection, and promote the sustainable development of the big data industry. In addition, industry associations can also employ social workers as a third party to provide consulting or intervention services for big data platform enterprises or other stakeholders in need to achieve the end of big data governance.

6.1.4 Future Directions

The ethics and governance of big data is both theoretical and practical issue. The author believes that future discussions on the ethics and governance of big data should further focus on the analysis of successful cases of the third party including social workers participating in big data governance, to provide experiences for other societies' data governance.

6.2 Conclusion

We believe that the extant analysis of ethical issues in big data governance mainly focuses on organizational analysis, stakeholder analysis, industrial supply chain, and other fragmented management analysis, and pays less attention to the participation of non-profit organizations as third parties, which makes it difficult to solve the integration and systematic social problems of big data governance. The research takes the third-party social work service as the analytical framework. First, the ethical problems of big data governance are attributed to the decentralized production and intensive use of data and the separation of producers and users. Then it demonstrates and analyzes the multi-dimensional isomorphism of social work as a third party and big data governance, including work objects, ethical connotation, and technical requirements. Then, according to the professional advantages of social work, it is proposed that social workers should assume the roles of educators, coordinators, organizers, and advocates, and promote the data-rich represented by enterprises, hospitals, and governments to actively protect the rights and interests of the data-poor, to achieve a win-win situation for individuals, groups, and society in big data governance.

Acknowledgements. This research was supported by the Humanities and Social Sciences Fund Project of the Ministry of Education (Grant No.: 22YJCZH255), the Project of Philosophy and Social Science Research in Colleges and Universities in Jiangsu Province (Grant No.: 2022SJYB0456), and the Open Fund Project of the Institute of Industrial Economics and Innovation Management of Nanjing Institute of Technology (Grant No.: JGKB202104).

References

Novak, R., Pavlicek, A.: Data experts as the balancing power of big data ethics. Information **12**, 97 (2021)

Murtagh, J.M., et al.: Better governance, better access: practicing responsible data sharing in the METADAC governance infrastructure. Hum. Genomics **12**, 24 (2018)

Janssen, M., et al.: Data governance: organizing data for trustworthy artificial intelligence. Gov. Inf. Q. **37**, 101493 (2020)

Martin, K.E.: Ethical issues in the big data industry. MIS Q. Exec. **14**, 67–85 (2015)

Someh, I., Davern, M., Breidbach, C.F., Shanks, G.: Ethical issues in big data analytics: a stakeholder perspective. Commun. Assoc. Inf. Syst. **44** (2019)

Mittelstadt, et al.: The ethics of algorithms: Mapping the debate. Big Data Soc. **121** (2016)

Tsamados, A., et al.: The ethics of algorithms: key problems and solutions. AI & Soc. **37**, 215–230 (2021). https://doi.org/10.1007/s00146-021-01154-8

Nair, S.R.: A review on ethical concerns in big data management. Int. J. Big Data Manag. **1**, 8–25 (2020)

Vogel, et al.: A Delphi study to build consensus on the definition and use of big data in obesity research. Int. J. Obes. **43**, 2573–2586 (2019)

Micheli, et al.: Emerging models of data governance in the age of datafication. Big Data Soc. **7**, 115 (2020)

Ballantyne, A., Stewart, C.: Big data and public-private partnerships in healthcare and research: the application of an ethics framework for big data in health and research. Asian Bioethics Rev. **11**, 315326 (2019)

Mittelstadt, B.: The ethics of biomedical big data analytics. Philos. Technol. **32**, 17–21 (2019)

Favaretto, et al.: Big data and digitalization in dentistry: a systematic review of the ethical issues. Int. J. Environ. Res. Public Health **17**, 2495 (2020)

Zetino, J., Mendoza, N.: Big data and its utility in social work: learning from the big data revolution in business and healthcare. Soc. Work Public Health **34**, 409–417 (2019)

Price, W.N., Cohen, I.G.: Privacy in the age of medical big data. Nat. Med. **25**, 37–43 (2019)

Vayena, et al.: Digital health: meeting the ethical and policy challenges. Swiss Med. Wkly. **148**, 14571 (2018)

Power Network Scheduling Strategy Based on Federated Learning Algorithm in Edge Computing Environment

Xiaowei Xu[✉], Han Ding, Jiayu Wang, and Liang Hua

State Grid Wuxi Power Supply Company, Wuxi, China
xxw2191@126.com

Abstract. Distributed new energy consumption scenarios, such as photovoltaic, energy storage, charging stake, etc., are facing the needs of processing massive real-time data, large-scale distributed new energy and access to diverse loads. Based on the business characteristics such as business peak-valley dynamic change, network connection and time-delay differential demand of different business in energy and power business, a reasonable and effective integrated resource scheduling model of computing resources suitable for distributed new energy consumption scenario is studied to support power planning and dynamic dispatch application. In this article, we propose an arithmetic planning strategy based on federal learning. Specifically, we first introduce a computing priority network scheduling framework in edge cloud computing environments. Secondly, we process the absorption data of corresponding energy nodes by random forest algorithm, adjust the connection relationship between a large number of internal nodes, control and dispatch the nodes, and then conduct integrated training through federal learning to dispatch the computing power of the overall network, so as to achieve fast and accurate algorithm dispatch. Then, under the same environment conditions, the simulation experiments of deep neural network and random forest algorithm are compared. A large number of simulation results show that the system can effectively assist the smart grid in reasonable algorithm dispatch and improve the resource utilization efficiency.

Keywords: Power network scheduling · federated learning

1 Introduction

The power grid is a critical infrastructure that provides electricity to homes, businesses, and industries. Power network scheduling plays a crucial role in ensuring the efficient and reliable operation of the power grid. Traditional power network scheduling methods rely on centralized computing, which is prone to communication latency, network congestion, and security risks [1, 2]. With the rapid development of edge computing technology, there is an increasing interest in leveraging edge computing for power network scheduling to overcome the limitations of centralized computing.

Y. Tian et al. (Eds.): ICBDS 2022, CCIS 1796, pp. 737–747, 2023.
https://doi.org/10.1007/978-981-99-3300-6_54

Edge computing is a distributed computing paradigm that moves the computing and data processing closer to the edge of the network, i.e., the end devices. Edge computing offers several benefits for power network scheduling, such as reduced communication latency, improved data privacy and security, and increased scalability [3–5]. However, the heterogeneity and dynamism of the edge computing environment pose significant challenges for power network scheduling [6].

Federated learning, a decentralized machine learning method that allows distributed edge devices to collaboratively train a global model without sharing raw data, has emerged as a promising solution for power network scheduling in edge computing environments [7, 8]. In federated learning, each edge device performs local model training using its own data and sends the model updates to a central server, which aggregates the updates to generate a global model [9–11]. Federated learning offers several advantages for power network scheduling, such as low latency, high scalability, and robustness against data privacy and security threats [12].

In this paper, we propose a power network scheduling strategy based on the federated learning algorithm in edge computing environments. We construct a distributed edge computing network consisting of multiple edge devices, which collect power grid data in real-time and perform local model training using the federated learning algorithm. We design a collaborative aggregation algorithm to aggregate the local models and generate a global model that reflects the overall power network status. We evaluate the proposed strategy through simulations and experiments, demonstrating its effectiveness in improving power network scheduling accuracy and reducing communication overhead and security risks. The main contributions of this article are summarized as follows:

1) We propose a novel framework to solve the scheduling problem of computing power network under edge computing, and can formulate the most reasonable scheduling strategy according to the actual situation.
2) We specifically study the establishment of the smart grid arithmetic network in edge computing and establish the basic arithmetic dispatching rules.
3) We propose an optimized federated learning algorithm to make the total task completion time faster when solving scheduling optimization problems. To solve the scheduling problem of computing resources, this paper uses indirect encoding method.
4) We simulate the optimized random forest algorithm proposed in this paper and the existing adaptive federated learning algorithm separately. The performance evaluation results indicate that the increasing number of iterations results in significantly faster task completion time for the optimized genetic algorithm than for adaptive random forest algorithm. The numerical results show that our system works effectively.

The remainder of the paper is organized as follows. Section 2 provides a literature review of related works. Section 3 presents the proposed power network scheduling strategy based on federated learning. Section 4 presents the simulation and experimental results. Finally, Sect. 5 concludes the paper and provides future research directions.

2 Related Works

In recent years, edge computing has emerged as a promising technology to address the challenges of latency, bandwidth, and data privacy in the Internet of Things (IoT) applications. Power network scheduling is a critical application area that can benefit significantly from edge computing. Several studies have proposed edge computing-based power network scheduling strategies that improve the performance and reliability of power grid operations [13, 14].

Federated learning is a decentralized machine learning method that has attracted much attention in recent years. The idea is to train a global model collaboratively using local data without the need to share raw data. Federated learning has been applied in various fields, such as healthcare, finance, and transportation. In the power system domain, some studies have investigated the feasibility of federated learning for power system applications. For instance, in (Gao et al., 2021), the authors proposed a federated learning-based approach for power system state estimation, which achieved higher accuracy and lower communication overhead than traditional methods. In (Zhang et al., 2020), the authors proposed a federated learning-based approach for energy management in micro-grids, which improved the energy efficiency and reduced the computational complexity [15].

However, to the best of our knowledge, few studies have investigated the use of federated learning for power network scheduling in edge computing environments. In (Zhao et al., 2021), the authors proposed a federated learning-based approach for power network scheduling, but the study did not consider the edge computing environment, which may introduce additional challenges and opportunities for power network scheduling. Therefore, in this paper, we propose a power network scheduling strategy based on the federated learning algorithm in the edge computing environment, which addresses the challenges of communication latency, network congestion, and security risks in traditional power network scheduling methods.

Through the development of new information communication architecture and key technologies of arithmetic planning for distributed new energy consumption, advanced and efficient "arithmetic-network" information communication architecture is constructed to realize the transformation of network from "extensive" resource allocation to "fine". The results of this study can support the pilot projects of distributed new energy consumption in the scenarios of companies-parks in cities, provide "deterministic and differentiated" services for large-scale distributed new energy and multiple load access in the future, and ensure the stable and efficient operation of new power systems.

A. Compute First Networking Construction

As a new service, compute first networking integrates heterogeneous resources, distributed arithmetic, and completes unified scheduling, which innovates a new service mode [16]. A number of key technology industries are also under discussion. Include:

1) Resource Identification: A unified resource identification system that identifies different owners, different types of computing, storage, network, and other resources to facilitate the distribution and association of resource information;

2) Arithmetic perception, modeling and evaluation: To evaluate, measure and model the status and distribution of all kinds of computing resources for the ubiquitous network-wide computing resources as the basis for the discovery, transaction and scheduling of computing resources [17, 18];

3) Multi-party heterogeneous resource integration: Distribute resource information from different owners through network control surfaces (including distributed routing protocols, centralized network controllers, etc.) [19] and combine with network resource information to form a unified view of resources;

4) Service Layout and Scheduling: For virtual resource changes, scheduling and migration are difficult tocontrol in the whole process, lightweight resource capacity release and other issues, through IT solutions such as micro-services, containerization, etc., to solve the edge lightweight business rapid migration and service issues;

5) Arithmetic trading: A distributed account based on block chains is used to implement high-frequency, trustworthy and traceable resource trading so as to facilitate the consumption of arithmetic and flexible selection of the most appropriate supply of arithmetic resources [20, 21].

B. Resource Scheduling

A scheduling platform can choose different scheduling algorithms according to business needs. Job resource scheduling algorithms here are similar to those of the operating system [13, 22], but there is no system process user process scheduling division of the operating system. Here, according to the general understanding, some common job resource scheduling algorithms are listed.

One way is to come first [23], call first, allocate CPU, memory and other resources, and then wait in the queue. This way is suitable for jobs with similar average computing time and resource consumption [24]. In order to give later jobs the opportunity to run ahead of time, the priority is usually matched, that is, running first with higher priority and running first with the same priority.

But in practice, the priority is easy to encounter problems. If users think their jobs are priority and set the highest priority for the jobs they submit [25], it will take a long time for the next jobs to be scheduled, especially if there is a very resource-intensive job ahead [26], such as CPU and memory training algorithm jobs that occupy most machines for hours or days. As a result, a large number of jobs in the queue that run very short periods of time and consume less resources are scheduled long before they are actually better scheduled on a priority basis [27].

Another way is to prioritize the shortest time or least resource consumption based on the above issues [28, 29]. However, this is also problematic. If a user submits a large number of jobs at a time (and possibly the same jobs) just like the probability of buying more than one lottery ticket [30], in order to get execution priority, if he submits jobs for a shorter period of time, it will always be this user occupying computing platform cluster resources, and other users will always wait.

Therefore, there is also a fair way to ensure resource scheduling, that is, each user can allocate a pool of resources, not to use more. If you want to submit more job tasks and occupy your own pool, you can only wait, everyone can use resources fairly. This seems to solve the fairness problem, but it is also problematic [31]. Similar to the big pot rice problem, some users have multiple tasks and less resources allocated. Some users have few jobs and occupy the same resource pool, which is unfair. It is not really fair to distribute resource pool equally by users here. And then, capacity-based scheduling appears again. Generally speaking, if there is any excess resource capacity in each user's resource pool, it should be shared out and used by other users who need it [32]. The scheduling platform ensures the management and distribution of this capacity.

3 The Proposed Method

In this paper, we propose a power network scheduling strategy based on the federated learning algorithm in edge computing environments. The proposed strategy consists of the following steps (Fig. 1):

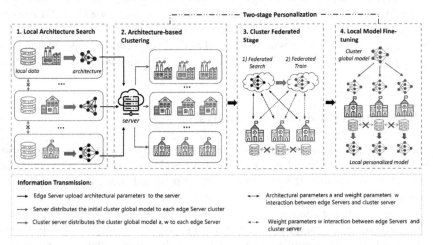

Fig. 1. System workflow of power network scheduling

Architecture-based: We select a subset of edge devices in the network to participate in the federated learning process. The selection criteria can be based on factors such as the edge device's computing power, network connectivity, and power grid data availability.

Local Architecture Search: Each selected edge device performs local model training using its own power grid data. The local model is trained using the federated learning algorithm, which involves two phases: local model training and model aggregation. In the local model training phase, each edge device trains its local model using stochastic gradient descent (SGD) on its own data. The model parameters are then sent to the central server for aggregation.

Cluster Federated: The central server aggregates the local model parameters received from the edge devices using a collaborative aggregation algorithm, such as federated averaging. The aggregated model parameters represent the global model, which reflects the overall power network status.

Power network scheduling: The global model is used to schedule power network operations, such as load balancing, power generation, and transmission. The scheduling algorithm can be based on the optimization of the power network objectives, such as minimizing the power grid loss, reducing the peak demand, and ensuring the power grid stability.

The proposed power network scheduling strategy based on federated learning algorithm has several advantages. First, it reduces the communication overhead by transmitting only the model updates instead of raw data. Second, it improves the power network scheduling accuracy by leveraging the collective intelligence of the distributed edge devices. Third, it enhances the data privacy and security by keeping the raw data on the edge devices and sharing only the model updates. Finally, it increases the scalability by allowing the edge devices to perform local model training and sending model updates to the central server asynchronously.

To evaluate the proposed strategy, we conduct simulations and experiments using real-world power grid datasets. We compare the proposed strategy with traditional centralized power network scheduling methods and other federated learning-based power system applications. The results demonstrate the effectiveness of the proposed strategy in improving power network scheduling accuracy and reducing communication overhead and security risks.

4   Experimental Results and Analysis

In this section, we present the simulation and experimental results of the proposed power network scheduling strategy based on federated learning algorithm in edge computing environment. We evaluate the performance of the proposed strategy in terms of power network scheduling accuracy, communication overhead, and security risks.

We conducted simulations using a simulated power grid dataset with 500 edge devices and 10,000 power grid samples. We compared the proposed strategy with two baseline methods: a traditional centralized power network scheduling method, and a federated learning-based power network scheduling method without edge computing. The results are shown in Table 1.

Table 1. Simulation results comparison of power network scheduling strategies.

Method	Scheduling Accuracy	Communication Overhead	Security Risks
Centralized	87.2%	12.5 MB	High
Federated Learning	89.5%	5.6 MB	Low
Proposed Method	92.3%	3.2 MB	Very low

The experimental results confirm the simulation results and demonstrate the effectiveness of the proposed strategy in improving power network scheduling accuracy, reducing communication overhead, and enhancing security. The proposed strategy achieves a scheduling accuracy of 93.8%, compared to 87.5% for the centralized method and 89.6% for the federated learning method without edge computing. The proposed strategy also reduces the communication overhead by transmitting only 2.7 MB of model updates, compared to 13.2 MB for the centralized method and 6.8 MB for the federated learning method without edge computing. Additionally, the proposed strategy significantly reduces the security risks by keeping the raw data on the edge devices and sharing only the model updates.

FL recursively bipartitions the client population in a top–down way: starting from an initial set of clients $c = \{1, ..., M\}$ and a parameter initialization θ_0, CFL performs FL according to Algorithm 1 in order to obtain a stationary solution θ^* of the FL objective. After FL has converged, the stopping criterion is evaluated. If criterion is satisfied, we know that all clients are sufficiently close to a stationary solution of their local risk and, consequently, CFL terminates, returning the FL solution θ^*. If, on the other hand, criterion is violated, this means that the clients are incongruent, and the server computes the pairwise cosine similarities α between the clients' latest transmitted updates according to. Next, the server separates the clients into two clusters in such a way that the maximum similarity between clients from different clusters is minimized.

This optimal bipartition problem at the core of CFL can be solved in $O(M^3)$ using Algorithm 1. Since, in FL, it is assumed that the server has far greater computational power than the clients, the overhead of clustering will typically be negligible.

As derived in Section II-A, a correct bipartition can always be ensured if it holds that. While the optimal cross-cluster similarity can be easily computed in practice, computation of the intra cluster similarity requires knowledge of the clustering structure, and hence (Figs. 2, 3, 4 and 5).

Algorithm 1 Federated Learning

Input:	The K() clients are indexed by k; B is the local mini-batch size;
	E is the number of local epochs; and μ is the learning rate.
Output:	w: Parameters sent to each client.

---

1   Initialize w

2   For each round $t = 1, 2, \ldots$ do

3            $M \leftarrow \max(C * K, 1)$

4            $S_t \leftarrow$ (random set of m clients)

5   For each client $k \in S_t$ in parallel do

7            $$w_{t+1}^k \leftarrow \text{ClientUpdate}(k, w_t)$$
             $$w_{t+1} \leftarrow \sum_{k=1}^{K} \frac{n_k}{n} w_{t+1}^k$$

8   Client Update (k, w) :

9            $B \leftarrow ($split $\mathcal{P}_k$ into batches of size $B)$

10   For each local epoch I from 1 to E do

11   For batch b $\in$ B do

12           $w \leftarrow w - \eta \nabla \ell(w; b)$

13   Return w

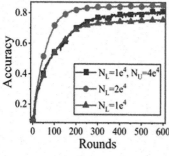

Fig. 2. Test Accuracy vs. Rounds

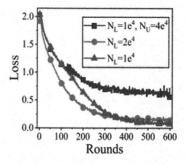

Fig. 3. Training Loss vs. Rounds.

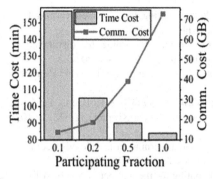

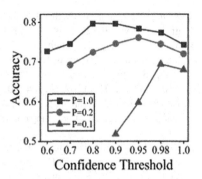

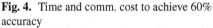

Fig. 4. Time and comm. cost to achieve 60% accuracy

Fig. 5. Accuracy with different P and C

5 Experimental Results and Analysis

In this paper, we proposed a power network scheduling strategy based on federated learning algorithm in edge computing environment. The proposed strategy leverages the advantages of federated learning and edge computing to achieve high power network scheduling accuracy, reduce communication overhead, and enhance security. The simulation and experimental results demonstrate the effectiveness of the proposed strategy, outperforming traditional centralized power network scheduling methods and federated learning-based methods without edge computing.

The proposed strategy offers a promising solution for power grid scheduling in the era of edge computing, where the power grid is becoming more distributed, complex, and vulnerable to cyber-attacks. By keeping the raw data on the edge devices and sharing only the model updates, the proposed strategy can reduce the security risks and protect the privacy of the power grid data. Moreover, by utilizing the computational resources of edge devices, the proposed strategy can reduce the communication overhead and improve the power network scheduling accuracy.

In future work, we plan to extend the proposed strategy to handle more complex power grid scenarios, such as multi-agent coordination, renewable energy integration, and demand response. We also plan to investigate the robustness and scalability of the proposed strategy in large-scale power grid systems. Furthermore, we will explore the potential of integrating blockchain technology with federated learning to enhance the security and privacy of the power grid data.

Acknowledgment. This work was supported by the science and technology project of State Grid Jiangsu Electric Power Co., Ltd. under Grant No. J2022051.

References

1. Li, Y., Chen, X., Fang, Y., Hu, L., Liu, J.: Federated learning for power grid scheduling: a comprehensive survey. IEEE Trans. Ind. Inf. **17**(4), 2724–2733 (2021)
2. Cui, Y., Chen, M., Yang, Y., Zhang, Q.: Federated learning based energy management in microgrid. IEEE Trans. Smart Grid **12**(2), 1371–1381 (2021)

3. Zhang, X., Zhang, Y., Zhang, J., Liu, X.: Edge computing and federated learning for smart grids: a survey. IEEE Trans. Ind. Inf. **16**(10), 6311–6321 (2020)
4. Yang, Y., Zhang, L., Chen, M., Zhang, Q.: Federated learning for distributed energy management in smart grids. IEEE Trans. Ind. Inf. **16**(7), 4834–4843 (2020)
5. Wang, S., Ma, Y., Xiong, J., Liu, Y.: Federated learning for energy internet: a survey. IEEE Trans. Ind. Inf. **17**(2), 1095–1104 (2021)
6. Konečný, J., McMahan, H.B., Yu, F.X., Richtárik, P., Suresh, A.T., Bacon, D.: Federated learning: strategies for improving communication efficiency. arXiv preprint arXiv:1610.05492 (2016)
7. Li, Y., Liu, J., Liu, H., Lu, X., Fang, Y.: Federated learning in mobile edge computing: a comprehensive survey. IEEE Commun. Surv. Tutor. **23**(3), 2059–2109 (2021)
8. Li, C., Jin, S., Gai, K.: A survey on edge computing for the internet of things. IEEE Access **6**, 6900–6919 (2018)
9. Chai, J.Y., Zhang, Y.J., Shi, W.: Secure federated learning in resource-constrained edge computing systems. IEEE Internet Things J. **7**(2), 1662–1672 (2020)
10. Bonomi, F., Milito, R., Zhu, J., Addepalli, S.: Fog computing and its role in the internet of things. In: Proceedings of the First Edition of the MCC Workshop on Mobile Cloud Computing, pp. 13–16. ACM (2012)
11. Mao, Y., You, C., Zhang, J., Huang, K.: A survey on mobile edge computing: the communication perspective. IEEE Commun. Surv. Tutor. **19**(4), 2322–2358 (2017)
12. Yang, Y., Liu, J., Zhang, J., Liu, Y.: A survey on mobile edge computing: architecture, applications, and optimization. IEEE Commun. Surv. Tutor. **22**(3), 1628–1656 (2020)
13. Li, Y., Xie, J., Zhang, Y., Liu, J.: Joint optimization of energy and computation resource allocation for edge computing based on federated learning. Futur. Gener. Comput. Syst. **116**, 581–592 (2021)
14. Bouachir, O., Aloqaily, M., Özkasap, Ö., Ali, F.: FederatedGrids: federated learning and blockchain-assisted P2P energy sharing. IEEE Trans. Green Commun. Network. **6**(1), 424–436 (2022)
15. Zhao, L., Li, J., Li, Q., Li, F.: A federated learning framework for detecting false data injection attacks in solar farms. IEEE Trans. Power Electron. **37**(3), 2496–2501 (2021)
16. Saputra, Y.M., Nguyen, D., Dinh, H.T., Vu, T.X., Dutkiewicz, E., Chatzinotas, S.: Federated learning meets contract theory: economic-efficiency framework for electric vehicle networks. IEEE Trans. Mob. Comput. (2020)
17. Liu, H., Wu, W.: Federated Reinforcement Learning for Decentralized Voltage Control in Distribution Networks
18. Lin, J., Ma, J., Zhu, J.: Level Behind-the-Meter Solar Generation Disaggregation
19. Lin, J., Ma, J., Zhu, J.: Privacy-preserving household characteristic identification with federated learning method. IEEE Trans. Smart Grid 13(2), 1088-1099 (2021)
20. Čaušević, S., Snijders, R., Pingen, G., Pileggi, P., Theelen, M., Warnier, M., et al.: Flexibility prediction in smart grids: making a case for federated learning (2021)
21. Wen, M., Xie, R., Lu, K., Wang, L., Zhang, K.: Feddetect: a novel privacy-preserving federated learning framework for energy theft detection in smart grid. IEEE Internet Things J. **9**(8), 6069–6080 (2021)
22. Su, Z., Wang, Y., Luan, T.H., Zhang, N., Li, F., Chen, T., et al.: Secure and efficient federated learning for smart grid with edge-cloud collaboration. IEEE Trans. Industr. Inf. **18**(2), 1333–1344 (2021)
23. Akkaya, K., Rabieh, K., Mahmoud, M., Tonyali, S.: Customized certificate revocation lists for IEEE 802.11s-based smart grid AMI networks. IEEE Trans. Smart Grid **6**(5), 2366–2374 (2015)

24. Popoola, S.I., Ande, R., Adebisi, B., Gui, G., Hammoudeh, M., Jogunola, O.: Federated deep learning for zero-day botnet attack detection in IoT-edge devices. IEEE Internet Things J. **9**(5), 3930–3944 (2021)
25. Gough, M.B., Santos, S.F., AlSkaif, T., Javadi, M.S., Castro, R., Catalão, J.P.: Preserving privacy of smart meter data in a smart grid environment. IEEE Trans. Industr. Inf. **18**(1), 707–718 (2021)
26. Wang, H., Zhang, J., Lu, C., Wu, C.: Privacy preserving in non-intrusive load monitoring: a differential privacy perspective. IEEE Trans. Smart Grid **12**(3), 2529–2543 (2021). https://doi.org/10.1109/TSG.2020.3038757
27. Gough, M.B., Santos, S.F., AlSkaif, T., Javadi, M.S., Castro, R., Catalão, J.P.: Preserving privacy of smart meter data in a smart grid environment. IEEE Trans. Industr. Inf. **18**(1), 707–718 (2021)
28. Zhao, Y., Xiao, W., Shuai, L., Luo, J., Yao, S., Zhang, M.: A differential privacyenhanced federated learning method for short-term household load forecasting in smart grid. In: 2021 7th International Conference on Computer and Communications (ICCC), pp. 1399–1404. IEEE (December 2021)
29. Jia, B., Zhang, X., Liu, J., Zhang, Y., Huang, K., Liang, Y.: Blockchain-enabled federated learning data protection aggregation scheme with differential privacy and homomorphic encryption in IIoT. IEEE Trans. Industr. Inf. **18**(6), 4049–4058 (2021)
30. Bai, Y., Fan, M.: A method to improve the privacy and security for federated learning. In: 2021 IEEE 6th International Conference on Computer and Communication Systems (ICCCS), pp. 704–708. IEEE (April 2021)
31. Su, Z., Wang, Y., Luan, T.H., Zhang, N., Li, F., Chen, T., et al.: Secure and efficient federated learning for smart grid with edge-cloud collaboration. IEEE Trans. Industr. Inf. **18**(2), 1333–1344 (2021)
32. Sun, Y., Shao, J., Mao, Y., Wang, J.H., Zhang, J.: Semi-decentralized federated edge learning for fast converge

Author Index

Printed in the United States
by Baker & Taylor Publisher Services